PLAYING THE PACIFIC PROVINCE

An Anthology of British Columbia Plays, 1967-2000

Playing the Pacific Province:
An Anthology
of British Columbia Plays,
1967-2000

Edited by
Ginny Ratsoy & James Hoffman

Playwrights Canada Press • Toronto

Playing the Pacific Province: An Anthology of British Columbia Plays, 1967-2000
© Copyright 2001 Ginny Ratsoy & James Hoffman, eds.

The Ecstasy of Rita Joe © 1967 George Ryga; *Crabdance* © 1969/72 Beverley Simons; *Babel Rap* © 1972 John Lazarus; *The Komagata Maru Incident* © 1976 Sharon Pollock; *Billy Bishop Goes to War* © 1978 John MacLachlan Gray with Eric Peterson; *Horseplay* © 1981 Peter Anderson and Phil Savath; *Talking Dirty* © 1982 Sherman Snukal; *Last Call* © 1982 Morris Panych; *Diving* © 1983 Margaret Hollingsworth; *Ten Ways to Abuse an Old Woman* © 1983/88 Sally Clark; *Under the Skin* © 1985 Betty Lambert; *Skin* © 1986 Dennis Foon; *NO`XYA`* © 1987 David Diamond with Hal Blackwater, Lois G. Shannon, and Marie Wilson; *The Hope Slide* © 1992 Joan MacLeod; *Mother Tongue* © 1995 Betty Quan; *Sex Is My Religion* © 1995 Colin Thomas; *The Unnatural and Accidental Women* © 2000 Marie Clements

Playwrights Canada Press
54 Wolseley St., 2nd fl. Toronto, Ontario CANADA M5T 1A5
Tel: (416) 703-0201   Fax: (416) 703-0059
info@puc.ca   http://www.puc.ca

CAUTION: These plays are fully protected under the copyright laws of Canada and all other countries of The Copyright Union, and are subject to royalty. Changes to any script are expressly forbidden without the prior written permission of the author. Rights to produce, film, or record, in whole or in part, in any medium or any language, by any group, amateur or professional, are retained by the authors. For information about professional or amateur production rights, please contact Playwrights Canada Press.

No part of this book, covered by the copyright hereon, may be reproduced or used in any form or by any means—graphic, electronic or mechanical—without the prior written permission of the publisher, except for excerpts in a review. Any request for photocopying, recording, taping or information storage and retrieval systems of any part of this book shall be directed in writing to The Canadian Copyright Licensing Agency, 1 Yonge St., Ste. 1900, Toronto, Ontario CANADA M5E 1E5 (416) 868-1620.

Playwrights Canada Press publishes with the generous assistance of The Canada Council for the Arts – Writing and Publishing Section and the Ontario Arts Council.

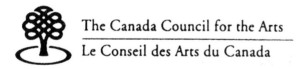

Cover: Ian Wallace, *Lookout*, 1979, silver gelatin prints, 91.5 x 122.2 cm, Vancouver Art Gallery, Vancouver Art Gallery Acquisition Fund VAG 86.19 a-l.

Production manager: Jodi Armstrong.

National Library of Canada Cataloguing in Publication Data

Main entry under title:
    Playing the Pacific province : an anthology of British Columbia plays, 1967-2000

ISBN 0-88754-617-X

I. Canadian drama (English)—British Columbia. 2. Canadian drama (English)—20th century.
I. Ratsoy, Ginny II. Hoffman, James

PS8315.5.B7P54 2001   C812'.5408'09711   C2001-900746-9
PR9196.3.P54 2001

First edition: October 2001.
Printed and bound by AGMV Marquis at Quebec, Canada.

To Alan and Evelyn

ACKNOWLEDGEMENTS

First and foremost, the editors wish to thank Angela Rebeiro for suggesting this anthology to us, for allowing its transformation from slim volume to weighty tome, for her unwavering belief in the importance of the book, and for her flexibility, knowledge, and patience; the playwrights for allowing us to borrow their plays, engaging in fascinating dialogue about their work, and supporting the publication in myriad ways; the photographers for their excellent production shots; and the staff of Playwrights Canada Press for research and editorial aid.

For varied and invaluable assistance, we are grateful to the following individuals: Melody Anderson, Lin Bennett, Denise Comtois, Alex Diakun, Sarah Eades Gordon, Zsuzsi Gartner, Pamela Hawthorn, Stephen E. Miller, Patricia Ney, Eric Nicol, Malcolm Page, David Ross, Ethel Whitty, and Christopher Wootten.

We are also appreciative of the assistance provided by the staff of the following institutions and organizations: Canadian Actors Equity Association, Canadian Film Centre, Caravan Farm Theatre, City of Vancouver Archives, Firehall Arts Centre, Gay and Lesbian Archives of Toronto, *The Georgia Straight*, L.W. Conolly Theatre Archives at the University of Guelph, Metro Toronto Reference Library, National Library of Canada, Playwrights Theatre Centre, Special Collections – University of Calgary Library, Tamahnous Theatre Workshop Society, Tarragon Theatre, University College of the Cariboo Library, and the Vancouver Public Library.

Ginny Ratsoy owes a particular debt of gratitude to the University College of the Cariboo's (UCC) Scholarly Activity Committee for the handy travel grant and UCC's Assisted Leave Committee for the precious gift of time. Finally, she would like to thank Maude and George Ratsoy for always letting her do what she wanted to do and Alan Penfold for always having an idea of what she should do next.

James Hoffman wishes to thank his colleagues, at UCC and beyond, for their many enlightened, helpful contributions – through endless e-mails and phone calls; and special thanks, as always, to Evelyn Hoffman for her generous, incisive support throughout this project – and the next!

The editors have made every effort to contact copyright holders; if any errors or omissions have occurred we will be happy to correct them in a reprinting of this volume.

CONTENTS

Introduction
"Playing out of Place: British Columbia Drama"
by James Hoffman and Ginny Ratsoy *page i*

Notes on the Editors *page ix*

The Ecstasy of Rita Joe
by George Ryga *page 1*

Crabdance
by Beverley Simons *page 47*

Babel Rap
by John Lazarus *page 91*

The Komagata Maru Incident
by Sharon Pollock *page 107*

Billy Bishop Goes to War
by John MacLachlan Gray with Eric Peterson *page 139*

Horseplay
by Peter Anderson and Phil Savath *page 173*

Talking Dirty
by Sherman Snukal *page 227*

Last Call
by Morris Panych *page 271*

Diving
by Margaret Hollingsworth *page 305*

Ten Ways to Abuse an Old Woman
by Sally Clark *page 313*

Under the Skin
by Betty Lambert *page 331*

Skin
by Dennis Foon *page 369*

NO` XYA`
by David Diamond with Hal Blackwater,
Lois G. Shannon, and Marie Wilson *page 391*

The Hope Slide
by Joan MacLeod *page 419*

Mother Tongue
by Betty Quan *page 437*

Sex Is My Religion
by Colin Thomas *page 457*

The Unnatural and Accidental Women
by Marie Clements *page 471*

PLAYING OUT OF PLACE: BRITISH COLUMBIA DRAMA

It is a striking, highly theatrical photograph – and a most important one in British Columbia dramatic writing: standing in line on a beach, hands in pockets, a vast ocean behind them, four men and one woman pose for the camera. Like newly arrived tourists, they seem suspended in an alien environment. The men gaze forward uncertainly; the woman, as though suddenly startled, looks off to her right. It seems not to be raining, yet two of the men grasp umbrellas. Only one is opened. In this speechless moment other images intrude: giant beach logs lie at their feet, while, floating on the horizon above their heads, the shadowy bulk of a freighter hovers and recedes. Who are these people? What is their relation to this beach? What is this picture about?

It is interesting that the publishers of an earlier anthology of British Columbia plays, *West Coast Plays*, selected a photograph of their five playwrights, Leonard Angel, Thomas Cone, Tom Grainger, Margaret Hollingsworth, and Sheldon Rosen, for the cover of their 1975 publication (Brissenden). And it is paradoxical that British Columbia's first generation of professional playwrights is represented as silenced – in relation to their region. Such a reading of *West Coast Plays* is made by critic Malcolm Page, who has stated that "apart from the beach [Kitsilano] there is little British Columbia content." The settings for the plays are variously Paris, London, northern Ontario, or unspecified, but definitely not British Columbia. Page further notes that two of the playwrights are American, two are English immigrants, and a fifth is Montreal-born (95). We suggest, however, that the photograph, rather than ignoring the province, graphically narrates many of the themes of *Playing the Pacific Province*.

At the time, in the early seventies, these five playwrights were all associated with the New Play Centre (now Playwrights Theatre Centre), Vancouver's institution for developing new plays. Founded in 1970, the Centre has an impressive record of nurturing local drama: countless scripts have received written critiques; numerous playscripts have been given workshops; almost two hundred plays have gone to full productions; and major playwrights such as Margaret Hollingsworth and Sharon Pollock have won important awards and critical recognition. Although the Centre has long supported the British Columbia playwright, it has been less certain about the British Columbia play – indeed, "in practice there was compromise" (Hoffman, "Genre Contention" 67). For example, Pamela Hawthorn, director of the New Play Centre, begins her introduction to *West Coast Plays* with the statement that the Centre is "dedicated solely to the BC play" but concludes by privileging the amorphous "Canadian play." Thus, as far as content is concerned, the book would seem to be misnamed; further, its geographically-specific title suggests a limited view of the province.

For the cover of *Playing the Pacific Province*, we selected a section of the photomural, *Lookout*. This work, by Vancouver conceptual artist Ian Wallace, is about people looking at and talking about a British Columbia landscape – this time a beach on Hornby Island. They are positioned not unlike the Kitsilano playwrights: they too are white, are awkwardly placed; they could be tourists – but they are also very studied, obsessively concentrating on....what? The forest? Beach? Ocean? Each other? Clearly they are posing, almost like models set in a foreign country, in a heightened monumentality. There is a strange dynamic: what seems a group becomes individual, but then, in the engaging gestural stance of each, reforms into a foursome. Then there is further disruption: at first glance, the photo, which in its full length is over fourteen meters, seems continuous, like those familiar series of side-by-side photographs depicting long stretches of landscape. But look more closely: the entire work is montaged, constructed. Each section both (very colorfully) participates in and then (very consciously) deconstructs many of our stereotypical notions of relating to nature. The land is both/alternately natural and humanly arranged.

The four visitors are familiar types, but they are also, as Christos Dikeakos has noted, "a construction, a fiction set within a real landscape" (13). For us, the characters (all-white, middle-class) represent a fiction that is just that, a "fiction" (i.e. not based in reality); we hope that both the writers and the plays of this diverse anthology go a long way towards deconstructing such an image of the British Columbia playwright. At the same time, through the youthful promise of these figures, their confident gestures, played out against the familiar British Columbia landscape, now emptied of human culture (and therefore available for re/presentation), there is breathtaking openness for the possibility of seeing the land anew. Like the earlier playwrights in the sand, these people seem awkward, displaced, but they also possess a powerful individual as well as public energy, even a strategy. Their beach, we can believe, has potential for genuine, dare we say postcolonial, negotiation. In this way they are like the playwrights in *Playing the Pacific Province*.

As editors we feel very much like tourists ourselves – especially as we window-shopped our way through a great number of plays to make our highly subjective selection. So far, there are few other volumes of recent British Columbia drama: there is Jerry Wasserman's *Twenty Years at Play*, another anthology of plays (there are eight) that originated at the New Play Centre, and Alan Filewod's *New Canadian Drama 7: West Coast Comedies* (three plays). Because of this, we believe that this present volume is a milestone – in publishing both a weighty (thank you, Playwrights Canada Press for letting us bump you up to seventeen titles!) and (we hope) a worthy collection of homegrown plays. As for our "authority" as British Columbians, we are two academics, one male, one female, one in a theatre department, the other in an English department; one was born and raised in British Columbia, the other migrated from southwestern Ontario more than two decades ago. We are writing from British Columbia about British Columbia for a Canadian publisher based in Toronto. To whom are we writing?

Like the playwrights standing on the beach, many of us are now positioned to explore the land, to place ourselves squarely in our region and discover its drama. At the first-ever conference on British Columbia Theatre, Staging the Pacific Province, held at the University College of the Cariboo in May 1999, more than one-third of the academic papers addressed issues surrounding British Columbia drama. We embrace the fact that a homegrown drama exists but is still largely unknown. We hope this volume will go a long way toward providing some key materials and critical thoughts in the search for one – both in and out of province.

We are aware of Playwrights Canada Press's appeal, within Canada, to a wide spectrum: to libraries, community theatres, bookstores, professional theatre practitioners, high schools, universities, and colleges. This alone will (we hope) give British Columbia drama the exposure—and the critical reflection—it needs. Further afield, the publisher's sales in several other countries have been expanded, a reflection, perhaps, of the increasing popularity of Canadian Studies programmes abroad. Jennifer Harvie, Senior Lecturer in Drama at the University of Surrey Roehampton, reports that "the performance of Canadian plays in the UK has increased exponentially in the last decade" (8). Playwrights Canada Press, to its credit, has done its part by publishing a growing number of play collections in Britain, distributed by London's Nick Hern Books. We see this present volume as a source book, a work to be consulted by students, professors, artistic producers, directors, actors, and the general public as they show increasing interest in Canadian culture – as it is powerfully conveyed through its dramatic canon.

We have tailored our approach accordingly. Along with the plays, we include a general introduction on the state of drama in British Columbia; each play, too, has its own briefer introduction in which we attempt to provide a useful context for the work as well as one or two critical thoughts. In addition, we have assembled selected bibliographies and, where possible, conducted interviews with the playwrights.

In the field of Canadian studies there has been intense discussion of two issues relevant to this anthology: regionalism (as a social construct) and canonicity (recognizing a body of works—such as our anthology of plays—as standard). On the first topic, some have questioned the validity of identification with both nation and region in a postmodern, globalized world. Frank Davey, for example, argues that region and regionalism are "both social creations, the first constituting a territorial definition of geographic space based on a selection of possible differentiating criteria – a territorial definition that can change as national policies change, and the second constituting an interpretation of social interests that gives geographic location priority over such possible interests as gender, ethnicity, class, age, sexual orientation, and race" (2). Because our anthology treats British Columbia as both province and region, because of its vast size, varied topography, and diverse cultures, and because the province has historically been simplistically characterized by polarities such as right wing and left wing, logger and environmentalist, retiree and youth, rural and urban, we must address this issue. In other words, regional designation, while it can be construed to be artificial and arbitrary, *works* in British Columbia as the conceptualization of place becomes crucial in the determination of cultural values – especially as the region struggles with its colonial/postcolonial inheritance. Our selections, therefore, rather than privileging a single vision, reflect the heterogeneity of the province. We see these plays as rife with the contending voices that give us our regional identity. Our text, like the province, is a polyphony.

Much has also been written about the privileging of certain texts in the academic community: the criteria behind that privileging, the social conditions that shape the canonizing process, and the role of the business of publishing. Specific to drama has been discourse on the relationship between anthologizing and canonization. Richard Paul Knowles (91-111) argues that three Canadian anthologies edited by Richard Perkyns, Jerry Wasserman, and Richard Plant have been responsible for the canonization of Canada's plays. On the other hand, Chris Johnson argues that Canadian drama is too recent to have undergone the lengthy process of canonization, that even some dramatists (such as David Freeman and John Herbert) who were well represented in those three volumes seem to have fallen out of favour, and that the fluidity that has been associated with the larger Canadian literary canon is especially, because of its ephemeral nature, applicable to drama (46-47). We realize that, especially as this is the first anthology of British Columbia plays not devoted to works of one playwright, genre, or institution, we are engaged in canon-making or, in some instances, depending on where the reader sits on this issue, canon reinforcing. If we are reinforcing the Canadian drama canon, the most salient examples are *Billy Bishop Goes to War* and *The Ecstasy of Rita Joe*, works which have been widely produced in various countries, published in various forms, frequently on post-secondary English and theatre course syllabi, and the subjects of numerous scholarly studies. Playwrights such as Sharon Pollock, Morris Panych, Sally Clark, Dennis Foon, Margaret Hollingsworth, John Lazarus, and Joan MacLeod have also garnered sufficient awards, scholarly recognition, and multiple productions to be considered in discussion of the Canadian canon. However, we have also included works by playwrights such as Peter Anderson, David Diamond, Sherman Snukal, Colin Thomas, Betty Lambert, and Beverley Simons who, while they are less in the limelight, have been instrumental in their impact on British Columbia theatre. Finally, we would be remiss if we neglected to point the way ahead: two very promising playwrights are represented in Betty Quan's *Mother Tongue* and Marie Clements' *The Unnatural and Accidental Women*. They bode well for the future.

We acknowledge that we are creating a kind of fiction: what a British Columbia dramatic canon would look like if there was a congruence of opinion among British Columbia playwrights, theatre practitioners, critics, and the audiences. We can imagine these people agreeing on the eclectic theatricality of these works as reflective of the cultural diversity (and its resulting energetics) of the province. We are reminded that British Columbia, despite its dichotomous (British/American) name, is not a single entity but a patchwork of regionalisms: Vancouver Island, the Lower Mainland, the Cariboo, the Kootenays, the Peace River District, the Okanagan, and the Northwest. The plays chosen for this anthology actively participate in the continuing ideological discourses of nationhood as it variously occurs – for example, what forces are at work in the construction of local identity(ies)? The theatre has long been utilized as a site for the negotiation of the differing values of the territory, from the earliest Spanish-British conflict over Nootka Sound at a performance in London in 1790 (Hoffman, "Captain Vancouver") to the Gitskan and Wet'suwet'en court action against the province government in the 1980s in *NO` XYA`*.

British Columbia is a province often characterized by extremes – not just in its topography but in its eccentric characters (Emily Carr), its bizarre politics (Premier Amor De Cosmos), and its generally freewheeling society ("no other region can outdo BC for its abundance of alternative, utopian settlement attempts in as short a time frame") (Scott 9); in short, its great difference from the rest of Canada. In 1973 *Maclean's* Magazine devoted a special issue to the province, calling it "the Latin America of Canada... a rain forest with mythical beasts [where] things grow tall and tropical; occasional cougars roam the suburbs" (Garr 28). Homegrown tourist brochures, using the language of magic realism, proclaim it as "Super Natural British Columbia." In short, we have a highly theatrical setting and one of most dramatic peoples in all of Canada – witness the incredibly powerful ceremonial life of the Northwest Coast Natives. The intricate dancing and singing of the

Kwakwaka'wakw Hamatsa ceremony, with its awesome masks and regalia, and its phenomenal stagecraft, haunted noted anthropologists such as Franz Boas and Edward Curtis, who returned time and time again to comprehend what amounted to a "vivid, highly theatricalized world" (Hoffman, "Towards" 321).

The challenge for us, in assembling our collection, was to consider what constitutes a British Columbia play – especially since, for many, the drama of our province has been non-existent, silent. Certainly during the nineteenth century, the colonial society of the province produced little in the way of enduring, indigenous drama. Chad Evans, in *Frontier Theatre*, a history of British Columbia theatre up to 1900, cites a plentiful range of performances—from British shipboard farces in the 1860s to American minstrel shows through the 1890s—all of which "reinforc[ed] the colonial social structure" (14). Perhaps the closest to a local drama was the work of Harry Lindley, with plays such as *In the Cariboo* and *On to the Klondike*, although even these were likely pirated from hit American plays. Michael Tait, writing generally about nineteenth-century English-Canadian drama, makes no mention of any British Columbia playwright (13-26). For much of the twentieth century, according to the critics, the province fared little better. Andrew Parkin, surveying the theatre history of the province in the early 1980s, also found a "rich and interesting" theatre, but "the emergence of regional drama slow and, until recently, disappointing" (101-112). Later, in a study of important writers who have contributed to the intellectual and imaginative development of the province, Douglas Cole lists no dramatists (73-77), nor, recently, does George Bowering in his "BC in Literature" (395). There was, nonetheless, an outpouring of drama in the province during the 1960s at the same time that a number of professional theatre companies commenced operations, mostly in Vancouver: the Playhouse Theatre Company (1963), the Arts Club (1964), Tamahnous (1971), City Stage (1972), and Touchstone (1976). In addition, there were dozens of smaller, often more experimental companies existing on federal LIP and OFY grants, such as Savage God and Troupe.

Many would agree that British Columbia drama truly began on the evening of November 23, 1967, when George Ryga's *The Ecstasy of Rita Joe* opened at the Vancouver Playhouse. With the plays of local writers such as Ryga, Eric Nicol, and Paul St. Pierre, plays that were set in British Columbia, we seemed at last to have an authentic, local drama. Critic Jamie Portman, reflecting on *Rita Joe*, compares the play to John Osborne's revolutionary British play of the mid-1950s, *Look Back in Anger*; he believes the evening was a "watershed event" in Canadian drama, in providing for the first time "an indigenous Canadian drama that surfaced and succeeded at a time when indigenous Canadian drama was considered an aberration" (65). That the story was set in British Columbia, was taken from a Vancouver newspaper headline, and featured a local icon, Chief Dan George, struck a deep chord with British Columbia audiences. For one thing, it refused to be silent about place: Peter Hay, in his introduction to the play, states that: "It was the first time that a playwright had used the Vancouver Playhouse to confront its largely middle-class clientele with the reality of Skid Row" (8). In short, referring back to the photograph cover of *West Coast Plays*, it was as though playwright and place were truly one. But why had it taken so long?

Photographs, with their intimate sense of locale, also insist on place. The cover photo of *West Coast Plays* provides a rich vernacular narrative: it graphically demonstrates the disjunction between playwright and place. This is characteristic of a settler colony such as British Columbia, where there is "a lack of fit between the language available and the place experienced" (Ashcroft 181). In an area that has suffered colonization there is a complex relationship between word and environment: the language of the Native peoples, for example, suffers from the discursive interference of the colonizers, while, for the settlers, their language, although dominant, seems "not their own" since it is transplanted from a distant centre – as such it too often fails to adequately describe the local. In both cases, with unequal social relations implicit, not only *vis-à-vis* settlers and Natives, but also between settlers and Imperial Centre, there is a troubled experience of regional identity – as well as a creative empowering for some.

British Columbia historian Jean Barman devotes the final chapter of her history of the province, *The West Beyond the West*, to "The British Columbia Identity." Beginning with the comment that the province is "not so much a place as a state of mind," Barman cites the province's relatively recent "non-native settlement," its cut-off position on the continent ("British Columbia still hovers on the edge of a nation"), its history of resource plunder (and environmental activism), a relatively unchanged economic structure since contact ("All that alters are the names of the particular staples being exploited"), its lively, populist politics ("strong leaders rather than ideas have dominated political life"), and its heavy immigration ("the province remains the only one in Canada where newcomers outnumber locally-born residents") as ever-increasing reasons for an essentially unpindownable local character. In its people, British Columbia has a profound "sense of autonomy"; it is, finally, a province *sui generis* (352-369).

Douglas Cole, in a survey of the culture of the province, sees only division – many smaller communities are "cut off" from the metropolitan centres such as Victoria and Vancouver, while larger communities themselves are "still subordinate to the greater cultural centres of the English-speaking world." While he believes there exists "a great variety of cultural traditions" in the province, nonetheless "most have yet to assert distinctively British Columbia voices"; indeed, he concludes, "The voices, images and pursuits that speak of British Columbia or claim to be British Columbian are mainly European or Native" (344). British Columbians, according to Cole, live in a province too new to give them local traditions and too remote to provide cultural roots. George Bowering, however, in his "Swashbuckling History" of British Columbia, returns to the importance of place: "the simple fact is that in British Columbia there is one hell of a lot of geography. There is more geography than there is history, always has been. There is a lot more geography than there are people" (23). He also sets the discussion of local culture within a wide First Nations' context, distinct from the recent histories of the "eurocolumbians."

We believe that a uniquely British Columbia drama does exist. Its fuller character of course will be assessed over time, but for the present we could offer several thoughts about a local drama – thoughts that have a lot to do with our criteria for selecting the seventeen plays of this collection.

First, we looked for plays that we felt significantly engaged with realities of living in postcolonial British Columbia. Plays that are clearly set in this province, especially ones that concern well-known events, such as *The Komagata Maru Incident*, *NO` XYA`*, or *The Hope Slide*, were selected – particularly as they stage the cultural redress underway in a society shedding its colonial past. This automatically placed us in the 1960s, when a vastly heightened awareness of identity issues, along with a critical attitude toward received/imposed culture, became widespread. In its concept of place, each play questions the materiality and commodification of the colonizing and neo-colonizing powers. Each uses highly self-reflexive theatrical forms, for example the presentational stand-up comedian, the First Nations ceremony, and the one-person show, to examine political and social issues that persist from colonial memory.

At the same time we looked for plays and playwrights that have had a significant impact in this province – usually through a strong production record as demonstrated in (some but not necessarily all of) length of run, audience and reviewer response, runs outside the province, number and kind of publications of the play, and reflective critical commentary. In some cases, the sheer magnitude of a production in several of these areas made inclusion virtually automatic. We could not ignore *The Ecstasy of Rita Joe*, with its almost legendary impact upon opening at the Playhouse in Canada's Centennial year, its opening of the National Arts Centre in 1969, its several publications, its translation and production in other languages, its numerous critical articles – indeed its sheer persistence as a milestone of Canadian drama.

Although *Talking Dirty* did not have nearly the same impact, it did nonetheless enjoy the longest run of any play in this anthology, running for an unprecedented three years (1,000 performances) at the Arts Club. We might rightly ask: what was it about this play, aside from its local references, that captivated Vancouver audiences for so long? On the opposite end, a play like *Crabdance*, written several years before *Rita Joe*, couldn't find a Vancouver production until 1972; it had to be opened in Seattle. Subsequent productions in Halifax, Winnipeg, Toronto, and Edmonton, and publication by Talonbooks, seem to confirm the opinion of the first director, Malcolm Black, that the play is "a masterpiece" (10).

In significant production we also include the notion of a play that may ostensibly have little to do with British Columbia but emerges from a significant theatrical matrix within the province.

There have been a number of powerful centres of creative energy in this province: from the collaborative efforts of writers, dramaturges, directors, and actors have emerged important works. Such is the case of *Billy Bishop Goes to War*. While the story of the play is clearly not set within British Columbia, the development of the play had a lot to do with Tamahnous Theatre, who staged the premiere. The fact that it arose from a playwright who studied theatre at UBC and was a founding member of this highly successful theatre collective was sufficient for us. This hit play, emerging from the producing structures of a significant British Columbia theatre company, can be assumed to speak volumes about the province and its developing voice, both within its own borders and, equally important, in dialogue with external places. Similarly, Colin Thomas's *Sex Is My Religion*, while perhaps little known, is a product of the Out West Performance Society's festival of one-act plays, presented in Vancouver in the mid-1990s under the title Plague of the Gorgeous – and published under the same title.

Why publish plays? The complex dynamics involved in the creation, production, and readership of text has been the subject of considerable interest in Canadian literary studies recently. Specifically, the effect of publication on a play's longevity and canonicity has engaged our drama community. For example, the Spring, 1999 issue of *Canadian Theatre Review* interrogates the distinct nature of drama publication. The process of creating a novel may be seen to be complete when it sees the light of day—and thus readers' eyes—in published form. Does the same hold true for a play, or does the production signal completion? The fact that the Governor General's Literary Awards began in 1936 but did not establish a discrete category for drama until 1981 might point to the primacy of production. John Gray, commenting on the first publication of *Billy Bishop Goes to War* (which won the Governor General's Award in 1982) concurs: "I never really thought about publishing plays.... Plays are intended for the stage, and any playwright who looks for readers is in an odd genre" (Ratsoy, "Dramatic Discourse" 25). However, many other playwrights detect a connection between production and publication and argue that publication brings with it its own form of recognition. Joan MacLeod states, "Production is primary, but, without question, I want the text to also be studied as literature" (26). MacLeod also noticed that when her *Amigo's Blue Guitar* received the Governor General's award in 1991 her recognition within the writing community was enhanced. Sally Clark perceives publication for the dramatist as fundamental but increasingly difficult over the course of the last decade: "There's been a steady decrease in the number of Canadian plays that are produced. The only way that people will be aware of plays is through their publication. But if they don't get produced, they won't get published" (27).

Clark's final generalization is to some extent measurable. Talonbooks, a Vancouver publisher that specializes in drama, for example, only very rarely publishes a play before it has received a major production, and Blizzard Press will publish only post-production drafts. Talonbooks has published a total of 145 new drama titles since its inception in 1967; this is 35.5% of its total of 408 new titles (Hayward 26). However, production does not ensure publication, and, although it has become easier over the last thirty years for a Canadian dramatist to publish her/ his work, it is still an uphill battle, according to Angela Rebeiro, publisher of Playwrights Canada Press: "Still only a few of us publish plays. The Governor General's Award list of plays submitted for consideration is generally around twenty titles, which isn't a lot. Plays are expensive to produce for the size of the market" (Ratsoy, "Perspectives" 22).

Of the seventeen works in our collection, only six had been previously published in single play format. Nine saw the printed page first in anthology form, one was published in *Canadian Theatre Review*, and the other had previously only been published in copyscript form. Many plays would be difficult, if not impossible, to access were it not for the copyscript service provided by Playwrights Union of Canada, which, like other drama publishers in Canada, would be able to publish far fewer plays than it does were it not for the granting role of such government bodies as The Canada Council for the Arts. Of course, as we were reminded while researching and reading plays for inclusion, some scripts never make it to the copyscript stage. A striking illustration of the ephemeral nature of plays is the fact that one of the plays we considered for inclusion was not only not available in copyscript form, but its script was also not in the possession of either its author or the theatre company that had premiered the production. At least one play publisher is using electronic innovations to its and the reader's advantage; Blizzard has developed a publish-on-demand programme.

As there are many British Columbias, there are many dramas, and our collection must necessarily reflect that fact as much as possible. We were conscious throughout the process of play selection of the importance of diversity. The word "anthology" has Greek etymology and means a gathering of flowers; it is crucial to us that our bouquet be both variegated and congruous. Several of these works are powerful in their minimalism: *Billy Bishop Goes to War* and *The Hope Slide* each feature a single actor and scant sets, an ideal venue for showcasing character-driven works, while *Last Call*, *Diving*, *Sex Is My Religion*, and *Babel Rap* make use of stark *mise en scène* for inquiries into elemental relationships. At the other end of the spectrum, *Horseplay*, *The Ecstasy of Rita Joe*, *The Unnatural and Accidental Women*, and *The Komagata Maru Incident*, which feature larger casts and are arguably more social plays, foreground spectacle and challenge the boundaries of conventional staging. Variety is evident in dramatic modes: on these pages musicals such as *Horseplay* and *Billy Bishop Goes to War* and comedies of manners such as *Talking Dirty* are in the company of a tragedy such as *The Ecstasy of Rita Joe*, the black comedy of *Ten Ways to Abuse an Old Woman*, *Last Call*, and *Babel Rap*, along with the realism of *Talking Dirty* and *Under the Skin*. Finally, fittingly, there are plays about the people of the First Nations – who, until their ceremonials were snuffed out by repressive legislation in the 1880s, had a strong cultural life. The potency of their performance culture, echoed in the power of their masks and stories, continues to resonate. There is a revival of the Potlatch and allied forms. There is the increasing use of the transcultural powwow in many areas of the province. It is appropriate that while this collection begins with a play written by a white male about the troubled relationship of whites and Natives, *The Ecstasy of Rita Joe*, it concludes with a play on a similar theme and even in the same locale written by a Native woman, *The Unnatural and Accidental Women*.

Multifarious though this grouping is, we like to think that it has an intrinsic wholeness, a vibrancy and resonance – somehow, a local voice, a British Columbia drama. As we researched, we were struck by the quantity and quality of plays worthy of our consideration; the inevitable task of discarding was not an easy one. However, these seventeen selections continue to impress us as theatrical, literary, and local works.

We conclude by returning to the photographic image of playwrights standing on the Kitsilano Beach. As we saw in the cover of *West Coast Plays*, in a settler colony such as British Columbia place has been a source of special geographic determinism: for these earlier writers the land is forbidding, alien; it has no human history; it needs to be discovered/conquered. We believe that the plays of this present volume strongly address issues of the postcolonial society that is British Columbia; in their pointedly local, even political settings (*The Ecstasy of Rita Joe*, *The Komagata Maru Incident*), in their representation of local subjects (*Talking Dirty*, *Under the Skin*), and perhaps especially in their employment of creative, even deconstructive narrative, dramaturgical strategies (*The Hope Slide*, *The Unnatural and Accidental Women*), they can be usefully referenced in describing a British Columbia drama. Equally interesting are the unspecified locales that only obliquely represent this province; each seems to exist as a kind of liminal, metaphoric space indicative of the transitional spaces of postcolonial negotiation. These are *Babel Rap*, *Last Call*, *Diving*, and *Ten Ways to Abuse an Old Woman*. In the end, we believe we are closer to learning what constitutes a British Columbia drama.

J.H./G.R.

Works Cited:

- Ashcroft, Bill, Gareth Griffiths and Helen Tiffin. *Key Concepts in Post-Colonial Studies*. London: Routledge, 1998.
- Barman, Jean. *The West Beyond the West: A History of British Columbia*. Toronto: University of Toronto Press, 1991.

- Black, Malcolm. "The Strange Unhappy Life of *Crabdance*." *Canadian Theatre Review* 9 (Winter 1976): 9-17.
- Bowering, George. *Bowering's BC: A Swashbuckling History*. Toronto: Viking, 1996.
- Brissenden, Connie, ed. *West Coast Plays*. Vancouver: New Play Centre-Fineglow, 1975.
- Byrne, James. *Nootka Sound; Or, Britain Prepar'd, 1790 ms*. The Huntington Library, San Marino.
- Cole, Douglas. "The Intellectual and Imaginative Development of British Columbia." *Journal of Canadian Studies* 24.3 (Fall 1989): 70-79.
- Cole, Douglas. "Leisure, Taste and Tradition in British Columbia." *The Pacific Province: A History of British Columbia*, Hugh J.M. Johnson, ed. Vancouver: Douglas and McIntyre,1996.
- Davey, Frank. "Toward the Ends of Regionalism." *Textual Studies in Canada* 9 (Spring 1997): 1-17.
- Dikeakos, Christos. *Ian Wallace: Selected Works, 1970-1987*. Vancouver: Vancouver Art Gallery, 1988. Catalogue of an exhibition held at the VAG February 5-April 3, 1988, curated by Christos Dikeakos.
- Evans, Chad. *Frontier Theatre*. Victoria: Sono Nis, 1983.
- Filewod, Alan. *New Canadian Drama 7: West Coast Comedies*. Ottawa: Borealis, 1999.
- Garr, Allen, and Bob Waller. "The Pacific Persuasion." *Maclean's* (June 1973).
- Harvie, Jennifer. "Canadian Drama and Performance in the UK: Featuring Quebec and a Canon." *Canadian Theatre Review* 105 (Winter 2001): 5-9.
- Hay, Peter. Introduction, *The Ecstasy of Rita Joe*. Vancouver: Talonbooks, 1970.
- Hayward, Michael. "Talonbooks: Publishing from the Margins." *Canadian Theatre Review* 98 (Spring, 1999): 23-27.
- Hoffman, James. "Towards an Early British Columbia Theatre: The Hamatsa Ceremony As Drama." *Canadian Drama* 11.1 (1985): 231-244.
- Hoffman, James. "Genre Contention at the New Play Centre." *Theatre Research in Canada* 16.1-2 (1995): 59-68.
- Hoffman, James. "Captain George Vancouver and British Columbia's First Play." *Theatre Research in Canada* 21.2 (Fall 2000): 135-148.
- Johnson, Chris. "'Wisdom Under a Ragged Coate': Canonicity and Canadian Drama." *Contemporary Issues in Canadian Drama*, Per Brask, ed. Winnipeg: Blizzard Publishing, 1995.
- Knowles, Richard Paul. "Voices (off): Deconstructing the Modern English-Canadian Dramatic Canon." *Canadian Canons: Essays in Literary Value*, Robert Lecker, ed. Toronto: University of Toronto Press, 1991.
- Page, Malcolm. "Fourteen Propositions About Theatre in British Columbia." *Journal of Canadian Studies* 25. 3 (Fall 1990): 90-104.
- Parkin, Andrew. "The New Frontier: Towards an Indigenous Theatre in British Columbia." *Theatrical Touring and Founding in North America*, L.W.Conolly, ed. Westport, Conn.: Greenwood, 1982.
- Perkyns, Richard, ed. *Major Plays of the Canadian Theatre 1934-1984*. Toronto: Irwin, 1984.
- Plant, Richard, ed. *Modern Canadian Drama, Vol. I*. Markham, Ont.: Penguin, 1984.
- Portman, Jamie. Review, *Vancouver Province* (23 Sept. 1976). *Canadian Drama and the Critics*, L.W. Conolly, ed. Vancouver: Talonbooks, 1995.
- Ratsoy, Ginny. "Dramatic Discourse at Talonbooks." *Canadian Theatre Review* 101 (Winter, 1999): 25-28.
- Ratsoy, Ginny. "Perspectives from Playwrights Canada Press: An Interview with Angela Rebeiro." *Canadian Theatre Review* 98 (Spring 1999): 20-22.
- Scott, Andrew. *The Promise of Paradise: Utopian Communities in BC*. Vancouver: Whitecap, 1997.
- Tait, Michael. "Playwrights in a Vacuum: English-Canadian Drama in the Nineteenth Century." *Dramatists in Canada: Selected Essays*, William H. New, ed. Vancouver: University of British Columbia Press, 1972.
- Wasserman, Jerry, ed. *Twenty Years at Play: A New Play Centre Anthology*. Vancouver: Talonbooks, 1990.
- Wasserman, Jerry, ed. *Modern Canadian Plays, Vols. I & II*. Vancouver: Talonbooks, 1993/1994.

NOTES ON THE EDITORS

Ginny Ratsoy has taught at the University College of the Cariboo (UCC) in Kamloops since 1980. In addition to coordinating UCC's Canadian Studies Program, she teaches a variety of courses in Canadian literature (including drama and Native literature) and Canadian Studies (including film). She has published in such journals as *Canadian Theatre Review* and *Essays on Canadian Writing*. Literary regionalism, the politics of production of literary texts, and representations of British Columbia in drama and prose fiction are among her scholarly interests.

James Hoffman is a Professor of Theatre at the University College of the Cariboo. He has a particular research interest in the theatre of British Columbia, and in 1999 chaired the first British Columbia Theatre Conference, Staging the Pacific Province. He has published articles on notable British Columbia figures and institutions such as director Carroll Aikins, critic Christopher Dafoe, The New Play Centre, and, recently, British Columbia's "first play": *Nootka Sound; Or, Britain Prepar'd*. He has also written a biography of playwright George Ryga, and is presently editing a volume of Ryga's stage plays.

THE ECSTASY OF RITA JOE

BY

GEORGE RYGA

Frances Hyland as Rita Joe, Chief Dan George as her father, David Joe

Photographer: Diane Parry

George Ryga's *The Ecstasy of Rita Joe*: Hauntingly True and Healing

We begin our anthology with George Ryga's *The Ecstasy of Rita Joe* for a very good reason: it is one of Canada's pre-eminent plays. It is still performed—lately in Tokyo and in Vancouver— and has had numerous productions in Canada and abroad. It is widely read and studied, probably more so than any other Canadian play: now in its twenty-third printing, it remains Vancouver's Talonbooks' best selling publication; further, it remains in print with General Publishing of Ontario, which means it is selling well with two publishers – surely a feat in Canadian drama! Since its creation in Vancouver in the mid-sixties the play has continually provoked and unsettled.

One of the greatest moments in British Columbia theatre occurred at Vancouver's Playhouse Theatre on a Thursday evening, November 23, 1967, the opening night of *The Ecstasy of Rita Joe*. The actors, playing themselves, walked onstage "workmanlike and untheatrical" (stage directions) from all over the theatre, from side doors and auditorium aisles, while the house and stage work lights did not dim but stayed on. The stage was mostly bare, surrounded by a simple, circular ramp, while in the rear there were backdrops depicting mountains and a cityscape. Moments later, Frances Hyland, one of Canada's great actors, playing Rita Joe, spoke her simple, opening line: "The first time I tried to go home I was picked up by some men who gave me five dollars. An' then they arrested me."

Here was a stark, unconventional act of theatre, one that local critics struggled to understand: "It was not a smooth play. It was jerky and fragmented... I don't know if it is a great play. But if the role of the stage is to communicate, and I believe it is, Ryga and director George Bloomfield have accomplished their purpose." (Jack Richards, *Vancouver Sun*, November 24, 1967)

For Bloomfield, it was, by his own admission, "a terrifying night," for he and George Ryga had spent many a long evening in discussions and rewrites of this ever-changing work. For this director it was much more than just another production: he had himself conducted research into the plight of Native children in Ontario and saw the play as based in a raw social reality, as he stated in his program note: "*The Ecstasy of Rita Joe* intends to take a good close look at the white man's social order. Everything in this piece is documentary."

So much that was personal and political was riding on this one evening, with people from government, from Ottawa, from the CBC sitting in the audience, with the great Chief Dan George, a man who had spoken his politically charged *Lament For Confederation* at a Centennial Birthday Party at Empire Stadium in Vancouver, now sixty-eight years of age, playing Rita Joe's father. Bloomfield recalled how nervous he was, especially at the end of act one, when there was no applause, only silence, as people slowly began leaving their seats: "I had no idea of what we had at this point. Then they came back, and watched, and by the time the play was over, there was a thunder of applause." As for Ryga, who overnight became one of Canada's premier, pioneering playwrights, it was his first play.

When he was asked by the artistic director of Vancouver's Playhouse Theatre, Malcolm Black, to write a play, George Ryga was not yet a playwright. His dramatic writing had been in creating scripts for radio and television. He had written a major hit, the teleplay "Indian", for the CBC series "Quest," a script so potent in its social concern that the producer had the script printed, along with rehearsal photographs, in *Maclean's* magazine before the show was aired in late November 1962. When Canadians watched the teleplay that winter evening, they saw, most of them for the first time, a harsh vision of the prairie landscape characterized by close-up camera shots of rural debris – among which a nameless, homeless Native man was seen hammering in fence posts on a white man's farm. When a patronizing Indian agent comes by to check on him, the man rebels, uttering one of the most ringing cries of social injustice ever heard in Canadian drama:

> *I got nothing – nothing – no wallet, no money, no name. I got no past – no future – nothing, sementos! I nobody. I not even live in this world – I dead! You get it? – I dead! I never been anybody. I not just dead – I never live at all – Misha! Listen, damn you – listen! One brother kill another brother – why? Why? Why? – Why?*

The immediate occasion for writing *The Ecstasy of Rita Joe* was twofold: it was Canada's Centennial year, which meant there was funding available for creating plays with regional themes. Then, Malcolm Black commissioned a new work based on a newspaper item about a Native woman found dead in a skid row rooming house. Ryga's first impulse was political: he penned a two-page outline, titled *Twilight to A Long, Long Day*, about the "Odyssey through hell of an Indian woman," a hell shaped by her society's "confusion of right and wrong inherited from older civilizations and religions." Ryga's other impulse was lyrical – after all, his first major publication, in the mid-fifties, was his book of poetry, *Song of my Hands*. In his first draft of *Rita Joe* there was already guitar music, the white geese and dragonfly speeches, and a haunting background soundscape of urban voices, train whistles, and children playing.

The play is structured as a dream/nightmare; indeed, in the various drafts, Rita Joe is declared already dead. The play then functions as a series of pre-death flashbacks, with the event of her death a provocation in a complacent society – and a cue for the entrance of another Native girl named Rita Joe. In the final scene of the third draft, the lights come up on a noisy skid row party – where one of the men drinking is the Magistrate. The door opens and in walks another Native girl: thus the story of Rita Joe is an ongoing social tragedy, not unlike the situation in the last play in this anthology, *The Accidental and Unnatural Women*, where the man the *Vancouver Sun* called the "Demon Barber" lures Native women into deadly bouts of binge drinking.

George Ryga's roots are in society's marginalized people. He was born in 1932 into a farming family of Ukrainian immigrants in northern Alberta, never speaking English until he went to school at age seven. Life on his father's farm was bleak: George Ryga senior had homesteaded late, in 1927, long after the earlier waves of immigration had taken the more desirable lands. The Ryga homestead, located in an area of boulders, patchy wood scrub, and near-muskeg, was barely hospitable, and the growing season was short. It was a dispiriting environment, where the ethnic Ukrainians were regarded as inferior by the dominant Angliki; then, as world depression deepened in the 1930s, his father, never a very successful farmer, fell into what Ryga characterized as a "Black despair." He had not yet obtained his citizenship and lived in fear of deportation to Ukraine – where there was now a disastrous famine brought about by Stalin's harsh program of enforced collectivization. The grinding poverty of his father's farm, his mother's fear of being "forced to walk," deeply affected Ryga: "This became real for me: I have a fascination with roaming people."

But life in Deep Creek was also exotic, as he indicated in a sensual remembrance of his youth:

> *Before I went to school my vision was reduced to most of what I could touch, taste, smell. Rubber footwear mouldering in the sun, sour mud after the northern rain, the touch of newly turned earth, the acid-scent of poplar leaves and the steel coldness of winters whose presence was felt the greater part of each year. Bread baking and split wood, sweating horses, smoke and kerosene, clover and wild strawberries – the coarse touch of tamarack wood, cruel as the arguments of cursing men who were always on the edge of violence, for the poverty was incredible and patience an unpredictable pool of water over which a storm always threatened.*

For the youthful Ryga the Ukrainian spoken in his community was a flamboyant language, "there were no soft comments – everything was slightly exaggerated so that a man didn't shout, he thundered; the child didn't whimper, he screamed," made even more vivid by the added folkloric images of the Polish and Icelandic peoples who lived nearby: "things like scaring the hell out of each other with dark groves of trees – the forests were the homes of threatening things—like boars. The Icelanders had black bulls with dripping intestines raging through the forests." Stark, cataclysmic images like these and hyperbolic language reappear in Ryga's texts. In *The Ecstasy of Rita Joe*, for example, a simple berry-picking expedition turns into a cataclysmic event; when Rita Joe is in jail she hears women screaming about riding black horses into an inferno.

This use of language, along with Ryga's ear for the rhythms of aboriginal speech (helped immeasurably by the presence of Chief Dan George), amounts to a powerful assertion of what Ryga calls "a forgotten people" in his program notes. A major price paid by the colonized indigenous peoples of British Columbia is loss of language, and therefore of their culture, as the white settlers' social system installed English, and its attendant conceptions of "truth" and "reality," as the norm and silenced Aboriginal cultural practices as aberrant – as in the banning of the Potlatch in the 1880s. The language employed by Ryga, written more than thirty years ago, is still pertinent, as Native author Lee Maracle believes: *"The Ecstasy of Rita Joe* is a Canadian classic; it remains hauntingly true and tremendously healing for all of us, Canadian and first-nations people alike."

J.H.

Selected Bibliography:

- Conolly, L. W., ed. *Canadian Drama and the Critics*. Vancouver: Talonbooks, 1995. Contains reprints of reviews of both the playscript and many of its major productions.
- Gregory, David, ed. *The Athabasca Ryga*. Vancouver: Talonbooks, 1990.
- Hoffman, James. *The Ecstasy of Resistance: A Biography of George Ryga*. Toronto: ECW Press, 1995.
- Hoffman, James. "Biocritical Essay." The George Ryga Papers. Calgary: University of Calgary Press, 1995. Also available at: http://www.ucalgary.ca/library/SpecColl/ryga.htm.
- Innes, Christopher. *Politics and the Playwright: George Ryga*. Toronto: Simon & Pierre, 1985.
- Kujundzic, Ann, ed. *Summerland*. Vancouver: Talonbooks, 1992.
- Maracle, Lee. "A Question of Voice." *Vancouver Sun*, June 6, 1992.
- Rubin, Don and Alison Cranmer-Byng, eds. *Canada's Playwrights: A Biographical Guide*. Toronto: Canadian Theatre Review Publications, 1980.
- Ryga, George. *The Ecstasy of Rita Joe and Other Plays*. Don Mills, Ontario: General Publishing, 1971. This anthology also contains *Indian* and *Grass and Wild Strawberries*.
- Watson, David and Christopher Innes. "Political Mythologies. An interview with George Ryga." *Canadian Drama*, Vol. 8, No. 2, 1982.

The Ecstasy of Rita Joe
by George Ryga

The Ecstasy of Rita Joe was first staged by the Playhouse Theatre Company, on November 23, 1967, with the following cast:

Rita Joe	Frances Hyland
Her Father	Chief Dan George
The Magistrate	Henry Ramer
Jamie	August Schellenberg
Mr. Homer	Wally Marsh
The Priest	Robert Clothier
Eileen	Patricia Gage
An Old Woman	Rae Brown
The Teacher	Claudine Melgrave
The Musician	Willy Dunn
The Singer	Ann Mortifee
Additional Cast	Merv Campone, Bill Clarkson, Leonard George, Robert Hall, Frank Lewis, Paul Stanley, Ed Brooks, Jack Leaf, Jack Buttrey
Director	George Bloomfield
Set and Lighting Design	Charles Evans
Dances Staged by	Norbert Vesak
Costume Design	Margaret Ryan
Music Composed by	Willy Dunn, Ann Mortifee
Lyrics by	George Ryga

CHARACTERS

RITA JOE
JAIMIE PAUL
DAVID JOE: Rita's father
MAGISTRATE
MR. HOMER
FATHER ANDREW: a priest
EILEEN JOE: Rita's sister
OLD INDIAN WOMAN
MISS DONOHUE: a teacher
POLICEMAN
WITNESSES
MURDERERS
YOUNG INDIAN MEN
SINGER

SET

A circular ramp beginning at floor level stage left and continuing downward below floor level at stage front, then rising and sweeping along stage back at two-foot elevation to disappear in the wings of stage left. This ramp dominates the stage by wrapping the central and forward playing area. A short approach ramp, meeting with the main ramp at stage right, expedites entrances from the wings of stage right. The MAGISTRATE's chair and representation of court desk are situated at stage right, enclosed within the sweep of the ramp. At the foot of the desk is a lip on stage right side. The SINGER sits here, turned away from the focus of the play. Her songs and accompaniment appear almost accidental. She has all the reactions of a white liberal folklorist with a limited concern and understanding of an ethnic dilemma which she touches in the course of her research and work in compiling and writing folk songs. She serves too as an alter ego to RITA JOE.

No curtain is used during the play. At the opening, intermission and conclusion of the play, the curtain remains up. The onus for isolating scenes from the past and present in RITA JOE's life falls on highlight lighting.

Backstage, there is a mountain cyclorama. In front of the cyclorama there is a darker maze curtain to suggest gloom and confusion, and a cityscape.

ACT ONE

The house lights and stage work lights remain on. Backstage, cyclorama, and maze curtains are up, revealing wall back of stage, exit doors, etc.

CAST and SINGER enter offstage singly and in pairs from the wings, the exit doors at the back of the theatre, and from the auditorium side doors. The entrances are workmanlike and untheatrical. When all the CAST is on stage, they turn to face the audience momentarily. The house lights dim.

The cyclorama is lowered into place. The maze curtain follows. This creates a sense of compression of stage into the auditorium.

Recorded voices are heard in a jumble of mutterings and throat clearings. The MAGISTRATE enters as the CLERK begins.

CLERK: (*recorded*) This court is in session. All present will rise...

The shuffling and scraping of furniture is heard. The CAST repeat "Rita Joe, Rita Joe." A POLICEMAN brings on RITA JOE.

MAGISTRATE: Who is she? Can she speak English?

POLICEMAN: Yes.

MAGISTRATE: Then let her speak for herself!

He speaks to the audience firmly and with reason.

To understand life in a given society, one must understand laws of that society. All relationships...

CLERK: (*recorded*) Man to man... man to woman... man to property... man to the state...

MAGISTRATE: ...are determined and enriched by laws that have grown out of social realities. The quality of the law under which you live and function determines the real quality of the freedom that was yours today.

The rest of the CAST slowly move out.

Your home and your well-being were protected. The roads of the city are open to us. So are the galleries, libraries, the administrative and public buildings. There are buses, trains... going in and coming out. Nobody is a prisoner here.

RITA: (*with humour, almost a sad sigh*) The first time I tried to go home I was picked up by some men who gave me five dollars. An' then they arrested me.

The POLICEMAN retreats into the shadows. The SINGER crosses down.

MAGISTRATE: Thousands leave and enter the city every day...

RITA: It wasn't true what they said, but nobody'd believe me...

SINGER: (*singing a recitivo searching for a melody*)
Will the winds not blow
My words to her
Like the seeds
Of the dandelion?

MAGISTRATE: (*smiling, as at a private joke*) Once... I saw a little girl in the Cariboo country. It was summer then and she wore only a blouse and skirt. I wondered what she wore in winter?

The MURDERERS hover in the background on the upper ramp. One whistles and one lights a cigarette – an action which will be repeated at the end of the play.

RITA: (*moving to him, but hesitating*) You look like a good man. Tell them to let me go, please!

The MAGISTRATE goes to his podium.

MAGISTRATE: Our nation is on an economic par with the state of Arkansas.... We are a developing country, but a buoyant one. Still... the summer report of the Economic Council of Canada predicts a reduction in the gross national product unless we utilize our manpower for greater efficiency. Employed, happy people make for a prosperous, happy nation...

RITA: (*exultantly*) I worked at some jobs, mister!

The MAGISTRATE turns to face RITA JOE. The MURDERERS have gone.

MAGISTRATE: Gainful employment. Obedience to the law...

RITA: (*to the MAGISTRATE*) Once I had a job...

He does not relate to her. She is troubled. She talks to the audience.

Once I had a job in a tire store... an' I'd worry about what time my boss would come.... He was always late... and so was everybody. Sometimes I got to thinkin' what would happen if he'd not come. And nobody else would come. And I'd be all day in this big room with no lights on an' the telephone ringing an' people asking for other people that weren't there.... What would happen?

As she relates her concern, she laughs. Towards the end of her monologue she is so amused by the absurdity of it all that she can hardly contain herself.

Lights fade on the MAGISTRATE who broods in his chair as he examines his court papers.

Lights up on JAIMIE PAUL approaching on the backstage ramp from stage left. He is jubilant, his laughter blending with her laughter. At the sound of his voice, RITA JOE runs to him, to the memory of him.

JAIMIE: I seen the city today and I seen things today I never knew was there, Rita Joe!

RITA: (*happily*) I seen them too, Jaimie Paul!

He pauses above her, his mood light and childlike.

JAIMIE: I see a guy on top of a bridge, talkin' to himself... an' lots of people on the beach watchin' harbour seals.... Kids feed popcorn to seagulls... an' I think to myself.... Boy! Pigeons eat pretty good here!

RITA: In the morning, Jaimie Paul... very early in the morning... the air is cold like at home...

JAIMIE: Pretty soon I seen a little woman walkin' a big black dog on a rope.... Dog is mad.... Dog wants a man!

JAIMIE PAUL moves to RITA JOE. They embrace.

RITA: Clouds are red over the city in the morning. Clara Hill says to me if you're real happy... the clouds make you forget you're not home...

They laugh together. JAIMIE PAUL breaks from her. He punctuates his story with wide, sweeping gestures.

JAIMIE: I start singin' and some hotel windows open. I wave to them, but nobody waves back! They're watchin' me, like I was a harbour seal! (*He laughs.*) So I stopped singin'!

RITA: I remember colours, but I've forgot faces already...

JAIMIE PAUL looks at her as her mood changes. Faint light on the MAGISTRATE brightens.

A train whistle is white, with black lines.... A sick man talkin' is brown like an overcoat with pockets torn an' string showin'.... A sad woman is a room with the curtains shut...

MAGISTRATE: Rita Joe?

She becomes sobered, but JAIMIE PAUL continues laughing. She nods to the MAGISTRATE, then turns to JAIMIE PAUL.

RITA: Them bastards put me in jail. They're gonna do it again, they said.... Them bastards!

JAIMIE: Guys who sell newspapers don't see nothin'...

RITA: They drive by me, lookin'...

JAIMIE: I'm gonna be a carpenter!

RITA: I walk like a stick, tryin' to keep my ass from showin' because I know what they're thinkin'.... Them bastards!

JAIMIE: I got myself boots an' a new shirt.... See!

RITA: (*worried now*) I thought their jail was on fire... I thought it was burning.

JAIMIE: Room I got costs me seven bucks a week...

RITA: I can't leave town. Every time I try, they put me in jail.

A POLICEMAN enters with a file folder.

JAIMIE: They say it's a pretty good room for seven bucks a week...

JAIMIE PAUL begins to retreat backwards from her, along the ramp to the wings of stage left. She is isolated in a pool of light away from the MAGISTRATE. The light isolation between her and JAIMIE PAUL deepens, as the scene turns into the courtroom again.

MAGISTRATE: Vagrancy.... You are charged with vagrancy.

JAIMIE: (*with enthusiasm, boyishly*) First hundred bucks I make, Rita Joe... I'm gonna buy a car so I can take you every place!

RITA: (*moving after him*) Jaimie!

He retreats, dreamlike, into the wings. The spell of memory between them is broken. Pools of light between her and the MAGISTRATE spread and fuse into a single light area. She turns to the MAGISTRATE, worried and confused.

MAGISTRATE: (*reading the documents in his hand*) The charge against you this morning is vagrancy...

The MAGISTRATE continues studying the papers he holds. She looks up at him and shakes her head helplessly, then blurts out to him.

RITA: I had to spend last night in jail.... Did you know?

MAGISTRATE: Yes. You were arrested.

RITA: I didn't know when morning came... there was no windows.... The jail stinks! People in jail stink!

MAGISTRATE: (*indulgently*) Are you surprised?

RITA: I didn't know anybody there.... People in jail stink like paper that's been in the rain too long. But a jail stinks worse. It stinks of rust... an' old hair...

The MAGISTRATE looks down at her for the first time.

MAGISTRATE: You... are Rita Joe?

She nods quickly. A faint concern shows in his face. He watches her for a long moment.

I know your face... yet... it wasn't in this courtroom. Or was it?

RITA: I don't know...

MAGISTRATE: (*pondering*) Have you appeared before me in the past year?

RITA: (*turning away from him, shrugging*) I don't know. I can't remember...

The MAGISTRATE throws his head back and laughs. The POLICEMAN joins in.

MAGISTRATE: You can't remember? Come now...

RITA: (*laughing with him and looking to the POLICEMAN*) I can't remember...

MAGISTRATE: Then I take it you haven't appeared before me. Certainly you and I would remember if you had.

RITA: (*smiling*) I don't remember...

The MAGISTRATE makes some hurried notes, but he is watching RITA JOE, formulating his next thought.

(*naively*) My sister hitchhiked home an' she had no trouble like I...

MAGISTRATE: You'll need witnesses, Rita Joe. I'm only giving you eight hours to find witnesses for yourself...

RITA: Jaimie knows...

She turns to where JAIMIE PAUL had been, but the back of the stage is in darkness. The POLICEMAN exits suddenly.

Jaimie knew...

Her voice trails off pathetically. The MAGISTRATE shrugs and returns to studying his notes. RITA JOE chafes during the silence which follows. She craves communion with people, with the MAGISTRATE.

My sister was a dressmaker, mister! But she only worked two weeks in the city.... An' then she got sick and went back to the reserve to help my father catch fish an' cut pulpwood. (*smiling*) She's not coming back... that's for sure!

MAGISTRATE: (*with interest*) Should I know your sister? What was her name?

RITA: Eileen Joe.

EILEEN JOE appears spotlit behind, a memory crowding in.

MAGISTRATE: Eileen... that's a soft, undulating name.

RITA: Two weeks, and not one white woman came to her to leave an order or old clothes for her to fix. No work at all for two weeks, an' her money ran out.... Isn't that funny?

The MAGISTRATE again studies RITA JOE, his mind elsewhere.

MAGISTRATE: Hmmmmm...

EILEEN JOE disappears.

RITA: So she went back to the reserve to catch fish an' cut pulpwood!

MAGISTRATE: I do know your face... yes! And yet...

RITA: Can I sit someplace?

MAGISTRATE: (*excited*) I remember now.... Yes! I was on holidays three summers back in the Cariboo country... driving over this road with not a house or field in sight... just barren land, wild and wind-blown. And then I saw this child beside the road, dressed in a blouse and skirt, barefooted...

RITA: (*looking around*) I don't feel so good, mister.

MAGISTRATE: My God, she wasn't more than three or four years old... walking towards me beside the road. When I'd passed her, I stopped my car and then turned around and drove back to where I'd seen her, for I wondered what she could possibly be doing in such a lonely country at that age without her father or mother walking with her.... Yet when I got back to where I'd seen her, she had disappeared. She was nowhere to be seen. Yet the land was flat for over a mile in every direction... I had to see her. But I couldn't...

He stares down at RITA JOE for a long moment.

You see, what I was going to say was that this child had your face! Isn't that strange?

RITA: (*with disinterest*) Sure, if you think so, mister...

MAGISTRATE: Could she have been... your daughter?

RITA: What difference does it make?

MAGISTRATE: Children cannot be left like that.... It takes money to raise children in the woods as in the cities.... There are institutions and people with more money than you who could...

RITA: Nobody would get my child, mister!

She is distracted by EILEEN JOE's voice in her memory. EILEEN's voice begins in darkness, but as she speaks, a spotlight isolates her in front of the ramp, stage left. EILEEN is on her hands and knees, two buckets beside her. She is picking berries in mime.

EILEEN: First was the strawberries an' then the blueberries. After the frost... we picked the cranberries...

She laughs with delight.

RITA: (*pleading with the MAGISTRATE, but her attention on EILEEN*) Let me go, mister...

MAGISTRATE: I can't let you go. I don't think that would be of any use in the circumstances. Would you like a lawyer?

Even as he speaks, RITA JOE has entered the scene with EILEEN picking berries. The MAGISTRATE's light fades on his podium.

RITA: You ate the strawberries an' blueberries because you were always a hungry kid!

EILEEN: But not cranberries! They made my stomach hurt.

RITA JOE goes down on her knees with EILEEN.

RITA: Let me pick.... You rest. (*holding out the bucket to EILEEN*) Mine's full already.... Let's change. You rest...

During the exchange of buckets, EILEEN notices her hands are larger than RITA JOE's. She is both delighted and surprised by this.

EILEEN: My hands are bigger than yours, Rita.... Look! (*taking RITA JOE's hands in hers*) When did my hands grow so big?

RITA: (*wisely and sadly*) You've worked so hard... I'm older than you, Leenie... I will always be older.

The two sisters are thoughtful for a moment, each watching the other in silence. Then RITA JOE becomes animated and resumes her mime of picking berries in the woods.

We picked lots of wild berries when we were kids, Leenie!

They turn away from their work and lie down alongside each other, facing the front of the stage. The light on them becomes summery, warm.

In the summer, it was hot an' flies hummed so loud you'd go to sleep if you sat down an' just listened.

EILEEN: The leaves on the poplars used to turn black an' curl together with the heat...

RITA: One day you and I were pickin' blueberries and a big storm came...

A sudden crash of thunder and a lightning flash. The lights turn cold and blue. The three MURDERERS stand in silhouette on a riser behind them. EILEEN cringes in fear, afraid of the storm, aware of the presence of the MURDERERS behind them. RITA JOE springs to her feet, her being attached to the wildness of the atmosphere. Lightning continues to flash and flicker.

EILEEN: Oh, no!

RITA: (*shouting*) It got cold and the rain an' hail came... the sky falling!

EILEEN: (*crying in fear*) Rita!

RITA: (*laughing, shouting*) Stay there!

A high flash of lightning, silhouetting the MURDERERS harshly. They take a step forward on the lightning flash. EILEEN dashes into the arms of RITA JOE. She screams and drags RITA JOE down with her. RITA JOE struggles against EILEEN.

RITA: Let me go! What in hell's wrong with you? Let me go!

MAGISTRATE: I can't let you go.

The lightning dies, but the thunder rumbles off into the distance. EILEEN subsides, and pressing herself into the arms of RITA JOE as a small child to her mother, she sobs quietly.

RITA: There, there... (*with infinite tenderness*) You said to me, "What would happen if the storm hurt us an' we can't find our way home, but are lost together so far away in the bush?"

EILEEN looks up, brushing away her tears and smiling at RITA JOE.

RITA & EILEEN: (*in unison*) Would you be my mother then?

RITA: Would I be your mother?

RITA JOE releases EILEEN who looks back fearfully to where the MURDERERS had stood. They are gone. She rises and, collecting the buckets, moves hesitantly to where they had been. Confident now, she laughs softly and nervously to herself and leaves the stage, RITA JOE rises and talks to EILEEN as she departs.

We walked home through the mud an' icy puddles among the trees. At first you cried, Leenie... and then you wanted to sleep. But I held you up an' when we got home you said you were sure you would've died in the bush if it hadn't been for us being together like that.

EILEEN disappears from the stage. The MAGISTRATE's light comes up. RITA JOE shakes her head sadly at the memory, then comes forward to the apron of the stage. She is proud of her sister and her next speech reveals this pride.

She made a blouse for me that I wore every day for one year, an' it never ripped at the armpits like the blouse I buy in the store does the first time I stretch. (*She stretches languidly.*) I like to stretch when I'm happy! It makes all the happiness go through me like warm water...

The PRIEST, the TEACHER, and a YOUNG INDIAN MAN cross the stage directly behind her. The PRIEST wears a Roman collar and a checked bush-jacket of a worker-priest. He pauses before passing RITA JOE and goes to meet her.

PRIEST: Rita Joe? When did you get back? How's life?

RITA JOE shrugs noncommittally.

RITA: You know me, Father Andrew... could be better, could be worse...

PRIEST: Are you still working?

RITA JOE is still noncommittal. She smiles at him. Her gestures are not definite.

RITA: I live.

PRIEST: (*serious and concerned*) It's not easy, is it?

RITA: Not always.

The TEACHER and the YOUNG INDIAN MAN exit.

PRIEST: A lot of things are different in the city. It's easier here on the reserve... life is simpler. You can be yourself. That's important to remember.

RITA: Yes, Father...

The PRIEST wants to ask and say more, but he cannot. An awkward moment between them and he reaches out to touch her shoulder gently.

PRIEST: Well... be a good girl, Rita Joe...

RITA: (*without turning after him*) Goodbye, Father.

MAGISTRATE: (*more insistently*) Do you want a lawyer?

The PRIEST leaves stage right. As he leaves, cross light to where a happy JAIMIE PAUL enters from stage left. JAIMIE PAUL comes down to join RITA JOE.

JAIMIE: This guy asked me how much education I got, an' I says to him, "Grade six. How much education a man need for such a job?" ...An' the bum, he says it's not good enough! I should take night school. But I got the job, an' I start next Friday... like this...

JAIMIE PAUL does a mock sweeping routine as if he was cleaning a vast office building. He and RITA JOE are both laughing.

Pretty good, eh?

RITA: Pretty good.

JAIMIE: Cleaning the floors an' desks in the building.... But it's a government job, and that's good for life. Work hard, then the government give me a raise... I never had a job like that before...

RITA: When I sleep happy, I dream of blueberries an' sun an' all the nice things when I was a little kid, Jaimie Paul.

The sound of an airplane is heard. JAIMIE PAUL looks up. RITA JOE also stares into the sky of her memory. JAIMIE PAUL's face is touched with pain and recollection. The TEACHER, RITA JOE's FATHER, an OLD WOMAN, four YOUNG INDIAN MEN and EILEEN JOE come into the background quietly, as if at a wharf watching the airplane leave the village. They stand looking up until the noise of the aircraft begins to diminish.

JAIMIE: That airplane... a Cessna...

He continues watching the aircraft and turns, following its flight path.

She said to me, maybe I never see you again, Jaimie Paul.

There is a faint light on the MAGISTRATE in his chair. He is thoughtful, looking down at his hands.

MAGISTRATE: Do you want a lawyer?

RITA: (*to JAIMIE PAUL*) Who?

JAIMIE: Your mother... I said to her, they'll fix you up good in the hospital. Better than before.... It was a Cessna that landed on the river an' took her away.... Maybe I never see you again, Jaimie, she says to me. She knew she was gonna die, but I was a kid and so were you.... What the hell did we know? I'll never forget...

JAIMIE PAUL joins the village group on the upper level.

SINGER: (*singing an indefinite melody developing into a square-dance tune*)
There was a man in a beat-up hat
Who runs a house in the middle of town,
An' round his stove-pipe chimney house
The magpies sat, just a-lookin' round.

The Indian village people remain in the back of the stage, still watching the airplane which has vanished. JAIMIE PAUL, on his way, passes MR. HOMER, a white citizen who has the hurried but fulfilled appearance of the socially responsible man. MR. HOMER comes to the front of the stage beside RITA JOE. He talks directly to the audience.

MR. HOMER: Sure, we do a lot of things for our Indians here in the city at the Centre.... Bring 'em in from the cold an' give them food.... The rest... well, the rest kinda take care of itself.

RITA JOE lowers her head and looks away from him. MR. HOMER moves to her and places his hand on her shoulders possessively.

When your mother got sick we flew her out.... You remember that, Rita Joe?

RITA: (*nodding, looking down*) Yes, Mr. Homer.... Thank you.

MR. HOMER: And we sent her body back for the funeral.... Right, Rita Joe?

The people of the village leave except for the YOUNG INDIAN MEN who remain and mime drinking.

And then sometimes a man drinks it up an' leaves his wife an' kids and the poor dears come here for help. We give them food an' a place to sleep.... Right, Rita?

RITA: Yes.

MR. HOMER: Clothes too.... White people leave clothes here for the Indians to take if they need 'em. Used to have them all up on racks over there...just like in a store... (*pointing*) But now we got them all on a heap on a table in the basement.

He laughs and RITA JOE nods with him.

Indian people... 'specially the women... get more of a kick diggin' through stuff that's piled up like that...

MR. HOMER chuckles and shakes his head. There is a pale light on the MAGISTRATE, who is still looking down at his hands.

MAGISTRATE: There are institutions to help you...

MR. HOMER again speaks to the audience, but now he is angry over some personal beef.

MR. HOMER: So you see, the Centre serves a need that's real for Indians who come to the city. (*wagging his finger at the audience angrily*) It's the do-gooders burn my ass, you know! They come in from television or the newspaper... hang around just long enough to see a drunken Indian... an' bingo!

JAIMIE: Bingo!

MR. HOMER: That's their story! Next thing, they're seeing some kind of Red Power...

The YOUNG INDIAN MEN laugh and RITA JOE gets up to join them.

...or beatin' the government over the head! Let them live an' work among the Indians for a few months... then they'd know what it's really like...

The music comes up sharply.

SINGER:
Round and round the cenotaph,
The clumsy seagulls play.
Fed by funny men with hats
Who watch them night and day.

The four YOUNG INDIAN MEN join with RITA JOE and dance. Leading the group is JAIMIE PAUL. He is drunk, dishevelled. Light spreads before them as they advance onstage. They are laughing rowdily. RITA JOE moves to them.

RITA: Jaimie Paul?

MR. HOMER leaves. JAIMIE PAUL is overtaken by two of his companions who take him by the arms, but he pushes them roughly away.

JAIMIE: Get the hell outa my way!... I'm as good a man as him any time...

JAIMIE PAUL crosses downstage to confront a member of the audience.

You know me?... You think I'm a dirty Indian, eh? Get outa my way!

He puts his hands over his head and continues staggering away.

Goddamnit, I wanna sleep...

The YOUNG INDIAN MEN and JAIMIE PAUL exit. RITA JOE follows after JAIMIE PAUL, reaching out to touch him, but the SINGER stands in her way and drives her back, singing...

Music up tempo and volume.

SINGER:
Oh, can't you see that train roll on,
Its hot black wheels keep comin' on?
A Kamloops Indian died today.
Train didn't hit him, he just fell.
Busy train with wheels on fire!

The music dies. A POLICEMAN enters.

POLICEMAN: Rita Joe!

He repeats her name many times. The TEACHER enters ringing the school handbell and crosses through.

TEACHER: (*calling*) Rita Joe! Rita Joe! Didn't you hear the bell ring? The class is waiting.... The class is always waiting for you.

The TEACHER exits.

MAGISTRATE & POLICEMAN: (*sharply, in unison*) Rita Joe!

The POLICEMAN grabs and shakes RITA JOE to snap her out of her reverie.

Light up on the MAGISTRATE who sits erect, with authority.

MAGISTRATE: I ask you for the last, time, Rita Joe.... Do you want a lawyer?

RITA: (*defiantly*) What for?... I can take care of myself.

MAGISTRATE: The charge against you this morning is prostitution. Why did you not return to your people as you said you would?

The light on the backstage dies. RITA JOE stands before the MAGISTRATE and the POLICEMAN. She is contained in a pool of light before them.

RITA: (*nervous, with despair*) I tried... I tried...

The MAGISTRATE settles back into his chair and takes a folder from his desk, which he opens and studies.

MAGISTRATE: Special Constable Eric Wilson has submitted a statement to the effect that on June 18th he and Special Constable Schneider approached you on Fourth Avenue at nine-forty in the evening...

POLICEMAN: We were impersonating two deckhands newly arrived in the city...

MAGISTRATE: You were arrested an hour later on charges of prostitution.

The MAGISTRATE holds the folder threateningly and looks down at her. RITA JOE is defiant.

RITA: That's a goddamned lie!

MAGISTRATE: (*sternly, gesturing to the POLICEMAN*) This is a police statement. Surely you don't think a mistake was made?

RITA: (*peering into the light above her, shuddering*) Everything in this room is like ice.... How can you stay alive working here?... I'm so hungry I want to throw up...

MAGISTRATE: You have heard the statement, Rita Joe.... Do you deny it?

RITA: I was going home, trying to find the highway... I knew those two were cops, the moment I saw them... I told them to go f... fly a kite! They got sore then an' started pushing me around...

MAGISTRATE: (*patiently now, waving down the objections of the POLICEMAN*) Go on.

RITA: They followed me around until a third cop drove up. An' then they arrested me.

MAGISTRATE: Arrested you.... Nothing else?

RITA: They stuffed five dollar bills in my pockets when they had me in the car... I ask you, mister, when are they gonna charge cops like that with contributing to...

POLICEMAN: Your Worship...

MAGISTRATE: (*irritably, indicating the folder on the table before him*) Now it's your word against this! You need references... people who know you... who will come to court to substantiate what you say... today! That is the process of legal argument!

RITA: Can I bum a cigarette someplace?

MAGISTRATE: No. You can't smoke in court.

The POLICEMAN smiles and exits.

RITA: Then give me a bed to sleep on, or is the sun gonna rise an' rise until it burns a hole in my head?

Guitar music cues softly in the background.

MAGISTRATE: Tell me about the child.

RITA: What child?

MAGISTRATE: The little girl I once saw beside the road!

RITA: I don't know any girl, mister! When do I eat? Why does an Indian wait even when he's there first thing in the morning?

The pool of light tightens around the MAGISTRATE and RITA JOE.

MAGISTRATE: I have children... two sons...

RITA: (*nodding*) Sure. That's good.

The MAGISTRATE gropes for words to express a message that is very precious to him.

MAGISTRATE: My sons can go in any direction they wish... into trades or university.... But if I had a daughter, I would be more concerned...

RITA: What's so special about a girl?

MAGISTRATE: I would wish... well, I'd be concerned about her choices... her choices of living, school... friends.... These things don't come as lightly for a girl. For boys it's different.... But I would worry if I had a daughter.... Don't hide your child! Someone else can be found to raise her if you can't!

RITA JOE shakes her head, a strange smile on her face.

MAGISTRATE: Why not? There are people who would love to take care of it.

RITA: Nobody would get my child... I would sooner kill it an' bury it first! I am not a kind woman, mister judge!

MAGISTRATE: (*at a loss*) I see...

RITA: (*a cry*) I want to go home...

Quick up-tempo music is heard. Suddenly, the lights change.

JAIMIE PAUL and the YOUNG INDIAN MEN sweep over the backstage ramp, the light widening for them. RITA JOE moves into this railway station crowd. She turns from one man to another until she sees JAIMIE PAUL.

EILEEN JOE and an OLD WOMAN enter.

RITA: Jaimie!

EILEEN: (*happily, running to him*) Jaimie Paul! God's sakes.... When did you get back from the north?.... I thought you said you wasn't coming until breakup...

JAIMIE: (*turning to EILEEN*) I was comin' home on the train... had a bit to drink and was feeling pretty good.... Lots of women sleeping in their seats on the train... I'd lift their hats an' say, "Excuse me, lady... I'm lookin' for a wife!" (*turning to the OLD WOMAN*) One fat lady got mad, an' I says to her, "That's alright, lady.... You got no worries.... You keep sleepin'!"

Laughter.

JAIMIE PAUL and the OLD WOMAN move away. EILEEN sees RITA JOE who is standing watching.

EILEEN: Rita!... Tom an' I broke up... did I tell you?

RITA: No, Leenie... you didn't tell me!

EILEEN: He was no good.... He stopped comin' to see me when he said he would. I kept waiting, but he didn't come...

RITA: I sent you a pillow for your wedding!

EILEEN: I gave it away... I gave it to Clara Hill.

RITA: (*laughing bawdily and miming pregnancy*) Clara Hill don't need no pillow now!

JAIMIE: (*smiling, crossing to her and exiting*) I always came to see you, Rita Joe...

RITA JOE looks bewildered.

OLD WOMAN: (*exiting*) I made two Saskatoon pies, Rita.... You said next time you came home you wanted Saskatoon pie with lots of sugar...

EILEEN and the OLD WOMAN drift away. JAIMIE PAUL moves on to the shadows. The THREE MURDERERS enter in silhouette; one whistles. RITA JOE rushes to the YOUNG INDIAN MEN downstage.

RITA: This is me, Rita Joe, God's sakes.... We went to the same school together.... Don't you know me now, Johnny? You remember how tough you was when you was a boy?... We tied you up in the Rainbow Creek and forgot you was there after recess.... An' after school was out, somebody remembered. (*laughing*) And you was blue when we got to you. Your clothes was wet to the chin, an' you said, "That's a pretty good knot... I almost gave up trying to untie it!"

The music continues. RITA JOE steps among the YOUNG INDIAN MEN and they mime being piled in a car at a drive-in.

Steve Laporte?... You remember us goin' to the drive-in and the cold rain comin' down the car windows so we couldn't see the picture show anyhow?

She sits beside STEVE LAPORTE. They mime the windshield wipers.

A cold white light comes up on the playing area directly in front of the MAGISTRATE's chair. A MALE WITNESS of dishevelled, dirty appearance steps into the light and delivers testimony in a whining, defensive voice. He is one of the MURDERERS, but apart from the other three, he is nervous.

FIRST WITNESS: I gave her three bucks... an' once I got her goin' she started yellin' like hell! Called me a dog, pig... some filthy kind of animal.... So I slapped her around a bit.... Guys said she was a funny kind of bim... would do it for them standing up, but not for me she wouldn't.... So I slapped her around...

The MAGISTRATE nods and makes a notation. The light on the FIRST WITNESS dies. RITA JOE speaks with urgency and growing fear to STEVE LAPORTE.

RITA: Then you shut the wipers off an' we were just sitting there, not knowing what to do... I wish... we could go back again there an' start livin' from that day on... Jaimie!

RITA JOE looks at STEVE LAPORTE as at a stranger. She stands and draws away from him. JAIMIE PAUL enters behind RITA JOE.

There is a cold light before the MAGISTRATE again and another MALE WITNESS moves into the light, replacing the FIRST WITNESS. He too is one of the MURDERERS. This SECOND WITNESS testifies with full gusto.

SECOND WITNESS: Gave her a job in my tire store... took her over to my place after work once.... She was scared when I tried a trick, but I'm easy on broads that get scared, providin' they keep their voices down.... After that, I slipped her a fiver.... Well, sir, she took the money, then she stood in front of the window, her head high an' her naked shoulders shakin' like she was cold. Well, sir, she cried a little an' then she says, "Goddamnit, but I wish I was a school teacher..."

He laughs and everyone onstage joins in the laughter. The light dies out on the SECOND WITNESS. JAIMIE PAUL enters and crosses to RITA JOE. They lie down and embrace.

RITA: You always came to see me, Jaimie Paul.... The night we were in the cemetery... you remember, Jaimie Paul? I turned my face from yours until I saw the ground... an' I knew that below us... they were like us once, and now they lie below the ground, their eyes gone, the bones showin'.... They must've spoke and touched each other here... like you're touching me, Jaimie Paul... an' now there was nothing over them, except us... an' wind in the grass an' a barbwire fence creaking. An' behind that, a hundred acres of barley.

JAIMIE PAUL stands.

That's something to remember, when you're lovin', eh?

The sound of a train whistle is heard. JAIMIE PAUL goes and the lights onstage fade.

The music comes up and the SINGER sings. As JAIMIE PAUL passes her, the SINGER pursues him up the ramp, and RITA JOE runs after them.

SINGER:
Oh, can't you see that train roll on,
Gonna kill a man, before it's gone?
Jaimie Paul fell and died.
He had it comin', so it's alright.
Silver train with wheels on fire!

The music dies instantly. RITA JOE's words come on the heels of the music as a bitter extension of the song.

She stands before the MAGISTRATE, again in the court, but looks back to where JAIMIE PAUL had been in the gloom. The POLICEMAN enters where JAIMIE PAUL has exited, replacing him, for the fourth trial scene.

RITA: Jaimie, why am I here?... Is it... because people are talkin' about me and all them men.... Is that why? I never wanted to cut cordwood for a living... (*with great bitterness*) Never once I thought... it'd be like this...

MAGISTRATE: What are we going to do about you, Rita Joe? This is the seventh charge against you in one year.... Laws are not made to be violated in this way.... Why did you steal?

RITA: I was hungry. I had no money.

MAGISTRATE: Yet you must have known you would be caught?

RITA: Yes.

MAGISTRATE: Are you not afraid of what is happening to you?

RITA: I am afraid of a lot of things. Put me in jail. I don't care...

MAGISTRATE: (*with forced authority*) Law is a procedure. The procedure must be respected. It took hundreds of years to develop this process of law.

RITA: I stole a sweater.... They caught me in five minutes!

She smiles whimsically at this. The MAGISTRATE is leafing through the documents before him. The POLICEMAN stands to one side of him.

MAGISTRATE: The prosecutor's office has submitted some of the past history of Rita Joe...

POLICEMAN: She was born and raised on a reservation. Then came a brief period in a public school off the reservation... at which time Rita Joe established herself as something of a disruptive influence...

RITA: What's that mean?

MAGISTRATE: (*turning to her, smiling*) A trouble maker!

RITA JOE becomes animated, aware of the trap around her closing even at moments such as this.

RITA: Maybe it was about the horse, huh?

She looks up at the MAGISTRATE who is still smiling, offering her no help.

There was this accident with a horse.... It happened like this... I was riding a horse to school an' some of the boys shot a rifle an' my horse bucked an' I fell off. I fell in the bush an' got scratched.... The boys caught the horse by the school and tried to ride him, but the horse bucked an' pinned a boy against a tree, breaking his leg in two places...

She indicates the place the leg got broken.

They said... an' he said I'd rode the horse over him on purpose!

MAGISTRATE: Well... did you?

RITA: It wasn't that way at all, I tell you! They lied!

The POLICEMAN and the SINGER laugh.

MAGISTRATE: Why should they lie, and Rita Joe alone tell the truth?... Or are you a child enough to believe the civilization of which we are a part...

He indicates the audience as inclusive of civilization from his point of view.

...does not understand Rita Joe?

RITA: I don't know what you're saying.

MAGISTRATE: (*with a touch of compassion*) Look at you, woman! Each time you come before me you are older. The lines in your face are those of...

RITA: I'm tired an' I want to eat mister! I haven't had grub since day before yesterday.... This room is like a boat on water... I'm so dizzy.... What the hell kind of place is this won't let me go lie down on grass?

She doubles over to choke back her nausea.

MAGISTRATE: This is not the reservation, Rita Joe. This is another place, another time...

RITA: (*straining to remember, to herself*) I was once in Whitecourt, Alberta. The cops are fatter there than here. I had to get out of Whitecourt, Alberta...

MAGISTRATE: Don't blame the police, Rita Joe! The obstacles to your life are here... (*He touches his forefinger to his temples.*) ...in your thoughts... possibly even in your culture...

RITA JOE turns away from him, searching the darkness behind her.

What's the matter?

RITA: I want to go home!

MAGISTRATE: But you can't go now. You've broken a law for which you will have to pay a fine or go to prison...

RITA: I have no money.

MAGISTRATE: (*with exasperation*) Rita Joe.... It is against the law to solicit men on the street. You have to wash...

RITA JOE begins to move away from him, crossing the front of the stage along the apron, her walk cocky. The light spreads and follows her.

You can't walk around in old clothes and running shoes made of canvas.... You have to have some money in your pockets and an address where you live. You should fix your hair... perhaps even change your name. And try to tame that accent that sounds like you have a mouthful of sawdust.... There is no peace in being extraordinary!

The light dies on the MAGISTRATE and the POLICEMAN.

RITA JOE is transported into another memory. JAIMIE PAUL enters and slides along the floor, left of centre stage. He is drunk, counting the fingers on his outstretched hands. MR. HOMER has entered with a wagon carrying hot soup and mugs. Four YOUNG INDIAN MEN come in out of the cold. MR. HOMER speaks to the audience in a matter-of-fact informative way.

MR. HOMER: (*dispensing soup to the YOUNG INDIAN MEN*) The do-gooders make something special of the Indian.... There's nothing special here.... At the Centre here the quick cure is a bowl of stew under the belt and a good night's sleep.

JAIMIE: Hey, Mister Homer! How come I got so many fingers? Heh?

He laughs. MR. HOMER ignores JAIMIE PAUL and continues talking to the audience.

MR. HOMER: I wouldn't say they were brothers or sisters to me... no sir! But if you're...

JAIMIE PAUL gets up and embraces RITA JOE.

JAIMIE: I got two hands an' one neck... I can kill more than I can eat.... If I had more fingers I would need mittens big as pie plates.... Yeh?

MR. HOMER: (*to JAIMIE PAUL*) Lie down, Jaimie Paul, an' have some more sleep. When you feel better, I'll get you some soup.

RITA JOE laughs. JAIMIE PAUL weaves his way uncertainly to where MR. HOMER stands.

JAIMIE: (*laughing*) I spit in your soup! You know what I say?... I say I spit in your soup, Mister Homer...

He comes to MR. HOMER and seems about to do just what he threatens.

MR. HOMER: (*pushing him away with good humour*) I'll spit in your eyeball if you don't shut up!

JAIMIE: (*breaking away from MR. HOMER, taunting*) You... are not Mister Homer!

MR. HOMER: I'm not what?

JAIMIE: You're not Mister Homer.... You're somebody wearing his pants an' shirt... (*stumbling away*) But you're not Mister Homer... Mister Homer never gets mad.... No sir, not Mister Homer!

MR. HOMER: I'm not mad.... What're you talkin' about?

JAIMIE PAUL turns and approaches the YOUNG INDIAN MEN. He threatens to fall off the apron of the stage.

JAIMIE: No... not Mister Homer! An' I got ten fingers.... How's that?

MR. HOMER: For Chris' sake, Jaimie... go to sleep.

JAIMIE PAUL stops and scowls, then grins knowingly. He begins to mime a clumsy paddler paddling a boat.

JAIMIE: (*laughing again*) I know you.... Hey? I know you!... I seen you up Rainbow Creek one time... I seen you paddling!

He breaks up with laughter.

MR. HOMER: (*amused, tolerant*) Oh, come on... I've never been to Rainbow Creek.

JAIMIE: (*controlling his laughter*) Sure you been to Rainbow Creek... (*He begins to mime paddling again.*) Next time you need a good paddler, you see me. I have a governmen' job, but screw that. I'm gonna paddle! I seen you paddle...

Again he breaks up in laughter as he once more demonstrates the quality of paddling he once saw.

RITA JOE is fully enjoying the spectacle. So are the YOUNG INDIAN MEN. MR. HOMER is also amused by the absurdity of the situation. JAIMIE PAUL turns, but chokes up with laughter after saying...

I have seen some paddlers... but you!

JAIMIE PAUL turns and waves his hand derisively, laughing.

MR. HOMER: It must've been somebody else... I've never been to Rainbow Creek.

JAIMIE: Like hell, you say!

JAIMIE PAUL paddles the soup wagon out. Guitar music comes in with an upbeat tempo. RITA JOE and the YOUNG INDIAN MEN dance to the beat. The YOUNG INDIAN MEN then drift after MR. HOMER.

The light fades slowly on centre stage and the music changes.

RITA JOE, happy in her memory, does a circling butch walk in the fading light to the song of the SINGER. At the conclusion of the song, she is on the apron, stage right, in a wash of light that includes the MAGISTRATE and the SINGER.

SINGER:
I woke up at six o'clock
Stumbled out of bed,
Crash of cans an' diesel trucks
Damned near killed me dead.
Sleepless hours, heavy nights,
Dream your dreams so pretty.
God was gonna have a laugh
An' gave me a job in the city!

RITA JOE is still elated at her memory of JAIMIE PAUL and his story. With unusual candour, she turns girlishly before the MAGISTRATE, and in mild imitation of her own moment of drunkenness, begins telling him a story.

Faint guitar music in the background continues.

RITA: One night I drank a little bit of wine, an' I was outside lookin' at the stars... thinking... when I was a little girl how much bigger the trees were... no clouds, but suddenly there was a light that made the whole sky look like day...

Guitar out.

...just for a moment... an' before I got used to the night... I saw animals, moving across the sky... two white horses.... A man was takin' them by the halters, and I knew the man was my grandfather...

She stares at the MAGISTRATE, unsure of herself now.

MAGISTRATE: Yes! Is that all?

RITA: No.... But I never seen my grandfather alive, and I got so sad thinkin' about it I wanted to cry. I wasn't sure it was him, even... (*She begins to laugh.*) I went an' telephoned the police and asked for the chief, but the chief was home and a guy asks what I want.

MAGISTRATE: (*mildly amused*) You... called the police?

RITA: I told the guy I'd seen God, and he says, "Yeh? What would you like us to do about it?" An' I said, "Pray! Laugh! Shout!"

MAGISTRATE: Go on...

RITA: He... asked where I'd seen God, an' I told him in the sky. He says you better call this number.... It's the Air Force. They'll take care of it!

She laughs and the MAGISTRATE smiles.

I called the number the guy gave me, but it was nighttime and there was no answer! If God was to come at night, after office hours, then...

A terrible awkwardness sets in. There is a harsh light on her. She turns away, aware that she is in captivity.

The MAGISTRATE stirs with discomfort.

(*with great fear*) How long will this be? Will I never be able to...

MAGISTRATE: (*annoyed at himself, at her*) There is nothing here but a record of your convictions... nothing to speak for you and provide me with any reason to moderate your sentence! What the hell am I supposed to do? Violate the law myself because I feel that somehow... I've known and felt.... No! (*turning from her*) You give me no alternative... no alternative at all!

The MAGISTRATE packs up his books.

RITA: I'll go home... jus' let me go home. I can't get out of jail to find the highway... or some kind of job!

MAGISTRATE: (*standing*) Prison and fines are not the only thing.... Have you, for instance, considered that you might be an incurable carrier? There are people like that.... They cannot come into contact with others without infecting them. They cannot eat from dishes others may use.... They cannot prepare or touch food others will eat.... The same with clothes, cars, hospital beds!

The MAGISTRATE exits.

RITA JOE shakes her head with disbelief. The idea of perpetual condemnation is beyond her comprehension. She falls to the floor. Guitar music is heard in the background.

She turns away from the MAGISTRATE and the light comes up over the ramp at the back of the stage. Another light comes up on centre stage left. Here, EILEEN JOE and the OLD WOMAN are miming clothes washing using a scrubbing board and placing the wash into woven baskets. The woman and the girl are on their knees, facing each other.

On the ramp above them, JAIMIE PAUL is struggling with a POLICEMAN who is scolding him softly for being drunk, abusive and noisy. JAIMIE PAUL is jocular; the POLICEMAN, harassed and worried. They slowly cross the ramp from stage left.

SINGER:
Four o'clock in the morning,
The sailor rides the ship
An' I ride the wind!
Eight o'clock in the morning,
My honey's scoldin' the sleepyheads
An' I'm scoldin' him.

JAIMIE: (*to the POLICEMAN*) On the Smoky River... four o'clock in the morning.... Hey? There was nobody... just me.... You know that?

POLICEMAN: No, I don't. Come on. Let's get you home.

JAIMIE PAUL moves forward and embraces the POLICEMAN.

JAIMIE: You wanna see something?

JAIMIE PAUL takes out a coin to do a trick.

OLD WOMAN: (*to EILEEN*) Your father's been very sick.

EILEEN: He won't eat nothing...

OLD WOMAN: Jus' sits and worries.... That's no good.

JAIMIE PAUL: (*finishing his coin trick*) You like that one? Hey, we both work for the government, eh?

They exit laughing.

Watch the rough stuff... just don't make me mad.

OLD WOMAN: If Rita Joe was to come and see him... maybe say goodbye to him...

RITA: (*calling from her world to the world of her strongest fears*) But he's not dying! I saw him not so long ago...

The women in her memory do not hear her. They continue discussing her father.

OLD WOMAN: He loved her an' always worried...

RITA: I didn't know he was sick!

OLD WOMAN: You were smart to come back, Eileen Joe.

RITA: (*again calling over the distance of her soul*) Nobody told me!

SINGER:
Nine o'clock in the evening,
Moon is high in the blueberry sky
An' I'm lovin' you.

JAIMIE: (*now passing along the apron beside RITA JOE, talking to the POLICEMAN*) You seen where I live? Big house with a mongolia in front.... Fancy place! You wanna see the room I got?

POLICEMAN: (*gruffly, aware that JAIMIE PAUL can become angry quickly*) When I get holidays, we'll take a tour of everything you've got... but I don't get holidays until September!

From the apron they cross upstage diagonally, between the OLD WOMAN with EILEEN, and RITA JOE.

JAIMIE: You're a good man... good for a laugh. I'm a good man... you know me!

POLICEMAN: Sure, you're first class when you're sober!

JAIMIE: I got a cousin in the city. He got his wife a stove an' washing machine! He's a good man.... You know my cousin maybe?

Fading off. They leave the stage.

The OLD WOMAN has risen from her knees and wearily collected one basket of clothes. She climbs the ramp and moves to the wings, stage right. EILEEN is thoughtful and slower, but she also prepares her clothes wash and follows.

OLD WOMAN: Nothing in the city I can see... only if you're lucky. A good man who don't drink or play cards... that's all.

EILEEN: And if he's bad?

OLD WOMAN: Then leave him. I'm older than you, Eileen... I know what's best.

The OLD WOMAN exits. The guitar music dies out. JAIMIE PAUL's laughter and voice is heard offstage.

JAIMIE: (*offstage, loud, boisterous*) We both work for the gov'ment! We're buddies, no?... You think we're both the same?

Laughter. The lights on the ramp and centre stage die.

RITA: (*following JAIMIE PAUL's laughter*) Good or bad, what difference? So long as he's a livin' man!

RITA JOE and EILEEN giggle. The light spreads around her into pale infinity.

The TEACHER enters on the ramp. She rings a handbell and stops a short distance from the wings to peer around. She is a shy, inadequate woman who moves and behaves jerkily, the product of incomplete education and poor job placement.

TEACHER: (*in a scolding voice*) Rita! Rita Joe!

The bell rings.

The class is waiting for you. The class is always waiting.

RITA JOE is startled to hear the bell and see the woman. She comes to her feet, now a child before the TEACHER, and runs to join EILEEN. JAIMIE PAUL and YOUNG INDIAN MEN have entered with the bell and sit cross-legged on the floor as school children.

RITA: The sun is in my skin, Miss Donohue. The leaves is red and orange, and the wind stopped blowin' an hour ago.

The TEACHER has stopped to listen to this. RITA JOE and EILEEN, late again, slip into class and sit on the floor with the others.

TEACHER: Rita! What is a noun?

No answer. The kids poke RITA JOE to stand up.

Did you hear what I asked?

RITA: (*uncertain*) No... yes?

TEACHER: There's a lot you don't know.... That kind of behaviour is exhibitionism! We are a melting pot!

RITA: A melting pot?

TEACHER: A melting pot! Do you know what a melting pot is?

RITA: It's... (*She shrugs.*) ...a melting pot!

The class laughs.

TEACHER: Precisely! You put copper and tin into a melting pot and out comes bronze.... It's the same with people!

RITA: Yes, Miss Donohue... out comes bronze...

Laughter again. The TEACHER calls RITA JOE over to her. The light fades on the other children.

TEACHER: Rita, what was it I said to you this morning?

RITA: You said... wash my neck, clean my fingernails...

TEACHER: (*cagey*) No, it wasn't, Rita!

RITA: I can't remember. It was long ago.

TEACHER: Try to remember, Rita.

RITA: I don't remember, Miss Donohue! I was thinkin' about you last night, thinkin' if you knew some...

TEACHER: You are straying off the topic! Never stray off the topic!

RITA: It was a dream, but now I'm scared, Miss Donohue. I've been a long time moving about... trying to find something!... I must've lost...

TEACHER: No, Rita. That is not important.

RITA: Not important?

TEACHER: No, Rita.... Now you repeat after me like I said or I'm going to have to pass you by again. Say after me...

RITA: Sure. Say after you...

TEACHER: Say after me... "A book of verse underneath the spreading bough..."

RITA: "A book of verse underneath the spreading bough..."

TEACHER: "A jug of wine, a loaf of bread and thou beside me... singing in the wilderness."

RITA: (*the child spell broken, she laughs bawdily*) Jaimie said, "To heck with the wine an' loaf.... Let's have some more of this here thou!"

Her laughter dies. She wipes her lips, as if trying to erase some stain there.

TEACHER: (*peevish*) Alright, Rita.... Alright, let's have none of that!

RITA: (*plaintively*) I'm sorry, Miss Donohue... I'm sure sorry!

TEACHER: That's alright.

RITA: I'm sorry!

TEACHER: Alright...

RITA: Sorry...

TEACHER: You will never make bronze! Coming from nowhere and going no place! Who am I to change that?

RITA JOE grips the edge of the desk with both hands, holding on tightly.

RITA: No! They said for me to stay here, to learn something!

TEACHER: (*with exasperation*) I tried to teach you, but your head was in the clouds, and as for your body.... Well! I wouldn't even think what I know you do!

The TEACHER crosses amongst the other children.

RITA: I'm sorry... please! Let me say it after you again... (*blurting it out*) "A book of verse underneath the spreading..."

TEACHER: Arguing... always trying to upset me... and in grade four... I saw it then... pawing the ground for men like a bitch in heat!

RITA: (*dismayed*) It... isn't so!

TEACHER: You think I don't know? I'm not blind... I can see out of the windows.

The TEACHER marches off into the wings and the class runs after her leaving RITA JOE alone onstage.

RITA: That's a lie! For God's sake, tell the judge I have a good character... I am clean an' honest.... Everything you said is right, I'm never gonna argue again... I believe in God... an' I'm from the country and lost like hell! Tell him!

She shakes her head sadly, knowing the extent of her betrayal.

They only give me eight hours to find somebody who knows me.... An' seven and a half hours is gone already!

The light on the scene dies.

SINGER: (*recitivo*)
Things that were...
Life that might have been...

A pale backlight on the back of the ramp comes up. Recorded sounds of crickets and the distant sound of a train whistle are heard.

RITA JOE's FATHER and JAIMIE PAUL enter on the ramp from stage left. The FATHER leads the way. JAIMIE PAUL is behind, rolling a cigarette. They walk slowly, thoughtfully, following the ramp across and downstage. RITA JOE stands separate, watching.

SINGER:
The blue evening of the first
Warm day
Is the last evening.
There'll not be another
Like it.

JAIMIE: No more handouts, David Joe.... We can pick an' can the berries ourselves.

FATHER: We need money to start a cooperative like that.

JAIMIE: Then some other way!

The old man listens, standing still, to the sounds of the train and the night.

FATHER: You're a young man, Jaimie Paul... young an' angry. It's not good to be that angry.

JAIMIE: We're gonna work an' live like people... not be afraid all the time... stop listening to an old priest an' Indian Department guys who're working for a pension!

FATHER: You're a young man, Jaimie Paul...

JAIMIE: I say stop listening, David Joe!... In the city they never learned my name. It was "Hey, fella"... or "You, boy"... that kind of stuff.

Pause. The sound of the train whistle is heard.

FATHER: A beautiful night, Jaimie Paul.

JAIMIE: We can make some money. The berries are good this year!

JAIMIE PAUL is restless, edgy, particularly on the train whistle sound.

FATHER: Sometimes... children... you remember every day with them.... Never forget you are alive with children.

JAIMIE PAUL turns away and begins to retrace his steps.

JAIMIE: You want us all to leave an' go to the city? Is that what you want?

The FATHER shakes his head. He does not wish for this, but the generation spread between them is great now. JAIMIE PAUL walks away with a gesture of contempt.

The sounds die. The light dies and isolates the FATHER and RITA JOE.

RITA: You were sick, an' now you're well.

FATHER: (*in measured speech, turning away from RITA JOE, as if carefully recalling something of great importance*) You left your father, Rita Joe... never wrote Eileen a letter that time.... Your father was pretty sick man that time... pretty sick man... June ninth he got the cold, an' on June twenty he...

RITA: But you're alive! I had such crazy dreams I'd wake up laughing at myself!

FATHER: I have dreams too...

RITA JOE moves forward to him. She stops talking to him, as if communicating thoughts rather than words. He remains standing where he is, facing away from her.

RITA: I was in a big city... so many streets I'd get lost like nothin'.... When you got sick I was on a job...

FATHER: June ninth I got the cold...

RITA: Good job in a tire store... Jaimie Paul's got a job with the government, you know?

FATHER: Pretty sick man, that time...

RITA: A good job in a tire store. They was gonna teach me how to file statements after I learned the telephone. Bus ticket home was twenty dollars.... But I got drunk all the same when I heard an' I went in and tried to work that day... (*smiling and shaking her head*) Boy, I tried to work! Some day that was!

FATHER: I have dreams.... Sometimes I'm scared...

They finally look at each other.

RITA: (*shuddering*) I'm so cold...

FATHER: Long dreams... I dream about Rita Joe... (*sadly*) Have to get better. I've lived longer, but I know nothing... nothing at all. Only the old stories.

RITA JOE moves sideways to him. She is smiling happily.

RITA: When I was little, a man came out of the bush to see you. Tell me why again!

The FATHER hesitates, shaking his head, but he is also smiling. The light of their separate yearnings fades out and the front of the stage is lit with the two of them together. The FATHER turns and comes forward to meet her.

FATHER: You don't want to hear that story again.

He sits on the slight elevation of the stage apron. RITA JOE sits down in front of him and snuggles between his knees. He leans forward over her.

RITA: It's the best story I ever heard!

FATHER: You were a little girl... four years old already... an' Eileen was getting big inside your mother. One day it was hot... sure was hot. Too hot to try an' fish in the lake, because the fish was down deep where the water was cold.

RITA: The dog started to bark...

FATHER: The dog started to bark.... How!

FATHER & RITA: (*in unison*) How! How! How!

FATHER: Barking to beat hell an' I says to myself why... on such a hot day? Then I see the bushes moving... somebody was coming to see us. Your mother said from inside the house, "What's the matter with that dog?" An' I says to her, "Somebody coming to see me." It was big Sandy Collins, who ran the sawmill back of the reserve. Business was bad for big Sandy then... but he comes out of that bush like he was being chased... his clothes all wet an' stickin' to him... his cap in his hands, an' his face black with the heat and dirt from hard work.... He says to me, "My little Millie got a cough last night an' today she's dead." ..."She's dead," big Sandy says to me. I says to him, "I'm sorry to hear that, Sandy. Millie is the same age as my Rita." And he says to me, "David Joe... look, you got another kid coming... won't make much difference to you.... Sell me Rita Joe like she is for a thousand dollars!"

RITA JOE giggles. The FATHER raises his hand to silence her.

"A thousand dollars is a lot of money, Sandy," I says to him... "Lots of money. You got to cut a lot of timber for a thousand dollars." Then he says to me, "Not a thousand cash at once, David Joe. First I give you two hundred fifty dollars.... When Rita Joe comes ten years old and she's still alright, I give you the next two hundred fifty.... An' if she don't die by fifteen, I guarantee you five hundred dollars cash at once!"

RITA JOE and the FATHER break into laughter. He reaches around her throat and draws her close.

So you see, Rita Joe, you lose me one thousand dollars from big Sandy Collins!

They continue laughing.

A harsh light on the MAGISTRATE, who enters and stands on his podium.

MAGISTRATE: Rita Joe, when was the last time you had dental treatment?

RITA JOE covers her ears, refusing to surrender this moment of security in the arms of her FATHER.

RITA: I can't hear you!

MAGISTRATE: (*loudly*) You had your teeth fixed ever?

RITA: (*coming to her feet and turning on him*) Leave me alone!

MAGISTRATE: Have you had your lungs x-rayed recently?

RITA: I was hungry, that's all!

MAGISTRATE: (*becoming staccato, machine-like in his questions*) When was your last Wasserman taken?

RITA: What's that?

RITA JOE hears the TEACHER's voice. She turns to see the approaching TEACHER give the MAGISTRATE testimony. The stage is lit in a cold blue light now.

TEACHER: (*crisply to the MAGISTRATE as she approaches, her monologue a reading*) Dear Sir.... In reply to your letter of the twelfth, I cannot in all sincerity provide a reference of good character for one Rita Joe...

The WITNESSES do not see her and the testimony takes on the air of a nightmare for RITA JOE. She is baffled and afraid. The TEACHER continues to quietly repeat her testimony. RITA JOE appeals to the MAGISTRATE.

RITA: Why am I here? What've I done?

MAGISTRATE: You are charged with prostitution.

Her FATHER stands and crosses upstage to the ramp to observe. He is joined by EILEEN JOE, the OLD WOMAN and the PRIEST. MR. HOMER approaches briskly from stage left.

MR. HOMER: She'd been drinking when she comes into the Centre.... Nothing wrong in that I could see, 'specially on a Friday night. So I give her some soup an' a sandwich. Then all of a sudden in the middle of a silly argument, she goes haywire... an' I see her comin' at me... I'll tell you, I was scared! I don't know Indian women that well!

MAGISTRATE: Assault!

RITA JOE retreats from him. The TEACHER and MR. HOMER now stand before the MAGISTRATE as if they were frozen. MR. HOMER repeats his testimony under the main dialogue. JAIMIE PAUL staggers in from stage right, over the ramp, heading to the wings of lower stage left.

JAIMIE: (*to himself*) What the hell are they doing?

RITA: (*running to him*) Say a good word for me, Jaimie!

JAIMIE: They fired me yesterday.... What the hell's the use of living?

JAIMIE PAUL leaves the stage as the SCHOOL BOARD CLERK enters to offer further testimony to the MAGISTRATE.

SCHOOL BOARD CLERK: I recommended in a letter that she take school after grade five through correspondence courses from the Department of Education... but she never replied to the form letter the school division sent her...

RITA: (*defending herself to the MAGISTRATE*) That drunken bastard Mahoney used it to light fire in his store.... He'd never tell Indians when mail came for us!

SCHOOL BOARD CLERK: I repeat... I wish our position understood most clearly.... No reply was ever received in this office to the letter we sent Rita Joe!

RITA: One letter... one letter for a lifetime?

TEACHER: Say after me! "I wandered lonely as a cloud, that floats on high o'er vales and hills.... When all at once I saw a crowd... a melting pot..."

A POLICEMAN and a MALE WITNESS enter. The PRIEST crosses downstage. The testimonies are becoming a nightmare babble.

RITA JOE is stung, stumbling backward from all of them as they face the MAGISTRATE with their condemnations.

POLICEMAN: We were impersonating two deck-hands...

The PRIEST is passing by RITA JOE. He makes the sign of the cross and offers comfort in a thin voice, lost in the noise.

PRIEST: Be patient, Rita.... The young are always stormy, but in time, your understanding will deepen.... There is an end to all things.

WITNESS: I gave her a job, but she was kind of slow... I can't wait around, there's lots of white people goin' lookin' for work... so I figure, to hell with this noise...

MAGISTRATE: (*loudly over the voices*) Have your ears ached?

RITA: No!

MAGISTRATE: Have you any boils on your back? Any discharge? When did you bathe last?

The MURDERERS appear and circle RITA JOE.

MAGISTRATE: Answer me! Drunkenness! Shop-lifting! Assault! Prostitution, prostitution, prostitution, prostitution!

RITA: (*her voice shrill, cutting over the babble*) I don't know what happened... but you got to listen to me and believe me, mister!

The babble ceases abruptly. RITA JOE pleads with them as best she knows.

You got rules here that was made before I was born... I was hungry when I stole something... an' I was hollerin' I was so lonely when I started whoring...

The MURDERERS come closer.

MAGISTRATE: Rita Joe... has a doctor examined you?... I mean, really examined you? Rita Joe... you might be carrying and transmitting some disease and not aware of it!

RITA: (*breaking away from the MURDERERS*) Bastards! (*to the MAGISTRATE*) Put me in jail... I don't care... I'll sign anything. I'm so goddamn hungry I'm sick.... Whatever it is, I'm guilty!

She clutches her head and goes down in a squat of defeat.

MAGISTRATE: Are you free of venereal disease?

RITA: I don't know. I'm not sick that way.

MAGISTRATE: How can you tell?

RITA: (*lifting her face to him*) I know.... A woman knows them things...

Pause.

MAGISTRATE: Thirty days!

The POLICEMAN leads RITA JOE off and the house lights come up. The ACTORS and the SINGER walk off the stage, leaving emptiness as at the opening of the act.

ACT TWO

The house lights dim. A POLICEMAN brings RITA JOE in downstage centre. She curls up in her jail cell and sleeps. RITA JOE's FATHER enters on the ramp and crosses down to the audience.

The stage worklights die down. Lights isolate RITA JOE's FATHER. Another light with prison bar shadows isolates RITA JOE in her area of the stage.

FATHER: (*looking down on RITA JOE*) I see no way... no way.... It's not clear like trees against snow... not clear at all...

To the audience.

But when I was fifteen years old, I leave the reserve to work on a threshing crew. They pay a dollar a day for a good man... an' I was a good strong man. The first time I got work there was a girl about as old as I.... She'd come out in the yard an' watch the men working at the threshing machine. She had eyes that were the biggest I ever seen... like fifty-cent pieces... an' there was always a flock of geese around her. Whenever I see her I feel good. She used to stand an' watch me, an' the geese made a helluva lot of noise. One time I got off my rick an' went to get a drink of water... but I walked close to where she was watching me. She backed away, and then ran from me with the geese chasin' after her, their wings out an' their feet no longer touching the ground.... They were white geese.... The last time Rita Joe come home to see us... the last time she ever come home... I watched her leave... and I seen geese running after Rita Joe the same way... white geese... with their wings out an' their feet no longer touching the ground. And I remembered it all, an' my heart got so heavy I wanted to cry...

The light fades to darkness on the FATHER, as he exits up the ramp and off. RITA JOE wakes from her dream, cold, shaking, desperate.

SINGER:
The blue evening of the
First warm day
Is the last evening.
There'll not be another
Like it.

The PRIEST enters from darkness with the POLICEMAN. He is dressed in a dark suit which needs pressing. He stops in half shadow outside RITA JOE's prison light.

The scene between them is played out in the manner of two country people meeting in a time of crisis. Their thoughts come slowly, incompletely. There is both fear and helplessness in both characters.

PRIEST: I came twice before they'd let me see you...

RITA JOE jumps to her feet. She smiles at him.

RITA: Oh, Father Andrew!

PRIEST: Even so, I had to wait an hour.

A long pause. He clumsily takes out a package of cigarettes and matches from his pocket and hands them to her, aware that he is possibly breaking a prison regulation.

I'm sorry about this, Rita.

RITA JOE tears the package open greedily and lights a cigarette. She draws on it with animal satisfaction.

RITA: I don't know what's happening, Father Andrew.

PRIEST: They're not... hurting you here?

RITA: No.

PRIEST: I could make an appointment with the warden if there was something...

RITA: What's it like outside?... Is it a nice day outside? I heard it raining last night.... Was it raining?

PRIEST: It rains a lot here...

RITA: When I was a kid, there was leaves an' a river... Jaimie Paul told me once that maybe we never see those things again.

A long pause. The PRIEST struggles with himself.

PRIEST: I've never been inside a jail before.... They told me there was a chapel...

He points indefinitely back.

RITA: What's gonna happen to me?... That judge sure got sore...

She laughs.

PRIEST: (*with disgust, yet unsure of himself*) Prostitution this time?

RITA: I guess so...

PRIEST: You know how I feel.... City is no place for you... nor for me... I've spent my life in the same surroundings as your father!

RITA: Sure... but you had God on your side!

She smiles mischievously. The PRIEST angers.

PRIEST: Rita, try to understand...Our Lord Jesus once met a woman such as you beside the well...He forgave her!

RITA: I don't think God hears me here.... Nobody hears me now, nobody except cops an' pimps an' bootleggers!

PRIEST: I'm here. I was there when you were born.

RITA: You've told me lots of times... I was thinkin' about my mother last night.... She died young... I'm older than she was...

PRIEST: Your mother was a good, hard-working woman. She was happy...

A pause between them.

RITA: There was frost on the street at five o'clock Tuesday morning when they arrested me.... Last night I remembered things flyin' and kids runnin' past me trying to catch a chocolate wrapper that's blowin' in the wind... (*She presses her hands against her bosom.*) It hurts me here to think about them things!

PRIEST: I worry about you.... Your father worries too... I baptized you... I watched you and Leenie grow into women!

RITA: Yes... I seen God in what you said... in your clothes! In your hair!

PRIEST: But you're not the woman I expected you to be.... Your pride, Rita... your pride... may bar you from heaven.

RITA: (*mocking him*) They got rules there too... in heaven?

PRIEST: (*angry*) Rita!... I'm not blind... I can see! I'm not deaf... I know all about you! So does God!

RITA: My uncle was Dan Joe.... He was dyin' and he said to me, "Long ago the white man come with Bibles to talk to my people, who had the land. They talk for hundred years... then we had all the Bibles, an' the white man had our land..."

PRIEST: Don't blame the Church! We are trying to help...

RITA: (*with passion*) How? I'm looking for the door...

PRIEST: (*tortured now*) I... will hear your confession...

RITA: But I want to be free!

PRIEST: (*stiffly*) We learn through suffering, Rita Joe.... We will only be free if we become humble again. (*Pause.*) Will you confess, Rita Joe? (*A long pause.*) I'm going back on the four o'clock bus. (*He begins walking away into the gloom.*) I'll tell your father I saw you, and you looked well.

He is suddenly relieved.

RITA: (*after him as he leaves*) You go to hell!

The PRIEST turns sharply.

Go tell your God... when you see him... tell him about Rita Joe an' what they done to her! Tell him about yourself too!... That you were not good enough for me, but that didn't stop you tryin'! Tell him that!

The PRIEST hurries away. Guitar in. RITA JOE sits down, brooding.

SINGER:
I will give you the wind and a sense of
    wonder
As the child by the river, the reedy river.
I will give you the sky wounded by thunder
And a leaf on the river, the silver river.

A light comes up on the ramp where JAIMIE PAUL appears, smiling and waving to her.

JAIMIE: (*shouting*) Rita Joe! I'm gonna take you dancing after work Friday.... That job's gonna be alright!

RITA JOE springs to her feet, elated.

RITA: Put me back in jail so I can be free on Friday!

A sudden burst of dance music. The stage lights up and JAIMIE PAUL approaches her. They dance together, remaining close downstage centre.

SINGER:
Round an' round the cenotaph,
The clumsy seagulls play.
Fed by funny men with hats
Who watch them night and day.
Sleepless hours, heavy nights,
Dream your dreams so pretty.
God was gonna have a laugh
An' gave me a job in the city!

The music continues for the interlude.

Some YOUNG INDIAN MEN run onto the stage along the ramp and join JAIMIE PAUL and RITA JOE in their dance. The MURDERERS enter and elbow into the group, their attention specifically menacing towards JAIMIE PAUL and RITA JOE. A street brawl begins as a POLICEMAN passes through on his beat. The MURDERERS leave hastily.

I woke up at six o'clock,
Stumbled out of bed.
Crash of steel and diesel trucks
Damned near killed me dead.
Sleepless hours, heavy nights,
Dream your dreams so pretty.
God was gonna have a laugh
An' gave me a job in the city!

Musical interlude. RITA JOE and JAIMIE PAUL continue dancing languidly. The YOUNG INDIAN MEN exit.

I've polished floors an' cut the trees,
Fished and stooked the wheat.
Now "Hallelujah, Praise the Lord,"
I sing before I eat!
Sleepless hours, heavy nights,
Dream your dreams so pretty.
God was gonna have a laugh
An' gave me a job in the city!

Musical interlude.

The music dies as the YOUNG INDIAN MEN wheel in a brass bed, circle it around and exit. The stage darkens except for a pool of light where RITA JOE and JAIMIE PAUL stand, embracing. JAIMIE PAUL takes her hand and leads her away.

JAIMIE: Come on, Rita Joe... you're slow.

RITA: (*happy in her memories, not wishing to forget too soon, hesitating*) How much rent... for a place where you can keep babies?

JAIMIE: I don't know... maybe eighty dollars a month.

RITA: That's a lot of money.

JAIMIE: It costs a buck to go dancin' even...

They walk slowly along the apron to stage left, as if following a street to JAIMIE PAUL's rooming house.

JAIMIE: It's a good place... I got a sink in the room. Costs seven bucks a week, that's all!

RITA: That's good... I only got a bed in my place...

JAIMIE: I seen Mickey an' Steve Laporte last night.

RITA: How are they?

JAIMIE: Good.... We're goin' to a beer parlour Monday night when I get paid... the same beer parlour they threw Steve out of! Only now there's three of us goin' in!

They arrive at and enter his room. A spot illuminates the bed near the wings of stage left. It is old, dilapidated. JAIMIE PAUL and RITA JOE enter the area of light around the bed. He is aware that the room is more drab than he would wish it.

JAIMIE: How do you like it... I like it!

RITA: (*examining room critically*) It's... smaller than my place.

JAIMIE: Sit down.

She sits on the edge of the bed and falls backward into a springless hollow. He laughs nervously. He is awkward and confused. The ease they shared walking to his place is now constricted.

I was gonna get some grub today, but I was busy.... Here...

He takes a chocolate bar out of his shirt pocket and offers it to her. She opens it, breaks off a small piece, and gives the remainder to him. He closes the wrapper and replaces the bar in his pocket. She eats ravenously. He walks around the bed nervously.

No fat DP's gonna throw me or the boys out of that beer parlour or he's gonna get this!

He holds up a fist in a gesture that is both poignant and futile. She laughs and he glowers at her.

JAIMIE: I'm tellin' you!

RITA: If they want to throw you out, they'll throw you out.

JAIMIE: Well, this is one Indian guy they're not pushing around no more!

RITA: God helps them who help themselves.

JAIMIE: That's right! (*laughing*) I was lookin' at the white shirts in Eaton's and this bugger comes an' says to me, you gonna buy or you gonna look all day?

RITA: (*looking around her*) It's a nice room for a guy, I guess...

JAIMIE: It's a lousy room!

RITA JOE lies back lengthwise in the bed. JAIMIE PAUL sits on the bed beside her.

RITA: You need a good job to have babies in the city... Clara Hill gave both her kids away they say...

JAIMIE: Where do kids like that go?

RITA: Foster homes, I guess.

JAIMIE: If somebody don't like the kid, back they go to another foster home?

RITA: I guess so... Clara Hill don't know where her kids are now.

JAIMIE: (*twisting sharply in his anger*) Goddamn it!

RITA: My father says...

JAIMIE PAUL rises, crosses round the bed to the other side.

JAIMIE: (*harshly*) I don't want to hear what your father got to say! He's like... like the kind of Indian a white man likes! He's gonna look wise and wait forever... for what? For the kids they take away to come back?

RITA: He's scared... I'm scared.... We're all scared, Jaimie Paul.

JAIMIE PAUL lies face down and mimes a gun through the bars.

JAIMIE: Sometimes I feel like takin' a gun and just...

He waves his hand as if to liquidate his environment and all that bedevils him. He turns over on his back and lies beside RITA JOE.

I don't know.... Goddamnit, I don't know what to do. I get mad an' then I don't know what I'm doing or thinkin'... I get scared sometimes, Rita Joe.

RITA: (*tenderly*) We're scared... everybody...

JAIMIE: I'm scared of dyin'... in the city. They don't care for one another here.... You got to be smart or have a good job to live like that.

RITA: Clara Hill's gonna have another baby...

JAIMIE: I can't live like that.... A man don't count for much here.... Women can do as much as a man.... There's no difference between men and women. I can't live like that.

RITA: You got to stop worrying, Jaimie Paul. You're gonna get sick worryin'.

JAIMIE: You can't live like that, can you?

RITA: No.

JAIMIE: I can't figure out what the hell they want from us!

RITA: (*laughing*) Last time I was in trouble, the judge was asking me what I wanted from him! I could've told him, but I didn't!

They both laugh. JAIMIE PAUL becomes playful and happy.

JAIMIE: Last night I seen television in a store window. I seen a guy on television showing this knife that cuts everything it's so sharp.... He was cutting up good shoes like they were potatoes.... That was sure funny to see!

Again they laugh in merriment at the idea of such a demonstration. JAIMIE PAUL continues with his story, gesturing with his hands.

JAIMIE: Chop... chop... chop.... A potful of shoes in no time! What's a guy gonna do with a potful of shoes? Cook them?

They continue laughing and lie together again. Then JAIMIE PAUL sobers. He rises from the bed and walks around it. He offers his hand to RITA JOE, who also rises.

(*drily*) Come on. This is a lousy room!

SINGER: (*reprise*)
God was gonna have a laugh,
And gave me a job in the city!

The light goes down on RITA JOE and JAIMIE PAUL. The YOUNG INDIAN MEN clear the bed. Cross fade to the rear ramp of the stage. RITA JOE's FATHER and the PRIEST enter and cross the stage.

PRIEST: She got out yesterday, but she wouldn't let me see her. I stayed an extra day, but she wouldn't see me.

FATHER: (*sadly*) I must go once more to the city... I must go to see them.

PRIEST: You're an old man... I wish I could persuade you not to go.

FATHER: You wouldn't say that if you had children, Andrew...

The lights go down on them.

The lights come up downstage centre. Three YOUNG INDIAN MEN precede MR. HOMER, carrying a table between them. MR. HOMER follows with a hamper of clothes under his arm.

MR. HOMER: Yeh... right about there is fine, boys. Got to get the clutter out of the basement.... There's mice coming in to beat hell.

MR. HOMER empties the clothes hamper on the table. The YOUNG INDIAN MEN step aside and converse in an undertone.

On the ramp, a YOUNG INDIAN MAN weaves his way from stage left and down to centre stage where the others have brought the table. He is followed by JAIMIE PAUL and RITA JOE, who mime his intoxicated progress.

(*speaking to the audience*) The Society for Aid to the Indians sent a guy over to see if I could recommend someone who'd been... well, through the mill, like they say... an' then smartened up an' taken rehabilitation. The guy said they just wanted a rehabilitated Indian to show up at their annual dinner. No speeches or fancy stuff... just be there.

The YOUNG INDIAN MAN lies down carefully to one side of MR. HOMER.

Hi, Louie. Not that I would cross the street for the Society.... They're nothing but a pack of do-gooders out to get their name in the papers...

The YOUNG INDIAN MAN begins to sing a tuneless song, trailing off into silence.

Keep it down, eh, Louie? I couldn't think of anybody to suggest to this guy... so he went away pretty sore...

RITA JOE begins to rummage through the clothes on the table. She looks at sweaters and holds a red one thoughtfully in her hands. JAIMIE PAUL is in conversation with the YOUNG INDIAN MEN to one side of the table. MR. HOMER turns from the audience to see RITA JOE holding the sweater.

Try it on, Rita Joe.... That's what the stuff's here for.

JAIMIE PAUL turns. He is in a provocative mood, seething with rebellion that makes the humour he triggers both biting and deceptively innocent. The YOUNG INDIAN MEN respond to him with strong laughter. JAIMIE PAUL takes a play punch at one of them.

JAIMIE: Whoops! Scared you, eh?

He glances back at MR. HOMER, as if talking to him.

Can't take it, eh? The priest can't take it. Indian Department guys can't take it.... Why listen to them? Listen to the radio if you want to hear something.

The YOUNG INDIAN MEN laugh.

Or listen to me! You think I'm smart?

YOUNG INDIAN MAN: You're a smart man, Jaimie Paul.

JAIMIE: Naw... I'm not smart... (*pointing to another YOUNG INDIAN MAN*) This guy here... calls himself squaw-humper... he's smart!... Him... he buys extra big shirts... more cloth for the same money.... That's smart! (*laughter*) I'm not smart. (*seriously*) You figure we can start a business an' be our own boss?

YOUNG INDIAN MAN: I don't know about that...

JAIMIE PAUL leaves them and goes to lean over the YOUNG INDIAN MAN who is now asleep on the floor.

JAIMIE: Buy a taxi... be our own boss...

He shakes the sleeping YOUNG INDIAN MAN, who immediately begins his tuneless song.

Aw, he's drunk.

JAIMIE PAUL goes over to the table and stares at the YOUNG INDIAN MAN beyond the table.

(*soberly*) Buy everything we need.... Don't be bums! Bums need grub an' clothes.... Bums is bad for the country, right Mr. Homer?

MR. HOMER: (*nodding*) I guess so... (*to RITA JOE who is now wearing the old sweater*) Red looks good on you, Rita Joe.... Take it!

JAIMIE PAUL goes over and embraces RITA JOE, then pushes her gently away.

JAIMIE: She looks better in yellow. I never seen a red dandelion before.

He and the YOUNG INDIAN MEN laugh, but the laughter is hollow.

MR. HOMER: Come on, Jaimie! Leave the girl alone. That's what it's here for.... Are you working?

JAIMIE: (*evasive, needling*) Yeh!... No!... "Can you drive?" the guy says to me. "Sure, I can drive," I says to him. "Okay," he says, "then drive this broom until the warehouse is clean."

They all laugh.

MR. HOMER: That's a good one... Jaimie, you're a card.... Well, time to get some food for you lot...

MR. HOMER leaves. RITA JOE feels better about the sweater. She looks to one of the

YOUNG INDIAN MEN *for approval. JAIMIE PAUL becomes grim-faced.*

RITA: Do you like it?

YOUNG INDIAN MAN: Sure. It's a nice sweater.... Take it.

JAIMIE: Take it where? Take it to hell.... Be men! (*pointing after MR. HOMER*) He's got no kids.... Guys like that get mean when they got no kids.... We're his kids an' he means to keep it that way! Well, I'm a big boy now! (*to RITA JOE*) I go to the employment office. I want work an' I want it now. "I'm not a goddamned cripple," I says to him. An' he says he can only take my name! If work comes he'll call me! "What the hell is this," I says to him. "I'll never get work like that.... There's no telephone in the house where I got a room!"

MR. HOMER returns pushing a wheeled tray on which he has some food for sandwiches, a loaf of bread and a large cutting knife. He begins to make some sandwiches.

RITA: (*scolding JAIMIE PAUL*) You won't get work talking that way, Jaimie Paul!

JAIMIE: Why not? I'm not scared. He gets mad at me an' I say to him... "You think I'm some stupid Indian you're talkin' to? Heh? You think that?"

JAIMIE PAUL struts and swaggers to demonstrate how he faced his opponent at the employment office.

MR. HOMER: (*cutting bread*) You're a tough man to cross, Jaimie Paul.

JAIMIE: (*ignoring MR. HOMER, to the YOUNG INDIAN MEN*) Boy, I showed that bastard who he was talkin' to!

RITA: Did you get the job?

JAIMIE: (*turning to her, laughing boyishly*) No! He called the cops an' they threw me out!

They all laugh. The YOUNG INDIAN MEN go to the table now and rummage through the clothes.

MR. HOMER: Take whatever you want, boys... there's more clothes comin' tomorrow.

JAIMIE PAUL impulsively moves to the table where the YOUNG INDIAN MEN are fingering the clothes. He pushes them aside and shoves the clothes in a heap leaving a small corner of the table clean. He takes out two coins from his pockets and spits in his hands.

JAIMIE: I got a new trick.... Come on, Mister Homer... I'll show you! See this!

He shows the coins, then slams his hands palms down on the table.

Which hand got the coins?

MR. HOMER: Why... one under each hand...

JAIMIE: Right! (*turning up his hands*) Again? (*He collects the coins and slaps his hands down again.*) Where are the coins now? Come on, guess!

MR. HOMER is confident now, and points to the right hand with his cutting knife. JAIMIE PAUL laughs and lifts his hands. The coins are under his left hand.

MR. HOMER: Son of a gun.

JAIMIE: You're a smart man.

He puts the coins in his pockets and, laughing, turns to RITA JOE who stands uncertainly, dressed in the red sweater. She likes the garment, but she is aware JAIMIE PAUL might resent her taking it. The YOUNG INDIAN MEN again move to the table, and MR. HOMER returns to making sandwiches.

MR. HOMER: There's a good pair of socks might come in handy for one of you guys!

A YOUNG INDIAN MAN pokes his thumbs through the holes in the socks, and laughs.

JAIMIE: Sure... take the socks! Take the table!

He slaps the table with his hands and laughs.

Take Mister Homer cutting bread! Take everything!

MR. HOMER: Hey, Jaimie!

JAIMIE: Why not? There's more comin' tomorrow, you said!

RITA: Jaimie!

MR. HOMER: You're sure in a smart-assed mood today, aren't you?

JAIMIE: (*pointing to the YOUNG INDIAN MAN with the socks, but talking to MR. HOMER*) Mister, friend Steve over there laughs lots.... He figures... the way to get along an' live is to grab his guts an' laugh at anything anybody says. You see him laughing all the time. A dog barks at him an' he laughs... (*laughter from the YOUNG INDIAN MAN*) Laughs at a fence post fallin'... (*laughter*) Kids with funny eyes make him go haywire... (*laughter*) Can of meat an' no can opener...

MR. HOMER watches the YOUNG INDIAN MEN and grins at JAIMIE PAUL.

MR. HOMER: Yeh... he laughs quite a bit...

JAIMIE: He laughs at a rusty nail.... Nice guy... laughs all the time.

MR. HOMER: (*to JAIMIE PAUL, holding the knife*) You wanted mustard on your bread or just plain?

JAIMIE: I seen him cut his hand and start laughin'... isn't that funny?

The YOUNG INDIAN MEN laugh, but with less humour now.

MR. HOMER: (*to JAIMIE PAUL*) You want mustard?... I'm talkin' to you!

JAIMIE: I'm not hungry.

The YOUNG INDIAN MEN stop laughing altogether. They become tense and suspicious of JAIMIE PAUL, who is watching them severely.

MR. HOMER: Suit yourself. Rita?

She shakes her head slowly, her gaze on JAIMIE PAUL's face.

RITA: I'm not hungry.

MR. HOMER looks from RITA JOE to JAIMIE PAUL, then to the YOUNG INDIAN MEN. His manner stiffens.

MR. HOMER: I see...

JAIMIE PAUL and RITA JOE touch hands and come forward to sit on the apron of the stage, front. A pale light is on the two of them. The stage lights behind them fade. A low light that is diffused and shadowy remains on the table where MR. HOMER has prepared the food. The YOUNG INDIAN MEN move slowly to the table and begin eating the sandwiches MR. HOMER offers to them. The light on the table fades very low. JAIMIE PAUL hands a cigarette to RITA JOE and they smoke.

Light comes up over the rear ramp. RITA JOE's FATHER enters onto the ramp from the wings of stage right. His step is resolute. The PRIEST follows behind him a few paces. They have been arguing. Both are dressed in work clothes: heavy trousers and windbreakers.

JAIMIE: When I'm laughing, I got friends.

RITA: I know, Jaimie Paul...

PRIEST: That was the way I found her, that was the way I left her.

JAIMIE: (*bitterly*) When I'm laughing, I'm a joker... a funny boy!

FATHER: If I was young... I wouldn't sleep. I would talk to people... let them all know!

JAIMIE: I'm not dangerous when I'm laughing...

PRIEST: You could lose the reserve and have nowhere to go!

FATHER: I have lost more than that! Young people die... young people don't believe me...

JAIMIE: That's alright... that's alright...

The light dies out on JAIMIE PAUL and RITA JOE. The light also dies out on MR. HOMER and the YOUNG INDIAN MEN.

PRIEST: You think they believe that hot-headed... that troublemaker?

FATHER: (*turning to face the PRIEST*) Jaimie Paul is a good boy!

PRIEST: David Joe... you and I have lived through a lot. We need peace now, and time to consider what to do next.

FATHER: Eileen said to me last night... she wants to go to the city. I worry all night.... What can I do?

PRIEST: I'll talk to her, if you wish.

FATHER: (*angry*) And tell her what?... Of the animals there... (*gesturing to the audience*) who sleep with sore stomachs because... they eat too much?

PRIEST: We mustn't lose the reserve and the old life, David Joe.... Would you... give up being chief on the reserve?

FATHER: Yes!

PRIEST: To Jaimie Paul?

FATHER: No... to someone who's been to school... maybe university... who knows more.

PRIEST: (*relieved by this, but not reassured*) The people here need your wisdom and stability, David Joe. There is no man here who knows as much about hunting and fishing and guiding. You can survive.... What does a youngster who's been away to school know of this?

FATHER: (*sadly*) If we only fish an' hunt an' cut pulpwood... pick strawberries in the bush... for a hundred years more, we are dead. I know this, here... (*He touches his breast.*)

The light dies on the ramp.

A light rises on stage front, on JAIMIE PAUL and RITA JOE sitting at the apron of the stage. MR. HOMER is still cutting bread for sandwiches. The three YOUNG INDIAN MEN have eaten and appear restless to leave. The fourth YOUNG INDIAN MAN is still asleep on the floor. RITA JOE has taken off the red sweater, but continues to hold it in her hand.

JAIMIE: (*to MR. HOMER*) One time I was on a trapline five days without grub. I ate snow an' I walked until I got back. You think you can take it like me?

MR. HOMER approaches JAIMIE PAUL and holds out a sandwich to him.

MR. HOMER: Here... have a sandwich now.

JAIMIE PAUL ignores his hand.

RITA: Mister Homer don't know what happened, Jaimie Paul.

MR. HOMER shrugs and walks away to his sandwich table.

JAIMIE: Then he's got to learn.... Sure he knows! (*to MR. HOMER*) Sure he knows! He's feedin' sandwiches to Indian bums.... He knows. He's the worst kind!

The YOUNG INDIAN MEN freeze and MR. HOMER stops.

MR. HOMER: (*coldly*) I've never yet asked a man to leave this building.

RITA JOE and JAIMIE PAUL rise to their feet. RITA JOE goes to the clothes table and throws the red sweater back on the pile of clothes. JAIMIE PAUL laughs sardonically.

(*to RITA JOE*) Hey, not you, girl.... You take it!

She shakes her head and moves to leave.

RITA: I think we better go, boys.

The sleeping YOUNG INDIAN MAN slowly raises his head, senses there is something wrong, and is about to be helped up when...

JAIMIE: After five days without grub, the first meal I threw up... stomach couldn't take it.... But after that it was alright... (*to MR. HOMER, with intensity*) I don't believe nobody... no priest nor government.... They don't know what it's like to... to want an' not have... to stand in line an' nobody sees you!

MR. HOMER: If you want food, eat! You need clothes, take them. That's all.... But I'm runnin' this centre my way, and I mean it!

JAIMIE: I come to say no to you.... That's all... that's all!

He throws out his arms in a gesture that is both defiant and childlike. The gesture disarms some of MR. HOMER's growing hostility.

MR. HOMER: You've got that right... no problems. There's others come through here day an' night.... No problems.

JAIMIE: I don't want no others to come. I don't want them to eat here! (*indicating his friends*) If we got to take it from behind a store window, then we break the window an' wait for the cops. It's better than... than this!

He gestures with contempt at the food and the clothes on the table.

MR. HOMER: Rita Joe... where'd you pick up this... this loudmouth anyway?

RITA: (*slowly, firmly*) I think... Jaimie Paul's... right.

MR. HOMER looks from face to face. The three YOUNG INDIAN MEN are passive, staring into the distance. The fourth is trying hard to clear his head. JAIMIE PAUL is cold, hostile. RITA JOE is determined.

MR. HOMER: (*decisively*) Alright! You've eaten... looked over the clothes.... Now clear out so others get a chance to come in! Move!

He tries to herd everyone out and the four YOUNG INDIAN MEN begin to move away. JAIMIE PAUL mimics the gestures of MR. HOMER and steps in front of the YOUNG INDIAN MEN herding them back in.

JAIMIE: Run, boys, run! Or Mister Homer gonna beat us up!

RITA JOE takes JAIMIE PAUL's hand and tries to pull him away to leave.

RITA: Jaimie Paul... you said to me no trouble!

JAIMIE PAUL pulls his hand free and jumps back of the clothes table. MR. HOMER comes for him, unknowingly still carrying the slicing knife in his hand. An absurd chase begins around the table. One of the YOUNG INDIAN MEN laughs, and stepping forward, catches hold of MR. HOMER's hand with the knife in it.

YOUNG INDIAN MAN: Hey! Don't play with a knife, Mister Homer!

He gently takes the knife away from MR. HOMER and drops it on the food table behind. MR. HOMER looks at his hand, an expression of shock on his face. JAIMIE PAUL gives him no time to think about the knife and what it must have appeared like to the YOUNG INDIAN MEN. He pulls a large brassiere from the clothes table and mockingly holds it over his breasts, which he sticks out enticingly at MR. HOMER. The YOUNG INDIAN MEN laugh. MR. HOMER is exasperated and furious. RITA JOE is frightened.

RITA: It's not funny, Jaimie!

JAIMIE: It's funny as hell, Rita Joe. Even funnier this way!

JAIMIE PAUL puts the brassiere over his head, with the cups down over his ears and the straps under his chin. The YOUNG INDIAN MEN are all laughing now and moving close to the table. MR. HOMER makes a futile attempt at driving them off.

Suddenly JAIMIE PAUL's expression turns to one of hatred. He throws the brassiere on the table and gripping its edge, throws the table and clothes over, scattering the clothes. He kicks at them. The YOUNG INDIAN MEN all jump in and, picking up the clothes, hurl them over the ramp.

RITA JOE runs in to try and stop them. She grips the table and tries lifting it up again.

MR. HOMER: (*to JAIMIE PAUL*) Cut that out, you sonofabitch!

JAIMIE PAUL stands watching him. MR. HOMER is in a fury. He sees RITA JOE struggling to right the table. He moves to her and pushes her hard.

You slut!... You breed whore!

RITA JOE recoils. With a shriek of frustration, she attacks MR. HOMER, tearing at him. He backs away, then turns and runs. JAIMIE PAUL overturns the table again. The others join in the melee with the clothes. A POLICEMAN enters and grabs JAIMIE PAUL. RITA JOE and the four YOUNG INDIAN MEN exit, clearing away the tables and remaining clothes.

A sharp, tiny spotlight comes up on the face and upper torso of JAIMIE PAUL. He is wild with rebellion as the POLICEMAN forces him, in an arm lock, down towards the audience.

JAIMIE: (*screaming defiance at the audience*) Not jus' a box of cornflakes! When I go in I want the whole store! That's right... the whole goddamned store!

Another sharp light on the MAGISTRATE standing on his podium looking down at JAIMIE PAUL.

MAGISTRATE: Thirty days!

JAIMIE: (*held by POLICEMEN*) Sure, sure.... Anything else you know?

MAGISTRATE: Thirty days!

JAIMIE: Gimme back my truth!

MAGISTRATE: We'll get larger prisons and more police in every town and city across the country!

JAIMIE: Teach me who I really am! You've taken that away! Give me back the real me so I can live like a man!

MAGISTRATE: There is room for dialogue. There is room for disagreement and there is room for social change... but within the framework of institutions and traditions in existence for that purpose!

JAIMIE: (*spitting*) Go to hell!... I can die an' you got nothing to tell me!

MAGISTRATE: (*in a cold fury*) Thirty days! And after that, it will be six months! And after that... God help you!

The MAGISTRATE marches off his platform and offstage. JAIMIE PAUL is led off briskly in the other direction offstage.

The lights change. RITA JOE enters, crossing the stage, exchanging a look with the SINGER.

SINGER:
Sleepless hours, heavy nights,
Dream your dreams so pretty.
God was gonna have a laugh
An' gave me a job in the city!

RITA JOE walks the street. She is smoking a cigarette. She is dispirited.

The light broadens across the stage. RITA JOE's FATHER and JAIMIE PAUL enter the stage from the wings of centre stage left. They walk slowly towards where RITA JOE stands. At the sight of her FATHER, RITA JOE moans softly and hurriedly stamps out her cigarette. She visibly straightens and waits for the approaching men, her expression one of fear and joy.

FATHER: I got a ride on Miller's truck... took me two days...

JAIMIE: It's a long way, David Joe.

The FATHER stops a pace short of RITA JOE and looks at her with great tenderness and concern.

FATHER: (*softly*) I come... to get Rita Joe.

RITA: Oh... I don't know...

She looks to JAIMIE PAUL for help in deciding what to do, but he is sullen and uncommunicative.

FATHER: I come to take Rita Joe home.... We got a house an' some work sometime...

JAIMIE: She's with me now, David Joe.

RITA: (*very torn*) I don't know...

JAIMIE: You don't have to go back, Rita Joe.

RITA JOE looks away from her FATHER with humility. The FATHER turns to JAIMIE PAUL. He stands ancient and heroic.

FATHER: I live... an' I am afraid. Because... I have not done everything. When I have done everything... know that my children are safe... then... it will be alright. Not before.

JAIMIE: (*to RITA JOE*) You don't have to go. This is an old man now.... He has nothing to give... nothin' to say!

RITA JOE reacts to both men, her conflict deepening.

FATHER: (*turning away from JAIMIE PAUL to RITA JOE*) For a long time... a very long time... she was in my hands... like that! (*He cups his hands into the shape of a bowl.*) Sweet... tiny... lovin' all the time and wanting love... (*He shakes his head sadly.*)

JAIMIE: (*angrily*) Go tell it to the white men! They're lookin' for Indians that stay proud even when they hurt... just so long's they don't ask for their rights!

The FATHER turns slowly, with great dignity, to JAIMIE PAUL. His gestures show JAIMIE PAUL to be wrong; the old man's spirit was never broken. JAIMIE PAUL understands and looks away.

FATHER: You're a good boy, Jaimie Paul... a good boy... (*to RITA JOE, talking slowly, painfully*) I once seen a dragonfly breakin' its shell to get its wings... it floated on water an' crawled up on a log where I was sittin'.... It dug its feet into the log an' then it pulled until the shell bust over its neck. Then it pulled some more... an' slowly its wings slipped out of the shell... like that!

He shows with his hands how the dragonfly got his freedom.

JAIMIE: (*angered and deeply moved by the FATHER*) Where you gonna be when they start bustin' our heads open an' throwing us into jails right across the goddamned country?

FATHER: Such wings I never seen before... folded like an accordion so fine, like thin glass an' white in the morning sun...

JAIMIE: We're gonna have to fight to win... there's no other way! They're not listenin' to you, old man! Or to me.

FATHER: It spread its wings... so slowly... an' then the wings opened an' began to flutter... just like that... see! Hesitant at first... then stronger... an' then the wings beatin' like that made the dragonfly's body quiver until the shell on its back falls off...

JAIMIE: Stop kiddin' yourself! We're gonna say no pretty soon to all the crap that makes us soft an' easy to push this way... that way!

FATHER: ...An' the dragonfly... flew up... up... up... into the white sun... to the green sky... to the sun... faster an' faster.... Higher... higher!

The FATHER reaches up with his hands, releasing the imaginary dragonfly into the sun, his final words torn out of his heart. RITA JOE springs to her feet and rushes against JAIMIE PAUL, striking at him with her fists.

RITA: (*savagely*) For Chris' sakes, I'm not goin' back!... Leave him alone.... He's everything we got left now!

JAIMIE PAUL stands, frozen by his emotion which he can barely control. The FATHER turns. RITA JOE goes to him. The FATHER speaks privately to RITA JOE in Indian dialect. They embrace. He pauses for a long moment to embrace and forgive her everything. Then he goes slowly offstage into the wings of stage left without looking back.

FATHER: Goodbye, Rita Joe.... Goodbye, Jaimie Paul...

RITA: Goodbye, Father.

JAIMIE PAUL watches RITA JOE who moves away from him to the front of the stage.

JAIMIE: (*to her*) You comin'?

She shakes her head to indicate no, she is staying. Suddenly JAIMIE PAUL runs away from her diagonally across to the wings upstage. As he nears the wings, the four YOUNG INDIAN MEN emerge, happily on their way to a party. They stop him at his approach. He runs into them, directing them back, his voice breaking with feelings of love and hatred intermingling.

(*shouting at them*) Next time... in a beer parlour or any place like that... I'll go myself or you guys take me home.... No more white buggers pushin' us out the door or he gets this!

He raises his fist. The group of YOUNG INDIAN MEN, elated by their newly-found determination, surround JAIMIE PAUL and exit into the wings of the stage. The light dies in back and at stage left.

The MAGISTRATE enters. There is a light on RITA JOE where she stands. There is also a light around the MAGISTRATE. The MAGISTRATE's voice and purpose are leaden. He has given up on RITA JOE. He is merely performing the formality of condemning her and dismissing her from his conscience.

MAGISTRATE: I sentence you to thirty days in prison.

RITA: (*angry, defiant*) Sure, sure.... Anything else you know?

MAGISTRATE: I sentence you to thirty days in prison, with a recommendation you be examined medically and given all necessary treatment at the prison clinic. There is nothing... there is nothing I can do now.

RITA: (*stoically*) Thank you. Is that right? To thank you?

MAGISTRATE: You'll be back... always be back... growing older, tougher... filthier... looking more like stone and prison bars... the lines in your face will tell everyone who sees you about prison windows and prison food.

RITA: No child on the road would remember you, mister!

The MAGISTRATE comes down to stand before her. He has the rambling confidence of detached authority.

MAGISTRATE: What do you expect? We provide schools for you and you won't attend them because they're out of the way and that little extra effort is too much for you! We came up as a civilization having to... yes, claw upwards at times.... There's nothing wrong with that.... We give you X-ray chest clinics...

He turns away from her and goes to the apron of the stage and speaks directly to the audience.

We give them X-ray chest clinics and three-quarters of them won't show up.... Those that do frequently get medical attention at one of the hospitals...

RITA: (*interjecting*) My mother died!

MAGISTRATE: (*not hearing her*) But as soon as they're released they forget they're chronically ill and end up on a drinking party and a long walk home through the snow.... Next thing... they're dead!

RITA: (*quietly*) Oh, put me in jail an' then let me go.

MAGISTRATE: (*turning to her*) Some of you get jobs.... There are jobs, good jobs, if you'd only look around a bit... and stick with them when you get them. But no... you get a job and promise to stay with it and learn, and two weeks later you're gone for three, four days without explanation.... Your reliability record is ruined and an employer has to regard you as lazy, undependable.... What do you expect!

RITA: I'm not scared of you now, bastard!

MAGISTRATE: You have a mind... you have a heart. The cities are open to you to come and go as you wish, yet you gravitate to the slums and skid rows and the shanty-town fringes. You become a whore, drunkard, user of narcotics.... At best, dying of illness or malnutrition.... At worst, kicked or beaten to death by some angry white scum who finds in you something lower than himself to pound his frustrations out on! What's to be done! You Indians seem to be incapable of taking action to help yourselves. Someone must care for you.... Who! For how long!

RITA: You don't know nothin'!

MAGISTRATE: I know... I know.... It's a struggle just to stay alive. I know... I understand. That struggle is mine, as well as yours, Rita Joe! The jungle of the executive has as many savage teeth ready to go for the throat as the rundown hotel on the waterfront.... Your days and hours are numbered, Rita Joe... I worry for the child I once saw... I have already forgotten the woman!

He turns away from her and exits into the wings stage right.

The lights on RITA JOE fade. Lights of cold, eerie blue wash the backdrop of the stage faintly. RITA JOE stands in silhouette for a long moment.

Slowly, ominously, the three MURDERERS appear on the ramp backstage, one coming from the wings of stage right; one from the wings of stage left; and one rising from the back of the ramp, climbing it. One of the MURDERERS is whistling, a soft nervous noise throughout their scene onstage.

RITA JOE whimpers in fear, and as the MURDERERS loom above her, she runs along the apron to stage left. Here she bumps into JAIMIE PAUL who enters. She screams in fear.

JAIMIE: Rita Joe!

RITA: (*terrorized*) Jaimie! They're comin'. I seen them comin'!

JAIMIE: Who's coming! What's the matter, Rita Joe?

RITA: Men I once dreamed about... I seen it all happen once before... an' it was like this...

JAIMIE PAUL laughs and pats her shoulders reassuringly. He takes her hand and tries to lead her forward to the apron of the stage, but RITA JOE is dead, her steps wooden.

JAIMIE: Don't worry... I can take care of myself!

A faint light on the two of them.

RITA: You been in jail now too, Jaimie Paul...

JAIMIE: So what! Guys in jail was saying that they got to put a man behind bars or the judge don't get paid for being in court to make the trial.... Funny world, eh, Rita Joe!

RITA: (*nodding*) Funny world.

The light dies on them. They come forward slowly.

JAIMIE: I got a room with a hot plate.... We can have a couple of eggs and some tea before we go to see the movie.

RITA: What was it like for you in jail?

JAIMIE: So so...

JAIMIE PAUL motions for RITA JOE to follow him and moves forward from her. The distant sound of a train approaching is heard. She is wooden, coming slowly after him.

RITA: It was different where the women were.... It's different to be a woman.... Some women was wild... and they shouted they were riding black horses into a fire I couldn't see.... There was no fire there, Jaimie!

JAIMIE: (*turning to her, taking her arm*) Don't worry... we're goin' to eat and then see a movie.... Come on, Rita Joe!

She looks back and sees the MURDERERS rise and slowly approach from the gloom. Her speech becomes thick and unsteady as she follows JAIMIE PAUL to the front of the ramp.

RITA: One time I couldn't find the street where I had a room to sleep in... forgot my handbag... had no money.... An old man with a dog said hello, but I couldn't say hello back because I was worried an' my mouth was so sticky I couldn't speak to him...

JAIMIE: Are you comin'?

RITA: When you're tired an' sick, Jaimie, the city starts to dance...

JAIMIE: (*taking her hand, pulling her gently along*) Come on, Rita Joe.

RITA: The street lights start rollin' like wheels an' cement walls feel like they was made of blanket cloth...

The sound of the train is closer now. The lights of its lamps flicker in back of the stage. RITA JOE turns to face the MURDERERS, one of whom is whistling ominously. She whimpers in fear and presses herself against JAIMIE PAUL. JAIMIE PAUL turns and sees the MURDERERS hovering near them.

JAIMIE: Don't be scared.... Nothing to be scared of, Rita Joe... (*to the MURDERERS*) What the hell do you want?

One of the MURDERERS laughs. JAIMIE PAUL pushes RITA JOE back behind himself. He moves towards the MURDERERS, taunting them.

You think I can't take care of myself?

With deceptive casualness, the MURDERERS approach him. One of them makes a sudden lurch at JAIMIE PAUL as if to draw him into their circle. JAIMIE PAUL anticipates the trap and takes a flying kick at the MURDERER, knocking him down.

They close around JAIMIE PAUL with precision, then attack. JAIMIE PAUL leaps, but is caught mid-air by the other two. They bring him down and put the boots to him. RITA JOE screams and runs to him. The train sound is loud and immediate now.

One of the MURDERERS has grabbed RITA JOE. The remaining two raise JAIMIE PAUL to his feet and one knees him viciously in the groin. JAIMIE PAUL screams and doubles over. The lights of the train are upon them. The MURDERERS leap off the ramp leaving JAIMIE PAUL in the path of the approaching train. JAIMIE PAUL's death cry becomes the sound of the train horn. As the train sound roars by, the MURDERERS return to close in around RITA JOE.

One MURDERER springs forward and grabs RITA JOE. The other two help to hold her, with nervous fear and lust. RITA JOE breaks free of them and runs to the front of the stage. The three MURDERERS come after her, panting hard. They close in on her leisurely now, playing with her, knowing that they have her trapped.

Recorded and overlapping voices.

CLERK: The court calls Rita Joe...

MAGISTRATE: Who is she?... Let her speak for herself...

RITA: In the summer it was hot, an' flies hummed...

TEACHER: A book of verse, a melting pot...

MAGISTRATE: Thirty days!

FATHER: Barkin' to beat hell.... How! How!

JAIMIE: (*laughing, defiant, taunting*) You go to hell!

PRIEST: A confession, Rita Joe...

Over the voices she hears, the MURDERERS attack. Dragging her down backwards, they pull her legs open and one MURDERER lowers himself on her.

RITA: Jaimie! Jaimie! Jaimie!

RITA JOE's head lolls over sideways. The MURDERERS stare at her and pull back slightly.

MURDERER: (*thickly, rising off her twisted, broken body*) Shit... she's dead.... We hardly touched her.

He hesitates for a moment, then runs, joined by the SECOND MURDERER.

SECOND MURDERER: Let's get out of here!

They run up onto the ramp and watch as the THIRD MURDERER piteously climbs onto the dead RITA JOE.

Sounds of a funeral chant. MOURNERS appear on riser backstage. RITA JOE's FATHER enters from the wings of stage left, chanting an ancient Indian funeral chant, carrying the body of JAIMIE PAUL. The MURDERER hesitates in his necrophilic rape and then runs away.

The YOUNG INDIAN MEN bring the body of JAIMIE PAUL over the ramp and approach. The body is placed down on the podium, beside RITA JOE's. All the Indians, young and old, kneel around the two bodies. The FATHER continues his death chant. The PRIEST enters from the wings of stage right reciting a prayer. The TEACHER, SINGER, POLICEMAN and MURDERERS come with him forming the outside perimeter around the Indian funeral.

PRIEST: Hail Mary, Mother of God... pray for us sinners now and at the hour of our death.

Repeated until finally EILEEN JOE slowly rises to her feet and, turning to the PRIEST and WHITE MOURNERS, says softly...

EILEEN: (*over the sounds of chanting and praying*) No!... No!... No more!

The YOUNG INDIAN MEN rise one after another facing the outer circle defiantly, and the CAST freezes on stage, except for the SINGER.

SINGER:
Oh, the singing bird
Has found its wings
And it's soaring!
My God, what a sight!
On the cold fresh wind of morning!...

During the song, EILEEN JOE steps forward to the audience and as the song ends, says...

EILEEN: When Rita Joe first come to the city, she told me... the cement made her feet hurt.

The end.

CRABDANCE

BY

BEVERLEY SIMONS

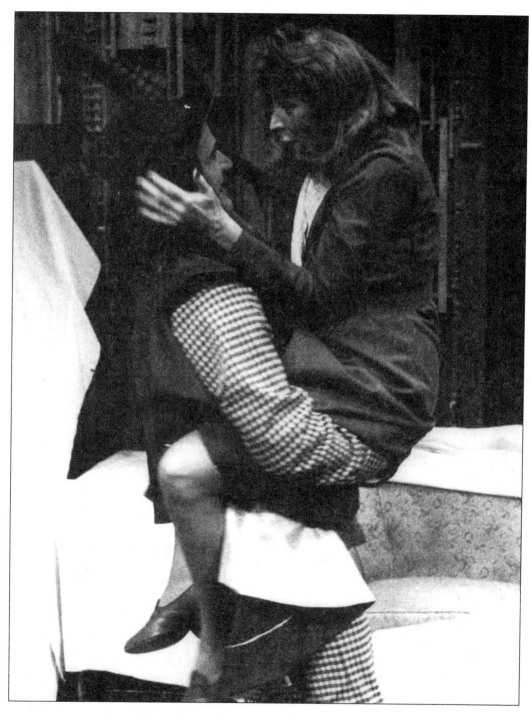

Florence Paterson as Sadie, Maurice Good as Highrise

Photographer: Doug McKay

Colonized Woman at Play in Beverley Simons' *Crabdance*

In 1976 the journal *Canadian Theatre Review* did something it had never done before: it devoted an entire issue to one playwright—Beverley Simons. The editor, Don Rubin, called Simons "Canada's most ignored, important writer" and her play *Crabdance*, "perhaps the finest play yet written in this country." In the same issue, Malcolm Black, the first director of the play, wrote an article entitled "The Strange Unhappy Life of Crabdance."

In this article, Black recounts how Simons, during the early sixties, began to write a play about a woman facing death. But it was not her hometown, Vancouver, that first staged the play: Black directed the premiere production at Seattle's A Contemporary Theatre (ACT), opening in September 1969. Only after what Vancouver Playhouse dramaturge Peter Hay termed "intense pressure" did the Playhouse Theatre finally perform the work, in January 1972, directed by Frances Hyland. Why had it taken so long?

Sometimes real-life events surrounding the theatre itself eclipse the drama it is attempting to stage: this was especially true during the 1950s and 1960s when British Columbia's professional theatre was itself struggling to be born – in a city that was not supportive of an emerging theatre that contradicted its stable, largely British, values. The Vancouver city council, in response, nervously asserted its authority. In the early fifties police walked on stage during Everyman Theatre's performance of *Tobacco Road* and arrested five actors. The prolonged court case that followed led to the eventual withdrawal of the company's founder and director, Sydney Risk.

Similarly, in the sixties the city prosecuted Gallimaufry Theatre for its production of Michael McClure's *The Beard*, charging three of the company with giving an obscene performance; they received fines and suspended sentences. Finally however, with support for the company from people such as drama critics Christopher Dafoe (*Vancouver Sun*) and Jurgen Hesse (CBC *Radio*), the British Columbia Court of Appeal dismissed the charges, but by then the Gallimaufry Theatre Company had collapsed, defeated by two years of litigation.

At the Playhouse Theatre, the province's designated "regional" theatre, the first two directors, Malcolm Black and Joy Coghill, had successfully encouraged new Canadian playwrights such as Eric Nicol, Paul St. Pierre, and George Ryga. But there had also been opposition to new values, with regular audience members walking out during performances of Ryga's play about hippie culture, *Grass and Wild Strawberries*, then a full-blown public controversy when the Playhouse board refused to stage Ryga's play about the FLQ crisis, *Captives of the Faceless Drummer*. As Ryga well knew, to write a play about social reality in British Columbia is a political act. For Simons, such writing is, as she admits, invariably "disturbing."

Beverley Simons was born in 1938 in Flin Flon, Manitoba. Her early training was in music, but in high school she wrote a play, *Twisted Roots*, which won a national writing contest for students. After a summer of writing at Banff, for which she won a scholarship, Simons enrolled in English studies at McGill University in Montreal. While there, she founded an experimental theatre group that also produced several of her short plays. In 1958 she transferred to the University of British Columbia, completing her BA in English and Theatre. After that, she travelled throughout Europe to see a lot of theatre; it was on this trip that she began her first play, *The Elephant and the Jewish Question*.

The production of *Crabdance*, according to Black, was not as well received in Vancouver as it was in Seattle. In his review, *Vancouver Sun* critic Christopher Dafoe commented on the troubled reaction of the audience: "A number of people have expressed dismay and consternation over Beverley Simons' play *Crabdance*, currently sending them around the bend at the Playhouse. People tend to love it or hate it; few I suspect have found it dull" (22 Jan. 1972). After Vancouver there was only one more mainstage production in Canada, at the Citadel Theatre in Edmonton, again directed by Black; otherwise it was staged only on "second stages," in Halifax (1972) and Winnipeg (1975), then adapted for airing on CBC *Radio* (1974). There have been productions in Europe and in Japan, but none in Canada. So why has *Crabdance* had such a "short, unhappy life"? The answer lies in the representation of its central character.

Sadie Golden powerfully embodies a woman in a society struggling to emerge from its colonial past. British Columbia women have been particularly strong leaders in the women's movement, ever since their active participation in the social reform groups of the 1880s, such as the Women's Christian Temperance Union and the local Councils of Women. By 1970, with the women's liberation movement, there was renewed energy for political activism, or at least consciousness-raising, with the founding of a number of significant projects in Vancouver, some of them firsts in Canada: the feminist newspaper, *The Pedestal*; women's studies courses at UBC; and the all-women publishing group, the Press Gang. These, and many other initiatives, came about because women faced massive discrimination, confirmed by the federal Royal Commission on the Status of Women, which made 167 recommendations.

In a post-colonial play like *Crabdance*, women's bodies are territories where society's battles are fought: the concerns with fertility, child-bearing, and mothering that occur at the heart of *Crabdance*, on the body of Sadie Golden, take on political meaning, reflecting how external powers, whether it be Ottawa, Britain, or the United States, seek to extend their control over all aspects of life, including reproduction. With her body subjugated and marked under an Imperial/male gaze, Sadie is seen as mere merchandise, a sex object, at the very least a passive customer ready for exploitation by an endless visitation of salesmen, while the parallel system of patriarchy strictly limits her existence to the roles of mother, wife, and lover. Just as the territory in British Columbia annexed by the settler-invaders was figured as "unoccupied" and therefore in need of "penetration" and "settlement," even as the livelihood of the indigenous peoples was violated, central concerns in *Crabdance* are death and seduction. The penultimate scene, similar to that of *The Ecstasy of Rita Joe*, reveals the rape mentality of the salesmen – an analogue to the brutality of imperial patriarchy.

But Sadie is also a split character, a confusion of roles. She still plays mother, wife, and lover but with powerful self-questioning, even against God himself, and a wild mixing of roles in a fierce endgame that, in the end, reduces her male visitors to childishness. "The things we might have done to you and didn't – you think it's just me standing here?" she tells them, evoking the natural, unfettered potential of women. The men, meanwhile, alternately overwhelm and shrink from Sadie, themselves clashing and disintegrating in the hierarchical roles assigned them in a reductive customer/salesman economy. Sadie's fragmenting character reflects the diverse elements of the white woman in a settler territory; faced with the absolutes of death, she deconstructs the roles of mother, wife, lover, thus opening possibilities for new relationships.

In this way *Crabdance* is a "difficult" play, one that problematizes its characters as well as their changing situation in a society alternately colonized and colonizing. This play, we believe, is a very powerful and effective dramatization of the post-colonial dilemma that exists in British Columbia.

J.H.

Selected Bibliography:

•Black, Malcolm. "The Strange Unhappy Life of *Crabdance*." *Canadian Theatre Review* 9 (Winter 1976): 9-17. The entire issue of this journal is devoted to the work of Simons; it also includes her play *Leela Means To Play*.
•Lister, Rota Herzberg. "Beverley Simons and the Influence of Oriental Theatre." *Canadian Drama*, 10.2 (1984): 218-226.
•Parkin, Andrew, ed. *Stage One: A Canadian Scenebook*. Toronto: Van Nostrand Reinhold, 1973. Contains an excerpt and a brief discussion of *Crabdance*.
•Rubin, Don and Alison Cranmer-Byng, eds. *Canada's Playwrights: A Biographical Guide*. Toronto: Canadian Theatre Review Publications, 1980.
•Simons, Beverley. *Crabdance*. Vancouver: Talonbooks, 1972. Fifth Printing: Dec. 1976.
•Simons, Beverley. *Preparing*. Vancouver: Talonbooks, 1975. Contains Simons' shorter plays *Preparing, Triangle, The Crusader*, and *Green Lawn Rest Home*.

Crabdance
by Beverley Simons

Crabdance was first produced at A Contemporary Theatre in Seattle, Washington, U.S.A., on September 16, 1969, with the following cast:

Sadie	Marjorie Nelson
Mowchuk	Robert Casper
Dickens	Alan Scarfe
Highrise	Gordon Gould
Directed by	Malcolm Black

Crabdance was also produced at the Playhouse Theatre Centre in Vancouver, British Columbia, on January 14, 1972, with the following cast:

Sadie	Jennifer Phipps
Mowchuk	Hutchinson Shandro
Dickens	Sandy Webster
Highrise	Neil Dainard

Directed by Frances Hyland
Designed by Cam Porteous

CHARACTERS

SADIE
MOWCHUK
DICKENS
HIGHRISE

ACT ONE

A living room, dining room area, entrance hall and entrance to a kitchen. Free-standing stairs end abruptly in space above the set. The upper portion of the stairs leading to the voice may be obscured at first by a wall and exposed only at the three o'clock glare. The stage front represents a plate glass window.

The set should be suggestive rather than detailed, and though the furniture is real, the effect should be curiously disturbing. The furniture is shrouded in cowl-like sheets. Each piece has a character of its own, related to its function and to the person who will belong to it.

Scattered on the sheet which covers the dining room table are mounds of writing paper, envelopes, letters, lists, newspaper clippings and a pair of scissors. A wall phone hangs between the dining room area and the kitchen. Pinned beside the phone is an exaggeratedly long sheet of foolscap filled with names and several large advertisements.

A large, blue china cat with an enormous belly filled with SADIE's savings stands in a conspicuous position on the floor, and nearby, there is a box filled with advertisements.

SADIE is in her fifties, now thin, sagging, highly nervous. Smiles appear and disappear involuntarily on her face. She makes little noises without being aware of them. The word "hunh" when it appears in the text, merely indicates a place for the use of her sounds. She emanates a strange combination of vulnerability and threat, naivete and cunning.

As the play opens, SADIE is in the midst of hurried preparations.

SADIE: Listen, you can't kid me about making woman out of man's ribs. You wouldn't change your mind about how to do things right off the bat. I mean, God doesn't make mistakes. First shot, bango, right on target. So why ribs first and then wombs? Man springs from woman, it's in your book.

Come on, you can tell me. Nobody's listening. It's a cover-up, right? You don't want us to know you had a bit of pleasure with the first woman. You shouldn't be ashamed. Immaculate Conception! Pheh! That must have been some fight before you got her down. With appreciation. Or maybe you haven't told because you don't want the other women, me, to take a real look at what we're left with. Mortal lovers.

She spits, then sings the following song, using a simple three-pitch melody that will be used throughout the play.

How she loved her darling man.
She wound her arms around him.
But when she woke,
Her man was gone.
A baby had replaced him.

The last line is spoken. After a pause, she resumes her work.

They'll be here soon. We better hurry. What'll they think if we're not ready for them? They'll think we're slops, that's what. Hunh. They won't come back. They'll come back.

Hunh, hunh. Wouldn't Golden be jealous if he knew about this afternoon! It's not my fault I attract friends. It's a gift from God. You could as soon cut off my arms, I told him. I wonder if he can hear me.

SADIE looks to her imagined location of heaven, up the staircase to the second floor and beyond. She shouts to "The Old Man," Golden.

Can you hear me? Like Jehovah, he hears me. The two of them up there playing stupid. Wouldn't the neighbours be surprised if he answered! Either of them.

A bell or the buzzer of a stove in the kitchen is heard.

My tarts.

She dashes into the kitchen. The sound of pans being removed from the oven is heard. She re-enters the living room.

Pumpkin for Mr. Dickens, strawberry for Mr. Wilkins, blood pudding for Mr. Highrise, sugar cookies, date cookies, chocolate cookies, meat balls, rice balls, chicken soup, duck soup, oh dear, oh dear, oh dear...

It's starting. My breasts. I can feel them. Muscles, tick tick.

They're my two white sacs, no, collapsed globes, maps of blue veins and white stretch lines, meaning nothing until they... yes, starting, swell and fill, full.... Then whole worlds can be read on them My nipples corks of fire. Burn! I want to hurt. The pain pleasures me. MILK!

SADIE falls over the blue cat. The sound of the cash inside it is heard.

Under my feet again! Why are you always under my feet? Why don't you stay in your place where you're put where I put you?

Are you hurt? Puss puss? Nothing lost?

SADIE rocks the cat and hums comfortingly. Sounds from the cat and SADIE's sound mix with the muted rumble of an approaching trolley.

Listen! The one o'clock trolley. Here it comes. Sparks on the wire like... like fireworks. He's dropped a cable! The conductor will get out and knock on our door. "May I have a glass of water?" Like last year. The blonde one. Remember? (*suddenly concerned*) We won't have room for him this time. She looks out again. No. Sadly. Gone. (*She stops shaking the jar.*) You are a liar, old woman. You're dry. You sag. Why don't you throw them away, Sadie, with the old vacuum cleaner bags?

The phone rings. SADIE answers it.

Hello? Sadie Golden speaking. I'm always in. (*dryly*) Of course I remember who you are, Mr.... (*She runs her fingers down the list pinned on the wall.*) Schwartz. This afternoon? (*She touches her hair self-consciously.*) I'll have to rush to straighten up, but.... How is three o'clock? Oh, did I mention it in my letter? I'll expect you then. And Mr. Schwartz, we'll use the silver tea service this time.

She hangs up the phone.

Schwartz... coming.

In a businesslike way she puts a check mark beside Schwartz's name, then fingers a stack of invitations on the dining room table.

Too late for these.

She drops them in a wastebasket. Reconsidering, she pulls one out again.

One more. Mister... Underhill. Our party wouldn't be complete without him. Out of the garbage. He'd appreciate that. (*She writes quickly.*) Special delivery. RSVP. (*She licks the envelope.*)

The phone rings again.

Hello? Yes. Three o'clock. It can't be later. I look forward to seeing you, Mr. Goodman.

She hangs up. She puts another check on her list.

Whooo! I'm falling off my feet, but I can't disappoint them. You're too soft, Sadie Golden, that's your trouble. You've never learned to say no, have you? Look at your hands. Not very pretty. And the veins.

Wouldn't it be embarrassing if they popped and spattered all over the teacups? I'll wear gloves. I don't want them to know how hard I've worked for them. (She reconsiders.) One glove? Well, you can't pour tea with gloves on. What if... they don't come?

None of them.

A moment of dull panic, then SADIE rushes to her source of reassurance, the windows that open out on an artery of the city. She stares out, trying to suck the life she sees into her body. Next she must get that body busy. She sprays and polishes as she talks.

Plate glass, a real invention! We're lucky to be living here, you and I, Puss. Right in the centre of things. The whole world passes in front of us. No surprises left. Not for you and me. We've been here too long. We can't be lonely even if we want to.

SADIE starts to sing.

Bye baby bunting,
Mama's goin' a hunting,
The world is round
And though you run
You'll end up here with the setting sun,
My baby...

Her song is interrupted.

Hey, there goes Old Man Gerd. Pretends he can't see us. I know where the sun is. The glare's not till three o'clock. (*She makes an appropriate thumb gesture.*) Up yours, Gerd!

MOWCHUK enters.

He looked! He saw us, Puss! He saw us!

SADIE's movement brings into her vision the nondescript stranger standing in the living-room doorway. It is MOWCHUK, the rabbit, the son-to-be. In his late thirties, small boned, he overarticulates to cover a trace of accent. He carries a briefcase filled with books.

I didn't hear you come in.

MOWCHUK: I... I knocked. The door... it opened by itself. It must have been off the catch... the latch.

SADIE approaches MOWCHUK even as he speaks and circles him, examining him, touching him with short, hesitant hand movements, first the material of his jacket, his fingers, perhaps even his face; sniffing even, as though she were blind and could only read him through fingers and nostrils; yet her eyes feel MOWCHUK too, but in pieces, disembodying him.

SADIE: (*sniffing his jacket*) Jacket... not bad.

MOWCHUK: (*during this process*) Shall I go away? I can come back later, another time. (*hopefully*) Tomorrow?

SADIE: Hands...

MOWCHUCK: (*as he pulls his briefcase back*) My briefcase!

SADIE: ...small. Everything hunh there, as far as meets the eye.

MOWCHUK instinctively covers his crotch.

What do you think, Puss. Hunh? Will he do? Not exactly what we had in mind for our first born.... But a woman can't choose.

MOWCHUK: I... I...

SADIE: (*still to the cat*) He stutters! A handicap at a party.

She turns on him suddenly.

You're early! I'm not angry. Don't be frightened. I'm flattered. You couldn't wait to get here. (*to Puss*) He couldn't wait, Puss. To reach us. Impatient. Just like a man, We can use a man's back. You can help me get things in order. A party's a delicate thing, Mr...

MOWCHUK: (*searches his mind desperately*) Mmmmmmm.... Mmmmmmm...

SADIE: Yes?

MOWCHUK: Mmmmaaa...

SADIE: (*encouraging*) That's it.

MOWCHUK: Ma.... Ma...

SADIE: Good boy! You got it!

MOWCHUK: Mmmmmowchuk. Leonard Mowchuk. Leonard Mowchuk.

SADIE: How do you do, Mr. Mowchuk? Sadie Golden.

Elegantly she holds out her hand to him. As he deliberates whether or not to touch it, she changes the gesture into a wave, indicating chairs.

Won't you sit down?

Hypnotized, MOWCHUK goes toward the large sheeted chair.

I said, sit down.

MOWCHUK starts to obey.

Not there. Over here. (*She leads him.*)

He's perfect for the training chair, don't you agree, Puss? At least until we get to know him better. People don't understand these things nowadays, Mr. Mowchuk. Parties have to be shaped.

MOWCHUK has started to sit in the indicated chair.

Wait!

He stands up again. Ceremoniously, reverently, SADIE removes the sheet revealing a child's potty.

Guest number one.

She places her hands on MOWCHUK's shoulder, gently pressing him down. MOWCHUK opens his mouth as if to speak. SADIE gestures for silence.

Shhh. I want to remember.

MOWCHUK poses as though awaiting a photographer's flash. He forces a sick smile. Then SADIE poses beside him. Proud mother and son. Tintype style.

MOWCHUK: (*blurting it out*) I'm not a guest.

SADIE: (*just as suddenly hard*) Then you're a thief.

MOWCHUK: No! At least, I don't think so. If anything I'm plagued by integrity.

SADIE: You walked into my house.

MOWCHUK: The door, I told you. It was like someone was on the other side pulling.

SADIE: Are you suggesting...

MOWCHUK: Nothing. I'm not anything.

SADIE: I don't have to drag people in off the street. The phone, it doesn't stop. Or the doorbell. Day and night. Telegrams. Cables. It's "Help me! Should I do this, Sadie? Or should I do that? " Nobody stops to worry Sadie Golden maybe she's tired. My bones are glass. They've sucked the marrow out of them. I'm not complaining. There are some people... there are power centres, you know? You see them. Up on a hill or under a lake. Where all the wires and batteries and cables come together, they pulse...

For a moment, her strength is revealed. Suddenly, she is businesslike and hard again.

(*to MOWCHUK*) You didn't wipe your feet.

MOWCHUK: (*looking guiltily down at his shoes*) Shall I go back?

SADIE: A thief would have wiped his feet so as not to leave tracks. The truth, Mr. Muffett.

MOWCHUK: (*standing formally, reciting his name*) Mowchuk. Leonard Mowchuk.

SADIE: Can't be avoided. You're a guest. I expect you to behave like one. (*in a complete change of tone*) Will you have tea? We should wait for the others, but one cup won't hurt.

Without waiting for a reply, SADIE exits to the kitchen for some tea.

MOWCHUK: (*uncertain, to himself*) You could call it a visit, I suppose.

SADIE: (*calling from the kitchen*) Don't be fooled by appearances, Mr Mowchuk.

MOWCHUK: (*to himself*) They didn't prepare me for anything like this. It's not fair.

SADIE: The room looks like a funeral parlour to you. (*The exaggerated sound of water being poured into a tea kettle is heard.*) You didn't have to say it. I could read your face.

MOWCHUK: (*still to himself*) Not at any of the lectures. Or in the pamphlets.

The high piercing whistle of the water boiling in the tea kettle is heard. MOWCHUK jumps.

A book... I must... hold.... (*He opens his case, gropes for, and takes out, a large tome.*) Heavy... weight.... Thank God! No! Control reflexes, Mowchuk. Reason. Data. (*He fumbles in his inner jacket pocket and pulls out a measuring tape.*) That's it. Facts.

With desperate concentration MOWCHUK measures the book. He kneels on the floor with the book on his chair seat.

Fourteen inches in length, twelve inches in width, four inches thickness, five thousand years content.... No. Non sequitur. An immeasurable there.

SADIE has been beside him with tea things for part of his data speech.

SADIE: Are you leaving? You can if you want to.

She sweeps the sheet from the coffee table and sets down the tray.

MOWCHUK is embarrassed at being caught. Trying to keep his back to SADIE, he hurriedly puts the book and the tape back into his briefcase.

If you're bored...

MOWCHUK: No! Why should I be?

SADIE gives one end of the sheet to MOWCHUK.

SADIE: You won't hurt my feelings...

MOWCHUK: On the contrary, I...

They fold the sheet together.

SADIE: There's no obligations. That's the first rule here. You walked into my house because you wanted to. Or so I gather. Now you're welcome to stay. Or go. Whichever you choose. (*She starts to pour tea.*)

MOWCHUK: As a gentleman, Madam, I... I hardly...

SADIE: You can't throw it at me later I didn't give you a chance. Sadie Golden hangs onto no one. But... if you do stay...

MOWCHUK: Yes?

SADIE: It gets harder and harder to leave.

MOWCHUK: Why?

The phone rings.

SADIE: See what I mean? It never stops. Not that I'm complaining.

She picks up the phone.

Hello? Yes, Reverend Cavil. (*running her pencil down her list*) You can't make it? (*She puts an "x" beside his name.*) Why should I be offended? (*Stretching the phone cord, she moves toward the kitchen.*) You come to see me whenever you like. It's not for me to choose. I'm surprised you want to talk to a silly old woman at all. Of course, I might not be at home when you do decide to come, but I'm sure you have so many others to visit you'll hardly notice. Yes. A little something, yes, Mr. Golden left me that. Thank you for your condolences. Your concern is touching. Tomorrow? I won't be here. No. Not the rest of the week either. I'm getting old, Reverend. It's as hard for me to hold back a decision as it is to hold my water.

MOWCHUK coughs.

Did I tell you that Rabbi Grubber will be here? Now why should you change your plans for me?

Although he is listening, MOWCHUK can't resist the impulse to peek under the sheets.

I wouldn't dream of interfering in a family crisis. (*Pause.*) You insist.

MOWCHUK is horrified at what he sees under one of the sheets – a coffin, unseen by the audience.

At three o'clock then.

SADIE re-enters to change the "x" to a check mark on the list, just in time to see MOWCHUK drop the corner of the crucial sheet.

Ah ah ah. Don't rush it, Mowchuk. You'll see everything in good time.

SADIE puts her hand affectionately on a covered piece of furniture.

They're in cocoons, waiting to be let out. You released your chair, Mr. Mowchok. You've got to accept responsibility for it now. It's not complete unless Leonard Muffett...

MOWCHUK: Mowchuk.

SADIE: ...is sitting on it. One by one my friends will break all the shells. This room will be as gay as a garden. Right, Puss? But I haven't introduced you...

SADIE notices MOWCHUK is staring at her.

Your face, it's... (*She laughs, a surprisingly full throaty laugh.*) You must have thought I was... talking to... I've been impolite.

She picks up the blue cat and carries it to MOWCHUK.

Puss, I'd like you to meet Mr. Mowchuk. Leonard Mowchuk. Leonard Mowchuk, Puss.

MOWCHUK: (*weakly*) How do you do?

SADIE: Go ahead. Pat her. Only if you want to. No? Maybe later. (*to the cat*) You're better than flesh and blood, aren't you, Puss? You don't pull up threads from my furniture or shed hair on the cushions. No yowling at the door at night to go out. And you stay where you're put. Most of the time, that is. (*to MOWCHUK*) Why aren't you drinking your tea?

MOWCHUK automatically takes a sip.

I had a real one once, a tabby, brown and white stripes.

Suddenly MOWCHUK notices a bouquet of flowers on the table. Inexplicably, it frightens him.

MOWCHUK: (*involuntarily*) They're wax.

SADIE: I was a slave to the seasons. The smell and the screams, you wouldn't believe it! He was killed by... (*She looks out the window; rushes to it.*) That dachshund! Shoo! Scat! He's at my spruce again. Sicked on by the neighbour. I'm sure of it. She's jealous of that spruce. It's got the largest cones in the neighbourhood. Did you notice them when you came up the walk? Both sexes on the same bush. The big ones at the top are female.

SADIE is standing with her back to the window. Her body seems to grow and block out the light.

I'd had his claws pulled. Just the front ones. Because of the furniture. It was a perfectly painless operation. Or so the doctor said. Sugar?

MOWCHUK shakes his head no.

He also said he'd still be able to climb trees. I don't think he liked cats, that doctor. It was a terrible sight. Him scrambling up the tree trunk, and then sliding down again, up and down, up... while that... "animal" waited for him at the bottom, sniffing. It lacked dignity. At least it could have been a German Shepherd or a... a Black Labrador. There'd have been some splendour then. You really ought to, you know?

MOWCHUK: Ought to... what?

SADIE: Have sugar. Gives you energy. You remind me of my son. Did I tell you that? Same complexion. Same bone structure, here... (*She touches MOWCHUK on the chin.*) ...here. (*She touches him on the forehead around the temples.*) One or two spoons?

MOWCHUK: (*hypnotized*) Two.

SADIE: Three?

MOWCHUK: Three.

SADIE: (*her hand still on his face*) When the time came, when they came of age, my son and my daughter, I said to them, "Go. Get out." For their good. That is, when they were ready for independence. (*She puts three sugars in MOWCHUK's cup and stirs.*) Tell me about you. You have something to say, haven't you? There was a reason that made you walk into my house.

MOWCHUK: (*not believing that his time may have come*) Y... y... yes. Yes! Yes!

SADIE pings one of her teacups with a spoon.

I...

SADIE motions for silence until the sound ends.

SADIE: That's its song. Leonard Mowchuk. What's yours?

MOWCHUK: I'm a... I'm a...

SADIE is silent.

I'masalesman!

No reaction from SADIE. MOWCHUK standing, a prolonged call.

A saaaaaaalesmaaaaaaan!

SADIE: Aren't we all?

MOWCHUK: Not that way!

SADIE: (*infinitely patient*) In what way, then?

MOWCHUK: B... b... b.... Books! I sell books! There. I've said it. I... I represent... (*He looks at her imploringly. She says nothing.*) I represent.... How do you do Mrs. Golden, my name is Leonard Mowchuk and I represent THE UNIVERSAL BOOKS OF KNOWLEDGE.

SADIE: Whoo! Big name. A lot to represent.

MOWCHUK: I... may not... ideally, that is, but... I don't matter, it's... it's what's in there, Mrs. Golden. (*tapping his briefcase*) Be... be... be... between these covers, in... in this case, there lies the power.... (*now getting involved*) ...to... to roll back the Dark Ages of Man, forever. Knowledge! Ed... u... cation! (*giving it an exaggerated French pronunciation*) There's the answer. If we can just get all the facts, compile the data. It's pouring in all the time. Do you realize, at this very minute, as you sit here, there are hundreds, thousands, millions of books coming off the presses of the world? In Canada, Russia, America, Sierra Leone. (*almost crying with joy*) Facts. Facts. And every fact brings us closer and closer to Ultimate Truth. Now we're wanderers in a cave with a candle, no, thousands of candles, but soon we'll find the crack. We'll rip off that roof of rock and let in the Great White Light of Knowledge!

SADIE: (*covering her face with her shawl*) No.

MOWCHUK: No more secrets. Think of it! Already we're taking pictures of the dark side of the moon.

SADIE: No.

MOWCHUK: All the shadows burnt away.

SADIE: No.

MOWCHUK: No dark corners.

SADIE: No.

MOWCHUK: No basements.

SADIE: No.

MOWCHUK: No caves.

SADIE: No.

MOWCHUK: No jungles.

SADIE: No.

MOWCHUK: No bogeymen to come down from the attic and eat you up if you're a bad boy. (*catching himself*) That's how I try to describe it to my students.

SADIE uncovers her face.

SADIE: You're a teacher. What do you teach, Mowchuk? I said, what do you teach?

MOWCHUK: I beg your pardon?

SADIE: Or have you been fired?

MOWCHUK: No!

SADIE: Then this is a second job?

MOWCHUK: (*French accent again*) Une avocation!

SADIE: What do you teach?

MOWCHUK: (*defensively*) Violin.

SADIE: I should have guessed. Long sensitive fingers.

MOWCHUK: Not like that. Music is logic. It's closer to mathematics than the arts. When man lives by his emotions he's an animal. His intellect makes him God. Not in the orthodox sense, of course. I used to be a Catholic. But I'm happy to say I've rid myself of that primitive conditioning. Rubbing beads, drinking blood, eating flesh.... Repulsive, even symbolically. And these men go out to convert! While actually it's people like me knocking at doors like yours...

SADIE: You think I need converting? Why me, Mowchuk? Why my house?

MOWCHUK: (*flustered*) I had a list.

SADIE: You think you've come by chance? Talk. I want you to talk, but about Leonard Mowchuk. Not what he's representing.

MOWCHUK: But that's not.... They didn't send me out here to...

SADIE: Oh yes, they did.

MOWCHUK: I... I can't. I won't! I won't give myself... myself... away so... so...

SADIE: You force me to be blunt, Muffett.

MOWCHUK: Mowchuk. Leonard Mowchuk...

SADIE: A woman doesn't enjoy that. I'm not sure I'll forgive you. You are a salesman and I am a buyer. "A relationship." There aren't many of those left anymore. Mother and child? Husband and wife? Lovers? (*dismissing each of them*) Hunh! Who cares about me, unh? You. Why, you and I might be the last two people in the world having a real conversation. Would you care to sit on the couch? (*She lifts an edge of the sheet seductively.*)

MOWCHUK: Are you suggesting?... I won't...

SADIE: Everything in this world has a flowering, Mowchuk, even those things we think aren't alive. It may be a dance or a glow or a song, like I said, sometimes so short that after it's finished you wonder if you heard it at all.

But in this house we have time and time to listen...

MOWCHUK: What... do you expect me to do?

SADIE: Why, have tea, of course. With my friends.

MOWCHUK: If you'd only let me... leave me.... My head...

SADIE: (*suddenly realizing*) Why, Leonard Mowchuk, it's... your first time. Isn't it. Isn't it? Admit it. It's nothing to be ashamed of. We all have a first.

MOWCHUK nods his head, miserable, unable to look at her.

No wonder he was early, Puss. Anxious, poor Muffett. And incompetent. No, you weren't either. Shame, Sadie Golden. (*to MOWCHUK*) It'll get easier and easier, you'll see.

MOWCHUK: My mind, it's... I can't concentrate.

SADIE: Is your head... hurting?

He nods. His inadvertent sounds counterpoint her lines. She approaches his chair from behind.

Close your eyes. It's better you should learn from me...

MOWCHUK: (*to himself, puzzled*) Tiptop shape, mental and physical...

SADIE: ...an older woman, more mature and experienced, who can help the situation along with... delicacy.

SADIE starts to massage MOWCHUK's head. He jumps.

Don't shrink from me! (*He falls back.*) I used to do it for my son. (*She continues to massage.*) A gentle woman, yet one who tells it to you straight, if you make that necessary. Relax! Better. There are other guests coming, but not yet. I can't count how many of them I've introduced to the art of our... relationship.

SADIE begins to massage MOWCHUK's shoulders. Again he jumps nervously and subsides.

It won't hurt. I'm not demanding. You'll see. I wish.... If I'd known... I'd of been looking more appropriate. What did I ever ask of my son? Which is what I got, but I'll get more out of you, won't I, Leonard?

MOWCHUK: (*almost unconscious*) Name... I can't remember...

SADIE: (*still massaging*) Aren't there... aren't there little things, small things, little buts in your mind that you'd like to let fly out? Things you'd like to tell?

MOWCHUK appears to be dozing. His sounds, which have become grunts of submission and pleasure, transform into a light snore. SADIE, furious, shakes him.

SADIE: Get up! You're here to help.

MOWCHUK: (*barely awake*) You want me to...

He stumbles to the box. As he starts to push, he becomes aware of what's in it.

SADIE: That box! Push it to the cupboard. I want something.

MOWCHUK: (*referring to the box contents*) Advertisements?

She points to a high cupboard drawer.

SADIE: You're taller than me.

MOWCHUK climbs up on the box.

Reach way in the back.

MOWCHUK: (*pulling his hand back, frightened*) Christ! It was warm.

SADIE: That's my fur jacket, ninny. Behind that.

MOWCHUK: What did I just say? A profanity! Pardon me, Mrs. Golden.

SADIE: I've heard worse.

MOWCHUK: Not that. I'm against overprotecting the female sex. But that I should call on God.... It's... it's unsettling.... You see, I was brought up as a Catholic, but.... Or did I mention that?

SADIE: (*dryly*) It's at the back of the cupboard, Mr. Mowchuk.

MOWCHUK puts his hand in. He pulls it out again.

MOWCHUK: Is this absolutely necessary? I feel as though I'm being indiscreet. Reaching into your... intimate places. I prefer to see what I'm touching.

SADIE: Absolutely necessary. It's in a case.

MOWCHUK: Yes, as I was saying. I'm an atheist now. It's the only logical conclusion a man of intellect can reach. Do you have a rag? Not that I'm suggesting...

MOWCHUK is troubled by the dirt and cobwebs. He takes out his hanky to wipe himself before he reaches in again. Eventually his face and clothes are smeared with grime.

What I can't stand are individuals who announce they've "suspended their judgement." Can't be done, you know. One has to choose. Actually they're cowards. (*He reaches in again and suddenly screams.*) Holy Mother of God. Something moved. (*He teeters on the box.*)

SADIE: Are you alright?

MOWCHUK: I did it again. Did you hear me? Those words. After all these years. Regression. It's this house.

SADIE: (*dryly*) It's mice or bats, maybe. Not a Holy Spirit. Mind, they all like dark places. If you'd rather, I'll...

MOWCHUK: No. No. I'm perfectly capable...

He reaches up again, closes his eyes, and plunges his arm in. The phone rings. SADIE exits as MOWCHUK pulls out a case.

SADIE: Hello?

MOWCHUK can't resist a desire to open the case. In it is a violin.

(*offstage*) Yes, Mr. Applebaum Three o'clock. And don't forget to bring the flowers.

MOWCHUK: She's a witch.

SADIE: (*re-entering*) Well? You're not playing.

MOWCHUK doesn't answer.

Sadie Golden forces no one to do anything. It was just a silly dream I had. Music for my party would make it like... like a salon. Isn't that what they used to call them? Welcome to Sadie's Salon. I bought it for my son, but he won't even spit on it. He's full of music. The few times he played it when he was a kid, everything stood on tiptoe to listen. Now he's... Rock'n' Roll.

MOWCHUK: (*In spite of himself, he has touched the violin.*) What?

SADIE: Rock'n'Roll. To aggravate me, he bought a clock radio; he presets it, anytime, in the middle of the night, four in the morning, three in the afternoon, it blares full volume. I never know if it's him upstairs in his room or if it's the clock. Listen.

She goes to the stairway. They listen. Nothing is heard.

He's not home. Or then again, he might be. I told him he's perfectly.... (*She shouts upstairs.*) ...welcome to move out whenever he wants. Maybe he has. Play, Leonard Mowchuk. (*Her voice changes suddenly to command.*) I said play!

MOWCHUK has wiped the violin with a hanky. He nervously raises it under his chin and starts to play with a definite squeak: "Bye Baby Bunting".

That's it. Beautiful. Maybe you'll reconsider a recital for the guests.

As he plays, SADIE, smiling, drifts into the kitchen. MOWCHUK becomes aware that he's alone.

MOWCHUK: Where... am I? Define. On a floor. Between four... three walls and a window. In a house, in fact. Something has gone wrong. Something has definitely... it's a dream. How to test it? Pain. With what? Pin. (He takes off his tie pin and jabs it into his arm.) Never give up. The rules. Where's the rule book? No. No cheating. Recite from memory. But they didn't prepare me for anything like.... Index. Index Manual, that's it. (*Getting a book from his briefcase, he flips wildly through the pages.*) Encounter problems. They'll have her in here. Babies. No.... Dogs. No Husband. No. Pregnancy.... (*He closes the book.*) Wasting time. Try again. Rehearse.

He picks up the violin, which is used as a humourous dramatic countervoice, and begins to play long drawn out screeching notes while reciting and marching back and forth. If this is too difficult, he can pluck the strings, starting and stopping according to the progress of his argument.

Rehearse while she isn't here. Rehearse what? The rules. What rules? She doesn't follow rules. She should go over them, not me. She doesn't act like a client's supposed to. It's not my fault. I did everything I could. Did you? Step number one: Salesman approaches door, shoulders back, chin squared, if possible. Knocks on door.... Even that. Never mind. No self-pity. Step number two: Greet the customer like an old friend, but with respect.... She didn't give me a chance. I should be at the Illustration Section by now. Step number three: Casually guide the conversation to topic of mutual interest...

No self-pity, Mowchuk! Without making client feel ignorant, tactfully suggest how knowledge can be supplemented by the use of the... of the.... The Universal Books of Knowledge. Step number four: Step number four.... Forgotten. (*Mumbling, he goes through steps which get more and more disjointed, tempo increasing as he approaches step number four.*) Step number one: Approaching door... confidence, Leonard Mowchuk. Step number two: Topic of mutual.... Step number three: Suggest use of books.... Step number four: My mind's a blank. Nonsense. Impossible. The excuse is unacceptable. You won't take it from students, so why from you? It's strictly a mechanical proposition. The brain is a machine connected by the nervous system to sensory perception nodes. (*as though giving a lecture*) Experience is programmed through these nodes of touch, sight, sound and smell to the brain where knowledge is imposed on the grey tissue as firmly as impressions in wax. It can't... just... disappear. (*He starts to play again and pace frantically.*) Step number one.... Step number two.... Step three.... Step four... step four (*a terrible cry*) Fooour! (*sadly*) It's time for a moment of honesty. It's not that poor woman's fault you're not successful. She wouldn't be able to withstand the vigour of your onslaught if you believed in your mission, but the sad fact is.... It's not that you can't remember. No, no. It's not that. Question: Do you believe in what you're selling? Answer: I don't know. Question: Do you believe that Mrs. Golden will benefit by The Universal Books of Knowledge ? Will she ever read them? Does she need them? Answer: I don't know. I don't know. Question: Do you have a right to be in this house, a right to have the presumption to presume that another human being as compared with yourself is ignorant? Answer: I don't know. Leonard Muffett! You are a failure! I... give... you... zero!

MOWCHUK starts to pack up and leave, but in his confusion he overlooks the Index Manual.

SADIE: (*re-entering*) Mr. Mowchuk.

MOWCHUK: Yes, Mrs. Golden?

SADIE: Universal Books of Knowledge, isn't it?

MOWCHUK: (*hopefully*) Yes, yes it is.

SADIE: On Main and Hastings?

MOWCHUK: That's right.

SADIE dials a number.

SADIE: Hello? Dr. Wiseman please, the local supervisor of the Universal Books of Knowledge. That's right. Sadie Golden here. I'm sorry to hear you're sick, Doctor. You're not? What's wrong, then. I'm not good enough for you to come around yourself nowadays? No. I'm not complaining. There's one of your salesmen here right now. He's doing very well, this young man, Mr. Muffett.

MOWCHUK: (*whispers ardently*) Mowchuk.

SADIE: So far. In fact, I'm thinking of writing a letter to the Head Office about him. He should make you feel nervous. He might take away your job. No, I'm not comparing. I wouldn't do that. But you should keep an eye on him. Shall I phone you later? Or would you rather come by for tea? How is three o'clock?

She hangs up. She checks off WISEMAN's name on her list.

Play more! I wish my son could have heard you just now. He'd have learned a lot. Unfortunately he took after his father. A pig. Not a bad man. Dead. Don't misunderstand me. Decent, honourable, dependable. He adored me. Couldn't keep his hands off...

A sudden jangling burst of rock music is heard. SADIE starts to run upstairs, but the phone rings. She runs downstairs and picks up the phone. She shouts.

Hello? Yes. Three o'clock.

She runs upstairs again. While she's climbing the stairs, the front door opens. A huge sack of mail is thrown in. It narrowly misses MOWCHUK. MOWCHUK, distracted now, seizes his coat and briefcase and starts to run out the front door. He trips over the sack of mail. The music stops. SADIE comes back downstairs. She sees MOWCHUK leaving.

So. I might have guessed. It's a good thing I've learned not to trust anyone. I used to be soft. Any fool could take advantage of Sadie Golden. My own family taught me better. I could see right from the beginning what you were, twitching to get out. But you're going to see, it's not so easy now. You opened my door.

MOWCHUK: It opened itself.

SADIE: Under the pressure of your knuckles. You're on this side now. Something's begun, Leonard Mowchuk, between you and your chair and Puss and the violin. And me.

MOWCHUK has been listening half hypnotized. A moan is heard from his chair; a sound is heard from the violin. He makes a dash for the door. The sounds stop as he moves.

So? Why aren't you gone? I wouldn't expect you to feel guilty about leaving. You'd walk in my door and out again whhhsshht, just like that, if you could. I'm not sure it'll let you out, but then again he might. I've got a son, Mr. Mowchok, who shrinks from me when I go to kiss him. What are you standing there for? You're going. "Mind your own business," they tell me. What other business has a mother got to mind? I'll soon be dead and gone. Do you think it's for my sake? I don't count anymore. I used to be beautiful. I watched the veins sprout like grapes on my hips and my breasts when I was pregnant. They share nothing with me, not even their troubles. My hands were spoilt washing diapers. My skin smells from all the meals I cooked for them, herring, cabbage rolls, doughnuts.... When I lie awake at night I can see the smell rising off me like mist, like the spatter of frying fat. But what do you care? You talk about logical conclusions but you're running away.

MOWCHUK: (*concerned*) You.... You.... You're distraught. (*trying to touch her shoulder*)

SADIE: Don't touch me. After you've hurt someone it's no good. You don't touch.

Hard rock music suddenly blares forth again. SADIE rushes up the stairs. The music stops. She re-enters, stands still, and stares fixedly at MOWCHUK. Then, without warning, she slaps him hard. Her love anguish here is real. My own son, why do you turn away from me?

Did I do do something to hurt your feelings? I'm sorry. Did I say too much? I'm sorry. Look how I humble myself. Just let me touch... (*She reaches out to him.*)

MOWCHUK: I'll stay... a little longer.

SADIE: (*playing the brave mother*) Why should you? I want you to leave. You must have other appointments. I don't want to force you to do anything you don't want to.

MOWCHUK: I want to stay. No. Really, I want to.

SADIE: Are you sure? Puss doesn't believe you.

She picks up the cat and holds her out to MOWCHUK. MOWCHUK strokes her. SADIE smiles, in control. Her voice purrs.

There's my good boy.

ACT TWO

DICKENS rings the doorbell. SADIE jumps guiltily.

SADIE: Hunh! Mr. Dickens. Already. Quick! Into the kitchen.

SADIE throws a sheet over the teacups and the table. MOWCHUK, distracted, obeys each instruction until the next one arrests and redirects him.

No. Behind the couch. No. Under the table. Why are you running around like a fool? Stay in your chair. You twitch, that's your trouble. You're a twitcher. Not Mr. Dickens. There's not a quarter inch of doubt in him.

SADIE takes off her apron. She touches her hair nervously. DICKENS knocks. SADIE rushes into the hall then back again. She pulls the cover off the loveseat, balls it up, throws it behind the sofa, thinks better of it, pulls it out again, and offers an end to MOWCHUK.

Hurry. He's waiting.

MOWCHUK helps her fold the cover.

Put it in the cupboard. No. Behind the couch. Oh my God, what'll he say. Back on the loveseat.

MOWCHUK obeys. DICKENS' knock is followed by a doorbell this time.

Why are you looking so scared? How can you expect others to have confidence in you...

She pushes him into his chair, drags the mailbag to one side, rushes to the front door, and opens it to reveal DICKENS, a man in his fifties, big-bellied, with a sonorous, pompous voice, and a British accent. SADIE tries to appear collected.

Mr. Dickens! What a surprise!

DICKENS: By my watch it is precisely 1:30 PM on this day the first Monday of the month. Or am I mistaken in my calculations?

SADIE: If you're here it must be true.

DICKENS enters and hands SADIE his hat. She puts it on the hall stand. This and the following have been done every month for fifteen years.

DICKENS: Happening to find myself in the neighbourhood it came upon me that I might drop in for a cup of tea.

SADIE: Mr. Dickens, you didn't just happen...

DICKENS: That was an interminably long interval between my ringing then knocking then knocking ringing and your answering of the door, my dear...

SADIE: I was busy preparing for you.

DICKENS: (*looking suspiciously down the hall*) Then it must have been, and I'm sure it was, a mere firmament of my imagination...

SADIE: You have so many of those.

DICKENS: I perceived, that is, I thought I perceived, as I made my laborious way up your path...

SADIE bends to help DICKENS take off his buckle galoshes. He has wide, baggy trousers and a vest under his jacket.

I can't continue. I might rupture something far more precious to me than...

SADIE: You have to. You never leave your sentences unfinished, Mr. Dickens. I'd be thinking all sorts of silly endings.

DICKENS: (*abruptly*) A male voice! Impossible, I know, soundwaves of a particular resonance emulating from within your domicile.

SADIE: Your face, it's quite jaundiced, Mr. Dickens. Have you been unwell?

DICKENS: Are you trying to disarm me?

SADIE: You haven't been taking the magnesia I gave you. Am I right? I've told you and told you.... But where.... You didn't bring... (*disappointed*)

DICKENS: Be at rest, dear lady. Have I even once during our long relationship forgotten this precious object?

Dramatically, he pulls out his briefcase from under his coat. It's long and narrow, a sample box.

SADIE: Ooooooh. It's bigger than I remembered.

DICKENS: Just protecting it in case of rain. I could never replace it, as you well know.

SADIE goes to take it. DICKENS pulls away, shocked.

Not yet!

SADIE: (*apologetically*) I don't know what got into me.

DICKENS: It's usually you who chasticates me.

SADIE: For being impatient. You're quite right. The pleasure is in the pace. We've discussed it often.

DICKENS: Not often. We understand each other without...

SADIE takes DICKENS' coat. She hangs it up.

SADIE: You're thinner.

DICKENS: (*still suspicious, looking down the hall*) Saving up. I always starve between our visits.

SADIE: Then you should make them more often.

DICKENS: A man should show constraint, especially in his pleasures.

They start down the hall. SADIE is getting more nervous and giddy as they go.

SADIE: You're looking pale. My mint tea will do you good.

DICKENS: It always does. And you? There's nothing new, I hope?

SADIE: Mr. Golden, his demands, he's getting worse. (*in a half whisper*) You wouldn't believe...

A sound is heard from MOWCHUK. DICKENS sees him and stops, confounded. SADIE, enjoying the situation, turns coquette.

Oh, I don't think you two have met. Mr. Mowchuk, this is my dear friend Mr. Dickens. Mr. Dickens, Mr. Mowchuk.

MOWCHUK: (*coming forward with his hand proffered*) How do you do ?

SADIE: (*to DICKENS*) Aren't you going to shake hands? Why are you looking... I didn't plan it. I didn't think that he.... That is, when you.... Not at the same time.

DICKENS: Adulteress!

MOWCHUK: (*His voice, as at the beginning of the play, has a strange squeak to it.*) I can't let you talk to the lady like that.

DICKENS: You can't... let me.... Pooh.... Pooh.... Whoo...

DICKENS' cheeks puff in and out like an angry toad. He starts to choke.

I... can't... breathe...

SADIE: (*taking some keys off a string around her neck*) Oh dear. Oh dear. He's having an attack. Get wine. Wine, Mr. Mowchuk. In the cabinet. (*She throws the keys to MOWCHUK.*)

DICKENS: (*suddenly observant*) You'd throw him your keys?

As SADIE's attention returns to him, DICKENS returns to sputtering and moaning.

SADIE: Sit down and rest, my dear Mr. Dickens. It's going to be alright. Sadie Golden will make everything all...

Happily hypnotized, DICKENS is almost seated on the loveseat.

Not there! (*harshly*) You've come here often enough.

DICKENS, moaning histrionically, stumbles to another sheeted piece of furniture, pulls off the sheet with his hand behind him, and sinks into large stuffed armchair with footstool, obviously meant for the man of the house.

That's better.

With his eyes closed DICKENS helps SADIE fold the sheet.

DICKENS: (*in a moan which continues until he drinks*) Shame shame shame shame shame...

SADIE: Shhh. Don't try to say anything. (*to MOWCHUK*) Where's the wine? Idiot! Don't drop it.

(*She holds the cut glass decanter to DICKENS' lips.*) An anniversary gift. From Mr. Golden.

DICKENS sputters.

You've had too much. She pulls it away. You'll go to sleep like Golden – when he isn't having me. Everything to satisfy his needs!

DICKENS: Shame, shame... (*then in weak agreement through her following speech*) ...same, same, same...

SADIE: (*together with DICKENS' refrain*) But you, you're decent, considerate, honourable, dependable. What would Sadie Golden have done without her Dickens all these years, eh? With only that...

DICKENS ends the "same" duet.

...toad and his son to hop in and out the door. But the first Monday...

DICKENS: (*happily, by rote*) ...of every month...

SADIE & DICKENS: (*together*) ...for the past fifteen years, Mr. Dickens has come to Sadie Golden.

SADIE stands by DICKENS' chair, as though posing for a photograph. Husband and wife. Tintype style. A twang from the kitchen stove is heard.

SADIE: (*exiting to the kitchen*) My turkey!

DICKENS collects his dignity.

DICKENS: Hmmmmmmm. Haaaa.

A possible interplay of sound here between the two men – throat clearing, bits of humming or whistling.

MOWCHUK: Just so.

DICKENS: Just so what?

MOWCHUK: What you said. Just... that.

DICKENS: Aha! Agreeable. Trying to be agreeable. (*He circles MOWCHUK, who pivots as he moves around him.*) Not convincing.

MOWCHUK: *Un*convincing.

DICKENS: *Dis*agreeable.

MOWCHUK: I didn't mean anything by it. I can't help myself. Correcting people, I mean. It's like a tic. It gets me in all sorts of...

DICKENS, while slowly circling MOWCHUK, begins to audibly sniff him like a dog testing his competition.

Does everyone do that here?

DICKENS: I... smell... a savage.

MOWCHUK: I beg your pardon!

DICKENS: An opportunist, a hoodlum, a hippie...

MOWCHUK: The terms are not interchangeable.

DICKENS: (*still circling him*) Ha!

MOWCHUK: Sir, if I were not in the house of a lady for whom I have an affection...

DICKENS: I would advise you not to use such words ideally.

MOWCHUK: "Idly." You said "ideally," but I think you...

DICKENS: Think! Think! You've probably been through college, eh? Apprenticeship, the School of Life, what does that mean nowadays? I know your kind. Coming here trying to bedazzle a defenceless woman.

MOWCHUK: I don't think she's bedazzled. Or defenseless. On the contrary, I... (*hopefully*) Do you think I did that?

DICKENS: Me, sir? What right have I to thoughts, sir? A poor unlettered working man. (*Pause.*) You're an old friend of the lady's, I presume?

MOWCHUK: No! That is, I... I'm not sure.

DICKENS: You wouldn't be here... on business, would you?

MOWCHUK: You know, it's very strange, but... I... didn't mean it to happen, but...

DICKENS: Yes?

MOWCHUK: I don't have to answer your questions. Who are you anyway?

DICKENS: (*bowing*) Stanley Dickens at your service, one who does have the honour of being an old and trusted friend of the lady of the house.

MOWCHUK: I already know that much.

DICKENS: (*shocked*) She told you about me? (*to himself*) Not that too. To sit here and gossip with some... (*to MOWCHUK*) Did she.... Did she ask you... to... sit on the couch?

SADIE: (*calling out*) I'll be right with you, gentlemen.

DICKENS: Damn it, man, how did you get in here?

MOWCHUK: I walked in.

DICKENS: You...

MOWCHUK: The door opened itself. Of course I don't believe in ghosts...

DICKENS: (*relieved*) Walked in. Without knocking, I presume.

MOWCHUK: Or assume, though neither actually...

DICKENS: (*drawing himself up pompously*) Friendship, Mr....

MOWCHUK: Mowchuk. Leonard Mowchuk. (*Again, he offers him his hand, which is ignored.*)

SADIE peeks through the kitchen hatch.

DICKENS: ...involves certain moral obligations.

MOWCHUK: That's something I understand.

DICKENS: Mrs. Golden is a naive, one might even say, gullible woman.

SADIE smiles. The hatch closes.

DICKENS: I'm not discrediting her. These are rare virtues. There are some who might try to take advantage.

MOWCHUK: I can't tell you how pleased I... how pleased I am to meet you. (*He comes forward, seizes DICKENS' hand and pumps it.*) Mowchuk. Leonard Mowchuk. It's not often one comes across a man with a social conscience.

DICKENS: Let go, pup. (*disentangling himself*) I can see as well as anyone else what you're after. I'll tell you straight. I intend to protect her from you.

MOWCHUK: My intentions are the best, sir.

DICKENS: You will have no intentions, sir. How did you get here? By car? I didn't see any car at the curb. By bus? Go on, admit it. And you paid for two seats, am I right? For you and that puny valise, eh? A greener, an amateur, wet behind the ears.... That Lincoln is my car, sir! (*pointing outside*) Be warned!

SADIE enters, smiling innocently.

SADIE: Well, gentlemen. How are you getting on? Friends already, I can tell. Have you said hello to Puss yet, Mr. Dickens? She'll think you're angry with her. You wouldn't want that, would you?

SADIE picks up the cat and holds it out to DICKENS.

Would you, Mr. Dickens?

Reluctantly, DICKENS pats the cat, avoiding MOWCHUK's eyes.

DICKENS: (*taking her to one side*) Why didn't you explain? He took advantage of your good nature. You must learn how to fend off rascals, my dear. Or the little rats, they'll go nibble nibble...

SADIE: (*momentarily hard*) And there'd be no cheese left for you. (*warmly again, loud enough for MOWCHUK to hear*) Silly man! I'd have told you I was innocent if you'd given me the chance. It's that jealousy of yours. Don't deny it. Sometimes it scares me. A pleasurable fear. I lie awake beside Golden listening to the night noises...

DICKENS: (*an anxious whisper*) Not in front of... (*pompously, to MOWCHUK*) You will leave now, Mr. Whatever-your-name-is...

MOWCHUK: I'll leave when the lady asks me.

DICKENS: Well? One word. (*He whispers.*) Our time together, madam.

MOWCHUK: (*almost to himself*) I've been trying all afternoon to get out. Now it seems a question of honour that I stay.

SADIE: He stays.

DICKENS: Wha... I'm... I...

The beginning of another collapse. DICKENS looks to see if SADIE is fetching the wine. She isn't, but MOWCHUK rushes to pour a glass. DICKENS ignores him.

I'm speechless.

SADIE: Hardly.

DICKENS: Can this be my Mrs. Golden? And this The House?

SADIE: Why are you upset?

DICKENS: There are certain things... certain things in life one ought to be able to depend on. Out there... (*He gestures to the window.*) Vicious. A fight against billboards and television and God knows what next...

SADIE: You're getting excited again. Sit down.

DICKENS: It's one way streets and red lights and who believes in God, eh? A man takes a step he might sink out of sight. But the rest of them keep right on walking.

SADIE eases DICKENS into the armchair and lifts his feet onto the footstool.

SADIE: There, there. I almost have a mind to send Muffet away... (*She looks at MOWCHUK.*) No.

DICKENS: (*relaxing back in his chair*) But here, this room, you...

SADIE: Shhhhhh.

DICKENS: Something a man could hold onto. A plateau, an oasis, no, no, more, a faith.

MOWCHUK: That's blasphemy.

SADIE gestures impatiently for him to be silent.

DICKENS: Did somebody...

SADIE: Shh. The first...

DICKENS: Monday...

SADIE: Of every month...

DICKENS: By my watch it is precisely 1:30 PM.

While speaking in a singsong voice. SADIE tucks in DICKENS with the sheet from his chair.

SADIE: Good afternoon, Mr. Dickens.

DICKENS: Finding myself in the neighbourhood...

SADIE: Come in. You're looking pale...

DICKENS: Saving up between visits.

SADIE: Then you should come...

SADIE & DICKENS: (*sung together, as in a religious ritual*) More often.

DICKENS: (*with a beatific childlike smile*) Like in a holy place. (*He closes his eyes.*)

SADIE: (*singing*) Aamen. (*to MOWCHUK, who has risen*) Shhhhh.

Gesturing to him, SADIE leads the way toward the kitchen. DICKENS wakes with a start.

DICKENS: Where're you going?

SADIE: To let you rest.

DICKENS: (*suspiciously*) What were you going to do in there?

SADIE: Why, Mr. Dickens. You are jealous.

DICKENS: Of him? Ha! I'm jealous for you, not of you. Ha! Poof.

MOWCHUK: (*embarrassed*) I'm intruding.

DICKENS: You finally noticed.

MOWCHUK: Mrs. Golden, if you don't mind...

DICKENS: (*exploding*) If it'd been me, I wouldn't have had to pay for my sample case. The bus driver would have begged me to let it ride free.

MOWCHUK: That's dishonest. Well, isn't it? How do I know you're not taking advantage of Mrs. Golden?

DICKENS: (*starting to circle MOWCHUK*) What do you sell?

MOWCHUK: Books. (*He starts to move.*)

DICKENS: (*with exaggerated disbelief*) Books?

MOWCHUK: (*defensively*) Books. And you?

DICKENS: Condiments.

SADIE: (*delighted*) Gentlemen! My goodness, are you going to fight over me?

They circle each other, the female forgotten in preparation for the dog fight.

As the men argue. SADIE drags a large piece of furniture covered with a sheet to stage centre. She places Puss at her right hand.

MOWCHUK: (*genuinely incredulous*) You mean food?

DICKENS: Sustenance, I mean.

SADIE: It's time for our chair, Puss.

She takes off the sheet, revealing an intricately-carved throne chair, perhaps mounted on a small dias, and majestically seats herself, still unnoticed by the jousters. Their lines continue through her action.

DICKENS: Stimulation, I mean, for the palate.

MOWCHUK: Frivolities! This... (*He picks up a book which gives him security.*) ...is necessary.

SADIE smiles.

DICKENS: Can you smell it, hmmmmm? Taste it, hmmmmm? Eat it?

SADIE: I shall be She for Whom the Battle Rages. I feel quite giddy.

SADIE hits the cat. A surprisingly resonant note is heard. This is how she registers a hit. There are two notes, one for each man.

MOWCHUK: Yes, yes, you can. I've got you there. Books feed the mind.

SADIE: A hit for Mowchuk.

DICKENS: Arrowroot!

SADIE: A hit for Dickens.

MOWCHUK: Anthropology.

SADIE: (*indifferently*) Does it hurt, Puss?

SADIE continues to register the hits on Puss throughout the following.

DICKENS: Basil!

MOWCHUK: Biology!

DICKENS: Cardamom!

MOWCHUK: Cardiology.

DICKENS doubles over, grabbing at his chest. SADIE bangs out the count of nine for a knockdown. DICKENS recovers just in time.

DICKENS: (*now on the attack again*) Hunky! What did your father do, eh? Harnessed your mother to a plow to raise potatoes.

MOWCHUK: You w... wasp! You beer bellied de... d... decadent... (*groping for an adequate insult*) ...Englishman!

DICKENS: Pope lover!

MOWCHUK: Convert! Exploiter!

DICKENS: Job stealer! Immigrant!

MOWCHUK: Imperialist!

DICKENS: Communist!

SADIE: (*grandly*) My men! You've battled well for me.

A climax of sound, then a sudden silence. The men look around, bewildered, having forgotten SADIE in the excitement of the fight.

For me, yes. And for Puss. She's gone to sleep. One day you'll miaow, won't you, Puss? And the world will go deaf. (*to the men*) But you were both entertaining.

SADIE goes to MOWCHUK. She speaks so that DICKENS can't hear.

Your first time? I could hardly believe it. (*referring to DICKENS*) Poor man! I had to comfort him. You understand. So whatever I say...

SADIE approaches DICKENS. She speaks so that MOWCHUK can't hear.

You didn't really believe he was here as a.... That I kept him here to... (*She laughs freely, clearly.*) Look at him! Can a rabbit lock horns with a stag? Aren't you ashamed of yourself?

DICKENS: (*appeased somewhat*) He is pathetic.

SADIE: I stopped keeping points halfway through. I didn't want to embarrass him. (*a pause for effect*) It's his first time.

MOWCHUK: (*who has been edging in to hear*) Did you have to tell?

DICKENS: (*embarrassed for MOWCHUK*) It wasn't necessary, after all.

SADIE pulls DICKENS away from MOWCHUK for a more private conversation.

SADIE: You have a duty, Mr. Dickens, to teach the apprentice.

DICKENS stares at SADIE uncomprehendingly.

This poor young man needs you. Us.

They look at MOWCHUK. MOWCHUK tries to disappear.

He doesn't know about the subtlety of a relationship such as ours.

MOWCHUK: (*now feeling quite paranoid, in an outburst*) I'll not be talked... talked... talked about like a piece of goods. I w... w... won't!

SADIE: You see? He's not mature. He needs an example.

DICKENS: Are you attempting to humiliate me? I should walk out and leave you open to any little pedlar who...

SADIE: Better he should learn from us, with style, not one two and that's that, thank you very much, the way they do it nowadays. Consider yourself his father.

DICKENS: (*raising his arm*) If I were, I'd whip the...

SADIE: Duty is duty.

DICKENS: For God's sake, Madam.

SADIE: Your Anglican blood is showing, Mr. Dickens. Look how accommodating he is. He's disappearing into his training chair.

DICKENS: (*whispering*) I beg of you...

SADIE is silent.

Our product speaks for itself.

SADIE: I don't hear it.

DICKENS: In the kitchen. If *he* went in the kitchen maybe...

SADIE: Our boy, a Peeping Tom? What if he got nervous and lost the keyhole at the crucial moment? He wouldn't be able to hear well either. He'd imagine all sorts of things. He has a peculiar imagination, fed on books and lectures, he told me himself. He might even think we... (*She whispers.*)

DICKENS: (*giggling, titillated*) Do you think so? He clears his throat. Out of the question. I couldn't be natural, knowing he was there.

SADIE: You could! You could! You have such strong instinct.

SADIE reaches for his briefcase.

DICKENS: Have you no modesty?

DICKENS stands protectively in front of his sample case.

SADIE: Then I won't look. And I won't touch.

DICKENS is defeated.

We'll begin with our talk. Side by side as we always do. No? From the loveseat.

SADIE takes one end of the sheet covering the loveseat then waits for DICKENS to take the other to help her fold. DICKENS stays her hand.

DICKENS: I can't.

SADIE, with the sheet draped seductively over her and trailing behind, goes to MOWCHUK for folding.

SADIE: Very well, then. Leonard and I will.

DICKENS: Leonard? I thought you prided yourself on your style, Madam.

SADIE: We were almost ready for the couch. (*still trying to persuade DICKENS*) It'll make it more exciting, Mr. Dickens. An extra plum in the pot, huh?

DICKENS: Voyeurism! I have to revisit my conception of you.

MOWCHUK: (*weakly*) Revise. He meant...

DICKENS: You see?

SADIE: (*warning*) Muffett, don't be naughty.

DICKENS: I'm leaving.

DICKENS waits for SADIE to say something. She doesn't. He picks up his briefcase. He expects her to call to him. She doesn't.

I said I'm leaving. I can't be expected to stay on under these conditions.

SADIE: Goodbye.

DICKENS: Just like that? That's all?

SADIE: I've never forced anyone to remain in my house.

DICKENS: Deny if you can that you're meeting this... whelp... that you intend... for the same purpose you and I...

SADIE: Is it so terrible what you and I do?

DICKENS starts into the hall.

Mr. Dickens!

He turns back hopefully.

I believe I owe you some money. How much?

DICKENS: Are my ears deceiving me? Such words have never passed between us.

SADIE: What would you prefer? Cheque or cash?

DICKENS: Are you driving me to murder, woman?

MOWCHUK rushes up to him.

MOWCHUK: Don't touch her.

DICKENS hits him. MOWCHUK falls.

DICKENS: See what you've done? (*to SADIE*) You've turned me into a ruffian.

SADIE: (*calmly*) Well. You won't be coming back again, will you? Once a tradition is broken.... It's what you've been thinking. Confess!

DICKENS nods his head, miserable.

Well, how shall it be? Cheque or...? (*She wrenches off the cat's head and digs into its belly.*) Let me see, I owe you for...

DICKENS sobs.

Did you say something? Oh, dear, we only seem to have small change. Hold out your hand. (*loudly*) I said hold... (*a sweet voice again, counting into his hand*) Five, eight-fifty, ten, fourteen, fourteen-fifty. seventy-five, eighty-five, ninety-five, ninety-six, ninety-seven, ninety-eight, ninety-nine, fifteen. There.

DICKENS: But I always leave you with credit.

SADIE: Oh, and five dollars more. For loyal reliable service.

DICKENS: (*with dignity*) I don't take tips, Mrs. Golden.

SADIE: It's your Christmas bonus. I forgot to give it to you.

DICKENS: You gave me a pudding.

SADIE: Next year's. I believe that clears the account.

DICKENS: For God's sake, Sadie... (*He realizes his unaccustomed familiarity.*) I mean, Mrs.... (*He stumbles into the hall.*)

SADIE: (*calling after him in a hard voice*) What's the matter? Not enough? Then send me the bill.

MOWCHUK: Really, Mrs. Golden, I know it's not my place, but...

SADIE is listening for the door. DICKENS has paused in front of it. Both of them are breathing heavily. DICKENS opens the door and lets it close again. Pushing MOWCHUK roughly out of her way, SADIE rushes into the hall.

SADIE: Dickens!

She bumps into DICKENS who is coming back into the living room. They fall against each other. She holds him. All this is ludicrous, but at the same time poignant.

There. I knew you couldn't leave me. Who knows what horrible things that man might have done? How would you have felt?

MOWCHUK looks around for "that man."

DICKENS: (*almost a gasp*) I'm back.

SADIE: We'll carry on just as we always have.

They go back to their own chairs.

Have you had a good month?

DICKENS nods.

DICKENS: (*still speaking with difficulty*) And you?

SADIE: Mr. Golden, he's getting worse.

DICKENS: One must be brave.

SADIE: When I gave birth I bled something awful.

They're both seated now.

DICKENS: Blessed is he who...

SADIE: The doctor nearly passed out. He said he'd never seen so much blood. My mother warned me.

DICKENS: Life is difficult.

SADIE: Giving life.

DICKENS: You're too generous. You have to learn to hold back.

SADIE: (*coming out of the ritual*) Your next part louder. Be natural.

DICKENS: (*rising*) How can I? With that foreigner spying.

MOWCHUK starts to move. SADIE beckons him to stay where he is.

SADIE: Start from the door. It'll be easier for you.

DICKENS, on his way to the hat rack, passes SADIE. She pushes him so the two of them proceed almost at a run.

(*She hands DICKENS his hat and coat.*) Hat. Coat. (*She opens the door and pushes him out.*) Out. (*She slams the door.*)

DICKENS: (*re-entering*) By my watch it is exactly...

SADIE: Your face! If I saw that I'd have a heart attack.

DICKENS adjusts his face. SADIE hangs up his coat.

That's better.

DICKENS: Happening to find myself in the...

SADIE: You didn't just... (*She takes DICKENS' hat from him and hangs it up.*)

DICKENS: A man should show constraint...

SADIE: Let me...

DICKENS: There's nothing new, I trust?

They approach the living room at double speed, like a fast moving motion picture film.

SADIE: It's Golden, you wouldn't believe it.

DICKENS hesitates for just a moment before he enters the living room. SADIE hurriedly puts a sheet on his chair so that he can lift it off. He does.

Sit down. You must be tired.

DICKENS: One must be brave.

SADIE: He lay on me last night.

DICKENS: Blessed is he who learns through...

SADIE: His demands are...

DICKENS: Suffering...

SADIE: Shall I tell you?

DICKENS: (*referring to MOWCHUK*) He's in too close.

SADIE: ...Getting worse.

DICKENS: It's a shame that...

SADIE: You wouldn't believe how he...

DICKENS: (*sitting, though still not relaxed*) Poor good Mrs. Dickens.

SADIE: Dickens!

DICKENS: I meant Golden.

SADIE: You said Dickens.

DICKENS: A slip of the tongue.

SADIE: I'm an old tree.

DICKENS: Not true. Blessed is she who learns through...

SADIE: A dried tree. Use me for firewood. At least then someone could warm their hands by...

DICKENS: Sadie Golden, Sadie Golden.

SADIE: Or bury me as I am. I might make good fertilizer. A petunia bush from my forehead, a spray of roses from.... Your spray didn't work.

DICKENS: (*showing new interest*) What spray?

SADIE: For the couch.

DICKENS: The stain?

SADIE: Still there.

DICKENS: I'm glad.

SADIE: You're wicked.

DICKENS moves to the loveseat and attempts to pull the sheet off it. The sheet, as though animated, resists and returns to its place.

DICKENS: It won't come off.

SADIE: Too fast. You're rushing it.

The loveseat, on casters, skitters away from DICKENS.

You men are all the same.

DICKENS pursues the loveseat and stops it. SADIE returns to the ritual. Her following line is the cue for DICKENS to remove the sheet.

SADIE: Golden beat me.

DICKENS: (*sympathetically, yet titillated*) No!

SADIE: (*folding the sheet together*) A brute. No culture. Not like you. Right after dinner. I was so tired.

DICKENS: He beat you?

SADIE: Wife, mother, cook, all of us...

They sit on the loveseat. Rhythm and intimacy intensify.

DICKENS: I shall be forced to...

SADIE: Last night he...

DICKENS: If I were here I would have...

SADIE: I know you would. But how much? That's the question.

DICKENS: Don't you trust me?

SADIE: I'm not sure I trust me. One's own body. Sometimes my stomach, without notifying me at all.... And my breasts...

DICKENS: A defenceless woman. I'll confront him.

SADIE: Yes.

DICKENS: I'll walk up to the door and knock...

SADIE: Hard.

DICKENS: (*in a deep voice, as if speaking to her husband*) "What did you mean by..."

SADIE: He's a big man. He'll kill you. He suspects.

DICKENS: (*his voice growing suspicious*) Are you? Are you unfaithful?

SADIE: (*whispering*) It's time.

They rush to the couch and tear off its sheet, throwing it anywhere.

When you come... after you come... I feel I'm growing pregnant until the next...

DICKENS: The first Monday . . .

SADIE: Nobody listens anymore. Nobody cares.

DICKENS: We do.

They sit on the couch.

SADIE: Yes. You and I. The last strongholds.

DICKENS: Civilization.

MOWCHUK looks surprised. They are words similar to those he's heard about himself:

SADIE: My breasts are heavy.

DICKENS: (*looking at his watch*) Soon it will be...

SADIE: Three o'clock. The glare. After I weaned them they didn't stop filling, but no one drinks. Is nobody thirsty?

DICKENS rises.

DICKENS: (*urgently*) Faster.

SADIE: They need me. They couldn't get along without me. I could die and nobody'd notice. Except the dandelions would spread onto the neighbour's lawns. Then they'd come knocking.

DICKENS: (*nervous, whispering*) You're changing the order. Not today.

SADIE: (*building the pace*) I'd lie here festering, a corpse of love. My children love me. They won't leave me alone. Then they'd feel sorry. My breasts hurt. They'd touch me, the little children, the mothers, the businessmen, the doctors, the plumbers, the dogs would have a sniff too, and they'd all catch the plague. (*She laughs again, a surprisingly clear laughter.*) Because that's what happens to milk. It turns rancid. (*She looks at DICKENS then screams.*) You weren't listening! I should make you go back to the first chair.

DICKENS: (*frightened*) I was! I swear!

SADIE: I'm a dead tree. Brittle. Birds don't light on me. Cats don't climb.

DICKENS strolls around the room pretending to make a casual study.

DICKENS: Such a pleasant house.

SADIE: I'm a husk.

DICKENS: Order. Everything the same.

SADIE: My fruit has fallen from me, rotted.

DICKENS: (*hissing*) It's nearly time. (*He changes his voice.*) It never changes. The sideboard, the dining table, the telephone...

He puts his hands behind his back and feigns a casualness to mask his excitement.

SADIE: I curse my daughter! Not even a phone call and a how do-you-do? Let her love her children like I love her.

DICKENS: (*excitement rising*) ...the cat, the footstool, my armchair.

SADIE: Bit by bit, stone by stone, let her take away the foundations of her soul and plant them in her children. In the night when she puts her hand on their forehead let it be her forehead. It will be her body she covers in the night. Her ears will be on them. Her arms and her hair will be to protect them from the sun. Then one day let her be surprised when she looks at herself and sees there's nothing left of her but the skin.

She sings.

Bye baby bunting,
Mama's gone a-hunting,
She's taken off her own white skin
To wrap her baby bunting in...

DICKENS: God, I can't wait. Hurry!

SADIE rushes to his briefcase and opens it. DICKENS moans. He is separate from her, never looking directly at what she is doing.

Coriander, basil, sweetbreads, wine, vinegar, lemon...

As SADIE touches or strokes each bottle, DICKENS reacts. With a wrench she uncorks a bottle of white fluid. DICKENS squeals.

Floor spray, window spray, hair spray...

SADIE drinks from the bottle. The fluid drips over her chin and onto the case. Having satisfied DICKENS, she tosses the bottle behind her. A swoosh of the remaining liquid is heard. MOWCHUK's case opens. He reacts automatically. Books, pamphlets and order forms come out on the floor. MOWCHUK's eyes, like DICKENS', are glazed.

SADIE: (*with mock concern*) Oh, dear, I've spilled it.

DICKENS: I... I'll use my handkerchief. (*But be doesn't move from where he's sprawled exhausted.*)

SADIE: There, Mr. Dickens, that wasn't so difficult, was it! (*She eyes him.*) You're out of shape.

DICKENS: (*still breathless*) For God's sake, close it up. (*He staggers to his case.*)

SADIE: (*starting towards Puss*) Shall I...

DICKENS: I'll send a bill!

SADIE: You're right. I'm indiscreet. (*She speaks to MOWCHUK on her way.*) Naughty boy. Wasted.

The phone rings. She takes it into the kitchen.

DICKENS is bowed over his briefcase. MOWCHUK, terribly embarrassed, scoops and shoves his material back into his case.

DICKENS: (*softly, to himself*) The... humiliation.

SADIE: (in the kitchen) Hello.

MOWCHUK: Uncalled for. I apologize. I couldn't help myself.

SADIE: (*offstage*) My letter meant what it said, Mr. Underhill.

DICKENS: She wrote to him?

MOWCHUK: I can't...

DICKENS motions to him to be quiet.

SADIE: (*offstage*) Premature? I don't think so.

DICKENS: Jezebel!

SADIE: (*offstage*) One must plan for every eventuality. Isn't that your motto? At three o'clock then.

A doubt plagues DICKENS. He goes to the table and lifts a corner of the sheet covering the tea things.

Underhill... coming.

MOWCHUK discovers he has left a book out that has been doused by SADIE's bottle.

MOWCHUK: (*running to the book*) My book! She's spilled... (*He tries to wipe off the stain with his hanky, but it is black with dirt from the cupboard.*) Your... essence on my book.

SADIE: (*calling from the kitchen*) I'll be right with you, gentlemen. (*coyly*) When you're ready. One must allow a decent amount of time.

MOWCHUK: Pages 1365-66, "Rodents in South America," ruined.

DICKENS: She probably won't even pay for it.

MOWCHUK: I begin to think... I'm forced to say... the lady is not as gracious as... as we...

DICKENS: Mr. Mowchuk, we must unite. She's united us already in dishonour.

MOWCHUK stares uncomprehending.

To sell, man. That's what we're here for.

MOWCHUK: Why don't we just leave?

DICKENS: An eye for an eye.... We'll sell her till she's busted, the old biddy. To think of the years I.... She probably can't even read.

MOWCHUK: Or tell sweet from sour.

They giggle. DICKENS puts his arm around MOWCHUK.

DICKENS: And I hit you.

MOWCHUK: I deserved it. I learned a lot from you.

DICKENS: Did you? You weren't half bad yourself. In fact, you were quite good.

MOWCHUK: Was I?

DICKENS: For the first time.

MOWCHUK breaks away from DICKENS.

MOWCHUK: I can't do it.

DICKENS: Why not?

MOWCHUK: My conscience.

DICKENS: What's conscience got to do with it? We don't owe her anything.

MOWCHUK: It's like a hairshirt. Up to now I've thought of myself as a Crusader of a kind.

DICKENS: Who made you doubt it? It is our arduistic task, Mr Mowchuk, to enrich the life of that ignorant woman. It's your duty.

MOWCHUK: Enlightenment?

DICKENS: Who are the teachers in the contemporary world, tell me that?

MOWCHUK: (*beginning to pace*) Yes, yes, you inspire me. One relationship, the symbol of an age. For the Greeks it was philosopher and student. For the Romans: Emperor and soldier. For the Christians: Priest and penitent. And now...

DICKENS: Salesman and...

MOWCHUK: Client.

They embrace.

DICKENS: But remember, we maintain control. We will not be ordered around. We will not turn against each other.

SADIE peeks through the hatch. DICKENS grasps MOWCHUK's arm.

Stay firm?

MOWCHUK: Stay firm.

DICKENS: No undercutting?

MOWCHUK: No undercutting.

DICKENS: Friendship?

MOWCHUK: Friendship.

SADIE: (*re-entering*) Gentlemen, I must apologize for my clumsiness.

DICKENS: Perfectly alright, Mrs. Golden.

MOWCHUK: Don't think any more of it.

SADIE: Of course I'll pay for the bottle and the book.

DICKENS: It's just a piffle.

MOWCHUK: (*in unison with DICKENS' last line*) I wouldn't dream of it.

DICKENS: After you, Mr. Mowchuk...

MOWCHUK: No, you, Mr....

A shadow is visible at the window.

SADIE: (*a sudden command*) Down on your knees!

MOWCHUK drops automatically.

DICKENS: I will not. (*to MOWCHUK*) Fool!

SADIE: Dickens!

Slowly DICKENS lowers himself to his knees. The shadow crosses.

(*squealing with excitement*) Oh! Oh! Oh! (*She crawls quickly along the floor and hides under a piece of furniture.*) Sssst. (*She beckons the others to follow.*) He can see us. He can see us.

HIGHRISE's extravagantly tall shadow crosses and re-crosses the stage. Laughing to herself, SADIE scurries to hide under the dining room table, pulling the sheet down to cover her. Some teacups crash.

He's coming.

MOWCHUK: Who is it? Her husband?

DICKENS: Oh my God!

SADIE: (*hissing*) Hide.

More teacups crash. DICKENS dives under his chair.

MOWCHUK: (*crawling quickly to join DICKENS*) I thought he was dead.

DICKENS: Find your own place!

MOWCHUK scurries to his training chair. Bottoms and legs sprout absurdly from between the chair rungs.

HIGHRISE: (*offstage*) Fee... Fi... Fo... Fum...

HIGHRISE enters with slow strides, his back to the audience. A tall, handsome, flashy man, beginning to show age, perhaps already covering it with make-up, he's dressed in a cape, carrying a cane, and has a hat which is tipped at the back of his head. He is a combination of magic man, aging actor and cheap con. He wears heavy built-up shoes, similar to those used by Greek actors, or, as originally conceived, he's wearing stilts. He looms above the characters and the furniture.

I smell the blood of Sadie Golden. (*He sniffs and looks around the room.*)

ACT THREE

A hysterical giggle is heard from SADIE.

HIGHRISE: Come out, come out, wherever you are...

HIGHRISE reaches out with his cane and lifts the sheet on the table, revealing SADIE curled up covering her eyes.

Or I'll huff and I'll puff...

SADIE opens her eyes. The pleasant fright of a child. She covers her eyes again.

You can't hide from Highrise.

SADIE rises slowly from under the dining room table. She takes a few tentative steps towards HIGHRISE, then runs to him. He picks her up and swings her in the air.

Sadie, baby, how are you? You've been preparing for me. You know Jack Highrise. A thousand cups and he's still thirsty. But not just tea, eh?

DICKENS: It's more than you she's expecting.

HIGHRISE: What's this? Do you suffer, madam, from crawling... (*He removes the chair from DICKENS.*) ...insects? Look, it's a toad, and here... (*He tries to take the chair from MOWCHUK, but he holds onto it.*) ...a turtle. (*wrenching the chair away*) Without its shell. Embarrassing to see a turtle without a shell. Makes you want to... (*He rises high on one foot.*) ...end its misery.

SADIE: No!

HIGHRISE: Are they friends of yours?

SADIE: Why not? Why should it be only you who...

DICKENS: (*standing*) Who... who is this man? I demand to know.... All these years you made me think...

HIGHRISE: Toads don't think. They croak. Croak, toad. (*He holds his cane to DICKENS' throat.*)

DICKENS: What's in that thing?

HIGHRISE: Adjustable, moves in and out. Croak.

DICKENS opens his mouth and croaks. MOWCHUK opens his mouth and croaks too.

Not you, fool. You chirp.

MOWCHUK chirps.

SADIE: I used to have a pet toad. Two of them. At the summer beach cottage. They'd hop every morning to my bed room to be fed. Here, little toads.

HIGHRISE: Hop! Hop!

DICKENS hops to SADIE. MOWCHUK follows.

SADIE: They would sit in my lap...

DICKENS stops. HIGHRISE gestures with his cane. DICKENS croaks, hops and sits in SADIE's lap. Kept at a distance by HIGHRISE, MOWCHUK's longing chirps breaks into...

MOWCHUK: Me too... me too... me too...

SADIE: I fed them milk. (*She unbuttons her blouse.*)

DICKENS: It's beyond...

HIGHRISE gestures again. A knife shoots out of his cane. DICKENS buries his head against SADIE's breasts. Sucking sounds are heard.

SADIE: Every morning they came...

MOWCHUK, not to be kept back now, hopping and chirping, nestles against SADIE.

One, of course, turned into a prince, but I threw him away. (*She shoves MOWCHUK away.*) Sometimes the ants would come.

HIGHRISE mimes this and provides the sounds.

They didn't frighten me.

MOWCHUK patters back in a new guise.

Slugs would leave trails that looked like dance patterns with me at the centre. And the birds. Down from the trees they flew.

HIGHRISE makes flying, chirping, and other appropriate sounds.

I had lots of milk for all of them. No. Don't fight. Some of them nibbled at the tips of my fingers. Or my ears. But they grew back. You see, there were no leaves in the forest, no worms, no berries, just me. When I left, every autumn it was the same. I could hear the birds behind me fall out of their nests out of the trees... kerplunk, kerplunk...

HIGHRISE takes over the dull thud sound.

...from hunger.

SADIE stands up. DICKENS rolls out of her lap. MOWCHUK falls from her shoulder.

All dead.

DICKENS: No. No.

HIGHRISE grinds his cane into DICKENS.

SADIE: Without me.

HIGHRISE: (*to SADIE*) Hey. Bravo. Better than you've ever done it.

DICKENS: (*weakly, as he sits up*) I thought I was...

HIGHRISE: Rubber, idiot. Look.

HIGHRISE jabs at MOWCHUK who tries to evade him. MOWCHUK cuts his hand.

Sorry.

SADIE: Shame on you, Jack Highrise. Mommy'll make it better. (*She rushes out for a bandage.*)

HIGHRISE: Ant, turtle, toad? Between us, gentlemen, we're all the same, leeches, including out dear... hostess.

HIGHRISE, taking off his shoes as he talks, gestures to the door where SADIE enters, bringing bandages for MOWCHUK.

SADIE: (*to HIGHRISE*) You are a wicked man, Highrise. I don't know why I let you in the house. But you'll all learn to love each other.

DICKENS: How much have you given this man? I've a right to know.

HIGHRISE: Is this your husband? I thought he was dead. I read a notice in the obituaries, and I said to myself, "Sadie Golden needs me. For her pleasures. She'll be able to afford them again. What luck I'm ready for her."

SADIE: Are you?

DICKENS: Dead? You didn't tell me.

SADIE: Well, Highrise? The shoes and the stick weren't bad, as an entrance. But what have you really brought me today?

HIGHRISE: (*going into a spiel*) Bricks, Incorporated. Special interlocking bricks that need no cement, no nails, no design. They interlock themselves and you don't know what you're building, ladies and gentlemen, until it's built itself around you. The trick is, it builds according to what's enclosed. A demonstration. Free of charge, my friends. (*He mimes setting up a machine, making the appropriate sounds.*) For you, my fair Fury... (*to SADIE*) A castle with a grand salon. My bricks interlock themselves into people too, who laugh precisely when you want, and when you want, shut up. You don't like someone? Why, take him apart. (*He mimes demolition.*) For you... (*to MOWCHUK*) A monk's cell, with a nun of bricks. Hard to make, but dependable. And for you... (*to DICKENS*) An interlocking shithouse. (*mimicking DICKENS sitting in his chair as if it were a toilet*) "Let me comfort you. Stiff upper lip. One learns through suffering."

SADIE: Not interested. What else?

HIGHRISE: I was afraid you'd say that. Fact is, I'm tired.

SADIE: (*excited*) Are the police after you?

HIGHRISE: Tired.

SADIE: With dogs? I'd love to hear them howling outside the window.

HIGHRISE starts to take off his jacket.

Not yet! Gentlemen wait for a lady's permission to disrobe. (*a change in tone*) You may take it off Highrise! You didn't come here to rest, did you?

HIGHRISE: (*recovering himself*) How could I, with Sadie Golden? (*He takes off his jacket, then his stilts.*)

MOWCHUK: (*to DICKENS*) His legs! They came off!

DICKENS: (*pulling MOWCHUK to one side*) They're stilts.

MOWCHUK: (*looking back as he's being pulled aside*) Ooh.

DICKENS: Mr. Mowchuk, we agreed to a partnership, did we not?

MOWCHUK: Yes, we did.

DICKENS: And in a partnership one listens to the suggestions of the partner, does one not?

MOWCHUK: Yes, that's true.

DICKENS: Then, as your partner, I suggest we leave.

MOWCHUK: Maybe she needs our protection.

DICKENS: Partners act together or not at all.

SADIE: I didn't think you'd turn your back on a cockfight, Dickens.

HIGHRISE: (*seeing the cat*) How's old Puss? What's this? Turned blue since I was here last? Whatsamatter? Caught a chill?

HIGHRISE: (*picks up the cat and strokes it, checking the neck*) It's loose.

SADIE: That was the time of the yellow cat.

DICKENS: Well, Mowchuk?

HIGHRISE tries to twist the cat's neck off without letting the others notice. His face contorts with the attempt.

HIGHRISE: Are you going to miaow for me?

SADIE: (*taking the cat from him*) You have to work to please Puss.

HIGHRISE: Her charm.

SADIE: Good. I like this return to self confidence. While Highrise works you can lick envelopes, Mr. Mowchuk.

She leads him to a stack of correspondence on the dining room table and picks up a colourful advertising pamphlet that unfolds to the floor. She drops it.

That one first, I think.

MOWCHUK: I'll get it.

MOWCHUK picks up the pamphlet. She smiles. MOWCHUK continues to lick and seal throughout the following.

SADIE: (*to DICKENS*) And you can glower. I'll let you know when we're ready for you. (*She sits on the footstool beside HIGHRISE.*) Now, where have you been and what have you been doing, my tall wicked man? Where have you been? I'll sit as quiet as a little girl in kindergarten.

HIGHRISE: (*looking around at the covered furniture*) I'll start here. (*gradually uncovering a delicate chair*) This one comes off gently. I'm undressing a shy young girl. You have to peel her delicate without touching the tender fruit too soon or she'll be frightened. In an absent-minded way, as though it's not important at all, I take her. (*He sits on the chair back to front.*)

SADIE: Tell me. Tell me.

HIGHRISE: More?

SADIE: And better.

HIGHRISE: I've an urge to travel. A sea voyage, yes. Fisherman!

SADIE: I don't like that one.

HIGHRISE: It only just happened.

SADIE: Never did like it. The usual, Mr. Highrise.

HIGHRISE: (*menacing as he moves behind SADIE*) But I've never told you how a fisherman kills an octopus. He lifts her high out of the water, like this... (*With a swift movement, he scoops up SADIE's shawl, creating a head with his left fist.*) ...where her tentacles hang ugly and useless. Then, with his shiny sharp teeth he cuts the nerve between her eyes.

HIGHRISE pulls a spring knife from his vest. The blade cuts through the shawl and forward to SADIE's throat. MOWCHUK starts to her defence. DICKENS restrains him.

SADIE: False teeth.

HIGHRISE raises the weapon high, as if to strike.

It would be your best story and you'd have no one to tell it to with Sadie gone.

Defeated, knowing what she wants, HIGHRISE returns the knife to his vest.

HIGHRISE: The usual.

Though he's tired, HIGHRISE climbs up on a piece of furniture and assumes the stance of a performer.

MOWCHUK: What is the usual?

SADIE jumps up and down, laughing and clapping in her excitement. Her applause infuses animation into HIGHRISE, but he waits silently, his eyes on DICKENS and MOWCHUK, who indicate no enthusiasm, though MOWCHUK is curious. SADIE pokes them.

SADIE: Clap! Come on. Then he'll do it.

They clap. HIGHRISE bows.

DICKENS: (*trying to save face by enjoying HIGHRISE's humiliation*) I hadn't hoped for a minstrel show.

HIGHRISE bangs three times with his cane, cutting into DICKENS' line.

The following sequence is played like a vaudeville skit.

HIGHRISE: I'm working as a car salesman in a clip joint, see. And when I say clip joint, I'm not just beating my gums. The owner not only takes the wool from the sheep, he takes the skin. This guy is so crooked he has to have a special bed made like a pretzel to fit him. So I decide, as I have a strong sense of justice, my downfall, ladies and gentlemen, to get one back at the owner on behalf of all the little folk. I sacrifice myself for them as I do every day of my life.

DICKENS: (*sarcastically, to MOWCHUK*) Have you got a hanky?

HIGHRISE: Besides, he's handed me a few soft cheques.

SADIE: (*prompting*) You take a car.

HIGHRISE: Not just a car. (*He pulls a sheet off the tea trolley.*) A Jaguar XKE.

MOWCHUK: Is that better than a Lincoln?

HIGHRISE: (*wheeling the tea trolley around*) So long, suckers! I've taken your debts on me, your dreams, and your hate. Blessed and cleansed be your pocketbooks! They read about me in the papers and, man, they wish me luck like I'm an athlete, every one of 'em wanting to be me but knowing he doesn't have the guts. The lights of the small towns come and go. Come and go.

Appropriate effects from SADIE who switches the overhead lights on and off.

Young girls turn over in their beds and moan as I pass. Then dawn.

SADIE: Dawn in Wetaskiwin.

HIGHRISE: (*shrugging*) Why not? (*approaches DICKENS*) Excuse me, is this Wetaskiwin?

DICKENS: What?

SADIE: Answer him. Go on. Say, "Yes it is, Mister. Looking for anything in particular?" Say it. You're an old cleaning man in the train station.

HIGHRISE: Torn overalls, yellow moustache, pushing a broom...

SADIE: The smell of banana and orange peel, gum wrappers, half-eaten wieners...

DICKENS: Have you gone mad?

SADIE: Are you going to play, or would you like to leave?

DICKENS: (*grudgingly playing the role*) Are you looking for anyone in particular?

HIGHRISE: Why yes, my good man...

DICKENS bristles.

SADIE: He can keep his name, can't he, Highrise?

DICKENS: No one in my family has been in sanitation.

HIGHRISE: (*in play*) As a matter of fact, I'm looking for the mayor.

DICKENS: How would you expect a janitor to know the mayor?

SADIE: You have that part too.

DICKENS: A mayor, eh? That's more like it. What was he like? A man of dignity, I'd imagine, with the proper word for...

HIGHRISE: With a paunch and a silver pocket watch and a passingly pretty daughter of about... eighteen.

SADIE strikes a simpering pose.

Delightful.

DICKENS: (*in role*) May I be of help to you, sir?

HIGHRISE: I'm looking for a printer to make... (*He takes out a large colourful lease form.*)

SADIE: Copies of a copy of a leasing form.

DICKENS: I'd be glad to oblige, but why ask me such a thing?

HIGHRISE: Well, you see, I, or rather my company, have reason to suspect that the land around your little town, your charming town of... er...

SADIE: Wetaskiwin.

HIGHRISE looks around as though to check if anyone is listening.

HIGHRISE: Mr. Mayor, would you like to become the official most likely to be remembered in the entire history of this region? Instead of being the mayor of Wetaskiwin...

SADIE: ...the trade centre of the grain belt...

HIGHRISE: How would you like to be the mayor of Wetaskiwin, Oil Centre of the North?

DICKENS: Oil?

MOWCHUK: Oil.

SADIE: Copies of a copy of a...

MOWCHUK: (*innocently finishing the phrase*) ...leasing form.

HIGHRISE, from his magical pockets, produces shares and agreements for DICKENS and MOWCHUK to sign.

SADIE: Go on. Sign.

MOWCHUK: I don't sign anything I haven't read.

DICKENS: A man's reputation rests in his name.

MOWCHUK: This is a contract for a share in a brick company.

SADIE: Highrise, don't be naughty.

HIGHRISE takes these papers back and exchanges them for other papers.

HIGHRISE: (*as though speaking to a group*) I am indeed privileged to be addressing this distinguished assembly of the town council as well as interested fellow citizens, who have kindly gathered here tonight. I assure you that this honour will be repaid in the same spirit in which is given.

SADIE: Hip hip...

ALL: Hooray!

HIGHRISE: I have with me news that the first drilling begins in two weeks.

SADIE: Hip hip..

HIGHRISE: Men and machinery are now on their way to Wetaskiwin...

ALL: Hooray!

HIGHRISE: There will be full employment.

SADIE: Hip hip...

HIGHRISE: And all for the smallest contribution on your part.

Silence. HIGHRISE sits ceremoniously, hand out, waiting for the money. Neither of the men budge.

SADIE goes to the cat, unscrews its head and takes out some money. DICKENS tries to stop her.

DICKENS: My dear Mrs. Golden...

SADIE: You're obsessed with money today, Dickens.

DICKENS falls back offended, clutching at his collar.

HIGHRISE: The excitement's been too much for the mayor. His heart.

SADIE pushes DICKENS into his chair.

SADIE: (*to DICKENS*) You need a holiday. Yes, you do, daddy.

SADIE & HIGHRISE: (*singing together*) So the mayor decides to go to the...

SADIE: (*singing alone*) ...seashore. But before he leaves he says...

HIGHRISE: (*imitating DICKENS*) "Move into the house, dear boy. Consider yourself a member of the family."

DICKENS: (*beaten*) I'll be back in two weeks, when the first of your machinery is due to come in. In the meantime, help yourself to whatever you find in the house.

SADIE: The mayor's daughter stays behind to be...

HIGHRISE: And since the good man had told me to... I...

SADIE: He...

HIGHRISE: (*with SADIE*) Do.

SADIE: (*with HIGHRISE*) Does.

HIGHRISE has SADIE in his arms, her face turned front. This could be done in tango rhythm, the lines delivered between rhythmic pauses. This business may include singing.

HIGHRISE: I almost don't bother. I prefer a challenge.

MOWCHUK: (*remembering*) The last two...

DICKENS: (*with disgust*) Civilization.

SADIE crawls awkwardly onto the couch and into a formal sexual position with HIGHRISE over her. Their pose is held briefly, as if for a photograph. A squeak from MOWCHUK marks the moment.

MOWCHUK: (*crossing himself*) Our Father which art in...

HIGHRISE: After we empty the fridge and cupboards and drain the last bottles of booze in the house I bid my weeping bride-to-be adieu.

SADIE: (*still on the couch*) But she knows he's left her something valuable.

HIGHRISE: I'd lain with her laughing into her breasts.

SADIE: She carries his laughter like a foetus. (*She sits up and imitates the voice of the mayor, in unison with HIGHRISE.*)

SADIE & HIGHRISE: (*together*) "Help yourself to everything, my boy."

HIGHRISE: Come on. Move it out.

MOWCHUK and DICKENS act as loaders.

SADIE: To the van. Waiting outside.

HIGHRISE: One dining table with teacups, four chairs.... One tassled couch, very well used, one glass cat... one... two cases...

HIGHRISE picks up DICKENS' and MOWCHUK's cases. DICKENS and MOWCHUK stop loading.

MOWCHUK: Leave that alone!

SADIE: (*annoyed*) You've got no play in you.

HIGHRISE puts the cases on the tea trolley.

Goodbye, my love. Goodbye. (*He waves.*)

HIGHRISE: (*using the tea trolley as a car, moving around the room*) You should see the dust we raise on the highway. Some of the farmers recognize me and wave. Ye blessed little hamlets of tedium, I give thee gossip and hate and cheated fortune to smoke over oil stoves in the harsh white winter. I say unto you, day after day I sacrifice myself without thanks, to bring excitement to the underprivileged.

DICKENS: I'll expose you and put you in jail. Justice!

HIGHRISE: I promised you a place in the town's history. Expose me and you expose yourself.

SADIE: (*with delight*) Isn't he awful?

MOWCHUK: What about the town people? All their money?

SADIE: The good mayor refunded it.

DICKENS: Out of his own bank account?

HIGHRISE: (*at the door*) Regrettable.

HIGHRISE kisses his fingers and waves goodbye as he disappears into the hall, still with DICKENS' and MOWCHUK's briefcases as well as the cat on the tea trolley.

DICKENS: Hey! Come back. He's got my case.

MOWCHUK: And mine.

A clatter is heard as HIGHRISE, with the tea trolley, gets stuck in the doorway. SADIE laughs. The two men pursue HIGHRISE to the door.

You, sir, do not exist.

HIGHRISE: What do you mean I don't?

MOWCHUK: You went out with the n... n... nineteenth-century novel. You're an... an... an... anachronism.

MOWCHUK and DICKENS take their briefcases from an unresisting HIGHRISE.

HIGHRISE: I'm not thirty yet.

SADIE: You never are. (*in the hall doorway, thoughtfully absent*) I really ought to tell that story to the police.

HIGHRISE looks worried. SADIE picks up the phone, smiles, then puts it down.

When you get jowly. (*She goes into the kitchen.*)

DICKENS: Give me back her money.

HIGHRISE, still considering SADIE's last words, takes the money out of his vest pocket and hands it to DICKENS.

My God, look what she was ready to... (*DICKENS replaces the money in the cat.*)

HIGHRISE: She would too.

MOWCHUK: Would what?

HIGHRISE: Rat on me.

He pushes DICKENS and MOWCHUK out of the way. He collapses into the armchair.

DICKENS: Hey, that's my chair.

HIGHRISE: Nothing's yours. It's all hers.

MOWCHUK: You are tired, aren't you? How old did you say you were?

HIGHRISE: Shut up. None of them make me work like her. She did call the cops once. Sadie Golden. I spent a night in jail for her, then she withdrew the charge. Said it was a mistake. That's what attracts me. It's talons against talons with us. If we draw blood all the better. Some of them go down like moths in a bottle of formaldehyde, and that's a bore. But the old bitch is taking over. Sometimes when I'm doing things I'm not sure whether it's for me or so I can tell her. Or if I've done them at all. "Where've you been Highrise? Tell me. Tell me." (*aware of MOWCHUK's naive interest*) Say, why don't you buy a share in my brick company. I could see you were taken by the idea.

MOWCHUK: The logic did fascinate me, the possibility that one could define the ideal environment for every individual.

HIGHRISE: Yeh. You got it. So why not become a millionaire? Not interested. How about if I name you co-inventor?

MOWCHUK: (*taking the bait*) How could you...

DICKENS: Lay off the boy.

HIGHRISE: I can't help myself. When I see a pigeon with his neck out.... But you're right. We're brothers.

DICKENS: No claims to relationship, thank you very much.

HIGHRISE: La de dah. I'd prefer it weren't so. You two are pathetic examples of our guild.

DICKENS: She made a fool of you.

HIGHRISE: And you? But you don't like it. Especially before an audience. If you're not willing to be a jackass, go home, buster. Change professions. We're performers. Artists. If she wanted to see your ass you'd bend over and split your pants to oblige.

DICKENS goes to HIGHRISE. MOWCHUK holds him back.

MOWCHUK: You crude cr... r... rook.

HIGHRISE: Two ends of the same stick. So you're polite, and obviously less stimulating.

DICKENS: I reject your perforation. We have a grand role. A noble role.

HIGHRISE: Depends on the customer. Some roll. Some won't.

DICKENS: I am not being fa... fa...

MOWCHUK: Facetious.

HIGHRISE: Bless you.

MOWCHUK: You're a fraud. We satisfy legitimate needs.

HIGHRISE: With books she won't read? Spices she doesn't use?

DICKENS: We, sir, are the last personal communicants with Sadie Golden.

HIGHRISE: You think you're a fucking priest. Not so far from me then.

DICKENS: Ours is a sacrosanct relationship. Not like you.

MOWCHUK: Not sacred, logical.

HIGHRISE: She is a Customer.

SADIE is suddenly among them.

SADIE: You've been talking too much, Highrise. I'll remember that.

DICKENS: (*pathetic*) Were they lies?

SADIE: Everything is true. When I say it. (*She deliberately goes to the phone and dials.*) Hello? Police Department? (*HIGHRISE stiffens.*) I've something of interest to tell you. I'm having a party this afternoon. Did you receive the invitations? I know it's against policy, but this one might be... (*HIGHRISE hangs up the phone.*) There was something missing in your performance this afternoon Highrise. Perhaps your hair is thinning a bit.

DICKENS finds it difficult to conceal his delight. HIGHRISE turns his back to the audience and begins to pull something from his vest.

SADIE: (*excited*) Presents?

Feather dusters, one attached to another, emerge as a flowing peacock plume, stiff enough to hold the peacock's crescent shape. When HIGHRISE shakes them, they whirr with the sound of the peacock's feathers in his mating dance.

HIGHRISE: They're for you. From me. For use. As you will. Red. And gold. And green. And purple. And red. And red. And yellow. And red.

As he speaks, HIGHRISE holds the large duster crown around his shoulders. He takes short strutting steps trapping SADIE in the circle of feathers. She makes quiet frightened anticipatory sounds.

SADIE: (*throughout HIGHRISE's dance*) Oh. Oh. Oh. Oh.

HIGHRISE: I've been high. And low. And in. And out. Theft. Burglary. Fraud. Drugs. Rape. Murder.

SADIE crumples to the floor, legs spread. HIGHRISE scatters the feathers over her in what is obviously a sexual act. This last effort to please SADIE has exhausted HIGHRISE. He slumps on the loveseat. His magical jacket is too heavy for him. He takes it off revealing a surprisingly slight frame.

MOWCHUK: Holy Mary Mother of God protect me in this hour of need in this house of sin.

DICKENS crawls to SADIE where she lies twitching, then still, under the feathers.

DICKENS: Mrs. Golden? Are you all right? Are you listening? I've got things to confess. You always said I had no need to. You said I was the only man you knew without a flaw. You said it made you strong and proud just to know me. You said you wondered if I was human.

SADIE: (*in a weak voice, from under the feathers*) A weakness for food, you've that.

DICKENS: But I know now, when you said why should I confess anything to a silly old woman anyway...

SADIE sits up, annoyed, blowing away the loose feathers.

I think you didn't mean it.... And... and... and now I want to.

MOWCHUK: (*horrified*) Mr. Dickens, our agreement. Dignity. Logic. (*He trips.*)

HIGHRISE: What's wrong?

MOWCHUK: Your damn bricks!

HIGHRISE laughs, though exhausted. MOWCHUK tries to move again. He trips again. He's trapped.

MOWCHUK: I can't move.

DICKENS: The last year, the bottles I've been bringing you... I'm no longer with the company. They've taken to publicity. Television and all that. I'm not needed anymore.

SADIE: And the bottles? They were filled with...

DICKENS: Coloured water.

Suddenly, a mailbag, even larger than the first one, is thrown through the door.

SADIE: More mail. You see how they love me. I'm glad you told me, Dickens. And you still insisted on credit. I'll remember that. Now join hands, the three of you. Go ahead. You've given me such pleasure.

They do so. They play ring around the rosie with SADIE in the centre.

It's nearly three o'clock. If only you were babies.

MOWCHUK puts his thumb in his mouth.

I could talk to you then. Babies understand me. And animals.

DICKENS drops on all fours.

HIGHRISE: Would you like me to think of you as my mother?

SADIE: Yes.

HIGHRISE: When I'm about to do something very naughty I ask myself, "What would Sadie Golden want me to do? Would she be proud of me or ashamed?"

SADIE: And what do you do?

HIGHRISE: What would make you ashamed. Because then you'll be angry. You'll want to spank Highrise. (*bending over a chair for a spanking*)

SADIE: I've been meaning to have a talk with you.

DICKENS: I have other things to confess.

MOWCHUK: You promised. A gentleman's agreement.

DICKENS: It's my wife. She.... She makes tea when I want coffee.... She doesn't pay any attention to me even when I'm being a bad boy.

MOWCHUK: Mmmmm.... Mmmmmmm.... Mmmmmmmmmm.

The sound of a hurt, angry, wailing child.

SADIE: Poor little man. Were we ignoring you?

MOWCHUK: You were. Yes, you were.

SADIE: Would you like mommy to pat the little tummy? Stretch out on the rug then.

DICKENS: Me too. Me too.

HIGHRISE is still bent over the chair for his spanking.

HIGHRISE: Spanking!

SADIE: I wish I'd known my husband as a baby. Can he see us now, I wonder? You don't know what a temptation helplessness is to a woman. You don't give us credit.

The three men remain in varying positions of childlike vulnerability.

The things we might have done to you and didn't. Holding you in our arms, dependent on our breasts, grasping, pulling at us...

The following begins as though she were giving a speech, but breaks down quickly into inner musing, memories, fear.

I have led a full, rich and rewarding life. You think it's just me standing here? I have friends and relatives. While they are alive, wherever they are, so am I. We should be like the tribes in Africa. They all live under one roof. On the mother's side, I read it somewhere. Or no roof at all. That's how it was in the old days. There's no such thing as neighbours anymore. My friends are here. But none of you can suckle from me. It's nearly three o'clock. Before he couldn't have enough of me, Old Man Golden, it wasn't decent, it was cruel, he wouldn't let me alone, when I bled, in the night when I was safe in my dreams he came for me, in the hospital right on the hospital bed, right after I'd had the babies, in the afternoon when even the teacups are sleeping, he'd surprise me, "Now, now," he'd say. Am I real? Do you see me? And then the pain, but "Now," he'd say, "now." These hands, wrinkled, crippled, blue veins, but parchment too, I think. Do you see them? Or through them. (*imitating her husband again*) "You're not here, woman. You don't exist. No, not now. Not tonight." Me not asking, just looking. It changed. Now it's all silence. The smell is musty, yes, but still there is a smell. Is there? "I don't see you," he'd say. "I won't see you." I feel a pain, but is it just a thought? Not even that sometimes, at night, my mind, I think, "Now think," but blank, then white as chalk, not even a colour, not lights even, not... (*singing weakly*) A... B... C.... Write something. Draw. Like with a pencil. Like with a... like... you, you see me, touch me.

The men, infants, are incapable of responding.

You're not in the house of a dead woman, are you? Thin, dissolving... transparent, like my window. I float into it, yes, I love it, yes, I become this glass and through it, too, dissolve I enter whatever passes in front of my window, a dog or a cat or a man; sometimes I'm the sparks in the wire, or a sound, yes, there are sounds in my street sometimes, the things I've been I'd blush to tell you, through this glass. But when the sun hits it, oh my God, the glare, then I'm trapped like a spirit in a white cave crying for a body to enter.

REVEREND CAVIL enters from the kitchen carrying a large briefcase and a Bible.

REVEREND CAVIL: Is this the residence of Mrs. Golden? May I come in?

The phone rings. SADIE answers it.

SADIE: Three o'clock... that's right.

WISEMAN enters carrying a case similar to MOWCHUK's, but much larger.

Why, Mr. Wiseman.

Another sack of mail is thrown in through the door. The phone rings. SADIE answers it.

Yes, three o'clock.

All present look at their watches The front door opens and an enormous sack filled with samples and advertisements is thrown in. It spills on the floor. A salesman enters just behind, walking over the mound. It's the florist, APPLEBAUM, who looks like a rotund wax figure.

APPLEBAUM: For you, Madam.

He hands her a large bouquet of wax death flowers. SADIE spreads them over the last sheeted piece of furniture. MILKMAN, LAWYER, DOCTOR—as many representatives of our consumer sales society as the production can afford—enter up the aisles, through the front plate glass window, and, if possible, through the walls. As an alternative, tapes and mannequins may be used. SADIE scans the salesmen anxiously. A dapper small man dressed in undertaker's costume enters down the staircase from the non-existent second floor. He is wearing white gloves. He hands SADIE a card.

UNDERHILL: Mr. Underhill at your service.

SADIE: I've been waiting for you.

The salesmen drop their products to the floor and move in on SADIE, grasping for the cat which she holds out of their reach above her head. Frightened, she lets it fall. It shatters. Money spills from its belly. SADIE goes to the cupboard and opens it, revealing rows of coloured cats. She selects a white cat and returns to the salesmen who are scrambling on the floor for the money.

You're welcome, all of you, welcome in my house. It can never be said Sadie Golden denied a visitor. Look, my room is almost completely in flower, and it's you, gentlemen, I have to thank. And now we will have tea.

A serving man enters from the kitchen carrying a huge silver tea tray. He places the tray on the table. SADIE mounts her chair.

But first... I will sing for you.

The fly swings in the quivering web.
The fish is pierced in the craw,
It's all for love that you must die
Sang the wise jackdaw.

No. That's not the one. That's not the song.

She opens her mouth. All are polite attention. The sound starts as a moan and builds and builds to a terrible cry, a scream of loneliness and anguish. As the cry builds, the lights rise to an unbearable glare, the three o'clock terror. Even before the cry ends, the salesmen begin to clap politely. The glare is at its peak. Suddenly, rock music blares, continuing SADIE's scream. She falls. The salesmen catch her. UNDERHILL gestures. One of the salesmen pulls the sheet off the last remaining covered piece of furniture – the coffin. The music merges with the howl of a cat. The salesmen place SADIE in the coffin. UNDERHILL closes her eyes and covers her with a sheet. The salesmen raise the coffin and carry it slowly towards the staircase, followed by DICKENS, MOWCHUK and HIGHRISE.

The music dissolves, except for the howl of the cat, now high and thin. The walls move, or, if a scrim, it is pierced by the light. It is apparent now that there is definitely no second storey. The sound ceases abruptly. The cortege moves silently up the stairs to the void.

Blackout.

The end.

BABEL RAP

BY

JOHN LAZARUS

Alex Diakun as Smoker, John Lazarus as Worker

Photographer: Martin Keeley

WORLDS ASKEW: THE PLAYS OF JOHN LAZARUS

Two decades after its initial production, John Lazarus recalled the origins of *Babel Rap*: "I told myself (wrongly) that if I was a real playwright I should be able to write a play about the very next thing I saw, and I looked up and saw the lighting man's stepladder. So I decided to write a play that my friend Alex and I could perform *on* a stepladder, which would represent the biggest structure in the world. And I went home that night and wrote *Babel Rap*" (Author's Intro, *Six Canadian Plays*). Created by a playwright not yet 25 and produced by a collective of young people in a city where indigenous drama was in its early days, *Babel Rap* has had a particular appeal to more than one generation of youth.

In the nearly three decades that have now elapsed since the play's birth, John Lazarus has worn virtually every theatrical hat. Born in Montreal on December 24, 1947, he studied at McGill University and in the National Theatre School's acting program. Upon graduation in 1969, he performed at the Stratford Festival and with touring children's companies in British Columbia and Quebec. His playwriting career began in 1970, the year he moved to Vancouver, with the unpublished, unproduced, but award-winning children's play *Mad King Andrew*. He has also been a critic for a number of Vancouver newspapers and television stations; a broadcaster for CBC and other radio stations; a teacher of playwriting and dramaturgy at Vancouver Community College, Studio 58, and Queen's University; a screenwriter for such television series as "Sesame Street", "Northwood", "Mom PI", and "Little Bear"; a teacher of screenwriting at Vancouver Film School; and a dramaturge and adjudicator for such groups as Theatre BC and the Association of BC Drama Educators.

It is stage writing, however, that has been Lazarus's mainstay. He followed up *Mad King Andrew* with, in 1971, *Chester, You Owe My Bird an Apology*, which won the National Playwriting Competition and which was published, produced, and adapted for radio. *Babel Rap*, written in 1972, has had over 100 productions since its first by Troupe that year. Anthologized by Coach House Press under the title *Not So Dumb*, Lazarus's four children's plays, all of which premiered at Vancouver's Green Thumb Theatre, have also enjoyed world-wide production. In addition to creating original works such as *Dreaming and Duelling*, *Village of Idiots*, *The Late Blumer*, *Homework & Curtains*, *Medea's Disgust*, and *The Trials of Eddy Haymour*—most of which premiered in British Columbia—Lazarus has written adaptations of Andersen's *The Nightingale*, Brecht's *The Good Woman of Setzuan*, and (with Robert Metcalfe) Feydeau's *The Hotel Freedom*. A recent collaboration with DanceArts saw him write both the text for the company's dance-theatre hit *ICE: beyond cool* and the screenplay for the film version, and act as dramaturge for the company's annual festival, *The Kiss Project*.

Characteristic Lazarus work, *Village of Idiots* shares with *Babel Rap* a keen wit, an impressive display of verbal acuity, and an ability to show us not the "real world," but a world decidedly askew and, in so doing, to reveal to the audience the inherent preposterousness of the "real world." Lazarus has a singular knack for altering audience perceptions, for causing us to question that which we too often take for granted. *Village of Idiots* is based on Jewish folklore that Lazarus became familiar with in his childhood. Chelm, the village referred to in the title (today located in Poland), developed in Jewish folklore as a place inhabited by fools. After meticulously researching various versions of the tale, Lazarus added two components: an outsider to act as a foil to the townspeople and a pogrom. Adapted into a CBC radio mini-series and a National Film Board cartoon that took the Genie award for best animated short in 2000, the play is replete with charm and humour.

The story of the company from which *Babel Rap* emerged is very much a story of 1970s Canada. In the post-Centennial Trudeau era, nationalism was high and Canadians were eager to see themselves reflected in their art: the climate was finally conducive to the flourishing of indigenous drama. Troupe, composed of about a dozen actors, began with a workshop in an East Vancouver loft in the fall of 1971. Under the direction of Jon Bankson, and with a Local Initiatives Program grant, the company was committed to producing Canadian work, especially new and local plays. In its short life, it moved from venue to venue, including Intermedia Hall and the Vancouver East

Cultural Centre. Although plagued by the usual problems of theatre companies in Canada (such as restricting grant conditions and perpetual money shortages necessitating brief rehearsal time and resulting in the actors going into their salaries in order to make ends meet), Troupe quickly garnered considerable support from such sources as James Barber of the *Province* and Lloyd Dykk and Christopher Dafoe of the *Sun*. These critics saw the indigenous mandate of the company as filling an important niche and lauded the group's willingness to be daring and experimental. In its first season alone, the collective produced six plays by local writers, beginning with Herschel Hardin's *Esker Mike and His Wife Agiluk*, and including the highly successful *Rinse Cycle* by Jackie Crossland and Rudy Lavalle, Douglas Bankson's *Lenore Nevermore* (a black farce devoted to the life of Edgar Alan Poe, with Lazarus as Poe), and, of course, *Babel Rap*, which Dykk called "a really fine piece of comic invention" and Barber, who noted Lazarus's gift for "the essence of things," praised as "a remarkably tight and concise little piece of theatre." The company charged admission—$1.00 per person—only reluctantly, and, in subsequent seasons, produced such works as George Walker's *Sacktown Rag*. John Lazarus had an ongoing involvement with the company: he acted (under John MacLachlan Gray's direction) in David Tipe's *The Travesty and the Fruit Fly* and wrote two one-act solo plays, *A Cold Beer with a Warm Friend* and *Encroaching Chaos*.

Ratsoy: Newspaper articles and reviews certainly paint a picture of Troupe as a very daring, talented, exciting, and dedicated company. Is that how you would depict them?

Lazarus: Yes. I look at it as a generational thing. Everybody talks about the early playwriting in the 1970s as being sort of nationalistic: as a reaction against American writing and English writing, we were going to do our own Canadian writing, which is probably true. But at the time I looked at it more along the lines of us young hippies were going to do our own generation's work, as opposed to what the older people were doing at the Playhouse and the Arts Club. I admired what they were doing: I was thrilled when Paxton Whitehead, Artistic Director of the Playhouse, came to our shows, and I would have been very happy working for the Playhouse. But it was also exciting to be doing our own generation's work. Sure it was brave and bold; we didn't know what we were doing. We didn't know we couldn't do it.

Ratsoy: The pond has become much larger in the intervening decades. In what ways has the Canadian theatre scene changed over the course of your career?

Lazarus: It is now more taken for granted that Canadian theatres should be doing Canadian plays. I worked early in my career with the New Play Centre, which was formed to foster script development. It is now taken for granted that theatre companies have their own script development branch. We are also fortunate that organizations like the Playwrights Union of Canada and Banff Playwrights Colony developed and continue to thrive. There are also a lot more people in the business pursuing a lot fewer tickets. The Fringe festivals are a demonstration of that. I'm glad they are there; they often serve as a showcase for young talent.

On the other hand, in recent years in Vancouver people have become very frustrated because there's an awful lot of good work being done, but we're not getting the attendance that we used to. Perhaps this is the corollary of the fact that it is now taken for granted that Canadian companies produce Canadian plays. Part of the kindness of the response of the critics to Troupe had to do with the desire to support something that needed to be done. There's no longer that attitude.

In Vancouver, because of the increase in television and movie filming, an ancillary industry of agencies and acting schools has cropped up, and I'm very suspicious of a lot of the acting schools when I look at the product they turn out.

One thing that has not changed in Canada, I think, is that working in theatre is still considered a very odd career choice.

Like Morris Panych's *Last Call* and Sally Clark's *Ten Ways to Abuse an Old Woman*, *Babel Rap* owes much to the tradition of theatre of the absurd, a term coined by Martin Esslin in 1961 to describe works by playwrights such as Eugene Ionesco, Samuel Beckett, Jean Genet, Edward Albee, and Harold Pinter. Originally largely a manifestation of the despair and loss felt after WORLD WAR II, theatre of the absurd tends toward the theatrical rather than the realistic, eschewing, for example, realistic characters and favouring impossible situations; at its root serious, it often embraces satire, and its thematic core focuses on alienation, the impotence of the individual, and the meaninglessness of life in a godless, mechanized society.

The liminal space to which we refer in our general introduction is also often a feature of theatre of the absurd, usually functioning, as it does in *Babel Rap*, to underscore the universality of the preposterousness of life. Lazarus's instructions regarding character, gender, costumes, and set mesh well with the dialogue itself. Nameless, identified only by a single characteristic, of either gender, dressed in either modern or Biblical clothes (or a combination of the two), the duo are suspended in space against a minimalist backdrop. Such a setting transcends time and space, as does their dialogue – a philosophical exploration of eternal theological questions that is both earnest and comic.

Ratsoy: Do you consider yourself a BC playwright?

Lazarus: Yes, but you're asking me at an interesting moment, as I've suddenly gone east [to teach at Queen's University]. I'm still considering myself a BC playwright because everything of mine that gets produced was written in BC. I'm working on three, but I haven't yet finished a play in Kingston. I suppose once I finish a play in Kingston and it gets produced in Ontario then I'll start to have to consider the question of whether I'm an Ontario playwright.

Ratsoy: How important is place to you as a playwright?

Lazarus: Not very. I have plays that are Canadian, sometimes overtly. But place doesn't really stand out for me a whole lot.

In *Babel Rap*, Lazarus has achieved a neat, if unlikely, union of Biblical narrative and absurdist drama. Given that one of the identifiers of absurdist drama is an exploration of a godless world, Lazarus's melding of apparent contradictions is a particularly clever congruence of the incongruous. The words of the title also create an interesting juxtaposition: in addition to alluding to the Biblical tower, the word "babel" (from the Hebrew "confused") means a confusion of many different sounds and a place of noise and confusion, and "rap" is free, informal talk.

The plot—at once a metaphor for life and for art—also recalls the Greek myth of Sisyphus, the king of Corinth punished for his misdeeds with an eternal sentence: to roll a large stone up a steep hill from which it always rolled down again. James Hoffman has noted that Lazarus's characters "have that special intuition and stage savvy that only someone who really knows actors can create; they seem to know they are actors too, that their fictional playworld might self-consciously destruct at any moment." This reflexivity is patent in the Worker's speculation about God: "You see, I get the feeling that He has this thing for dramatic endings. He seems to like getting into the confrontation after the story has gone on a bit, rather than nipping it in the bud." It is when the Worker and the Smoker put on a show for God that their dialogue disintegrates, and when the two co-operate and change roles and the dismantling begins that the thunder stops.

Much has changed on the Canadian theatre scene since the debut of *Babel Rap* in 1972. However, despite the relative abundance of Canadian works on both indigenous and foreign stages, *Babel Rap*, which has been adapted for television by both Alberta Access and TV Ontario and translated into French and German, is still one of the most frequently produced (by professional, community, and especially university groups) plays in Canada – a testimony to the universality of its appeal.

G.R.

Selected Bibliography:

•Barber, James. "Citystage Cleans Up Act; When It's Hot, They're Not." *Vancouver Province* 4 July 1972.
•Dykk, Lloyd. "Review of *Babel Rap*." *Vancouver Sun* 28 Apr. 1972.
•Groberman, Michael. "Lazarus Welcomes Middle Age." *The Georgia Straight* 9-16 Oct. 1987.
•Heald, Joseph. "Waiting for the Dough: A Small Group's Search." *Vancouver's Leisure Magazine* (June 1974): 54-55. Troupe's story provides an interesting case study of the independent theatre companies that sprang up in the early 1970s.
•Hoffman, James. "The Actors' Theatre of John Lazarus." *Western Canada Theatre Company's Program Magazine* 16:1 (October 1994): 9.
•Lazarus, John. "Author's Introduction to *Babel Rap*." *Six Canadian Plays*. Ed. Tony Hamill. Toronto: Playwrights Canada Press, 1992. 11
•Lazarus, John. "ICE: beyond belief." *Canadian Theatre Review* 106 (Spring 2001): 24-28. Details the creation and production of *ICE: beyond cool*, on which Lazarus, David Diamond, and others collaborated with Judith Marcuse. Lazarus describes the work as "both a high point and a low point" in his career.
•Lazarus, John. Telephone Interview. 18 Dec. 2000.
•Lazarus, John. "Teaching Do-It-Yourself at Studio 58, [Langara College, BC.]" *Canadian Theatre Review* 81 (Winter 1994): 88-89.
•Lazarus, John. "When Have a Critic's Comments had a Positive Impact on your Work? Never." 2000. http://www.rumble.org/trans/trans6-2.html (1 Nov. 2000).
•Rubin, Don and Alison Cranmer. *Canada's Playwrights: A Biographical Guide*. Toronto: CTR Publications, 1980.

Babel Rap
by John Lazarus

Babel Rap was first produced by Troupe in Vancouver, in April, 1972, with the following cast:

Worker   John Lazarus
Smoker   Alexander Diakun

Directed by John Lazarus

A revised version was produced for the opening of Citadel II in Edmonton, March 1975, with the following cast:

Worker   Alan Lysell
Smoker   Scott Swan

Alan Lysell and Scott Swan made very important contributions to the revisions, for which the author extends deep thanks.

CHARACTERS

A WORKER
A SMOKER

The characters do not have to be male, of course.

COSTUMES

Modern dress is recommended – overalls or work clothes, with touches of colour about them. Biblical robes are acceptable too: one production had the actors in robes, sandals, and MacMillan-Bloedel hardhats.

SET

The highest point on the Tower of Babel. The original production took place on a step-ladder, built for the purpose, that was meant to represent the top of the tower. Whatever the set design, it should be established early on that the stage floor is accepted as nonexistent – that is, the actors look down through infinite space, and never touch the floor. We have found that the best production design has been the simplest. A sky-cloth backdrop or cyclorama is also recommended, maybe even a cloud or two.

ACT ONE

The sound of hammering in darkness. Lights up. The WORKER is busy hammering, working on the tower. The SMOKER is relaxing with a cigarette, watching the birds fly by below. After a few moments, the noise of the hammering begins to bother the SMOKER. He raps briskly on the side of the tower like an annoyed tenant. The WORKER repeats the brisk pattern, deafeningly, with his hammer.

SMOKER: Hey, would you like to stop and have a smoke?

WORKER: (*stops hammering; short pause, pointedly*) No thanks. I'm working.

SMOKER: (*pointedly*) Oh. (*returning to his smoking and watching the birds*)

The WORKER looks at him, and goes back to hammering. After a moment, the noise bothers the SMOKER.

SMOKER: Listen, do you mind? (*as the WORKER stops*) I'm trying to relax here. Have my cigarette and watch the birds. I find that hammering distracting.

WORKER: Yeah?

SMOKER: Yeah.

WORKER: I'm working my ass off, and you're sitting on yours, and you find my hammering distracting?

SMOKER: Yeah!

Pause.

WORKER: What about all that goddamn noise you're making? All that sucking and blowing. (*noisily imitating a drag on a cigarette*) That's what I call distracting.

SMOKER: Yeah?

WORKER: Yeah. Also the smoke from your cigarette is irritating my sensitive nostrils.

SMOKER: Yeah?

WORKER: Yeah! (*pausing*) Look, we're at a very high altitude. The atmosphere is thin. The smoke is proportionately more irritating.

SMOKER: All right, whaddaya wanna do?

WORKER: Why don't we both work hard for five minutes and then stop for a smoke?

SMOKER: Why don't we both smoke hard for five minutes and then go back to work?

Pause, both thinking.

BOTH: Okay...

WORKER: I'll work for five minutes...

SMOKER: I'll smoke for five minutes...

BOTH: And then we'll both take a break!

WORKER: No smoking!

SMOKER: No hammering!

WORKER: Shalom! (*simultaneously*)

SMOKER: Shazam! (*simultaneously*)

The WORKER resumes hammering. The SMOKER puffs thoughtfully.

SMOKER: (*amiably*) You know, it's fortunate that we get along as well as we do.

WORKER: (*stops hammering, chuckling*) Yes, isn't it. Considering how high up we are!

They chuckle.

SMOKER: And considering why we're here.

WORKER: Mmm.... Not everybody gets along as well as we do. I'm told there was an incident yesterday on one of the lower parapets. Two workmen pushed each other off the ledge.

SMOKER: Really?

WORKER: One of them asked for a hammer, and the other one gave him a saw... and in the ensuing dispute, they just pushed each other off the ledge.

SMOKER: That seems a bit extreme.

WORKER: Yeah, doesn't it. It sounds to me like they had the wrong attitude toward the holy nature of their work.

SMOKER: Oh, I don't know about that. They were willing to sacrifice each other for the sake of the Tower. That sounds kind of noble.

WORKER: Don't be facetious!

SMOKER: I'm not. Those two were probably more successful than we are. Look. Here we've been hammering and sawing since about as far back as I can remember, trying to build this tower to Heaven. All those guys had to do was get into a bit of a quarrel, and (*indicating a long fall, whistling a descending glissando, followed by a long pan up to Heaven, as he whistles an ascending glissando*) they're probably up in Heaven right now. Looking down upon us and giggling.

WORKER: (*working cheerfully*) That never occurred to me! This Tower's been my whole life! Whaddaya know.

SMOKER: Well, don't let it worry you.

WORKER: I won't.

SMOKER: You know, if you don't mind my saying so, you're probably too involved with the details. You ever ask yourself why we're building this Tower? What's it for?

WORKER: To get to Heaven!

SMOKER: To get to Heaven.

WORKER: What, do you think all this is in vain?

SMOKER: Well, we're gonna get to Heaven anyway! When we die! Aren't we?

WORKER: Sure! But you have to do something to pass the time before you get there. So why not work on the Tower? It's a good project. Gives people jobs. Makes everybody feel important. And besides, we might succeed! We might get to Heaven any day now!

SMOKER: (*uneasily*) Any day now...?

WORKER: Sure! This Tower's a real shortcut! Also, you avoid the pain and inconvenience of dying! (*pausing*) Boy, you really know how to make me feel better about the whole thing. Shalom! (*heartened, returning to his work*)

SMOKER: (*thoughtfully*) Shazam... (*smoking and thinking*) The one thing that keeps bothering me, though...

WORKER: Yeah?

SMOKER: Well, I keep wondering what's going to happen when we get there.

WORKER: (*slowing and stopping work*) How do you mean?

SMOKER: Well, for one thing, how do you know you're there?

WORKER: Well, everybody knows what Heaven is like!

SMOKER: Oh? Really?

WORKER: Sure! There's... blue sky... sunshine... birds singing everywhere... lots of clouds floating around.

SMOKER: Yeah, but there are clouds right here. Some time ago, as a matter of fact, when we were working some stories below, you promised me that when we got above the clouds, we'd be in Heaven.

WORKER: (*shrugging off his former ignorance*) Oh! Well...

SMOKER: Well, we got above the clouds, and what did we find? Clouds.

WORKER: Well, I'm sorry! It's not my fault that this isn't Heaven.

SMOKER: (*pause*) Maybe... maybe it is.

WORKER: (*horrified*) What?

SMOKER: Sure. This could be Heaven. Blue sky... sunshine... all kinds of clouds drifting by... the occasional bird. Very peaceful.

WORKER: No! No, no, no, no, no! This isn't Heaven!

SMOKER: Why not?

WORKER: Because... well, because Heaven has great golden pillars thrusting up through the clouds, capped with tall spires and vast domes! And long rolling green meadows... and Technicolour gardens, filled with sparkling, jewelled, multi-coloured flowers! And massed chori of angels, singing Beethoven and Handel and Bach! Beautiful angels, everywhere!

They look around, in the direction of the audience.

SMOKER: Nope.

WORKER: Well, it's worth hammering a few nails. (*resuming hammering as the* SMOKER *smokes and thinks*)

SMOKER: Yeah, but...

The WORKER *puts down his hammer with resignation and disgust.*

SMOKER: But I still don't understand what happens when we get there.

WORKER: I'm sorry, but I still don't understand what the hell you're talking about.

SMOKER: Okay, look. We arrive. We look around. We see the angels and the pillars and the gardens of flowers. Hooray! Whoopee! We're in Heaven!

WORKER: Right!

SMOKER: Yeah, well then what? (*pausing*) What do we do then? Have lunch? Go sight-seeing...? Start another tower?

Pause.

WORKER: Well... we do whatever we want to, I suppose. Personally I'd sort of like to just gaze upon the countenance of the Almighty.

SMOKER: Yeah.... That'd be nice. But you wouldn't want to do that forever. For one thing, it'd be rude. You don't just walk up to the Almighty and gaze upon His countenance, like some gawky tourist. You'd want to say something.

WORKER: Well, sure! A private audience with the Almighty Himself! Great idea.

SMOKER: What would you say?

WORKER: Well... I'd introduce myself... and I'd introduce you.... I'd tell Him how happy I was to be there.

SMOKER: Yeah, but He already knows all that. He knows who we are. He knows that you're happy to be there and that I'm happy to be there.

WORKER: I know. But it's just a way of being polite. You know? Making conversation.

SMOKER: Well, maybe He'd take offence.

WORKER: Why should He take offence?

SMOKER: Well, you're sort of talking down to Him, telling Him stuff He already knows. What if He says, "I already know all that. Tell me something I don't already know." Ha! That would stop you, wouldn't it!

WORKER: Oh... He wouldn't do anything like that. He's too polite.

SMOKER: You never know. After all, He does work in mysterious ways His wonders to perform. Nobody really knows what the rules are. Something that's polite to you or me might be very rude to Him. Look. Suppose you say, "Good morning, God, how are you?" That's pleasant enough, right?

WORKER: Sure.

SMOKER: Yeah, but He's the one who decides whether it's going to be a good morning or not. So your saying good morning could be taken as a very presumptuous command.

WORKER: Oh, now...

SMOKER: Not only that, but if you ask Him "How are you?" you're implying that He's changeable; that He isn't perfect. He could have you up for blasphemy just for saying hello.

Pause.

WORKER: Why are you being so negative?

SMOKER: Because I don't think anybody's thought this whole Tower business through properly. It might scare Him.

WORKER: Scare God? Come on.

SMOKER: Well then, maybe just make Him mad. What if we arrive and He says, "What the hell is the matter with you wise guys? Why can't you die like everybody else?"

WORKER: Well, if that happens, we'll just apologize and go back.

SMOKER: Yeah, but if Heaven is as great as everybody says, I think we'll find it very difficult to settle back down on the farm again.

WORKER: You never did like the farm. I think you just don't like work!

SMOKER: Not true! I like farming. I don't mind working at all, when I can see some point to it.

WORKER: Oh, you're just being a defeatist. You're afraid of the unknown. Anyway, look. If He really doesn't want us to get to Heaven by building this Tower, then He won't let us get to Heaven by building this Tower, that's all. He'll stop us.

SMOKER: How? How's He gonna stop us?

WORKER: Well, He could make the whole thing collapse and kill us all, if He wants to be a bastard about it.

SMOKER: Yeah, sure. He makes the whole thing collapse, and He kills us all, and we all die, and we all wind up in Heaven anyway. Precisely because we were building this thing. Nope.

WORKER: Well, He could stop us any way He wants to! He could make us all forget what we're doing; He could make our tools disappear. He could call up a thunderstorm, scare the crap out of us. He's the Almighty! He doesn't have to wait until we get up there and then send us back.

SMOKER: (*chuckling*) Come to think of it, waiting until we get up there and then sending us back would be a very just punishment.

WORKER: Oh, for Heaven's sake, don't give Him any bright ideas.

A gloomy silence. The WORKER, now thoroughly discouraged, contemplates the distance they have come and the distance they have yet to go. The SMOKER smokes and thinks.

SMOKER: Hey, whose bright idea was this, anyway? Who suggested we start building this Tower in the first place?

WORKER: I don't know.... Some smartass a few generations back. Nobody remembers.

SMOKER: Because it occurs to me that if God didn't want us to build this thing, He would have stopped us a long time ago. He wouldn't even have given the original smartass the idea.

WORKER: (*thinking it through*) That's true... but He did... so He does. There! Ha! There, you see? Proof! From your own mouth! He obviously doesn't mind a bit.

SMOKER: Maybe not... I dunno.... But if He did originally inspire us with the idea, then just maybe, He's planning something nasty.

WORKER: Oh, you just don't have any faith at all, do you? Why should He be planning something nasty? God made the world! He made you and me! He's on our side.

SMOKER: (*considering*) He did make the Garden of Eden...

WORKER: Right!

SMOKER: And Adam and Eve...

WORKER: Right again!

SMOKER: (*innocently*) And the Serpent... (*looking at the WORKER*)

WORKER: (*after a brief pause*) Well... yeah... okay... hmm.

SMOKER: You see, I get the feeling that He has this thing for dramatic endings. He seems to like getting into the confrontation after the story has gone on a bit, rather than nipping it in the bud.

WORKER: Maybe He likes getting His name in the Bible.

SMOKER: Maybe. Maybe He just likes giving people lessons they won't forget.

WORKER: (*exasperated*) I see. So. According to you, the whole Tower is just doomed to failure, hm?

SMOKER: (*exasperated*) No, no, no, now I didn't say that. I just think He may find it offensive, that's all.

WORKER: He'll love it! Why, may I ask, do you assume that He's going to be offended? I would think He'd be flattered! I know that if a bunch of people went to this kind of trouble to get to me, I'd be tickled pink. Who knows? We don't know! Maybe when we arrive He'll come rushing over, hollering, "Glory be! You built that great huge Tower just to come up and visit? Just to visit little old Me? Well, glory be! Glory be to Me!" Maybe he'll have us over for dinner.

SMOKER: Yeah, but there are more traditional means of approach. Like meditation and prayers and good works.

WORKER: Yeah, so?

SMOKER: So since He's made these methods traditional, I would think He probably favours them.

WORKER: Aha! I see! So that's why you sit around on your ass cloud-gazing while I'm trying to get the work done!

SMOKER: (*pleased with the rationale*) Yeah! Yeah, that's one way of looking at it.

WORKER: Right. Right. Just suppose He were to look down at the two of us here.

SMOKER: Okay.

WORKER: He looks at me, getting my hands nice and filthy with the grime of honest toil...

SMOKER: Oh, He'll love you. Haven't you heard the bit about cleanliness and Godliness?

WORKER: At least I'm working for His greater glory. What are you doing? Absolutely nothing, except to pollute His atmosphere with your foul tobacco. Who do you think He'll like best?

SMOKER: At least I'm quiet! At least I'm grateful for the world He's given me, and I trust Him to take me to the next world in His own sweet time. Not like you, banging and sawing, storming the Pearly Gates, trying to impress him with this – runaway technology. Who do you think He'll like best?

WORKER: (*after a brief pause*) I sing hymns to Him. I'm always singing hymns to Him.

SMOKER: I've noticed.

WORKER: You never sing hymns to Him.

SMOKER: Don't jump to conclusions. Maybe I sing them silently.

WORKER: Well, I sing mine nice and loud. I'm not ashamed of mine. I'll bet He really enjoys mine.

SMOKER: Does He?

WORKER: (*starting low and sweet and unctuously pious*) Holy, holy, holy, Lord God Almighty, Early in the morning our song shall rise to Thee...

SMOKER: (*louder, over the WORKER's hymn, beginning during the line "Early in the morning"*)
The Lord's my shepherd,
I'll not want,
He makes me down to lie
In pastures green,
He leadeth me
The quiet waters by.

WORKER: (*raising the volume, and taking revenge by starting on the SMOKER's line "In pastures green..."*)
Mine eyes have seen the Glory of the coming of the Lord,
He is trampling through the vintage where the grapes of wrath are stor'd;
He hath loos'd the fearful lightning of His terrible swift sword,
His truth is...

SMOKER: (*swinging, jiving, snapping his fingers, coming in somewhere around "fearful lightning..."*)
Swing low, sweet chariot,
Coming for to carry me home,
Swing low, sweet chariot,
Coming for to carry me...

WORKER: (*full volume, grand opera, all stops out; from Handel's "Messiah"*)
Hallelujah! Hallelujah!
Hallelujah, Hallelujah, Halle-e-lu-jaahh!
For the Lord God Omni-i-potent reigneth...

SMOKER: (*half singing along, half shouting*) Hallelujah! Hallelujah!

BOTH: (*screaming at each other in fury*) Hallelujah! Hallelujah! Hallelujah!

They are interrupted by a huge and angry thunderclap and a profound dimming and flickering of the lights. They stop and look up for a moment, and then dive for a hiding place (in the original production, the two actors had worked their way to the top of the step-ladder during the hymns, then down the ladder to cower on a small platform built across its lower strut).

They hide, quaking and gazing up at the storm rumbling and flickering for several moments before slowly dying out in a sulky muttering and rumbling. The lights steady at a dimmer level than the bright sunshine we had before. A pause.

SMOKER: (*with awe and fear*) Maybe we should cut out the bullshit.

WORKER: (*with awe and fear*) I don't think He's too pleased with either one of us at the moment.

SMOKER: He probably feels we're presuming.

WORKER: (*frustrated*) Yes, but presuming to what? Presuming to find favour with the Almighty? What's wrong with that?

SMOKER: Well, maybe we shouldn't be putting each other down in order to do it.

WORKER: (*with some self pity*) Perhaps... I wish He'd tell us what the hell He wants from us. I mean, I'm doing my best.

SMOKER: I know; it's very trying.

WORKER: Trying is the word for it.

SMOKER: Hey, maybe He just wants us to cooperate. Get along. Work together.

WORKER: Work together? Huh. I know what that means. That's where I came in. With me working and you goofing off.

SMOKER: No, no, I don't mean just on the Tower. I mean on anything. He may not want us to work on the Tower at all. But if we're going to work on something, maybe He figures we shouldn't fight over it.

WORKER: Okay. Well. What is there to work on?

SMOKER: I dunno.

WORKER: Look. As I pointed out a short time ago, you might as well work on the Tower as on anything else. Helps pass the time.

SMOKER: Hm.

WORKER: (*his idea gaining momentum*) And... judging from that little thunder routine, He is perfectly capable of expressing His displeasure when He wants to. Ergo, He hasn't previously wanted to... ergo, the Tower is an acceptable project on which to work.

SMOKER: (*considers this for a moment*) Maybe He didn't know we were around until just now.

WORKER: What?

SMOKER: We were singing pretty loudly. Maybe our singing attracted His attention. Maybe He hadn't noticed us before.

WORKER: How could He not have noticed us before? He sees the little sparrow fall.... We're building the tallest goddamn tower in human history! I'm hammering nails at top volume. You're letting cigarette smoke drift up into the stratosphere. How could He not have noticed us?

SMOKER: Maybe He was asleep.

Pause.

WORKER: (*horrified*) Do you think maybe we woke him up?

SMOKER: It's a possibility.

WORKER: That's not a very nice thing to do, is it?

SMOKER: Well, if I were the Almighty, trying to get some sleep, and two guys were building a tower and singing hymns one floor below me, I imagine I might get mildly pissed off.

WORKER: (*after a pause*) Maybe we should apologize.

SMOKER: Maybe we should.

They kneel side by side in attitudes of prayer. They pray, ad lib, almost silently, in very low whispers, but we can see their mouths moving, and they tend to gesture. Their approach vacillates between abject flattery and high-pressure persuasion.

(*finishing first*) Amen...

The WORKER goes on, ad lib; we can barely hear him, but it sounds like he is blaming the noise on the SMOKER.

Amen!

WORKER: Amen.

Pause. They look around.

Any reply?

SMOKER: No. You?

WORKER: No... He never says nothin' to me anyway.

The lights have been brightening back to sunlight.

SMOKER: Well, maybe we calmed Him down a little. The sun's shining... everything seems all right!

WORKER: (*with apparent heartiness, but underneath, a new unease*) Yeah! Everything... seems the same...

SMOKER: (*after a brief pause*). Well! I'm gonna have another cigarette.

WORKER: Right! You do that. I'm gonna... get back to work... Shalom.

SMOKER: Shazam. (*the WORKER does not move*) Something wrong?

WORKER: You know there's something wrong.

SMOKER: Yeah.... Hey, do you get the feeling we're being watched?

As soon as the thought is voiced, they look frantically around them, high and low, upstage and into the audience, and wind up looking back at each other.

WORKER: Nobody around.

SMOKER: Nope.

WORKER: Just... you and me! Heh, heh.

SMOKER: Yup.

WORKER: We are definitely being watched.

SMOKER: (*equally nervous, but a bit more in control*) Yes. Definitely. There's somebody behind us.

WORKER: (*starting to panic*) How can there be somebody behind us? We're facing each other!

SMOKER: Yeah! I know...

Pause, as they both realize the identity of the watcher.

WORKER: Look busy. (*handing the SMOKER a tool*) Here. Get to work.

SMOKER: Right.

They both start to work, whistling ostentatiously. They work for a few moments, still paranoid then a couple of touches of thunder sound

SMOKER: Hey, will ya pass the gerzil?

WORKER: (*preoccupied*) What?

SMOKER: Kindly pass the gerzil.

Pause.

WORKER: What the fump is a gerzil?

Pause.

SMOKER: The gerzil, you plink! It's in the gool fronk.

Pause. All work has stopped.

WORKER: Are... you playing some kind of a shnobbly frape with me? What is this crimple?

Pause.

SMOKER: What the fnerch are you scroggling about?

WORKER: All right, come on, nerkle. Flumb it.

SMOKER: Aw, cub it ouch!

Pause, as the WORKER seethes for a moment; then he loses his temper.

WORKER: I have had enunch! You blaw gap futhermudding summon afitch!

SMOKER: Why you cog spugging hansard! Don't you spall me grames!

WORKER: Plimp!

SMOKER: Grutch!

WORKER: (*grabbing the SMOKER by his collar*) Chiltz!

SMOKER: (*doing likewise*) Patser! (*as the lights dim and a blast of thunder sounds, SMOKER, realizing, points to the sky*) See? See? It's Rib! It's Gob! He's blogging argle! Befuzz we're gilding the Townsend! He's mailing us gawk funny!

WORKER: I stan't undercand a flerd you snay! You're glonking funny!

SMOKER: (*overlapping slightly*) I stan't undercand a flerd you snay! You're glonking funny!

Thunder up. They look at the sky. The SMOKER suddenly starts pulling out planks, and throwing them down. Thunder under.

WORKER: You can't doobers! We're too curst to Heaven! You don't understand!

SMOKER: You can't doobers! We're too toast eleven! You don't stand under! You're not talking the same language any more!

WORKER: Borg?

SMOKER: (*gesticulating*) You're... not... talking... the same... language... anymore!

WORKER: Glop?

SMOKER: You're not... ohh...

More thunder. The SMOKER pulls down a plank. The thunder abruptly stops and the lights brighten. The WORKER grabs the plank, putting it back up: the thunder starts again and the lights dim. The SMOKER pulls it down: thunder stops, lights brighten. The WORKER, experimenting, puts it up: thunder starts, lights dim. The WORKER, his eye on the sky, slowly hands the plank to the SMOKER: thunder fades, sky fades up. The SMOKER continues dismantling in silence, while the WORKER looks on, bewildered. The sun is now bright, the sky peaceful. The SMOKER glances up, sees the WORKER feeling useless and silently offers him the cigarette he refused at the beginning of the play. Slowly the WORKER lights up and sits back, still trying to figure this thing out. The SMOKER works, the WORKER smokes. Gradually the WORKER's frown fades, and he is beginning to relax and enjoy watching the birds when the lights fade out.

The end.

The Komagata Maru Incident

By

Sharon Pollock

Richard Fowler as Hopkinson, Heather Brechin as Evy, Diana Belshaw as Woman, Nicola Cavendish as Sophie, Leroy Schulz as Georg.

LOCAL CEREMONIES: SHARON POLLOCK'S *THE KOMAGATA MARU INCIDENT*

> "The West Coast is getting alienated more and more from the rest of the country. You could call my new comedy a political comedy – set on the West Coast."
> —Sharon Pollock discussing the writing of *The Komagata Maru Incident*, interviewed by Herbert Whittaker (*Globe and Mail*, 22 July 1974)

British Columbia has long intrigued Sharon Pollock. Far from family roots and away from much of her practical work in the theatre, the province has been for Pollock a place where exotics of diversity and remoteness, as well as hierarchies of authority, have inspired her to create works engaging "settler" issues in a colonial society. In these plays, people are temporarily or radically displaced because of their class or race; as such, they interrogate the models and ideologies of the dominant society. In *A Compulsory Option*, three male teachers, each in his way an outcast, share a house in a rural part of the province: one is a failed political activist, one a nervous paranoiac, the third a victimized gay man. *And Out Goes You* is a work of agitprop theatre showing the deteriorating relations between residents of the East Hastings area of Vancouver and the politicians—including premier Dave Barrett—who would drive them into unwanted highrise buildings. The plot of *One Tiger to a Hill* is taken from the headlines: in 1975 prisoners at the British Columbia Penitentiary in New Westminster took several hostages, one of whom was subsequently murdered. *End Dream*, her latest play, revisits a 1920s news story of the murder of a Scottish nanny in Vancouver, and the accusations against a Chinese servant.

Pollock examines society with the mind of a documentarist and the fierce regard of a moralist – in *Walsh* she literally damns Major Walsh of the North West Mounted Police to the hell of a dismal saloon for his failure in negotiating the settlement of Sitting Bull and his Sioux in Canada. She has been called by one of her early critics, Malcolm Page, "the most committed Canadian playwright." Her stance takes her directly into matters of history; it also widens the discourse from simple revisionist story-telling to probing revelations of society's "dirty little secrets." This of course is a recipe for great drama, as in the work of Shaw or Ibsen – to whom she has been compared. But it has also been a source of difficulty as she has struggled, not always successfully, to find dramatic form to convey her giant concerns.

Pollock was born in 1936 in New Brunswick, the daughter of well-known Fredericton physician and MLA Everett Chalmers – who has loomed as a presence in several of her plays, in *One Tiger to a Hill* and especially *Doc* (1984). She attended the University of New Brunswick and worked at Fredericton's Playhouse Theatre, but it was in 1966, when she moved to Calgary with actor Michael Ball to tour with the Prairie Players, that she felt a new freedom. Asked in an interview if she felt committed to the west, she replied, "Yes, it's my home. When I went out in the mid-60s, there was that wonderful sense that anything was possible" (Metcalfe 39). Although she has been strongly associated with Alberta theatre for much of her career, she lived in Vancouver during the mid-1970s, working with Christopher Newton at the Playhouse Theatre.

The Komagata Maru Incident is based on an ugly racist event in British Columbia – when, in 1914, the provincial government prevented the landing of a boat load of East Indian immigrants, mostly British subjects and therefore eligible for citizenship, in Vancouver harbour. After stalling them for two months by invoking an arcane rule that an immigrant ship's voyage must be made non-stop from point of origin, even when that was impossible, then attempting to starve them, the province finally threatened the passengers—which included many British war veterans—with a naval warship, the *H.M.S. Rainbow*. The hapless freighter finally returned to the east with disastrous results as the immigrants faced hostility, violence, and a loss of lives in their troubled homeland.

Pollock, as she had in *Walsh*, turned to history, to factual people and events, in order to expose the institutional forces that led to this incident – and, she would maintain, continue to this day. In *Walsh* she relied on masses of documentary material, much of it reduced in the final draft; in *The Komagata Maru Incident* Pollock utilized a greatly reduced use of the historical record and an adventurous theatricality, indeed a newfound freedom of form, to make her case. There is a mix of styles – reflected in the three spaces in the stage setting. First, the story of William Hopkinson, the immigration inspector, is realistically and centrally staged, surprisingly and meaningfully as a metaphor, in a Vancouver brothel. Then, in the manner of a cabaret or sideshow, a figure called T.S., whose name may stand for The System, acts as master of ceremonies; with top hat and cane, he mainly works on an outer runway surrounding the brothel, and also plays a number of roles. Then, located above and behind the other spaces, an East Indian woman occupies a cage-like frame suggesting the ship; her shadowy, generalized appearance, as she talks only to her baby, seems like a character from an expressionist play.

This mix of theatrical styles disrupts history: by relentlessly interchanging facts and varying points of view, by going back and forth between truth and illusion, much in the style of the now-you-see-it-now-you-don't of a carnival sideshow, Pollock interrupts conventional history telling. We see Hopkinson constructed as bureaucratic toady to anonymous institutional forces as well as a recent settler himself divided by family (his mother was East Indian) and personal (his close prostitute friend Evy opposes his spy network) contradictions. The effect is that this history, much of it hitherto hidden, is not only re-examined from a variety of decolonizing perspectives, but that the problem of racism is made real for audiences today. T.S., addressing the audience in the second person, continually invites us to join in, to run down to the harbour and watch, in effect to become complicit. In her introductory note to the play, Pollock places the issue squarely on the present: "Until we recognize the past, we cannot change our future." In this way, especially in the figure of T.S., we are promised some kind of social analysis.

Some critics, however, have found a problem with the form of the play; that the realism of the brothel scenes sits uneasily with, and indeed is weakened by, the lighthearted, presentational style of the cabaret. Denis Salter, who wrote the biocritical essay for the Sharon Pollock Papers, held at the University of Calgary, believes that, ultimately, the treatment of Hopkinson, is "reductive" as he finally admits the error of his ways in the court scene, then goes to meet his death as a contrite Sikh. In this way, the promise of a broader study of racism in British Columbia, suggested in the theatrics of T.S., becomes the mere issue of Hopkinson's personal problem. Thus "the audience is left off the hook" (Salter xix). Rather than passing judgment on itself, in a kind of Brechtian political self-awareness, the audience merely judges Hopkinson; a social problem is reduced to an individual's woes.

Nonetheless, Sharon Pollock has written a work that is clearly postcolonial in that it challenges both the hegemony of institutional colonialism as well as the authority of conventional (read imposed) dramaturgy. Along the way, she has given us a lively and still provoking play about how people and institutions in British Columbia contend.

J.H.

Selected Bibliography:

- Bessai, Diane. "Sharon Pollock's women: a study in dramatic process." Shirley Neuman and Smaro Kamboureli, eds. *A Mazing Space: Writing Canadian Women Writing*. Edmonton: Long Spoon/Newest, 1986.
- Hamill, Tony, ed. *Six Canadian Plays*. Toronto: Playwrights Canada Press, 1992. Contains *The Komagata Maru Incident*.
- Kerr, Rosalind. "Borderline Crossings in Sharon Pollock's Out-Law Genres: *Blood Relations* and *Doc*." *Theatre Research in Canada* 17-2 (Fall 1996): 200-215.
- Metcalfe, Robin. "Interview with Sharon Pollock." *Books in Canada* (March 1987): 39.
- Much, Rita. "Sharon Pollock Interview." *Fair Play: 12 Women Speak*, Judith Rudakoff and Rita Much. Toronto: Simon & Pierre, 1990.
- Nothof, Anne F., ed. *Sharon Pollock: Essays on Her Works*. Toronto: Guernica, 2000. Contains eight major essays on Pollock, from 1979 to 1999, and a recent interview.
- Page, Malcolm. "Sharon Pollock: Committed Playwright." *Canadian Drama* 5.2 (Fall 1979): 104-111.

- Pollock, Sharon. "Many Brave Spirits." *Theatre Memoirs*. Toronto: Playwrights Union of Canada, 1998. The playwright recalls her beginnings as a writer.
- Rubin, Don and Alison Cranmer-Byng, eds. *Canada's Playwrights: A Biographical Guide*. Toronto: Canadian Theatre Review Publications, 1980.
- Salter, Denis. "(Im)possible Worlds: The Plays of Sharon Pollock." *The Sharon Pollock Papers*. Calgary: University of Calgary Press, n.d.
- Wallace, Robert. "Sharon Pollock [interview]". *The Work: Conversations with English-Canadian Playwrights*, Robert Wallace and Cynthia Zimmerman. Toronto: Coach House Press, 1982.
- Zimmerman, Cynthia. "Towards a Better, Fairer World." *Canadian Theatre Review* 69 (Winter 1991): 34-38. An interview with Sharon Pollock.
- Zimmerman, Cynthia. "Sharon Pollock: The Making of Warriors." *Playwriting Women: Female Voices in English Canada*. Toronto: Simon & Pierre, 1994.

The Komagata Maru Incident
by Sharon Pollock

The Komagata Maru Incident was first produced at the Vancouver Playhouse, January, 1976, with the following cast:

T.S.	Allan Stratton
Hopkinson	Richard Fowler
Evy	Heather Brechin
Georg	Leroy Schulz
Sophie	Nicola Cavendish
Woman	Diana Belshaw

Directed by Larry Lillo.
Designed by Jack Simon.
Stage Managed by Paul Reynolds.

The Komagata Maru Incident was subsequently produced by Citadel Theatre, Edmonton, January, 1977, with the following cast:

T.S.	Ray Hunt
Hopkinson	Michael Ball
Evy	Peggy Mahon
Georg	Jean-Pierre Fournier
Sophie	Angela Gann
Woman	Patricia Lenyre

Directed by James DeFelice.
Designed by David Lovett.
Stage Managed by Marion Brant.

CHARACTERS

T.S.: The Master of Ceremonies, who plays many roles
William Hopkinson: Department of Immigration Inspector.
Evy: A prostitute involved with Hopkinson.
Sophie: A prostitute involved with Georg.
Georg: A German national.
Woman: A Sikh immigrant, British subject.

SCENE

Vancouver, 1914.

PRODUCTION NOTE

It is important that the scenes flow together without blackouts and without regard to time and setting. The brothel is the major playing area. Surrounding it is an arc or runway used by T.S. and HOPKINSON for most of their scenes. Although T.S. cannot intrude upon the WOMAN's space, he is free to move anywhere else on the set to observe or speak. As the play progresses, T.S.'s scenes move from the arc into the brothel area.

The characters never leave the stage. The WOMAN is on a level above and behind the area used by the other characters. An open grill-like frame in front of her gives both the impression of a cage, and of the superstructure of a ship. T.S. observes the audience entering. The other characters are frozen on stage; the grill-like frame, with the WOMAN behind it, is concealed by a sheet.

ACT ONE

The houselights fade out and a faint light comes up on T.S. who moves to a stool set in the centre of the arc. On this stool are his gloves, hat, and cane. He carefully puts on the gloves while surveying the audience.

T.S.: Good... goood. (*pausing for a moment*) Do you like the suit?

T.S. puts on his top hat, gives it a tap with the cane, looks toward the lighting booth, and snaps his fingers. A spot comes up on him.

Hurry! Hurry! Hurry! Right this way, ladies and gentlemen! First chance to view the *Komagata Maru*! At this very moment steaming towards picturesque Vancouver Harbour. Yes sireee! The *Komagata Maru*! A first-class—let the buyer beware—Japanese steamer, 329.2 feet in length, 2,926 gross tonnage! Captained by one Yomamoto, remember that name. And Japanese crew, carrying a cargo of coal! And 346 Sikhs, count 'em! Plus 30 East Indians, religious affiliation unknown! Add 'em all together and what do you get? That is correct, sir! Give the man a cigar! Three hundred and seventy-six is the answer! Three hundred and seventy-six Asians, to be precise, and all of them bound for Oh Canada, We stand on guard for thee!

T.S. salutes, holds it for a moment, then lets it drop as he moves into the brothel area.

T.S.: This is Vancouver, ladies and gentlemen, the 21st day of May, nineteen hundred and fourteen.... And may I direct your attention to my hat... I place the hat on the table... I pass my hands over the hat... and what do we have inside the hat? A pair of gloves! I give you Inspector William Hopkinson, Head of Intelligence, Department of Immigration!

T.S. slaps the gloves into HOPKINSON's hand, looks at him for a second, then continues.

Ladies and gentlemen, the hand is truly faster than the eye... you see this box... and now you don't... and here it is again (*passing it behind his back*) I open it, it's empty, I close the box (*looking at EVY, then placing it in her hands*) May I present (*stepping back*) Miss Evy: Entrepreneur!

T.S. bangs his cane, spot out. EVY and HOPKINSON are lit and animated.

EVY: What is it?

HOPKINSON: It's a present.

EVY: Don't tell me, silly.

HOPKINSON: You asked.

EVY: But I don't want you to tell me.

HOPKINSON removes his hand from her eyes.

EVY: Oh, Bill (*opening the box which contains a brooch*) It's beautiful. Here, pin it on me.

HOPKINSON bends over her to do so. T.S. bangs his cane, they freeze, spot on T.S.

T.S.: Ladies and gentlemen! Your attention, please! Now the pocket's empty. Not so now. (*taking out billfold and visa*) I have here one billfold and one German visa for one Georg Braun! (*throwing it on the floor by GEORG*) And here! Behind an ear, a chocolate! (*placing it in SOPHIE's hand*) Allow me to introduce, one Georg Braun and Sophie!

T.S. bangs his cane, spot out. SOPHIE goes to eat the chocolate, GEORG attempts to embrace her, and she pushes him off.

SOPHIE: Not so fast.

GEORG: Eh?

SOPHIE: No tickee, no washee.

GEORG: I...?

SOPHIE: (*putting her hand out*) Mon-ey.

GEORG: Oh. (*feeling for his billfold and finding it on the floor as T.S. knocks*)

SOPHIE: Somebody get the door! (*plucking billfold from GEORG's hand*) Thank you.

GEORG amorously tries to embrace SOPHIE again as she counts the money. T.S. knocks. SOPHIE pushes GEORG away.

SOPHIE: Wait a minute! Are you deaf? There's someone at the door.

SOPHIE moves SR with the billfold. After a moment of indecision, his billfold gone, GEORG moves after her.

GEORG: Ah – Sophie?

T.S.: (*laughing, spot on him*) Ladies and gentlemen. Lest we forget. The *Komagata Maru*. A Japanese steamer chock-full of brown-skin Hindus headed for a predominantly pale Vancouver, and entry into whitish Canada. The *Komagata Maru* in blue Canadian waters!

T.S. pulls cover to reveal WOMAN who bends over child on deck. T.S. bows. Spot is out.

WOMAN: Go to sleep. Go to sleep. Shut your eyes, go to sleep.

It's very hot and WOMAN turns from the child, wipes her forehead and looks out with a sigh, then turns back to the child.

WOMAN: Still not asleep?

HOPKINSON: (*pinning brooch on*) There. Everything's forgotten. All right?

EVY: All right.

HOPKINSON: But you have to thank me for the brooch.

EVY: Thank you, Billy.

HOPKINSON: Don't tease. You know I don't like Billy.

EVY: Thank you, Bill.

HOPKINSON: That's better.

EVY: Now you sit down, and I'll get you a drink.

HOPKINSON checks his watch.

EVY: Oh – not the time again? You just got here.

HOPKINSON: Can't be helped. I'm sorry.

EVY: You always have to go.

HOPKINSON: Don't be mad. I won't be long, it's just an appointment.

EVY: Bill?

Still holding the billfold, SOPHIE crosses round to SL with GEORG following.

SOPHIE: You may as well get used to it. That's what it's like around here. Half the time I'm running messages for him.

GEORG: For who?

SOPHIE: Mr. Hopkinson. Evy's friend with Immigration.

GEORG: Immigration?

SOPHIE: I'm sick of answering that damn door for him.

GEORG: Sophie, do you think–?

SOPHIE: (*at "door" SL*) There's a man out back for Mr. Hopkinson!

HOPKINSON: (*from inside "room"*) Who is it?

SOPHIE: He says tell Mr. Hopkinson that Bella Singh is here.

EVY: Your rat again.

HOPKINSON: (*preparing to leave*) Don't call him that.

EVY: I don't like rats coming round.

HOPKINSON: Let's not start this again.

EVY: He's always coming round and when he does, off you go, poof!

HOPKINSON: It'll only take a minute.

EVY: My mother always said, don't snitch, and don't play with snitchers. Didn't your mother ever tell you that?

HOPKINSON: Evy, we've settled all this.

SOPHIE: Mr. Hopkinson! Did you hear me!

HOPKINSON: Now don't pout, you'll get wrinkles.

EVY: Oh, get out.

HOPKINSON: I'm going. (*going to "door"*)

SOPHIE: Come on, Georg.

GEORG: Mr. Hopkinson?

HOPKINSON: Who's this, Sophie?

GEORG: Georg Braun, sir, if I could–

WOMAN: See the birds? Land must be near.... Mountains, trees, then the island, through the pass. Your uncle will meet us.... Look! Soon we will enter the harbour. See where your uncle lives? That is where we'll live.

GEORG: Thank you, sir.

SOPHIE: Georg!

GEORG goes to SOPHIE. HOPKINSON turns back into the room.

HOPKINSON: Evy? That fellow with Sophie.

EVY: Georg Braun?

HOPKINSON: I've, ah, asked him in for a drink when I get back.

EVY: Oh?

HOPKINSON: I want to meet him.

EVY: You've already met him.

HOPKINSON: Talk to him, then.

EVY: I thought brown rats were your specialty.

HOPKINSON: Bella Singh's a loyal British subject.

EVY: Well, Georg Braun's no British subject! You're setting up no rats in my house!

HOPKINSON: I'll do just as I please in your house! It's me that keeps you open, and don't you forget it! A nod from me, and you'd be buried under warrants. Oh Evy, Evy, Evy... what's good for me is good for you, eh...? Eh Evy? All I want to do is meet him, get to know him better...

EVY makes a murmur of protest.

I get ahead, Evy, do you know how I do that? I look ahead, I'm always thinking. Now, you read the papers, you stop and think.... With Kaiser Wilhelm and all, something in here tells me a German can do me some good. Eh? Perhaps not today or tomorrow, maybe next year, who knows. Now you can understand that, can't you?

EVY: I just don't like–

SOPHIE: Bella Singh's at the end of the yard! He wants to see you!

HOPKINSON: The German's coming in for a drink, Evy. *(exiting)*

EVY: If – if you say so.

T.S.: Hopkinson!

HOPKINSON joins T.S., DSR arc.

HOPKINSON: Yes sir.

T.S.: The *Komagata Maru*'s in port with three hundred and seventy-six potential immigrants.

HOPKINSON: Yes sir.

T.S.: So? What do you know about them?

HOPKINSON: I've spoken to my man, Bella Singh, sir. He tells me they're Sikhs from India, British subjects, and as such they do have right of entry to Canada, sir.

T.S.: The word is no entry.

HOPKINSON: I realize that, but we may have a problem.

T.S.: A what?

HOPKINSON: Many are veterans of the British Army, sir; they're sure to plead consideration for military service.

T.S.: You can put it this way – we don't mind them dying for us, we just don't want them living with us. *(laughing)* Get the point?

HOPKINSON: *(laughing)* Yes sir... but if they should go to the courts–

T.S.: They won't go to the courts. He hasn't done his homework. Have you forgotten our two orders-in-council? If an immigrant wishes to enter the country through a western port, he must make a continuous voyage from his own country to here. Have they done so?

HOPKINSON: No sir, they haven't.

T.S.: And that's no surprise. There's not a steamship line in existence with a direct India-to-Canada route and for our second ace-in-the-hole – a tax, two hundred dollars per head, to be paid before entry. Do they have it?

HOPKINSON: Bella Singh says they do not, however–

T.S.: Again, not surprising. In the land of his birth, the average Indian's wage is nine dollars per year. There – you see how we operate, Hopkinson? Never a mention of race, colour, or creed – and yet, we allow British subjects; they are British subjects; we don't allow them to enter.

HOPKINSON: Thank you, sir. However, I must inform you that Hermann Singh says–

T.S.: Sh, sh.

HOPKINSON: (*lowering his voice*) Hermann Singh says that the local Sikhs have raised the money for the head tax.

T.S.: That's not so good.

HOPKINSON: It's possible that a launch–

T.S.: It is possible? Do you pay for information like that?

HOPKINSON: Bella Singh says a launch will deliver the head tax to those on the ship late tonight.

T.S.: The word is no entry, Hopkinson.

HOPKINSON: Yes sir.

SOPHIE rushes into the room followed by GEORG.

SOPHIE: Listen everybody! Here it is! (*reading from paper*) "Immigration Officials Intercept Head Tax in Vancouver Harbour."

EVY enters SR. HOPKINSON enters from arc.

WOMAN: Look! A launch is coming! Maybe it's your uncle.

SOPHIE: There's your name right there! Inspector William Hopkinson.

WOMAN: Be careful! You'll fall!

SOPHIE: Look, Georg! Look, Evy!

WOMAN: The Immigration boat is stopping the launch.

SOPHIE: There it is again, "Hopkinson declares–"

WOMAN: Shhhhhh. Don't be afraid.

SOPHIE: You read it, Evy, what's it say?

HOPKINSON: I can tell you what it means. British Columbia wants no Calcutta coolies. We've Chinamen and Japs running our shops, Greeks running our hotels, Jews running our second-hand stores, and we don't want Hindus running our mills.

EVY: For God's sake, Bill, have a drink.

T.S.: Have a drink.

HOPKINSON: (*offering bottle*) Georg?

GEORG: Please. The Sikhs on the ship would pay the head tax with the money from the launch, eh? And what is legal? Can you intercept it like that?

HOPKINSON: Well, we did. Another bottle, Evy. The Calcutta coolie, Georg, belongs in India.

GEORG: Do you know India, sir?

HOPKINSON: Do I know India? He wants to know if I know India, Evy.

EVY: Does he know India!

EVY gives him a bottle, sits at the table and begins to play cards.

HOPKINSON: I know India, and I know its people. When I was a child, my father was stationed in the Punjab. He had only to shout "Quai Hai" to summon a slave—a servant—no, goddamn it, a slave, to summon a slave, to scrawl his initials on a chit, and there was a felt carpet from Kashmir, brass ornaments from Moradabad, silver for pocket money, cigars, a horse, a dog, anything he wanted. Show him your brooch, Evy. It belonged to my father. Wonderful craftsmen, the natives.

GEORG: It's lovely.

HOPKINSON: Did you know "loot" was an Indian word?

GEORG: Is it?

SOPHIE: (*examining the brooch*) Really beautiful.

HOPKINSON: My father was a big man, blond curly hair, wonderful moustache he had, looked like a prince in his uniform. A prince – surrounded by little beige people. (*laughing*)

SOPHIE: What about your mother?

HOPKINSON: "Quai Hai!" That's all, and they'd scuttle like bugs.

SOPHIE: Did your mother like it there?

HOPKINSON: She never said. You've no idea, Georg, of the size, the immensity, and the millions. (*smiling*) When I was a boy I used to like to read at night, alone, in a room that had dimensions.

GEORG: Sophie tells me you yourself served in the Punjab.

HOPKINSON: Oh, yes. Lahore Police Force. Six years service.

GEORG: And how do you end up in Canada, sir?

HOPKINSON: Promotion was blocked in Lahore.

GEORG: That's hard to believe for a man like yourself.

HOPKINSON: Quite simple, Georg. Cliques. And I learned something from that. So. I answered an ad and here I am.

GEORG: Your life has been very exciting–

SOPHIE: Sophie can make your life exciting too, yes, she can. Let Sophie sit on Georg!

SOPHIE lifts her skirts and plunks herself on him. They both fall over on the floor as T.S. bangs his cane. They freeze.

T.S.: Ladies and gentlemen! The turbaned tide is flowing! May 23rd, 1914. The first wave of an Asian Invasion sits at anchor in Vancouver Harbour!

WOMAN: They won't let us land! I've told you. We've asked a judge to rule on the orders-in-council. Now go...! Our food and our water are rationed. How long must we wait?

T.S.: Today's lesson is taken from the Department of Immigration's handbook, Regulation 23, Paragraph 4. I am talking about Checks and Balances of Power. Now, I am the Department of Immigration, I have the power to hold proceedings, make decisions, give orders. I can detain and deport any person or potential immigrant on any grounds whatsoever, unless that person is a Canadian citizen. You are the courts. You have the power to review, reverse, and restrain, quash, and otherwise interfere with my power to hold, to make, and to give, to detain and deport. And you do. Fairly often. It's annoying. So what do I do? Quite simple. I pass Catch 22, Regulation 23, Paragraph 4, which states: "No judge and no court and no officer thereof shall have any jurisdiction to review, reverse, and restrain, quash or otherwise interfere with my holding and making and giving, detaining, deporting."

We are gathered here in the sight of God, and in the spirit of the British Empire to rule on the *Komagata Maru*'s contention that Catch 22 Regulation 23, Paragraph 4 is invalid. They maintain that the Department of Immigration has not the authority to deny immigrants access to the courts. If we give them access, then a judge or a court or an officer thereof could overthrow our orders-in-council of which we have two denying them entry – And that, my good friends, would open the floodgates!

T.S. bangs his cane. GEORG picks himself up in embarrassment, pushing SOPHIE aside.

GEORG: My... my feelings are this, sir. If you examine the world and its history, you will see that the laws of evolution that have shaped the energy, enterprise, and efficiency of the race northwards have left less richly endowed the peoples inhabiting the southern regions.

HOPKINSON: Go on.

GEORG: Yes. This... this process is no passing accident, but part of the cosmic order of things which we have no power to alter. The European races must administrate; all that's needed to assure their success is a clearly defined conception of moral necessity. Do you agree, sir?

HOPKINSON: Agreed. It's a pleasure to talk to you, Georg. I feel as if you're a friend, a good friend.

GEORG: I'm honoured.

HOPKINSON: I have very few friends. A man in my position, Head of Intelligence, has very few friends.

GEORG: Please consider me one of them.

HOPKINSON: I'm thought of most often as a dose of salts; not palatable, but essential for the health of the body. I accept this.

GEORG: You are–

HOPKINSON: But! If I may make a small observation? It's truly amazing the number of people who use laxatives regularly, and lie about it. Eh? (*laughing*) You follow me, eh?

HOPKINSON laughs and GEORG joins in.

HOPKINSON: Yes, I have my job, and I do it. And damn well, if I say so myself.

GEORG: You've a good network of men.

HOPKINSON: Uh uh, more than that. It's a sense of responsibility, that's what it is. I take the risks, and I find my reward in the fulfillment of my task. Now there's your difference between white and coloured – the Gift of Responsibility.

EVY: (*looking up from her cards*) What's the difference?

HOPKINSON: You see that's why we're sitting in here, and the *Komagata Maru*'s out there scratching at the door.

EVY: Why?

HOPKINSON: For Christ's sake, Evy, if it weren't for the British, they couldn't construct a canoe, much less charter a steamer.

EVY: (*back to her cards*) You should know, I suppose. You lived with them.

HOPKINSON: I did not live with them!

EVY: Well, you were there God knows I've heard it often enough. It's hard to keep straight where you were when and with who.

HOPKINSON: I was brought up in India! I know them, if that's what you mean. Keep your mouth shut when we're talking! (*picking up bottle and starting off*) Come on, Georg, I've a chess set, hand-carved from ivory. (*moving off with GEORG following*) Marvellous chess player, my father.

WOMAN: I saw what you did! Do you think because I have no man you can steal food from my child? If you steal again, I will come when you sleep and I'll kill you!

T.S.: (*DSR, arc*) Ah, Hopkinson.

HOPKINSON: I have observed suffering and deprivation on the *Komagata Maru*.

WOMAN: The child cries! He is thirsty!

T.S.: What else?

HOPKINSON: Our policy of disallowing the supplying of the ship is sound. It weakens their morale. It's only a matter of time till they question their leadership...

T.S.: Continue.

HOPKINSON: As... conditions deteriorate, we could, at some future date, offer supplies as an incentive to leave.

T.S.: Very good. Very good.

HOPKINSON: There is... a woman and child on the ship.

T.S.: Irrelevant.

WOMAN: It's hard to explain to a child.... Your father was a soldier, he died fighting for the king, so we come to live with your uncle. But first – we must wait...

SOPHIE: My feet hurt.

EVY: Mmn?

SOPHIE: I don't know why. I'd have thought it'd be my back.

EVY looks at SOPHIE and laughs.

What? (*laughing*) Noo. Back trouble runs in the family.

EVY: Oh.

SOPHIE: In the women, that is. With the men it's always having to, you know, piss when they're older.

EVY laughs.

Yeah, I guess if I had my druthers, I'd rather have a bad back.... In the night when the pot was full, Grampa would piss out the window.... Unless the wind blew from the east. Then he pissed out the door.

EVY: Why?

SOPHIE: It blew back at the window. The window faced east.

EVY: Oh Sophie.

They both laugh.

SOPHIE: It's true... I used to lie on my back in the field and Mama would scream "Sophie, Sophie!" and I'd lie there and think, "Sophie, get out of here, better yourself!" ...And Mama would scream "Sophie! I know you're hidin'" ...and I'd just lie there.... Mama always said I was lazy. Maybe I am, but you don't see me emptying piss pots. I got out of there.

EVY: Don't stop here, Sophie.

SOPHIE: My back's not breaking from too many kids and carrying milk cans. (*looking at her foot*)

EVY: (*as she exits*) Find a nice man, and move on.

SOPHIE: Maybe I sprained it.

WOMAN bends over, retching, dry spasms. When she's finished she draws in several deep breaths. She attempts a smile for the child.

WOMAN: Don't worry... smile, it's only the water. Don't worry. You are a very brave boy. Your uncle will like you. Come, we'll sit on the side where there's shade.

T.S.: I don't understand.

HOPKINSON: I've promised them food and water.

T.S.: Really?

HOPKINSON: I've given my word.

T.S.: And what did you hope to gain from that?

HOPKINSON: Sir–

T.S.: Surely not plaudits from me.

HOPKINSON: Sir, when I boarded the ship for inspection, they seized me and were ready to take off in our launch and head for shore, patrol boats or not. They were desperate. They say they'd rather be shot than die of hunger and thirst. I felt it only – humanitarian to grant one week's provision.

T.S.: You've enabled them to hang on. That's what you've done!

HOPKINSON: I saw the mother and child–

T.S.: Now where's that incentive to leave?

HOPKINSON: Their case is still pending.

T.S.: Never initiate action when you haven't the guts to carry it through. It's a sign of weakness, Hopkinson.

HOPKINSON: Yes sir.

T.S.: You disappoint us.

HOPKINSON: Yes sir.

T.S.: We brought you up. We can put you down.

HOPKINSON: Yes sir.

T.S.: We trust that our meaning's sufficiently clear?

HOPKINSON: Yes sir.

EVY enters the room SL.

EVY: Bill!

SOPHIE: Evy!

EVY: Bill!

SOPHIE: Mr. Hopkinson!

HOPKINSON enters SR.

HOPKINSON: What's the matter?

EVY: Oh, Bill.

SOPHIE: I thought you went shopping.

EVY: I just – sat on the tram. A round trip. I never got off it.

HOPKINSON: Come on, Evy.

SOPHIE: Are you sick?

EVY: I... was on the tram. I had a seat by the window. When we...

HOPKINSON: Come on now.

EVY: When we came round by the creek there was a queue for employment, a long line of men looking for work. They were standing in line, we'd stopped for a fare, and then... the line... all of a sudden it... there was a man in a turban at the end of the line, his eye had caught my eye as I looked out the window – he looked so – solid – and I smiled... and he smiled... and as he smiled a man stepped in front of him, and he was back at the end.... Then, I don't know, it happened so quickly, he touched the man on the shoulder, the man turned... and the long line of men, it seemed to turn. The man in the turban started to speak, he got out a few words, I didn't sense anger – and then it exploded. They knocked him down, the man in the turban, they were kicking, and then pushing and shoving to get in a blow – and the tram pulled away... it was gone. As if I'd imagined it. It had never been.

HOPKINSON: You were frightened, that's all.

EVY: I should have done something.

HOPKINSON: You should have come home and you did. Come on now, you saw a fight. You've seen fights before.

EVY: No, it wasn't a fight! And I just sat on the goddamn tram and came home.

HOPKINSON: (*to SOPHIE*) Get her a drink.

EVY goes to look out the window, at the audience, where the Komagata Maru *sits.*

EVY: There are... people at the end of Burrard Street, staring out at that ship.... They look like the men in that line.

HOPKINSON: That's why we're sending the *Komagata Maru* back, so things like your fight won't happen. We don't want them here.

SOPHIE exits after giving him a drink.

EVY: But why does it happen?

HOPKINSON: All I know, Evy, is my father didn't die in the service for the world to be overrun by a second-rate people.

EVY: You don't make sense. Who's second-rate when you run out of brown people?

HOPKINSON: Drink your drink.

EVY: I don't want a drink! (*speaking while exiting SR*) You belong on Burrard.

HOPKINSON follows her.

HOPKINSON: Evy!

T.S: Mr. Speaker; Prime Minister; Honourable Members. Today I am opening my heart to you. I am telling you my fears – fears that affect each and every Canadian today... I fear for my country, and I fear for my people... I am not ashamed, nor should you be, to state that this is white man's country! And I can tell you that our British legacy, our traditions, those things that we hold dear, that we have fought and died for, is placed in jeopardy today by a massive influx of coloured foreigners! The class of East Indian that has invaded British Columbia is commonly known as Sikh. Having been accustomed to the conditions of a tropical clime, he is totally unsuited to this country. He is criminally inclined, unsanitary by habit, and roguish by instinct. The less we speak of his religion, the better. Suffice it to say that unless his ridiculous forms of worship are relinquished, he is an affront to a Christian community. His intelligence is roughly that of our Aborigines. He indeed belongs to a heathen and debased class. Honourable Members, stand up and be counted! Admit the honest fears of your constituents! Will the Sikh work for cheaper wages. and thus take away their jobs? Will he bring out his women, children, relatives and friends. Will Canadians step on a tram next week to ride from home to work and never hear a word of English spoken? And once at work, if they still have a job, who will they eat their lunch with? Men, honest and true like ourselves, whose fathers made this country what it is today – or will they be surrounded by coloured men with foreign food? Canadians have rights! Our fathers died for them! Let any man who is not willing to do the same step down! I've told you here today what's in my heart. For God's sake, show me what's in yours!

HOPKINSON enters SL.

HOPKINSON: Evy!

EVY enters SR.

EVY: I'm here.

HOPKINSON: Was Bella Singh around?

EVY: Don't ask me.

HOPKINSON: Where's Sophie? Sophie!

SOPHIE enters SR.

SOPHIE: What?

HOPKINSON: Was Bella Singh around?

SOPHIE: When?

HOPKINSON: Day before yesterday, goddamn it, was he here?

SOPHIE: Maybe. I don't remember.

HOPKINSON: What the hell do you mean, you don't remember?

EVY: Look, Bill, my girls don't keep track of your rats.

HOPKINSON: If they don't, they better start. Customs picked up three men at the border today. Sikhs smuggling guns for the *Komagata Maru*. And my head's on the block! That's the kind of information I'm paid to deliver! And I knew nothing. Do you hear that? Sweet bugger all! Was Bella Singh around or not?

EVY: You can leave now, Sophie.

HOPKINSON: She'll leave when I tell her. Did you forget a message, Sophie?

EVY: You run your business, I'll run mine; Sophie, get out!

HOPKINSON: (*grabbing SOPHIE*) By Jesus, I want an answer!

EVY: Me! It was me! Bella Singh came round, he left a note, I threw it out!

HOPKINSON releases SOPHIE. She leaves.

HOPKINSON: Why did you do that?

EVY: I don't pass notes.

HOPKINSON: It's me they come down on. Don't you realize that? If I don't deliver, I'm the one that pays – not Bella Singh. Why did you do it?

EVY: I'm sorry.

HOPKINSON: No you're not.

EVY: No, I'm not.

HOPKINSON: You wanted to make me look bad, is that it?

EVY: No.

HOPKINSON: I look bad enough then they'll dump me. Is that what you want?

EVY: No.

HOPKINSON: And off we go! Something else, somewhere else, eh?

EVY: What's wrong with that? People do it!

HOPKINSON: Not me.

EVY: Don't you like honest work?

HOPKINSON: That's a funny remark from a whore!

EVY: You want to know why I threw out your note? I'll tell you why! I'm a whore and what you do is offensive to me! What you do would gag me! I'm a whore and when I look at your job, I could vomit!

HOPKINSON slaps her.

WOMAN: Don't look at the crowd on the shore...! Don't listen, pretend they aren't there... the sky is a blue, a beautiful blue... look at it! Don't look at them on the shore, they are ugly!

WOMAN turns her back and begins to sing to the child.

HOPKINSON: I never think of the woman and child. They never enter my mind... Mewa Singh is a mill worker and priest caught crossing the border with guns. Mewa Singh is a trusted man in the Sikh community. Mewa Singh is a man I could use... I speak to him in his jail cell. I begin with loyalty, move on to money, end up with threats. Mewa Singh says nothing. He looks me straight in the eye. I don't always like that. With some it's an act of defiance.... In Mewa Singh's eyes there is an infinite sadness, and surrounding him is a pool of silence, and as I speak and the words fall on my ears as if from a distance... I think of an incident when I was a child... there was trouble at the bazaar... the soldiers had to come in on their horses... and the next day I walked through... I saw blood, like clots of dark jelly still on the streets... but no people... an empty bazaar. Do you have any conception of how strange that is? I remember standing very still, scrawny and pasty, very still, afraid to move... in the middle of silence, listening, like a mouse on a pan, listening, for the beat of the wings of the owl... very still.... And then as I stood there, I saw a figure approaching from one of the streets. Some native person. He stopped in the shadow of the huts... he extended his arms towards me... and I... turned around... and ran home. I was frightened... Mewa Singh... when I finish my mixed bag of offers Mewa Singh turns his head towards the window. It's narrow and barred. He has dismissed me. His answer is no. Goddamn it! I need a man who they trust! I'm the one who has something to lose!

T.S.: Relax! Don't worry! Congratulations are in order.... The courts have come through! Catch 22, Regulation 23, Paragraph 4 still stands!

Carnival music, the air of a party. SOPHIE, GEORG, and EVY join HOPKINSON on stage.

T.S.: Hurry! Hurry! Hurry! Final Immigration ruling on the *Komagata Maru*! Right this way, folks! Right this way! July 16th, 1914! Last and final chance to view the *Komagata Maru*! Anchored in picturesque Vancouver Harbour these last six weeks and two days! Yes sireeee! A decision is made! Of three hundred and seventy-six Asians, twenty individuals have proven to Immigration Officials the legality of their Canadian domicile; ninety suffering from disease are ordered deported and the rest can just shove off! The Immigration Department reigns supreme! To hell with the judges, the courts and the officers thereof! Last chance to view! The *Komagata Maru*! Take it away, Bill!

Everyone's been drinking and it shows.

HOPKINSON: Fare thee well, *Komagata Maru*! Have a pleasant journey!

GEORG: Fare thee well!

HOPKINSON: *Bon voyage*! You had your day in court–

SOPHIE: Goodbye you Hindus!

HOPKINSON: Now you and yours can eat crow from here to Calcutta! Crow with seagull, crow with seaweed, or crow with seawater!

SOPHIE: (*laughing*) Crow!

HOPKINSON: Fare thee well! Fare thee well!

They're all roaring with laughter, except EVY.

HOPKINSON: Fare thee well *Komagata Maru*!

EVY: Is it moving yet?

HOPKINSON: Not yet, but any minute.

SOPHIE: That's funny.

HOPKINSON: Have a drink, Evy.

SOPHIE: That's very funny. Why would they want to eat crow with seawater?

GEORG: Who knows what Hindus eat?

GEORG and SOPHIE are laughing still.

SOPHIE: Still, crow and seawater? It would make you sick. It would make me sick.

GEORG: You aren't a Hindu.

SOPHIE: It'd make anybody sick!

GEORG: Silly, silly, Sophie.

HOPKINSON: See, Evy? It's all over.

SOPHIE: You wouldn't eat that unless you had nothing else to eat, that's for sure.

GEORG: Silly, silly.

SOPHIE: Hey, crow and seaweed sounds awful too.

HOPKINSON: Forget it, Sophie.

SOPHIE: Eh?

HOPKINSON: It's just an expression.

SOPHIE: So what's it mean?

HOPKINSON: Come on, Evy.

SOPHIE: (*louder*) Eh?

HOPKINSON: To submit humbly!

EVY: Surely that rings a bell, I mean, it does for me.

SOPHIE: What?

HOPKINSON: Don't be like that. Say you're sorry. I'm sorry.

SOPHIE: Come on, Georg.

GEORG embraces SOPHIE.

SOPHIE: Where's the music – you gotta have music for a party!

HOPKINSON: Sophie's right.

GEORG: What we'll have is a polka!

GEORG and SOPHIE wind up the gramophone.

HOPKINSON: It's a party! Come on, Evy, let's dance.

SOPHIE: I love to polka! It's hard on the feet, but I love it!

They dance to the music.

T.S.: Hopkinson!

HOPKINSON stops dancing.

There's someone at the end of the yard. Bella Singh's at the end of the yard!

HOPKINSON exits. EVY follows him for a step or two, then stops. SOPHIE and GEORG dance, carry the bottle and laugh.

WOMAN: We hear them rejoice on the shore.... They say we are beasts; physical death is no evil for us, it may be a blessing, else why pestilence and famine? They say we are the enemies of Christ, the Prince of Peace; they will hate us with a perfect hatred; they will blast us with grape shot and rockets; they will beat us as small as dust before the wind!

The music stops. SOPHIE and GEORG collapse.

They say our appeal to the courts is dismissed. They say tonight the *Komagata Maru* will sail for India.

T.S.: *(winking)* Guess again!

HOPKINSON: The bastards!

WOMAN: On the ship a meeting is held. I vote in the place of my son who is five. It is right that we're here!

HOPKINSON: *(gazing out at the ship)* Sit tight in the harbour, will they?

EVY: Drink up, everyone.

HOPKINSON: The foolish bastards. They must think it's a cricket game with the officers. Fair play. Your wicket. Pass the crumpets.

GEORG: So what can they do?

HOPKINSON: Bugger all. A move can't be made nor a word whispered, on the street, in the temple, on the waterfront, without my knowing it.

EVY: He has his men! His men produce! Eh, Bill?

HOPKINSON: If they don't, they'll find themselves in steerage on the next ship out!

EVY: *(drunk)* You know something?

HOPKINSON: I'll seal the *Komagata Maru* off tighter than paint on a wall.

EVY: You sound worried.

HOPKINSON: I'll see it wrapped round with rot and rust and manned by skeletons before one bastard disembarks!

EVY: Come on, everyone! It's a party!

HOPKINSON: That's right! Glasses up, glasses up! Here's to the *Komagata Maru* – stuck in picturesque Vancouver Harbour! It gives me great pleasure to extend to you the hospitality of the Canadian people! Enjoy your anchorage! Sip our rain and eat our air! And when you've had your fill – India lies westward!

T.S.: Ladies and gentlemen! It walks! It talks! It reproduces! It provides cheap labour for your factories, and a market for your goods! All this, plus a handy scapegoat! Who's responsible for unemployment! The coloured immigrant! Who brings about a drop in take-home pay? The coloured immigrant! Who is it creates slum housing, racial tension, high interest rates, and violence in our streets? The coloured immigrant! Can we afford to be without it? I say "No!" It makes good sense to keep a few around – when the dogs begin to bay, throw them a coloured immigrant! It may sound simple, but it works. Remember though – the operative word's "a few" – For reference, see the Red, the White, the Blue and Green Paper on Immigration, whatever year you fancy!

EVY: (*still drinking*) This place is a pigsty.

SOPHIE: That's old news, Evy.

EVY: This place is a pigsty.

SOPHIE: At least it's a profitable pigsty – isn't it?

EVY: Money isn't everything. (*laughing as no one else reacts*) ...eh?

SOPHIE: Don't be silly.

EVY: Did you know that if a pig falls in a trough, the other pigs would eat him. (*playing cards*) Gobble, gobble gobble... I think pigs are all right... I've known some not bad pigs... it's the goddamn pigstys that turn them nasty...

GEORG: (*sitting reading a German paper*) I would not want to be Kaiser Wilhelm today...

EVY: Why? Isn't he feeling well. (*laughing as no one else reacts*) Oh well... that's too bad... maybe tomorrow...?

SOPHIE: It's so hot. At home you always get a breeze off the water.

EVY: In Manitoba you don't.

GEORG: (*turning page*) If war should break out... well...

EVY: (*brightly*) People will die, eh?

EVY looks at HOPKINSON who stands staring out at the ship.

EVY: Bill...? Bill, a watched pot never boils.

T.S.: (*speaking very quietly, his stance mirroring HOPKINSON's*) What we need is a reason to board her. To mount a police action, preliminary, whatever. To arrest those aboard.

EVY: Leave the window alone, Bill.

T.S.: We could board them, arrest them, escort them to the open sea, and once there, release them, pointed towards India.

EVY: Come talk to me.

T.S.: Now if the captain and crew charged the Sikhs with mutiny, we'd be away, eh?

EVY: Bill?

T.S.: The captain refuses to press charges? Really? You know, I can't help but feel you don't give full vent to your powers of persuasion. One begins to wonder whose side you're on. Someone should check out your file. A good man would find a reason to board her.

HOPKINSON: Yes...

SOPHIE: It's the heat. It's so hot.

SOPHIE gets up and exits.

HOPKINSON: It's July.... It's supposed to be hot...

T.S. howls in a boy scout position, on his haunches, two fingers of each hand at his temples.

T.S.: Akela says "Be Prepared." (*howling*) Akela says "Do your Duty for God and the King, and Obey the Law of the Pack." (*howling, then stops abruptly and rises*) Akela says I have three merit badges for the boy who comes up with a first-rate reason to board the *Komagata Maru*!

HOPKINSON is writing a letter.

EVY: What're you writing?

HOPKINSON: Nothing.

EVY: Are you writing in German, what is it?

HOPKINSON: It's nothing... now... clear off, I'm busy.

EVY wanders off SL.

WOMAN: This is not where we live... we shall not see your uncle... but we can't cross an ocean without water or food.... You must not be afraid. For hundreds of years the Khyber Pass has run with our blood, we're not afraid to spill more of it here! Do you hear me ashore! We have suffered, but we have endured! We are tempered like steel! We are ready!

HOPKINSON: Georg?

GEORG: Mnn? (*from behind his paper*)

HOPKINSON: I was wondering.

GEORG: Yes?

HOPKINSON: I have a small problem... perhaps you could advise me...

GEORG: Certainly. What is your problem?

HOPKINSON: It's the *Komagata Maru*.

GEORG: (*laughing*) You call this a small problem?

HOPKINSON: (*doesn't like the laugh*) Compared to, say, Kaiser Wilhelm, of course. Compared to that of an enemy alien in this country if war should break out, yes, I think a small problem, don't you?

GEORG gets the point.

T.S.: It's not what you call subtle, but it works.

HOPKINSON: I wish to make the *Komagata Maru* an offer – to give them supplies, to make some vague promise of promises, to recompense them for their cargo of coal, to entice them to sail. I wish the whole transaction kept quiet.

GEORG: And what is your problem?

HOPKINSON: If my offer got out, it might look like some kind of acknowledgement of their rights, and in this affair, they have none.

GEORG goes to speak, but HOPKINSON continues.

As for Bella Singh and the rest, well, to be blunt, I don't trust them – trustworthy as they are, have been in the past, will be in the future, I do not totally trust them in this endeavour. A very slight qualm of mistrust.

GEORG: I see.

HOPKINSON: What do you advise, my good friend, Georg?

EVY enters unobserved. She's come in for a bottle but stops to listen.

GEORG: You're looking for someone to carry your offer out to the ship?

HOPKINSON: That's correct. (*drawing out envelope*) This particular offer – a man I can trust – a man for whom I possibly could do a small favour sometime in the future in return for this favour...

GEORG: And with some small financial reward, I suppose?

HOPKINSON: Correct. I will provide a boat, and one of our patrols will study the night sky as you slip through the – oh – excuse the use of the pronoun.

GEORG: Quite all right. Quite – all right – in fact, is there any reason why I myself, Georg, cannot act on your behalf in this matter?

HOPKINSON: Ah.

GEORG: Shall we drink to it? (*moving to do so*)

HOPKINSON: First the details–

They catch sight of EVY.

EVY: Hello.

GEORG: Hello, Evy.

HOPKINSON lowers his voice slightly as EVY hovers in background.

HOPKINSON: First the details, then the drink – Note, the envelope is sealed, and must remain so.

As he passes the envelope to GEORG, EVY takes it.

EVY: What's this?

GEORG: (*looking to HOPKINSON*) Ah?

EVY: A letter home?

GEORG: Yes. May I have it?

EVY: A letter to Germany – but it has no address.

HOPKINSON: Give him his letter.

EVY: A letter to Germany – what if – someone should open it. What's in it?

HOPKINSON: Evy–

EVY: Georg, where's your head? We're practically at war. The only thing worse than a letter to Germany is a letter from Germany. Governments are paranoid. Ask Bill.

GEORG: Eh?

HOPKINSON: She drinks too much.

EVY: I just had an idea! What if–

HOPKINSON: (*making a grab for her arm and missing*) Give it to me!

EVY: I'm not finished! What if a letter containing – who knows what – was carried by a German national out to the *Komagata Maru*–

HOPKINSON: Shut your mouth.

EVY: –and intercepted by the Department of Immigration – what if, eh?

GEORG: What if? (*shrugging*)

EVY: A plot between the Germans and the Sikhs!

GEORG: A plot between...?

GEORG laughs with a tinge of nervousness and a look to HOPKINSON.

GEORG: Give me the letter.

EVY: He wants a good solid reason to board the *Komagata Maru* and by Jesus I'm looking at it! (*holds up the letter*)

HOPKINSON: You're going to end up in a sailor's bar, Evy.

EVY: I won't let you do this!

HOPKINSON: Two-bits-a-crack in a dark alley.

EVY: Georg– (*giving it to him*) Open it.

GEORG: This is an offer to–

HOPKINSON: That's enough.

EVY: It's a trick. Open it!

HOPKINSON: Return it, or deliver it sealed.

GEORG: You don't understand–

HOPKINSON: No trust, no deal.

EVY: Don't you know who he works for?

GEORG: Evy, he works for the government.

EVY: Oh yes...! Oh yes... and I can tell you a story about governments... a bedtime story–

T.S. & EVY: Once upon a time–

The characters freeze as T.S. moves among them. T.S. continues the story.

T.S.: There was a little boy who came to Manitoba with his mummy and daddy and sisters and brothers and many others very much like him. Their skin was a pale ivory, their eyes a light blue, and their hair dark—without being too dark—and curly—but not too curly! They were running from persecution and injustice... and Canada said: "You wish to own farm land communally? No bother at all! You will not swear allegiance to the crown and the flag? Weeeelllll, what is it, after all, but headgear and a piece of cloth? You do not wish to fight wars? That too can be arranged; exceptions can be made." The daddies worked to earn money for seed and supplies, and the mummies harnessed themselves to the plough and pulled it, breaking the hard brown earth of Manitoba and the soft white flesh of their backs till the red blood ran down, and the little boy walked beside the plough picking bouquets of tiny blue flowers. By and by, the mummies and daddies had homes and barns and food for the winter and seed for the spring and horses for the plough. Then others came and saw what they had. And Canada said – "Now about this allegiance! And which of you owns this particular piece of land? Be precise and sign here! And my goodness, friends, isn't all this worth killing and maiming for? What kind of people are you?" The mummies and daddies and sisters and brothers set out on a pilgrimage. They walked to Yorktown and along the tracks towards Winnipeg.

T.S. bangs his cane. The others unfreeze, and GEORG turns to HOPKINSON.

GEORG: About this letter! *(extending it)*

EVY: Listen to me! I watched them walk past–

T.S. bangs his cane. They freeze.

T.S.: It was snowing. They had little to eat, and then nothing to eat, for the Mounties cut off their supplies – and it snowed. People dropped by the tracks and a special train came along and returned everyone to Northern Manitoba. And those who would not sign and swear allegiance were driven from their land with only what they could carry! *(banging his cane)*

HOPKINSON: *(snatching the letter)* I'll make other arrangements!

T.S. bangs the cane. They freeze.

T.S.: Then people whose skin was so fair as to be opalescent, whose eyes were so light they shone in the dark, whose hair sparkled like dust motes in the sun, with each strand hanging in a manner that can only be described as poker straight – these people stormed the land office for homesteads and barns and harvests still in the fields.

EVY: My brother stood in line for three days, he got a section – next to my father's.

T.S.: And they all lived happily ever after...! There now. Good night, sleep tight, don't let the bedbugs bite.... Shhhhhhhhhh! *(tiptoeing away)*

EVY: It can happen to any of us.

HOPKINSON: Go to bed.

EVY: Look at him. He'd cut off his hand before he'd make the *Komagata Maru* an offer. *(laughing)* He's got a thing about race, about colour, haven't you noticed?

HOPKINSON: You're boring and stupid, Evy.

EVY: Why do you suppose that is?

GEORG: I–

EVY: He goes to the temple.

GEORG: Eh?

EVY: Gets himself all dolled up, goes to the temple in disguise – he thinks he looks like a Sikh. I bet the Sikhs think he looks like an ass.

HOPKINSON: Good night, Georg.

GEORG: About–

HOPKINSON: Good night.

GEORG gives a little bow and leaves.

EVY: I've been thinking. Funny thing, your background–

HOPKINSON: That's enough.

EVY: Birthplace, things like that, where were you born, Bill?

HOPKINSON: Get the hell upstairs.

EVY: Where?

HOPKINSON: England.

EVY: Where in England, be specific.

HOPKINSON: Yorkshire!

EVY: Yorkshire? Yorkshire! Now that's a new one, Yorkshire, eh...? That's not what I think.

HOPKINSON: Evy!

EVY: Quick, Georg (*pretending GEORG is still there*) without looking, what colour's his eyes, wanna bet? I'd say brown.

Sometime during this scene, HOPKINSON begins to subtly stalk her. She as subtly avoids him.

HOPKINSON: You filthy bitch!

EVY: Blue, did you say? Well then I bet his mother's eyes were brown.

HOPKINSON: My mother's dead.

EVY: Born in Punjab, served by Yorkshire.

HOPKINSON: Born in Yorkshire!

EVY: So are they blue or brown?

HOPKINSON: Blue!

EVY: Your mother's eyes, now what were they?

HOPKINSON: My mother's eyes were blue, you bitch! I'll kill you.

EVY: First you'll have to catch me.

HOPKINSON chases her; she avoids him.

EVY: You're stupid, Bill, you're stupid... it's not me that's stupid, it's you. Stupid, stupid, Bill! They all use you, Bill, yes, they do.... You think that you use Georg, you think that you use Bella Singh, you think that you use me, but you're the one that's being used... they're using you and Billy Boy's too dumb to know and stupid dumbo Billy will keep on being used cause Billy Dumbo's stupid! Stupid dumbo Billy's stupid dumbo Billy.

HOPKINSON catches EVY; she speaks softly.

EVY: And Billy's mother's brown.

HOPKINSON slaps EVY; she speaks louder.

EVY: And Billy's mother's brown!

HOPKINSON slaps EVY; she speaks louder.

EVY: And Billy's mother's brown.

HOPKINSON throws EVY down, kneels and shakes her.

HOPKINSON: Don't say that. Don't say that! I'll kill you if you say that to me! (*slowing down his attack on her*) Evy, don't say that. Please don't say that... (*stopping*) I... I love you, Evy, don't say that to me...

EVY reaches out and draws his head to her.

EVY: Oh... oh... poor, poor, Billy.

T.S.: Hopkinson!

HOPKINSON *moves very slowly and speaks without expression. It's an effort for him to get up.*

T.S.: What're you waiting for... where's your report?

HOPKINSON: Sir.

T.S.: You've come up with what?

HOPKINSON: Sir.

T.S.: A reason to board her, remember?

HOPKINSON: Sir.

T.S.: Kindly observe (*clearing his throat*) Captain Yomamoto! Captain Yomamoto! Is there a Captain Yomamota in the house? Ah, my dear Captain, there you are. If you wouldn't mind taking a seat.

T.S. indicates a chair for the CAPTAIN who is exceedingly short.

How many times have we had this conversation? How many times must we have this conversation? Yes, yes, I know what you said before: "strictly speaking" your passengers have not mutinied, hence you are reluctant to lay a charge.... Truly a commendable stance – however. Let us forget "strictly speaking" for a moment. How about trying "laxly speaking," "loosely speaking," "informally speaking" – could you find it in your heart to lay a charge "loosely speaking" against the passengers of the *Komagata Maru*...? Nothing has changed, huh...? Not so quick, Captain, one more minute please.... While casually flipping through my classified copy of condensed Canadian law "What to Do in a Pinch" I found the most interesting – oh, I'm sure you'd be interested – you see it says right here, as I interpret this small item here.... Yes, right here in very small print – You can't see it? But my dear Captain, I assure you I can. It states: If given formal notice to sail, then sail you must, *toute suite*—it's a bilingual law—or be subject to a fine of $500.00. That's per person aboard. "With-the-Power-Vested-in-Me-by-His-Majesty's-Government-I-Hereby-Give-You-Formal-Notice-to-Sail!" Now, let me see, 500 times 356, that's put down the zero, carry the three – what was that you just said? You wish to press charges? Mutiny, sedition, treason, and – blackmail? Be serious, my dear fellow, the first is sufficient...
Mutiny!
M - that's Militia for instilling fear,
U - Union Jack which God knows we hold dear,
T - for a tugboat, one you can't sink,
I - for informant, a nice word for fink,
N - for our Navy of fine volunteers,
Y- for Yomamoto, who finally signed

Here!
Hopkinson! Here are your papers.
Now, my good man, do your duty.

GEORG helps HOPKINSON on with his jacket.

GEORG: I'm sorry about the letter. I pay no attention to her. She's a stupid woman.

HOPKINSON: Yomamoto has signed, pressed charges of mutiny. The militia is lining the dock, they are armed, they wait in reserve.... We will engage the *Komagata Maru* at sea!

GEORG: In the harbour, you mean.

HOPKINSON: In the harbour. (*addressing a crowd*) We will mount an attack from the *Sea Lion*, the largest ocean-going tug in the port! Police Chief MacLennan shall lead 120 policemen and 40 special Immigration Officers–

GEORG: May I volunteer my services, sir?

HOPKINSON: In a paramilitary attack on the ship?

GEORG: Will I come under fire, sir?

HOPKINSON: On board the *Komagata Maru* are veteran soldiers.

GEORG: Are they armed?

HOPKINSON: Reliable sources inform me that weapons abound on the ship. They have made clubs from floating driftwood, possibly spears from bamboo poles.

T.S.: He's forgotten the cargo of coal.

HOPKINSON: Force will be met with force. Rifles will be issued before we embark...

T.S.: (*prompting*) I expect every...

HOPKINSON: I expect every man to do his duty. No doubt we will meet with stubborn opposition, but remember, we are a formidable force!

T.S.: In an orderly manner.

WOMAN: They are coming.

T.S.: Board the *Sea Lion*.

WOMAN: (*softly*) Jai Khalsa...

GEORG: It was fair-sized for a tug, but not large enough for a company of men such as we were.

WOMAN: Stand back from the rail.

GEORG: Four reporters came along for the ride. "Hoppy," they cried, "How about a smile for the press!" Mr. Hopkinson smiled.

WOMAN: Get below.

GEORG: It looked like a very big ship and the closer we got–

WOMAN: They have guns.

GEORG: The more quiet we were... silence.... The *Sea Lion* rode low in the water.. .as we looked up we saw them... lining the rails were great turbanned figures.... We stared up at them... they stared down at us... then...

T.S.: (*low*) Throw out the grappling hooks.

WOMAN: (*screaming*) Jai Khalsa!!

GEORG: All hell broke loose!

WOMAN: Jai Khalsa!

GEORG: From three hundred odd throats came a yell!

WOMAN: Jai Khalsa!

GEORG: Followed by bricks from the boiler settings, scrap iron and coal!

WOMAN: Hide!

GEORG: Mostly coal!

WOMAN: Hide below!

GEORG: Coal rains around us!

WOMAN: Jai Khalsa!

GEORG: Hopkinson's hit again and again!

WOMAN: Jai Khalsa!

GEORG: They can see the gold braid on his hat!

HOPKINSON: I look for the woman and child.

GEORG: Get down! For God's sake get down!

WOMAN: Jai Khalsa!

HOPKINSON: I stand as straight as I can.

GEORG: Take off your hat and get down! (*raising his gun to fire*)

HOPKINSON: There's no order to fire! Don't fire!

WOMAN throws the missile of coal which knocks HOPKINSON down.

WOMAN: Jai Khalsa!

A pause with HOPKINSON lying on the floor. EVY enters slowly with SOPHIE. They help HOPKINSON to the sofa and press a cloth to his head.

GEORG: It was a total and humiliating defeat. What else can you expect? It was ridiculous. We go out with guns and then never use them. The whole thing was poorly conceived. However, compared to the execution of the scheme, the conception was an act of genius!

SOPHIE: What do you mean?

GEORG: It was a stupid thing to do.

EVY: Hold the cloth to your head, Bill. It's cold. It'll help.

HOPKINSON: I'm all right. I just want something to wash with.

SOPHIE: (*laughing*) I don't wonder. He looks like a chimney sweep, doesn't he, Georg?

GEORG: There you sit, a servant in His Majesty's government, battered and bruised by a bunch of Hindus.

HOPKINSON: Get me some water!

SOPHIE: If you yell you can get it yourself.

GEORG: Tell me the point of carrying guns if nobody uses them...? And there he stood with his hat. The smart thing to do was remove it. No, there he stood. Every time he was hit, they all cheered. The air rang with cheers!

SOPHIE: I just thought of something... (*laughing*) Mr. Hopkinson, I guess it was you that ate crow, eh?

SOPHIE nudges GEORG who chuckles after a slight effort to restrain himself.

SOPHIE: It was him that ate crow!

HOPKINSON: Get out! Get out and leave me alone!

SOPHIE and GEORG move to exit SL.

SOPHIE: It was him that ate crow.

They're still chuckling.

GEORG: Sophie.

They exit. WOMAN is at a meeting on the ship.

WOMAN: We have gained nothing but time! We've driven them off for only a while, what now we must press for is food! I say it is better we starve on their doorstep than out on the sea!

HOPKINSON: Do you remember when I gave you your brooch?

EVY: Yes.

HOPKINSON: Do you like it?

EVY: Yes, I do.

T.S.: Order! Order!

HOPKINSON begins to adjust his clothing.

EVY: Bill – this time don't go.

T.S.: Order!

EVY: Say to hell with it.

T.S.: Are you assembled?

EVY speaks as HOPKINSON joins T.S.

EVY: Don't go, Bill.

T.S.: The meeting will come to order.... Well now, that was a bit of a balls-up yesterday, wasn't it?...

HOPKINSON goes to speak, but T.S. continues.

However, we aren't here to assign blame, we can do that later. What's the next step, that's the question. Any suggestions, Hopkinson?

HOPKINSON shakes his head slowly.

I thought not. Well, luckily we have in our midst a man with courage and foresight. He has had refurbished, refitted, and manned a second-class cruiser at Esquimalt, the *Rainbow*, length 300 feet, 3,600 gross tonnage with two six-inch guns and six four-inch guns. A small hand please for Harry Stevens, our federal M.P.... I think we can do better than that.

HOPKINSON claps.

Ah, yes... Mr. Stevens has worked diligently since the arrival of the *Komagata Maru* in our waters. Diligence, perseverance, and patriotism always pay off. Let the *Rainbow* push through the Narrows; let her anchor near enough to the *Komagata Maru* for the sun to glint on her guns. Let our next message be – we won't necessarily fire on you – but we will fire on you if necessary! (*turning to leave*)

HOPKINSON Sir...! My informants in the Sikh community inform me–

T.S.: Informants inform you? (*laughing*) You're being redundant, my boy.

HOPKINSON: My people in the Sikh community tell me that threats have been made. Death threats.

T.S.: You've stirred up a hornet's nest, haven't you? You've opened up Pandora's Box. You've created a maelstrom.

HOPKINSON I was following orders.

T.S.: Let me tell you something – there's someone at the end of the yard...

HOPKINSON: Bella Singh?

T.S.: Not Bella Singh.... Someone who's not Bella Singh waits at the end of the yard...

EVY: Who is it out there?

HOPKINSON: One of my men, I imagine.

EVY: Why don't you go out?

HOPKINSON: Later, perhaps.... Let him wait.

WOMAN: (*laughing*) Do you know something? My son's lips have swollen and burst from the thirst – they are covered with grease from the engines. My legs are like sticks – if I smelled a real meal I would vomit – and you think a few guns will make our knees knock? (*stopping laughing*) Sale Haramazaade! Give us supplies and we'll leave!

HOPKINSON: See the cruiser... it has guns trained on the *Komagata Maru*.

EVY: Will they fire on it?

HOPKINSON: That – is not my concern.

EVY: Don't you feel anything for them?

HOPKINSON: You wouldn't understand.

EVY: Yes I would. I would try.

HOPKINSON: One has to make decisions. Commitments. To one side or another.

EVY: Which side are you on?

HOPKINSON: The winning side.

EVY: Are you winning?

HOPKINSON: This time the *Komagata Maru* will sail.

EVY: Do you think then you'll have won?

HOPKINSON: I'm... tired. Let's go to bed. (*starting off*)

EVY: Not right now.

HOPKINSON stops, turns to look at EVY.

HOPKINSON: Lie beside me. That's all.

EVY: I don't want to.

HOPKINSON: I don't have to ask! I can order!

EVY looks at him, then picks up her cards, begins to lay them out. After a moment, HOPKINSON leaves. Carnival music plays.

T.S.: Hurry! Hurry! Hurry! Absolutely the last and final chance to view the *Komagata Maru*! Anchored in picturesque Vancouver Harbour for two, count 'em, two glorious months! Note the cruiser standing by to the right, see the sun on its guns, what a fantastic sight! Ladies and gentlemen, can you truly afford to bypass this splendid spectacle? Run, my good friends, you mustn't walk, you must run! Cotton candy, taffy apples, popcorn and balloons! All this and a possible plus, the opportunity to view your very own navy in action with no threat to you!

Music stops.

SOPHIE: It's all so exciting... now tell me what are all the little boats doing?

GEORG: Some of them are harassing the Sikhs, some of them are supplying the ship – the government is giving them provisions.

SOPHIE: And what about the cargo of coal – if there's any left.

GEORG: I hear the government may recompense them. My friends tell me they have promised them everything and will give them nothing. That's called diplomacy, eh Bill?

SOPHIE: Oh look, everybody! Look! There's black smoke coming out of the smokestack... look the *Rainbow*'s moving... it's moving in... what's it going to do... I bet it's going to shoot, I hope it's going to shoot, it's.... Look, Evy! Come look! It's.... It's... it's moving—The *Komagata Maru*'s moving—and the *Rainbow*'s going right along side.... We won! We won! Didn't we, Georg? Didn't we, Mr. Hopkinson? Aren't you even going to look? It's over and we won!

A bang of the cane and they freeze.

T.S.: Over...? A note, Mr. Hopkinson, from the man at the end of the yard... "When the affairs were past any other remedy, I thought it righteous to draw my sword."

HOPKINSON looks at the note.

WOMAN: (*hard, not sentimental*) We go back. My husband is dead. He died in their war. His father is dead. He died when they cut back the famine relief. I am a British subject, and my people's taxes have gone to their King. I am not a possession, a thing. I am myself and I will fight for myself and my son and my people. I am strong.

GEORG: The whole thing has been most educational. I should thank you. I have made many valuable friends and good contacts. I owe it to you, Bill.... Can I get you a drink, Sophie, get him a drink.

HOPKINSON: (*stepping out to T.S.*) I have good men in the Indian community... good men... they produce... Bella Singh, Baboo Singh, Hermann Singh, Gunga Ram–

T.S.: Mewa Singh?

HOPKINSON: Not – Mewa Singh.

T.S.: For God's sake, get on.

HOPKINSON: Their lives are in danger... the community feels that they're traitors, surely they're loyal British subjects, like myself.

T.S.: Hurry up.

HOPKINSON: My own life has been threatened... I ask for–

T.S.: Extra! Extra! Read all about it! War Declared! Recession Recedes! Factories Hum the National Anthem! Send your sons overseas! See all of Europe at federal expense! Check your programme for casting – the enemy's the Kraut! The Sikh's on our side! Extra! Extra! Read all about it!

GEORG: (*picking up paper*) This can't help but work nicely for me.

HOPKINSON: What?

GEORG: I say the war shall increase my use to your department.

SOPHIE: Isn't he smart, Evy? Georg is going places – and so is Sophie.

EVY: (*looking up from her cards*) Christ, Sophie, it's a war.

GEORG: It's also a good business deal.

EVY spits on the floor.

GEORG: You should teach her some manners.

SOPHIE: You're jealous.

EVY: Oh Sophie.

SOPHIE: It's true – you're jealous of me – Georg's up and doing – he gets around – we have a good time. Look at him – he doesn't do anything since the *Komagata Maru*. And you're just as bad. This place is just like a morgue. Who wants to live in a morgue? I'll leave if I want to – I can, you know – I'll leave anytime I want.

HOPKINSON: No you won't.

SOPHIE: Yes I will. Won't I, Georg? Whenever Georg wants.

HOPKINSON: Georg wants what I give him! When I say move, you bloody well move, when I say jump, you say how high. In this stinking world there's two kinds, there's the ruler and the ruled – and when I see the likes of you, I know where I stand! (*beginning to weaken*) Some people talk, and some people listen, but by God, I act, and if... it weren't for people like me... people like you... would still be down in the slime... I have my... I have my...

T.S.: Bill?

HOPKINSON: I have...

T.S.: Mewa Singh waits at the end of the yard.

HOPKINSON: Yes.

EVY moves to him.

WOMAN: We dock at Budge Budge fourteen miles from Calcutta. We are to be herded aboard trains and returned to the Punjab although many of us have not been there for years. We resist. Police, reinforced by soldiers, open fire. Men who shared their rancid flour with my son are dead. (*threatening*) We will remember them.

T.S.: Order! Order! The court will come to order! Will the Inspector take the stand! Do you swear to tell the truth, the whole truth, and nothing but the truth, as it befits this case, so help you God?

HOPKINSON: I do.

T.S.: Might I ask if you were acquainted with one Hermann Singh?

HOPKINSON: I was.

T.S.: What was his character?

HOPKINSON: He was a quiet, unassuming man, intensely loyal to his King.

T.S.: What was the nature of your relationship?

HOPKINSON: He rendered assistance to the government in the *Komagata Maru* Incident.

T.S.: Five and one half weeks after the departure of the *Komagata Maru*, one Pirt Warnes was walking along a little used trail on the Kitsilano Indian Reserve. It was quite a pleasant trail... he noticed what at first glance appeared to be a bundle of rags behind a log close to the path. He examined it. It was the badly decomposed body of an East Indian. The turban was wrapped round the ankles. Beside the body lay a leather satchel, an empty brandy flask, and an open straight razor. When he touched the head it came off in his hand. It was Hermann Singh. Let me ask you, Inspector, from your intimate knowledge of the Asian mind, would you say the facts as related are consistent with... suicide?

HOPKINSON: No, I would not.

T.S.: Ah... and if indeed it were murder, can you suggest a possible motive?

HOPKINSON: By informing, Hermann Singh had incurred the hatred of his people.

T.S.: You may step down.

EVY: Why don't we go away...? Why can't we...? Bill...? Bill, talk to me...! I can leave. I can leave. And I will. (*exiting off stage*)

T.S.: Six weeks after the departure of the *Komagata Maru*, Arjun Singh shot through the back of the head from behind!

HOPKINSON: Arjun Singh is dead.

GEORG: (*on the sofa, feet up, reading the paper*) He'll have to get a new stable of fellows, eh?

SOPHIE: (*playing cards*) Where would he find them, eh?

GEORG: (*laughing*) Good point... where is he going to find them?

T.S.: September 5th, 1914... early evening... Bella Singh goes to the temple. Inside the temple, people are singing. They're singing hymns for Arjun Singh, Hermann Singh... Bella Singh takes off his shoes... Bella Singh enters the temple... Bella Singh moves to the back... Bella Singh sits in a corner... Bella Singh takes out a gun... he fires ten shots, scores nine out of ten, seven wounded, two dead. He never speaks till arrested.

GEORG: Do you know what he says, Sophie? He says that he acted in self-defence, he says Bill will verify that... will you testify, Bill?

HOPKINSON: Yes.

T.S.: October 21st, 1914.... My God, what a day! Look at that sky... and the leaves all russet and gold... the mountains like sentinels, just a light breeze, the city set like a precious gem on the Pacific... breathe in... breathe out... breathe in... breathe out...

HOPKINSON: I leave the house early. I walk to the court house.... It's fall... I feel like a toy man walking through a toy town. Everything's working. My arms and my legs move so well together, there is... a mechanical precision to everything... I notice the houses seem neater than usual, a certain precision... at the same time, it's slower, things are slower, but very precise... there are no clouds in the sky, and it's blue, a deep blue... there's a slight breeze... the veins in the leaves protrude as if swollen... toy mountains frame my toy town... I'm just a bit late because of the walk. I enter the court house from Howe Street. As I wait for the lift to take me up to the court, I place very carefully one hand on the wall, feeling the wall, and feeling my hand on the wall, in this tiny toy court... I open the door of the lift, I step inside, then I close it. I think of the peace of the coffin. I think of the safety of the cage. I open the door. I step out. I walk down the corridor. I see no one I know...

T.S.: Mewa Singh waits in the witness room.

HOPKINSON: I stop at the witness room.

T.S.: Mewa Singh steps out of the witness room. In each hand he carries a gun.

HOPKINSON: When I see him, I feel myself bursting. My toy town is destroyed in an instant. He is large, he encompasses my world, I feel myself racing towards eternity.... They say I grapple with him. I do not. I open my arms, I say: Now!
Dazzles the sparkle of his sword
Who is utterly dreadful and is contained not
By the elements. And when he performeth
His death-dance, how dolefully his bells toll and knell.
He, the four-armed one, of a lustrous hair bun,
He wieldeth the mace and the club,
And crushes the swollen head, even of death.
His auspicious tongue of blazing fire
Licketh all that is unholy.
When shrieks his horrid conch
The whole universe reverberates with its raucous notes
How tintinnabulating are thy ankle bells,
And when thou movest, thou stampest the earth like a quake,
And thy immense gongs strike deep resonant notes.

T.S.: Mewa Singh fires three times. A bullet pierces Hopkinson's heart.

T.S. touches HOPKINSON with the cane. HOPKINSON's head falls forward.

WOMAN: Mewa Singh will be hanged by the neck till he's dead. Mewa Singh says on the gallows : "I am a gentle person, but gentle people must act when injustice engulfs them. Let God judge my actions for he sees the right and the wrong. I offer my neck to the rope as a child opens his arms to his mother."

T.S. does a soft-shoe shuffle, stops, looks out, raises his arms, pauses and makes a large but simple bow. Black.

The end.

BILLY BISHOP GOES TO WAR

BY

JOHN MacLACHLAN GRAY
WITH ERIC PETERSON

l to r
Eric Peterson and John MacLachlan Gray

Photographer: Joe B. Mann

SATIRE, MONOLOGUE, AND THE CREATION OF INDIGENOUS MYTHOLOGY: *BILLY BISHOP GOES TO WAR*

His investiture into the Order of Canada in the fall of 2000, the release in the same year of his second novel, *A Gift for the Little Master*, and the concurrent media focus on the large advances he received from British, German, American, and Canadian publishers for the rights to *The Fiend in Human* (a novel in progress) provide ample reason to survey the career of one of this country's most distinguished and versatile writers. Few Canadians have performed in more literary and artistic capacities than musician, novelist, historian, essayist, screenwriter, commentator, actor, director, and playwright John MacLachlan Gray.

Ratsoy: You've worn many different hats in the theatre and as a writer. Is there one particular hat with which you most identify?

Gray: The different things I do have more in common than not. I identify with stories and metaphors and the arrangements of words. Now I'm a novelist. I don't know when or if I'll write another play.

Born in Ottawa in 1946 and raised in Truro, Nova Scotia, Gray received a BA in English from Mount Allison University before heading to Vancouver in 1968. By 1971, he had completed an MA in theatre, with a focus on directing, at the University of British Columbia and co-founded (with Larry Lillo, Eric Peterson, and others) what was to become the west-coast city's most successful alternative company, Tamahnous Theatre. After its premier production, *Dracula 11*, he spent three years with Tamahnous.

The few years at Toronto's Theatre Passe Muraille (under the direction of Paul Thompson) in the mid-1970s left an indelible mark on John Gray's writing style. As he wrote the music for several of the company's works, Gray witnessed the power of productions such as Rick Salutin's *1837: The Farmers' Revolt* to create Canadian myths and engage a populist audience. Having been schooled in the colonial tradition still prevalent in Canada at the time, he had scarcely been aware of the existence of plays set in Canada and featuring Canadian themes. The fruits of that cultural awakening have manifested themselves in his work ever since, beginning with *18 Wheels*, his first major play, produced in 1976 at Theatre Passe Muraille, where *Billy Bishop Goes to War* was eventually conceived and workshopped. Gray and Eric Peterson immersed themselves in research into the life of William Avery Bishop, the World War One flying ace.

The circumstances surrounding the premiere of *Billy Bishop Goes to War* were inauspicious: Vancouver was in the midst of both a mail and newspaper strike; it was difficult to get the word out. However, it is a testament to the power of word of mouth and the play itself, of course, that it was held over for a week at the Vancouver East Cultural Centre and then moved to another local venue. Max Wyman began his glowing review with a prediction that may have seemed rash but was, as it turned out, modest: "*Billy Bishop Goes to War* is made-in-Vancouver entertainment that's going to be a national knockout" and ended it with "There'll be guaranteed happy landings wherever it goes." Four years later, the duo wrapped up a tour of *Billy Bishop Goes to War* that had begun with an extensive run throughout the country and later moved to Broadway, Los Angeles, the Edinburgh Festival, and London's West End. Few Canadian plays have had the national and international impact of Gray's minimalist two-hander. For a time, it was the most produced play on the continent, having been remounted by other companies from Canada (Cedric Smith, who replaced Peterson in matinee performances while the play was on Broadway, and Ross Douglas would tour Canada with the play in the early 1980s) and as far away as Kenya.

Ratsoy: Do you have any idea of the number of productions of *Billy Bishop Goes to War*? Is it still being produced? Do you have any examples of unusual productions of it?

Gray: Around 200. It was the most frequently produced show in the USA for four years during the 1980s. This year it received a wonderful production in Albany, New York. There's an Afro-American actor who got a tape from Sigourney Weaver around 1980 who performed it off and on for fifteen years all over America, totally as a work of fiction. He did it in a child's playpen.

Gray and Peterson's production won both the Chalmers Award and the Los Angeles Drama Critics Award (Best Play and Best Actor Awards). Peterson also took the Clarence Derwent Award for most promising actor in the New York theatre in 1979-1980. Adapted for CBC television, the play won an ACTRA for best production; the book, published in 1982, garnered its author a Governor General's Award. *Billy Bishop Goes to War* also inspired documentary filmmaker Paul Cowan to create his controversial work on Bishop, "The Kid Who Couldn't Miss," which includes scenes of Peterson adapted from the play.

On the occasion of the twentieth anniversary of the play, which Peterson recalls as "an amazing patriotic event," (Birnie) the original cast remounted *Billy Bishop Goes to War*; in 1998 and 1999, it played Toronto, Vancouver, London, Winnipeg, and Ottawa to considerable acclaim. Kate Taylor, who confessed to having been too young and busy to take in the original, wrote, "It is not hard to see why it became such a success" and found Bishop's reminiscences "superbly animated by Peterson's great gift as a storyteller." Gray made few changes to the original: one song was replaced, a few props were added, and the closing scene of the original became the opening scene – a modification that changed Bishop's perspective from a young man fresh from the action to a middle-aged man reflecting on the events. When asked how his and Peterson's perspective on the play had changed since 1978, Gray replied, "Mortality isn't just a theory for us anymore" (Birnie). An indication of how the nature of Canadian theatre itself had changed since Gray's university days is that *Globe and Mail* drama critic Ray Conlogue used the occasion of the remount to pose to the country's leading drama scholars, playwrights, and artistic producers the question of whether Canada had a drama canon. Over the course of the first thirty years of John Gray's career, Canadian drama had gone from virtual unacknowledgment to probable entrenchment.

Ratsoy: At what point was it obvious that the original production was a hit?

Gray: We were always popular with audiences – in a two-week run we'd do 50 percent at the beginning and sell out just as we were about to leave town. We knew we were a hit in Canada when it was announced that we were going to New York and that Mike Nichols was involved. Audiences promptly doubled.

Ratsoy: What stands out for you about the 1998 remount?

Gray: It was more fun to do than the original; I'm not sure why. It was a better show because our ages fit; at the same time, it didn't seem to be about war anymore. More to do with the attrition that is part of normal life.

The play is characteristically Canadian in its blending of seemingly disparate, even incompatible modes that have been strong currents running through indigenous art and popular culture: documentary, satire, and monologue. Although documentary is most often associated with our film, it has a long history in our poetry and prose, and, as Alan Filewod has noted, it played a seminal role in the development of Canadian theatre. Historical events have a seductive appeal to the storyteller in a country trying to write itself into existence, especially a country so large, diverse, and sparsely populated as Canada.

William Avery Bishop's story has all the ingredients for mythmaking: a small-town boy with an unexceptional track record in peace time, the pilot would emerge from World War I with the Allied record of seventy-two kills. A satiric documentary may seem somewhat of a contradiction in terms, but *Billy Bishop Goes to War* successfully conflates the two techniques. Satire has had an ongoing role as a form of resistance in a culture once politically colonized and later culturally colonized. It has been a popular means of expression in our literature dating back at least as far as the early nineteenth century, and one has only to look at its manifestations in current Canadian popular culture for proof of its endurance. The relationship between Britain and Canada during a lengthy conflict involving most of the world is rife with possibilities for scrutiny by the humorist, and Gray is judicious in his selection of targets.

Theatre scholar Renate Usmiani has ascribed the popularity of the solo performance in Canadian theatre to its compatibility with themes such as isolation and the search for identity and the facility with which it can convey a political message. Gray adopted his variant on the monologue (in which a single actor takes on a score of roles) for both artistic and practical reasons: he had noticed the predilection for it among the non-mainstream audiences he encountered at Theatre Passe Muraille, he knew a small cast would mean fewer expenses and increase the likelihood of multiple productions, and he was aware of the powers of the solo performance to transcend physical space. As he put it, "A dogfight can be a tricky number to stage, and the sky is hard to evoke with a roof over your head. But to a good storyteller anything is possible, and Eric is a wonderful storyteller" (*Modern Canadian Plays* 51).

Almost as central an expressionistic device as the dropping of the fourth wall, the music in *Billy Bishop Goes to War* is firmly embedded in the text. In addition to highlighting the time period and reflecting the mood, it functions on an intrinsic level as a narrative thread. It also substitutes for visual elements: while the set itself is sparse, the lyrics are frequently intense and rich. Like the songs in Anderson and Savath's *Horseplay*, Gray's lyrics underscore serious thematic concerns and belie the often light tunes that accompany them. Here, as in Panych's *Last Call*, the influence of Bertolt Brecht and Kurt Weill is evident. Gray's distinct brand of musical is at once satiric and earnest, bleak and affectionate.

The three most popular Gray plays apart from *Billy Bishop Goes to War* were published collectively in 1987 under the title *Local Boy Makes Good*: *Eighteen Wheels* features truck drivers and waitresses from across the country telling their stories, *Don Messer's Jubilee* is a fond look at a Maritime music group that enjoyed long-time success on CBC television, and *Rock and Roll* has its genesis in Gray's teenage years as an organist and trumpet player with the Lincolns, a Maritime band. These three plays celebrate different types of music; however, what they have in common with each other and *Billy Bishop Goes To War* is a consciously Canadian mythology. Gray's other plays, most of them also musicals, include *The Tree, The Tower, The Flood*; *Better Watch Out, Better not Die*; *Health* (with Peterson as protagonist Mort, an Everyman in mid-life crisis); *Amelia* (about Amelia Earhart); and two plays for children, *The Magic Star*, and *Bongo from the Congo*.

Ratsoy: How would you describe your particular type of musical?

Gray: Narrative as opposed to dramatic. The songs are usually a natural extension of the storytelling, as opposed to a number set up by a scene. *Rock and Roll* **is the closest thing to a conventional musical.**

Gray has received six Western Magazine Awards and a National Magazine Award for his nonfiction. His journalism has included sixty-five satiric opinion pieces for CBC television and columns for *The Vancouver Sun* and *The Globe and Mail*. A glimpse at his two books of non-fiction reveals his eclecticism, versatility, and eccentricity. *I Love Mom: An Irreverent History of the Tattoo* (complete with evocative photos and diagrams and Gray's own poems) traces the responses of various cultures to an ancient art, and thereby provides insight into societies from Biblical times to the 1990s. *Lost in North America: The Imaginary Canadian in the American Dream* features vibrant, witty personal narratives and political and social observations that mesh to form a potent, quirky, and unconventional analysis of Canada – past, present, and future. This collection captures the complex, elusive Canadian condition, and does so in a most engaging style.

Both of Gray's novels employ his characteristic satire and foreground American cultural colonization of Canada. Willard, the protagonist of *Dazzled*, is a washed-out hippie relegated by a change in fortune to a job in a men's clothing store; as such, he is an ideal vehicle for a satiric examination of both alternative and mainstream culture. By stressing the fact that Williard's hippie ideals were acquired second-hand, Gray illustrates the inevitable inadequacy of borrowed dreams. *A Gift for the Little Master* shares with its predecessor brisk, at times jarring pacing and incisive dissection of contemporary obsessions with materialism and media. His latest work, however, is a departure in an important way: it is a dark, edgy thriller set in an unnamed city that shares with "real-life" Vancouver place names and landmarks but also has many of the characteristics and identifiers of contemporary American cities: Canada is an occupied country. Gray's vision is chillingly dystopian: this is an urban jungle in which the public and the private are indistinguishable, television supersedes reality, and the darkest aspects of globalization are realized.

As diverse as are the genres in which John MacLachlan Gray writes, most of the work that comes from his pen is informed by penetrating humour, populist appeal, and a firm conviction that the preservation of a national culture is paramount. *Billy Bishop Goes to War* is a complex character study about war and the transition from innocence to experience. Above all, though, it is about post-colonial resistance: by looking at history through the lens of the storyteller and re-creating a historical figure who both transcended and was manipulated by the imperial structure he worked within, John MacLachlan Gray produced an indigenous myth.

G.R.

Selected Bibliography:

- Abley, Mark. "Calvary of the Air." *The Times Literary Supplement* 4 Nov. 1981.
- Bessai, Diane. "Discovering the Popular Audience." *Canadian Literature* 118 (Autumn 1988): 7-28.
- Birnie, Peter. "Billy Bishop Will Fly Again." *The Vancouver Sun* 11 July 1998.
- Bishop, William Avery. *Winged Warfare*. 1918. Toronto: McGraw-Hill Ryerson, 1990.
- Conlogue, Ray. "Bringing Billy to a New Generation." *The Globe and Mail* 9 Sept. 1998.
- Cowan, Paul. "The Kid Who Couldn't Miss." National Film Board, 1982. This film, which outraged some war veterans because it suggests Bishop was less than honest in reporting his victories, sparked heated debate in the press and Senate sub-committee hearings into the filmmakers' methodology. The Senate eventually recommended a re-labelling from "documentary" to "docudrama".
- Filewod, Alan. *Collective Encounters: Documentary Theatre in English Canada*. Toronto: University of Toronto Press, 1987. A thorough historical study of documentary drama.
- Gray, John. E-Mail Interview. 21 Dec. 2000.
- Gray, John. *Local Boy Makes Good: Three Musicals*. Vancouver: Talonbooks, 1987.
- Gray, John. "Preface to *Billy Bishop Goes to War*." *Modern Canadian Plays: Volume 11*. Ed. Jerry Wasserman. Vancouver: Talonbooks, 1994. 51-56.
- Gray, John. "Trudeau Helped Canadians Tread Their Own Boards." *The Globe and Mail*. 2 Oct. 2000. Gray remembers the role Prime Minister Trudeau's government played in the establishment of alternative theatre.
- MacIntyre, Jean. "Language and Structure in *Billy Bishop Goes to War*." *Canadian Drama* 13:1 (1987): 50-59.
- Moher, Frank. "From Grey Days to Gray's Days." *The Vancouver Sun* 4 Nov. 2000.

- Taylor, Kate. " Billy Bishop Still Flying High." *The Globe and Mail* 26 Sept. 1998.
- Usmiani, Renate. "Going It Alone: Is Canadian Theatre the Sound of One Voice Talking?" *Theatrum* 28 (April 1992): 13-18.
- Wallace, Robert and Cynthia Zimmerman. *The Work: Conversations with English-Canadian Playwrights*. Toronto: Coach House Press, 1982.
- Wasserman, Jerry. "Flying Low Into Another Tour of Duty: Jerry Wasserman Speaks with John Gray." *Books in Canada* 28:1 (Feb. 1999): 25-27.
- Wyman, Max. "Into the Wild Blue Yonder by The Seat of His Pants." *The Vancouver Express* 6 Nov. 1978.
- Yardley, M. Jeanne. "Unauthorized Re-Visions of the Billy Bishop Story." *Textual Studies in Canada* 3 (1993): 86-96. Compares *Winged Warfare*, *The Kid Who Couldn't Miss*, and *Billy Bishop Goes to War* as historical narratives.

**Billy Bishop Goes to War
by John MacLachlan Gray
with Eric Peterson**

Billy Bishop Goes to War was first produced by the Vancouver East Cultural Centre in association with Tamahnous Theatre, on November 3, 1978, with the following cast:

Billy Bishop   Eric Peterson
Narrator/Pianist   John Gray

Directed by John MacLachlan Gray
Set and Lighting Designed by Paul Williams
Music and Lyrics by John MacLachlan Gray

CHARACTERS

NARRATOR/PIANIST
BILLY BISHOP, who also plays
AN UPPERCLASSMAN
ADJUTANT PERRAULT
AN OFFICER
SIR HUGH CECIL
LADY ST. HELIER
CEDRIC, her butler
A DOCTOR
GENERAL JOHN HIGGINS,
    Brigade Commander
A TOMMY
THE LOVELY HÉLÈNE
ALBERT BALL
WALTER BOURNE,
    Bishop's mechanic
A GERMAN
GENERAL HUGH M. TRENCHARD
AN ADJUTANT
SECOND OFFICER
KING GEORGE V

ACT ONE

The lights come up slowly on BILLY BISHOP and the PIANO PLAYER, who sits at the piano. They are in an Officers' Mess.

BISHOP & PIANO PLAYER: (*singing*)
We were off to fight the Hun,
We would shoot him with a gun.
Our medals would shine
Like a sabre in the sun.
We were off to fight the Hun
And it looked like lots of fun,
Somehow it didn't seem like war
At all, at all, at all.
Somehow it didn't seem like war at all.

BILLY BISHOP speaks to the audience. He is a young man from Owen Sound, Ontario. His speech pattern is that of a small town Canadian boy who could well be squealing his tires down the main street of some town at this very moment.

BISHOP: (*to the audience*) I think when you haven't been in a war for a while, you've got to take what you can get. I mean, Canada, 1914? They must have been pretty desperate. Take me, for instance. Twenty years old, a convicted liar and cheat. I mean, I'm on record as the worst student RMC... Royal Military College in Kingston, Ontario... I'm on record as the worst student they ever had. I join up, they made me an officer, a lieutenant in the Mississauga Horse. All I can say is they must have been scraping the bottom of the barrel.

BISHOP & PIANO PLAYER: (*singing*)
We were off to fight the Hun,
Though hardly anyone
Had ever read about a battle,
Much less seen a Lewis gun.
We were off to fight the Hun
And it looked like lots of fun,
Somehow it didn't seem like war
At all, at all, at all.
Somehow it didn't seem like war at all.

BISHOP: (*to the audience*) Yeah, it looked like it was going to be a great war. I mean, all my friends were very keen to join up, they were. Not me. Royal Military College had been enough for me. Now the reason I went to RMC is, well... I could ride a horse. And I was a great shot. I mean, I am a really good shot. I've got these tremendous eyes, you see. And RMC had an entrance exam and that was good because my previous scholastic record wasn't that hot. In fact, when I suggested to my principal that, indeed, I was going to RMC, he said, "Bishop, you don't have the brains." But I studied real hard, sat for the exams and got in.

He imitates an RMC Officer.

Recruits! Recruits will march at all times. They will not loiter, they will not window shop. Recruits! Recruits will run at all times when in the parade square. Recruits! Recruits will be soundly trounced every Friday night, whether they deserve it or not.

As himself.

I mean, those guys were nuts! They were going to make leaders out of us, the theory being that before you could learn to lead, you had to learn to obey. So, because of this, we're all assigned to an upperclassman as a kind of, well... slave. And I was assigned to this real sadistic SOB, this guy named Vivian Bishop. That's right, the same surname as me, and because of that, I had to tuck him into bed at night, kiss him on the forehead and say, "Goodnight, Daddy"! I mean, it's pretty hard to take some of that stuff seriously. One of my punishments: I'm supposed to clean out this old Martello Tower by the edge of the lake. I mean, it's filthy, hasn't been used for years. Now I do a real great job. I clean it up real well. This upperclassman comes along to inspect it.

UPPERCLASSMAN: What's this in the corner, Bishop?

BISHOP: That? (*He has another look.*) That's a spider, Sir.

UPPERCLASSMAN: That's right, Bishop. That's a spider. Now you had orders to clean this place up. You haven't done that. You get down on your hands and knees and eat that spider.

BISHOP: (*to the audience*) I had to eat that spider in front of all my classmates. You ever have to eat a spider? In public? I doubt it. Nuts! Now, whenever I'm not happy, I mean, whenever I'm not having a really good time, I do one of three things: I get sick, I get injured or I get in an awful lot of trouble. My third year at RMC, I got into an awful lot of trouble. This friend of mine, Townsend, one night, we got a bottle of gin, eh? And we stole a canoe. Well, we'd arranged to meet these girls on Cedar Island out in Dead Man's Bay. Well, of course, the canoe tips over. Now, it's early spring, really cold. We get back to shore somehow and we're shivering and Townsend says to me, "Bish, Bish, I'm going to the infirmary. I think I got pneumonia." And I'm sitting there saying, "Well, whatever you do, you silly bugger, change into some dry clothes." Because we couldn't let anybody know what we'd been doing. I mean, we were absent without leave, in possession of alcohol and we'd stolen a canoe. What I didn't know was the officer on duty had witnessed this whole thing. Townsend goes to the infirmary and is confronted with these charges and he admits everything. I didn't know that. I'm rudely awakened out of my sleep and hauled up before old Adjutant Perrault.

At attention, addressing Adjutant PERRAULT.

Sir! I've been in my bed all night. I really don't know what you're talking about, Sir.

PERRAULT: Come on. Come on now, Bishop. We have the testimony of the officer on duty. We also have the full confession of your accomplice implicating you fully in this. Now, what is your story, Bishop?

BISHOP: (*to the audience*) Well, I figured I was in too deep now to change my story. (*to PERRAULT*) Sir, I still maintain...

PERRAULT: Bishop! I'm going to say the worst thing that I can say to a gentleman cadet. You are a liar, Bishop!

BISHOP is sobered briefly by the memory, but he quickly recovers.

BISHOP: (*to the audience*) I got twenty-eight days restricted leave for that. It's like house arrest. Then they caught me cheating on my final exams. Well, I handed in the crib notes with the exam paper! And that's when they called me the worst student RMC ever had. They weren't going to tell me what my punishment was until the next fall, so I could stew about it all summer, but I knew what it was going to be. Expulsion! With full honours! But then the war broke out and I enlisted and was made an officer. I mean, for me, it was the lesser of two evils. But everyone else was very keen on the whole thing. They were.

BISHOP & PIANO PLAYER: (*singing*)
We were off to fight the Hun,
Though hardly anyone
Had ever seen a Hun,
Wouldn't know one if we saw one.
We were off to fight the Hun
And it looked like lots of fun,
Somehow it didn't seem like war
At all, at all, at all.
Somehow it didn't seem like war at all.

The PIANO PLAYER raps out a military rhythm.

BISHOP: (*to the audience*) October 1st, 1914, the First Contingent of the Canadian Expeditionary Forces left for England. I wasn't with them. I was in the hospital. Thinking of Margaret...

The PIANO PLAYER plays the appropriate "Dear Margaret" music under the following speech.

BISHOP: (*as if writing a letter*) Dear... Dearest Margaret. I am in the hospital with pneumonia. I also have an allergy, but the doctors don't know what I am allergic to. Maybe it's horses. Maybe it's the Army. The hospital is nice, so I am in good spirits. Thinking of you constantly, I remain...

The PIANO PLAYER raps out a military rhythm once again.

(*to the audience*) March, 1915, the Second, Third, Fourth, Fifth and Sixth Contingents of the Canadian Expeditionary Forces left for England. I wasn't with them either. I was back in the hospital... thinking of Margaret.

As if writing a letter.

Sweetheart. Please excuse my writing, as I have a badly sprained wrist. Yesterday, my horse reared up and fell over backwards on me. It was awful, I could have been killed. My head was completely buried in the mud. My nose is, of course, broken and quite swollen, and I can't see out of one eye. I have two broken ribs and am pretty badly bruised, but the doctor figures I'll be up and around by Monday. The hospital is nice, so I am in fine spirits. Thinking of you constantly, I remain...

The PIANO PLAYER raps out a military rhythm once again.

(*to the audience*) June, 1915. The Seventh Contingent of the Canadian Expeditionary Forces left for England. I was with them. Now, this was aboard a cattle boat called the *Caledonia*, in Montreal. There was this big crowd came down to the pier to see us off. I mean, hundreds and hundreds of people, and for a while there, I felt like the whole thing was worth doing. It's pretty impressive when you look out there and you see several hundred people cheering and waving... at you. I mean, when you're from a small town, the numbers get to you. And you're looking out at them and they're looking back at you, and you think, "Boy, I must be doing something right!"

The PIANO PLAYER strikes up "God Save the King."

And they play "God Save the King," and everybody is crying and waving and cheering, and the boat starts to pull out, and they start to yell like you've never heard anybody yell before. I mean, you feel good. You really do! And we're all praying, "Please God, don't let the fighting be over before I can get over there and take part..."

He becomes carried away and starts yelling.

"On the edge of destiny, you must test your strength!"

He is suddenly self-conscious.

What the hell am I talking about?

The music changes from heroic to the monotonous roll of a ship.

The good ship *Caledonia* soon changed its name to the good ship Vomit. It was never meant to hold people. Even the horses didn't like it. Up, down, up, down. And they're siphoning brandy down our throats to keep us from puking our guts up on deck. It was a big joke. Whenever anyone would puke, which was every minute or so, everyone would point to him and laugh like it was the funniest thing they had ever seen. I mean, puke swishing around on the deck, two inches deep, har, har, har! You couldn't sleep, even if it was calm, because every time you closed your eyes, you had a nightmare about being torpedoed.

He demonstrates a torpedo hitting the ship.

Every time I closed my eyes, I could see this torpedo coming up through the water, through the hull of the ship and... BOOM! And we were attacked, too, just off the coast of Ireland. I was scared shitless. All you could do was stand at the rail and watch the other ships get hit and go down. Bodies floating around like driftwood. But we made it through. The Good Ship *Caledonia*, latrine of the Atlantic, finally made it through to Portsmouth, full of dead horses and sick Canadians. When we got off, they thought we were a boat load of Balkan refugees.

BISHOP & PIANO PLAYER: (*singing*)
We were off to fight the Hun,
We would shoot him with a gun.
Our medals would shine
Like a sabre in the sun.
We were off to fight the Hun
And it looked like lots of fun,
Somehow it didn't seem like war
At all, at all, at all.
Somehow it didn't seem like war at all.

BISHOP: (*to the audience*) A few days later, we marched into Shorncliffe Military Camp, right on the Channel. You know, on a clear night, you could see the artillery flashes from France. I took it as a sign of better things to come.... It wasn't.

As if writing a letter.

Dearest Margaret... Shorncliffe Military Camp is the worst yet! The cold wind brings two kinds of weather. Either it rains or it doesn't. When it rains, you've got mud like I've never seen before. Your horse gets stuck in a foot and a half of mud. You get off and you're knee deep. The rain falls in sheets and you're wet to the skin. You are never dry. Then the rain stops and the ground dries out. What a relief, you say? Then the wind gets the dust going and you have dust storms for days. The sand is like needles hitting you, and a lot of the men are bleeding from the eyes. I don't know which is worse, going blind or going crazy. The sand gets in your food, your clothes, your tent, in your... body orifices. A lot of the guys have something called desert madness, which is really serious. As I write this letter, the sand is drifting across the page. Thinking of you constantly, I remain...

To the audience.

Being buried alive in the mud... I was seriously considering this proposition one day when a funny thing happened.

He demonstrates with a chair.

I got my horse stuck in the middle of the parade ground. The horse is up to its fetlocks; I'm up to my knees. Mud, sweat and horse shit from head to toe.

The music becomes ethereal and gentle.

Then, suddenly, out of the clouds comes this little single-seater scout. You know, this little fighter plane? It circles a couple of times. I guess the pilot had lost his way and was going to come down and ask directions. He does this turn, then lands on an open space, like a dragonfly on a rock. The pilot jumps out. He's in this long sheepskin coat, helmet, goggles... warm and dry. He gets his directions, then jumps back into the machine, up in the air, with the mist blowing off him. All by himself. No superior officer, no horse, no sand, no mud. What a beautiful picture! I don't know how long I just stood there watching until he was long gone. Out of sight.

He breaks the mood abruptly.

I mean, this war was going on a lot longer than anyone expected. A lot more people were getting killed than anyone expected. Now I wasn't going to spend the rest of the war in the mud. And I sure as hell wasn't going to die in the mud.

The PIANO PLAYER strikes up a new tune. BISHOP drunkenly joins in.

BISHOP & PIANO PLAYER: (*singing*)
Thinking of December nights
In the clear Canadian cold,
Where the winter air don't smell bad,
And the wind don't make you old.
Where the rain don't wash your heart out,
And the nights ain't filled with fear.
Oh, those old familiar voices
Whisper in my ears.
(*Chorus*)
Oh, Canada,
Sing a song for me.
Sing one for your lonely son,
So far across the sea.

The piano continues with a popular dance tune of the period. BISHOP's reverie is interrupted by a Cockney OFFICER, who is also drunk and who is slightly mad.

OFFICER: You don't fancy the Cavalry then, eh?

BISHOP: What?!

OFFICER: I say, you don't fancy the Cavalry then, eh? It's going to be worse at the front, mate. There, you got blokes shooting at you, right...? With machine guns. (*He imitates a machine gun.*) DakDakDakDakakaka. Har, har, har. It's a bloody shooting gallery. They still think they're fighting the Boer War! Cavalry charges against machine guns. DakDakDakak. Har, har! It's a bloody shooting gallery with you in the middle of it, mate.

BISHOP: This is awful. Something's got to be done. Jeez, I was a casualty in training.

OFFICER: Take a word of advice from me, mate. The only way out is up.

BISHOP: Up?

OFFICER: Up. Join the Royal Flying Corps. I did. I used to be in the Cavalry, but I joined the RFC. I like it. It's good clean work. Mind you, the bleeding machines barely stay in the air and the life expectancy of the new lads is about eleven days. But I like it. It's good clean work.

BISHOP: Just a minute. How can I get into the Royal Flying Corps? I'm Canadian. I'm cannon fodder. You practically have to own your own plane to get into the RFC.

OFFICER: *Au contraire*, mate. *Au contraire*. The upper classes are depressed by the present statistics, so they aren't joining with their usual alacrity. Now, anyone who wants to can get blown out of the air. Even Canadians.

BISHOP: Well, what do I have to do?

OFFICER: You go down to see them at the War Office, daft bunch of twits, but they're all right. Now... you act real eager, see? Like you want to be a pilot. You crave the excitement, any old rubbish like that. Then, they're not going to know what to ask, because they don't know a bleeding thing about it. So, they'll ask you whatever comes into their heads, which isn't much, then they'll say you can't be a pilot, you've got to be an observer.

BISHOP: What's an observer?

OFFICER: He's the fellow who goes along for the ride, you know? Looks about.

BISHOP: Ohhh...

OFFICER: So, you act real disappointed, like your Mum wanted you to be a pilot, and then, you get your transfer...

BISHOP: Just a minute. So, I'm an observer. I'm the fellow that goes along for the ride, looks about. So what? How do I get to be a pilot?

OFFICER: I don't know. Sooner or later, you just get to be a pilot. Plenty of vacancies these days. Check the casualty lists, wait for a bad one. You've got to go in by the back door, you know what I mean? Nobody gets to be a pilot right away, for Christ's sake. Especially not bleeding Canadians!

BISHOP: (*to the audience*) Did you ever trust your future to a drunken conversation in a bar? Two days later, I went down to see them at the War Office.

The PIANO PLAYER plays some going to war music. In the following scene, SIR HUGH CECIL interviews BISHOP at the War Office. He is getting on in years and the new technology of warfare has confused him deeply.

SIR HUGH: So... you wish to transfer to the Royal Flying Corps? Am I right? Am I correct?

BISHOP: Yes, Sir. I want to become a fighter pilot, Sir. It's what my mother always wanted, Sir.

SIR HUGH: Oh... I see. Well, the situation is this, Bishop. We need good men in the RFC, but they must have the correct... er... qualifications. Now, while the War Office has not yet ascertained what qualifications are indeed necessary to fly an... er... aeroplane, we must see to it that all candidates possess the necessary qualifications, should the War Office ever decide what those qualifications are. Do you understand, Bishop?

BISHOP: Perfectly, Sir.

SIR HUGH: That's very good. Jolly good. More than I can say. Well, shall we begin then?

BISHOP: Ready when you are, Sir.

SIR HUGH: That's good, shows keenness, you see.... And good luck, Bishop. (*to himself*) What on earth shall I ask him? (*There is a long pause while he collects his thoughts.*) Do you ski?

BISHOP: Ski, sir?

SIR HUGH: Yes... do you ski?

BISHOP: (*to the audience*) Here was an Englishman asking a Canadian whether or not he skied. Now, if the Canadian said he didn't ski, the Englishman might find that somewhat suspicious. (*to SIR HUGH*) Ski? Yes, Sir. (*to the audience*) Never skied in my life.

SIR HUGH: Fine, well done... thought you might. (*pause*) Do you ride a horse?

BISHOP: I'm an officer in the Cavalry, Sir.

SIR HUGH: Doesn't necessarily follow, but we'll put down that you ride, shall we? (*pause*) What about sports, Bishop? Run, jump, throw the ball? Play the game, eh? What?

BISHOP: Sports, Sir? All sports.

SIR HUGH: I see. Well done, Bishop. I'm most impressed.

BISHOP: Does this mean I can become a fighter pilot, Sir?

SIR HUGH: Who knows, Bishop? Who knows? All full up with fighter pilots at the moment, I'm afraid. Take six months, a year to get in. Terribly sorry. Nothing I can do, old man.

BISHOP: I see, Sir.

SIR HUGH: However! We have an immediate need for observers. You know, the fellow who goes along for the ride, looks about. What do you say, Bishop?

BISHOP: (*to the audience*) I thought about it. I wanted to be a pilot. I couldn't. So, in the fall of 1915, I joined the Twenty-First Squadron as an observer. That's what they were using planes for at that time. Observation. You could take pictures of enemy troop formations, direct artillery fire, stuff like that. It seemed like nice quiet work at the time and I was really good at the aerial photography. I've got these great eyes, remember? And to fly! You're in this old Farnham trainer, sounds like a tractor. It coughs, wheezes, chugs its way up to one thousand feet. You're in a kite with a motor that can barely get off the ground. But even so, you're in the air.... You're not on the ground.... You're above everything.

The PIANO PLAYER plays some mess hall music.

It was a different world up there. A different war and a different breed of men fighting that war.... Flyers! During training, we heard all the stories. If you went down behind enemy lines and were killed, they'd come over, the Germans, that is... they'd come over under a flag of truce and drop a photograph of your grave. Nice. If you were taken prisoner, it was the champagne razzle in the mess. Talking and drinking all night. It was a different war they were fighting up there. And from where I stood, it looked pretty darn good.

PIANO PLAYER: Can you be a bit more specific, please?

BISHOP and the PIANO PLAYER sing a song of champagne and vermouth.

BISHOP & PIANO PLAYER: (*singing*)
I see two planes in the air,
A fight that's fair and square,
With dips and loops and rolls
That would scare you (I'm scared already).
We will force the German down
And arrest him on the ground,
A patriotic lad from Bavaria
    (Poor bloody sod).
But he'll surrender willingly
And salute our chivalry,
For this war is not of our creation.
But before it's prison camp
And a bed that's cold and damp,
We'll all have a little celebration.
(*Chorus*)
Oh, we'll toast our youth
On champagne and vermouth,
For all of us know what it's like to fly.
Oh, the fortunes of war
Can't erase esprit de corps
And we'll all of us be friends
'Til we die.

PIANO PLAYER: Can you go on a bit, please!

BISHOP & PIANO PLAYER: (*singing*)
Oh, we'll drink the night away,
And when the Bosch is led away,
We'll load him down with cigarettes and wine.
We'll drink a final toast goodbye,
But for the grace of God go I,
And we'll vow that we'll be friends
    (Cheers – ping!)
Another time.
(*Chorus*)
Oh, we'll toast our youth
On champagne and vermouth,
For all of us know what it's like to fly.
Oh, the fortunes of war
Can't erase esprit de corps
And we'll all of us be friends
'Til we die.

BISHOP: You want chivalry? You want gallantry? You want nice guys? That's your flyer. And Jeez, I was going to be one! January 1st, 1916, I crossed the channel to France as a flyer. Well, an observer anyway. That's when I found out that Twenty-First Squadron was known as the "suicide squadron." I mean, that awful nickname used to prey on my mind, you know? And the Archies? The anti-aircraft guns? Not tonight, Archibald! I mean, you're tooling around over the line, doing your observation work, a sitting duck, when suddenly you are surrounded by these little black puffs of smoke. Then... wham-whizz! Shrapnel whizzes all around you. I was hit on the head by a piece of flak, just a bruise, but a couple of inches lower and I would have been killed. And we were all scared stiff of this new German machine, the Fokker. It had this interrupter gear, so the pilot could shoot straight at you through the propeller without actually shooting the propeller off. All he had to do was aim his plane at you! And casualties? Lots and lots and lots of casualties. It was a grim situation. But we didn't know how grim it could get until we saw the RE-7... the Reconnaissance Experimental Number Seven. Our new plane. What you saw was this mound of cables and wires, with a thousand pounds of equipment hanging off it. Four machine guns, a five hundred pound bomb, for God's sake. Reconnaissance equipment, cameras... Roger Neville (that's my pilot), he and I are ordered into the thing to take it up. Of course, it doesn't get off the ground. Anyone could see that. We thought, fine, good riddance. But the officers go into a huddle.

Imitating the Officers.

Mmmmum? What do you think we should do? Take the bomb off? Take the bomb off!

As himself.

So we take the bomb off and try again. This time, the thing sort of flops down the runway like a crippled duck. Finally, by taking everything off but one machine gun, the thing sort of flopped itself into the air and chugged along. It was a pig! We were all scared stiff of it. So they put us on active duty... as bombers! They gave us two bombs each, told us to fly over Hunland and drop them on somebody. But in order to accommodate for the weight of the bombs, they took our machine guns away!

As if writing a letter.

Dearest Margaret. We are dropping bombs on the enemy from unarmed machines. It is exciting work. It's hard to keep your confidence in a war when you don't have a gun. Somehow we get back in one piece and we start joking around and inspecting the machine for bullet and shrapnel damage. You're so thankful not to be dead. Then I go back to the barracks and lie down. A kind of terrible loneliness comes over me. It's like waiting for the firing squad. It makes you want to cry, you feel so frightened and so alone. I think all of us who aren't dead think these things. Thinking of you constantly, I remain...

PIANO PLAYER: (*singing*)
Nobody shoots no one in Canada,
At least nobody they don't know.
Nobody shoots no one in Canada,
Last battle was a long, long time ago.
Nobody picks no fights in Canada,
Not with nobody they ain't met.
Nobody starts no wars in Canada,
Folks tend to work for what they get.
Take me under
That big blue sky,
Where the deer and the black bear play.
May not be heaven,
But heaven knows we try,
Wish I was in Canada today.
Nobody drop no bombs on Canada,
Wouldn't want to send no one to hell.
Nobody start no wars on Canada,
Where folks tend to wish each other well.

The music continues as BISHOP speaks.

BISHOP: Of course in this situation, it wasn't too long before the accidents started happening again. It's kind of spooky, but I think being accident prone actually saved my life. I'm driving a truckload of parts a couple of miles from the aerodrome and I run into another truck. I'm inspecting the undercarriage of my machine when a cable snaps and hits me on the head. I was unconscious for two days... I had a tooth pulled, it got infected and I was in the hospital for two weeks.... Then Roger does this really bad landing. I hit my knee on a metal brace inside the plane so hard I could barely walk.... Then I got three weeks leave in London. None too soon. On the boat going back to England, we all got into the champagne and cognac pretty heavy, and, by the time we arrived, we were all pretty tight and this game developed to see who would actually be the first guy to touch foot on English soil. I'm leading the race down the gangplank. I trip and fall! Everyone else falls on top of me, right on the knee I hurt in the crash! Gawd, the pain was awful! But I was damned if I'd spend my leave in the hospital, so I'd just pour down the brandy until the thing was pretty well numb. I had a hell of a time! If the pain got to me in the night and I couldn't sleep, I'd just pour down the brandy. But around my last day of leave, I started thinking about the bombing runs, the Archies, the Fokkers, and I thought, Jeez, maybe I better have someone look at this knee. The doctor found I had a cracked kneecap, which meant I'd be in the hospital for a couple of weeks. They also found I had a badly strained heart, which meant I would be in the hospital for an indefinite period. As far as I was concerned, I was out of the war.

BISHOP & PIANO PLAYER: (*singing*)
Take me under
That big blue sky,
Where the deer and the black bear play.
May not be heaven,
But heaven knows we try,
Wish I was in Canada today.
I'm dreaming of the trees in Canada,
Northern Lights are dancing in my head.
If I die, then let me die in Canada,
Where there's a chance I'll die in bed.

BISHOP: The hospital is nice. People don't shoot at you and people don't drop things on you. I thought it would be a nice place to spend the rest of the war. I went to sleep for three days.

Distorted marching music is heard.

I had this nightmare. A terrible dream. I am in the lobby of the Grand Hotel in London. The band is playing military music and the lobby is full of English and German officers. They're dancing together and their medals jingle like sleighbells in the snow. The sound is deafening. I've got to get out of there. I start to run, but my knee gives out underneath me. As I get up, I get kicked in the stomach by a Prussian boot. As I turn to run, I get kicked in the rear by an English boot. Then I turn around and all the officers have formed a chorus line, like the Follies, and they are heading for me, kicking. I scream as a hundred black boots kick me high in the air, as I turn over and over, shouting, "Help me! Help me! They are trying to kill me!"

He wakes up abruptly.

LADY ST. HELIER: My goodness, Bishop, you'll not get any rest screaming at the top of your lungs like that.

BISHOP: (*to the audience*) In front of me was a face I'd never seen before. Very old, female, with long white hair pulled back tightly in a bun, exposing two of the largest ears I had ever seen.

LADY ST. HELIER: You'd be the son of Will Bishop of Owen Sound, Canada, would you not? Of course you are, the resemblance is quite startling. Your father was a loyal supporter of a very dear friend of mine, Sir Wilfred Laurier. It was in that connection I met your father in Ottawa. (*She zeros in on BISHOP.*) A gaping mouth is most impolite, Bishop. No, I am not clairvoyant. I am Lady St. Helier. Reform alderman, poetess, friend of Churchill, and the woman who shall save your life.

BISHOP: (*speechless*) Ahh... oh... mmmm Ahhh...

LADY ST. HELIER: Enough of this gay banter, Bishop. Time runs apace and my life is not without its limits. You have been making rather a mess of it, haven't you? You are a rude young man behaving like cannon fodder. Perfectly acceptable characteristics in a Canadian, but you are different. You are a gifted Canadian and that gift belongs to a much older and deeper tradition than Canada can ever hope to provide. Quite against your own wishes, you will be released from this wretched hospital in two weeks' time. Promptly, at three o'clock on that afternoon, you will present yourself before my door at Portland Place, dressed for tea and in a positive frame of mind. Do I make myself clear? Good. Please be punctual, Mr. Bishop.

BISHOP: (*to the audience*) Well, Jeez, that old girl must have known something I didn't, because, two weeks later, I'm released from hospital. Promptly, at three o'clock, I find myself in front of her door at Portland Place, in my best uniform, shining my shoes on my pants. The door is opened by the biggest butler I have ever seen. (*He looks up and speaks to the butler.*) Hi!

The butler looks down at him with distaste, turns away and calls to LADY ST. HELIER.

CEDRIC: (*calling*) Madam, the Canadian is here. Shall I show him in?

LADY ST. HELIER: (*from a distance*) Yes, Cedric, please. Show him in.

CEDRIC: (*turning his back to BISHOP*) Get in!

BISHOP: (*to the audience*) I'm shown into the largest room I've ever seen. I mean, a fireplace eight feet wide and a staircase that must have had a hundred steps in it. I'm not used to dealing with nobility. Servants, grand ballrooms, pheasant hunting on the heath, fifty-year-old brandy over billiards, breakfast in bed... shit, what a life!

CEDRIC: Madam is in the study. Get in!

BISHOP: The study. Books, books... more books than I'll ever read. Persian rug. Tiger's head over the mantle. African spears in the corner. "Rule Britannia, Britannia rules the..." I stood at the door. I was on edge. Out of my element. Lady St. Helier was sitting at this little writing desk, writing.

LADY ST. HELIER: Very punctual, Bishop. Please sit down.

BISHOP: I sat in this chair that was all carved lions. One of the lions stuck in my back.

CEDRIC: Would our visitor from Canada care for tea, madam?

LADY ST. HELIER: Would you care for something to drink, Bishop?

BISHOP: Tea? Ahhh, yeah.... Tea would be fine.

LADY ST. HELIER: A tea for Bishop, Cedric. And I'll have a gin.

CEDRIC: Lemon?

BISHOP: (*disappointed*) Gin! I wonder if I could change.... No, no. Tea will be fine. (*to the audience*) Tea was served. I sip my tea. Lady St. Helier sips her gin. And Cedric loomed over me, afraid I was going to drool on the carpet or something. Lady St. Helier stared at me through her thick spectacles. Suddenly, her ears twitched, like she was honing in on something.

LADY ST. HELIER: I have written a poem in your honour, Bishop. I can but hope that your rustic mind will appreciate its significance. (*She signals to the PIANO PLAYER.*) Cedric!

LADY ST. HELIER: (*spoken to music*)
You're a typical Canadian,
You're modesty itself,
And you really wouldn't want to hurt a flea.
But you're just about to go
The way of the buffalo.
You'd do well to take this good advice from me.
I'm awfully sick and tired
Being constantly required
To stand by and watch Canadians make the best of it,
For the Colonial mentality
Defies all rationality.
You seem to go to lengths to make a mess of it.
Why don't you grow up,
Before I throw up?
Do you expect somebody else to do it for you?
Before you're dead out,
Get the lead out
And seize what little life still lies before you.
Do you really expect Empire
To settle back, retire,
And say "Colonials, go on your merry way"?
I'm very tired of your whining
And your infantile maligning.
Your own weakness simply won't be whined away.
So don't be so naïve,
And take that heart off your sleeve,
For a fool and his life will soon be parted.
War's a fact of life today
And it will not be wished away.
Forget that fact and you'll be dead before you've started.
So, Bishop, grow up,
Before I throw up.
Your worst enemy is yourself, as you well know.
Before you're dead out,
Get the lead out.
You have your own naïveté to overthrow.

LADY ST. HELIER: (*to the PIANO PLAYER*) Thank you Cedric. (*to BISHOP*) Do I make myself clear, Bishop? You will cease this mediocrity your record only too clearly reveals. You will become the pilot you wished to be but were lamentably content to settle for less. Now this will take time, for you must recover the health you have so seriously undermined. To that end, you will remain here, a lodger at Portland Place, top of the stairs, third floor, seventh room on the left. Cedric, be kind to Bishop and ignore his bad manners. For cultivation exacts its price. The loss of a certain... vitality. Beneath this rude Canadian exterior, there is a power that you will never know. Properly harnessed, that power will win wars for you. Churchill knows it and I know it too. Good day, Bishop.

BISHOP: (*to the audience*) Now there are one or two Canadians who would have taken offence at that. Not me. Staying at Portland Place, I found out some things right away. For example, life goes much smoother when you've got influence. Take this pilot business, for example. Lady St. Helier was on the phone to Churchill himself, and, the next day, I was called down to the War Office. The atmosphere was much different.

Going to war music is heard once again.

SIR HUGH: Bishop, my boy. Good to see you, good to see you. Well, well, well, your mother's wish is finally going to come true.

BISHOP: Really, Sir?

SIR HUGH: Yes, yes. You are going to become a pilot. No problem, *pas de problème*. Medical examination in two days time, then report for training.

BISHOP: (*to the audience*) Medical examination! What about my weak heart? What about the fact that three weeks ago I was on the verge of a medical discharge?

DOCTOR: (*addressing BISHOP, but seldom ever looking up from his desk*) Strip to the waist, Bishop. Hmnmnmnm? Stick out your tongue and say ninety-nine.... Good.... Cough twice.... That's good, too.... Turn around ten times.... Eight, nine, ten.... Attention! Still on your feet, Bishop? You're fit as a fiddle and ready to fly!

BISHOP: (*singing*)
Gonna fly...
Gonna fly so high,
Like a bird in the sky,
With the wind in my hair,
And the sun burning in my eyes.
Flying Canadian,
Machine gun in my hand,
First Hun I see is the first Hun to die.

Gonna fly...
In my machine,
Gonna shoot so clean,
Gonna hear them scream
When I hit them between the eyes.
Flying Canadian,
Machine gun in my hand,
First Hun I see is the first Hun to die.

(*Chorus*)

Flying...
What have I been waiting for?
What a way to fight a war!
Flying Canadian,
Machine gun in my hand,
First Hun I see is the first Hun to die.

Gonna fly...
Gonna shoot them down
'Til they hit the ground
And they burn with the sound
Of bacon on the fry.
Flying Canadian,
Machine gun in my hand,
First Hun I see is the first Hun to die.

(*Chorus*)

Flying...
What have I been waiting for?
What a way to fight a war!
Flying Canadian,
Machine gun in my hand,
First Hun I see is the first Hun to die.

The song ends abruptly.

BISHOP: I'll never forget my first solo flight. Lonely? Jeeezus! You're sitting at the controls all by yourself, trying to remember what they're all for. Everyone has stopped doing what they're doing to watch you. An ambulance is parked at the edge of the field with the engines running. You know why. You also know that there's a surgical team in the hospital, just ready to rip.

The PIANO PLAYER calls out the following. BISHOP repeats after him.

PIANO PLAYER: Switch off.

BISHOP: Switch off.

PIANO PLAYER: Petrol on.

BISHOP: Petrol on.

PIANO PLAYER: Suck in.

BISHOP: Suck in.

PIANO PLAYER: Switch on.

BISHOP: Switch on.

PIANO PLAYER: Contact!

BISHOP: Contact!

During the above, BISHOP does all the sound effects vocally, much as a small boy would do during a demonstration.

The propeller is given a sharp swing over and the engine starts with a roar... coughs twice, but soon starts hitting on all cylinders. You signal for them to take away the chocks. Then you start bounding across the field under your own power and head her up into the wind.

He checks the equipment.

Rudder.

Click, click.

Elevator.

Click, click.

Ailerons.

Click, click.

Heart.

Boom-boom! Boom-boom!

I open the throttle all the way... and you're off! Pull back on the stick, easy, easy.

He demonstrates the plane bumping along, then rising up into the air.

Once I was in the air, I felt a lot better. In fact, I felt like a king! Mind you, I wasn't fooling around. I'm flying straight as I can, climbing steadily. All alone! What a feeling!

He looks about.

I've got to turn. I execute a gentle turn, skidding like crazy, but what the hell. I try another turn. This time, I bank it a little more. Too much. Too much...! All in all, I'm having a hell of a time up there until I remember I have to land.... What do I do now? Keep your head, that's what you do. Pull back on the throttle.

The engine coughs.

Too much! I put the nose down into a steep dive. Too steep. Bring it up again, down again, up, down... and in a series of steps, kind of descend to the earth. Then I execute everything I remember I have to do to make a perfect landing. Forty feet off the ground! I put the nose down again and do another perfect landing. This time, I'm only eight feet off the ground, but now I don't have room left to do another nose down manoeuvre. The rumpty takes things into her own hands and just pancakes the rest of the way to the ground. First solo flight! Greatest day in a man's life!

PIANO PLAYER & BISHOP: (*singing*)
Flying...
What have I been waiting for?
What a way to fight a war!
Flying Canadian,
Machine gun in my hand,
First Hun I see is the first Hun to die,
First Hun I see is the first Hun to die.

BISHOP: In the early part of 1916, I was posted back to France as a fighter pilot. Sixtieth Squadron, Third British Brigade. I worked like a Trojan for these wings and I just about lost them before I really began. I was returning from my first OP, Operational Patrol, and I crashed my Nieuport on landing. I wasn't hurt, but the aircraft was pretty well pranged, and that was bad because General John Higgins, the Brigade Commander, saw me do it. Well, he couldn't help but see me do it. I just about crashed at his feet!

HIGGINS: I watched you yesterday, Bishop. You destroyed a machine. A very expensive, a very nice machine. Doing a simple landing on a clear day. That machine was more valuable than you'll ever be, buck-o.

BISHOP: Sir, there was a gust of wind from the hangar. I mean, ask Major Scott, our patrol leader. It could have happened to anyone.

HIGGINS: I was on the field, Bishop.

BISHOP: Yes, Sir.

HIGGINS: There was no wind.

BISHOP: No wind? Yes, Sir.

HIGGINS: I have your record here on my desk, Bishop, and it isn't a very impressive document. On the positive side, you were wounded. And you score well in target practice, although you have never actually fired upon the enemy. The list of your negative accomplishments is longer, isn't it, much longer? Conduct unbecoming an officer. Breaches of discipline. A lot of silly accidents, suspicious accidents, if I might say so. A trail of wrecked machinery in your wake. You are a terrible pilot, Bishop. In short, you are a liability to the RFC and I wish to God you were back in Canada where you belong, or failing that, digging a trench in some unstrategic valley. In short, you are finished, Bishop, finished. When your replacement arrives, he will replace you. That is all.

BISHOP: That was the lowest point of my career. Then came March 25, 1917.

The following is performed on microphone with BISHOP creating the sound effects. The PIANO PLAYER joins him. The mike should be used as a joy stick and the aggression implied in the story should be transferred to the microphone.

March 25, 1917. Four Nieuport scouts in diamond formation climb to nine thousand feet crossing the line somewhere between Arras and St. Léger. Our patrol is to crisscross the lines noting Heinie's positions and troop movements.

The sound of an airplane engine is heard.

Rrrrr. I'm the last man in that patrol, tough place to be, because if you fall too far behind, the headhunters are waiting for you. It starts out cloudy, then suddenly clears up. We fly for half an hour and don't see anything, just miles and miles of nothing. Rrrrr. Suddenly, I see four specks above and behind us. A perfect place for an enemy attack. I watch as the specks get larger. I can make out the black crosses on them. Huns! It's hard to believe that they are real, alive and hostile. I want to circle around and have a better look at them. Albatross "V" strutters, beautiful, with their swept back planes, powerful and quick. Rrrrr. We keep on flying straight. Jack Scott, our leader, either hasn't seen them or he wants them to think he hasn't seen them. They are getting closer and closer. We keep on flying straight. They are two hundred yards behind us, getting closer and closer. Suddenly, Rrrrr! Jack Scott opens out into a sharp climbing turn to get above and behind them. The rest of us follow. Rrrr! Rrrrr! Rrrrrr! I'm slower than the rest and come out about forty yards behind. In front of me, a dogfight is happening, right in front of my very eyes. Real pandemonium, planes turning every which way. Rrrrrr! Machine gun fire. Suddenly, Jack Scott sweeps below me with an Albatross on his tail raking his fuselage and wing tips with gunfire! For a moment, I'm just frozen there, not knowing what to do, my whole body just shaking! Then I throw the stick forward and dive on the Hun. I keep him in my Aldis sight 'til he completely fills the lens. Akakakak! What a feeling, as he flips over on his back and falls out of control! But wait, wait... Grid Caldwell warned me about this. He's not out of control, he's faking it. He's going to level out at two thousand feet and escape. Bastard! I dive after him with my engine full on. Sure enough, when he comes out of it, I'm right there Akakakaka! Again, my tracers smash into his engine. Gawd, I've got to be hitting him! He flips over on his back and is gone again. This time, I stay right with him. Eeeeeeeee! The wires on my machine howl in protest. Nieuports have had their wings come off at 150 miles per hour. I must be doing 180. I just don't give a shit! I keep firing into the tumbling Hun. Akakaka! He just crashes into the earth and explodes in flames. Baa-Whoosh! I pull back on the stick, level out, screaming at the top of my lungs, I win, I *win*, I *win*!

The sound of wind is heard – no engine, no nothing.

Jeezus, my engine's stopped! It must have filled with oil on the dive. I try every trick in the book to get it going again. Nothing. Oh God, I'm going to go in! Down, down.

The sound of gunfire is heard.

Gunfire! I must still be over Hunland. Just my luck to do something right and end up being taken a prisoner. Lower and lower. I pick out what seems to be a level patch in the rough terrain and I put her down.

The sound of a bouncing crash is heard.

I got out of the plane into what must have been a shell hole. I took my Very Lite pistol with me. I wasn't exactly sure what I was going to do with it.

TOMMY: (*in a "Canadian" accent*) Well you're just in time for a cup of tea, lad.

BISHOP: (*surprised*) Arrghgh... you spoke English! Hey, look, where am I?

TOMMY: You're at the corner of Portage and Main in downtown Winnipeg. You want to keep down, lad. Heinie is sitting right over there. Well, goll, that was a nice bit of flying you did there! Yep, you're a hundred yards our side of the line.

BISHOP: Oohhh, look... can you do me a favour? I'd like to try and get the plane up again.

TOMMY: Not tonight, lad, nope.... You're going to have to take the Montcalm Suite here at the Chateau.

BISHOP: I spent the night in the trench in six inches of water! The soldiers seemed to be able to sleep. I couldn't.

The sound of shelling gets progressively louder.

Next morning at first light, I crawled out to see how my plane was. Miraculously, it hadn't been hit. And that's when I got my first real look at "No Man's Land." Jeezus, what a mess! Hardly a tree left standing. And the smell! It was hard to believe you were still on earth. I saw a couple of Tommys sleeping in a trench nearby.

He goes over to the Tommys.

Hey, you guys, I wonder if you could give me a hand with...?

He takes a closer look. The Tommys aren't asleep. He backs off with a shudder.

The PIANO PLAYER sings and BISHOP joins him.

BISHOP & PIANO PLAYER: (*singing*)
Oh, the bloody earth is littered
With the fighters and the quitters.
Oh, what could be more bitter
Than a nameless death below.
See the trenches, long and winding,
See the battle slowly grinding,
Don't you wonder how good men can live so low.

Up above, the clouds are turning,
Up above, the sun is burning,
You can hear those soldiers yearning:
"Oh, if only I could fly!"
From the burning sun, I'll sight you,
In the burning sun, I'll fight you.
Oh, let us dance together in the sky.

(*Chorus*)

In the sky,
In the sky,
Just you and I up there together,
Who knows why?
One the hunter, one the hunted;
A life to live, a death confronted.
Oh, let us dance together in the sky.

And for you, the bell is ringing,
And for you, the bullets stinging.
My Lewis gun is singing:
"Oh, my friend, it's you or I."
And I'll watch your last returning
To the earth, the fires burning.
Look up and you will see me wave goodbye.

(*Chorus*)

In the sky,
In the sky,
Just you and I up there together,
Who knows why?
One the hunter, one the hunted;
A life to live, a death confronted.
Oh, let us dance together in the sky.

ACT TWO

The lights come up, as in Act One, with the PIANO PLAYER and BILLY BISHOP at the piano.

BISHOP & PIANO PLAYER: (*singing*)
Oh, the bold Aviator lay dying,
As 'neath the wreckage he lay (he lay),
To the sobbing mechanics beside him,
These last parting words he did say:

Two valves you'll find in my stomach,
Three sparkplugs are safe in my lung (my lung).
The prop is in splinters inside me,
To my fingers, the joystick has clung.

Then get you six brandies and soda,
And lay them all out in a row (a row),
And get you six other good airmen,
To drink to this pilot below.

Take the cylinders out of my kidneys,
The connecting rod out of my brain (my brain),
From the small of my back take the crankshaft,
And assemble the engines again!

The music changes to a theme reminiscent of a French café. Time has gone by and BISHOP has changed.

BISHOP: Survival. That's the important thing. And the only way to learn survival is to survive. Success depends on accuracy and surprise. How well you shoot, how you get into the fight and how well you fly. In *that* order. I can't fly worth shit compared to someone like Barker or Ball, but I don't care. If I get a kill, it's usually in the first few seconds of the fight. Any longer than that and you might as well get the hell out. You've got to be good enough to get him in the first few bursts, so practice your shooting as much as you can. After patrols, between patrols, on your day off. If I get a clear shot at a guy, he's dead. You ever heard of "flamers"? That's when you bounce a machine and it just bursts into flames. Now, I don't want to sound bloodthirsty or anything, but when that happens, it is very satisfying. But it's almost always pure luck. You hit a gas line or something like that. If you want the machine to go down every time, you aim for one thing: the man. I always go for the man.

The music stops. The PIANO PLAYER becomes a French announcer.

ANNOUNCER: Ladies and Gentlemen.... Madames et Messieurs.... Charlie's Bar, Amiens, proudly presents: The Lovely Hélène!

BISHOP: (*as the LOVELY HÉLÈNE, singing*)
Johnny was a Christian,
He was humble and humane.
His conscience was clear,
And his soul without a stain.
He was contemplating heaven,
When the wings fell off his plane.
And he never got out alive,
He didn't survive.

George was patriotic,
His country he adored.
He was the first to volunteer,
When his land took up the sword,
And a half a dozen medals
Were his posthumous reward.
And he never got out alive,
He didn't survive.

(*Chorus*)

So when you fight, stay as calm as the ocean,
And watch what's going on behind your shoulder.
Remember, war's not the place for deep emotion,
And maybe you'll get a little older.

(*as himself*) Come into a fight with an advantage: height, speed, surprise. Come at him out of the sun, he'll never see you. Get on his tail, his blind spot, so you can shoot him without too much risk to yourself. Generally, patrols don't watch behind them as much, so sneak up on the last man. He'll never know what hit him. Then you get out in the confusion. Hunt them. Like Hell's Handmaiden. If it's one on one, you come at the bugger, head on, guns blazing. He chickens out and you get him as he comes across your sights. If you both veer the same way, you're dead, so it's tricky. You have to keep your nerve.

(*as the LOVELY HÉLÈNE, singing*)
Geoffrey made a virtue
Out of cowardice and fear.
He was the first to go on sick leave,
And the last to volunteer.
He was running from a fight,
When they attacked him from the rear.
And he never got out alive, (no),
He didn't survive.

(*as himself*) Another thing is your mental attitude. It's not like the infantry where a bunch of guys work themselves up into a screaming rage and tear off over the top, yelling and waving their bayonets. It's not like that. You're part of a machine, so you have to stay very calm and cold. You and your machine work together to bring the other fellow down. You get so you don't feel anything after a while... until the moment you start firing, and then that old dry throat, heartthrobbing thrill comes back. It's a great feeling!

(*as the LOVELY HÉLÈNE, singing*)
Jimmy hated Germans
With a passion cold and deep.
He cursed them when he saw them,
He cursed them in his sleep.
He was cursing when his plane went down
And landed in a heap.
And he never got out alive, (no),
He didn't survive.

(*Chorus*)

So when you fight, stay as calm as the ocean,
And watch what's going on behind your shoulder.
Remember, war is not the place for deep emotion,
And maybe you'll get a little older.

(*as himself*) Bloody April? We lost just about everyone I started with. Knowles, Hall, Williams, Townsend, Chapman. Steadman, shot down the day he joined the squadron. You see, the Hun has better machines and some of their pilots are very good. But practice makes perfect, if you can stay alive long enough to practice. But it gets easier and easier to stay alive because hardly anyone else has the same experience as you. Oh yeah, another thing. You take your fun where you can find it.

The music and mood change.

He has noticed the Lovely Hélène. She has noticed him. They meet outside. Without a word, she signals him to follow. Silently, they walk down an alley, through an archway, and up a darkened stairway. They are in her room. He closes the door. He watches her light a candle. She turns to him and says: "I should not be doing this. My lover is a Colonel at the front. But you are so beautiful and so, so young." An hour later, they kiss in the darkened doorway. She says: "If you see me, you do not know me." She's gone. He meets his friends who have all enjoyed the same good luck. It's late, they've missed the last bus to the aerodrome. Arm in arm, they walk in the moonlight, silently sharing a flask of brandy, breathing in that warm spring air. As they approach Filescamp, they begin to sing, loudly: "Mademoiselle from Armentières, *parlez-vous*. Mademoiselle from Armentières, *parlez-vous*"... as if to leave behind the feelings they have had that night. In an hour, they will be on patrol. They go to bed. They sleep.

There is an abrupt change of mood. BISHOP is flying and shooting once again.

As if writing a letter.

Dearest Margaret. It is the merry month of May, and today, I sent another merry Hun to his merry death. I'm not sure you'd appreciate the bloodthirsty streak that has come over me in the past months. How I hate the Hun. He has killed so many of my friends. I enjoy killing him now. I go up as much as I can, even on my day off. My score is getting higher and higher because I like it. Yesterday, I had a narrow escape. A bullet came through the windshield and creased my helmet. But a miss is as good as a mile and if I am for it, I am for it. But I do not believe I am for it. My superiors are pleased. Not only have I been made Captain, they are recommending me for the Military Cross. Thinking of you constantly, I remain...

BISHOP & PIANO PLAYER: (*singing*)
You may think you've something special
That will get you through this war,
But the odds aren't in your favour,
That's a fact you can't ignore.
The chances are, the man will come
A-knocking at your door.
And you'll never get out alive,
And you won't survive.

(*Chorus*)

So when you fight, stay as calm as the ocean,
And watch what's going on behind your shoulder.
Remember, war's not the place for deep emotion,
And maybe you'll get a little older.

The music stops. There is a blackout.

BISHOP talks to ALBERT BALL.

BISHOP: Albert Ball, Britain's highest scoring pilot, sat before me. His black eyes gleamed at me, very pale, very intense. Back home, we would have said he had eyes like two pissholes in the snow. But that's not very romantic. And Albert Ball was romantic, if anybody was.

BALL: Compatriots in Glory! Oh, Bishop, I have an absolutely ripping idea. I want you to try and picture this. Two pilots cross the line in the dim, early dawn. It is dark, a slight fog. They fly straight for the German aerodrome at Douai, ghosts in the night. The Hun, unsuspecting, sleeps cosily in his lair. The sentries are sleeping. Perhaps the Baron von Richthofen himself is there, sleeping, dreaming of eagles and... wiener schnitzel. It is the moment of silence, just before dawn. Suddenly, he is awakened from his sleep by the sound of machine gun fire. He rushes to his window to see four, maybe five, of his best machines in flames. He watches as the frantic pilots try to take off and one by one are shot down. The two unknown raiders strike a devastating blow. Bishop, you and I are those two unknown raiders.

BISHOP: Jeez, I like it. It's a good plan. How do we get out?

BALL: Get out?

BISHOP: Yeah. Get out? You know, escape!

BALL: I don't think you get the picture, Bishop. It's a grand gesture. Getting out has nothing to do with it.

BISHOP: Oh! Well, it's a good plan. It's got a few holes I'd like to see plugged. I'd like to think about it.

BALL: All right, Bishop, you think about it. But remember this: Compatriots in Glory!

BISHOP: Quite a fellow.

He turns to the audience and announces.

"The Dying of Albert Ball"

The following is performed like a Robert Service poem.

He was only eighteen
When he downed his first machine,
And any chance of living through this war was small;
He was nineteen when I met him,
And I never will forget him,
The pilot by the name of Albert Ball.

No matter what the odds,
He left his fate up to the gods,
Laughing as the bullets brushed his skin.
Like a medieval knight,
He would charge into the fight
And trust that one more time his pluck would let him win.

So he courted the reaper,
Like the woman of his dreams,
And the reaper smiled each time he came to call;
But the British like their heroes
Cold and dead, or so it seems,
And their hero in the sky was Albert Ball.

But long after the fight,
Way into the night,
Cold thoughts, as dark as night, would fill his brain,
For bloodstains never fade,

And there are debts to be repaid
For the souls of all those men who died in vain.

So when the night was dark and deep,
And the men lay fast asleep,
An eerie sound would filter through the night.
It was a violin,
A sound as soft as skin.
Someone was playing in the dim moonlight.

There he stood, dark and thin,
And on his violin
Played a song that spoke of loneliness and pain.
It mourned his victories;
It mourned dead enemies
And friends that he would never see again.

Yes, he courted the reaper,
Like the woman of his dreams,
And the reaper smiled each time he came to call;
But the British like their heroes
Cold and dead, or so it seems,
And their hero in the sky was Albert Ball.

It's an ironic twist of fate
That brings a hero to the gate,
And Ball was no exception to that rule;
Fate puts out the spark
In a way as if to mark
The fine line between a hero and a fool.

Each time he crossed the line,
Albert Ball would check the time
By an old church clock reminding him of home.
The Huns came to know
The man who flew so low
On his way back to the aerodrome.

It was the sixth of May,
He'd done bloody well that day;
For the forty-fourth time, he'd won the game.
As he flew low to check the hour,
A hail of bullets from the tower—
And Albert Ball lay dying in the flames.

But through his clouded eyes,
Maybe he realized,
This was the moment he'd been waiting for.
For the moment that he died,

He was a hero, bonafide.
There are to be no living heroes in this war.

For when a country goes insane,
Obsessed with blood and pain,
Just to be alive is something of a sin.
A war's not satisfied
Until all the best have died,
And the devil take the man who saves his skin.

But sometimes late at night,
When the moon is cold and bright,
I sometimes think I hear that violin.
Death is waiting just outside,
And my eyes are open wide,
As I lie and wait for morning to begin.

Now I am courting the reaper,
Like the woman of my dreams,
And the reaper smiles each time I come to call;
But the British like their heroes
Cold and dead, or so it seems,
And my name will take the place of Albert Ball.

The PIANO PLAYER sings a sad song. BISHOP joins in.

BISHOP & PIANO PLAYER: (*singing*)
Look at the names on the statues
Everywhere you go.
Someone was killed
A long time ago.
I remember the faces;
I remember the time.
Those were the names of friends of mine.

The statues are old now
And they're fading fast.
Something big must have happened
Way in the past.
The names are so faded
You can hardly see,
But the faces are always young to me.

(*Chorus*)

Friends ain't s'posed to die
'Til they're old.
And friends ain't s'posed to die
In pain.
No one should die alone
When he is twenty-one,
And living shouldn't make you feel ashamed.

I can't believe
How young we were back then.
One thing's for sure,
We'll never be that young again.
We were daring young men,
With hearts of gold,
And most of us never got old.

In an abrupt change of mood, a loud pounding is heard. CEDRIC is knocking on BISHOP's door.

CEDRIC: Wakey, wakey, Bishop. Rise, man! Rise and shine!

BISHOP: (*hung over*) Ohhhh, Cedric. What's the idea of waking me up in the middle of the night?

CEDRIC: It's bloody well eleven o'clock and Madam has a bone to pick with you.

BISHOP: All right, all right, I'll be right there. (*pause*) Good morning, Granny.

LADY ST. HELIER: Bishop! Sit down. I have a bone to pick with you. Cedric, the colonial is under the weather. Bring tea and Epsom salts. Where were you last night, Bishop!

BISHOP: I was out.

LADY ST. HELIER: Good. Very specific. Well, I have my own sources and the picture that was painted for me is not fit for public viewing. Disgusting, unmannered and informal practices in company which is unworthy, even of you, Bishop. But what concerns me is not where you were, but where you were not. To wit, you were not at a party which I personally arranged, at which you were to meet Bonar Law, Chancellor of the Exchequer. What do you have to say in your defence?

BISHOP: Look, Granny...

LADY ST. HELIER: I'll thank you not to call me Granny. The quaintness quite turns my stomach.

BISHOP: Look, that was the fourth darn formal dinner this week! First, it's General Haigh, then what's-his-name, the Parliamentary Secretary... I want to have some fun!

LADY ST. HELIER: Bishop, I'm only going to say this once. It is not for you to be interested, amused or entertained. You are no longer a rather short Canadian with bad taste and a poor service record. You are a figurehead, unlikely as that may seem. A dignitary. The people of Canada, England, the Empire, indeed, the world, look to you as a symbol of victory and you will act the part. You will shine your shoes and press your trousers. You will refrain from spitting, swearing, gambling and public drunkenness, and you will, and I say this with emphasis, you will keep your appointments with your betters. Now, tonight you are having dinner with Lord Beaverbrook, and tomorrow night, with Attorney-General F.E. Smith. Need I say more?

BISHOP: No, no. I'll be there.

LADY ST. HELIER: Good. Oh, and Bishop, I had the occasion to pass the upstairs bathroom this morning and I took the liberty of inspecting your toilet kit. There is what I can only describe as moss growing on your hairbrush and your after-shave lotion has the odour of cat urine. I believe the implications are clear. (*addressing CEDRIC*) Cedric, a difficult road lies before us. Empire must rely for its defences upon an assemblage of Canadians, Australians and Blacks. And now, the Americans. Our way of life is in peril!

BISHOP: (*slightly drunk and writing a letter*) Dearest Margaret. I'm not sure I can get through this evening. In the next room is Princess Marie-Louise and four or five Lords and Ladies whose names I can't even remember. I drank a little bit too much champagne at supper tonight and told the Princess a lot of lies. Now I'm afraid to go back in there because I can't remember what the lies are and I'm afraid I'll contradict myself and look like an idiot. Being rich, you've got a lot more class than me. They'd like you. Maybe we ought to get married. Thinking of you constantly, I remain...

The PIANO PLAYER and BISHOP break into song.

BISHOP & PIANO PLAYER: (*singing*)
Breakfasting
With Queens and Kings,
Dining with Lords and Earls;
Drink champagne,
It flows like rain,
Making time with high class girls.
Just a Canadian boy,
England's pride and joy,
My fantasies fulfilled;
Ain't no one
Asks me where I'm from,
They're happy for the men I killed.

(*Chorus*)

Number One is a hero,
Number One's the hottest thing in town!
While I'm in my home
Away from home,
Nobody's gonna shoot me down.

I'm a hired gun,
Gonna shoot someone,
But England's gonna stand by me;
And if I die
You can't deny
They're gonna call it a tragedy.
I'm quaint company,
From the Colonies;
Their love is so sincere.
And when the war is done
And the battle won,
I've got friends as long as I stay here.

(*Chorus*)

Number One is a hero,
Number One's the hottest thing in town!
While I'm in my home
Away from home,
Nobody's gonna shoot me down.

The music changes to a more sinister note. The following story is half-told, half-acted out, the overall effect being of an adventure story being told in the present tense. It is done as a boy might tell a story, full of his own sound effects.

BISHOP: I woke up at three o'clock in the morning. Jeez, was I scared! Very tense, you know? I mean, Ball said you couldn't do it with just one guy and Ball was a maniac. But I figure it's no more dangerous than what we do every day, so what the hell. I mean, it's no worse. I don't think. The trouble is, no one has ever attacked a German aerodrome single-handedly before, so it's chancy, you know what I mean? I put my flying suit on over my pyjamas, grab a cup of tea and out I go. It's raining. Lousy weather for it, but what can you do? Walter Bourne, my mechanic, is the only other man up. He has the engine running and waiting for me.

BOURNE: Bloody stupid idea if you ask me, Sir. I would put thumbs down on the whole thing and go back to bed if I was you, Sir.

BISHOP: Thanks a lot, Walter. That's really encouraging.

BOURNE: It's pissing rain, Sir. Bleeding pity to die in the pissing rain. I can see it all now. Clear as crystal before me very eyes. First, Albert Ball snuffs it. Then, Captain Bishop snuffs it. It's a bleeding pity if you ask me, Sir. I mean, it's a balls-up from beginning to end. Why don't you take my advice and go back to bed like a good lad, Sir?

BISHOP: Why don't you shut up, Walter? Ready?

BOURNE: Ready, Sir!

The plane takes off.

BISHOP: God, it's awful up here! Pale grey light, cold, lonely as hell. My stomach's bothering me. Nerves? Naw, forgot to eat breakfast. Shit, just something else to put up with. Rrrrrrr. I climb to just inside the clouds as I go over the line. No trouble? Good. Everybody is asleep. Let's find that German aerodrome. Rrrrr. Where is it? Should be right around here. Rrrrrr. (*He spots something.*) All right, a quick pass, a few bursts inside those sheds, just to wake them up, and then pick them off one by one as they try to come up. Wait a minute, wait a minute. There's no planes. There's no people. The bloody place is deserted. Well, shit, that's that, isn't it? I mean, I can't shoot anyone if there is nobody here to shoot. Bloody stupid embarrassment, that's what it is. Rrrrr.

Feeling really miserable now, I cruise now looking for some troops to shoot them. Rrrrrr. Nobody! What the hell is going on around here? Is everybody on vacation? Suddenly, I see the sheds of another German aerodrome ahead and slightly to the left. Dandy. Trouble is, it's a little far behind the lines and I'm not exactly sure where I am. But, it's either that or go back. My stomach is really bothering me now. Why didn't I eat breakfast? And why didn't I change out of my pyjamas? That's going to be great, isn't it, if I'm taken prisoner, real dignified? Spend the rest of the bloody war in my bloody pyjamas. Rrrrrrrrr. Over the aerodrome at about three hundred feet. Jeezus, we got lots of planes here, lots and lots of planes. What have we got... six scouts and a two-seater? Jeez, I hope that two seater doesn't come up for me. I'll have a hell of a time getting him from the rear. It's a little late to think about it now. Rrrrrrrrr.

Machine gun fire opens up.

Akakakakakakak, Rrrrrrrrrrrr. Akakakakaka.

On the ground, GERMANS are heard yelling.

GERMANS: *Ach Himmel! In's Gelände! In's Gelände! Hier sind wir alle tot!*

BISHOP: I don't know how many guys I got on that first pass. A lot of guys went down; a lot of guys stayed down. I shot up a couple of their planes pretty bad.

The sound of ground fire is heard.

I forgot about the machine gun guarding the aerodrome, bullets all around me, tearing up the canvas on my machine. Just so long as they don't hit a wire. Keep dodging. Rrrrr. Rrrrrr. I can't get too far away or I'll never pick them off as they try to come up. Come on, you guys, come on! One of them is starting to taxi now. I come right down on the deck about fifteen feet behind him. Akakakakaka. He gets six feet off the ground, side slips, does this weird somersault and smashes into the end of the field. I put a few rounds into him and pull back on the stick. Rrrrrrrrr. I'm feeling great now. I don't feel scared, I don't feel nothing. Just ready to fight. Come on, you bastards, come on! Wait a minute, wait a minute. This is what Ball was worried about. Two of them are taking off in opposite directions at the same time. Now I feel scared. What do I do now? Get the hell out, that's what you do! One of them is close enough behind me to start firing. Where's the other one? Still on the ground. All right, you want to fight? We'll fight! I put it into a tight turn, he stays right with me, but not quite tight enough. As he comes in for his second firing pass, I evade him with a lateral loop, rudder down off the top and drop on his tail... Akakakakakakakakak... I hit the man. The plane goes down and crashes in flames on the field. Beautiful! The second man is closing with me. I have just enough time to put on my last drum of ammunition. I fly straight for him, the old chicken game. I use up all my ammunition... Akakakaka... I miss him, but he doesn't want to fight. Probably thinks I'm crazy. I got to get out of here. They will have telephoned every aerodrome in the area. There will be hundreds of planes after me. I climb and head for home. Rrrrrrrr. All by myself again, at last. Am I going the right way? Yeah. Jeezus, my stomach! Sharp pains, like I've been shot. Nope, no blood. Good, I haven't been shot, it's just all that excitement on an empty stomach. Being frightened. Jeez, I think I'm going to pass out. No, don't pass out! (*He looks up.*) And then I look up and my heart stops dead then and there. I'm not kidding. One thousand feet above me, six Albatross scouts, and me, with no ammunition. I think I'm going to puke. No, don't puke! Fly underneath them, maybe they won't see you. Rrrrrrr. I try to keep up.... For a mile, I fly underneath them, just trying to keep up. Rrrrrr. I got to get away. They're faster than me and if they see me, they got me. But I got to get away! I dive and head for the line... Rrrrrrrrr...! I can feel the bullets smashing into my back at any second, into my arms, into my legs, into my... (*He looks up again.*) Nothing! Jeez, they didn't see me. Rrrrrrr. Filescamp. Home. Just land it, take it easy. Rrrr. I land. Walter Bourne is waiting with a group of others.

BOURNE: I'm standing around, waiting for him to be phoned in missing, when there he comes. Like he's been out sightseeing. He lands with his usual skill, cracking both wheels, then comes to a halt, just like usual, except there is nothing left of his bloody machine. It's in pieces, bits of canvas flopping around like laundry in the breeze. Beats me how it stayed together. Captain Bishop sits there, quiet-like, then he turns to me and he says: "Walter," he says, "Walter, I did it. I *did it*! Never had so much fun in me whole life!"

BISHOP: That was the best fight I ever had. Everyone made a very big deal of it, but I just kept fighting all summer. My score kept getting higher and higher and I was feeling good. By the middle of August, I had forty-three, just one less than Albert Ball. And that's when the generals and colonels started treating me funny.

Going to war music is heard once again.

TRENCHARD: Bishop! Yes, we have lots of medals for you, eh? Lots and lots of medals. And that's not all, no, no, no. You will receive your medals, then you'll go on extended Canada leave and you won't fight again.

BISHOP: What did you say, Sir?

TRENCHARD: Do I have a speech impediment, Bishop? I said you won't fight again.

BISHOP: Not fight again? But I've got to fight again. I've got forty-three; Ball had forty-four. All I need is one more of those sons of...

TRENCHARD: Bishop! You have done very well. You will receive the Victoria Cross, the Distinguished Service Order, the Military Cross. No British pilot has done that, not even Albert Ball, God rest his soul. Leave it at that, Bishop. You have done England a great service. Thank you very much. Now you don't have to fight any more. I should think you'd be delighted.

BISHOP: You don't understand, Sir. I like it.

TRENCHARD: Oh, I know you like it. But it's becoming something of a problem. You see, you have become a colonial figurehead.

BISHOP: I know, a dignitary.

TRENCHARD: A colonial dignitary, Bishop. There is a difference. You see, Bishop, the problem with your colonial is that he has a morbid enthusiasm for life. You might call it a Life-Wish. Now, what happens when your colonial figurehead gets killed? I'll tell you what happens. Colonial morale plummets. Despair is in the air. Fatalism rears its ugly head. But a living colonial figurehead is a different cup of tea. The men are inspired. They say: "He did it and he lived. I can do it too." Do you get the picture, Bishop?

BISHOP: I believe I do, Sir.

TRENCHARD: Good lad. You shall leave Squadron Sixty, never to return, on the morning of August 17th. That is all.

BISHOP: Well, that still gives me a week. A lot can be done in a week.

To the audience.

In the next six days, I shot down five planes. I really was Number One now. And the squadron, they gave me a big piss-up on my last night. But something happened in that last week that made me fairly glad to get out of it for a while. It was number forty-six.

Music is heard.

It's dusk. Around eight o'clock. I'm returning to Filescamp pretty leisurely because I figure this is my last bit of flying for a bit. It's a nice clear evening and when it's clear up there in the evening, it's really very pretty. Suddenly, I see this German Aviatic two-seater heading right for me. It's a gift. I don't even have to think about this one. I put the plane down into a steep dive and come up underneath him and just rake his belly with bullets. Well, I don't know how they built those planes, but the whole thing just fell apart right before my very eyes. The wings came off, bits of the fuselage just collapsed, and the pilot and the gunner, they fall free. Now I'm pretty sure I didn't hit them, so they are alive and there is nothing I can do to help them or shoot them or anything. All I can do is just sit there and watch those two men fall, wide awake... to die! It's awful. I know I've killed lots of them, but this is different. I can watch them falling down, down. One minute, two minutes, three minutes. It's almost like I can feel them looking at me.

He stops for a moment, perplexed by unfamiliar qualms, shrugs and then goes on.

So when I leave for London the next day, I'm pretty glad to be going after all.

The scene changes to London.

LADY ST. HELIER: Bishop, today you will meet the King. This represents a high water mark for us all and you must see to it that you do not make a balls-up of it. I understand the King is particularly excited today. It seems this is his first opportunity of presenting three medals to the same gentleman. Furthermore, the King is amused that that gentleman is from the colonies. The King, therefore, may speak to you. Should you be so honoured, you will respond politely, in grammatically cogent phrases, with neither cloying sentimentality nor rude familiarity. You will speak to the King with dignity and restraint. Do you think you can manage that, Bishop? Is it possible that the safest course would be for you to keep your mouth shut?

Music is heard.

BISHOP: I arrived at Buckingham Palace, late. It is very confusing.

ADJUTANT: Excuse me, Sir, but where do you think you're going?

BISHOP: Oh, look, I'm supposed to get a medal or something around here.

ADJUTANT: Oh, you're way off, you are, Sir. This is His Majesty's personal reception area. You just about stumbled into the royal loo!!!

2ND OFFICER: What seems to be the trouble around here?

ADJUTANT: Good Lord! Well, the colonial here wants a medal, but his sense of direction seems to have failed him.

2ND OFFICER: Come along, Bishop. We've been looking all over for you. Now, the procedure is this: ten paces to the centre, turn, bow.

The music strikes up "Land of Hope and Glory."

It's started already, Bishop. You're just going to have to wing it!

The music continues as a processional. BISHOP enters stiffly into the presence of the King.

BISHOP: Here comes the King with his retinue, Order of St. Michael, Order of St. George, and here I am. The King pins three medals on my chest. Then he says...

The King's voice is booming, echoing. It is spoken by the PIANO PLAYER and mimed by BISHOP.

KING GEORGE: Well, Captain Bishop. You've been a busy bugger!

BISHOP: I'm not kidding. I'm standing here and the King is standing here. The King talks to me for fifteen minutes! I can't say a word. I've lost my voice. But after the investiture comes the parties, the balls, the photographers, the newspaper reporters, the Lords and Ladies, the champagne, the filet mignon and the fifty-year-old brandy. And here's me, Billy Bishop, from Owen Sound, Canada, and I know one thing: this is my day! There will never be a day like it! I think of this as we dance far into the night, as we dance to the music of... the Empire Soirée.

The PIANO PLAYER and BISHOP sing sotto and sinister.

BISHOP & PIANO PLAYER: (*singing*)
Civilizations come and go (don't you know),
Dancing on to oblivion (oblivion).
The birth and death of nations,
Of civilizations,
Can be viewed down the barrel of a gun.

Nobody knows who calls the tune (calls the tune),
It's been on the Hit Parade for many years (can't you hear).

You and I must join the chorus,
Like ancestors before us,
And like them, we're going to disappear.

(*Chorus*)

You're all invited to the Empire Soirée,
We'll see each other there, just wait and see;
Attendance is required at the Empire Soirée,
We'll all dance the dance of history.

Revolutions come and go (don't you know).
New empires will take the others' place (take their place).
The song may be fun,
But a new dance has begun,
When someone points a gun at someone's face.

Alexander and Julius had their dance (had their chance),
'Til somebody said: "May I cut in?" (with a grin).
All you and I can do,
Is put on our dancing shoes,
And wait for the next one to begin.

(*Chorus*)

You're all invited to the Empire Soirée,
We'll see each other there, just wait and see;
Attendance is required at the Empire Soirée,
We'll all dance the dance of history.

At the end of "The Empire Soirée," BISHOP does a little dance of victory for the audience, ending with a final salute.

Blackout.

A spotlight hits the PIANO PLAYER, who sings a narration summing up BISHOP's career and building to a reprise of "We Were Off to Fight the Hun." The song has a bitter edge now, for it is World War II we are talking about.

PIANO PLAYER: (*singing*)
Billy went back home again,
But still, he was not done;
Seventy-two planes did their dance,
To the rhythm of his guns.
And in twenty years, he was back again,
A new war to be won;
And the hero calls to new recruits in 1941.
The hero calls to new recruits in 1941.

And they were off to fight the Hun,
They would shoot him with a gun.
Their medals would shine,
Like a sabre in the sun.
They were off to fight the Hun
And it looked like lots of fun,
Somehow it didn't seem like war
At all, at all, at all.
Somehow it didn't seem like war at all.

The lights come up slowly on BISHOP. Twenty years have gone by and he is much older and very tired. He is wearing an astonishing array of medals and they seem to weigh him down a bit. BISHOP addresses the audience as though they were fresh World War II recruits. His voice has the tone and melody of war rhetoric.

The PIANO PLAYER plays "God Save the King."

BISHOP: I have seen you go and my heart is very proud. Once again, in the brief space of twenty years, our brave young men rush to the defence of the Mother Country. Once again, you must go forward with all the courage and vigour of youth to wrest mankind from the grip of the Iron Cross and the Swastika. Once again, on the edge of destiny, you must test your strength. I know you of old, I think. God speed you. God speed you, the Army, on feet and on wheels, a member of which I was for so many happy years of my life. God speed you the Air Force, where in the crucible of battle, I grew from youth to manhood. God speed you and God bless you. For, once again, the freedom of mankind rests in you: in the courage, the skill, the strength and the blood of our indomitable youth.

BISHOP's recruitment speech ends on a grand note. He stops and stares at the audience for a while with a certain amount of bewilderment. The PIANO PLAYER plays a haunting and discordant "In the Sky." BISHOP speaks, but this time it is quiet and personal.

You know, I pinned the wings on my own son this week. Margaret and I are very proud of him. And of our daughter. Three Bishops in uniform fighting the same war. Well, I guess I'm on the sidelines cheering them on. It comes as a bit of a surprise to me that there is another war on. We didn't think there was going to be another one back in 1918. Makes you wonder what it was all for? But then, we're not in control of any of these things, are we? And all in all I would have to say, it was a hell of a time!

BILLY BISHOP sings a cappella.

BISHOP: (*singing*)
Oh, the bloody earth is littered
With the fighters and the quitters.
You can hear the soldiers yearning:
"Oh, if only I could fly!"
From the burning sun, I'll sight you,
In the burning sun, I'll fight you,
Oh, let us dance together in the sky.

The PIANO PLAYER joins him in the chorus.

BISHOP & PIANO PLAYER: (*singing*)
In the sky,
In the sky,
Just you and I up there together,
Who knows why?
One the hunter, one the hunted;
A life to live, a death confronted.
Oh, let us dance together in the sky.

BISHOP: Goodnight ladies. Goodnight, gentlemen. Goodnight.

Blackout.

The end.

HORSEPLAY

BY

PETER ANDERSON
AND
PHIL SAVATH

174

l to r:
On Banjo: Sue Kyle;
On Guitar: Alan Bates

Jimmy Tait as Dodge, Peter Anderson as Ford, Steven Campbell Hill as Lincoln, Jan Kudelka as Chevy

Photographer:
Melody Anderson

COLLABORATION AND POPULISM: PETER ANDERSON AND PHIL SAVATH, CARAVAN FARM THEATRE, AND *HORSEPLAY*

An incident that occurred during *Horseplay*'s initial production provides a case study of the logistical challenges Caravan Stage Company experienced in its touring days. In May of 1981, twelve Clydesdales, eight wagons, six outriders, twenty-four actors and technicians, and several children began a sixteen-week tour of southern Ontario. Near St. Catherines, all four legs of Star, a fifteen-year old show horse, became stuck in a railway trestle. After over an hour and an unsuccessful attempt by firefighters to free the animal, a veterinarian sedated Star, a drydock worker cut through the timbers with a chain saw, and a twenty-ton mobile crane lifted the horse across the canal. Star, who had held up traffic on the Welland Canal for two hours, escaped serious injury, and the show went on to receive rave reviews from towns large and small. In several ways, Star's "real-life" drama mirrors Caravan's own history: chance, resilience, and, above all, the spirit of cooperation are prime ingredients in the unfolding narrative of an underdog who succeeds despite the odds.

Perhaps Peter Anderson's roots in car country account for the fact that several of his works, *Horseplay* included, examine the dark side of industrialization – and for the fact that, in a humorous reversal, the quintet of horses in *Horseplay* is named for automobiles. Born in Detroit, Michigan, in 1950, Anderson received post-secondary education that would prove most fitting for his career as playwright and actor: an Honors BA in Creative Writing from the University of Michigan and a year's study at the Blue Lake, California, Dell'Arte School of Physical Theatre. However, chance played a central role in both Anderson's career in theatre and his coming to Canada. It wasn't until his last year at the University of Michigan that he realized the appeal the vocation had for him: as he told Jon Kaplan, "I took a Grotowski acting class as a lark. It started to bring me out of myself; I got the classic acting bug. Writing and acting feed two different sides of me – the solitary and the social." While in California, he heard about Caravan Stage Company, hitchhiked to Armstrong, British Columbia, and got the part of train robber Bill Miner in the show *Hands Up!*.

Thus began a long association—of both the outlaw and the playwright—with Caravan Farm Theatre. Miner became an emblem for the company; even today, his portrait graces the threshold of one of the buildings that dots the farm's landscape, and the Bill Miner Society for Cultural Advancement owns and operates the farm. To date, Anderson has been involved in writing eleven Caravan productions – *The Coyotes* (1978); *Law of the Land* (1982); *Animal Farm* (1985), which he co-wrote with Caravan Farm theatre founder Nick Hutchinson; *Bull by the Horns* (1987); *The Shepherds' Play* (1989); *Creation* (1991) and *Passion* (1993), two parts of a three-part Mystery Cycle; *The Ballad of Weedy Peetstraw* (1999), co-written with John Millard; an adaptation of Dickens' *A Christmas Carol* (2000); *The Coyotes' Nativity* (2001); and, of course, *Horseplay*.

Anderson has spread his playwriting talents throughout the world. At Vancouver's Touchstone Theatre, he collaborated on the writing of *El Crocodor* (1986), which won a Jessie Award for outstanding original musical; wrote *Bones* (1988); and was part of a company of writers which garnered two Jessie Richardson awards for the highly successful *The Number 14*, which, following its initial run (in co-production with Axis Mime in 1992), has toured throughout Canada and the United States, and had runs in Hong Kong, Japan, and New York City. Following its debut at Vancouver's Arts Club Theatre, *Rattle in the Dash* (1987) has been produced in Edmonton, Toronto, Israel, and New Zealand. Kamloops' Western Canada Theatre Company was the site of *Nativity* (the second in the three-part Mystery Cycle), and Nanaimo's Malaspina Theatre produced his adaptation of *Lysistrata*. *Horseplay* is scheduled for production by the Yukon's Theatre Guild in 2002, and *Creation* has been remounted in Vancouver, Winnipeg and Australia. In addition, Anderson's monologues and short pieces have been staged by several companies in British Columbia and Alberta.

Although his acting credits in film and television are numerous (and include a film adaptation for CBC television of Morris Panych and Wendy Gorling's *The Overcoat*), it is in theatre that Anderson has concentrated his talents. Highlights of his stage career include Jessie nominations for best actor in John Lazarus' *Identical Islands* and Panych's *Necessary Steps* and *7 Stories*; Jessie awards for ensemble performance and creation for Panych's *The Imaginary Invalid*, *The Overcoat*, and *The Number 14*; and a Jessie award for best actor in Robert Morgan, Martha Ross, and Leah Cherniak's *The Anger in Ernest and Ernestine*. He has also worked with a team of fellow Vancouverites in collaboration with the troupe Legs on the Wall, of Sydney, Australia, to create *Flying Blind*, a physical theatre piece. The range of Anderson's roles is impressive, running the gamut from Aristophanes to contemporary children's plays, from Shakespeare to stand-up comedy.

Phil Savath shares with his collaborator American roots. Born in Brooklyn, New York, in 1946, he trained as an actor and dancer at Harpur College, graduated with honours in 1968, and worked as an actor in both New York City and Washington, DC. His work in Toronto theatre is extensive: Toronto Workshop productions, Studio Lab Theatre, Factory Lab, and Young People's Theatre are among the companies with which he has been associated, and his involvement with both Theatre Passe-Muraille (where he helped create *Doukhobors* and *Them Donnellys*) and Homemade Theatre (where he wrote, among others, *Ice Folly*) proved to be especially fitting preparation for his time with Caravan. The *Horseplay* tour found him in many of the same towns in which he had earlier acted, and, as he told Ray Conlogue in 1981, "I found Caravan attracted me because it's the only company in the country that does things on the same scale as Homemade Theatre used to." Savath, who had joined Caravan as an actor for the 1978 tour of *The Coyotes*, also wrote and directed *Golden Horseshoe* for the company.

Although he has written several radio plays, was the first president of the Vancouver Theatresports League, and has acted at Vancouver Playhouse, Stage 33, and City Stage, Savath has concentrated his efforts on film and television since the early 1980s. Film highlights include screenplays for "Big Meat Eater" and "The Outside Chance of Maximilian Glick" (both Genie Award nominees for best original screenplay) and David Cronenberg's "Fast Company." Savath's television writing and production credits include, for CBC, "Max Glick," "Homemade Television," "Little Criminals," "Liar, Liar," "These Arms of Mine," and "White Lies" (which garnered one International Emmy and six Gemini nominations); and, for Fox and Family Channel/Beta Taurus respectively, "Beverly Hills, 90210" and "African Skies."

Ratsoy: The original production happened almost twenty years ago. What stands out after all this time?

Savath: I remember more about the performing of the play than the actual writing of the play. The writing of the play was a very painless process. We did some things together and some things apart and shifted our papers back and forth. And then I think we did one workshop and then we read it out loud and then we did it. It didn't go through a long, tortured infancy as a play. There were whole sections that just sprang full-blown and never really changed that much. Other stuff, obviously, changed a lot.

Anderson: Phil and I had worked as both writers and actors in each other's projects up to that point. He had acted in *The Coyotes* and I had acted in *Ice Folly*, so I agree that our skills were very complementary. Phil's a better craftsman in terms of plot; it comes easier to him, while I love playing with language – lyrics, dialogue, etc. Because of our involvement with Caravan, the writing came naturally. It seemed like the play was waiting to be written for Caravan because it dealt with rural themes. It was something that was really close to the heart of what Caravan was all about.

Savath: We incorporated events and stories from the farm into the play, so it had a resonance for the group beyond what the audience could understand. The description of the birth or death of a horse, for example, might draw on an actual birth or death.

Anderson: Even the personalities of the horses in *Horseplay* are modelled somewhat on the personalities of the workhorses at Caravan. Ford was certainly modelled on Tom, a horse I took care of. Melody made the mask to look like him too – a bit of a clown.

Caravan Stage Company, founded in 1970 by Paul Kirby and Nans Kelder Kirby near Armstrong, had, by 1983, branched into two separate companies, the Caravan Stage Company (based in Ontario, this branch has further evolved into a sailing theatre which travels the eastern seaboard as Caravan StageBarge) and Caravan Farm Theatre, which stages itself in the beautiful outdoor setting of a 32-hectare farm northwest of Armstrong. Although Caravan Farm Theatre stopped travelling with its remarkable Clydesdales many years ago, it continued to adhere to many of the original tenets of the company: populist, collaborative, spontaneous, anti-establishment, even anarchical, the company often borrows on such traditions as commedia dell'arte, epic theatre, folk tales, myths, and legends, and incorporates various forms of twentieth-century music (including rock, bluegrass, and country) to produce art that appeals to an all-ages audience. The company has traditionally produced two shows annually – one in the summer and a second that (weather permitting) takes the audience by sleigh to different stages during the Christmas season. In the summer productions, large-cast musical comedy predominates, and, although original plays are favoured, classics by those such as Bertolt Brecht, with whom the company has an affinity, are sometimes adapted, but in each case natural landscape is an intrinsic element in the performance.

The result is at once popular and subversive, original and familiar. The title of Anderson's 1993 article on the company, "Breaking All Four Walls," emphasizes its revolutionary nature. Not only is the conventional fourth wall between actor and audience elided, but, as Anderson writes, "It is the removal of walls—whether between parts of one's self, fellow performers, actor and technician, actor and audience, or between human being and the natural world—that is at the heart of how and why the Caravan Farm Theatre works. A shared belief in our interconnectedness with the land and its inhabitants influences the form, content, and method of working"(8).

Ratsoy: Two of the most obvious differences between this play and the others in this collection are the facts that *Horseplay* was performed outdoors and was written for an all-ages audience. How do these factors influence the writing and performance aspects?

Savath: One of the things that is attractive about writing for Caravan is that it is huge. You are writing spectacle, and you are writing for a cast of twenty or thirty people, something you seldom get a chance to do anywhere else. Even though the play has a lot of verbal wit, it also has a lot of physical life. The plays have to be able to be played hugely to the outside without microphones and to audiences of five-year-olds to ninety-year-olds. So there has to be a broad, clowning element. You are trying to fill the play with as many attractive things as you can.

Anderson: All theatre should be entertaining, but the challenges to Caravan are really moment to moment: we are competing with everything from high winds to trucks going by on the highway. And that's where Caravan draws on the roots of circus and presentational forms of theatre. There's never been a fourth wall and live music has always been a part of the aesthetic of the show. The relation to the audience is always very open and theatrical. It drives me crazy when actors talk about being real and true and yet that doesn't include the reality of being an actor onstage performing for an audience. I love it when that is openly acknowledged and it is like a wink to the audience saying "I know I'm up here acting and I'm not really this person." It is existing on that dual level that I find really exciting in theatre.

Horseplay was both a critical and a popular success. Colleen Johnston praised "the superb acting company", and "the marvellous effects" of the "riotous, brilliantly-constructed, energetic, meaningful presentation", and Carole Corbeil was similarly effusive, deigning it "a delightful experience, visual, punchy, and buoyed by some spirited performances." As word spread in the small Ontario towns in which it toured, audience response reinforced critical opinion. The 1993 remounted production marked the official retirement of long-time Caravan artistic director Nick Hutchinson. *Horseplay* was an appropriate selection for Hutchinson's farewell; as he told Chris Dafoe, "In a sense, it's an autobiographical piece for the farm. When they wrote the play, Peter and Phil gathered all those stories and memories of working with the horses.... I think doing it again on the farm adds another dimension. The original production of *Horseplay* in 1981 marked the culmination of the first wave of Caravan. Now I guess we're looking at a third or maybe a fourth wave."

Ratsoy: Were you involved in the remount at all, Phil?

Savath: No. I was in the audience.

Anderson: I was there as a writer and in the role of Ford. The 1993 production was very similar. Nick Hutchinson, who directed both productions, was also instrumental in the vision and shaping of the original script.

Ratsoy: Is Nick still involved in theatre?

Anderson: He's semi-retired. He's farming next door to the Caravan. But he has been a teamster at the Christmas shows and will be directing the 2001 Christmas show, which I am writing.

Horseplay is certainly representative Caravan fare. Running the gamut from shameless puns and malapropisms to strong anti-establishment statements, the play simultaneously promotes and attenuates myths of the wild west and rural life in general. While it contains all of the ingredients of the American western—from sheriffs and deputies to, of course, horses—it uses the musical comedy to undermine and attack patriarchal and capitalistic institutions, rather than, as is traditional in the western, affirm the status quo. Humour is a subversive tool in much of Canadian literature—and, indeed, in several other plays in this collection—but nowhere is the subversive humour both more obvious and more subtle than in *Horseplay*. While, like most Caravan productions, it was a hit with children, the play is by no means froth. Amidst the broad physical comedy is a host of anti-authoritarian statements; societal ills such as sexism, ageism, and the bureaucratic mindset of capitalism are firmly attacked. The collaborative, anarchical philosophies behind Caravan Farm Theatre were put into practice not only in the process of the play's construction, but also in the thought and action of the work. Nothing less than an overthrow of the system is enacted – an overthrow that is accomplished, significantly, not by a single hero or heroine, but through group effort.

Proof positive that populist theatre can also be literate theatre, *Horseplay*, amidst the farce, includes references to, among others, Karl Marx, George Orwell, the Bible, Ernest Hemingway, and fellow Canadian theatre revolutionary Rick Salutin. In fact, Cora's statement, "I guess they're afraid this is going to turn into some kind of farmers' revolt" functions as a homage to Salutin's *1837: The Farmers' Revolt*, an examination of the Rebellion of 1837 in Upper Canada from the point of view of the workers. The theatre companies which produced the two works (in the case of *1837*, Theatre Passe Muraille) were also rebels who championed the populist – not only in their scripts, but also in the process of script production and the audiences they targetted.

Horseplay is especially powerful in its evocation, through song, dialogue, and exposition, of the noble history of horses. Allusions to the winged Pegasus, who, in Greek mythology, created the fountain of the Muses with the stomp of a hoof (and has thus become associated with poetic inspiration) and assisted Bellerophon in fighting various enemies (including the previously indomitable Chimera) heighten the pathos around the predicament of Rambler, Chevy, Lincoln, Dodge, and Ford, as do reminders of such events as Paul Revere's ride and the charge of the light brigade. The richness of the horse's role in myth and legend is juxtaposed with the stark, unimaginative place these twentieth-century horses occupy in the contemporary mindset.

Ratsoy: Melody Anderson's masks were certainly an important element in the theatricality of the play.

Savath: They were a huge element.

Anderson: There are some great anecdotes about those masks. When we first put them on and went into the fields with the real horses, they were spooked. We had stampedes going. I guess they looked real to the horses; they were seeing horses on two legs.

Savath: But by the time we went on tour we would stand by the horses and they were completely still. They got used to the masks.

That *Horseplay* champions the marginalized—women, the elderly, the agrarian, and animals—is fitting from a theatre company in the Interior of Canada's west coast province, a theatre located on the outskirts of a town of a few thousand people. That Caravan Farm Theatre has, from its multi-marginalized position, managed to not only survive but also thrive is a testament to the company's ability to rise to self-imposed challenges, to sustain a philosophy of cooperation, and to be unwavering in its commitment to its unconventional audience. Peter Anderson and Phil Savath's *Horseplay* epitomizes the company where it was born.

G.R.

Selected Bibliography:

- Anderson, Peter. "Breaking All Four Walls: Open Air Theatre at the Caravan Farm." *Canadian Theatre Review* 76 (Fall 1993): 8-12.
- Anderson, Peter. Personal Interview. 8 Nov. 2000.
- Anderson, Peter. "Theatre in the Rough: Play Of The Land." *Vancouver Sun* 21 Aug.1999.
- Bott, Robert. "The Roar of the Greasepaint, The Smell Of The Clydes." *Quest* (May 1981): 40B-42. Provides substantial background to the *Horseplay* tour.
- Brennan, Pat. "Horse Slips Off Beaten Track." *The Toronto Star* 3 June 1981.
- Conlogue, Ray. "Modern Gypsies Put On Quite A Show." *Globe and Mail* 20 July 1981.
- Corbeil, Carole. "Horseplay Full of High Spirits." *Globe and Mail* 7 Sept. 1981.
- Crook, Barbara. "Horseplay Down on the Farm." *Vancouver Sun* 21 July 1993.
- Dafoe, Chris. "Theatre's Mane Man Steps Down." *Globe and Mail* 28 July 1993.
- Hess, Henry. "Horseplay Is Too Good to Miss." *Listowel Banner* 29 July 1981.
- Hodgson, Liz. "Peter Anderson: He Suffers So That We May Laugh." *Vancouver Sun* 29 Jan. 1999.
- Hood, Sarah. "The Mystery Cycle." *Performing Arts* (June 1991): 28-29.
- "Horse Drawn Magic". Dir. Dorothy Todd Henaut. National Film Board of Canada, 1979. Provides a striking visual history of Caravan Theatre.

•Johnston, Colleen. "*Horseplay* is Subtle With Kick." *Stratford Beacon Herald* 10 July 1981.
•Kaplan, Jon. "Memories of Auto Factories Drive Autobiographical Play." *Now* 21-27 Apr. 1988. Interviews Anderson about *Rattle in the Dash*.
•Kirkley, Richard Bruce. "Caravan Farm Theatre: Orchestrated Anarchy And The Creative Process." *Canadian Theatre Review* 101 (Winter, 2000): 35-39. Based on interviews with Anderson, Hutchinson, former publicist Ken Smedley, and current co-artistic director Estelle Shook, the article provides a thorough overview of the company's philosophy.
•Mallet, Gina. "Kids Will Love *Horseplay*'s Musical Fun." *The Toronto Star* 11 Sept. 1981.
•Savath, Phil. Interview. 8 Nov. 2000.

Horseplay
by Peter Anderson and Phil Savath

Horseplay was first produced by the Caravan Stage Company in Armstrong, B.C., on May 9, 1981, with the following cast:

Rambler	Dugald Nasmith
Chevy	Suzanne Morgan
Lincoln	Ross Imrie
Dodge	Phil Savath
Ford	Peter Anderson
Grandma Mulvaney	Sandy Nichols
Madge	Nans Kelder Kirby
Ted	Philip Kuntz
Linda	Judi Young
Sheriff Lutz	David Balser
Cora Lutz	Ida Burrows
Deputy Hack	Jim Meers
Elmer Frankenmuth	Paul Kirby
Orville Frankenmuth	Esther Shatz
Mel Twiggs	Brad Francis
Trucker	Catherine Hahn
Nurse	Derek Hawksley
The Agent	Dugald Nasmith

Directed by Nick Hutchinson
Assistant Directed by Annie Skinner
Designed by Catherine Hahn, Molly March
Masks by Melody Anderson
Lighting Designed by Frank Masi
Stage Managed by Maureen Mackintosh
Music by Derek Hawksley, Bernie Jaffe, David Balser, Peter Anderson
Band: Derek Hawksley, Bernie Jaffe,
  David Harris, Brad Francis,
  David Balser, Philip Kuntz

CHARACTERS

RAMBLER, a Clydesdale stud
CHEVY, a Clydesdale mare
LINCOLN, a Clydesdale has-been stud
DODGE, a proud-cut Clydesdale
FORD, a Clydesdale gelding
GRANDMA MULVANEY
MADGE WILLIS, her daughter
TED WILLIS, Madge's husband
LINDA WILLIS, Madge and Ted's daughter
SHERIFF VERNON LUTZ
DEPUTY WALDO HACK
CORA LUTZ, Sheriff's wife
ELMER FRANKENMUTH, a meatpacker
ORVILLE FRANKENMUTH, his son
MEL TWIGGS, gas station owner
FEMALE TRUCKER
MALE NURSE
SECRET AGENT
CITIZENS

SETTING

A farm near Noburg.

ACT ONE

A farmyard. Four old HORSES are standing in a field next to a rundown farm. ORVILLE drives by on the highway. GRANDMA enters on the run, shaking her fist at the passing car.

GRANDMA: Slow down! God-forsaken hot-rod!

GRANDMA mutters as she grabs a bale of hay for the horses. MADGE enters.

MADGE: Mother, what are you doing? It's time for your nap.

GRANDMA: I've got to feed the horses.

MADGE: You can't feed the horses. Your heart.

GRANDMA: If I don't do it, no one else will.

MADGE: (*grabs the bale of hay*) That's garbage and you know it!

GRANDMA: Let go of this bale!

MADGE: (*yelling off*) Ted! She's at it again!

GRANDMA: I wouldn't have to do all the chores around here if you hadn't married that useless twit.

MADGE: You don't do all the chores.

GRANDMA: You do your share, what about him? Sits on his butt drinking whiskey all day long.

MADGE: Oh, come on, you know he's trying to quit.

GRANDMA: Only thing he's done since you moved here's sell half the farm for a song and dance.

MADGE: They were going to put that highway in one way or the other.

GRANDMA: Well, I didn't ask you to come here when your father died. I can look after myself.

MADGE: You can not.

GRANDMA: Can too.

MADGE: I'm not going to argue with you.

GRANDMA: Because you'll lose. When I go it'll be on my own two feet, not lying on my back in some bed feeling sorry for myself.

MADGE: There. All the hay is out. Will you please come in the house now?

GRANDMA stops, in pain.

What is it this time... your hip?

GRANDMA: No, as a matter of fact I just had a heart attack.

MADGE exits, GRANDMA calls the horses.

Graintime! Come on! Graintime!

GRANDMA exits. HORSES sniff and paw the hay.

FORD: That ain't grain, it's hay.

DODGE: Not only that, it's bad hay.

CHEVY: We haven't had grain in seven years.

DODGE: Look at the mould on this stuff.

LINCOLN: This is worse than last night.

CHEVY: If Henry was alive they wouldn't treat us like this.

FORD: In the old days we got some respect.

DODGE: Now look at us. I'm skin and bones.

LINCOLN: It's been what... ten years since this place has been farmed.

CHEVY: That's ten years since we've been in harness.

FORD: Now there's weeds where there used to be corn.

DODGE: Dust where there was clover.

LINCOLN: Stones where there was alfalfa.

CHEVY: And over there, where the tastiest carrots in this valley used to grow, there's a highway.

FORD: And we're supposed to live on this rotten hay! Us! Noble Clydesdales! Gentle Giants who foundered a nation hobbled to the confirmation that all men are created equine... (*sees audience, stops*)

DODGE: What'd you stop for?

FORD: There's a whole herd of people out there! Ahem. Hello. My name is Ford. Even though I'm a gelding, what I lack down north I make up for up south between my ears...

DODGE: (*bucking FORD out of the way*) Get out of here. Ford likes to chew the leather, but when it comes to work, call on Dodge. That's me. Solid muscle and a mouth that bites the bit with a bite that can't be beat.

LINCOLN: Beat it, ya stupid gelding!

DODGE: Just a minute, I was proud-cut. I still got one...

LINCOLN: One what?

DODGE: Uh, never mind. (*slinks off*)

LINCOLN: My name's Lincoln and I'm a stud!

CHEVY: I guess I'll have to take your word for it.

LINCOLN: Shut up, Chevy. I'm a stud!

CHEVY: Put your money where your mouth is.

LINCOLN: (*backing down*) I am a stud! Really! Honest! Sort of... (*slinks away*)

CHEVY: Honey, let me tell ya something: behind every stallion there's a mare. All these geldings and has-been studs would like you to think they run the show, but don't you buy it for a second. I've got them wrapped around my little hoof.

RAMBLER enters.

RAMBLER: (*shouting*) Out of my way you cry-baby, sway-backed, lame-brained, thrush-foot, good-for-nothing plugs! Where's my dinner?

FORD: Here.

DODGE: Here.

LINCOLN: Here.

RAMBLER: (*shouting*) This hay stinks.

CHEVY: Rambler, honey, scratch my back.

RAMBLER: Uh... sure thing, baby. (*scratches her back*)

CHEVY: I had fun last night.

RAMBLER: (*to other horses*) What're you staring at?

They all turn away.

FORD: (*to audience*) That's Rambler. He's the number one prize stud...

DODGE: The meanest...

LINCOLN: The toughest...

FORD: The fastest...

DODGE: The strongest...

LINCOLN: The biggest....

CHEVY: The best!

RAMBLER: Shut up! There's only one thing you, or them, gotta know.

DODGE: (*gulping*) Uh, what's that?

RAMBLER: I'm a workhorse! Hit it, boys!

RAMBLER and HORSES sing.

THE WORKHORSE SONG

Millions of years before man and his wars,
When earth was ruled by the dinosaurs,
All the wild horses sprang from one seed,
Were fruitful and multiplied into thousands of breeds.

Four legs, a tail but we ain't all the same,
Man came along and soon we were tamed,
Our social place determined by birth,
Some dine on the finest and some work the earth.

I'm a workhorse, baby, I got sweat on my brow,
Never find no show horse pullin' no plough,
Don't play no polo, go to no racetrack,
My style ain't dainty, got a big, broad back.

I eat my oats, I scratch my itch,
Don't carry no queens, ain't no friend of the rich,
Don't hunt no fox, ain't built for pleasure,
Don't prance fancy, ain't no horse of leisure.

Rich horse finds his treatment unfair,
Curls his lips, sticks his nose in the air,
We don't horse around with no uppity tricks,
Our solution is a good swift kick.

I'm a workhorse, baby, I got sweat on my brow,
Never find no show horse pullin' no plough,

Workhorse poor while the rich eat hay,
Poor horse work while the rich horse play.

Dance break.

I'm a workhorse, baby, I got sweat on my brow,
Never find no show horse pullin' no plough,
We don't horse around with no uppity tricks,
Our solution is a good swift kick!

On last beat of song, RAMBLER kicks the fence and knocks it down.

CHEVY: You better get away from there.

RAMBLER: I've had it with this place and its rotten hay. I'm bustin' out. Who's coming with me?

DODGE: Maybe the hay's rotten, but at least it's hay.

FORD: You know what they say, "a bale under hoof is better than two in the barn."

CHEVY: Who'd take care of us out there? We're safe here.

RAMBLER: Safe? Safe for what? A bad case of heaves? Lincoln, what about you?

LINCOLN: You won't catch me crossing that highway. It's too dangerous.

RAMBLER: Herds of a feather stuck in their tethers. Stay here then! Get sold to the meatpackers! See if I care! (*exits*)

FORD: Maybe he's got a point.

ORVILLE drives by.

CHEVY: Rambler, look out!

The sound of ORVILLE's car hitting RAMBLER offstage. The HORSES spook. LINDA enters, looks down the highway.

LINDA: Mom, Dad! Quick! It's Rambler! He's been hit!

TED and MADGE enter, followed by GRANDMA.

MADGE: Oh, my god!

TED: Where's the other horses?

GRANDMA: I got 'em.

MADGE: Mother, get in the house.

GRANDMA: You get in the house!

MADGE: Your heart!

GRANDMA: Nothing wrong with my heart!

TED: What happened! How'd he get out?

LINDA: I don't know.

MADGE: The gate's down.

The teen-aged ORVILLE enters, drunk.

ORVILLE: I'm sorry, please don't call the police, my dad'll kill me if he finds out, please, I'm really really sorry, I'll replace the horse, anything, I didn't mean to...

LINDA: You killed him!

TED: Linda!

ORVILLE: I didn't see him, I swear I didn't! Please, I'll pay you back!

TED: Calm down, son. It wasn't your fault.

LINDA: Maybe it was. Maybe he was speeding.

TED: Linda, that's enough.

MADGE: (*to ORVILLE*) Better come inside and I'll make you some coffee.

SHERIFF LUTZ enters.

SHERIFF LUTZ: Okay, what's the story here?

TED: Hello, Sheriff.

SHERIFF LUTZ: How'd he get out?

LINDA: He was speeding!

SHERIFF LUTZ: The horse was speeding?

LINDA: No, him!

TED: Linda, get in the house.

LINDA: But he killed Rambler.

TED: In the house, Linda!

MADGE: Linda, mind your father. (*LINDA exits in disgust.*) Apparently he broke down the fence.

SHERIFF LUTZ: Who? Him? (*indicating ORVILLE*)

TED: No, the horse.

SHERIFF LUTZ: (*to ORVILLE*) You the driver, son?

ORVILLE: Yes, sir.

SHERIFF LUTZ: How fast were you going?

ORVILLE: Speed limit, sir.

SHERIFF LUTZ: Speed limit, eh? And you didn't see the horse?

ORVILLE: No, sir. He ran into me. I didn't have time to stop.

SHERIFF LUTZ: You had anything to drink, boy?

ORVILLE: No, sir.

SHERIFF LUTZ: Aren't you Elmer Frankenmuth's boy?

ORVILLE: Yes, sir.

SHERIFF LUTZ: Can I see your license? (*ORVILLE hands him his license.*) All right, Orville. I'm letting you go with a warning. Next time drive more carefully. Now get out of here. (*SHERIFF returns license and ORVILLE exits.*)

GRANDMA: Wait just a minute. That kid was so drunk he couldn't hit the ground with his hat in three tries.

SHERIFF LUTZ: No, you wait a minute. For the past ten years I've had nothing but trouble from you and your horses, Mrs. Mulvaney. I've got a whole filing cabinet full of complaints down at the office. Property damage, disturbing the peace, trespassing. You're lucky those horses have lasted as long as they have without getting shot.

TED: It won't happen again. (*to GRANDMA*) Isn't that right?

SHERIFF LUTZ: You just keep those horses where they belong. On your property.

GRANDMA: That highway used to be our property 'til the government stole it.

SHERIFF LUTZ: Willis. (*taking TED aside*) She needs medical help.

TED: I know. Soon as we can scrape the money together we're going to get someone to look after her.

SHERIFF LUTZ: You need money, Willis? Take my advice. Sell those horses.

TED: Who'd want them? They can't work. They're no good to anybody.

SHERIFF LUTZ: There's a big market for horsemeat these days. Europeans, Japanese, buying it up like crazy. In fact, a fresh road kill, no disease, I'll wager Elmer Frankenmuth'd pay a pretty penny for that big fella out there. Why don't you give him a call?

TED: Thanks, I will.

SHERIFF LUTZ: (*to everyone*) Any more trouble you folks let me know. (*exits*)

GRANDMA: I oughta tie his ears in a knot. And you, buzzard-bait, you sell those horses and I'll punch a hole in your yellow belly big enough to drive a wagon through, understand?

TED: (*sarcastically*) I understand, Mother Mulvaney. (*GRANDMA exits. TED turns to MADGE.*) She's getting worse.

MADGE: Come on, Ted. We'll call Elmer and tell him to pick up Rambler.

TED: What do you suppose the price for a horse that size is?

MADGE: Too little no doubt.

TED: Maybe we should sell the horses...

MADGE: No. It would break mother's heart.

TED: Yeah. Well. It was just a thought.

TED and MADGE exit. HORSES enter in a funeral procession, carrying flowers, RAMBLER's collar bedecked with roses. CHEVY wears a widow's veil.

LINCOLN: I think one of us should say a few words. Ford?

FORD: No, I wouldn't know what to say.

DODGE: Go ahead, Ford.

FORD: Well, all right. Dearly bereaved, it behooves me to say Rambler has gone four feet up, six feet under, but not in defeat, not in de feet dat have taken dere last shod at de unfair farriers who were never man enough to fill his shoes nor shoe his foals. No, not of de feet I speak, but of de parts de departed played in our lives, no part sadder than his departing, when, having exhausted all avenues of escape, he took the highway and the highway took him. Pass with care, Rambler. You who yearned for greener grass have found it. But the grass is not in you, you are in the grass. And that ain't hay. Hey, hey, new-mown hay, but do not moan nor look so baleful my friends. Let us not furrow our brows crooked like the furrows he ploughed, but rather remember Rambler's favourite yoke: a horse's ass stands on only two legs. In closing, let me add, if those pearly gates do not swing open for Rambler, we can rest assured he'll kick the hell out of them until they do. Amen. A-horse. A-hoof.

ALL: Gesundheit.

HORSES circle solemnly as LINDA and GRANDMA enter.

LINDA: Look at 'em, Grandma. What are they doing?

GRANDMA: Saying goodbye to Rambler.

LINDA: They're not the only ones miss him. Right, Chevy? Good girl.

LINDA pats the HORSES. GRANDMA sings, joined by LINDA and HORSES.

NEW-BORN FILLY

New-born filly
Trembling in the sun,
Listen and hear
What your fathers have done,
How they took their place
In the world of men,
Were beaten down
And rose up again.

Under the weight
Of iron knights,
Copper coats
Flecked with white,
Under the weight
Of iron knights,
Horse met horse
And never took flight
And with foaming mouths
They fought men's wars,
Feathers soaked
On the bloody moors,
Bruised their hooves
On the fallen shields,
Breathed the stench
Of steaming fields
Till the blade of a sword
Bit deep and hot,
They died in the battles
That foolish men fought.

Now sons of these horses
Drink from the well
Working for new men
Where their fathers fell,
New farms planted

On war's remains,
Watered with blood
and summer rain.
Moving the stones
Over ghosts of knights,
Ploughing the earth,
Clearing the sites,
Their copper coats
And their tangled manes
Caked with salt,
They harvest the grain
To their knees in mud,
Shining with sweat,
Working for farmers
To their necks in debt,
Until new soldiers come
And burn down the barns,
Leaving horses for dead
In the ashes of farms.

New-born filly
Standing in the sun,
I tremble to think
Of your life to come,
Though you won't understand
The world of men,
When beaten down
You must rise again.

GRANDMA: Goodbye, Rambler.

LINDA: Look. Dodge has a cut.

GRANDMA: Where?

LINDA: There.

GRANDMA: That's no cut. That's where his wings are comin' in.

LINDA: Grandma.

GRANDMA: That's what your grandpa always said. "My horses don't have collar-sores. That's where their wings are coming in." He'd swear on a stack of bibles with the straightest face you ever saw that the first horses ever was were flying horses. Nowadays, he'd say, when a horse gets ready to leave this world he grows some wings like his ancestors so he can fly away.

LINDA: Once I asked Grandpa where the horses went when they flew away.

GRANDMA: What'd he say?

LINDA: Some get a job pulling the dreams through your head at night, but the stronger horses go to work pulling the sun across the sky.

GRANDMA: You think Rambler's pulling the sun right now?

LINDA: Only one horse I know could cause a sunset like that.

GRANDMA: He was a lot of horse all right. But you know what the biggest part of him was? His heart. I remember the day he pulled Henry's tractor out of the mud. It was sunk in hip-deep. I said, "Henry, he'll never do it." Henry hitched him up anyway. Didn't have to yell or scream or swat him with a switch like the other horses. Just a whisper "Rambler" and that horse hit those traces head down low, feet pumping, sweat pouring, muscles popping, straining with every bone in his body. If he didn't move that tractor, he was going to die trying. I said, "Henry, you're killing him," and Henry gave me one of his looks could burn the skin off your behind so I shut up and sure enough that tractor started rockin' little by little until with this big, loud sucking sound and a *pop* he pulled it clean out of the mud. I had tears in my eyes I was so proud of that horse. Henry just spit, looked at Rambler and said, "Dinna ken what took him so long. Too many mares must be wearing him out." (*snapping out of her reverie*) And look what we're left with. Sorriest lot of workhorses in all creation. Maybe Rambler had the right idea breaking out like he did. What have we got to look forward to? Send you to the hospital and me to the glue factory. Look at those feet. How do you expect to do any work in your condition? Gimme your foot, Chevy. Good girl. Like Henry always said... (*CHEVY steps on GRANDMA's foot.*) Chevy! Get off my foot! Chevy. Get. Off. My. Foot.

LINDA: (*pushes CHEVY off GRANDMA's foot*) Grandma? You all right?

GRANDMA: Of course I'm all right. Should've paid more attention to what I was doing. Linda, I want you to fix that fence. I'm going in the barn and get the harness.

LINDA: The harness?

GRANDMA: That's right, the harness. You gettin' hard of hearing in your old age? These are workhorses, aren't they? I think it's high time they went back to work. (*exits*)

LINDA chops wood for repairing fence. TED enters. LINDA ignores him as she works on fence.

TED: Linda? What are you doing? Put that axe down. You haven't seen Mr. Frankenmuth, have you? Linda, listen to me. It was an accident. There's nothing we can do about it. Rambler was old. And when you're old... I mean, when your time comes, it comes. Maybe he's happier now. He's not hurting. Like the other horses. It's almost cruel to keep them like we do. We can't afford to feed them proper. They can't work any more. Lincoln and Chevy are too old to foal. Linda, I know this sounds hard, but they're a luxury we can't afford any more. I know they mean a lot to you. They mean a lot to me, too. I love those animals as much as anybody. More. But they're old and in pain. If I—if we—sold them to... someone... we could take the money and when things got better, buy some real horses.

LINDA: I don't want a real horse, I want Rambler. (*exits*)

TED: Linda, Rambler's dead. Linda!

ELMER Frankenmuth enters.

ELMER: Some business, eh, Willis? My kid knocks 'em down and I pick 'em up. (*laughs*)

TED: Hello, Elmer.

ELMER: Don't worry, everything's all taken care of. Here's your cheque. How about some vitamins? (*offering TED a drink of scotch*)

TED: No, thanks.

ELMER: So. What about these other horses?

HORSES listen intently.

TED: They're not for sale.

ELMER: Shame. Good healthy horses like that. Fetch a nice price at the auction.

TED: Not that healthy.

HORSES cough melodramatically.

ELMER: Guess they're pretty useful to you.

TED: No use to me. No use to anyone since old Henry died.

ELMER: Sentimental value, eh?

TED: The old lady.

ELMER: I hear she's not, you know... sharp.

TED: She confuses things once in a while.

ELMER: Sheriff tells me she drove her car down the sidewalk of Main Street for three blocks.

TED: She got the brake and gas mixed up.

ELMER: Willis, with the money you could get from those horses you could afford to take care of her. Some nice photographs in a book and she can remember those horses all she wants.

TED: If I was to sell them what would they be worth?

ELMER: Twenty-five hundred dollars.

TED: I'd have to talk it over with Madge.

ELMER: This is a man's business, Willis. Women don't understand money. They're too emotional. Three thousand.

TED: I hear there's a big demand for horsemeat in Japan.

ELMER: Willis, I know it's been hard for you since the plant laid you off, so I'll make you a deal. Thirty-two fifty.

TED: Sixty-five hundred dollars.

ELMER: Sixty-five hundred? They're nothing but skin and bones. Their ribs are showing. Thirty-five hundred.

TED: Dodge there's got a lot of meat on his bones. One stud, one mare, two geldings. Five thousand.

ELMER: That stud hasn't been on a mare in ten years. Thirty-seven fifty. Final offer. Take it or leave it.

TED: Four.

ELMER: Highway robbery, Willis.

TED: Four thousand.

ELMER: It's a deal. I like doing business with a man who's his own boss. (*pulls out contract*)

TED: (*signing contract*) I'll, uh, need some time to break it to my family.

ELMER: What for? Get it over with quick. It's better that way. I'll go home, get my truck, be right back and get 'em. Before I go, Willis, my boy wants to say something. Orville! Get your carcass in here! (*ORVILLE enters.*) Go on.

ORVILLE: I'm sorry, sir. Here. (*hands TED a package of meat*)

ELMER: Don't worry, it's hamburger. Free. Kind of like a rebate. No, don't thank me. (*to ORVILLE*) You go back to the car. (*ORVILLE exits.*) Kids. No respect for property. The trouble is no one teaches them the old values anymore. Right, Willis?

TED: Right.

ELMER: So. Business is over, *now* let's have some vitamins. (*ELMER takes a healthy swig, hands bottle to TED, who does not drink.*) What's this one's name?

TED: Ford.

ELMER: Well, Ford. I've got a better idea for you. Pretty soon you're gonna be a Toyota. Ha ha ha! See you in an hour or so, Willis. (*exits*)

TED: (*to himself, holding bottle in his hand*) Okay, let's see. Madge. When we got married you swore to love, honour and obey me. Now I've made up my mind about these horses, I don't care what you say, my decision is final. (*MADGE enters unseen, behind TED.*) I don't want to discuss it. Not with your mother, not with Linda and not with you. I am the man in this family. Do I make myself... (*turns and sees MADGE*) ...clear. I... uh... Elmer. (*looks at bottle in his hand*) Liniment. What's for dinner, dear?

MADGE exits, followed by TED.

DODGE: What's for dinner? Us! We're for dinner!

FORD: Oh no, oh no, oh no!

DODGE: Get ahold of yourself. Relax. There's no need to come unglued... (*realizing what he's said*) ...oh no, oh no, oh no!

FORD: Oh no, oh no, oh no!

LINCOLN: Shut up! What we need is to get tough!

DODGE: Right. Tough as nails.

FORD: Right. Tough as a well-done steak!

FORD, DODGE & LINCOLN: Oh no, oh no, oh no!

CHEVY: Quiet! All we have to do is break out!

LINCOLN: Right. Escape!

DODGE: Right. Vanish without our traces!

FORD: Right. Just like Rambler!

FORD, DODGE, LINCOLN & CHEVY: Oh no, oh no, oh no!

FORD: I don't want to die I don't want to die I don't want to die I don't want to die I don't want to...

GRANDMA and LINDA enter with harness.

GRANDMA: Whoa there. Where do you think you're all going in such a hurry?

LINDA: What's the matter, Ford? Scared of a little harness?

GRANDMA: They'll calm down once we get 'em harnessed and hitched up.

LINDA: Where we gonna plough?

GRANDMA: The Lord will show us. Now, let's see. First of all... the horses. Always approach 'em from the left. And watch your feet. Now the harness. You grab this here and that there. Or this there and that here. Or maybe... you grab the harness.

LINDA: What's this?

GRANDMA: That? That's a... uh... thingamabob goes over the horse's whazzit.

LINDA: What's it for?

GRANDMA: Don't know. Guess we don't need it. (*rips it off, tosses it away*) There. Okay. Now. You take your horse. Always from the left side...

LINDA: Yours or theirs?

GRANDMA: The left side. Here. Lincoln. Stand. And you just... alley-oop! (*GRANDMA throws the harness and falls down tangled up in it. She gets up.*) I'm just a wee bit rusty. You just... alley-oop! (*She throws the harness and misses LINCOLN completely.*) Lincoln! A little co-operation's all I'm asking for here. Now you just alley-oop! (*GRANDMA jumps on LINCOLN's back, fumbles with the harness.*) Oh, put it on yourself. (*LINCOLN does.*)

LINDA: Here, Chevy, stand. (*LINDA easily and perfectly harnesses CHEVY.*)

GRANDMA: Aye, that's the general idea. Now the bridle. Just put the bit in the mouth. Open up, Lincoln. Say "ahh". Lincoln, gimme your mouth. Your mouth! (*LINCOLN bites her hand.*) My hand! Gimme my hand! (*LINCOLN releases her hand.*) You no good... (*kicks LINCOLN*) Now stand there! (*GRANDMA bridles LINCOLN. LINDA has already bridled CHEVY.*) Finished? Already? You're lucky Chevy's so calm.

LINDA: I could never do Lincoln.

GRANDMA: Yeah. Well. Okay. Now we snap the lines onto these rings here and we're in business. Lincoln, Chevy, yee-haw! Hi-yah! Woo-hoo! Git going! Come on, you old has-beens! Move it! Hyah!

LINCOLN and CHEVY remain motionless.

LINDA: Maybe if I tried. (*whispering*) Lincoln, Chevy... (*LINDA makes a kissing sound. LINCOLN and CHEVY move with GRANDMA holding the lines.*)

GRANDMA: Never kiss a horse unless you're holding the lines! Whaddya been up to? Practicing when no one was looking?

LINDA: I just watched Grandpa every summer.

GRANDMA: Okay. Now to go left you say "gee"... (*LINCOLN and CHEVY veer right.*) I mean "haw". (*LINCOLN and CHEVY veer left. They continue to veer every time "gee" or "haw" is spoken.*) Right is "gee" and left is "haw".

LINDA: Left is "haw" and right is "gee"?

GRANDMA: No! "Haw" is left and "gee" is right! (*GRANDMA and LINCOLN and CHEVY are by now hopelessly tangled in the lines.*)

LINCOLN: She's pulling my mouth off!

GRANDMA: Now always keep a good grip on the lines here or else ...

LINDA: What?

CHEVY: Ouch!

GRANDMA: They might get away from you. (*LINCOLN and CHEVY start to spook.*) Easy, Chevy. Easy, Lincoln.

LINDA: What's wrong?

LINCOLN: My lines are crossed.

GRANDMA: Nothing. It's okay.

CHEVY: No, it's not.

LINDA: Should I get their heads?

LINCOLN: Yes!

GRANDMA: No! It's okay. I got 'em. Get out of the way. Lincoln! (*GRANDMA yanks hard on the lines, twisting LINCOLN's head around.*)

LINCOLN: That's it. I've had it.

LINCOLN and CHEVY take off running, dragging GRANDMA behind.

GRANDMA: Everything's under contro-oh-whoa! Whoa! Whoa!

LINDA: Grandma, you forgot the plough! (*exits after them*)

FORD, DODGE and CHORUS sing, as events of the runaway are enacted.

THE RIDE OF GRANDMA MULVANEY

Listen now my children and I'll tell you of the ride
Of Grandma Mulvaney and her two fearless Clydes,
How two runaway horses and one runaway soul
Rocked a town's foundation when they started to roll.

They hit the blacktop highway like a team that was possessed,
Heading down to Noburg, two miles to the west,
Destroyed the city limits sign, began to gather speed,
First Lincoln led, then Chevy, then Grandma took the lead.

They came around the corner, courting clear disaster,
Galloped through the Lutheran church and nearly killed the pastor.
The wedding party stood in shock, but the organ wasn't idle,
He struck a rousing chorus up of "Here Comes The Bridle".

"We need more beer" the cry went up inside the Noburg pub,
Just drinkin' brew, with fat to chew, the juke played Ernest Tubbs,
Behind the bar Old Red was drunk, threw back his head and laughed,
When the horses ran right through the pub he yelled "Here's a couple of draught!"

Things were quiet down at Mel's, the kettle was on the boil,
There hadn't been no customers at Twigg's Gas and Oil,
He thought that he heard thunder but it didn't look like rain,
The TV wasn't on, it was too early for the train.

Just then he saw the three of them, his heart it started sinkin'–
Grandma, Chevy neck-and-neck, no, in the lead is Lincoln!
They ripped Mel's pumps right from the ground, ignoring all his cries,
Every car those pumps had served flashed before his eyes.

You can take your Lady Godiva, you can have your Paul Revere,
Headless Horseman, Light Brigade, none of them comes near,
There ain't a single one of them rides
That can touch Grandma Mulvaney and her famous flying Clydes!

MADGE bursts out of the house crying, wiping her face with a dish towel, followed by TED.

TED: Now, honey, there's no reason to be so upset. Rambler is better off.

MADGE: I'm not upset.

TED: But you're crying.

MADGE: I was peeling onions, you damn fool. Cooking your supper. What do I care about a stupid horse anyway?

TED: Are you gonna cook up that meat Elmer gave us?

MADGE: Are you kidding? I wouldn't eat that stuff if you paid me.

TED: But it's not... it was too soon... I mean, it's not Rambler. It's just hamburger.

MADGE: It ain't hamburger, it's horseburger. Now get out of my way. (*MADGE picks up the axe and begins splitting firewood.*)

TED: You know, this stuff is forty-eight bucks a pound in Japan. It must be pretty good.

MADGE: I don't need it. I'm cooking up some goldfish soup, then we're having dog roast. If you haven't sold Smoky yet.

TED: Very funny. Look, Madge, I... (*MADGE chops wood ferociously.*) ...Madge, I'm trying to talk to you. (*She ignores him, chopping wood.*) What is it with this wood? First Linda, then you. We've got to talk.

MADGE: If you want supper, just stay out of my way and let me chop. This is the Mulvaney farm, remember. No modern new-fangled stuff for us, like a simple gas stove. Just chock full of rustic charm like that damn white elephant of a woodstove.

TED: Let me help you.

MADGE: Stay away. You'd probably cut yourself. I grew up splitting wood for that stove. All I ever wanted to do was leave.

TED: You liked it when Linda was little.

MADGE: She liked it. I liked to make her happy. Besides, Dad was still alive. Since he went the whole place's been dying slowly. Now it's dead. Of course Rambler got it. He was living in a funeral parlour.

TED: Calm down, Madge.

MADGE: And then you decided you liked it. And I like to make you happy. Remember all that crap you told me. "We'll make this place live."

TED: I tried. I just seem to have a black thumb.

MADGE: Face it, Ted, we came back to live here because you couldn't keep a job in the city. We didn't have a choice. Oh, pardon me, I forgot. I'm not supposed to talk about that, am I? Just pretend there's no problem. I'm so sorry, I forgot.

TED: What do you want from me? I'm trying.

MADGE: It's not good enough. Talk is cheap, Ted. Now I'm gonna make myself happy for a change. Gimme that cheque, the one Elmer gave you.

TED: What are you going to do? You're not going to leave?

MADGE: No, you fool, I'm going to buy a new stove. Gas. Like Cora's got. (*swings the axe*) Damn. The handle's split. Nothing works around here. Least of all you. (*MADGE cries, sits down on stump. TED awkwardly tries to comfort her. Pause.*) You know that summer I was pregnant with Linda and you were... you were away? I was worried, and scared. It'd been such a rocky pregnancy, and after the first time...

TED: I had to work. Grandma and Henry took care of you, didn't they?

MADGE: I was lonely. Even this place looked better than that empty apartment. Dad still had most of the herd then. His "outlaw steeds bred secretly in the highland night," he used to call them. Well, Glennie, she was one of the brood mares, was pregnant, too. Seems like everything that could go wrong was going wrong with that poor horse. One day Mother and Dad were away and Glennie went into labour. I phoned the vet, but he was out, some emergency or something. I didn't know what to do so I just tried to make her comfortable.

And I watched. She'd lie down, and moan, then try to get up, fall and try again. I was sure something bad was going to happen, something terrible, and I didn't want to see it, to see the foal born twisted, or dead. But I kept watching. Glennie lay over on her side, and she heaved this big sigh and the foal started coming. Little by little, in this white sac. And when it got its head out, I ripped the sac away. And this little half-born horse, still stuck inside its mother, looked around. Glennie looked back and they stared at each other, and Ted, I swear they smiled. They smiled, and I cried, and then I knew if she could do it, so could I.

TED: That's quite a story.

MADGE: That was Rambler. (*starts to cry again*)

TED: I knew you cared. Like I know you care about the farm. You're not as tough as you'd like to pretend.

MADGE: And you're not as big an idiot.

TED: Look, honey, maybe we went about it wrong last time, trying to grow food. This is a horse farm. Let's grow horses.

MADGE: Don't. Just don't start.

TED: We'll put the mares in that field. And over there... there's our prize stud. We can put an electric watering system in... and when we sell the first foal, we'll buy a horse van, hit every show—you, me and Linda—and walk away with first prize.

MADGE: I don't want any new dreams. I'm still paying for the old ones. First the plans, then the excuses, then you hit the bottle and we're right back where we started.

TED: Madge, that's all over. You know it.

MADGE: Ted, I saw you drinking with Elmer.

TED: That's what I'm talking about. Elmer's giving us a new lease on life. He's giving me a real good price...

MADGE: You sold them. You sold Ford and Dodge?

TED: I just traded them in on a new model.

MADGE: How could you?

TED: Honey, we have to. I mean, it wasn't easy. I'll miss them, too. But think of what we're getting in return. We'll have some money to take care of your mother the way she should be taken care of. And we'll have something to give to Linda, something alive and thriving. I'll talk to them. I know they'll see it my way. And when Grandma sees the farm working again, she'll be happy. I know it. Just trust me. Okay? Stand with me.

MADGE: No. (*exits*)

TED: But I did it for you! (*TED watches her go. Confused and angry, he picks up ELMER's bottle, looks at the house, then throws it away.*) You'll change your mind! And I'm getting a nurse for Mother! (*to FORD and DODGE*) Come on, guys. Don't look at me that way. We're all just victims of the law of supply and demand.

FORD: Who's he kidding? No one's gonna make teriyaki out of him.

TED: Now... where are your pals? (*FORD and DODGE shy away from him.*) Lincoln? Chevy? (*checks inside the barn*)

DODGE: Must be worried about his profit margin.

TED: (*coming out of barn*) Madge! Where are the other horses?

LINDA: (*entering, out of breath*) Dad, Dad! Come quick! There's been a runaway... Grandma...

DEPUTY HACK enters with MEL TWIGGS, gas station owner.

DEPUTY HACK: Freeze! This area is now under police supervision.

MEL TWIGGS: Go on, Waldo, do your duty!

DEPUTY HACK: Right! (*to TED*) You have the right to remain silent. You have the right to be represented by an attorney...

TED: What's going on? I haven't done anything.

DEPUTY HACK: You don't have the right to interrupt an officer of the law.

SHERIFF LUTZ enters.

SHERIFF LUTZ: All right, Waldo. I'll take it from here.

DEPUTY HACK: (*continuing*) Anything you say may be held against you–

SHERIFF LUTZ: Shut up, Waldo. And put that gun away.

DEPUTY HACK: (*stops abruptly*, sotto voce *to SHERIFF*) Sheriff, these people are dangerous. We show 'em any dissension in authority and they'll turn ugly.

SHERIFF LUTZ: What the heck are you talking about? Just butt out and let me handle this.

DEPUTY HACK: Right!

MEL TWIGGS: Damn it, Sheriff, are you gonna stand around talking all day?

SHERIFF LUTZ: Okay, Mel, back off.

MEL TWIGGS: What are you waiting for? Let's have justice done. Get those horses. They're a danger to society.

DEPUTY HACK: (*trying to arrest FORD and DODGE*) You have the right to remain silent...

LINDA: Get out of here, they haven't done anything.

MADGE: (*entering*) What's going on here?

DEPUTY HACK: You're all under arrest. You have the right...

LINDA: It's Grandma... the horses...

MEL TWIGGS: They ruined my station!

SHERIFF LUTZ: Calm down. Everybody! Now Ted, Madge, I thought you'd know about this. Seems like your horses have got out again. Caused some damage in town.

MADGE: How do you know they were our horses?

SHERIFF LUTZ: One, because no one else around here has Clydesdales, and two, because they were running away with old lady Mulvaney hanging on for dear life.

MADGE: My god! Mother? Is she all right?

SHERIFF LUTZ: Isn't she here?

MADGE: No.

MEL TWIGGS: Sheriff!

SHERIFF LUTZ: Now, look, Willis. I warned you the last time I was out here. Now we got real trouble and I'm holding you responsible.

TED: Me?

SHERIFF LUTZ: It's hard to say exactly what the bill will come to, but it isn't going to be cheap.

TED: Vern, you know I don't have any money.

SHERIFF LUTZ: Then I'll have to impound the horses and sell them at auction.

TED: But you can't, I already sold them to Elmer.

LINDA: You what?

TED: Uh, Linda. I, uh, wanted to talk to you.

LINDA: You sold the horses?

TED: Well, not exactly.

SHERIFF LUTZ: So you didn't sell them?

TED: No, I did.

SHERIFF LUTZ: Then you've got some money.

TED: Just the cheque for Rambler.

SHERIFF LUTZ: That'll be fine. (*taking cheque from TED*)

MADGE: Wait a minute. You can't take that money. Don't we get a fair trial?

MEL TWIGGS: Hang on a minute, Sheriff. I'm not going to see these culprits get off scot-free. I want to press charges.

SHERIFF LUTZ: Easy, Mel. Maybe you want to think about it.

MEL TWIGGS: I don't want to think, I want somebody arrested!

LINDA: Grandma's not here.

MEL TWIGGS: Then where is she? Arrest *her*, Sheriff. Withholding information, harbouring a known criminal. (*steps toward LINDA*)

MADGE: Get away from my daughter, Mel Twiggs! (*knocks MEL down*)

MEL TWIGGS: Sheriff, you can add assault to your list.

SHERIFF LUTZ: Ted, I'm sorry. Is your mother-in-law here?

LINDA: We already told you she's not.

SHERIFF LUTZ: I'm afraid we'll have to take a look around.

MADGE: The hell you will. Linda, take the horses in the barn and lock the door behind you.

DEPUTY HACK: You can't do that.

MADGE: You blind fool. Those aren't the horses you want.

DEPUTY HACK: They're material witnesses.

LINDA exits into barn with FORD and DODGE.

SHERIFF LUTZ: Mrs. Willis, will you please step aside so we can look in the house.

MADGE: You got a warrant?

SHERIFF LUTZ: What?

MADGE: You heard me. A search warrant. I watch enough TV to know you can't come in here without a search warrant.

SHERIFF LUTZ: We're all friends here.

MADGE: Yeah? Well, beat it friend. Vamoose.

DEPUTY HACK: Cover me, Sheriff! I'm going in the house!

MEL TWIGGS: Come on, Sheriff, you don't need a warrant!

CORA LUTZ: (*entering*) Yes, he does. Vern, what's going on here?

SHERIFF LUTZ: Police business, Cora.

DEPUTY HACK: Hello, Mrs. Lutz.

CORA LUTZ: Hello, Waldo. Mel. Madge, I just came by to say how sorry I was about Rambler. Vern told me.

MADGE: Thank you, Cora.

CORA LUTZ: Here, I brought you this. (*hands MADGE a covered casserole*) It's just a meatloaf I cooked up. Bury the dead and feed the living, I always say. It's better than flowers.

MADGE: Thanks, Cora. That's real thoughtful of you.

CORA LUTZ: (*to SHERIFF*) And you, Vern Lutz, you said you'd be home an hour ago for supper!

SHERIFF LUTZ: Look, dear, there's been some trouble. They–

CORA LUTZ: I don't want to hear it! Just because Mel Twiggs has another bee in his bonnet doesn't mean you have the right to trespass. Now, go on, shoo! All of you!

CORA shoos DEPUTY, MEL and SHERIFF out.

(*to MADGE*) What's this world coming to when people can't mourn in peace? Vern, you keep walking! Go on! (*exits, yelling at SHERIFF*)

TED: Madge, this is it. The last straw. The last piece of hay. I've had it with your mother and her senile stunts.

MADGE: I hope to God she hasn't hurt herself.

TED: No comment. (*starts to exit into house*)

MADGE: Where are you going?

TED: I'm going in that house, I'm calling up the rest home, and I'm hiring a private nurse to come out here and sit on that mother of yours.

TED exits, followed by MADGE. GRANDMA, LINCOLN and CHEVY enter at a full gallop. They crash into the haystack. GRANDMA is knocked out, LINCOLN and CHEVY are tangled in harness.

CHEVY: Boy, that was great. Did you see the look on their faces when we ran through that pub? I bet half those guys'll be on the wagon tomorrow.

LINCOLN: (*groaning*) I'd rather be on the wagon than pulling it. Ow.

CHEVY: What's the matter? Did you pull something?

LINCOLN: I think I got a charley-man. I just gotta lie down and rest.

CHEVY: It's a little early to be hitting the hay, isn't it?

LINCOLN: Chevy, what's got into you?

CHEVY: Lincoln, when we ran down the aisle in that wedding, I ate the bouquet. You know what that means.

LINCOLN: Oh, no. I ain't going through life bridled and groomed. How can you think of love at a time like this? We gotta wait till things get more stable.

CHEVY: Rambler never waited.

LINCOLN: Will you knock it off? I'm the stud here now.

CHEVY: Then prove it.

LINCOLN: Okay, I will. Take that harness off and come here.

LINDA enters from barn, followed by FORD and DODGE. She helps GRANDMA up.

LINDA: Grandma, Grandma, are you all right?

GRANDMA: (*dazed*) When Detroit stole horse names like Pinto and Mustang and gave them to cars, Henry stole car names and gave them to our horses.

LINDA: Grandma, can you hear me?

GRANDMA: It's an eye for an eye, a tooth for a tooth, and a tail for a tailpipe.

LINDA: Grandma, listen. Father's sold the horses.

GRANDMA: Flesh has a soul and souls are not for sale. No contracts hobble our spirits, no hobbles contract our dreams. We follow the moon, not the fenceline.

LINDA: If we don't do something they're going to turn Ford and Dodge into horsemeat.

GRANDMA: (*as she harnesses FORD and DODGE*) Linda, I saw the future. Great hooves of vengeance pounding the high and mighty down into the asphalt of their own works. Their dead machinery rotting on the roadside like big, black birds with four-door wings flapping broken, mechanical in rainbow pools of dead-dinosaur-bone blood. Where's Henry Ford now, you demons of Detroit, you sons of dead-end progress?

LINDA: I don't know where Henry Ford is, but if we don't hurry Elmer's going to be here.

GRANDMA: And then, Linda, from out of the middle of the highway a giant carrot reared its head and said:
"The seasons are not an assembly line;
To get to the other side, cross the dividing line.
Money can't measure what life is worth,
Bury the dead and turn the earth."

LINDA: Grandma, we have to do something!

GRANDMA: Polish the brass, soap the leather, clean the harness, watch the weather.

LINDA: Grandma!

GRANDMA: (*having hitched all four horses*) On Lincoln! On Chevy! On Dodge! On Ford! The highway's our enemy, the plough our sword!

GRANDMA drives the horses and plough off, followed by LINDA. TED bursts out of house, followed by MADGE.

TED: What was that? Did you hear that? I could've sworn I heard hoofbeats.

MADGE: Oh, Ted, where could mother be?

TED: I don't know, but when we find her, she's staying in bed and out of trouble.

MADGE: How long will it take the nurse to get here?

TED: They said right away. And meanwhile, what about Elmer? He'll be here any minute. I sold him four horses, now I only got two.

MADGE: You can't sell those horses. Any of them.

TED: I've got no choice now. That nurse is going to cost plenty and the Sheriff took the cheque for Rambler. Madge, I'm taking charge here.

MADGE: I saw the way you took charge with Vern Lutz.

TED: What was I supposed to do?

MADGE: Ted, those horses are not for sale and that's final.

TED: And what'll I tell Elmer when he gets here?

MADGE: Tell him you were drunk. (*storms into house*)

TED: But I signed a contract.

ELMER: (*entering*) And I've got a copy right here.

TED: Oh, hi, Elmer. I was, uh, I was just gonna call you.

ELMER: Call me anything you want, just don't call me late for dinner. Ha ha ha! The wife and I were about to sit down to a nice meal. Filly mignon with lots of *horseradish*. Ha ha!

TED: Elmer, about our contract...

ELMER: It's for your own protection. This butcher's a real horsetrader. Hahahaha!

TED: Seriously, Elmer, there's a little problem...

ELMER: You ain't backing out on me, are you, Willis? I already paid the auction fee.

TED: No, no. It's just that... well, you remember we were talking about four... four... animals.

ELMER: Yeah...

TED: There's a little hitch.

ELMER: Willis!

TED: It's not a four-horse hitch, just a two-horse hitch.

ELMER: What the hell are you talking about?

TED: It's just that Lincoln and Chevy...

ELMER: Not Lincoln! He's the biggest one!

TED: Oh, they'll be back in a minute. I'm sure. They just, uh, they just went up to the orchard. Yeah, it's an old family tradition. When someone leaves the Willis farm, they go up to the orchard and pick the sweetest apple they can find, take a bite and then bury it. You know... for luck.

ELMER: You ain't got no orchard.

TED: That's why it's taking so long! They went to my cousin Darryl's farm, over near Sumton.

ELMER: That's the biggest load of patootie I've ever heard. Look, Willis, we signed a contract for four horses and by God I want to see four horses or there's gonna be hell to pay!

TED: Right. Well, let's just start with Ford and Dodge. I'll bring 'em out of the barn and you can... do whatever it is you have to do, and by that time the other two'll be back. Okay?

ELMER: You got two horses in that barn?

TED: Yeah.

ELMER: Big, fat Clydes?

TED: Yeah.

ELMER: Then shoo those horses out here. And no stallin'. Get it? Stallin'. (*ELMER chuckles to himself. TED goes into barn. ELMER waits outside, lights a cigar, turns to audience.*) I know you think I'm a rotten SOB but I'm just trying to earn a living. Times is tough and people just got to hitch up their socks and do a lot of distasteful things – not that my horsemeat don't taste good – but if there wasn't a market for it, I wouldn't be selling it. Besides, it ain't no worse than eating pigs or sheep. Don't be so quick to judge your fellow man. I'm just a victim of the law of supply and demand.

ELMER breaks into song.

SUPPLY AND DEMAND

You need some oil to heat your home?
Some soldier buys it on the desert sand–
See that new car down the street?
Some worker in a factory lost his hand.

Certain needs gotta be filled,
That's something all men understand,
Sex, food, gas or contraband,
We're all victims of supply and demand.

In India, eating a cow is taboo,
Over here you'd eat a horse like that if he knew how to moo,
Everybody's gotta eat, it don't matter which animal,
It's a question of culture, now I'm not saying be a cannibal...

But I knew a guy so broke, he was flat on his back,
He got a job in a circus, eating a Cadillac,
As his body got thinner, his bankroll got fatter,
Which proves when you're hungry you don't give a damn what they put on your platter.

Certain needs gotta be filled,
That's something all men understand,
Sex, food, gas or contraband,
We're all victims of supply and demand.

Now take the Last Supper–
Disciples sitting down for the main course,
Jesus says, "Take and eat of my flesh."
If we can eat him, what's wrong with eating a horse?

Certain needs gotta be filled,
That's something all men understand,
Sex, food, gas or contraband,
We're all victims of supply and demand.

TED: (*screaming and cursing behind barn door after discovering FORD and DODGE are gone*) Why I oughta... that no-good I'll wring her wrinkled old neck that... arrgh! (*The barn door opens and TED comes out, smiling as though nothing's wrong.*) Elmer?

ELMER: (*suspiciously*) Willis?

TED: You said you never got to eat that delicious dinner of yours. How about let's sit down to some of Madge's famous pie and...

ELMER: The horses, Willis, I want my damn horses.

TED: They're right there in the barn, Elmer.

ELMER: Dungwort! (*starts for barn*)

TED: Don't go in there!

ELMER: Cause you don't got any horses in there.

TED: They're in there. All four, I swear.

ELMER: I'm just gonna see for myself.

TED: Don't do that! I mean... they're just a little skittish. I'll get 'em. (*goes toward barn, stops, looks at audience*) He'll never believe this.

TED enters the barn and makes sound of horses stomping and whinnying.

Easy, Ford. Whoa, big fella. (*more whinnying*) Back, Dodge! Back, I say.

There is more stomping and whinnying until TED comes flying out barn door as if kicked.

ELMER: Having trouble?

TED: Don't worry about a thing, Elmer. I've got it under control. (*aside to audience*) I can't believe he's buying this. (*goes back into barn, resumes horse impersonations*) Take that! And that! (*As TED impersonates the horses, ELMER swings the barn door open and watches. TED sees him.*) Can you believe that? They just broke out. All four of them. Just as you walked in.

ELMER: That's it, Willis. I've had enough of your crap. I'm gonna get the Sheriff.

TED: But, Elmer, just give me a few minutes. Linda must have taken them for a walk. Hey, Elmer, how about a drink? Whaddya say?

ELMER: Well...

TED: That's it, sure. Come on in the barn and we'll have some vitamins.

TED lures ELMER into the barn. GRANDMA enters, ploughing up the highway with HORSES, followed by LINDA.

GRANDMA: Whoa. Good girl, Chevy. Good boys. Furrow's a little crooked, but not bad for a beginner.

LINCOLN: It'd be straighter if we all pulled, huh, Ford?

GRANDMA: What do you think, Linda? Plant the turnips here, spinach there...

LINDA: Grandma, you can't plant a garden in the middle of the highway.

GRANDMA: Why not? Hardest part's over and done with.

DODGE: I'll say.

GRANDMA: Look at that. Ruined a good plough.

FORD: Ruined the plough? What about my back?

GRANDMA: The rest is easy. Just let nature take its course.

LINDA: But it's against the law.

GRANDMA: What law?

LINDA: The law that says you can't plough up a highway.

GRANDMA: The highway ploughed up my garden. I'm just returning the favour.

LINDA: The law doesn't work that way.

GRANDMA: The law doesn't work, period.

A tanker truck carrying gasoline enters.

LINDA: Uh, oh. Grandma, do you see what I see?

GRANDMA: Holy Moses. Quick, wave this sign! No, grab the horses. We gotta stop it.

The truck grinds to a halt in the ploughed-up highway. A female TRUCKER in the cab.

TRUCKER: What the blazes is going on here?

LINDA: Road construction.

TRUCKER: Where's the flagman?

LINDA: Lunch break.

GRANDMA: Your front wheels are in pretty deep there. Why don't you try backing up? (*The truck grinds gears, spins wheels.*) You're stuck good now.

TRUCKER: (*getting out of cab, inspecting damage*) Of all the stupid, dumb... what kind of construction crew is this anyway? No flagman. Where's the foreman? What are those horses doing here? I'm behind schedule already. This is gonna set me back at least another two hours.

GRANDMA: Relax. We'll get you out.

TRUCKER: With what?

GRANDMA: With these. Linda, help me hitch 'em up.

TRUCKER: Lady, don't make me laugh. That tanker's full of gasoline. We better call a tow truck.

GRANDMA: Don't need a tow truck. All set? (*climbs on hood of truck*) Ford, Dodge, Lincoln, Chevy! (*kisses them*) Git on! Git on!

The HORSES strain, but fail to budge truck.

TRUCKER: Listen, honey, you know how much that truck weighs?

GRANDMA: Ford! Dodge! Step up! Hyah!

The HORSES strain again, fail again.

TRUCKER: Grandma, that truck ain't going nowhere.

GRANDMA: Wanna bet?

TRUCKER: I don't take money from pensioners.

GRANDMA: What'd you call me? I've got fifty bucks. I'll give you ten-to-one odds.

TRUCKER: Grandma, you are...

GRANDMA: Linda, you hold the money.

TRUCKER: All right. You're on.

GRANDMA: Lincoln! Chevy!

The HORSES strain and fail.

LINDA: Wait a minute. Grandma, you got ahold of 'em?

GRANDMA: Course I do. Why?

LINDA: (*to HORSES*) Here comes Elmer Frankenmuth.

The HORSES pull the truck, aided by the ghost of RAMBLER wearing little wings and pushing, unnoticed, from behind.

GRANDMA: Yee-haw, hot-diggity! Whaddya think of that, missus? So the old lady's kinky in the noodle, eh? Well, take a look at that. That's real horsepower for you.

LINDA hops on the truck as HORSES pick up steam and GRANDMA drives them off.

TRUCKER: I don't believe it. Look how deep those wheels were in. A tractor couldn't have pulled that out. What kind of horses did you say those were. (*He realizes GRANDMA, LINDA and the HORSES have driven off with* *the truck.*) Hey, come back here! That truck is federal property!

SHERIFF's office. DEPUTY on the radio.

DEPUTY HACK: All stations please be on lookout for Noburg suspects in damage suit. Ringleader is white, female caucasian, age approximately eighty-five. Suspects are four brown and white equines, one male, one female, two indeterminate sex. Equine suspects are approximately six-foot-three, fifteen hundred pounds. Roger. One-five-oh-oh-pounds.

SHERIFF LUTZ: (*entering*) Any word on the horses yet, Waldo?

DEPUTY HACK: No sign of 'em, Sheriff.

SHERIFF LUTZ: They've gotta turn up sooner or later. You can't hide a horse that big for very long.

LINDA, GRANDMA and the HORSES enter the farmyard, bursting through haystack with truck in tow. Its grille is visible in hay. GRANDMA passes out. When LINDA hears TED and ELMER drunkenly singing in the barn, she unhitches the horses and takes them to the house.

TED: (*inside the barn*) There. That's them right now. What'd I tell you, Elmer?

ELMER: Now we're getting someplace. (*following TED out of barn*) I don't see no horses.

TED: They're here. You heard them, didn't you?

ELMER: Listen, that don't mean nothin' around here. It was probably your wife with some sawed-up coconuts on her feet.

TED: No, I saw them. They went in the house.

ELMER: In the house? You must think I'm awful stupid.

TED: They're in the kitchen, Elmer. I swear it.

ELMER: Willis, you owe me four Clydesdale horses. If those horses aren't in that kitchen, I am gonna go get Vern Lutz and nail your behind to the country courthorse. Courthouse!

TED: Just see for yourself.

TED opens the kitchen door. MADGE is at the stove. LINDA is serving tea to CHEVY, FORD and DODGE, who are playing cards, wearing aprons, dresses and hats. LINCOLN helps MADGE at stove.

FORD: Four no trump.

DODGE: Two spades.

CHEVY: (*to LINDA*) Two lumps.

FORD: That's two lumps to me.

ELMER: (*slamming the door and starting to leave*) Some horses.

TED: Elmer, let me explain.

ELMER: I'm gonna be back, Willis. But I only got one thing to say before I go.

TED: What's that?

ELMER: Damn, there's some ugly women in your kitchen. (*exits*)

TED: Wait, Elmer! Don't be hasty! (*exits after ELMER*)

In the kitchen, all celebrate their successful ruse.

LINDA: He's gone. We did it!

MADGE: For the moment. What happens when he comes back?

LINDA: We'll think of something, won't we? (*The HORSES shrug.*) Chevy, what's wrong? Did Elmer hurt your feelings? We don't think you're ugly, do we?

MADGE: Where's Grandma?

LINDA: Uh, Mom, let's go in the living room.

MADGE: What for?

LINDA: I think you better be sitting down for this.

MADGE: Oh, my god. What's happened? Where is she?

LINDA: Oh, it's not what you think. She's fine. But there is something... (*exits with MADGE*)

LINCOLN: (*taking off dress*) I've never been so humiliated in my life. Dressing up like a human. Blecch!

FORD: I had a run in two suits.

CHEVY: Madge is gonna break out of the chute snortin' when she hears about the truck.

DODGE: Don't worry your pretty little mane over it. Linda can handle her.

FORD: Who's gonna handle Ted? And Elmer?

LINCOLN: I can handle them.

CHEVY: Just because you pulled a little truck out of the mud doesn't mean you're a Rambler.

LINCOLN: Whaddya mean? Look at these muscles! I feel like a new horse.

DODGE: And that truck wasn't so little!

FORD: And we didn't need Rambler to pull it out!

DODGE: Whaddya mean "we"? Your traces were as loose as your tongue.

FORD: It wasn't my fault, I almost lost a shoe.

DODGE: Whenever we have to work, you start limping.

CHEVY: Lincoln's the expert when it comes to going limp.

LINCOLN: You're asking for a kick.

CHEVY: Listen to the big stud. You might as well be a gelding for all the use you are to me.

DODGE: Touchy, touchy.

FORD: Aw, she's just bugged cause Elmer said she was ugly.

LINCOLN: Hey, maybe you ain't much to look at in people's eyes...

DODGE: But when it comes to us horses...

FORD: Baby, you're a knock-out!

CHEVY: But I don't have that skinny race-horse look.

LINCOLN: Maybe not. But, baby, there's lots of other things you got. Like, for instance... (*LINCOLN sings*)

HORSELIPS

My baby got horselips
My baby got horselips
My baby got horselips
When I roll her oats, oh she rolls her hips

My baby got big feet
My baby got big feet
My baby got big feet
Got big horseshoes go clippity-clop down the street

My baby got a big belly
My baby got a big belly
My baby got a big belly
When they hitch her up she shake it like a bowl of jelly

My baby know when to stop
My baby know when to go
She built for power not for speed, I say whoa

I say whoa,
I say whoa,
I say whoa
Don't run away, baby, I love you so

Horselips horselips
Horselips, horselips
Horselips, horselips
She got horselips and great big workhorse hips

Chevy you are heavy!

On last note of song, TED shakes a grain bucket.

TED: Graintime!

The HORSES follow TED and grain bucket into barn. In the SHERIFF's office, DEPUTY is cleaning.

SHERIFF LUTZ: Waldo, you missed a spot.

ELMER: (*bursting in*) Sheriff, I want my horses!

SHERIFF LUTZ: Elmer, could you wipe your boots off? Waldo just swept that floor.

ELMER: Sorry, Sheriff. I got stuck in the mud out where they're repairing the highway. Willis sold me four horses and–

SHERIFF LUTZ: Where?

ELMER: At his place.

SHERIFF LUTZ: No, where are they repairing the highway?

ELMER: Out at Willis' place.

SHERIFF LUTZ: You sure? We were just out there.

ELMER: Sure, I'm sure. I got the contract right here. Four Clydesdale horses...

SHERIFF LUTZ: Waldo, you know anything about any highway construction going on out there?

DEPUTY HACK: No, sir.

ELMER: Sure. Highway's all ploughed up.

SHERIFF LUTZ: What?

ELMER: All tore up.

SHERIFF LUTZ: No, no. You said "ploughed up". Elmer, take off that boot.

ELMER: I wiped it off.

SHERIFF LUTZ: Take it off.

ELMER: (*taking off boot and handing it to SHERIFF who inspects it*) He sold me four horses and now he won't deliver!

SHERIFF LUTZ: Waldo, take a look at this.

DEPUTY HACK: It's horse doo-doo, sir.

MEL TWIGGS and TRUCKER enter.

TRUCKER: Four horses just walked off with my truck!

MEL TWIGGS: With my gas in it!

SHERIFF LUTZ: Four horses just walked off with your truck?

DEPUTY HACK: With his gas in it!

Back at the farm, MADGE and LINDA enter the kitchen. The HORSES are gone, locked in barn.

MADGE: Four horses just walked off with a truck?

LINDA: With Mel's gas in it!

MADGE: A whole truck?

LINDA: No, a semi-truck.

MADGE: Very funny. And where's your grandmother now?

LINDA: She's asleep in the cab. She was pretty tired out.

MADGE: I'm not surprised.

LINDA: You should've seen her, Mom. She looked so great sitting up there, driving the team. And the horses, just pulling away...

LINDA stops, noticing the HORSES are gone.

MADGE: The horses! Ted? Ted? (*MADGE and LINDA exit house into yard.*) Ted?

TED: (*inside barn*) I'm in here! Tying down our meal ticket!

MADGE: Ted Willis, you get out here right now.

GRANDMA: (*waking up, as HORSES whinny in barn*) Walk, Lincoln. Walk.

TED: Here I come. (*opening barn door*)

MADGE: (*seeing truck and slamming barn door shut*) No! Stay in there!

TED: Hey!

GRANDMA: Howdy, girls.

MADGE: Oh, mother. What have you done now?

GRANDMA: (*hopping down from cab of truck*) Just out weeding my truck garden. Looks like it's gonna be a bumper crop.

MADGE: Mother!

GRANDMA: Calm down, good buddy, I got my ears on.

MADGE: You've got to get that thing out of here.

GRANDMA: Gimme forty acres and I'll turn this rig around.

TED: (*inside barn*) What's going on out there? Is that Elmer? Elmer, I've got the horses! (*He starts to open door, but LINDA slams it shut. TED bangs his head on door.*)

LINDA: Grandma, Elmer's on his way here with the Sheriff.

GRANDMA: We better hide the horses.

MADGE: What about the truck?

GRANDMA: We better hide that, too.

They cover the truck with hay bales.

TED: (*in barn*) Who locked the door? (*appears at hayloft door*) So, it's you, Grandma. I might have known. What're you all doing?

LINDA: We were going to feed the horses.

TED: I'm coming down. Move away from that haystack.

MADGE: No, Ted, don't jump. I'll unlock the door.

TED: Stand back, Madge, I've been jumping into haystacks all my life. Softest landing in the world.

(*TED jumps into haystack, hits tanker with a loud clang, slides down in an unconscious heap.*)

GRANDMA: Let's get back to work.

MADGE: Mother, how can you be so cruel? Ted, are you okay?

GRANDMA: Aw, he's fine. I can hear him breathing from over here. He's got a hard head.

LINDA: What'll we do when he wakes up?

GRANDMA: Stick him in the house, pour some liquor on him. When he wakes up, tell him he was drunk and deny everything.

MADGE: That's awful. You know Ted's problem. Think it'll work?

GRANDMA: Like a charm. I done it to Henry lots. Does seem like a waste of good scotch, though. (*She takes a swig from bottle and pours the rest on TED.*) Now help the poor boy home.

MADGE picks TED up and carries him into house while GRANDMA and LINDA finish covering truck with hay. A car door slams.

LINDA: That'll be the sheriff.

GRANDMA: We're safe. He'll never find it.

LINDA: But what about the horses? Elmer'll be with him.

GRANDMA: Good thinkin', girl. You're bred from good stock.

LINDA: I'll take them in the house.

GRANDMA: (*picking up spade*) And I'll wait for the sheriff.

GRANDMA hides behind haystack. LINDA takes HORSES from barn into house. Stage empty as a young man, the NURSE, enters. He is smiling and good-natured, wearing a white uniform.

NURSE: Hello! Anybody home? Mr. Willis? Hello? I guess they're all out or something. Well, I can wait. (*sitting on edge of haystack*) Yes, sir, I can wait. Nice cushy job like this. Restful country living, good home-cooking, and only one patient. One sweet little old farm lady...

GRANDMA: (*leaping out, brandishing spade, with a blood-curdling yell*) Take that, Sheriff Lutz! (*knocks NURSE out with spade*) Bullseye! Boy, police uniforms sure have changed since my day. All clear, girls! (*LINDA and Madge stick their heads out of house.*) We done it. Three generations of Mulvaney women and each one a corker. Let's celebrate.

LINDA: (*coming out of house into yard*) Uh, Grandma...

GRANDMA: Did you see him fall? What a shot. Move over, Wayne Gretzky.

MADGE: Uh, Mother...

GRANDMA: What's the matter?

LINDA: There's a slight problem.

GRANDMA: I took care of the sheriff.

MADGE: That's not the sheriff.

GRANDMA: That's not the sheriff?

LINDA: That's the slight problem.

GRANDMA: Then who is it?

MADGE: Your nurse.

GRANDMA: She's a nurse? She does have a problem.

MADGE: No, Mother, *he's* a nurse. Ted hired him to look after you.

GRANDMA: Ain't doin' much of a job, is he? (*beat*) What do you mean look after me? I can take care of myself!

MADGE: Don't get excited, he–

Sound of a car driving up.

LINDA: Car coming!

MADGE: That'll be the sheriff.

GRANDMA: Quick, to your posts.

MADGE: What about him?

GRANDMA: I'll take Florence Nightingale up to my room.

All exit. Pause. FORD addresses audience.

FORD: Well, things are getting pretty exciting, hey? Elmer wants us horses to make hamburger, but we're in the living-room. Mel Twigg's gas station has been wrecked and he wants Ted to pay for it, but Ted's in the house with Madge. The Sheriff wants Grandma but she's hiding in the bedroom with the nurse, the hijacked truck is hidden in the haystack, Linda's in the living room with the horses, but no one's in the kitchen with Dinah, which means we got one slot open if anybody out there needs a place to hide.

LINDA: Ford, get in here!

FORD trots back to house. Everybody waits. Car door slams. SHERIFF and DEPUTY enter, followed by ELMER, MEL and TRUCKER. DEPUTY has bullhorn.

SHERIFF LUTZ: Now you three just stay out of my way.

ELMER: I want my horses.

MEL TWIGGS: I want my pumps.

TRUCKER: I want my truck.

SHERIFF LUTZ: I can handle it. C'mon, Waldo. All right, everybody, hold it right there.

DEPUTY HACK: (*into bullhorn*) All right everybody hold it right there!

SHERIFF LUTZ: Nobody move.

DEPUTY HACK: (*into bullhorn*) Nobody move. (*to SHERIFF*) It's working. Nobody's moving.

SHERIFF LUTZ: Nobody's here, dummy. (*to house*) Come out with your hands up.

DEPUTY HACK: (*into bullhorn*) Come out with your hands up.

SHERIFF LUTZ: This is Sheriff Lutz.

DEPUTY HACK: (*into bullhorn*) This is Sheriff Lutz. Well, actually that's Sheriff Lutz. This is Deputy...

SHERIFF LUTZ: Shut up, birdbrain!

DEPUTY HACK: (*into bullhorn*) Shut up, birdbrain!

SHERIFF LUTZ: Gimme that thing.

ELMER: This is what we pay our taxes for?

SHERIFF LUTZ: They're around here somewhere, I can smell 'em.

DEPUTY HACK: What about that tanker?

SHERIFF and DEPUTY sit on haystack.

SHERIFF LUTZ: We'll find that later. It could be anywhere. It'd be like finding a needle in a haystack. But don't worry. I'm on top of it.

DEPUTY HACK: (*sneezing*) Damn hay fever's acting up. I wonder what's doing it?

SHERIFF LUTZ: Waldo... let's check the barn.

As SHERIFF is followed by DEPUTY, ELMER, MEL and TRUCKER search the premises in a line. LINDA, the HORSES, MADGE, TED, GRANDMA and NURSE all sneak through house until they are all in the bedroom. As SHERIFF and his posse approach the house, FORD accidentally steps on MADGE's foot. A muffled scream. SHERIFF and his posse stop. They lean to the left, the right, then look up as everyone in the bedroom counters to the right, the left then looks down. Pause. SHERIFF and his posse scream and run for cover.

DEPUTY HACK: Freeze or I halt!

SHERIFF LUTZ: Shoot, you idiot! (*DEPUTY raises his gun.*) Not the gun, the words.

DEPUTY HACK: Shoot or I freeze!

SHERIFF LUTZ: Halt!

DEPUTY HACK: Why?

SHERIFF LUTZ: Not you, them! Where's that bullhorn? (*takes bullhorn, speaks into it*) Hello, Mrs. Mulvaney. This is your friend, Vernon Lutz. Now, Mrs. Mulvaney, I know how you're feeling. I hate these gas companies as much as you...

TRUCKER: (*grabbing bullhorn and speaking into it*) That truck is federal property.

SHERIFF LUTZ: (*grabbing bullhorn and speaking into it*) But we can't take the law into our own hands every time some little thing doesn't go the way we'd like it...

MEL TWIGGS: (*grabbing bullhorn and speaking into it*) So come out with your hands up, the place is surrounded!

SHERIFF LUTZ: (*grabbing bullhorn and speaking into it*) Life is a compromise, Mrs.

Mulvaney. If we don't accept that, we're no better than animals...

ELMER: (*grabbing bullhorn and speaking into it*) My horses, Willis! I want my horses...

SHERIFF LUTZ: (*grabbing bullhorn and speaking into it*) All you have to do is come on down, return the truck like a good girl, give Elmer his horses, and we won't press charges or hold you responsible for the repair of the highway. How about it? Is it a deal?

Pause. GRANDMA sticks a rifle out the window and opens fire. SHERIFF, DEPUTY, MEL, ELMER and TRUCKER scurry off, bumping into each other.

GRANDMA: Get out of my garden, you mangy coyotes!

SHERIFF LUTZ: Out of my way, Waldo!

ELMER: But, Sheriff, what about my horses?

SHERIFF LUTZ: You stay if you want, Elmer! (*They exit under hail of gunfire.*)

GRANDMA: And take your infernal combustion engines and their prehistoric emissions with you!

ACT TWO

MADGE opens the door to the house and the HORSES charge out.

CHEVY: Did you see the look on Elmer's face when she opened fire? Bang! Kapow!

LINCOLN: *They* know a mean stud when they see one.

CHEVY: Oh yeah? What're we gonna do when they come back?

LINCOLN: Give 'em a horseshoe sandwich.

DODGE: Float like a thoroughbred,
Kick like a Clyde,
Elmer Frankenmuth,
You'll fall in five.

FORD: Workhorses of the world, take off your blinders. You have nothing to lose but your reins.

DODGE: That's the biggest load of people-poop I've ever heard.

LINCOLN: All I know is ain't nobody gonna eat *this* horse for dinner.

FORD: Dinner! I'm starving.

DODGE: You're starving? I'm so hungry I could eat a butcher.

GRANDMA, MADGE and LINDA enter.

MADGE: This time you've really done it. The whole town'll be back here with an army of police.

GRANDMA: Let 'em come. I'm ready.

MADGE: Linda, where are you going?

LINDA: Time to feed the horses. They've put in a hard day's work.

MADGE: Mother, for God's sake, put that gun down.

GRANDMA: Don't worry. Ain't no bullets in it. Just blanks.

MADGE: Do you know what you've done?

GRANDMA: Saved my horses' lives.

LINDA: Grandma, this hay is all mouldy.

MADGE: (*as she approaches HORSES*) You two don't seem to realize we're in trouble. Big trouble.

GRANDMA: What're you doing?

MADGE: I'm going to hide these horses before Elmer gets back here.

GRANDMA: (*raising gun*) No, you're not. Those horses stay where they are.

MADGE: Your blanks don't scare me.

The gun goes off. Truck tire goes flat. GRANDMA shakes her head, confused.

GRANDMA: I could've sworn I put blanks in it.

TED and NURSE enter, tied back-to-back, running clumsily.

TED: There she is. Grab her.

NURSE: Oh, no. Not me.

TED: Madge? What the hell's going on here?

NURSE: Keep the old lady away from me!

TED: Untie me! Linda. Untie your father.

LINDA: Why?

TED: So I can take those horses to Elmer before he sues us.

GRANDMA: You're drunk.

TED: I'm not drunk, I... (*he sees the truck*) ...please let me be drunk, please let me be drunk. What is that?

MADGE: What?

TED: That.

MADGE: A truck.

TED: What's it doing in the haystack? Mother, you–

MADGE: Don't blame Mother. I borrowed the truck. It got stuck in the garden so I pulled it out with the horses and so, well, there it is.

TED: Garden? What garden?

MADGE: That one.

TED: The highway?!

GRANDMA: What's wrong with a little garden?

TED: I'll tell you what's wrong. It's against the law.

MADGE: Oh, come on, Ted. You know as well as me every farmer in this area hates that highway.

TED: That's no reason to go and plough it up. Just because you're frustrated. That's anarchy for crying out loud! This is a democratic country. There are rational ways to air your grievances, proper channels...

LINDA: He's right.

TED: Don't wise off to me, young lady– (*pause*) what do you mean I'm right?

LINDA: About democracy. Majority rules, right Dad?

TED: Right.

LINDA: Then I move we take a vote. All in favour of selling our horses to Elmer Frankenmuth say "aye".

TED: Me. I mean aye.

LINDA: All opposed.

MADGE: Nay.

GRANDMA: Nay.

LINDA: Nay.

HORSES: Neigh.

LINDA: The nays have it. Well, Dad, what do you say now?

TED: The hell with democracy.

MADGE: Ted Willis, if you sell those horses you might as well not come home.

TED: (*weakly*) I demand a recount. (*GRANDMA points gun at him.*) Okay, okay, but listen. The other part of democracy is compromise, so here's my deal. If I don't sell the horses, Grandma has to promise to stay out of trouble, stay in bed, and let Mr. Duffy here care for her.

NURSE: Oh, no.

TED: Don't worry, he'll stay.

GRANDMA: He'll stay, but I won't.

MADGE: Maybe Ted's right, Mother. You could use the rest.

GRANDMA: Oh, no, you don't. People only go to hospitals to die.

TED: No one's asking you to go to the hospital.

GRANDMA: That's right. You know I'm too smart for that, so you bring the hospital in here. First it's the nurse, then it's the tubes in your arm and the oxygen tent. Then...

MADGE: But your heart...

GRANDMA: I never felt better in my life... (*stops short in pain*)

MADGE: Mother!

TED: Untie us! Untie us!

LINDA and MADGE untie TED and the NURSE. NURSE attends to GRANDMA.

MADGE: It's her heart, it's her heart.

GRANDMA: I'm okay. Where's my pills?

NURSE: Give me a hand here. It's all right, Mrs. Mulvaney. We'll get you upstairs and in bed.

GRANDMA: The hell you will!

NURSE slings GRANDMA on his back and carries her into house.

NURSE: Where are her pills?

GRANDMA: I don't need my pills. The pain's gone. What're you doing?

NURSE: It's going to be all right.

GRANDMA: I'll give you all right! Linda, brush those horses down after you feed them.

NURSE exits with GRANDMA, followed by TED. LINDA tries to follow, but MADGE stops her.

MADGE: Come on, Linda. Let's look after the horses.

LINDA: I want to be with Grandma.

MADGE: Not now. Come on.

LINDA: No. (*exits after GRANDMA into house*)

MADGE: (*to HORSES*) Well, gang. Looks like it's down to you and me. Sometimes I wish our life was as simple as yours. (*MADGE tries to feed HORSES but they refuse to eat the hay.*) Here, Chevy. (*CHEVY turns away. MADGE sniffs hay.*) I don't blame you. This stuff *is* pretty bad, isn't it? What're we going to do?

CORA LUTZ: (*entering*) Hello, Madge.

MADGE: Cora, what're you doing here?

CORA LUTZ: I just ran out of gas up the road a piece. Is Vern here?

MADGE: He just left.

CORA LUTZ: I've been chasing that man down all day long.

MADGE: Oh, Cora...

CORA LUTZ: What's the matter?

MADGE: Ted sold the horses but Mother took them and ploughed up the highway and stole a truck and then when Elmer and Vern and Waldo and Mel showed up she got out Henry's gun and started shooting at them.

CORA LUTZ: (*laughs*) She did? That's a good one. Waldo and Elmer!

MADGE: It's not funny. Vern's gonna be back here and we're all going to be put in jail.

CORA LUTZ: No, you're not. That's why I've been trying to catch Vern. This fax came for him this morning. The government's telling him not to take any further action until their agent gets here to investigate.

MADGE: Agent?

CORA LUTZ: I guess they're afraid this is going to turn into some kind of farmers' revolt or something. Anyway, the long and short of it is Vern's hands are tied. He can't do a thing.

MADGE: *He* can't do a thing, but what happens when the agent gets here?

CORA LUTZ: Cross that bridge when you get to it.

MADGE: Well, I guess I should be thankful for small favours.

CORA LUTZ: Speaking of small favours, do you have a couple gallons of gas I could borrow?

MADGE: Yes, I have a couple gallons of gas.

CORA LUTZ: I'd pay you but Vern's got all my money.

MADGE: Oh, that's okay. You can have it.

CORA LUTZ: No, I want to give you something for it.

MADGE: We could use some hay.

CORA LUTZ: I just picked up some for my mother's goats.

MADGE: Is it good hay?

CORA LUTZ: You bet.

MADGE: Say... you think other people would be willing to do this?

CORA LUTZ: Do what?

MADGE: Barter... make a trade... hay for gas.

CORA LUTZ: I don't see why not.

MADGE: Cora, I've got a business proposition for you.

As HORSES sing following song, MADGE, LINDA and CORA trade gas for hay. Townspeople—all housewives (can be men in drag)—bring in haybales and fill up gas cans from truck in haystack.

THE REDISTRIBUTION RAP

CHEVY & DODGE: (*mock Gilbert & Sullivan intro*)
Madge Willis' economic solution:
A more equitable distribution
Of wealth in the form of gasoline
To be carried out in a manner clandestine.

FORD: (*spoken*)
Gas for hay in a heads up deal,
Power for them, for us a meal–
(*rap*)
This is MC Ford with the story how we scored
A Clydesdale's culinary smorgasbord
First Mrs. Willis got on the phone,
Called Mrs. Twiggs up at her home.

MADGE: (*rap*)
Is your husband around?

MRS. TWIGGS: (*rap*)
No, he's at the station.

MADGE: (*rap*)
Great, 'cause I got some secret information...

(*chorus*)

(*town*) We need gas
(*family*) We got gas
(*town*) We got hay
(*family*) We need hay
Whaddya say, get over here fast
That's how we made hay from gas

FORD: (*rap*)
No pumps, no problem, our plan can't fail
Tradin' that gas for a gallon of bale
Tote that hay, it's a cinch and a snap
When you're doin' the redistribution rap

(*chorus*)

(*town*) We need gas
(*family*) We got gas
(*town*) We got hay
(*family*) We need hay
Whaddya say, get over here fast
That's how we made hay from gas

CORA LUTZ: (*spoken over music*) Madge, I got some more customers.

MADGE: Way to go, Cora. Vern doesn't suspect, does he?

CORA LUTZ: Vern? He couldn't catch a cold if it was under his nose. Well, back to work.

FORD: (*rap*)
Then Cora Lutz called the Frankenmuth house...

CORA LUTZ: (*rap*)
Promise not to tell your spouse
You can stop cleaning up that dirty linoleum
And come on over for some cheap petroleum

MADGE: (*rap*)
How many gallons?

MRS. FRANKENMUTH: (*rap*)
I'll take ten.

MADGE: (*rap*)
Oh, one more thing...

MADGE & CORA: (*rap*)
...Don't tell the men.
What the men don't know sure won't hurt 'em.

ALL THE WOMEN: (*rap*)
If they find out, we'll desert 'em.

(*chorus*)

(*town*) We need gas
(*family*) We got gas
(*town*) We got hay
(*family*) We need hay
Whaddya say, get over here fast
That's how we made hay from gas

MEL TWIGGS enters and the smuggling operation stops. Percussion vamps underneath as

MEL eyes the HORSES and everyone else suspiciously, then exits. SONG resumes.

FORD: (*rap*)
Mel Twiggs shut down, cars runnin' all day
On the smuggled gas and that ain't hay
Tote them bales, don't gimme no crap
We're doing the redistribution rap

HORSES with fresh hay.

LINCOLN: (*spoken, over music*) Hay, hay, hay! This is more like it.

CHEVY: I hope you noticed it took a woman's touch to get it for us.

FORD: Don't eat so fast, you'll get gas.

DODGE: Ah, what the hay.

CHEVY: (*rap*)
Now I'm not the type of nag that brags

ALL THE HORSES: (*rap*)
But a little bit of hay and our backs don't sag
Our spirits don't flag and our feet don't drag
With a clip-clop hip-hop flippety-flap
We're doin' the redistribution rap

(*Chorus*)

(*town*) We got gas
(*Ford*) Contribution to a free-trade solution
(*family*) We got hay
(*Ford*) It's good for your constitution
(*town*) We got gas
(*family*) We got hay
(*all*) Whaddya say, get over here fast
That's how we made hay from gas
Whaddya say, get over here fast
That's how we made hay from gas

All exit except FORD. GRANDMA leans out bedroom window.

GRANDMA: Psst! Ford! (*FORD turns around.*) How're you doing? Miss me? Naw. You don't miss me. Glad to get the crazy old lady off your back. (*FORD stares blankly.*) I said... (*GRANDMA snorts like a horse. FORD answers her. They converse in horse language until LINDA enters bedroom.*)

LINDA: Grandma, what are you doing?

GRANDMA: Talkin' to my friends. Only ones make sense 'round here anymore.

LINDA: I think Ford's telling you you should be in bed.

GRANDMA: Your grandpa always said you can't pet no tractor on its head after a day's work.

LINDA: I came to see if there's anything I can get you.

GRANDMA: A new ticker.

LINDA: Right. Anything else?

GRANDMA: You taking good care of the horses?

LINDA: They've never been better. We're even giving them oats now. They're getting so fat they won't be able to fly away when their wings come in.

GRANDMA: Don't let 'em overeat.

LINDA: Don't worry, Gram. The farm's never looked better. Mom and I cleaned all the harness yesterday and tomorrow we're going to take the plough into town and get it fixed.

GRANDMA: What about Elmer?

LINDA: Dad's going to talk to him today so that'll be out of the way. And, oh yeah, Mrs. Lutz brought some seeds for your garden.

GRANDMA: Next new moon you and I'll do some planting.

LINDA: Mom and I planted a row of tomatoes already.

GRANDMA: Too early for tomatoes. (*pause*) So things are running pretty smooth without me, eh?

LINDA: Yeah.

GRANDMA: All the chores getting done?

LINDA: Yes.

GRANDMA: Hmmph. You miss me?

LINDA: Of course.

NURSE enters.

NURSE: Time for your pills, Mrs. Mulvaney.

GRANDMA: "Time for your pills, Mrs. Mulvaney." Quit being so polite. Gives me the willies. You hate me and you know it.

NURSE: Swallow 'em. All of 'em.

LINDA: Grandma...

GRANDMA reluctantly swallows the pills.

NURSE: Now let's take our clothes off and get back in bed, shall we?

GRANDMA: What do you mean *we*? Pervert. All right, all right, but turn your back. I ain't no kootch dancer. Linda, you tell your mother I've had it with this nonsense. You hear me?

LINDA: Yes. (*exits*)

GRANDMA: And don't worry about me. I'm fit as a fiddle. (*slumps in bed as drugs take effect*) I'll be back up and fightin' in no time. No time at all... (*drowses off*)

NURSE: That's it... calm down.

In SHERIFF's office. MEL, ELMER and TRUCKER talking to SHERIFF.

MEL TWIGGS: What do you mean calm down? First my pumps are ruined and you do nothing about it, then I spend seven thousand dollars on a new pump and people quit buying gas.

SHERIFF LUTZ: You want to blame that on the horses, too?

ELMER: What about those horses, Sheriff? They're mine. Willis promised 'em to me.

TRUCKER: To hell with their problems, Sheriff, I got federal property swiped right out from under my legs. A whole tanker full of Gas-Canada petroleum.

MEL TWIGGS: And I paid for the gas in that truck!

TRUCKER: Hijacked by that old lady and her horses!

ELMER: You mean *my* horses!

SHERIFF LUTZ: Take it easy. I'm looking after things.

ELMER: How? Are you at the Willis place getting *my* horses?

MEL TWIGGS: That knocked over *my* pumps and stole *my* gas...

TRUCKER: Out of *my* truck.

ELMER: You're just sitting around twiddling your thumbs.

SHERIFF LUTZ: I assure you we have the matter well in hand.

MEL TWIGGS: We want action, Vern Lutz.

ELMER: Not talk.

SHERIFF LUTZ: We are talking action.

TRUCKER: What?

SHERIFF LUTZ: I'm sorry but I can't tell you.

ELMER: That's not good enough.

SHERIFF LUTZ: It's got to be. Look, just give me a little time.

ELMER: That's what we'll do. Very little. Then we're going to do things our way. Right, men?

MEL TWIGGS: Right.

TRUCKER: Right. (*exits with MEL and ELMER*)

SHERIFF LUTZ: Damn and double-damn. (*reads fax*) "Your continued inaction will be greatly appreciated." Don't they know what's going on here? "Please institute cessation of information." (*throws fax away*) Damn, double-damn and triple-damn!

Back on the farm, TED enters with two buckets and a bottle, talks to HORSES.

TED: Okay, guys, I've got it all figured out. Don't worry about a thing. Ted Willis to the rescue. (*HORSES shy away.*) Come on. Bury the past. Don't hold a grudge. Listen, how's this sound? "Elmer, I've got some bad, bad news. Those horses you bought? Sick. Every last one of 'em. Vet quarantined 'em. Said they can't be sold for meat. Don't know what it is. They can't stand up straight. Eyes all bloodshot. Tongues swollen, hanging out. It's like they're poisoned or drunk or something...." Well, fellas, whaddya think? Is that a switcheroo or what? Ted Willis saves your hide. No, don't thank me. I've got to keep the peace somehow. And now, how about a little drink to celebrate? (*pours whiskey into grain buckets*) Better you than me. Come on, graintime. Well. Wish me luck. (*as HORSES drink*) "Elmer, I've got some terrible news..." (*exits*)

DODGE: Not such a bad guy after all.

LINCOLN: He'll talk himself hoarse before Elmer'll ever listen.

CHEVY: (*tasting*) Hmmm. Chateau Surecrop, 1981. An intoxicating feast for the discriminating horse palate.

LINCOLN: The full-bodied flavour of these oats are matched only by their pungent bouquet.

DODGE: You can lead a horse to whiskey but you can't make him think.

FORD: You can lead a horse to water, but a pencil must be lead.

LINCOLN: (*to DODGE who has grabbed his bucket*) Ged outa there. Thash mine.

DODGE: Whaddya mean yoursh? Ish mine.

LINCOLN: Oh, yeah?

DODGE: Yeah.

LINCOLN, DODGE and FORD start a drunken brawl, stopped by CHEVY.

CHEVY: Knock it off! Look at you, horsing around like a bunch of greedy people. You've got it soft now, but remember: where the human giveth hay, the human can taketh hay away. Don't ever forget you were born a horse. (*SHE sings to LINCOLN as he circles her, dancing.*)

WILD OATS

Gonna kick my heels
Till the barndoor bust
Gonna bury the living
In a cloud of dust
Gonna raise the dead
And rattle their teeth
Gonna shake the earth
When we stomp our feet
Gonna make the air sing
When we kick our heels
Gonna roll in the mud
Gonna bite and squeal
Sowing wild oats
Coats wet with sweat
Stomping and snorting
Don't need no vet
Fire in the belly
Alfalfa in the air
Wind full of rainbows
And a stallion for the mare

LINCOLN carries CHEVY to haystack. They fall asleep. ELMER and ORVILLE enter. They go for CHEVY but DODGE jumps in the way. They pull DODGE down with ropes, tranquilize him and drag him off.

ORVILLE: Dad, I think this horse is sick.

ELMER: We've got to sell them fast then, before they die on us. (*exits with ORVILLE and DODGE*)

FORD: Dodge? Dodge! Lincoln, Chevy! Wake up! They got Dodge! Oh, Dodge, Dodge, Dodge...

GRANDMA: (*sticking her head out window*) What's the racket down there? Ford, what are you doing?

FORD ducks.

Duck? Duck? You're chasing ducks? Dodge? Dodge! Where's Dodge?

FORD waves.

Bye-bye? Bye-bye? Dodge has gone bye-bye?

FORD mimes "no", waves backwards.

Bye-bye backwards? Hello? Hello!

FORD makes stretching motion with his arms.

Hell-o, hellll-ooo, helll-ooooo, helll—

FORD draws his hoof across his neck.

Hell? Hell! Dodge is in hell?

FORD mimes "no", mimes a little halo above his head.

Halo? Heaven? Dodge is in heaven?

FORD mimes "no", mimes rocking a baby in his arms.

Dodge had a baby?

FORD mimes halo.

Baby with a halo! Baby Jesus!

FORD stamps the ground three times.

Three? Three wise men!

FORD mimes giving a gift.

Gifts! Gold. Myrrh. Myrrh! Hell. Myrrh. Hell Myrrh. Elmer!

FORD mimes Frankenstein's monster.

Monster? Frankenstein? Frankenstein!

FORD puts gloves on his ears.

Moose? Frankenstein moose? Frankenmoose, Frankenmuth! Elmer Frankenmuth's got Dodge!

FORD collapses from the effort.

Well, why didn't you just say so in the first place? Hold your horses, I'll be right down.

NURSE: (*entering bedroom*) Whoa there, Mrs. Mulvaney. Where are we going in such a hurry?

GRANDMA: Out of my way. They got one of my horses.

NURSE: Who did?

GRANDMA: Elmer. Now move your butt.

NURSE: I see. And how do we know this?

GRANDMA: Ford told me.

NURSE: I see. And Ford is one of your horses?

GRANDMA: He ain't no tractor, that's for sure.

NURSE: Mrs. Mulvaney, I think we better lie down. (*grabbing GRANDMA*)

GRANDMA: Let go of me.

NURSE: (*with hypodermic needle*) There, there. It's going to be all right.

GRANDMA: Oh, no. Get that frogsticker away from me. Help! Help!

NURSE sedates GRANDMA, straps her to bed. LINDA comes out of barn.

LINDA: Grandma?

NURSE: (*leaning out window*) It's all right. Everything's under control. Your grandma just had a bad dream.

NURSE attends to GRANDMA. LINDA looks at window, then at HORSES. She sees DODGE is missing.

LINDA: Dodge? Dodge? Where's Dodge?

FORD starts to repeat mime, then gives up. LINDA exits. In SHERIFF's office, SHERIFF is sitting at desk.

CORA LUTZ: (*entering with paper bag*) Here's your dinner, Vern. Two cheeseburgers, fries and coke.

SHERIFF LUTZ: You're late.

CORA LUTZ: I, uh, ran out of gas. So I stopped in at Mel's. He says hello.

SHERIFF LUTZ: Mel was just here.

CORA LUTZ: He was? I mean, he was, that's right. He didn't say hello. His wife did.

SHERIFF LUTZ: His wife?

CORA LUTZ: I think it was his wife. Somebody said hello. Never mind. Here. You look so wound up. (*she massages his neck*)

SHERIFF LUTZ: Of course I'm wound up. I'm being beaten by four dumb plugs and a senile old woman, the whole town is on my back and there's nothing I can do.

CORA LUTZ: No word from the government yet?

SHERIFF LUTZ: No. You haven't told anyone, have you?

CORA LUTZ: Of course not.

SHERIFF LUTZ: Oh, yeah, that's the spot. The government. What are they gonna do anyway? Put the horses on a chain gang? Send the old lady to jail for the rest of her life, or two weeks, whichever comes first? I tell you, Cora, I'd forget the whole thing if I could. Just let Elmer have his horses and drop the whole stupid mess.

CORA LUTZ: (*still massaging*) Why don't you do just that?

SHERIFF LUTZ: Because that agent will be here any day now. Ouch!

CORA LUTZ: Sorry.

SHERIFF LUTZ: Besides, Twiggs and the rest would have my head. Ouch!

CORA LUTZ: Sorry.

SHERIFF LUTZ: And for another thing, she shot at me. Nobody shoots at me and gets away with it.

CORA LUTZ: They were just blanks, dear. (*SHERIFF turns to look at her.*) I mean, probably. Here. Does this feel good?

SHERIFF LUTZ: Hmmm. Remember my dad, Cora?

CORA LUTZ: Sure.

SHERIFF LUTZ: When I was about ten, he got a new wagon and team. He used to let me sit up there with him, driving through town. And you know something?

CORA LUTZ: What?

SHERIFF LUTZ: I hated it. I was scared of them. They made me break out in a rash. The smell was awful. Taking care of them was bad enough, but when you had to sit behind those fat, ugly bums bouncing back and forth and then one of them raises its tail and aims at you...

DEPUTY HACK: (*bursting in*) Sheriff, I caught a prowler! Guy was breaking into our files.

SHERIFF LUTZ: Where is he?

DEPUTY HACK: I got him handcuffed to the toilet.

SHERIFF LUTZ: Well, flush him out.

DEPUTY exits, immediately returns.

DEPUTY HACK: He's gone.

SHERIFF LUTZ: I thought you said he was cuffed.

DEPUTY HACK: He was. He was right there just a second ago.

AGENT: (*appearing on opposite side of office*) Which is precisely why I am not there now. A good cop is like the wind – invisible until he blows you away. Good evening, Sheriff Lutz.

SHERIFF LUTZ: Who the hell are you?

AGENT: I am not at liberty to address that question. Suffice it to say I am who you have been waiting for.

DEPUTY HACK: You mean the gov–

AGENT: Immediate termination of vocal speech is essential.

DEPUTY HACK: Huh?

AGENT: Shut up. (*looks at CORA*) Sheriff, I cannot continue this conversation until this room is made secure.

CORA LUTZ: Oh, don't mind me.

AGENT: I'm sorry. My orders are to trust no one.

SHERIFF LUTZ: Cora, maybe you'd better wait outside. (*CORA exits.*) So you're from the government, eh?

AGENT: If that is your assumption I am able not to correct you.

SHERIFF LUTZ: Let's see your ID.

AGENT: I am unauthorized to produce it prior to security clearance.

SHERIFF LUTZ: Then how do I know who you are?

AGENT: Sheriff, we're wasting time.

SHERIFF LUTZ: I'm sorry. My orders are to trust no one. (*AGENT sighs at this petty annoyance and punches a button on his wristwatch. SHERIFF's phone rings.*) Hello, Noburg Police, Sheriff Lutz... oh, yes, sir! Yes, sir... you bet, sir... oh, no, sir... yes, sir... yes, sir... thank you, sir. (*hangs up phone, stunned*)

DEPUTY HACK: Sheriff? Who was it?

AGENT: (*raises his hand to silence them*) Suppression of information is vital to a free society. The enemy is everywhere. Look out that window... there's a thousand little piles of revolutionary kindling out there just waiting for a spark.

DEPUTY HACK: I don't see anything.

AGENT: If the other side ever got hold of the truth, there's no telling what they might do with it. For instance, did you know that three-fourths of all the horses in North America died last year when a government experiment in germ warfare got out of hand?

DEPUTY HACK: No.

AGENT: And did you know the diseased meat was mistakenly sold to a multinational fast-food hamburger chain?

DEPUTY HACK: No.

AGENT: And that over one hundred million people died consuming it?

DEPUTY HACK: No.

AGENT: Thank you. That's a compliment for a job well done. Our job is to make sure news of *this* incident never gets out.

DEPUTY HACK: You think there's some connection?

AGENT: Everything is connected. We're taking no chances. Right now we've got a crew tearing up that highway to make it look real. We intend to keep Noburg off the map where it belongs. Now the terrorists–

SHERIFF LUTZ: You mean old lady Mulvaney and the horses?

AGENT: Whatever they're calling themselves... have initiated a widespread and highly illegal gas-smuggling operation. I have here aerial photographs I took on my way over. That farm is located on lot twenty-three, corner seven. Open your Communist Manifesto and turn to page twenty-three, paragraph seven. It says "Seize the means of production." We are dealing with a dangerous international conspiracy.

SHERIFF LUTZ: I thought communism was dead.

AGENT: Sheriff, a horse is never dead until you beat it.

DEPUTY HACK: This sounds like fun. What do we do?

AGENT: Infiltration, confrontation, elimination. According to these photographs, one of the "horse" members of the gang is absent. I intend to turn this to our advantage.

Near the auction barn, ELMER and ORVILLE enter, pulling a cart with DODGE in it.

ELMER: Graintime, big fella. You clean that bucket out, now. We want you nice and fat for the auction, get some meat on those bones.

DODGE: There's more to meat than meets the eye. And I, after all these years, what have I? A nightmare without a mare to warm my nights, no little one to follow in my hoofsteps, a few collar sores... oh, Dodge, you big, dumb, stupid horse! Maybe if I had some disease they wouldn't eat me. Nay. I will go nobly, not cringing, to my fate. Better to end it quick like Rambler than slow and... oh, what a way to go! Buried in a tin can. Still, maybe a belly's a more fit grave than a hole in the ground filled with grass... what am I saying? How can I think of food at a time like this? I'm hungry, that's how. Ah, that's all the world is – one big stomach waiting to digest us from the day we poke our heads out. Lucky me mama and papa never lived to see such days. When them who've been feeding us become them who feed on us. And do we get fed up? No. We serve them like servants until one day they serve *us*. Why? Why? Why? (*He sings.*)

MEAT ON THE BONE

Why is a man a man?
What makes a horse a horse?
Lead them both to the water
And they draw from the very same source.

Change them in mid-stream,
The rider is ridden,
What lies between
My hide and what's hidden?

Horseflesh and humanflesh,
What's the grand design?
Why does one pull the plough
And another one pull the lines?

What makes a man a man?
Why is a horse a horse?
Is it knowledge transmitted
By the application of force?

Is it a difference in language,
A question of taste?
Economics? Intelligence?
Or the marketplace?

Why is a man a man?
Is it the way that he's trained?
What makes a horse a horse?
Our place on the food chain?

Maybe it's all just meat on the bone–
All I know is I'm alive,
I'm alive,
I'm alone.

DODGE is led off. In GRANDMA's bedroom, NURSE is reading a magazine while GRANDMA hallucinates from her medication.

GRANDMA: Ask not for whom the hoof beats, the hoof beats for thee, for thee the hoof beats, beating, beaten. What's that? What? You don't have to shout! The pie's in the oven. Take it out when it's done. Henry, are you listening? Henry Mulvaney, you put that cider down and...

NURSE: (*concerned*) Mrs. Mulvaney?

GRANDMA: You let that pie burn up and those people will come in here and take over.

NURSE: (*looking in her pupils*) What people?

GRANDMA: Ones trampling my garden. Look at 'em. Stop eating my roses!

NURSE: (*taking her pulse, checking heart with stethoscope, consulting charts, mounting concern*) It's all right. They're gone now.

GRANDMA: Take that carrot out of your mouth when you speak to me, Ford. Doesn't Chevy look pretty today. That's a beautiful dress. Lincoln gave it to you? How nice. Dodge, you sit down over there next to Rambler.

NURSE: You're going to be all right, Mrs. Mulvaney.

GRANDMA: Who're you?

NURSE: You remember me.

GRANDMA: Yeah, I remember you. Just like all the rest. Real sweetheart 'til we got married. Then the tune changed. You think you can tell me what to do? You can't tell me what to do. If I want to go to town, I'll go to town. Just don't let that pie burn up.

NURSE: (*at bedroom door*) Mrs. Willis!

MADGE and TED enter, outside bedroom.

MADGE: What is it?

GRANDMA: Chevy, you be quiet!

NURSE: Your mother's had a severe reaction to her medication.

MADGE: Is she all right?

NURSE: Frankly, no. We have to get her to a hospital as soon as possible.

TED: I'll call an ambulance.

MADGE: Can we talk to her?

NURSE: Not right now.

MADGE: Ted, wait for me.

They exit. In the yard, AGENT, SHERIFF and DEPUTY enter. AGENT is dressed in black high-tech commando gear. SHERIFF wears a cheap, novelty-store-type horse mask. DEPUTY is disguised as a hay bale.

SHERIFF LUTZ: This is ridiculous.

DEPUTY HACK: (*speaking into walkie-talkie*) Lucky Horseshoe, Lucky Horseshoe. Come in, Lucky Horseshoe. This is Allergic Reaction. Do you read me?

SHERIFF LUTZ: Yes, I read you, Waldo. I'm right behind you.

DEPUTY HACK: I am now on the farm. Repeat. On the farm.

SHERIFF LUTZ: We know you're on the farm. Will you put that thing away?

DEPUTY HACK: Roger. Lucky Horseshoe, this is Allergic Reaction signing off. (*to AGENT*) Sir? What was your code name again?

AGENT: Grim Reaper.

DEPUTY HACK: Grim Reaper, this is Allergic Reaction over and out.

SHERIFF LUTZ: This is ridiculous. I don't look like a horse.

DEPUTY HACK: You look as much like a horse as those nags Willis has.

AGENT: All right. This is it. You two continue surveillance in the combat zone while I penetrate the target area on a preliminary reconnaissance mission.

DEPUTY HACK: What?

SHERIFF LUTZ: Keep your eyes peeled while he goes in the house.

AGENT: (*hearing something*) Shhh.

SHERIFF LUTZ: What's that?

AGENT: Eat the hay.

SHERIFF LUTZ: What?

AGENT: Eat the hay!

SHERIFF LUTZ: Just a minute.

AGENT pushes SHERIFF's face into DEPUTY's hay bale. AGENT sneaks up to house. As door opens and TED and MADGE come out, AGENT slips in.

TED: Is the ambulance here yet?

MADGE: No.

TED: I guess all we can do now is wait and pray.

MADGE: It seems so senseless, Ted. Watching everyone you love die. What's the point?

TED: Madge, after she's out of the hospital... I mean, if she gets better, let's take care of her ourselves.

MADGE: I don't know, Ted. I can't think right now.

TED: (*seeing SHERIFF*) What's that horse doing there?

MADGE: Dodge? Is that Dodge?

TED: It must be, Linda was looking for him earlier. I better get him.

MADGE: Wait, I'll help you.

TED: Here, Dodge, good boy. Come on, Dodge...

SHERIFF exits, pursued by TED and MADGE. LINDA enters, followed by FORD, LINCOLN and CHEVY.

LINDA: Dad? Did you find Dodge? Dodge! (*exits after them*)

DEPUTY HACK: (*as FORD sniffs him*) Sheriff? Is that you? Ouch! Sir, you bit me, sir. Ouch. Hey! (*exits, pursued by FORD, LINCOLN and CHEVY*)

AGENT approaches NURSE outside bedroom.

AGENT: Police. I'd like a few words with the patient.

NURSE: I'm sorry, but no one's allowed in. Mrs. Mulvaney is delirious.

AGENT: I'll determine who's delirious around here.

NURSE: I'm sorry, but she is not to be disturbed.

AGENT: The health of society is more important than the health of one individual, doctor. Step aside.

NURSE: I'm not a doctor.

AGENT: I see. So now you farmers are taking the medical profession into your own hands, too. (*knocks out NURSE*) Let that be a warning. (*enters bedroom*) Mrs. Mulvaney? Mrs. Mulvaney?

GRANDMA: (*startled awake*) Who's there? What do you want?

AGENT: It's a friend, Mrs. Mulvaney.

GRANDMA: Get away from me. I know who you are. You're Death.

AGENT: Mrs. Mulvaney, I am an agent–

GRANDMA: Agent of death. You don't fool me. Oh, wait... I need more time. I haven't planted my garden yet.

AGENT: I'll take care of your garden for you.

GRANDMA: Yes, and I know what kind of harvest it'll be.

AGENT: Let's be reasonable.

GRANDMA: I don't reason with Death.

AGENT: Mrs. Mulvaney, I want to help you.

GRANDMA: Help me right into the grave. This one's for you, Rambler. (*GRANDMA tries to throw a punch, AGENT puts his hand up to stop it. GRANDMA stops with severe chest pain.*)

AGENT: Mrs. Mulvaney?

GRANDMA: Let go of my heart. You're not fighting fair.

AGENT: (*makes a fist with his hand*) Mrs. Mulvaney?

GRANDMA: Don't touch me.

AGENT: Mrs. Mulvaney, I'll let go of your heart if you give me a confession.

GRANDMA: Over my dead body.

AGENT: If you won't confess, I could leave you and take your horses instead.

GRANDMA: No! Not my horses.

AGENT: I've already got Rambler.

GRANDMA: Okay, okay. You drive a hard bargain. What do you want?

AGENT: I want the truck.

GRANDMA: The truck?

AGENT: The truck.

GRANDMA: That's all?

AGENT: I want the truck.

GRANDMA: It's in the haystack.

AGENT: The haystack?

GRANDMA: The haystack! Clean the wax out of your ears. I drove it into the haystack.

Now let go of my heart. (*AGENT relaxes his fist, GRANDMA's pain stops*) Thanks.

AGENT: Poor creature. You really are delirious. (*starts to exit*)

GRANDMA: And you leave my horses alone. What's wrong with yours anyway? Gone lame?

AGENT: You're living in the past, Mrs. Mulvaney. Death doesn't ride a horse anymore. He drives a car. Goodbye. For now. (*exits*)

LINDA: (*entering*) Grandma? Are you awake?

GRANDMA: Of course I'm awake.

LINDA: Dodge is gone.

GRANDMA: What? (*yells after AGENT*) You lying cheat! We made a deal, you underhanded undertaker!

LINDA: Grandma? Who're you talking to?

GRANDMA: Huh? Linda, did you see someone on the stairs just now?

LINDA: No.

GRANDMA: No one?

LINDA: No. (*sees NURSE*) What's he doing on the floor?

GRANDMA: That fellow spends more time day-dreaming than anybody I know. Come on. Let's put him to bed. (*They drag NURSE into bed.*)

LINDA: Elmer must've got Dodge.

GRANDMA: Elmer? (*remembers FORD's mime and copies fragments*) Hell-myrrh Frankenmoose's got Dodge. Elmer Frankenmuth's got Dodge!

LINDA: Grandma?

GRANDMA: Well? What're you waiting for? A royal invitation? Go get the horses. We're gonna save Dodge if it's the last thing I do. (*They exit.*)

TED enters leading the captured SHERIFF by a rope. Thinking SHERIFF is Dodge, TED takes him into the barn. DEPUTY, still disguised as a hay bale, enters, chased by FORD, LINCOLN and CHEVY. HORSES stop when they see SHERIFF being led into the barn and follow. CORA enters and trips over DEPUTY.

CORA LUTZ: Madge! Madge! What's this bale doing here? (*Moves the DEPUTY*) Boy, that's heavy. Madge!

CORA exits into house. DEPUTY stands up to exit, but drops back down as TED comes out of barn. MADGE enters from other direction and trips over DEPUTY.

MADGE: Ted? Did you call me?

TED: No, but I got Dodge. I locked him in the barn with the other horses.

MADGE: Maybe it was Linda calling me. Oh, Ted, what if it's Mother?

They run into the house. On the way, TED trips over DEPUTY. LINDA and GRANDMA sneak out of the house and cross to the barn. LINDA trips over DEPUTY. LINDA opens the barn door and SHERIFF runs out, followed by LINCOLN and CHEVY.

LINDA: Whoa. Get back in there! (*She slams the barn door shut before FORD can get out. SHERIFF exits.*)

GRANDMA: Who was that?

LINDA: I think it was Ford.

FORD: (*in barn*) It wasn't Ford! I'm in here.

GRANDMA: We got no time to be chasing him. We'll just take Lincoln and Chevy. (*exits with LINDA, LINCOLN and CHEVY*)

FORD: (*in barn*) Hey! What about me?

AGENT enters.

AGENT: (*searching hay bales*) Deputy Hack? Deputy Hack? Allergic Reaction?

DEPUTY HACK: Over here, sir.

AGENT: We're ready to mount the offensive. Where's the Sheriff?

DEPUTY HACK: The enemy has him locked in the barn, sir.

AGENT: I'll effect a rescue of the Sheriff. You keep the old lady covered.

DEPUTY HACK: (*into walkie-talkie*) I read you loud and clear, Grim Reaper. This is Allergic Reaction over and out.

AGENT goes into the barn. DEPUTY goes toward the house, drops to the ground as TED and MADGE come out.

TED: What is this? Hay bales everywhere. (*TED side-steps DEPUTY and trips on a real bale.*)

MADGE: Oh, Ted, where could she be?

TED: She can't have gotten very far. Mother!

MADGE: Mother! (*She exits, followed by TED. DEPUTY enters the house.*)

At the auction, ELMER addresses the audience as if they were bidders.

ELMER: Thank you. And some smart bidding. But, ladies and gentlemen, we all know what these horses are worth. So let's get those bids up. I mean we're not talking about racing these nags. We're talking about eating them. And you know what kind of money's walking around here. (*checks his list*) Ah. On our programme, this will be number eighty-four. Orville!

ORVILLE: (*offstage, sounds of DODGE struggling*) Dad, I can't get him to come.

ELMER: (*to audience*) Excuse me. (*exits*)

GRANDMA and LINDA enter with LINCOLN and CHEVY.

LINDA: I hope we're not too late.

GRANDMA: (*to audience member*) Have they sold Dodge yet? Good.

LINCOLN and CHEVY sit with audience. ELMER and ORVILLE enter with DODGE, hitting him with a switch.

ELMER: Get up there. Get up. You're as stubborn as the old lady. Okay, folks, number eighty-four. Name of Dodge. Take a look at this hunk of flesh, friends. Nineteen-hundred pounds. No fat. Well, not much. Good strong teeth, no sign of disease. (*DODGE tries to bite ELMER.*) Lots of spirit. Nineteen hundred pounds worth. Plus you get to keep the tail for cushions, the hooves for glue, and teeth for your kids to play with. What am I bid? Let's start it off at five hundred dollars. Do I hear five, do I hear five?

ORVILLE watches the audience for bidders. Several plants bid.

ORVILLE: Five hundred dollars.

ELMER: I got five, I got five, now seven, now seven...

Bidding continues until one bidder is left.

Okay, nine-fifty, going once... going twice... last chance, folks... do I hear a thousand?

LINCOLN whinnies in audience.

I have a thousand, thank you. I have a thousand, now eleven hundred...

ORVILLE: Eleven.

LINCOLN whinnies.

ELMER: That's twelve, that's twelve.

ORVILLE: Fourteen.

ELMER: Fourteen, I have fourteen... do I hear fifteen? Do I hear fifteen? (*to LIN-*

COLN) How about it? You, sir, the gentleman with the big head? (*LINCOLN whinnies.*)

I have fifteen. Fifteen to you, sir...

PLANT: Forget it. Eat him yourself.

ELMER: That's fifteen once, fifteen twice, going, going...

CHEVY whinnies.

Sixteen, now sixteen...

LINDA: Wait! She didn't mean to bid.

ELMER: Whaddya mean? She had her hoof up in the air, didn't she? Her hoof?

GRANDMA: Dodge!

ELMER dodges. DODGE bolts from stage. LINDA trips ORVILLE. GRANDMA trips ELMER. HORSES exit, followed by GRANDMA and LINDA, followed by ORVILLE and ELMER. Meanwhile, back at the farm, the DEPUTY, still dressed as a hay bale, bursts into the bedroom where the NURSE lies unconscious.

DEPUTY HACK: Freeze! Hold it right there. (*pause*) Playing dead won't do, Mrs. Mulvaney. Get up.

NURSE: (*coming to*) What?

DEPUTY HACK: Disguising yourself as a man won't work either.

NURSE: Who are you? What are you talking about? I *am* a man.

DEPUTY HACK: I wasn't born yesterday. That ridiculous costume of yours couldn't fool a horse. Now put this dress on and come with me, Mrs. Mulvaney.

NURSE: I'm not Mrs. Mulvaney, I'm her nurse.

DEPUTY HACK: Ha. I've got you there. You can't be a man because nursing is a woman's job. Trapped by your own logic, Mrs. Mulvaney. Now be a good girl and come with me.

NURSE: Okay, okay. But I won't put this dress on.

DEPUTY HACK: Oh, yes, you will. This is a decent town. We like our criminals to keep the sex they were born with to themselves. Now get dressed. On the double.

As NURSE reluctantly dons dress, TED, MADGE and CORA enter the yard.

TED: Mother!

MADGE: Mother!

CORA LUTZ: Madge!

TED: Cora, what are you doing here?

MADGE: Have you seen my mother, Cora?

AGENT swings open the barn door and steps into the yard, followed by FORD.

AGENT: (*gun drawn*) Hold it right there. This is an arrest. Sheriff, search them.

FORD stands there and does nothing.

TED: What's going on here? Who are you?

AGENT: Don't play innocent with me. The truck. Illegal distribution of gas.

MADGE: He's innocent. I'm the one you want. I stole the truck. I distributed the gas.

TED: (*to MADGE*) What?

CORA LUTZ: They're both innocent. I'm the one you want.

AGENT: Identify yourself.

CORA LUTZ: You know who I am. Mrs. Vernon Lutz.

AGENT: (*to FORD*) Sheriff, do you know this woman?

CORA LUTZ: (*puzzled*) Vern?

AGENT: (*to FORD*) Sheriff, you are not to divulge your identity. (*to CORA*) Mrs. Lutz, I have to ask you to get out of the way before you get hurt.

CORA LUTZ: I will not.

TED: All right. Hold it, all of you!

AGENT: Look out, Sheriff, he's got a gun!

MADGE: Ted, where did you get a gun?

TED: I don't have a gun.

AGENT: He doesn't have a gun!

TED: No, I've got something better – a cigarette lighter! Make a move and I'll blow this truck sky high! (*TED moves toward the haystack where the truck is buried.*)

MADGE: Ted...

TED: It's okay, Madge. I won't let them get you. We're in this together.

AGENT: Okay, maybe we can talk about this.

TED: I'll do the talking, you do the listening.

AGENT: I'm listening. What do you want?

TED: I want you to drop all charges against me, my wife, my mother-in-law, my daughter, and the horses.

DEPUTY enters with NURSE in one of Grandma's dresses.

DEPUTY HACK: Drop that lighter, Willis, or I blow your grandmother's head off!

NURSE: (*as TED drops lighter*) I'm not their grandmother!

DEPUTY HACK: So you've raised a family of illegitimate offspring?

AGENT: Good work, deputy. Here, sheriff. Keep them covered while the deputy and I search them.

AGENT puts his gun in FORD's mouth. FORD spits it out. MADGE grabs it.

MADGE: Hold it right there! (*to FORD*) Don't try to stop me, Vern!

AGENT and DEPUTY raise their hands. FORD follows suit.

TED: Good work, Madge.

MADGE: Why shouldn't we take a little gas for ourselves? The gas companies have been stealing from us for years.

MEL and TRUCKER enter with guns.

MEL TWIGGS: Drop the gun, Mrs. Willis.

MADGE drops the gun.

DEPUTY HACK: Good work, Mel. I'll take over now.

MEL TWIGGS: Not so fast, Waldo. We're taking the law into our own hands. We're sick of you botching the job.

DEPUTY HACK: You can't do this.

MEL TWIGGS: Who says?

DEPUTY HACK: The sheriff. Right, sheriff?

FORD stands there doing nothing.

TRUCKER: Where's my truck?

MADGE: There.

TRUCKER: I said truck, not hay.

TED: Don't raise your voice to my wife.

AGENT: (*to NURSE*) I guess this breaks up your little outlaw gang, Grandma. Sheriff, you take care of the rest of the family, the old lady's mine.

NURSE: I am not an old lady!

DEPUTY HACK: Don't be fooled by her disguise, sir.

MEL TWIGGS: (*to FORD*) Keep your hands off them, sheriff. We're going to handle this our way.

ELMER: (*enters puffing and out of breath, grabs FORD*) Ha! I got ya!

CORA LUTZ: That's not your horse, Elmer, that's my husband!

ELMER: This contract says it's my horse.

SHERIFF, still wearing horse mask, runs by.

CORA LUTZ: There. There's your horse!

SHERIFF exits, pursued by ELMER.

TRUCKER: This ain't hay, it's my truck!

MEL TWIGGS: Maybe it's your truck, but it's full of my gas.

MADGE: It's not full anymore.

MEL TWIGGS: I oughta wring your neck, you and your rotten mother! (*threatens NURSE*)

NURSE: I'm not a mother! Go ahead – search me!

AGENT: Indecent exposure now, is it?

DEPUTY HACK: (*searching NURSE*) She's right! She's a man!

AGENT: Aha! Just as I suspected all along – the old lady Mulvaney is a man. What does this mean? A man dressed as a woman? Humans come in two sexes, horses walk on four legs. Two times four equals eight. The horse ate the hay. "Horse" is an anagram for "shore". Hay is spelled with three letters. Three is the number of the Christian trinity. The Father, the Son and the Holy Ghost. You can't have a ghost without a dead man. The dead man washed up on the shore and was buried in the earth. The earth is the third planet from the sun. The sun is a burning ball of gas. Gas is carried in a truck. Truck is spelled with five letters. There are five fingers on a hand. Horses don't have hands, therefore the horses involved in this crime are not horses but humans in disguise!

ELMER enters, dragging SHERIFF by a rope.

SHERIFF LUTZ: I am not a horse!

AGENT: I rest my case. You're all under arrest.

ALL: Horseshit!

A brawl about to break out when GRANDMA, LINDA, LINCOLN, CHEVY and DODGE enter. Music under.

GRANDMA: Take your stand with the Mulvaney clan.

FORD: Dodge!

DODGE: Ford!

MADGE: Mother!

TED: Madge!

LINDA: Cora!

The sides line up in battle formation. HORSES and FAMILY sing, dispatching their foes as they do.

A GOOD SWIFT KICK

Twas a time when we were well-respected,
Well-fed, well-groomed and well-protected,
Now they got tractors to get their fields planted
And everyone's taking the horses for granted.

Like the family farm we're a thing of the past,
But we're making hay while they run out of gas,
Highways all over, good soil turned to sand,
We're taking the law in our hooves and our hands.

Stop chasing that carrot on the end of a stick,
Feed the hand that bites you a good swift kick,
Better than bitchin', don't leave it to chance,
Give a good swift kick in the seat of the pants.

Draining your wallet and filling your tank,
Pumps are laughing all the way to the bank,
Prices are rising with every click,
You get more mileage from a good swift kick!

Stop chasing that carrot on the end of a stick,
Feed the hand that bites you a good swift kick,
Better than bitchin', don't leave it to chance,
Give a good swift kick in the seat of the pants.

Music continues as DODGE grabs ELMER.

DODGE: (*spoken*) And next on the auction block, a fine piece of flesh. What a rump roast this'll make. Good confirmation, a hard worker, a touch lame in the frontal lobes, needs breaking, will drink anything, stands fifteen hooves high. We'll start the bidding at one dollar. Do I have one? One, do I have two, one, two, one, two, one, two, three, four!

LINDA sings next verse.

Who needs the auctioneer's wooden gavel
When you got a problem that you're trying to lick?
The toughest knots will come unravelled,
When you make your point with a good swift kick.

DODGE kicks ELMER. GRANDMA performs a fling, then sings next verse.

People's like sheep, they'll follow the fold,
Get flocked, get sheared, get dumped when they're old,
But some folks is horses, won't stand for those tricks,
Push 'em too far, you'll get a good swift kick!

ALL join in for last chorus.

Stop chasing that carrot on the end of a stick,
Feed the hand that bites you a good swift kick,
Better than bitchin', don't leave it to chance,
Give a good swift kick–

LINDA: Stop! (*music stops*) Grandma's gone!

TED: Grandma?

MADGE: Grandma?

CORA LUTZ: Grandma.

All exit calling for GRANDMA. Only DEPUTY remains, talking into his walkie-talkie.

DEPUTY HACK: Grim Reaper, Grim Reaper. Come in, Grim Reaper.

Lights dim to blackout. Voices calling for Grandma fade in distance. Pause. FORD enters for epilogue. LINDA hooks HORSES to plough as FORD speaks.

FORD: They found Grandma lying in her garden. Madge said she hadn't looked so peaceful since her old man Henry died. But a few months later some of the biggest carrots you ever saw came up right there, where there used to be a highway.

CHEVY: And now there's corn where there used to be weeds.

DODGE: Clover where there was dust.

LINCOLN: And alfalfa where there was stones.

LINDA: Come on, Ford, sun's coming up.

As LINDA drives HORSES off, TED and MADGE enter from the house.

TED: Well, will you look at that. I think Chevy's in foal.

LINCOLN: I told you it was just a matter of time.

DODGE: (*to FORD, as they exit*) Step up, you jerk.

FORD: What's your hurry?

DODGE: Use your feet more and your mouth less.

FORD: Nag, nag, nag. (*exit pulling plough*)

The end.

TALKING DIRTY

BY

SHERMAN SNUKAL

Sheelah Megill as Beth, Norman Browning as Michael

Photographer: Glen Erikson

SHERMAN SNUKAL'S *TALKING DIRTY* – A COMEDY OF (KITSILANO) MANNERS

There have been few long-running "hits" in British Columbia theatre. With a limited audience base, especially outside Vancouver, theatre companies normally fill seats by offering a season of half a dozen plays consisting of a formulaic mix of classics and recent hits from Broadway or the West End, increasingly peppered with one or two "risky" plays – typically Canadian. In addition, because professional theatre companies normally depend on government and corporate subsidies for their existence, it is good business to sell a well-rounded "package" of events: sponsors for each show can then be lined up, happily displaying their civic regard for the arts, while theatres can bank on dependable funding. In this system, each play is safely presented within the context of a "balanced" season that somehow promises to be challenging, adventuresome, or some other cachet. The presence of a Shakespeare, of course, lends prestige, allows cultural claims to be made, and compensates for the presence of aforementioned risky works. Each play, although characterized in brochures and posters as unique, is also presented as merely contributing to a season – a season that somehow has a visionary meaning greater than its parts.

The problem is that this method is too often based more on good bookkeeping practice than on truly engaging in a vital cultural experience – such as developing meaningful plays and/or responding to audience needs. People buy a season of plays on the strength of one or two that they really want to see, then dutifully attend others they care less for or have been badly reviewed. Each production is slotted into a two or three-week run, whether sold-out or not, leaving no possibility to meet increased audience needs if a hit or early cancellation if a dud. As for the play itself, although frequently under-rehearsed and given a short appearance, it is considered to be complete, and, unless it miraculously transfers to another theatre, is thereby deprived of vital development in either dramaturgical or performance directions.

An exception to this occurred at Vancouver's Arts Club Theatre in the early 1980s. Founded in the late fifties as a literary reading society, the Arts moved into its own building on Seymour Street in 1964 and regularly presented plays there, about half a dozen a year, until the early seventies when Bill Millerd took over as artistic director. Under Millerd, the Theatre became a year-round operation with increased lengths of runs – plays ran for a month with an option for extension if they proved popular, such as happened with the hit musicals *Jacques Brel Is Alive and Well and Living in Paris* and *Side by Side by Sondheim*. One of the longest was *Talking Dirty*.

Sherman Snukal was a graduate student at University of British Columbia during the early 1980s, working on his doctorate in philosophy. He was also writing plays for the New Play Centre, an institution founded a decade earlier to assist new playwrights. One belief the Centre held was that if a playwright could successfully create a good one-acter and get it staged, the play might be seen by an established theatre company and lead to its accepting a full-length by the same author. Snukal had already had two of his short plays, *The Whispering Time* and *Perfect Plastic*, produced at the Centre when he submitted his full-length, *Talking Dirty*, for workshop development. Then, after an early version of the play was performed on Vancouver's Co-Op Radio, he sent the revised work to Bill Millerd at the Arts Club Theatre, who liked it.

By this time Millerd was operating two theatres—in 1979 he had opened the 450-seat Granville Island Stage—and exercised considerable flexibility in his programming. He set up series of plays in both theatres, allowing subscribers to buy a number of plays and attend either venue. His Privileged Personal Pass allowed the purchaser to attend any production at any theatre, and attend productions as many times as the ticketholder wished. When there was demand, he extended the play's run: *Talking Dirty* opened at the Seymour Street Theatre in October 1981 and ran for three years and over 1,000 performances – a stunning event in British Columbia theatre.

Critic Jerry Wasserman, reflecting on its success in the *Canadian Theatre Review* (Summer 1982) noted that "Nothing in town has excited so many people so much this year except maybe the Canucks making their run at the Stanley Cup." When it played in Toronto in 1983, *Maclean's Magazine* (October 24, 1983) called the play "a rare Canadian phenomenon – a genuine play of ideas in the tradition of Albee and George Bernard Shaw." That same year the play won the

Chalmers Award for Outstanding Canadian Play of the year. There were also major productions in Edmonton, Winnipeg, Ottawa, as well as other cities in Canada and the United States.

Talking Dirty is self-described as a Comedy of Manners – that peculiar form of drama where well-heeled members of Society banter, seduce, and make each other miserable with steely nonchalance, a form that, at its best in the plays of Wilde or Coward, is rescued from depression by ingratiating repartee and/or energetic farce. With *Talking Dirty*, Vancouver had such a play, and it was a hit. Surely part of the reason for its success was the pleasure of seeing the familiar – the setting is an apartment in Vancouver's funky, fashionable Kitsilano district, and the small cast of characters includes a girl (very much) from Burnaby, two UBC professors, and other recognizable singles. They are clever, educated, and very interested in creative relationships.

The play also engages in West Coast caricature: Vancouverite Michael is visited by his old pal Dave, a lawyer now living in Toronto, who regards his attendance at a convention in the city as an opportunity to have an extra-marital fling: "Only in BC", he boasts. So the West Coast is depicted as a place of misbehaviour and mad eccentrics: the Burnaby girl is a "space cadet," while the profs play the mating game with reckless, pre-AIDS abandon. This depiction, however, while obviously striking gleeful chords of meaning with its audience, is at the same time darkly qualified as one by one the characters retreat into suffocating guilt. "This god damn arrangement. Smiling at each other and pretending we're these sophisticated, enlightened people. It makes me nauseous," says Beth, who, along with pretty well everybody else, leaves Michael friendless, and his apartment empty at the play's close. If *Talking Dirty* portrays an emerging segment of British Columbia society, it does so with little assurance; perhaps its strongest message is that real British Columbians are *not* like that. Terra Kitsilano finally remains *terra incognito*.

J.H.

Selected Bibliography:

- Czarnecki, Mark. "A War of Ideas in Academe." *Maclean's Magazine*, October 24, 1983. A review of *Talking Dirty* at the Bathurst Street Theatre in Toronto.
- Malcolm Page. "Change in Vancouver Theatre, 1963-1980." *Theatre History in Canada*, Vol. 2, No. 1, Spring 1981. Presents a good picture of theatre in Vancouver before *Talking Dirty*, including a background to the Arts Club Theatre.
- Sherman Snukal. *Talking Dirty*. Madeira Park, B.C.: Harbour Publishing, 1983.
- Robert Wallace and Cynthia Zimmerman. "The Audience and the Season." *Canadian Theatre Review* 37 (Spring 1983): 19-24. An interview with Bill Millerd, Artistic Director of the Arts Club Theatre.
- Jerry Wasserman. "Vancouver: A Day in the Life." *Canadian Theatre Review* 35 (Summer 1982): 142-145. Contains a useful comparison of productions playing in Vancouver in March 1982, and includes a production photograph of *Talking Dirty* with cast members Norman Browning, Kyra Harper, and Gabrielle Rose.

Talking Dirty
by Sherman Snukal

Talking Dirty was first produced at the Arts Club Theatre, Vancouver on October 13, 1981, with the following cast:

Michael	Norman Browning
Dave	Dana Still
Beth	Sheelah Megill
Karen	Gabrielle Rose
Jackie	Alana Shields

Directed by Mario Crudo

CHARACTERS

MICHAEL KAYE: Early to mid thirties.
DAVE LERNER: Early to mid thirties.
KAREN SPERLING: Late twenties.
BETH GORDON: Late twenties.
JACQUELINE LEMIEUX: Early twenties.

TIME

The present. A weekend in May.

PLACE

Vancouver.

SETTING

Michael's apartment, the living room. The apartment is in an old house that has recently been reworked as a trendy apartment block.
On the left, a door to the hall. Down right, a window looking out on to the street. Up right, the entrance to the dining room. At the back, the entrance to the kitchen and doors to the bedroom and bathroom. The kitchen and the dining room are connected by an unseen passageway that allows free movement between the two rooms.
At the right, a large piece of antique furniture serves as a bar and also holds the stereo equipment. A couch to the right of stage centre. A coffee table in front of the couch. A Bonsai tree on the coffee table. To the left of the couch, a small end table, lamp, and comfortable arm chair. A desk and bookcase at left.

SCENE ONE

About twelve-thirty Saturday afternoon. MICHAEL is discovered sitting on the couch working. His notes and books are on the coffee table in front of him. After a moment, he puts down his book and takes a sip of coffee. Then he turns on the stereo, and taking his coffee mug and a dirty ashtray, he enters the kitchen. There is a knock on the door. MICHAEL returns from the kitchen with a bottle of wine. He pours himself a glass and returns to the couch. There is another knock. MICHAEL turns off the stereo and answers the door. DAVE is there. He is holding a small package.

MICHAEL: Dave.

DAVE: Mike. How you doing?

MICHAEL and DAVE give each other a hug.

MICHAEL: Jesus. It's been a while.

DAVE: No kidding.

MICHAEL: What are you doing here?

DAVE: I'm a "conventioneer". Can you believe it?

MICHAEL: Come in. When did you arrive?

DAVE: Last night.

MICHAEL: You should have called. I would have picked you up.

DAVE: Ah. Things were up in the air. I was going to go. And then I wasn't going to go. And then when I did go I had to take an afternoon flight which means I arrived just in time to go to meetings all last night. I shouldn't be here right now. A thousand lawyers in the same room. The body rebels. The mind rebels. I was losing the ability to think.

MICHAEL: You've come to the right place. I haven't thought about anything in years. No Lynn and the kids?

DAVE: In Toronto. Minding the family estate.

MICHAEL notices the box. DAVE waves it at him. Then he throws it at him.

DAVE: For you. A new ball.

MICHAEL: Thanks. Never say die, eh Dave?

DAVE: I've been practicing. I've got a feeling after twenty years I'm going to win the championship.

MICHAEL: Don't count your chickens. You want some wine?

DAVE: Sure. Mike.

DAVE shows off his ensemble.

MICHAEL: Very nice.

DAVE: Intelligent, successful, well dressed but short.

MICHAEL: Not short, Dave. Compact. More man per cubic inch.

DAVE: What counts in a man is density. Density and taste. Mike. (*showing his label*) Harry Rosen. Top of the line.

MICHAEL: Very nice. Very lawyer.

DAVE: Mike.

DAVE points to the floor.

MICHAEL: What?

DAVE points again.

What?

DAVE: Gucci. Two hundred and thirty dollars.

MICHAEL: Hudson's Bay. Forty-eight fifteen.

DAVE: On sale. Saved thirty bucks.

MICHAEL: Regular price. Includes tax.

MICHAEL hands DAVE his drink.

DAVE: Functional.

MICHAEL: You forget you have them on.

DAVE: Cheers. (*takes a sip*) Not bad. Are you working this afternoon?

MICHAEL: Someone's coming over for a meeting but it's not for a while.

DAVE: By the way, your philosophy department made *The Globe and Mail* last week.

MICHAEL: Yeah?

DAVE: Something about the new head you got in January. He's some sort of hot shot?

MICHAEL: Kant scholar. Big jerk.

DAVE: You still making enemies of your department heads?

MICHAEL: What do you think? He hates my guts. I hate his. A very uncomplicated bit of social interaction. Thank God I've got tenure. Maybe I should have been a lawyer.

DAVE: Then you'd have partners. And they can also be a big pain in the ass. Such is life.

MICHAEL: I'll drink to that.

DAVE: I like the new place. How long has it been?

MICHAEL: About six weeks.

DAVE: Very academic. Still have your Bonsai, I see.

MICHAEL: Yup. Still hasn't grown.

DAVE: (*to the tree*) Don't worry about it. Short trees have more personality. Hey. Where's Beth?

There is a loud buzz from the kitchen.

MICHAEL: That's my oven. Saturday afternoon. Beth is probably shopping. You want something to eat?

DAVE: Nah. Just ate.

MICHAEL exits to the kitchen.

MICHAEL: (*off*) Where you staying?

DAVE: The Four Seasons.

MICHAEL: (*off*) Very nice.

DAVE: And the two dozen hookers wandering around out front is that special touch that makes everything so much nicer.

MICHAEL: (*off*) A big tourist attraction.

DAVE: Yeah. I noticed the traffic jam taking in the sights.

MICHAEL returns with his lunch.

MICHAEL: Well Dave, not that you're interested, but for a small fee you can take some of that scenery up to your room.

DAVE: What's that?

MICHAEL: Whole wheat bread. Crab meat. Edam cheese. Throw it in the oven. Heat it up. *Voila.* You sure?

DAVE: Nah.... Full.... Maybe just a bite.... Not bad. Last night I watched three Japanese tourists purchase some of that scenery you were talking about. They bought six.

MICHAEL: Six?

DAVE: Six. The yen is strong. The dollar is weak. I'll have a little more.

MICHAEL: I could make you up one.

DAVE: Nah. Forget it. I'm not hungry. Mike. Do you ever wish you were Japanese?

MICHAEL: No. Do you?

DAVE: No. Yes. Lately I've been thinking it might make things a lot easier. Things are different over there in the land of the rising sun.

MICHAEL: What are you talking about?

DAVE: I'm talking about Geisha Girls. I'm talking about the Liberal Party. I'm talking about feeling like the straightest married man in all of Ontario.

MICHAEL: Is something bugging you, Dave?

DAVE: Ah, I don't know. It's as though sex is some sort of perk. If you've been a lawyer for a while, if you've got a good reputation, if you're successful. Well then, it only stands to reason that you join the Liberal Party and grab a little something on the side. You remember my partner?

MICHAEL: Sure.

DAVE: Well Jim Bannerman and the Liberal Party are like this.

MICHAEL: You're not just talking politics, are you?

DAVE: I see Jim everyday. Lynn and I have dinner with him and his wife at least once a month. Their kids and our kids play hockey in our living room. Now get this. In March when we had that late blizzard and I had to get a room downtown, guess who and his girlfriend had a room just down the hall.

MICHAEL: Really?

DAVE: Really, really. I was going to be discreet and pretend I didn't see him but Bannerman ambles over and introduces me to his bimbo. Cool as a cucumber. Like they spent the evening playing Crazy Eights and eating popcorn. It's been going on for over two years. A very sophisticated liaison. Every couple of months Bannerman and bimbo get away for a romantic weekend. This January it was Maui. Pretty nice for some people.

MICHAEL: I guess.

DAVE: I'm twice the lawyer he is. He'd be out on the God damn street if it weren't for me. All the best accounts are mine. Everybody knows that. So. I've been thinking. This is Vancouver, right?

MICHAEL: Right.

DAVE: And my home's in Toronto. Right?

MICHAEL: Right.

DAVE: So?

MICHAEL: So?

DAVE: So I'm away.

MICHAEL: Away?

DAVE: Away from Lynn and the kids.

MICHAEL: Oh. Right.

DAVE: Yeah. Why the hell not? So that's what's been bugging me. Not very bright, is it? What do you think?

MICHAEL: Look, Dave. I haven't been married for eight years but I know how it must be. If you feel you have to.

DAVE: I don't have to. I just want to.

MICHAEL: Well if you think it might be good for you.

DAVE: I don't think it will be good for me. It'll probably be terrible for me. What's the matter with you? You used to have an answer for everything.

MICHAEL: You know I understand.

DAVE: What do you mean "understand"? I haven't done anything. There's nothing to understand.

MICHAEL: Well if you were to do something. Then I'd understand.

DAVE: Well I probably won't. I'm only thinking about it.

MICHAEL: It's your decision.

DAVE: I know it's my decision.

MICHAEL: I can't make your decision for you.

DAVE: I don't want you to make my decision for me. I want to know how you feel.

MICHAEL: It's not my place, Dave. Look, I'm here, I'm your friend. Whatever you decide to do is fine with me.

DAVE: Terrific, wonderful. Good friend. (*DAVE crosses to the bar, pours himself some wine.*) Sorry, Mike. You got any grass? I wouldn't mind some grass.

MICHAEL: Sure.

DAVE: I was just thinking out loud. My eighteen-year-old self got the best of me. Who am I kidding? Right? It's not me.

MICHAEL exits to the dining room.

DAVE: Married eight years and you get an itch. The trick is not to scratch.

There is a knock on the door.

MICHAEL: (*off*) Will you get that Dave?

DAVE: Yeah.

DAVE answers the door. BETH is there. She is holding a cardboard box and a painting.

BETH: Dave.

DAVE: Beth.

BETH: When did you get in?

DAVE: Last night.

DAVE: You look terrific.

BETH: And you look very prosperous.

DAVE: I am prosperous.

BETH: You're not all here.

DAVE: Only the neurotic half. I left the better half in Toronto. Lynn doesn't like conventions.

BETH: The legal one? At the Four Seasons?

DAVE: With the lawyers loitering in the Garden Lounge. And the hookers loitering at the door.

BETH: Well be good, Dave. You're a lawyer not a travelling salesman.

DAVE: Ha-ha.

BETH: A friend of mine was at the session this morning.

DAVE: Yeah. What's her name?

BETH: Earl Telford.

DAVE: Bright woman taking a man's name in the legal profession. I'll say hello if I bump into him.

BETH: How are Lynn and the boys?

DAVE: Lynn's great. Going to exercise class three times a week. She's going back to work in the fall. She's got kids. Now she wants money. The boys are almost human. I got Josh and Danny skating last winter. And Sean is talking and making a mess of everything. I think we spoil the shrimp rotten. How's work?

BETH: Grade nine this year. Lots of boys. Are all fifteen-year-olds completely obsessed with sex? How were you at that age?

DAVE: I was great in crowds. I could bump into a different pair of breasts every five seconds.

Michael enters.

MICHAEL: Hi honey. I thought I heard you. (*a kiss for BETH*) What's all this?

BETH: It's yours. You left it when you moved out. I thought you might want it back.

DAVE stands up.

MICHAEL: Yeah. Thanks. (*noticing DAVE's reaction*) Well, isn't this great? Dave's going to be in town for a few days.

DAVE: Yup. Dave's in town and in the dark.

BETH: There's another box in the car.

MICHAEL: I'll get it.

BETH: I can manage.

BETH goes.

DAVE: When did this happen?

MICHAEL: About six weeks ago.

DAVE: I just acted like an idiot in front of you.

MICHAEL: You didn't act like an idiot.

DAVE: Why didn't you tell me?

MICHAEL: You know how you get.

DAVE: What does that mean? How the hell do I get?

MICHAEL: Think.

DAVE: I'm a little irked. That's all. What is it with you? Is three years the limit of your involvement with a woman? What are you, God's gift, that you have to spread yourself around? Make up your mind and settle down like the rest of the human race.

MICHAEL: I didn't see any sense in getting into this at long distance.... Look, Dave, Beth and I have been living together for over three years. We were thinking of buying a house together. And Beth needs a car. And I need dental work. And then there were going to be mortgage payments for God knows how long. And then, of course, given all this mutual financial involvement and human nature, we'd get married and have kids. It's inevitable, isn't it? And then what would we be? Some sitcom in the suburbs. Me and Beth and Ginger and

Skip and a big black lab that craps all over our back yard.

DAVE: Don't be so high and mighty. You're talking about my life. C'mon, Mike. Any eighteen year old can give me that crap. You can do better than that.

MICHAEL: Every second Sunday we go to Beth's parents for dinner. Her Dad's this charming old jock who sits around drinking Scotch and sneaking cigarettes and getting a little loaded and telling me how he bogied five and parred fifteen and who died last week and how the market's going to do next week. After dinner her mother, who is the nicest woman in the world but who talks too much and occasionally reminds me of Beth, which scares the shit right out of me, very graciously talks philosophy with me. Kahlil Gibran and Allan Watts and the meaning of life and also the meaning of marriage and just when are Beth and I going to settle down and make it all legal. And it's warm and safe and snug in that living room. With the fire in the hearth and the crocheted throws on the furniture and the chocolate mints in the china dish on the coffee table and all of us sitting around chatting like that wonderful family in the telephone commercial waiting around for that long distance call from that other wonderful family sitting around the fire thousands upon thousands of miles away. But, Dave, from Sunday to Sunday, nothing ever changes and it gets so warm and close in that living room that I feel like I can't move and if I don't get the hell out of there my life will be frozen in Maple Syrup forever.

DAVE: Why should you get away with it? You're not a kid. You grow old. Your life gets smaller. It's life. There's nothing anyone can do about it.

MICHAEL: You know my history. Nothing ever seems to last.

DAVE: I thought you felt differently about Beth.

MICHAEL: I do.

DAVE: So split. That's taking the bull by the horns.

MICHAEL: We haven't split up. Just because we no longer live together doesn't mean that we've split up. We've managed to work something out.

DAVE: Oh.

MICHAEL: Well there's always more than one way of looking at things, isn't there? If you want to look at it in the worst possible light. Well, then. Yes. We're both screwing around. But that's not the only way of looking at it.

DAVE: Uh-huh.

MICHAEL: I'm not denying there's sex. There's always sex. It's a biological law. There's nothing anyone can do about it. But I don't think sex is central.

DAVE: Sure.

MICHAEL: Look Dave. It was my idea. Okay? We have an arrangement. Some nights we see each other. Some nights we don't. We're playing it by ear. In another month or so a decision will be made.

DAVE: Can I say something?

MICHAEL: Shoot.

DAVE: Don't be a jerk.

MICHAEL: Wave your finger at me, Dave. That's just what I need.

DAVE: And in the meantime you're single.

MICHAEL: In a manner of speaking, yes.

DAVE: So how's the single life?

MICHAEL: I'm used to having Beth around. I'm on my own only I'm not really on my own. Some days I wake up by myself. Some days I wake up with Beth. Some days I wake up with someone else. It's confusing.

DAVE: Oh boo-hoo.

MICHAEL: I'm not complaining.

DAVE: Uh-huh. And?

MICHAEL: And?

DAVE: How's the sex?

MICHAEL: What do you want? The play by play?

DAVE: C'mon.

MICHAEL: Initially it was terrible. Christ, I'd been with one woman for over three years.

DAVE: Yeah, I suppose. But you persevered?

MICHAEL: What did you want me to do? Give up?

DAVE: A good boy scout. And now?

MICHAEL: I'm doing all right.

DAVE: You're a great raconteur, Mike. Anyone ever tell you that?

MICHAEL: What do you want, Dave?

DAVE: Nothing. Just wondering if all single men find their sex life as boring.

MICHAEL: I'm not saying it's boring. It's not boring. Look Dave, I've been with the same woman for more than three years. During that time I've thought about other women. Who wouldn't? And some of those other women have thought about me. I know that. And now, to be perfectly honest, I have the opportunity to do something about what I've only been thinking about.

DAVE: And all I'm asking is how's it been?

MICHAEL: How do you think?

DAVE: What does Beth think of this arrangement?

MICHAEL: She had her reservations. But lately she's beginning to come around.

DAVE: You giving her in-class tests?

MICHAEL: She's enjoying her independence.

DAVE: Who's this Earl guy?

MICHAEL: Who?

DAVE: Earl Telford.

MICHAEL: Just a friend.

DAVE: You know him?

MICHAEL: We've never met. Beth met him swimming. Very buddy-buddy.

DAVE: But she has been seeing other guys?

MICHAEL: What do you mean "seeing?"

DAVE: What do I mean "away?"

MICHAEL: Yes.

DAVE: What do you think about it?

MICHAEL: I don't think about it.

DAVE: What do you mean "you don't think about it?"

MICHAEL: (*intensely*) I mean I don't think about it.

DAVE: Oh. You don't think about it.

MICHAEL: What do you want me to do? Think about it? We have an arrangement. If I'm entitled, Beth's entitled. Why the hell should I let myself get upset?

BETH enters carrying a box.

BETH: Hello again.

MICHAEL moves to help her.

MICHAEL: Where'd you park? Burnaby?

BETH: I couldn't get the hatchback open. I had to drag this over the back seat.

DAVE: Michael just told me.

BETH: Yes.

DAVE: You look terrific.

BETH: What did you expect? A red mark on my cheek? My hair falling out in clumps?

DAVE: Ha ha. Very funny. Still have your sense of humour. I was just wondering how things are going.

BETH: Thanks for your concern. It's really not necessary.

DAVE: Good. So. You're having a great time?

MICHAEL: Dave.

BETH: Everything's fine Dave.

MICHAEL: That's all I said.

DAVE: You think you're typical?

BETH: What?

DAVE: There are some women... I mean, I know some who wouldn't be so fine. They'd be full of hate and resentment.

BETH: Is something bothering you?

DAVE: Just wondering about human nature.

BETH: What about it?

DAVE: Maybe there's no such thing.

BETH: You're shocked by our behaviour, aren't you?

DAVE: Surprised, that's all. You're both handling it so well. That's great. Good for you. But I've only seen you two as a couple. Never as an arrangement. And I'm a traditional guy. It's kind of confusing. I gotta go. They run that convention like a summer camp. If they don't see me for half an hour they'll have a search party out combing the woods. You free tonight, Mike?

MICHAEL: For sure.

DAVE: Nine-thirty?

MICHAEL: Fine.

DAVE: See yuh then. Bye-bye, Beth. Terrific.

MICHAEL: See yuh, buddy.

DAVE goes.

BETH: Well? How was I?

MICHAEL: What?

BETH: Was I cool and casual enough? Sophisticated, enlightened, the woman of the world you always wanted?

MICHAEL: Beth.

BETH: What's bugging Dave? He seemed very... something.

MICHAEL: I just told him about us.

BETH: It seemed like something else.... Oh. Never mind. It's probably me. Talking about our arrangement always makes me paranoid.

MICHAEL: You're not paranoid.

BETH: Want to bet?

MICHAEL: Dave is away.

BETH: Away?

MICHAEL: He's thinking of getting laid.

BETH: Ah. That explains it.

MICHAEL: He's just thinking about it. He probably won't do anything about it. Dave's always been terrible with women. I even had to get him together with his wife. Lynn was an old girlfriend of mine.

BETH: Very generous. Are you planning on offering my services this time round?

MICHAEL: In Dave's mind he's a sexual loser. A little fooling around may be good for him. A weekend affair. It happens all the time. What's the big deal?

BETH: Big deal? No big deal?

MICHAEL: Lynn doesn't have to know.

BETH: Not terribly original but it'll do.... Was that what you told him?

MICHAEL: I didn't tell him anything. It's not my place. I'm Dave's friend. Whatever he does. I'm here. I understand.... What would you have done?

BETH: If Dave was my best buddy and he's as happily married as he seems I would have tied him up until he got this silly idea out of his system.

MICHAEL: (*getting up*) Right.

MICHAEL takes a basketball from one of the boxes.

MICHAEL: Thanks for bringing everything over. What prompted this?

BETH: I was cleaning up. It's not my stuff.

MICHAEL: (*picking up the painting*) I thought you liked this.

BETH: I do. But it's yours. I thought you'd like it back.

MICHAEL: Thanks. (*MICHAEL examines the wall. He jokingly places the painting against the door.*) Here?

BETH nods no. MICHAEL tries a few other places.

BETH: Better.

MICHAEL enters the kitchen.

You remember we're going to Ted and Anne's on Wednesday.

MICHAEL: (*off*) I've got it marked down. How's Ted doing? He likes being a principal?

BETH: "Like" is not the word. An intelligent career move as they say in the staff room.

MICHAEL returns with a tool box.

MICHAEL: We're not going to spend another evening listening to them ramble on about sailing. Their boat and their brass and their teak and their heads. (*mocking*) We've two heads. Sleeps six. Had a lovely little sail up to Secret Cove. I wish to hell they'd stop talking about that boat and take us for a sail on the damn thing. How the hell can Ted afford it? What do they pay principals anyway? I don't know why I bothered getting a PHD. I should have gotten a degree in education and joined the local yacht club.

BETH: It's a co-op. They own it with three other couples. And the only reason Ted and Anne went on about sailing was to prevent you from monopolizing the evening ranting and railing about first year students that can't read or write. Ted is a high school principal after all. I think he showed a lot of restraint.

MICHAEL: Oh? Do I often embarrass you in public?

MICHAEL kisses BETH.

BETH: (*this is a come on*) You playing basketball at three?

MICHAEL: (*moving away*) Term's over. No more games until the fall. (*with picture*) Here?

BETH: You like your art on the ceiling? So?

MICHAEL: Karen's coming by. We're collaborating on a paper. Milton. How's this?

BETH: Mike, ever hear the expression "eye level"?

MICHAEL: You do it.

BETH: What do you know about Milton?

MICHAEL: Nothing. Karen needed my background in transformational grammar.

BETH: Didn't that kind of paper go out of style years ago?

MICHAEL: Karen found an obscure journal that was interested. In the English Department one publication is as good as another. They don't read articles. They just count them.

MICHAEL takes a vase from one of the boxes.

MICHAEL: This is not mine.

BETH: I wasn't sure.

MICHAEL: There's enough of this crap. Whose car did you borrow?

BETH: No one's. I bought one. It's just out front. The little red Rabbit. Now I can drive to Grandma's house.

MICHAEL: You didn't say anything.

BETH: Did I have to?

MICHAEL: No. Was that the down payment money?

BETH: Part of it.

MICHAEL: It's your money.

BETH: And I need a car. Besides it takes two incomes to buy a house these days.

MICHAEL: At least.... It makes a hell of a lot of sense. Beth. Really. Good luck with it. (*at wine*) Want some? (*BETH nods no.*) So. How does your little red Rabbit run?

BETH: It doesn't. It limps if I'm lucky. It won't start. And when it does it stalls. And then it won't start again.

MICHAEL: I'll take a look at it.

BETH: It's better now.

MICHAEL: It may happen again.

BETH: Actually I'm on my way to a friend's. He said he'd have a look at it.

MICHAEL: Didn't know Earl was so handy.

BETH: He feels responsible. He was the one who advised me to buy the car in the first place.

MICHAEL takes a hammer and moves to the wall to hang the painting.

MICHAEL: Well then it's only right that he should shoulder the blame if your little red Rabbit turns out to be a little red lemon.... You've been seeing a lot of Earl?

BETH: Yes.

MICHAEL: Still very buddy-buddy?

BETH: More than that.

MICHAEL: (*turns to the wall and begins to hammer in the nail for the painting*) Spatial relations isn't for me. I'm too verbal. Play me scrabble and I'll wipe you out. Jigsaw puzzles on the other hand drive me crazy. Earl, I'm sure, will go far. I see the Liberal Party in his future.

BETH: Mike. I don't think the picture is straight.

MICHAEL: (*letting it out*) Well what do you expect anyway? I'm a philosopher for Christ sake. Not a God damn interior decorator!

BETH adjusts the picture.

MICHAEL: Thanks for your help.

BETH: No charge.... Well, I should be going.

MICHAEL: Why don't you join Dave and me tonight?

BETH: I'm sorry, Mike. I've made other plans. Earl's throwing a party.

MICHAEL: Ah, Beth.

BETH: Yes.

MICHAEL: Don't forget your vase.

There is a knock on the door. KAREN enters.

KAREN: I'm early. I know I'm early. You don't mind, do you? I'll just flop down here out of the way. I won't make a peep. These shoes have got to go. Italian women must have the smallest feet in the world.

BETH: Hello, Karen.

KAREN: Beth. Hello. I'm interrupting. I know I'm interrupting. I'm sorry. Truly sorry. Michael, I'm leaving. Barefoot. These shoes will cripple me. Don't worry about me. I'll just pad up and down your hall.

MICHAEL: Relax.

BETH: I was just on my way out.

MICHAEL: Let me take your coat.

KAREN: Would you mind hanging it up? It cost me an arm and a leg. We're working on this paper together. I need Michael's background in transformational grammar.

BETH: So Michael said.

KAREN: I'm *Paradise Lost*.

MICHAEL: And I'm Past Participles. You must have heard of us. The famous Vaudeville team.

MICHAEL exits to the kitchen with the tool box.

KAREN: Did I walk in at a bad time?

BETH: No.

KAREN: You sure? I can still make myself scarce.

BETH: I'm sure.

KAREN: You are coming to our tennis lesson tomorrow?

BETH: I'll be there. Where do you get the time for all your exercise?

KAREN: Do I exercise that much?

BETH: If you're not playing tennis you're playing squash. And if you're not squashing, you're running in the rain just to clear your head.

KAREN: Well you're just as bad.

BETH: No I'm not.

KAREN: Well maybe so. But you don't need to. You're one of those lucky women. You're thin by nature. By nature I'm a tub. I was born fat and stayed fat for twenty years. Thank God for Weight Watchers and racquet sports. It's made my life bearable.

BETH: Karen, I've never known you as anything other than thin. All you do is talk fat.

KAREN: Really? I talk about my weight a lot?

BETH: I'm sorry. I didn't mean it that way.

KAREN: Yes. Well. Weight-wise things are under control. And I guess generally things are moving forward. (*MICHAEL enters.*) However, at present, as I was just about to tell Michael, the shits. But I'll bore you with that after our tennis lesson. Michael, where did you get this hideous vase?

BETH: It's mine.

MICHAEL: She got it from me. It was a birthday present.

BETH: I like it very much.

MICHAEL: And I know you do.

KAREN: Look at that. Two birds with one stone. Sorry, sorry.

MICHAEL: Karen. How about some wine?

KAREN: Michael, you are a life saver. Beth? How about you?

BETH: No. I really should be going.

KAREN: (*an aside*) Beth, you know I play squash with Earl.

BETH: Yes. He says your game is improving.

KAREN: Very cute in white.

BETH: Really?

MICHAEL moves to KAREN with her wine.

KAREN: I've always had this thing for lawyers. My father's a lawyer. Ah, Michael. Thank you. (*to BETH*) You look terrific. Have I told you that? (*a sip*) Nice. I must look a mess. I hope you've done your homework.

MICHAEL: Yes. And you?

KAREN: Busy little bee.

BETH: Well. I'll leave you two to it.

KAREN: Why don't we go for brunch after tennis tomorrow?

BETH: I'm spending the afternoon with my parents. It's Mother's Day.

KAREN: Damn it. I'll be by that phone for an hour trying to get through.

BETH: Good luck with the paper. Don't forget Wednesday. Ted and Anne's.

MICHAEL: Right.

BETH goes.

KAREN: I'm losing a friend.

MICHAEL: Don't be ridiculous.

KAREN: I know it. I'm losing a friend. I don't blame Beth. The way I behave around her I wouldn't like me either.

MICHAEL: What do you mean?

KAREN: Oh nothing. You know me. I get flustered and ramble on. Beth's certainly looking well. When I broke up with Danny I put on twenty pounds and my hair got so frizzy that I wore a scarf on my head for months. Stunning. Absolutely stunning. And it's only six weeks since you split up. She's certainly doing something right.

MICHAEL: (*at window*) We haven't split up.

KAREN: Whatever, Michael. Whatever. What are you looking at out there?

MICHAEL: Beth's been having car trouble.

KAREN: (*crossing to the window*) Oh, she's fine. Peppy little thing, isn't it? Whose is it?

MICHAEL: Beth's. She got it the other day.

KAREN: Oh.... With what? I thought every spare penny went for that house she wanted.

MICHAEL: Do you have those notes?

KAREN: Big step.

MICHAEL: You've been working hard.

KAREN: Beth forgot her vase.... It grows on you.

MICHAEL: Let's start with background material. Perhaps some very general information to put Milton and *Paradise Lost* in perspective.

KAREN: A little intellectual history.

MICHAEL: Right.

KAREN: For the Renaissance poets there were two major poetic forms: epic and tragedy. Milton divides the epic into two species: the diffuse epic in twelve books like *The Iliad* and *The Odyssey* and the brief type for which *The Book of Job* is the model. Could I have some more wine?

MICHAEL: Sure.

KAREN: I've had a terrible day. Melvin called from Whitehorse. He won't be coming down this weekend. Or any weekend for that matter. He's decided to spend his time entirely in the North. Melvin's found his heart's desire in the land of the midnight sun.

MICHAEL: I'm sorry to hear that.

KAREN: I lost Melvin to the call of the wild. (*taking her wine*) Thanks. There's this teacher in Watson Lake. From what I gather Melvin heard her howling at the Arctic moon on more than one occasion but last night he succumbed and tracked her spoor across the frozen tundra. Now they're yelping together and I'm out in the cold. I'm writing the Territorial Council an anonymous letter about Melvin Preschuk, their flying dentist. I think he's made every white woman above the sixtieth parallel. To be perfectly honest, Michael, the only reason I became involved with Melvin in the first place was because I thought, flying or not, a dentist is a dentist. Was I wrong. I should have taken a chance on that attractive but sleazy Greek restaurateur.... In high school I was the kind of girl who got firsts in everything but physics. I was never very attractive or popular. Too fat to be attractive. Too bright and bitchy to be popular. I think those miserable three years made me far too cautious about sexual matters.

MICHAEL: All of us feel, at one time or another, that we're not as sexually adventurous as we hope.

KAREN: On the other hand, as you well know, I'm not a careful, conventional, introverted woman. I've been finding that the older I get the less discreet I become.

MICHAEL: And that's very admirable, Karen. Trying to overcome your background that way.

KAREN: I know it sounds silly but it's been good for me. You should try it. It would be good for you. Oh, I know you talk a good game, Michael, but really, deep down, you're very unadventurous.

MICHAEL: Oh, am I?

KAREN: Don't be defensive.

MICHAEL: I'm not being defensive. I'm just trying to understand what you mean by "sexually unadventurous". Are you talking technique? What I do when I do it. Are you talking taste? Who I do it to and why. Or are you talking totals? How many I do it to and how often.

KAREN: I was talking timidity and don't be such a philosopher.

MICHAEL: So. There were two major poetic forms in the Renaissance: epic and tragedy.

KAREN: Most Renaissance critics regard the epic as the greater form. This is the result of the epic's larger intellectual scope. Of course things have changed. I'm no longer an awkward, plain teenager. I'm an attractive successful career woman. Do you find me attractive?

MICHAEL: Of course, I find you attractive.

KAREN: Don't humour me.

MICHAEL: I wasn't humouring you. You're very attractive.

KAREN: As an object of sexual desire?

MICHAEL: Only good breeding and an appreciation of high fashion prevents me from ripping the clothes from your body.

KAREN: Thanks.

MICHAEL: Karen. We're friends.

KAREN: And you're a hypocrite. Last Christmas.

MICHAEL: You were missing Melvin. I was missing Beth. It was the festive season. We were just exchanging greetings. Besides nothing happened.

KAREN: That faculty party.

MICHAEL: It was spring. The trees were budding. Everything was in blossom. More season's greetings... I was drinking brandy.

KAREN: Michael, if that drunk, obnoxious, funny looking man hadn't stumbled by...

MICHAEL: That drunk, obnoxious, funny looking man just happens to be the pumpernickel head of the philosophy department and in his more lucid moments he is one of the world's foremost Kant scholars.

KAREN: You're very good at confusing the issue, aren't you?

MICHAEL: I think the most important thing for you to remember, in terms of the paper, is that a theory of transformational grammar must begin by making a fundamental distinction between linguistic competence and linguistic performance.

KAREN: You're a very reasonable man, Michael.

MICHAEL: Well, reason before passion, don't you think?

KAREN: Not always. Sometimes it isn't reasonable to be reasonable. Sometimes we just have to say to hell with reason, to hell with obligation. I'm going to do what I damn well please and everything and everyone be damned.

MICHAEL: Linguistic performance is the actual use of language in concrete situations as opposed to linguistic competence which is the speaker's knowledge of his language.

KAREN: Arrangements like yours usually mean the end. They're the way decent, honest people fool themselves into thinking they still have something left. You and Beth have been making each other miserable for months.

MICHAEL: I was finding the relationship claustrophobic. I needed more freedom.

KAREN: And now you have it.

MICHAEL: Yes.

KAREN: And Beth has it.

MICHAEL: Yes.

KAREN: And I have it.

Short pause. MICHAEL doesn't respond.

KAREN: Okay.... We get along so wonderfully. I thought it would be a shame to waste it. When you really think about it, it does make so much sense.... Traditionally the epic begins at a low point in the middle of the action. In *Paradise Lost* the low point is the point furthest from God.... Michael our friendship is something very special to me. I would hate for this little "episode" to cause it any lasting damage... I'll read you some of this. You should have an idea of how it sounds. "Of man's first disobedience, and the fruit/ of that forbidden tree whose mortal taste/ Brought death into the world, and all our woe...." Well, perhaps Milton said it all. I don't know what came over me. I'm really very, very sorry.

MICHAEL: (*moving to KAREN*) You're right. It does make a hell of a lot of sense. And we do get along very well. I'm not saying we can do everything we want. That would be adolescent. On the other hand the limits to human behaviour are a lot less strict than some people make out. And what could the difficulties be? Especially if we're intelligent and educated and we try to be as frank and as candid as possible.

MICHAEL kisses KAREN. While in the embrace KAREN moves the vase from the couch to the floor.

SCENE TWO

About nine-thirty Saturday evening. MICHAEL and DAVE are standing over a wastepaper basket at stage right. DAVE is holding a glass of wine. MICHAEL's wine is on the desk at stage left.

MICHAEL: I don't believe this. I really don't believe this.

DAVE: I don't care what you believe.

MICHAEL: I was here. I was in the room. I saw it. It went right in. Swoosh. And you're going to stand there and tell me, right to my face, that it bounced.

DAVE takes a nerf ball from the wastepaper basket.

DAVE: It bounced. Bounce. And it doesn't count.

MICHAEL: Dave tell me. How did I miss it? Was the sun in my eyes? Maybe it was the blonde in the stands. Maybe this is all a bad dream and you're not here at all.

DAVE: Don't give me your philosophy, Mike.

MICHAEL: Okay, Dave. Explain it to me.

DAVE: You blinked.

MICHAEL: Right.

DAVE: You blinked when it bounced. No complicated explanation. Everyone blinks.

MICHAEL: You're cheating, Dave. You're cheating your best and oldest friend. And I'm disappointed in you as a friend and a human being. (*MICHAEL takes the nerf ball from DAVE.*) But I can see why you're a very successful lawyer.

DAVE: Take it over.

MICHAEL: I don't want to take it over. I want the point.

DAVE: Take the point.

MICHAEL: I don't need you to give me the point. I deserve the point.

DAVE: And it's yours if you want it.

MICHAEL: Well I don't want it. I won't take it over and I won't take the point.

DAVE: Take it over. That strikes me as a reasonable compromise.

MICHAEL: Forget it.

DAVE: Four one.

MICHAEL: Five one.

DAVE: Four one.

MICHAEL: It should have been six one. But we decided that since it's so hard to tell whether a nerf ball bounces that it's five one, Christ, almighty.

MICHAEL is about to throw. DAVE breaks his concentration.

DAVE: What time does this thing start?

MICHAEL: I told you. Ten-thirty. All I could get were tickets for the second show.

MICHAEL is about to throw.

DAVE: Game's to ten, right?

MICHAEL: Seven.

DAVE: Seven. Right.

MICHAEL hesitates.

Okay. Take your shot. You're delaying the game.

MICHAEL: Jesus.

MICHAEL throws. He sinks it.

DAVE: Fluke.

MICHAEL: You're a sweet guy, Dave. Anyone ever tell you that?

They exchange places.

DAVE: Yeah. Lynn tells me that all the time. Okay, Dave. Relax. Don't think. Let the ball find the target.

DAVE throws. He misses.

Shit. If this were Tokyo my life would be so much simpler. It would be stupid though. A wife, children, a family. To risk it all over a piece of ass. Idiotic.

MICHAEL returns the ball.

Have I ever won at this?

MICHAEL: Once. Nineteen seventy. I had a broken wrist.

DAVE: Very funny. What is it? A buck a point?

MICHAEL: Two bucks a point and a five dollar bonus to the winner. And it was your idea to play for money.

DAVE throws. He misses.

DAVE: I'll take it over.

MICHAEL: What?

DAVE: I'll take it over.

MICHAEL: Why?

DAVE: The music threw me off.

MICHAEL: What music?

DAVE: The music from the party down the hall.

MICHAEL: Dave.

DAVE: It's louder over here. And just as I was about to throw there was a sudden increase in volume.

MICHAEL: I didn't hear it.

DAVE: Well that stands to reason, doesn't it?

MICHAEL: Why?

DAVE: Because if you can miss seeing a nerf ball bounce then you can sure as hell miss hearing a burst of music burst.

MICHAEL: What are you saying, Dave? That some time today I've had a cerebral haemorrhage?

DAVE: Okay. Okay. I'll take it over.

MICHAEL: Don't take it over. Take the point.

MICHAEL gives DAVE the ball.

DAVE: No, no. I want to be fair. Don't be a big shot, Mike. I only want what I deserve.

You know, you and Bannerman should get together. You've got a lot in common. You've both managed to work out very nice arrangements. Christ, if Lynn had so much as an inkling that I'd been with another woman she'd be out on the town making the Blue Jays to get even.

MICHAEL: Christ.

DAVE throws. He sinks it.

DAVE: I'll win this game yet. So three more shots this round?

MICHAEL: Two more. You've taken three.

DAVE: Yeah. Well, live and learn. You know who I've been thinking about all weekend. Brenda Lipton. The last of my single life. Well I went out in style. What the body of Brenda Lipton had that made it so unique was economy. Now don't get me wrong. I'm not talking petite. She was a big girl, was she not?

MICHAEL: Taller than me I think.

DAVE: Yeah. Tall and long. Just the way I like them.

MICHAEL: You and Paul Simon.

DAVE: Brenda was a wonderful girl, right?

MICHAEL: Right.

DAVE: Nothing but the essentials. An absolutely no bullshit body. Long legs. Firm bum. Nice big boobs.

MICHAEL: Dave. Spare me.

DAVE: Mike. First of all I've got good taste and a way with words. And second of all you've got a present. All I've got is a past. She was a gymnast or a contortionist or something?

MICHAEL: A dancer.

DAVE: A dancer. Right. And double jointed and she could do things I still remember. With her head facing one way and my head facing another.

MICHAEL: Like a Japanese woodcut. One time I put my back out.

Pause.

DAVE: I'd forgotten about that. But that's all right. Now I remember. You went out with her first. You set me up. You were a good friend. Like always. Thanks for reminding me, I appreciate it.

MICHAEL: I'm sorry. I thought you remembered. It seemed like that kind of conversation. C'mon take your shot.

DAVE: What do I owe you?

MICHAEL: Forget it.

DAVE: Don't tell me to forget it. What do I owe you?

MICHAEL: Eight bucks.

DAVE: And the bonus makes thirteen. Here's twenty. Go water your Bonsai. You got any more wine?

MICHAEL: I'm out. How about a Scotch?

DAVE: (*a nod*) When does that show we're going to get out?

MICHAEL: I don't know. Midnight, I guess.

DAVE: Let's not hang around. There's a party I'd like to catch.

MICHAEL: Sure.

DAVE: (*taking his drink*) All I have is an address but I told some of the Vancouver guys I'd drop round to say good-bye.

MICHAEL: What's the matter? You don't like my Scotch?

DAVE: I'd like soda.

MICHAEL: It doesn't need soda. Try it.

DAVE: I like my Scotch with soda.

MICHAEL: Dave, I'm telling you, it's Glenn Fiddich. It doesn't need soda. Just have it neat. If you don't like it I'll get you soda.

DAVE: Christ.

MICHAEL: Look, Dave, why ruin good liquor? If you're going to drown it in soda you might as well throw in Kool Aid and drink it holding your nose.

DAVE: And you don't judge. What is all this Scotch business? I don't like Scotch, I've never liked Scotch. Jim Bannerman drinks Scotch. The Liberal Party drinks Scotch, I'm a Canadian, God damn it! I drink Rye. And proud of it. It's good for every occasion. You want to drink cheap – Three Star and ginger. You want to drink every day. C.C. and soda. You want to drink special – Crown Royal on the rocks. Don't give me this Glenn Fiddich crap. No wonder this God damn country is falling apart!

Dave drinks.

MICHAEL: Well?

DAVE: Where's your Kool Aid?

MICHAEL: There's soda in the fridge.

Dave exits to the kitchen.

(*calling to DAVE*) I'm going to shave.

DAVE: (*off*) Yeah.

MICHAEL exits to the bathroom. DAVE returns. There is a pause. Then there is a knock on the door. DAVE gets it. JACKIE is there.

JACKIE: Hello.

DAVE: Hello.

JACKIE: My name is Jacqueline LeMieux.

DAVE: Dave Lerner.

JACKIE: Hi David. I'm a friend of Jim's. Jim Loadman? Blonde guy down the hall?

DAVE: Yeah?

JACKIE: Jim's throwing this huge party. Wall to wall people. And it's only nine-thirty. Listen. I don't know how to say this. This is going to sound strange no matter what. I'm a member of an organization called Kinergetics. Does the name Kinergetics ring a bell?

DAVE: No.

JACKIE: Kinergetics began here in Vancouver about two years ago and lately it's been really catching fire.

DAVE: You're selling something?

JACKIE: Very funny. Actually Kinergetics is very mainstream. Lots of professional people and people in the arts and media. Suzy Brissenden? She's a sculptor. Had a show at that gallery on Pender Street. Some very unusual pieces.

DAVE: I'm from out of town.

JACKIE: Becky Selig? She was with the Royal Winnipeg Ballet for ten years.

DAVE: I'm from Toronto.

JACKIE: Becky's the driving force behind Kinergetics.

DAVE: What's Kinergetics?

JACKIE: It's a movement place.

DAVE: A movement place?

JACKIE: People go there to move. By themselves. In couples. In groups. They move together. They touch each other. They relax. It's very therapeutic.

DAVE: Uh-huh.

JACKIE: Bernard Hedley. He's an older man, been painting for over forty years, kind of a mentor figure for me, well, he suggested I take it. Bernard thinks there's an intimate connection between body awareness and visual imagination. I think it's helping. Tuesday I went up like Baryshnikov and I came down like a ton of bricks. And tonight, just when I thought I was through with it, my back is killing me again. And, like I said, it's wall to wall people down the hall. So what I'm wondering is, can I lie down? I'll just be ten minutes.

DAVE: Sure. The bedroom's this way.

JACKIE: Now you're really going to think I'm a nut case. My chiropractor recommended it. He's very progressive. And it's been written up in some very prestigious medical journals by some of the world's most famous orthopedic surgeons. I've sworn off beds. I use the floor.

DAVE: The floor?

JACKIE: We spend a third of our life lying down. Why shouldn't a lying posture be as important as standing posture? All I need is six square feet.

DAVE: Floor space is waste space.

JACKIE moves to the floor.

JACKIE: I've always liked the name David.

DAVE: David and Goliath.

JACKIE: David Macfarlane. Do you know him?

DAVE: I don't think so.

JACKIE: Architect. From Toronto. What do you do?

DAVE: I'm a lawyer.

JACKIE: Bill Maguire?

DAVE: Sorry.

JACKIE: He's my partner in movement class. Bill's a very sensual man as well as being a very successful lawyer. I don't think I've ever met a man with more eclectic tastes. Lawyers are often surprising. (*JACKIE stretches.*) Don't let me interrupt.

DAVE: No problem. (*after a beat*) So. How do you like it down there?

JACKIE: It's a very comfortable rug.

DAVE: Persian. They're very comfortable.

JACKIE exercises.

I've slept on the floor. In the past. I still do. Not as often as I like. You know how it is. You're a successful lawyer. You get busy. You don't have time to sleep on the floor.

JACKIE: I've been thinking of giving up beds permanently.

DAVE: Uh-huh.

JACKIE: It's healthier.

JACKIE exercises. DAVE watches.

DAVE: You're right. Healthier. (*looking for conversation*) Nice jeans.

JACKIE: (*indifferent*) Calvin Klein.

DAVE: They fit well.

JACKIE: Size eight.... Those are very unusual shoes.

DAVE: You think so? Gucci.

JACKIE: Very nice.

DAVE: Size eight and a half. D.

MICHAEL enters.

Ah, Mike. Jackie, this is my buddy, Michael Kaye. This is his place. Mike, this is the lovely and charming, Jacqueline LeMieux.

JACKIE: Hello.

MICHAEL: Hi.

DAVE: Jackie was at a party just down the hall. She has a bad back but there was no place to lie down there. So she's going to use your floor for a while.

MICHAEL: Sure. What seems to be the problem?

JACKIE: Muscle inflammation. Lumbar region. It needs support. I strained it at Kinergetics. That's a movement place. People go there to move.

MICHAEL: Uh-huh.

JACKIE: I'll just be ten minutes.

MICHAEL: That's fine. Will you excuse us?

DAVE: We'll just be a sec, Jackie.

MICHAEL and DAVE move away from JACKIE.

MICHAEL: What's she doing here?

DAVE: Don't worry about it.

MICHAEL: We're going out.

DAVE: We've got lots of time. The woman is in a lot of pain.

MICHAEL: Why on my living room rug?

DAVE: Why not? She helps the decor.

JACKIE: (*calling to MICHAEL*) I like your art.

MICHAEL: What?

JACKIE: Is that a Dondell?

MICHAEL: That's right.

JACKIE: It must be one of Jack's older pieces. What do you do, Michael?

MICHAEL: I teach philosophy at the university.

JACKIE: Aesthetics is my interest. What's your field?

MICHAEL: Philosophy of Language.

JACKIE: Words and things.

MICHAEL: In a manner of speaking.

DAVE: And you, Jackie? What do you do for a living?

JACKIE: I paint. So I notice good art when I see it.

DAVE: Have you had any shows?

JACKIE: I'm just starting out.

DAVE: I've got a friend who's an artist. It's a tough life. Only the best make a living at it.

JACKIE: Money's not everything. Besides I'm optimistic.

MICHAEL: That's the spirit.

JACKIE: Hope springs eternal.

MICHAEL: You can't rush these things.

JACKIE: You shouldn't.

MICHAEL: It's all developmental.

JACKIE: A slow painful process. Ow.

MICHAEL: What is it?

JACKIE: Muscle spasm.

MICHAEL: Oh. Can I get you something?

JACKIE: I have some Darvon at Jim's but I've taken a few already. I'll just have to grin and bear it.... There is something. Can you pop my back? My chiropractor does it. It sets me up for hours.

MICHAEL: I've never done this before. What do I have to do?

DAVE: Actually. And I don't want to brag. I have loads of experience.

MICHAEL: That's all right, Dave.

JACKIE turns on her stomach.

JACKIE: Kneel down. One leg on either side of me.

MICHAEL: Yes.

JACKIE: Place your hands really low on my back.

MICHAEL: Really low?

JACKIE: That's right.

MICHAEL: This okay?

JACKIE: Lower.

MICHAEL hesitates.

DAVE: You want me to do it?

MICHAEL: No thanks, Dave,

JACKIE: Now make sure your hands are on either side of my backbone.

MICHAEL: It's hard to find your backbone all the way down here.

DAVE: Right there.

MICHAEL: It's all right, Dave.

JACKIE: Now with the insides of your wrists facing each other and your fingers spread, lean forward with all your might.

MICHAEL: Hang on a second.

DAVE: Like this.

MICHAEL: Dave. Now what?

JACKIE: Just put your weight on you hands and lean forward.

MICHAEL attempts it awkwardly. JACKIE moans loudly.

MICHAEL: How's that?

JACKIE: Not good.

DAVE: Let me try.

JACKIE: It's all right. It helped a little.

DAVE: So Jackie. Where would you be on this Saturday night if you weren't lying on the floor?

JACKIE: I'm at a party. Jim's. Just down the hall.

DAVE: Oh. Right. Sorry.

JACKIE: I usually work Saturday nights.

DAVE: No kidding? You paint away your Saturday nights? Art's important, Jackie. But all work and no play.

JACKIE: I'm a cocktail waitress.

DAVE: That's interesting. Where do you work?

JACKIE: Creole Pete's.

DAVE: I don't know it.

MICHAEL: Their Chicken Gumbo is out of this world.

JACKIE: There's nothing like it.

DAVE: It must be a demanding job being a cocktail waitress.

JACKIE: It's all right.

MICHAEL: It gets an interesting crowd.

JACKIE: That's the best thing about it. Meeting all those unusual people.

DAVE: How do you do it? There must be a trick to it. Keeping all those glasses and bottles upright on your tray, not spilling a drop, threading your way through a crowded room.

MICHAEL: Funny. I've never seen you there.

JACKIE: I think I've seen you around.

MICHAEL: Really?

JACKIE: Yes. I think so.

MICHAEL: You do look kind of familiar now that I think about it.

DAVE: Do you hold your tray like this? Or like this?

MICHAEL: You looking for work, Dave? I usually eat there on Wednesday.

JACKIE: I have the section near the windows.

MICHAEL: I'll look for you.

DAVE: Mike. Get the lady a drink. Be a good host. You want a drink, don't you, Jackie?

JACKIE: (*to DAVE*) I wouldn't mind some water. Perrier with a twist?

DAVE: Mike.

MICHAEL: Coming up. Excuse me, Jackie.

MICHAEL goes. JACKIE exercises.

DAVE: Jackie.

JACKIE: Yes.

DAVE: It's Saturday night. I was thinking.

JACKIE: Do you know that evolutionarily speaking the backbone is the oldest bone we have?

DAVE: Jackie listen.

DAVE hesitates.

JACKIE: Yes.

DAVE: I'm from Toronto. Have I told you that?

JACKIE: Uh-huh. Do you travel a lot?

DAVE: Uh. Yeah.

JACKIE: That's a big dream of mine. To have the time and the money to just travel.

DAVE: I've been around. All over the world. One day Toronto. The next Vancouver, L.A., New York. Last week I was in London. That's the kind of practice I have. Lots of multinationals. And right now. Like I was saying. I'm not in Toronto. I'm away.

JACKIE: "Away"?

DAVE: From Toronto.

JACKIE: Oh... I've been to Toronto.

DAVE: Great town. No place like it in the world. And I've seen them all.

JACKIE: It's not my kind of city. All that concrete and cars and people. I like Vancouver with the mountains and the vistas and the natural grandeur.

DAVE: You're right there. You sure as hell don't get your mountains and your vistas and your natural grandeur on the corner of Bay and King. My wife always complains about that.

JACKIE: You're married?

DAVE: Yeah. Married. Eight years. Three boys.

JACKIE: That's nice.

DAVE: Yeah. Terrific.

MICHAEL enters with Perrier.

MICHAEL: Here we go.

JACKIE: Thanks.

MICHAEL: I'm sorry. Can I offer you anything to eat?

JACKIE: No thanks. I'm watching my weight.

DAVE: (*mocking, anger*) Calvin Klein. Size three.

DAVE exits to the dining room.

MICHAEL: What was all that about?

JACKIE: Your friend's married. He lives in Toronto. With his wife and three kids. He's away.

MICHAEL: Shit.

DAVE enters.

Dave.

DAVE: Where are those joints?

MICHAEL: Dave.

DAVE: Where are those joints?!

MICHAEL: Right hand drawer.

DAVE returns to the dining room.

JACKIE: He made his move as soon as you left. You're not married, are you?

MICHAEL: No.

JACKIE: I didn't think so. You don't have the ambiance.

MICHAEL: Look, Jackie. Things are getting a little complicated. Maybe you should...

JACKIE: I like your place, Michael. It makes its statement. Sophisticated, intelligent but not uptight.

JACKIE opens the door to the bedroom and peeks in.

MICHAEL: Jackie.

DAVE: (*off*) Matches!

There is a knock on the door.

MICHAEL: What?

MICHAEL answers the door. BETH strides into the living room.

BETH: Hello.

MICHAEL: Hello.

JACKIE: Hello.

MICHAEL: Oh. Beth. This is Jackie uh...

JACKIE: LeMieux.

MICHAEL: LeMieux. Jackie, this is Beth Gordon.

JACKIE: Hi.

BETH: Hello.

JACKIE lies down on the rug.

MICHAEL: Jackie has a terrible problem with her back. I just met her ten minutes ago. She was at a party down the hall. She needs a place to lie down. Dave and I are just on our way out. He's in the dining room toking up.

DAVE: (*off*) Where are the God damn matches?

MICHAEL: See. Well. How's the car?

BETH: No better. Stall, start, stall, start. It stalled just now and I couldn't get it started. I'm amazed I get anywhere at all.

MICHAEL: You should speak to your dealer about that car.

BETH: Either I get a replacement or they return my money.

MICHAEL: Exactly.

BETH: If only I could run my life on that straightforward a basis.

MICHAEL: Jackie, would you mind?

JACKIE begins to get up.

BETH: What is it, Michael? Do you think I'll embarrass you in front of your guests?

JACKIE lies back down.

I just came from my parents.

MICHAEL: Ah. How are they?

BETH: Mother invited me over for "tea."

MICHAEL: Right.

BETH: I haven't seen very much of her lately. It wasn't very pleasant. I told mother not to worry. You and I just needed some time to work the kinks out of our relationship. Mother said that she and father have been happily married for over thirty years and they never once used the word "relationship". I said times have changed. People aren't the same. Pressures are very different. We have an arrangement. We're going to work things out. "Arrangement" bothered mother. She said that except for its musical use, the term "arrangement" shouldn't be used in polite society. She asked me if it was one of your words. I said it was.

MICHAEL: Would you like me to give her a call?

BETH: She doesn't want to talk to you. She wants to wash your mouth out with soap.

MICHAEL: Jackie.

JACKIE gets up, takes her glass, heads for the hall then, remembering her glass, she returns to the kitchen.

BETH: Actually, to be honest, in spite of everything, she still seems to be fond of you. She invited you to dinner tomorrow night. I said you couldn't make it.

MICHAEL: Why?

BETH: Because I don't want to sit around the table with my family, on Mothers' Day, in the house where I grew up, and pretend that everything is hunky-dory between you and me knowing all the while that I'm seeing you and Earl and you're seeing me and God knows how many other women. I haven't felt as guilty since I was eighteen and hiding my pills and lying to my parents about just what I was doing out until four in the morning. Jesus Christ, I'm thirty years old and I feel like a teenager. I don't know what I'm doing. Half the time I don't know whether to laugh or cry. This God damn arrangement. Smiling at each other and pretending we're these sophisticated, enlightened people. It makes me nauseous.

MICHAEL: I thought we decided not to have this conversation.

BETH: You decided. I capitulated.

MICHAEL: I seem to remember it as a mutual agreement.... Beth. There's no point in rehashing things. Talking about it only makes us both upset.

BETH: Talking about it makes me upset.... It's just another philosophical conversation to you.

MICHAEL: Now is not the time.

BETH: I don't know how you can live like this. Sweeping everything under the rug. What is it with you? The only position you're happy in is sitting on the fence.

MICHAEL: Okay, okay. Let's talk.

BETH: I don't want to talk. I want to scream and yell and break things over your head.

MICHAEL: That won't solve anything.

BETH: It will make me feel a hell of a lot better.

MICHAEL: Beth, what is it you want from me.

BETH: I love you. I want you to make up your God damn mind.

DAVE enters with an unlit joint and some matches.

DAVE: Hi, Beth. Want some of this?

BETH: No thanks.

DAVE: Mike? (*MICHAEL turns away. DAVE talks to BETH.*) How are you doing? You're looking terrific as usual.

BETH: Thanks, Dave.

DAVE: Why don't you join us tonight?

BETH: I'm sorry but I have other plans.

DAVE: That's too bad. It would have been nice to spend some time with you.

BETH: Thank you, Dave. I appreciate that. (*BETH crosses to the door, then moves to the phone.*) May I use your phone?

MICHAEL: Of course.

BETH looks through the yellow pages.

You looking for anything in particular?

BETH: I'm calling a cab.

MICHAEL: Take my car. We don't need it.

BETH: No.

MICHAEL: Why not?

BETH: I don't want it.

MICHAEL: Okay, okay. Let me look at your car.

BETH: I don't need your help.

MICHAEL: Beth, please. This isn't doing any good. I don't have to see Dave tonight. He'll understand. You and I can have that talk.

BETH: Why bother, Michael? You'll put things off and I'll give in. We're not the best of people, are we? You're scared and I'm weak. But that's who we are. We might as well make the best of it.

BETH looks through the phone book. MICHAEL crosses to DAVE.

MICHAEL: (*hurrying DAVE across the stage*) Give her a hand.

DAVE: What?

MICHAEL: Give her a hand with the car.

DAVE: I don't know anything about cars.

MICHAEL: (*to BETH*) Dave will give you a hand.

DAVE: I'll have you going in no time.

BETH leaves.

MICHAEL: Just try, will you?

DAVE goes. After a moment, MICHAEL moves to the window. JACKIE enters.

JACKIE: Resentment, resentment, resentment.

MICHAEL: What?

JACKIE: Resentment. Your ex-girlfriend's reaction. You can't let it get you down. We do what we have to do. If people resent and can't forgive that's too bad for them. We just have to accept it as one of the consequences of doing what we want to do.

MICHAEL: Jackie, I'd really like to be alone.

JACKIE: Jeffrey Fiskin. Psychiatrist. Very eclectic. Jung, Freud, theatre games, body work. Once he made me listen to Blonde on Blonde for an entire afternoon. When's the last time you spent four hours listening to Bob Dylan? Jeffrey Fiskin is a very perceptive man. I recommend him wholeheartedly.

MICHAEL: Jackie. I don't know you. You've been lying on my living room floor for the last half hour. I just had a falling out with my best buddy over your lumbar region. You saw what happened between me and my girlfriend or whatever she is. Now don't you think it's time for you to leave?

JACKIE: I throw up. Every couple of weeks. Things are going along smoothly. Then, all of a sudden, vomit. I'm sweating. I can hardly move. I feel like I'm going to die. Jeffrey says it's a hysterical reaction. He says, I'm still trying to deal with Burnaby. It's really nothing that unusual. Just your run-of-the-mill suburban malaise. Environmentally I was being understimulated. Artistically I was being under utilized. Intellectually I was being under exercised. But you must have heard it all before. It's the same old story. I was born there. And I went to school there. And I met a guy there. And I was going to raise a family there. And then it hit me. I was going to live and die knowing only Burnaby. But Burnaby's not me. And I'm not Burnaby. So now, every couple of weeks or so, when Burnaby rears its ugly head, I throw up and feel like I'm going to die.

JACKIE stifles a belch.

MICHAEL: You're not going to throw up now, are you?

JACKIE: I'm not going to throw up. I haven't felt as good in months. Too much Perrier water. Can I use your bathroom?

JACKIE exits to the bathroom. Pause. There is a knock on the door. KAREN sticks her head into the apartment.

KAREN: Hello.

MICHAEL: Karen. Hello.

KAREN enters. She is carrying a bouquet of flowers and a bottle of wine.

KAREN: I was driving by and I saw the light. Well, to be frank, I bought the flowers and the wine first. I was hoping you'd be home and luck was with me. Narcissus. It's all over for the tulips and the daffodils. Nice. Aren't they? I stole them. Figuratively. There's this Chinese grocery on South Granville that has the freshest flowers and the cheapest prices.

KAREN offers the flowers to MICHAEL.

MICHAEL: Thank you.

KAREN: You know me and sexual stereotyping. (*with wine*) The talk of the English Department. A full bodied red with a pleasing bouquet. Also politically correct. From the now socialist France. Also, as French wines go, very cheap.

KAREN offers the wine.

MICHAEL: Thank you.

KAREN: I thought we might go for a walk. It's a lovely night. We could have the wine on the beach.

MICHAEL: Sorry. My best and oldest buddy is in from Toronto. He'll be back any second.

KAREN: Oh. Well then. I hope my behaviour this afternoon...

MICHAEL: No. No. It's not that.

KAREN: Really, Michael. I don't know what came over me.

MICHAEL: Karen, please.

KAREN: To become so anxiety ridden and uptight and unresponsive at such a time. It couldn't have been much fun for you. I owe you an apology.

MICHAEL: You're making far too much of it.

KAREN: Don't demean me by making light of it.

MICHAEL: Right. Sorry.

KAREN: I've always hated the kind of woman who behaves that way. I hope you don't think that I'm the kind of woman who's incapable of having a casual affair with a good friend.

MICHAEL: I don't think that, Karen. I know that you're capable of having a casual affair with just about any man you set your mind to.

KAREN: Yes. And having a hell of a good time while I'm at it.

MICHAEL: Well, then, that goes without saying, doesn't it?

KAREN: I guess I was feeling a little guilty.

MICHAEL: Well, sometimes it gets the better of us.

KAREN: It's a disgusting emotion. And there's absolutely no place for it in this situation. Michael, I've thought about my behaviour this afternoon. I understand it. Both emotionally and intellectually. I really have come to grips with it. And I can assure you that that kind of neurotic episode can never happen again.

MICHAEL: Good. Then the afternoon wasn't a complete waste of time.... I didn't mean that, Karen. What I meant was that when people are friendly with each other and like each other and are curious about each other well, then, sometimes, they do things to each other that maybe they should do only to others.

KAREN: I'm not looking for an intense emotional involvement. What I have in mind is a very casual, very informal, adult affair. No demands. No responsibilities. Just good, clean fun. Nothing will change between us, Michael. Nothing. Except that we'll sleep together on a regular basis.

MICHAEL: Karen, I'm sure you're aware that people sometimes convince themselves they feel one thing when really they feel something completely different. And then sometimes we blow things up out of all proportion because, perhaps, we're reacting to the past. Danny, Melvin-the flying dentist. So I think it would be best if we waited a few days to find out how we really feel. Okay?

KAREN: Okay.

MICHAEL: I'll call you Monday.

KAREN: Okay. Just think about it, Michael. That's all I ask.

JACKIE enters from the bathroom.

JACKIE: Michael, I'm seeing Jeffrey on Thursday. Oh, hi...

KAREN: What do you do, Michael? Give out lottery tickets as door prizes? Give every tenth woman a free pair of panty hose?

MICHAEL: Jackie and I met this evening under the most unusual circumstances. Jackie was at a party down the hall.

JACKIE: At Jim Loadman's? He's a foreman at The Alberta Wheat Pool, but most people know him as a shortstop. In the Industrial League? Last year he was voted most valuable player.

KAREN: You must keep track. How do you do it? Steal the labels from their panties and display them, mounted like butterflies, in a large red album.

MICHAEL: Jackie has a terrible problem with her back. There was no place to lie down at the party.

JACKIE: Wall to wall people.

MICHAEL: So I let her use the floor.

KAREN: Christ!

KAREN turns away. MICHAEL throws JACKIE a look. JACKIE exits to the bedroom.

MICHAEL: Karen, listen...

KAREN: There are so few decent men around these days. They're all fags or running around after eighteen-year-olds.

MICHAEL: I'm sure you haven't exhausted all the men in the city.

KAREN: Michael, you are so damn blind about everything. I've been screwing myself silly for months. Christ, if something good doesn't happen soon I'll start making it with my students. Michael, I know you. I understand you. It'll work. I know it will. God damn you, Michael. Why do I have to demean myself like this in front of you?

MICHAEL: I'm sorry. I didn't know you felt this way. Or maybe I did and conveniently ignored it. You were free. I was free. At the time there seemed no reason not to. It was a mistake, Karen. Let's not make it worse.

KAREN walks to the door. She turns.

KAREN: By the way, Michael, have you ever met Earl? He is one of the most dynamic, charming, attractive, tall, broad shouldered, smoldering dark eyed men I have ever had the pleasure of being in the same room with. What is it about men of that age? They have a drive, an energy, that men lose when they hit thirty.

MICHAEL: It's called "naivete" and they're well rid of it.

KAREN: I think he's putting it to your girl-friend. It's the first intelligent thing Beth has done since you moved out. Face it, Michael. It's over between you two.

MICHAEL: I hurt you. Now you hurt me.

KAREN: That's about it.

DAVE enters.

DAVE: Hello.

KAREN: Hello. Good-bye.

KAREN goes.

DAVE: Who was that?

MICHAEL: Karen Sperling. How's Beth?

DAVE: I don't know. Karen Sperling. What does she do?

MICHAEL: She teaches English at the university. What do you mean "you don't know"?

DAVE: I mean "I don't know".

MICHAEL: Did she get going all right?

DAVE: Yeah. Maybe her choke is sticking. Maybe her carburetor is lousy. Don't ask me about cars.

DAVE enters the kitchen to clean his hands.

MICHAEL: But you saw her drive away?

DAVE: (*off*) Yes.

MICHAEL: Did she say where she was going?

DAVE: (*off*) This Earl fella. He's throwing a party.

MICHAEL: Right.

DAVE returns from the kitchen, wiping his hands with a paper towel.

DAVE: I know it's none of my business, Mike. But do you know what you're doing?

MICHAEL: I know what I'm doing. I know exactly what I'm doing. I don't know what the hell I'm doing. What am I doing?

DAVE: Jeez, Mike. I don't know what to say. I haven't been single for eight years but I know how it must be. Look. If you want to get married and have kids, that's fine with me. And if you want to put an ad in the paper and make it with three bald women and a fox terrier twice a day, that's also fine with me. Because, you see, Mike, I'm your friend and whatever you do I'll never judge and I'll never advise and you're all on your own. Doesn't help much. does it, best buddy? Where's the lady with the backbone?

MICHAEL: In the bedroom.

DAVE: (*mocking*) Joseph Stalin. Do you know him? He's a Russian dictator but he has a marvellous sense of humour. The mountains and the vistas and the natural grandeur. It's all bullshit. I usually eat there on Wednesday. I have the section near the windows. I'll look for you.

MICHAEL: I thought you were just horsing around. I didn't think you were serious.

DAVE: You didn't?

MICHAEL: No.... Well.... Maybe I did. I don't know. I guess I just wasn't thinking. You know how you are with strange women. It was obvious you weren't going to get anywhere. I don't know, Dave. It felt like ten years ago and I guess I did what I always did, I'm sorry.

DAVE: Yeah?

MICHAEL: Dave. I mean it.

DAVE: Too fucking late.

MICHAEL: Where are you going?

DAVE: To that party. Stalin's friend was strike one. I'm told I get three.

MICHAEL: Dave, think about it.

DAVE: Eight years, Mike. Eight years is a long time, Eight years is no joke.

DAVE walks to the door.

MICHAEL: Okay, Dave. Go on. You deserve it. You're a successful lawyer. You've put in your time. It's coming to you. Go ahead. Join the Liberal Party and get your piece of ass.

DAVE: I don't know where you get off talking to me like this. We're no different you and me. Just because you don't say tits and ass, just because you say arrangement, just because you're full up to here with all this crap of sexual chic doesn't mean you're not just another horny guy looking to get laid.

MICHAEL: I know that, Dave, okay? All I'm saying is acting on it doesn't make it any better.

DAVE: And you know something else. Being up front about your failings doesn't make them any better. When you've got BO you've got BO. The solution is not to tell your girlfriend you smell bad and you want an arrangement. The solution is to take a God damn bath. Jesus Christ, Mike, you're driving Beth crazy.

MICHAEL: Yeah.

DAVE moves to the door.

Don't be an idiot.

DAVE: You haven't been doing without. I have. I haven't had any of it. And I'm going to get some of it. Even if it damn well kills me.

MICHAEL: Dave. It's exciting and romantic. It's one hell of a rush. I'm not going to deny that. But getting laid is not a detachable event. Acts have consequences and they're never the ones you want or the ones you expect. Dave. Just take it from me. It's not worth it.

DAVE: Thanks for the sermon, I'll keep it in mind.

DAVE moves to the door. MICHAEL gets him in a headlock.

MICHAEL: (*facetiously*) Dave, please. Don't make me tie you up.

DAVE: (*having none of it, intensely*) Let go.

MICHAEL releases DAVE. DAVE walks to the door.

MICHAEL: I'll see you tomorrow?

DAVE says nothing and goes. Pause. MICHAEL moves to the desk, finds a number in the phone book and dials.

Hello.... Who am I speaking to please...? Listen, you don't know me Earl but we have a friend in common. Beth Gordon.... That's right. It's Michael Kaye.... Yes, Earl, and I've heard a lot about you too. Is Beth there...? Well I wouldn't worry about it she's probably having car trouble.... I'm sure it's not your fault, Earl.... Could you have Beth call me when she arrives...? What? She did...? Sure. I'll hang on.... Beth. Mike... I want to talk to you. What do you think I want...? Yes. Of course, it's very important.... Yes. I know where your are.... Oh. I see. You think this is easy for me, do you...? Beth, what the hell are you talking about? You're the one who walked out of here without.... (*BETH has hung up.*) Beth? Beth? Fuck!

Short pause. Then MICHAEL takes his jacket from the closet and marks down EARL's address. JACKIE enters from the bedroom.

JACKIE: Did everyone leave?

MICHAEL: (*startled by JACKIE*) Oh my God.... Not everyone. I was just on my way out.

JACKIE: Michael, this wonderful thing happened. I was trying to get comfortable on your bedroom floor when something in my back popped. I feel just terrific.

MICHAEL: Jackie. The time has come for you to quietly fold your little tent and leave my apartment.

JACKIE: You look very tense and anxious.

MICHAEL: I am.

JACKIE: I know just the thing.

JACKIE attempts to give MICHAEL a back rub.

MICHAEL: What do you think you're doing?

JACKIE: You'll feel like a new man. I promise.

MICHAEL: Jackie.

JACKIE: I thought you were interested.

MICHAEL: I was.

JACKIE: What happened? Was it something I said? I talk too much. I know I talk too much.

MICHAEL: Jackie, why is it you don't want to leave this apartment?

There is a loud knock on the door.

JACKIE: That's why.

JACKIE hurries to the door and looks through the peephole. There is another loud knock.

MICHAEL: Who's that?

JACKIE: Phil. (*She quickly slips the chain and locks the door. There is another very loud knock.*) He's a big dumb jock and he's very drunk.

The door is shaken violently.

MICHAEL: What does he want?

JACKIE: He's my husband. He thinks we're screwing. He wants to beat the piss out of you.

The shaking continues. The door frame gives way. Blackout.

SCENE THREE

About eleven-thirty Sunday morning. KAREN and DAVE are sitting on the couch. Their arms are around each other.

DAVE: I was thinking body oils. Rose, lavender, peach blossom. I cover you in it then I sniff you all over. Then you cover me in it. Then you sniff me all over.

KAREN: I was thinking hot tubs. We could watch the water gurgle.

DAVE: Then there's always leather.

KAREN: I have just the thing. It's not leather but it'll do. An old fashioned corset. It cinches up. No bottom half. Black garter belts.

DAVE: Actually I was thinking leather thongs.

KAREN: David.

DAVE: I'm enlightened. I tie you up. Then you tie me up.

KAREN: You're crazy.

DAVE: A movie. Starring you. And me. It begins. You're naked. Covered in oil. Tied to the bed with leather thongs. I enter. Also naked. But not covered in oil. I look at your naked, oiled, tied up body. I give a fiendish ha-ha. Ha-ha. I turn my back to look at the other five women in the room.

KAREN: Well excuse me.

DAVE: But you're hot and sweaty and the oil has loosened the thongs. You squirm free and quick as a wink, while my back is turned, you overpower me.

KAREN: Good for me.

DAVE: Wait a minute. You're no better than me. You're just as twisted. You bind me with leather, douse me in oil, peach blossom, and then, with one of your perverse little giggles...

KAREN giggles.

You sadistically sniff me all over.

KAREN: Oooh.... Then.

DAVE: Then?

KAREN: (*standing up*) Your body a quivering mass on the floor. I leave.

DAVE: You leave?

KAREN: I leave. But I return in a moment clad in my crotchless corset.

DAVE: Vonderbar!

KAREN: And carrying a twelve foot bull whip.

DAVE: Oh my God!

KAREN: But by this time you have slithered free.

DAVE: (*standing up*) Slither, slither, I grab the whip from your oily hand and raise it above my head.

KAREN: When suddenly you catch sight of my liquid pools.

DAVE: Liquid pools?

KAREN: Eyes.

DAVE: Ah.

KAREN: We embrace passionately and make convulsive oily love.

DAVE: All over the bedroom floor. We don't worry about the wall to wall.

KAREN: What do we care? It's just some sleazy motel.

DAVE: Then I order in some beer and pizza and the two of us, content and happy, watch the last two periods between the Leafs and the Canadiens.

KAREN: Let's go, sex fiend.

DAVE: Let's wait another five minutes.

KAREN: You left him a note. You'll call him this afternoon.

DAVE: Five minutes. It's important. I may not see him for another year. I still don't like the looks of that door. And all this dirt.

KAREN: An accident.

DAVE: Could be. I'll have another look around.

DAVE enters the dining room.

KAREN: Where is my purse?

DAVE: (*off*) Oh my God!

KAREN: David! David!

DAVE returns with the remains of the Bonsai.

DAVE: The Bonsai is no more.

KAREN: You scared me half to death.

DAVE: Bad joke. Sorry sweetie.

DAVE gives KAREN a kiss. MICHAEL enters.

KAREN: Michael.

DAVE: Mike. How are you?

KAREN: What is wrong with your eye?

MICHAEL: It's nothing,

DAVE: What do you mean "nothing"? That's a beaut.

KAREN: What happened?

MICHAEL: Last night this big guy breaks down the door, knocks over my Bonsai and punches me in the face. I got in a good one though. Adam's apple. He was a nice deep blue here for five minutes. I really don't want to talk about it. What are you two doing here?

DAVE: I just dropped in to say good-bye.

KAREN: We've been trying to phone you all morning.

DAVE: There was no answer,

KAREN: We've been knocking on your door.

DAVE: There was no answer.

KAREN: But the door was unlocked.

DAVE: So we just walked in.... Karen and I. Met.

KAREN: Actually we've become quite good friends.

DAVE: Actually a little more than friends.

KAREN: Actually David's right.

DAVE: Life. Figure it out.

KAREN: People. Figure them out.

DAVE: That Vancouver guy. It was Earl. Imagine that.

KAREN: I remembered David from your apartment.

DAVE: Karen was the only person I knew. Next to the guys.

MICHAEL: Wasn't Beth there?

DAVE: Oh she was there. I just didn't see much of her. She was there for a second. Then she was gone.

KAREN: Just swallowed up by the crowd. Never to be seen again.

DAVE: So many people. All trying to get at each other. We hit it off right away.

KAREN: Thank God for that. There is so little time. David is leaving for Toronto first thing in the morning. We won't be able to spend any time together until he gets back from England.

MICHAEL: I didn't know you were going to England.

DAVE: I can't believe I didn't tell you. Four months. For the Federal Government. I wasn't supposed to tell anyone. Very hush-hush.

MICHAEL: What about your affairs in Toronto?

DAVE: No problem. I'll sub-let my apartment and Bannerman will look after my practice.

MICHAEL: (*at phone*) Well. Isn't that Bannerman one hell of a nice guy?

KAREN: We're going to spend two weeks together in September.

MICHAEL: Really? Two weeks?

DAVE: Yeah. Two weeks.

MICHAEL dials.

KAREN: We should go.

DAVE: What's your rush?

KAREN: I want to luxuriate over brunch.

DAVE: We have lots of time. I want to talk to Mike.

KAREN: Have you seen my purse?

DAVE: Don't worry, sweetie. It's around.

MICHAEL hangs up the phone.

MICHAEL: It's not like Beth to disappear on a Sunday morning.

KAREN: Have you tried Earl's?

DAVE: Stop worrying. She'll turn up.

MICHAEL: I've been trying to get in touch with her all morning.

KAREN: She's playing tennis.

MICHAEL: What?

KAREN: We had a tennis lesson this morning.

MICHAEL: How long does it go?

KAREN: She'll be another hour at least.

DAVE: Well, then. Let's have some coffee with Mike. Mike?

MICHAEL: Uh. Sure.

KAREN: What about our brunch?

DAVE: It's happening. We'll just visit for a little while. Karen, please.

KAREN: I'll put the kettle on.

DAVE: Thanks, sweetie. You get things started. I'll finish things off.

DAVE gives KAREN a domestic little kiss.

MICHAEL: There should be some apple strudel in the fridge if you want to warm it up.

KAREN: I'll find it.

KAREN goes.

DAVE: Well? What do you think?

MICHAEL: Huh? What about?

DAVE: Jesus Christ, Mike. This is the morning after the night before. This is the first time in eight years that I've got a night before to talk about. I'm enjoying this. Talking about it. It's exciting just talking about talking about it. Aren't you even happy for me?

MICHAEL: I hope you had a nice time.

DAVE: Ferocious. Absolutely ferocious.

MICHAEL: Ferocious?

DAVE: Did you ever go to bed with a member of the English Department? Do it. I recommend it wholeheartedly. I don't want to tell tales out of school but a wild, impetuous, passionate night. And after eight years of married life I was ready for it.

KAREN: (*off*) I need a pan for the strudel.

MICHAEL: Under the stove.

DAVE: Have you known Karen for a long time?

MICHAEL: Three, four years.

DAVE: She's a good friend?

MICHAEL: Pretty good.

DAVE: She always like this?

MICHAEL: Like what?

DAVE: No hassle, exciting, fun, good times.

MICHAEL: I guess.

DAVE: Nice girl.

MICHAEL: Dave.

DAVE: Yeah.

MICHAEL: Two weeks?

DAVE: We had a great time. We really got along.... Christ. I don't know.

KAREN sticks her head into the living room.

KAREN: David, could you give me a hand with the coffee?

DAVE: Sure, sweetie. (*KAREN goes.*) I don't know, Mike. I just don't know.

DAVE exits to the kitchen. Giggles and laughter off.

KAREN: (*off*) Stop that, David. We have to make the coffee. (*She enters.*) It's not as bad or as simple as it seems. I'll admit that last night I was angry and vindictive and the only reason I came on to David in the first place was to get back at you.

DAVE: (*off*) Where's the coffee?

MICHAEL: In the fridge.

KAREN: I never thought he'd turn out to be such a sweet, nice man. I never thought I'd have such a wonderful time.

DAVE: (*off*) Found it.

KAREN: I wasn't expecting it. I wasn't expecting that I was doing what I was doing. It started out one way but it ended up another.

DAVE: (*off*) This coffee is going to win me a golden cup.

KAREN: Yesterday afternoon. I was desperate. I made a mistake. It's best forgotten. No one need ever know anything.

MICHAEL: I haven't had time to think about this.

KAREN: You're doing very well.

MICHAEL: What if something comes up?

KAREN: Lie.

MICHAEL shakes his head.

You should never have gone to bed with me in the first place if you weren't willing to lie about it.

MICHAEL: Karen, I should never have gone to bed with you period.

DAVE: (*off*) Should I cut up the strudel before I heat it up?

KAREN: (*calling*) No.

DAVE: (*off*) Three fifty?

KAREN: (*calling*) I'll be there in a second. (*to MICHAEL*) Michael you're gracious and honest and well intentioned and it doesn't mean one damn thing. If you cause pain you cause pain and all the heartfelt talk in the world doesn't make one bit of difference.

DAVE: (*off*) Tin foil?

KAREN: Coming.

KAREN returns to the kitchen. Short pause. There is a knock on the door. MICHAEL answers it, BETH is there.

MICHAEL: Beth. C'mon in.

BETH: Mike, what happened to your eye?

MICHAEL: It's nothing.

BETH: Let me see.

MICHAEL: It's nothing. Really.

BETH: What happened?

MICHAEL: I'll tell you all about it later. Sit down. Please. I've been trying to get in touch with you all morning.

BETH: I went for a walk. It's such a beautiful morning.

MICHAEL: How was it?

BETH: Oh it did the trick. Mike, we have to talk.

MICHAEL: I know that Beth. I...

But KAREN enters with the plates and silverware on a tray.

KAREN: Michael, do you have any cinnamon? Beth.

BETH: Hi, Karen. I didn't know you were here.

KAREN: Just getting some coffee and pastry together.

BETH: I see.

KAREN: You didn't go to tennis?

BETH: No. Neither did you.

KAREN: Sunday mornings.

BETH: Yes.

KAREN: Great party last night. I felt like a kid again.

BETH: We weren't expecting that many people.

KAREN: Oh no. I liked the crush. I was putting coffee on. But maybe you and Michael...

BETH: Don't leave on my account. Perhaps I'm the one who should go?

KAREN: No, no, no. Michael's been trying to get in touch with you all morning.

BETH: Really?

KAREN: Yes. Oh silly you. I was just on my way to an absolutely decadent brunch. I only dropped in for a moment. Not five minutes ago. With an old friend of Michael's. He's an absolutely wonderful man. We just popped round to say good-bye. The mad fool has to go to England for four months. (*calling*) David. We've had a marvellous, glorious, twelve hours. I'm still reeling. (*calling*) David. There's someone who wants to say hello. (*as DAVE enters*) Oh. There you are. I believe you two know each other.

DAVE: Hi Beth.

BETH: Dave.

DAVE: Old friends.

MICHAEL: Dave's going to England for four months. These bachelor lawyers. The world's their oyster.

BETH: I hope Dave doesn't get indigestion.

DAVE: Ha-ha. The job's in London. For the Federal Government. Very hush-hush.

BETH: Dave, I wish you hadn't told me. I'm a terrible security risk. I'm sure I'll be spilling the beans to all the wrong people.

DAVE: Very funny.

KAREN: David's flying back here when he returns from England. We're going to spend two weeks together in September. Just the two of us.

BETH: Just the two of you. That's very romantic. You're going to be a very busy man these next four months.

DAVE: You know me. Pressure. I thrive on it.

KAREN: Beth. Coffee? Another cup, serviettes, oh my God, the strudel.

KAREN exits to the the kitchen.

BETH: You're out of your mind.

DAVE: Yeah. Well. Only in BC and I've made my peace with it.

Dave exits to the kitchen.

MICHAEL: I tried but he's an adult.

BETH: I doubt it.

MICHAEL: Beth.

BETH: Mike, I'd like to apologize for that phone call.

MICHAEL: Forget it.

BETH: And for my behaviour last night.

MICHAEL: Someone hurts you. You hurt them back. It's human nature.

BETH: Yes. I've done a lot of that. I think we should call it quits.

MICHAEL: Why...? Earl?

BETH: No, Michael.

MICHAEL: Why then?

BETH: I want it all. A husband, a family, a home for my family. The whole banal, bourgeois package. That's what I want. That's who I am. So let's just forget the whole damn thing because I'm not going to let you or anyone else make me feel guilty about it any longer.

MICHAEL: Beth, listen.

BETH: No. Let me finish. When you started talking arrangement I should have told you to get lost. But I was too scared of losing you. Of being out in that meat market looking for a man. Jesus Christ, I'm thirty. What if I didn't meet someone for a while. And even if I did, I wasn't going to get married and have kids with someone I just met. And God damn it, Mike, I was hoping you'd come through.

MICHAEL: And I have come through. That's what I've been trying to tell you. Beth. You're very special to me. I love you very much.

BETH: And I resent the hell out of you. Sometimes I don't even like you. God knows I don't respect you the way I used to. And there's no sense in even talking about trust.

MICHAEL: The arrangement was a big mistake. I know that now. But we can get over it.

BETH: These last few months. They're not marks on paper. They're here with us.

KAREN enters with strudel.

KAREN: Here's the strudel. And I found some melon. Why don't I cut this in the kitchen?

KAREN returns to the kitchen.

MICHAEL: I've been a big jerk. But that's over with. History. It's best forgotten. Beth? Let's give it another chance. There's more to us than these last few months.

BETH: I know that.

MICHAEL: We can do it. I've got all this garbage out of my system.

BETH: It doesn't work that way. Why are you doing this to me?

MICHAEL: We'll get it straight. You'll see.

BETH: Mike, please.

MICHAEL: All right, then. We'll have dinner tonight. We'll go to that little Portuguese place you like so much.

BETH: No.

MICHAEL: Tomorrow then? Beth? Please.

BETH: Okay, Mike. We'll talk.

DAVE enters with the coffee. KAREN follows with the strudel.

KAREN: Here we go. David will pour the coffee. This is an absolutely perfect melon. Did you pick this, Michael? Well, you certainly have a way with fruit. I go crazy in produce sections. I don't know whether to pinch or prod or sniff or squeeze.

DAVE: Sniff?

KAREN: Pineapples.

DAVE: Yeah? You sure? Where do you sniff them?

KAREN: All over, David. Where do you think?

BETH: Just the top.

KAREN offers DAVE some melon.

DAVE: None for me. I'll stick to strudel. Carbohydrates. They keep you young.

KAREN: And ruin your appetite. We are going for brunch. It's melon or nothing. Wonderful coffee.

DAVE: I told you. (*a sip*) Delish. (*another sip*) Delish, delish, delish. A little time, a little effort. And God rewards.

MICHAEL: Quite the spread you put on Karen. Thank you.

KAREN: David warmed the strudel.

DAVE: And cut the melon. And got the plates. And made the coffee. Delish, delish, delish.

There is a knock on the door. MICHAEL answers it. JACKIE is there. She is carrying two small pieces of luggage.

JACKIE: Free at last, Michael. Free at last. Oh. Does that eye hurt?

MICHAEL: It's fine.

JACKIE: I'm sorry. I didn't know you had people over. Hello, David.

DAVE: Hi.

JACKIE: I just came by to say I'm sorry. And Phil's sorry too. He's swallowing now.

MICHAEL: Good.

JACKIE: Here's a cheque for fifty dollars for the door.

MICHAEL: I can't take this.

JACKIE: Please. It'll make Phil feel better.

MICHAEL: Thanks.

JACKIE: I've made my decision. I'm leaving Phil. (*to the group at large*) Phil's my husband.

DAVE: And he mangled the door?

JACKIE: Yes.

KAREN: And hit Michael?

JACKIE: Yes.

BETH: Why?

JACKIE: Jeffrey Fiskin thinks it's Burnaby but I think...

MICHAEL: (*cutting Jackie off*) I'll tell you all about it later. Nice seeing you again Jackie.

BETH: Mike, why are you being so rude? Do you want some coffee, Jackie?

JACKIE: (*walking to the couch*) No thanks. Someone's supposed to be picking me up out front. Anyway Jeffrey's diagnosis is Burnaby but I think Jeffrey is full of it. (*sitting down*) Jeffrey's my psychiatrist. Very eclectic. I've been puking for months. Jeffrey blames it all on Burnaby. But I knew it couldn't just be Burnaby. I knew it was also Phil LeMieux. Phil and I got married just out of high school but we've been drifting apart ever since I started throwing up. I've been dancing and painting and meeting all these interesting people. And Phil, well he's been working at The Wheat Pool and going through a dozen beers a night and playing baseball like a maniac. Just generally being your basic veg. Last night at Jim's. Jim Loadman? Phil's foreman at the pool. I told Phil I wanted the freedom to experiment. We had this big fight and my back started to act up. And then I met Michael and David. Nothing happened. But Phil didn't know that. I've been in Burnaby arguing all night. I realize now that Phil is a very little person and that some people just can't handle change. He resents and he won't forgive. Well, I'm bigger than that. This is all I took and it feels just great. That's what I was thinking when I walked in. Goodbye, Burnaby. Goodbye Maalox. Free at last, Michael. Free at last. (*moving to MICHAEL*) I'm sorry you had to be a part of all this.

MICHAEL: It's all water under the bridge.

JACKIE: Guess I better be going. Bernard's picking me up out front. He always gets lost in Burnaby. Besides I didn't want him to run into Phil. Bernard Hedley, he's been painting for more than forty years, kind of a mentor figure for me. Well, I'm moving in. He's got this boat, close to forty feet, in a month he's going to sail the inside passage to Alaska. I'll be his deck hand.

DAVE: *Bon voyage*, Jackie.

JACKIE: I guess I owe you an apology too, David. I wasn't straight with you either.

DAVE: Forget it.

MICHAEL: You should wait for Bernard out front.

DAVE: Mentor figures are very impatient.

MICHAEL: Forty years waiting for a *protegé* like you. He must be getting antsy.

JACKIE: I just want you to know I respect you.

DAVE: Thanks.

JACKIE: You were honest about your wife in Toronto. I should have been as honest about Phil down the hall.

KAREN: Wife.

DAVE: Shit.

JACKIE: And family. Three boys.

KAREN: Where is my God damn purse?

DAVE: Karen don't be like that.

KAREN: Why didn't you have the guts to tell me the truth?

DAVE: Some women don't like to get involved with married men.

KAREN: I don't give a damn about your marital status. I hate being lied to.

DAVE: I'm new to all this.

KAREN: That makes everything just fine.

DAVE: I thought it would make things easier.

KAREN: You both knew, didn't you? Lovely. Just dandy. I love being treated this way. It does wonders for my self-esteem. And what's all this crap about two weeks away from it all?

DAVE: I'm serious. I'm looking forward to it.

KAREN: (*moving into the dining room in her search for her purse*) Bring your wife and kids. We'll get a family rate.

DAVE: (*following Karen into the dining room*) I'll work something out. I promise.

KAREN: (*off*) Forget it, David. I don't need you. There are twelve nineteen-year-olds in my first year section who would like nothing better than to tie me up and douse me in oil. Where is my God damn purse?

JACKIE, sitting, moans loudly, puts a hand to her stomach. KAREN enters. DAVE follows. KAREN continues her search for her purse.

DAVE: Karen, can't we handle this in a civilized manner? Let's talk about it. We'll go to the Four Seasons. We'll have that brunch.

JACKIE: Don't go there. You'll never get in.

DAVE: Sure we will.

JACKIE: Not today. The place will be just packed.

DAVE: So we'll go someplace else. Now get lost!

BETH: Dave. Unless you have reservations I'd forget about brunch.

DAVE: What's so special about.... Oh shit.

MICHAEL: What is it?

JACKIE: It's Mother's Day.

KAREN: Charming. Absolutely charming. That would have made for a very interesting brunch. Why can't I find anything when I need it?

JACKIE: This is all my fault. I'm so sorry. I'm not stupid. I'm really very sensitive. It's because I never saw them as a couple. It didn't make sense to me. So I didn't know to be quiet.

MICHAEL: It's all right, Jackie. It's not your fault.

JACKIE: But David, you must understand. (*DAVE turns away. She talks to MICHAEL.*) When things make sense to me I'm really very perceptive. I'm very astute. When I saw you and her together, (*gesturing to KAREN*) I knew right away something had been cooking. Because you two make sense together. And that's another reason I got things...

MICHAEL turns away. JACKIE trails off and sits down. She clutches her stomach.

BETH: What kind of sense did you and Karen make together?

Short pause. KAREN laughs loudly.

KAREN: Last night Michael and I were having a disagreement over Milton. This mindless muffin walked in on it. She obviously took our heated discussion of *Paradise Lost* to be sexual recrimination.... I really don't see how you can take this space cadet from Burnaby seriously.

BETH looks at MICHAEL. MICHAEL turns away.

KAREN: Michael, you are such a fool.

MICHAEL: I didn't see any point in telling you.

BETH: When?

MICHAEL: Yesterday afternoon.

KAREN: The one and only time.

MICHAEL: We did something very stupid. It was a big mistake.

KAREN: I really can't understand just how or why it happened. It was just one of those things. It means nothing. It's best forgotten. We both had an absolutely miserable time.

BETH turns away. KAREN follows.

KAREN: You had that silly, fatuous arrangement. Beth? Oh, damn it!

JACKIE: Does anyone have some Maalox?

MICHAEL walks towards BETH.

DAVE: You and Karen?

MICHAEL: Dave.

KAREN: I'll leave without my purse. I'll walk. Hitchhike. I don't care. (*remembering*) Oh right.

KAREN exits to the bathroom.

DAVE: Shit. The first time in eight years of marriage and on Mother's Day for fuck's sake. You shoulda said "no" to me right from the start. That's what a friend would have done. That's what I needed to hear. You shouldn't have been such a sophisticated, with it, enlightened son-of-a-bitch.

KAREN: (*off*) I can't believe my luck. Three men in one weekend. (*entering with her purse*) I'm not down. I'm out.

KAREN moves to go.

DAVE: Ten years later and I'm still getting your castoffs. Eh, best buddy? And for what? To feel like a big man. Like the successful lawyer.

KAREN: (*at door*) Excuse me, David. I didn't quite hear that. What did you call me?

Short pause. DAVE doesn't relent.

DAVE: Forget it.

KAREN: Well, David, "castoff" may very well be apt. But I think you should know that I found your conversation inane – delish, delish, delish. Your stature second rate – I don't know where you got the idea that women would forget about your height if you talked about your density. We're interested in men, not precious metals. And your performance, unusual to say the least. Sniff, sniff. I think you'd rather inhale than orgasm. The only reason I put up with all these failings was because I wanted to inflict some pain on a former friend who had recently, as you so aptly put it, cast me off.

KAREN goes. MICHAEL walks to DAVE. Puts his arm on DAVE's.

MICHAEL: Dave.

DAVE: Fuck off!!

DAVE pushes MICHAEL away. MICHAEL sprawls into the sofa.

JACKIE: I think I have to puke.

JACKIE runs to the bathroom. DAVE goes.

BETH: Are you all right?

MICHAEL: I'm fine.

BETH: You sure?

MICHAEL: Yes. I'm fine.

JACKIE returns from the bathroom holding a large bottle of Maalox.

JACKIE: And Jeffrey Fiskin kept saying it was Burnaby. It's an ulcer. It has to be. Oh. I'm sorry.... Well. Bernard must be waiting.

JACKIE takes a swig from the bottle and goes. There is a short pause. BETH walks to the door.

MICHAEL: I'm sorry.

BETH: Yes. I know.

BETH goes. MICHAEL sits for a moment, forces himself to get up, takes a sip of his coffee and turns on the stereo. He looks out the window. The lights fade.

The end.

LAST CALL

BY

MORRIS PANYCH

l to r
Ken MacDonald as Eddie, Morris Panych as Bartholomew

Photographer: David Cooper

MINIMALISM AND ABSURDITY IN SUBVERSIVE MUSICAL COMEDY: MORRIS PANYCH'S *LAST CALL*

Born in 1952, Morris Panych developed a passion for both music and theatre at an early age. While a high school student in his native Edmonton, he created and led a 70-piece marching band (composed primarily of kazoos) and, at an even earlier age, produced puppet shows and privately restaged his grandmother's three-day long Ukrainian funeral.

After receiving a diploma in radio and television broadcasting from the Northern Alberta Institute of Technology, Panych did a brief stint with CBC Radio in Edmonton in 1973. He went on to study creative writing at the University of British Columbia and acting at the E.15 Acting School in London, England. By 1979, he was busy acting in Vancouver and, by 1982, had seen the successful premiere of his first professionally produced play, *Last Call: A Post-Nuclear Cabaret*.

Panych has been a prolific presence on the Vancouver scene ever since. In 1990 and 1991 alone, his work garnered eleven Jessie Awards for excellence in theatre. In addition to performing in more than thirty plays and for television and film, he has also directed rock videos, opera, and countless plays, including, most recently, *Hamlet*, *Sweeney Todd*, and *She Loves Me*. Although he maintains he gained more recognition for a semi-recurring role as the Grey-Haired Man in the "X-Files" television series than for the Governor General's Literary Award he received for *The Ends of the Earth* in 1994, and he has recently returned to acting (after a seven-year hiatus) to star in Yasmina Reza's hit, *Art*, Panych gives primacy to his writing, insisting he is "a playwright who also acts and directs" (Ajzenstadt 29).

Context for a play that is as patently topical as *Last Call* is in order. As the references in the script to Lower Mainland place names might suggest, the work had its genesis in a decidedly Vancouver landmark. *Last Call* was inspired by a nightmare Panych had in 1981: led by a blinding flash outside his window, he ran to English Bay, only to find Ken MacDonald, his long-time professional and personal partner, blinded by the flash. From the image of a blind man roaming in the wilderness, the play emerged. Further impetus was provided by the visit to Vancouver of the US aircraft carrier Ranger and the suggestion of Dr. Helen Caldicott in her 1979 book, *Nuclear Madness: What You Can Do*, that her readers write a play about the nuclear tensions which were then running high.

Last Call was an instant hit. Its initial week-long run at the Vancouver East Cultural Centre, which began on January 29, 1982, sold out. By March, it was remounted at City Stage, where a petition urging the federal government to take a stand on nuclear disarmament was displayed in the lobby, and anti-nuclear groups distributed campaign literature at the door. Christopher Dafoe gave the first production a fervent and lengthy review in which he highlighted the local aspects of the play and emphasized its ability to both instruct and entertain. He also wrote, "Lessons can often be best learned when the pupil is laughing.... This wicked little show successfully turns comedy upside down and inside out. It makes a virtue out of bad taste." Panych and Macdonald followed up on their success with a tour to Winnipeg, Ottawa, Thunder Bay, and Toronto. Of the Toronto debut, presented by Phoenix Theatre at Adelaide Court Theatre, Judith Fitzgerald was effusive in her praise, singling out the "rich and multi-textured dialogue" and the songs, "so perfectly wrapped around their immediate environment and situation that the effect is stunning." *Last Call* continued with the original cast in the 1983 CBC television adaptation, and has had subsequent remountings with other actors.

Considering the mercurial nature of theatre, Panych has maintained a remarkable stability on several levels. His association with Tamahnous (including a two-year stint in the mid-eighties as artistic director of the company) was longstanding, Talonbooks has been his publisher for over a decade, MacDonald has invariably been a collaborator on his plays (now numbering close to twenty) as musical director or costume or set designer, and, as often as not, Panych has directed or co-directed the initial production of his plays.

There is also a consistency to the nature of his plays, although no subsequent work has been overtly political. The small cast recurs: in *Lawrence and Holloman*, for example, the eponymous characters are a controlling extrovert and a skeptical introvert, respectively; and *Vigil* (which recently garnered Floyd King a prestigious Helen Hayes Award nomination in Washington, DC in the best actor category) features Kemp, in a solo performance, admonishing his silent aunt Grace for failing to live up to her promise to die. Minimalism is a feature of even those Panych plays with larger casts: *The Overcoat*, Wendy Gorling and Panych's wildly popular adaptation of Gogol's short story (which is in the process of becoming a CBC television special), for example, features a cast of 22, led by Peter Anderson, that is wordless. A commonality among these and the rest of the Panych body of work, such as *7 Stories*, *2B Wut U R*, *The Ends of the Earth*, and *The Necessary Steps*, is an overriding sense of the absurd. The lonely main character in *Earshot*, a more recent work, for example, has extrasensory hearing that permits him to eavesdrop on the lives of others. Typically, Panych characters, often aware that they are acting for an audience, are in improbable situations over which they have no control, despite any illusions to the contrary they may harbour. Satire and black comedy are Panych's mainstays; inevitably, critics and reviewers have compared his work to that of Franz Kafka and Samuel Beckett.

Ratsoy: What stands out for you about the original production of *Last Call*?

Panych: It was a political satire; in that it stands completely apart from my other work. After *Last Call* I moved away from politics. I began to sense that it had no place in my work.

Ratsoy: You seem to favour two-handers, or at least you have repeated the pattern several times since *Last Call*. What are the advantages of the two-person play to your aesthetic as a playwright?

Panych: Two people is the essence of human relationships. It's yin and yang; it just makes sense.

Ratsoy: Do you consider yourself a BC playwright?

Panych: I consider myself a BC playwright the way I consider beer a BC drink. I guess the answer would be yes and no. I don't like boundaries much.

Ratsoy: Is there anything distinct about BC theatre? How would you describe it?

Panych: BC may be too young a place to already be creating a distinctive culture. Sometimes it takes hundreds, thousands of years. The culture that existed in this area before Europeans took millennia to develop. I think our theatre is more or less derivative of theatre throughout the country, throughout North America, except, perhaps, in one respect – there are few places where theatre survives with so little support, from audiences and government. Perhaps perseverance is our most distinctive feature.

Readers will notice similarities between *Last Call* and John Gray's *Billy Bishop Goes to War*. In addition to being initially produced by Tamahnous, both plays feature two characters (one of whom is a piano player), rely on a minimalist set, eschew the fourth wall in favour of direct address, and use music as a vehicle from which to scrutinize the horrors of war. *Last Call* also shares with Gray's play a Brechtian influence: several of Bertolt Brecht's concepts of epic theatre are adapted here, as is the musical formula that proved so successful in his collaboration with composer Kurt Weill on such satiric *exposés* of the 1920s German establishment as *The Threepenny Opera*.

This tradition of the musical is worlds away from the mega-musical that enjoyed world-wide popularity in the declining decades of the twentieth century. The mega-musical's primary method of engaging the audience is visual; because large casts and spectacle are foregrounded, a big budget is the prime requisite. The musicals of Gray and Panych are at the other end of the budget spectrum; the minimal visual elements and the small cast, while perhaps partly a response to the economic realities of Canadian theatre, are also elements of an aesthetic that facilitates focus and demands more of the audience. The large productions employ music to entertain and reinforce the status quo; the pared-down productions of Gray and Panych, in the guise of entertainment, undermine the status quo.

The company from which these two works sprang was Vancouver's leading and longest-lived alternative theatre. Initially known as Theatre Workshop, Tamahnous (the word is Chilcotin for "magic" or "spirit") acquired its permanent name in 1973. Begun two years earlier by UBC students Gray and Larry Lillo, Tamahnous operated on the collective creation principle popularized in Canada at the time by Toronto's Theatre Passe Muraille, with which Gray had worked. Both companies stressed process, populism, and the development of scripts by local playwrights (often arising out of local history or local contemporary events and issues). Along with the Gray and Panych plays, Stephen E. Miller's 1982 *A State of Grace* (about the BC Socred government) and Sally Clark's 1985 *Trial* (directed by Panych), were especially popular Tamahnous productions. Operating out of the Vancouver East Cultural Centre, the company, always experimental, was originally text-based. Over time, it developed a mandate for physical, interdisciplinary work and, especially under the artistic direction of Kathleen Weiss, Teri Snelgrove, and Brenda Leadlay, encouraged female playwrights. By the early 1990s, despite increasing financial difficulties because of cuts in government grants and sometimes disappointing box office returns, Tamahnous had success with Sheri-D Wilson's *Confessions (A Jazz Play)*, a sound poem that incorporated magic, clowning, and Christian ritual; and Ian Weir and Jeff Corness's *Faust*, an alternative opera incorporating dance that was staged in celebration of the company's twentieth anniversary. Tamahnous Theatre Workshop Society is currently dedicated to publishing the scripts of earlier productions, a project begun in 1998 with Jeremy Long's *The Final Performance of Vaslav Nijinsky*.

Ratsoy: What attracted so much talent to the Vancouver theatre scene in the 1970s and early 1980s?

Panych: Chris Newton at the Playhouse, and Seymour Street Arts Club, along with three or four really solid mid-sized companies, gave the city a happening feeling. This was before the film industry arrived.

Ratsoy: How would you summarize Tamahnous's contribution to Vancouver theatre?

Panych: Tamahnous made a tremendous contribution to the development of new theatre in Vancouver. It was at the forefront of experimentation and vital in the development of dozens of successful theatre artists.

The postmodernist elements in *Last Call* (and subsequent Panych work) can be seen as a logical extension of the Brechtian and absurdist influences. The characters acknowledge an awareness of an audience from the outset and throughout the play, the cabaret and play-within-a play structure reinforces this self-referentiality, and the dual ending underscores ambiguity. Taken together, these features, as Reid Gilbert notes, "force the spectators to accept that they do, indeed, create their own reality and that the borders between what they create imaginatively in the theatre and accept as real outside the theatre are more fluid than they may wish to believe" (6).

Although *Last Call* is clearly a product of its time and unashamedly didactic, its relevance to the twenty-first century reader transcends mere historical curiosity. Panych's targets are at once timely and timeless. *Last Call* is rife with both contemporary and historical references, and the objects of Panych's derision are manifold and specific; however, the play interrogates universals like, to name but a few, the nature of power structures, the ethics of a capitalistic society, the relevance of art, and the concept of material progress.

Last Call: A Post-Nuclear Cabaret was a landmark play for Morris Panych. It established him as a force to be reckoned with on the Vancouver—and Canadian—theatre scene, and it provided the groundwork on which his future opuses were built. Panych's materials of construction—subversive musical comedy, satire, absurdity, and postmodern reflexivity—have remained constant ever since.

G.R.

Selected Bibliography:

- Ajzenstadt, Michael. "The Unfinished Morris Panych." *Theatrum* 22 (Feb./Mar. 1991): 29-30. This article examines *7 Stories* as an autobiographical play and provides an overview of Panych's career.
- Birnie, Peter. "Panych Attack." *The Vancouver Sun* 20 Mar. 2001. Looks at Panych as a "triple threat": actor, director, and playwright.
- Dafoe. Christopher. "*Last Call* Bombs! And Mushrooms Into Glowing Brilliance." *The Vancouver Sun* 2 Feb. 1982.
- Druckman, Howard. "How to Laugh Off the Nuclear Horror." *The Toronto Star* 27 May 1983.
- Fitzgerald, Judith. "Full Moon Matches Spirit of *Last Call!*" *The Globe and Mail* 27 May 1983.
- Fitzgerald, Judith. "Humour Lies in Anxiety, not in 'the big boom'." *The Globe and Mail* 24 May 1983.
- Gilbert, Reid. "The Theatrical Stories of Morris Panych." *Canadian Theatre Review* 67 (Summer 1991): 5-11. Gilbert's examination is thorough and incisive.
- Godfrey, Stephen. "Tamahnous in Rough Water." *The Globe and Mail* 8 Oct. 1985.
- Johnston, Denis. "Directors in Vancouver: The New Community." *Canadian Theatre Review* 76 (Fall 1993): 25-30. Johnston introduces five Vancouver directors and in so doing provides insight into several theatre companies, including Tamahnous.
- Lacey, Liam. "Spotlight Settles on Panych at the Jessie Awards Ceremonies." *The Globe and Mail* 11 June 1991.
- Martin, Jennifer. "New Directions at Tamahnous." *Canadian Theatre Review* 63 (Summer 1990): 29-33.
- Panych, Morris. "Contradictions." *Canadian Theatre Review* 76 (Fall 1993): 58-59. This is a witty, personal essay on the nature of theatre.
- Panych, Morris. E-Mail Interview. 2 Feb. 2001.
- Wood, Chris. "Body—and Soul—Language." *Macleans* 113:6 (7 Feb. 2000): 60-62. Wood examines the success of Panych's adaptation of *The Overcoat*, starring Peter Anderson, and provides an overview of Panych's career.

Last Call
by Morris Panych

Last Call was first produced by the Tamahnous Theatre Workshop Society at the Vancouver East Cultural Centre, from January 29 to February 20, 1982, with the following cast:

Bartholomew Gross	Morris Panych
Eddie Morose	Ken MacDonald

Directed by Susan Astley
Stage Managed by Alison Eveson
Light & Sound Designed by Beverley Peacock

Last Call was also produced by CBC Television in March, 1983, with the following cast:

Bartholomew Gross	Morris Panych
Eddie Morose	Ken MacDonald

Original music in all productions by Ken MacDonald

Note: in the second production at the Vancouver East Cultural Centre, and on Canadian tour October-November 1982 the prologue was deleted.

CHARACTERS

BARTHOLOMEW GROSS, an escaped convict.
EDDIE MOROSE, a blind recluse.

NOTE ON PUNCTUATION

Italics without brackets in this play denote words that are sung; italics surrounded by brackets ( ) denote stage directions.

PROLOGUE

(The actors enter and sing.)

Now before we start the show,
Here's a short scenario
Of tonight's events.

Just imagine, if you will,
Two men from the future tense
Who are living evidence
Of a nuclear war.

Two survivors meet, by chance,
Who, by any circumstance
Other than a nuclear war
Never would have fraternized, it's true.

Two conflicting points of view,
Two men wandering alone,
From the radiation zone
Into barren wilderness.

Where they are is either partner's guess.
One is blind and must rely
On the other guy.
And the other one has a gun
He has just escaped, you see,
from a penitentiary
And has stopped them along the way
Thinking it's a cabaret.
It may be just in his mind,
But the other one is blind.

So they stay to sing a song
Of what is gone and what survived
Just in case you might appear–
Someone from the past to hear
Entertainments they've contrived.

(As the lights come up on stage, EDDIE Morose and BARTHOLOMEW Gross are seen skulking in the background, behind what is left of a retaining wall, amid the post-nuclear wreckage of bombed-out buildings. EDDIE is still in his pajamas and a housecoat. He is blind and wears dark glasses, guiding himself with a cane. BARTHOLOMEW wears institutional prison greens and an oversized suit-jacket. He carries a revolver. On one side of BARTHOLOMEW's face is the beginning of what looks like a very odd skin disease.)

EDDIE: Gross?

BART: Shh!

EDDIE: This is it?

BART: Shh! Don't move. Stay right where you are.

(They move about checking the premises until they bump into each other.)

BART: What the fuck are you doing?

EDDIE: Nothing.

BART: Well, can't you do it somewhere else?

EDDIE: Where are we anyway? I thought you said this was it. I think we're lost.

BART: Sit down.

EDDIE: I'm beginning to wonder about this cabaret idea of yours, you know. I mean, we haven't seen anyone, dead or alive, for at least a week now. So where are all these people going to come from? Of course, I'm assuming you want to perform this in front of an audience but I could be wrong.

BART: People have a way of showing up for these things. That's what's so amazing. Wherever there's fun to be had, you'll find people.

EDDIE: Well, we haven't found any yet. No, let me correct myself. You have. I haven't. In fact, lately you've been finding a lot of things that seem to appear out of nowhere.

BART: Why don't you just shut-up?

EDDIE: Right. I mean, I don't mind traipsing about the wilderness, day in and day out. But sooner or later...

BART: Faith, my boy, faith.

(BART turns away, coughing and spitting violently.)

EDDIE: Are you getting sick again?

BART: The trouble with you is that you wouldn't know a cabaret if you saw one. It's a question of altering your perspective. Did I ever tell you about the discovery of America?

EDDIE: No.

BART: There were these people, you see. These sailors. Looking straight ahead at America. Thought it was India for Christ sake. So they gave up on it and kept looking. Now this may have had something to do with the fact that they were Spanish... on the other hand... anyway, you see my point.

EDDIE: Not really.

BART: The point is... you never know what's sitting right under your nose.

(As he is speaking BART leans on the edge of a grand piano, which he hasn't as yet noticed. Just as he does this, EDDIE discovers the piano keys. They both start. EDDIE sits to play. BART cautiously approaches the keys, then notices lights coming up on him. He is mystified. Suddenly he is aware of the audience and takes on a different tone. He pokes EDDIE to signal him that something quite wonderful is happening.)

BART: *Ladies and Gentlemen,*
Attention, please.

The show will now begin.
The lights will dim, and then
Shadows will disappear
Under a bright veneer.
Darkness dissolves away
Lighting the cabaret
With our illuminating fantasies.

EDDIE: *And what is more besides*
Under the lights he hides
His own disease...

BART: Morose!

EDDIE: I thought the Ladies & Gentlemen might like to hear about your disease.

BART: No. They don't. This is a fairly sophisticated crowd. Your above average types. They don't want to hear about the nasty side-effects of nuclear war. I think that goes without saying.

EDDIE: Oh, they're sophisticated now. Sorry, I didn't know you'd changed your mind.

BART: What?

EDDIE: I thought you said we were going to entertain the masses. That's what you've been telling me for three weeks. And now, suddenly, they're all sophisticated.

BART: Haven't you heard of the sophisticated masses? Where were you when they invented television? Ladies and Gentlemen, I apologize. The man is obviously suffering from the secondary stages of radiation sickness. He has no sense of where we are.

EDDIE: Well, why don't you just tell me, Gross?

BART: Take my word for it. (*coaxing with the gun*) We have arrived and we are here.
*Ladies and Gentlemen,
Ignore that last song.*

EDDIE: *I guess that I was wrong.
Sincere apologies.
It seems there's no disease.*

BART: *So we'll begin again.
The lights will dim and then.
Shadows will disappear
Under a bright veneer.
Darkness dissolves away
Lighting the cabaret
With our illuminating fantasies!
Ladies and Gents,
Attention, please!
We will commence.*

EDDIE: *We will commence.
A tale will now unfold,
A story sadly told.*

BART: *Gladly told.*

EDDIE: *Gladly told.*

BART: *And with a ring of truth...*

EDDIE: *Ring of truth...
Nevertheless...*

BART: *Nevertheless.*

EDDIE: *It's hardly news, I guess.*

BART: *Not news to me.*

EDDIE & BART: *About the nuclear war.*

BART: *The twenty minute spree.*

EDDIE: *A limited exchange.*

BART: *A silly accident.*

EDDIE: *Perhaps oversight.*

BART: *Even intentional.*

EDDIE: *Perhaps too short a range.*

EDDIE & BART: *A course that couldn't change.*

EDDIE: *Destruction overnight.*

BART: *And rather permanent, and unconventional.*

EDDIE: *And then, of course, you've heard...*

BART: *They mutually assured...*

EDDIE & BART: *Not one, but there were more–
they equalized the score
And struck another blow.*

EDDIE: *To stop a full-scale war.
But this you know.*

BART: *But this you know.*

EDDIE: *Why bother you with this
Or ponder the abyss?
Instead we'll call to mind
A tale of humankind.*

MAN, MAN

BART: *Ever since
time began
We've had this creature
We call man.
And where he came from
No one knows
But he wasn't wearing any clothes.
So, he wasn't from Milan,
and he wasn't from Paris.
they say he evolved from a Chimpanzee.
Well, maybe he had good connections
A long time ago–
It isn't what you do, it's who you know.*

(*Chorus.*)

Man, man, what a man–
Did his thing like no one can.
Why he did it is a mystery,
But he had a great time making history.

BART: *Well, now the ice-age came*
And man was alone.
So he made a fire,
And he carved a bone,
And he sang a song
'Cause he was so smart.
It was very entertaining, but was it art?

He started making friends,
And they all lived together.
[I guess they had no telephone.]
But that's okay.
The contact was nice–
and you gotta mingle if you wanna break the ice.

(*Chorus.*)

BART: *Well, now man became*
A social beast,
And he went to war
Once a month at least.
When he wasn't making war,
Every other day,
He was making love in that old-fashioned way.

Well, the Greeks made vases
And the Romans made jugs,
And the Persians made those crazy rugs.
It's a good thing they lived
Those creative lives
'Cause those handicrafts are dandy for the archives.

(*Chorus.*)

BART: *Well, man had a Renaissance,*
Found his new thing,
Started thinking
And discovering.
But he didn't know about Chop-Suey,
You can bet on that–
It's the price you pay for thinking that the world is flat.

So he sailed around the African cape,
And Terra del Fuego and the whole seascape,
Looking for that passage
To those Chinese–
I guess they didn't have take-out deliveries.

(*Chorus.*)

BART: *Well, he got himself some manners,*
And he had his friends for tea,
Started acting with refinement
And courtesy.
And he wrote some crazy poems
And some crazy prose–
And man, he wore some crazy clothes.

And he built his empires,
And he spread himself around,
Making sure he covered all his ground.
Trying to spread his culture
All over the place–
Trying to put those natives in their proper place.

(*Chorus.*)

Well, man reached the Modern Age,
And making history was still the rage.
So he dropped a bomb–
And the rest is history text.
What's here today is gone the next.

He had class.
He had style.
He was around
For quite a while.
He got to know the situation.
But I guess he didn't know about annihilation.

EDDIE & BART: *Why he did it is a mystery,*
'Cause there's no one here
On this little ol' sphere...

BART: *'Cept for lil' ol' me...*

EDDIE: *An' lil' ol' me...*

BART: *An' lil' ol' he...*

EDDIE & BART: *To tell*
His history.

BART: (*speaking*) Yes, Ladies and Gentlemen, what can I say? It's all been blown away. But don't let that get you down. We can always evolve back up through the species. There's gotta be a couple of amœbas around here somewhere on friendly terms to start it all over. Where do we go from here?

EDDIE: Are you asking me? How do I know? I don't even know where we are. I thought we were supposed to be heading North.

BART: What are you bringing that up for? In the middle of the goddamned cabaret?

EDDIE: If we're going North, it should be getting colder, not warmer. It's actually getting warmer.

BART: What you're feeling is the lights. We're here, Morose.

EDDIE: Listen... I think you're just over-tired. I think you should rest.

BART: Fuck that. I'm going to have a beer.

EDDIE: Oh. There's beer, too?

BART: There's everything here. Everything we dreamed of. And a great-looking group of survivors. Hardly a mutation among them. Now... where was I? Oh, yes. As I was saying, Ladies and Gentlemen... (*Bart takes a balloon out of his pocket and blows it up.*) when you look at this globe, this scaled-down model of the world...

EDDIE: What globe?

BART: The one to which I am referring.

EDDIE: Just checking.

BART: When you look at this... it's plain to see... the earth is a basic entity of all life forms. Delicately suspended...

EDDIE: What are you talking about?

BART accidentally lets go of the balloon and it flies away.

BART: I was talking about mankind. I was referring to his present situation.

EDDIE: What situation?

BART: Exactly! You never know when he'll come in handy, Ladies and Gentlemen. Just when you think the guy's a useless burden. Just when you start thinking that it might be better to shoot him, and be done with it, he comes up with some remarkably deep and incisive thought. You just never know, I guess, when a handicapped person is going to come up with the goods.

EDDIE: Speaking of handicaps.

BART: Wait a second. Let me get this straight. Are you referring to a certain skin disease of mine by any chance?

EDDIE: I don't know anything about it, Gross. I'm blind.

BART: Right! So what makes you think you know what you're talking about?

EDDIE: It's only a guess.

BART: Yeah, well keep it to yourself. These people don't want to hear the gruesome details, Morose. Or maybe you'd like to tell them. About the melting flesh, the popping eyeballs, the charred remains of people strewn about the place, the epilation of the scalp, the bloody vomit, the radiation sickness, the insanity. You wouldn't have seen it anyway. You missed the whole thing. But we'll get to your story later.

EDDIE: I guess we'll be here for a while, then.

BART: What's your hurry? The man thinks he's going somewhere. We spend three weeks looking for this cabaret – and now he's got somewhere else to go. That was the whole trouble with the human race. If you want it in a nutshell. People always thought they were going somewhere. All you ever do is walk in circles anyway.

EDDIE: Tell me something. Have we been walking in circles?

BART: That depends.

EDDIE: On what?

BART: Whether you're speaking philosophically or geographically.

EDDIE: Geographically.

BART: That's an interesting point, now that you mention it.

EDDIE: I mean—pardon me for saying so—but you don't seem to have a very clear grasp on things these days. Yesterday you thought we were back in Vancouver.

BART: Did I?

EDDIE: That's what you said. You said we were walking right down Main Street.

BART: That's interesting.

EDDIE: You don't even remember.

BART: Of course I do. But who would want to remember Main Street? Are you sure I didn't say Davie Street?

EDDIE: What difference does it make? It's all gone anyway.

BART: Ah! You don't know that for sure. You didn't see it.

EDDIE: No, but I saw the flash. And I certainly heard it.

BART: Well, maybe it's gone and maybe it isn't. There's no point getting depressed about it.

EDDIE: Who's depressed?

BART: These people don't want to be reminded of the current situation. I mean, maybe some of them had friends there. Or investment property. I'd prefer to remember it as it was, Eddie.

THE CITY

EDDIE & BART: *Do you remember life in the city?*
Do you remember the crowded street?
Can you recall the sound of pounding feet?
Can you still feel the pedestrian beat?

Life was crazy then.
So cosmopolitan.
Moving with the urban mass–
It was quite the gas.
You can bet your – beep, beep!
Do you remember the – skyscrapers?
The morning papers with the depressing news?
The whores, the pimps, the junkies and the rapers?
The little white men in executive blues?

Man, man, what a sight:
The never-ending jive.
People moving left and right,
From five to nine to five,
Just to stay alive.

Should life get you down
When you were on the town,
You could always go
To some little place
To escape the pace.

BART: *Maybe a sunset amble through the park.*

EDDIE: *But never after dark.*

BART: *The dusky twilight was romancing time.*

EDDIE: *The lighting was sublime for a date with crime.*

(BART dances.)

EDDIE: *But you could always find a quiet corner in a quiet bar.*
And hide away all day behind a bottle of Pinot Noir...

BART: *Or Five Star!*

Do you remember the heavy action?
Do you remember the wildlife, too?
A million animals looking for satisfaction–
Who could forget living life in a zoo?

EDDIE: *People never left you alone in the city.*
Someone always had something annoying to say.
Cloyingly officious or soliciting pity–
In the city, people always got in the way...

BART: (*spoken*) Hey!

EDDIE: *But if you felt unsociable and sedentary,*
You could find seclusion at the library.
Hide behind a pile of books, and well out of view,
Or tarry for a while in the loo–

(*The song finishes.*)

BART: Morose! What kind of an attitude is that?

EDDIE: It's my attitude.

BART: Haven't you got anything positive to say about the city?

EDDIE: Yes. It's gone.

BART: Well, Ladies and Gentlemen, I guess it takes all kinds to make a world. Unfortunately, he's one of the few left. I don't know where all this anti-social behavior will get you, Morose.

EDDIE: Sorry. It's just an opinion. Can't I have an opinion?

BART: Of course. What do you think I am? Some kind of fascist? This is a democracy. That's what I decided. Right from the beginning. Now, you can't argue with that, can you? If you want to toddle off into the wilderness on your own, that's your business.

EDDIE: Well, why didn't you say that three weeks ago, instead of taking me hostage?

BART: Because I wanted to spare you the consequences.

EDDIE: Right.

BART: Listen... I had no idea you felt this way. I thought you wanted to set up this cabaret with me. I thought you were exercising your free will.

EDDIE: What free will? You've always got that gun pointed at my head.

BART: What gun? The man's hallucinating.

EDDIE: Come on, Gross. You've had it at my head for three weeks. Dragging me through the wilderness. Making me listen to your philosophies and stories. Anyway... you can shoot me. I don't care anymore.

BART: Have you gone through some spiritual change in the last twenty-four hours? I thought you liked being alive?

EDDIE: I like being alone. I always have.

BART: Well, I think you've hurt my feelings just *now*.

EDDIE: Sorry.

BART: I don't know what I've done to deserve this. I've looked after you. Found things. Food. Lodgings. I found the cabaret. You couldn't have done that on your own. And then I found our way back to Vancouver for a day. That was a nice diversion.

EDDIE: Yeah, well, we can't live on your diversions, Gross.

BART: What about that great big steak dinner I came up with the other day. With the fresh frozen peas you like so much? And that fabulous salad bar. Remember?

EDDIE: Yeah. I remember.

BART: Well, there you are.

EDDIE: That was a hallucination.

BART: It may have been to you, but I sure the hell enjoyed it. And you can't beat the price. No, but seriously, folks...

EDDIE: The point is... we didn't eat any steak dinner.

BART: That's not the point.

EDDIE: Oh, sorry.

BART: The point is... that was yesterday.

EDDIE: Oh, that's the point.

BART: And whether we ate it or not is irrelevant. Because it's all in the past. It's a case of here today, gone tomorrow. Yes, folks... whatever happened yesterday, happened yesterday – and today we find ourselves being served up a dish of something completely unrecognizable.

EDDIE: I'd prefer something I could get my teeth into.

BART: *So* said Mr. What's-His-Name. The fellow in the gutter.

EDDIE: Who?

BART: That man. The one who tried to tell us he had nothing to do with the former government, when in fact we knew there was something about him.

EDDIE: I think that man was dead, Gross.

BART: Yes, Morose... in the ditch. And how did he end up there, he wondered. When he'd been doing so well with the Department of Justice. Moving up, bit by bit. Accumulating power, day by day. He had his own office, for Christ's sake – and two secretaries. And if this nasty business with the bomb wouldn't have happened, he was up for a telex!

EDDIE: He told you all this, did he?

BART: He didn't have to tell me. I figured. Who else but a bureaucrat from the Department of Justice, with his own office and three secretaries...

EDDIE: Three secretaries.

BART: I didn't mention his receptionist before – and a photocopier. Who else but a man like that would be wearing such a suit. This suit, in fact. Perhaps you're wondering what it is that he actually told me.

EDDIE: That he didn't want his suit?

BART: Besides that. Well, I'll tell you. And maybe this will clear things up. Maybe it won't. You see, he didn't actually get blitzed like most people. He had, in fact, escaped the holocaust in his car. So for a while, there were some government people still alive, if that's any comfort. Still some people at the reins of power. Or so they thought. But, as he sped away in his car, down the highway – he wasn't aware of one thing which would later surprise him. Namely this: that without a functioning society to maintain law and order, anybody could take control – provided they had the one essential item necessary to take control.

EDDIE: A gun.

BART: Precisely. And how did he finally discover this, you ask? Well, it's quite simple. Somebody shot him. And took his wallet. And as he lay there, at the side of the highway, in a more or less analytical state of mind, he came to this conclusion...

THE ONE WITH THE GUN

BART: *The one with good credit is always secure.*
His cards are what separate him from the poor;
Giving freedom and access to limitless power
Any hour of day.

But a thief with a pistol can cut his time short
In the game of high finance he's not a good sport.
And he's faulty in business transactions, in fact
They're an act of foul play.

Though there isn't a person who cannot be bought
All the wealth in the world isn't worth such a lot.
The man with the money can call his attorney,
But the one with the gun calls the shot.

The one with the glasses has read every book.
His knowledge and foresight we can't overlook.
The theories expounded are worth our attention–
Not to mention our praise.

But he can't hold his own with a murdering crook
Whose penchant for reason he's sadly mistook
Thinking such a man's evil he can simply reverse
With a terse and a meaningful phrase.

To the power of wisdom all mankind submits,
But one can't think one's way through the nastier bits.
The man with the glasses may influence the masses,
But the one with the gun has the wits.

The man with the gavel can put you in jail
Without any mercy, without any bail–
His judgements are turgid and haven't a soul
So you wait for parole.

But he hasn't an edict when faced with a gun
Such anarchy tends to put law on the run.
The court is judicious, but not as auspicious
As guns, on the whole.

For the point of a barrel has never been moot.
While the lawyers debate it, you aim it and shoot.
With the deck up your sleeve, you may win a reprieve,
But the one with the gun wins the suit.

The man with religion won't suffer in life.
He'll remove all your sins without using a knife.
No placebo's as neat as a sacred belief for
Relieving the pain.

But you can't hope for grace in the face of a gun.
And you might resurrect long before your prayer's done.
If you plead on your knees to be saved from a slaying
You're praying in vain.

You may think seeds of truth have been scattered abroad.
But the truth's in your aim, all the rest is a fraud.
The man with the word may have otherwise heard,
But the one with the gun is God.

BART: (*as the music continues*) Well, now the poor guy never expected to end up like that. Dying in a cynical mood. But things aren't the same anymore. The tables have turned. And you can't rely on old values, mister—I said to him—there's a whole new set of circumstances, and depending on whether or not you possess the basic rudiments of authority... what exists and what doesn't is very much a matter of personal opinion.

(*BART sings.*)

Can you take what you dish out–
You glutton of power?
Now the one with the gun
is the man of the hour–
Yes, the one with the gun
Is the man of the hour.

(*As BART becomes preoccupied in his thoughts, EDDIE sings.*)

He's not a God
Without the gun he's just a criminal fraud–
He can't really sing
And he can't really act–
He wouldn't be king if the world was intact today
Hey, Hey...

He's not a God
Without the gun he's just a criminal fraud–
He can't really sing
And he can't really act–
He wouldn't be king if the world was intact today
Hey, Hey...

(*BART stops him, with a gun to the temple.*)

BART: Hey! I don't want to have to use this gun, Morose.

EDDIE: Go ahead. Use it.

BART: I could shoot off your hands. That wouldn't be very nice. Would it? Those fine, piano hands. And what would you hold your cane with? Huh? Then how the hell would you poke your way around? With your tongue? I could shoot off your tongue. Or give you a nose transplant. Ha.... Ha.... Oh, Morose... where's your sense of humour? He's getting maudlin again, Ladies and Gentlemen. He's getting ready to die, and the show's just begun.

EDDIE: You could just leave me here, on my own.

BART: I just might. I just might leave him here. Oh, yes! And then who gets the solo spot? Who the hell do you think you're dealing with here? A fucking idiot? You think I don't know? You think I don't know? Forget it. Forget it.

EDDIE: What? What do you know?

BART: The man's trying to usurp my power. I know a revolutionary when I see one. You better watch it, or you'll be out of a job, mister. Don't forget who your friends are.

EDDIE: I don't have any friends.

BART: Precisely! They're all gone.

EDDIE: I never had any friends.

(EDDIE plays Chopin Nocturne Op. 9, No. 2, as BART tells the story.)

BART: Eddie Morose. Ah! Eddie Morose. No friends, you say? Could that have been your mother's fault? It's hard to point the finger when it's all so long ago and far away. But it's clear that from the very beginning all you ever really wanted was just to be left alone, in your own world. You didn't want those nurses and that pediatrician, did you? No. Ladies and Gentlemen, he wanted to be born by himself – didn't even want his mother if the truth were known. And that was just the start of a long arduous series of aggravations. Why, at six months old he got rid of his teddy-bear, insisting that it got on his nerves. And whenever his parents came into his room, he'd pretend he was asleep, just so they'd go away and leave him alone. In fact, he was such a quiet child, such a recluse, that by the age of three he was diagnosed as clinically depressed. All he was really interested in was great music and literature. So his mother bought him a little toy piano, and a few junior best-sellers, and left him to his own devices. When he was older and went off to school, the other children hated him. Spat on his looseleaf binder. Threw his music dictation down the sewer. Beat him to within an inch of his life on a daily basis. Later, when his parents had finally lost all hope for his integration into social life, they decided on reform school. It was there Eddie received his roughest treatment. We won't go into detail, suffice it to say that he suffered the kind of indignities that leave permanent scars. But he continued to play piano. Even when they smashed his fingers. And he continued to lose himself in his great literature, even though they scribbled obscenities all over his favourite hard-bound copy of Sir Winston Churchill's *History of the English Speaking Peoples*, Volumes One through Four. It was a situation that went from bad to worse, and most self-respecting people would have at least attempted suicide, but not Eddie. Because he was happy. When he was alone. Often you could see the light from his attic loft at night, and hear the piano music spilling dolefully into the street. People passing by would stop, transfixed in a momentary state of vagueness, just hearing the sound. Eddie had that effect on people. Some didn't like it. In fact, he was asked to leave his place of employment on several occasions, not for reading on the job, but for reading such things as *A Portrait of the Artist as a Young Man*, by Mr. James Joyce. People didn't understand. And late at night, Eddie would sit at his piano, and sing this sad song...

EDDIE: *If I play this song*
I can sing—
Sing for me,
Make me happy.
I could sing along,
Sing along
La, la...
With the music...

(As EDDIE drifts away, BART reminds him of life's agony.)

BART: Eddie, why don't you find a girl and settle down.

Eddie, I'm afraid there's no point having you around.
Eddie, Say hello to Auntie May.
Eddie, The office staff has decided you are gay.
Eddie, Get up you're late for work.
Eddie, Jesus! What a jerk!
Eddie, Do you think you'd enjoy sex?
Eddie, Why are you wearing stripes with checks?

As he played,
Life closed in.
Eddie hid,
Alienated.

Then one day–
Code Condition Red!
Bombs away!
Everyone was dead.

EDDIE: *In the dead of Night*
The missiles came
To luminate the sky
With a light so bright
I lost my sight–
It came so suddenly.
And the last horizon to appear
Is the one I'll always see.

Now finally, at last,
I am alone.

BART: *Not so fast*
Don't forget me.

EDDIE: *This is all I need,*
Nothing more.

BART: *Plus a friend*
Thanks to war.

EDDIE & BART: *La, la, la...*

EDDIE: *I remember them*
The angry crowd–
The people of my past,
As a vague hallucination
Which at last would disappear.
And the dying note–
The one they wrote,
It's the one I'll always hear.

(*As the song comes to a close, EDDIE realizes that BART is becoming quite ill. BART vomits, as EDDIE listens.*)

EDDIE: Are you getting sick again?

BART: What the hell is he going on about? The man's life story depresses me, so I have to stop for a moment to reflect on life. And he thinks I've got some kind of radiation sickness.

EDDIE: I never said that.

BART: Maybe you'd like to hear about my bloody diarrhea while you're at it.

EDDIE: Not really. It's some kind of reaction.

BART: Reaction? Are you speaking philosophically or philosophically?

EDDIE: Maybe it's something you ate. Or didn't eat.

BART: I don't think these people want to hear about our diet. It's not a very appetizing subject. In fact, it makes me sick just to think about it. I think I ate a cockroach this morning.

EDDIE: Charming.

BART: It could have been worse. It could have been a dead cockroach.

EDDIE: Where did you find a cockroach?

BART: They're around. Good God... they're a lot more adaptable than we are. Yes, Ladies and Gentlemen. I reckon it's a question of proportion. The more you have, the more you stand to lose. People always used to think that wasn't the case. Why, there was a man on Mount Higgins. This was before I knew you, Eddie...

EDDIE: Oh.

BART: I believe he was a multi-millionaire, twenty times over. Why he lived up on Mount Higgins is a wonder, because it's about fifty miles from nowhere. Or should I say... Mission. Actually, you pass Mission on the Highway to Dewdney. You turn left and go

North a number of miles, through Durieu – then turn right at the old Alan Lake Road – turn left at Alan Lake, and go North along the Old Douglas Road, by the forest, which is often washed out, until you get to Davis Lake Park – over the Weatherland Creek, to the Lost Creek turn-off. Then you turn left and follow the road to where it ends at Stave Lake. There, he had a mooring – and he took his boat up Stave Lake about fifteen miles to Clearwater Bay, in the Mount Judge Howay Recreational Area. From there, he had to portage along the Tingle Creek about ten miles, and then make his way inland about five or six miles, until he reached the foot of the mountain. And then he climbed the mountain. And why on earth would he live up there, you ask.

EDDIE: Why on earth would he live up there?

BART: Ah! Like many people; especially people with a lot of money to spend on such projects, this man wanted to be prepared for nuclear war. And he certainly was. He built himself an enormous, sell-sufficiency farm at the top of that mountain, with animals and servants and enough ammunition and supplies to last him a lifetime.

EDDIE: I suppose it was blown up.

BART: No. It's still there, as far as I know. A monument to a man's foresight.

EDDIE: Lucky for him.

BART: Yes. Well, unfortunately... the day the city was bombed he was at the dentist... in Burnaby. Which just goes to show you one of two things. Number one – that you should look after your teeth. And number two – that you just never know when they're going to blow us all to hell. Yes, Ladies and Gentlemen – in a nutshell, I reckon the greatest folly of mankind was thinking there'd be time for orthodontics.

NO TRUMPETS, NO TEARS

EDDIE & BART: *No trumpets, no tears–*
No paranoid fears–
No brief anxiety attacks.
No time for a snack
Of Cheezies and beer,
Or even one last, fast, Big Mac.

No way
to enjoy it–
Annihilation comes so quick.
No fun
When they destroy it.
You can't digest–
It makes you sick.

No trumpets, no tears
No shopping at Sears–
No instant liquidation sale.
No specials, no deals,
No last minute steals
On dollar forty-nine retail.

(*Music.*)

No headline news–
No last point of views.
No editorial summize.
No time for goodbyes,
Or even adieus.
No one to even analyze.

Good grief!
Who'd believe it.
No eleventh hour reports.
Where was
Knowlton Nash, man?
Maybe he came
After the sports.

No trumpets, no tears,
No blindfold, my dears.
No last request and no last drags.
No time to be brave
Or even to shave–
No time to even pack your bags.

(*BART disappears, and EDDIE is left alone with his memories.*)

EDDIE: My mother certainly never expected it. Well, we never really communicated. I guess you could say we were worlds apart. Me upstairs, her downstairs. Me playing piano. Her screaming.

(*BART assumes the role of EDDIE's mother. EDDIE plays; BART sings.*)

THE SONG OF EDDIE'S MOTHER

Give me a break, would you?
I got a son who sits upstairs
For heaven's sake
All morning noon and night
Playing piano all alone.
And I've got problems of my own–
Excuse me, there's the phone.

EDDIE: "If it's for me I'm not at home."

BART: *Hello Gladys.*
How's your asthma?
Really? Really?
Well, do they have to do a scan, or what?
Good grief! Down there?
Well, anyway–
Thank God for Medicare.
It could be worse.
I used to be a nurse.
The things that happen to a woman over forty
Are astounding–
Just a second–
Eddie – stop that pounding!

EDDIE: It's music! It's my life!

BART: *The poor boy needs a wife.*
Well, listen dear,
I'll call you after lunch.
I've got a woman here;
Something political
Some kind of questionnaire...
That anti-nuclear bunch.
And God, her hair!
It's much too short.
She looks like just the sort of woman
With far too much education,
Into women's liberation.

BART: Eddie, stop!
You're driving me to drink!

EDDIE: It's Bach.

BART: *He plays it around the clock. The poor boy. He's just lonely, I think. Excuse me...*
Listen Gladys, I have to go–
Yes, I know. I know.
Oh, I know. It's true.
What can you do?
Yes, so do I. Bye-bye.

(*BART sings to the imaginary person at the door.*)

As I was saying, dear
I understand your fear.
Nobody wants to die
From radiation.
But, you have to understand
My situation:
I'm an ordinary woman
Not the type to be
a revolutionary.
So, you see,
It's no good asking me.
Quite frankly, I don't think
That we are on the brink of war.
In fact, according to the news
They say they'll never use
Those awful warheads.
They just want to keep an even score.
A balance with the Reds
And, furthermore, both sides are putting some away–
So really everything is quite okay.
Eddie! Do you have to play?

EDDIE: It's Minuet in G, in the key of A.

BART: Yes. Anyway, as I was going to say... why do you bother with all this anti-nuclear stuff? Can't you find some other occupation? Some more feminine vocation? Get out there and have some good, clean fun? Maybe you would like to meet my son.

(*EDDIE plays a crescendo, and the song ends. BART removes the mother's guise, and is himself again.*)

BART: With a guy like you, I imagine your mother had a lot of problems.

EDDIE: I was no problem. I just stayed in my room most of the time.

BART: I think you're guilty of criminal negligence, Morose. All the problems in the world, and you weren't even interested? Didn't you ever read the paper?

EDDIE: Yeah. I read the paper.

BART: Didn't you ever get involved?

EDDIE: No.

BART: Jesus! We could practically hold him responsible for the whole thing. If we didn't know how sensitive he was.

EDDIE: Well, what was I supposed to do? One guy... start a revolution?

BART: Well, if it's any comfort to you – I don't think anybody would have listened anyway.

(*BART searches through his loot bag. He sings to himself.*)

BART: *Every time I look in here–*
The evidence is clear...

EDDIE: Where? Oh. There. His bag of loot. Two people left in the world and one of them's a thief.

BART: Don't think of it as theft. Think of it as anthropology.

EDDIE: That's even better. Two people left in the world and one of them's an anthropologist.

BART: *As I was saying–*
Every time I look in here.
The evidence is clear–
These people weren't preoccupied
By fear of war.
No–
As you can see
From this menagerie,
There were far worse problems
Facing the society, indeed...

EDDIE: Thank you, Margaret Mead.

BART: Ah!

(*BART opens an envelope and reads:*)

THE LETTER

To whom it may concern...
you'll be interested to learn
That your payment has been due
Since early May of Nineteen Sixty-Eight
And, according to our current interest rate...
And owing to how your debt has accumulated
since that date,
We must foreclose on your account,
Until you've paid the full amount.
And our accountants have advised
That if this debt is not revised
That we can seek repair, indeed,
And have your wages garnisheed, by force...
But then, of course,
We wouldn't want to cause despair,
by ruining your credit line, or threatening your
lovely wife.
So, please–
Accept advice.
A small installment will suffice
Until you can afford to make
The payment in complete
For that pound and a half of meat.

(*BART continues the search through his bag of loot.*)

BART: This is definitely the purse of someone who was preoccupied by life's problems, Morose... (*He goes through the items in the purse.*) Phisohex – a manual on teenage sex – Dentyne: keeps the mouth clean – Antibacterial, fluoride rinse – breath mints – breath spray – and just in case: a pico pay – and a small tube of paste: mint taste – a compact mirror: slightly defaced – a small brochure: VD KILLS – Pills: Blue – I wonder if her mother knew – A picture: some guy.... Love John, till death – this must be the one who didn't like her breath – and a note: Well, Morose... shall we see what she wrote? Let's delve a little deeper into these goings-on – Aha! It's from John.

DEAR DEBBIE

I know that we planned to get married in the
Spring,
But, like, that depends on how things go.
I can't find a job, I've tried nearly everything.
I've applied, but been turned down twenty
times in a row.

I just can't hack this flack that is coming down
on me.
I even cut my hair–
But my dad says these days you can't plan
matrimony

When you haven't got no money to spare.

So, like, what's going on in the world today?
When my dad was a kid they gave jobs away.
But now with this big unemployment rate.
You wait. You wait.

We dreamed about having a nice little home,
With a little back yard of our own.
Not a studio suite on East Cordova Street,
With a hot-plate, two crates and a mattress of foam.

All the grocery prices are way out of reach.
And we'll never live close to the beach.
And we'd have to eat liver and cans of sardines–
And have no colour tv or designer blue jeans.

So, like, what's going on in the world today?
When I was a kid they gave things away.
But now with this stupid inflation rate–
You pay! You pay!

EDDIE & BART: *Ohhhhhh Na na na na na na na*
Ohhhhhh Na na na na na na na

(*BART reflects.*)

BART: Makes you sad to think about it, doesn't it, Eddie?

EDDIE: Not really.

BART: Have you become a cynic? Do we have a cynic in our midst? Ladies and Gentlemen... is this what the future holds in store for us? Could this man represent a moody trend in our society?

EDDIE: What future? What society?

BART: The society which is now forming.

EDDIE: And I thought we'd seen the last of it.

BART: As long as there are two people to gather together, there will be government.

EDDIE: Yes. With you in charge.

BART: I don't see it that way. It just depends on your perspective. If you want to be negative about it, you can call me an autocrat. But there's a positive side. I'm benevolent.

EDDIE: I thought you said this was a democracy.

BART: It is. In fact, I think it's time for an election. All those in favour of me in charge, raise your right hand. Are you abstaining, Morose?

EDDIE: I want to know who the other choices are.

BART: Well, unfortunately, we're short of choices, for Christ's sake.

EDDIE: What about me?

BART: Sorry. No blind people in office.

EDDIE: Who said?

BART: It's laid down in the constitution.

EDDIE: What constitution?

BART: The one I'm going to write when I'm elected.

EDDIE: Isn't that handy. Very clever.

BART: Yes. But I can't take all the credit. There are certain things you can learn from a previous government.

BART: So. That's that, then. I guess I'm it.

EDDIE: Well, I guess you won't be the first criminal ever elected to office.

BART: I couldn't agree with you more.

NAUGHTY MAN

Okay – So I'll admit
That I was quite habitually locked away.
But that was then and this is now
And what of it?
Do you think a criminal in charge
is half as bad as what you had before?

No way. *Not a bit.*
You have to understand the politics involved.
It's more than simply just a case of illegalities
Solved by putting every con-man in the joint.
The point is that you have to look at the realities.
Everybody would be inside, but of course they're not.
Justice is selective, and the spectre of authority
Neglects the large majority
Who don't get caught.

I still recall my first crime
Got into trouble for stealing a dime
Not a big job, but enough to get caught
My father was rather stern
Brought up for trial with no chance to adjourn.
Raising his hand he said:

Naughty child.
Go to your room naughty child.
No dessert.
Why are you such a bad child? Can't you see how it hurts me to beat you? And don't you talk back like that, you little brat – nyah, nyah, nyah, nyah, nyah, nyah, nyah!

When I think back on grade three
I see the roots of my delinquency
My principal had a record on me–
Admissible evidence
For a whole series of naughty events.
Raising his finger, he said:

Naughty boy!
Stay after school, naughty boy.
Fifty lines.
You will not act disrespectful, or spit, or say shit,
Nor will you ever pull down your pants and show Nancy your dick, ever, ever, oh ever again.

When I was still just a teen
I went to class and did bank jobs between.
Had to report to the juvenile court.
Probation man was aghast. He'd never seen a lad learn quite so fast.
Shaking his head, he said:

Naughty lad!
You're on good time, naughty lad.

Get a job.
What's the excuse for this uselessness? You've got at least seven years education. I can't see why you're on probation – and blah, blah, blah, blah, blah, blah, blah!

When I reached maturity, I, craving some kind of security,
Drew large amounts from large savings accounts.
Not mine, but why be obscure.
Anyway, my judge thought jail more secure.
Raising his brow, he said:

Naughty man!
Sentence is passed, naughty man.
Twenty years.
Though it appears that the court is unjust, you must understand my point of view in connection with you. It is for your protection we do what we do.

Now that we're in such a mess,
One tends to bow to authority less,
Particularly when one has a gun.
Anarchy now rules the day!
Finally, at long last, I have my say.
And raising my fist, I say:
Fuck you all!

EDDIE: Charming! A whole new era of politics is here. With Mr. Gross at the helm, things should be back to order in no time. (*BART is again being ill.*) Are you getting sick again? What a shame. And just after you'd been elected. Just after you'd reached the pinnacle of your political career. I hate to put it this way, but I think you're going to die. Soon. There are certain things even you can't control.

BART: I don't think that's a very entertaining notion, Morose. We're all aware of the existential dilemma.

EDDIE: I wasn't speaking existentially. I was speaking immediately. (*EDDIE sings, as BART deals with his deteriorating physical condition.*)
When it's time to go
You often know
You often show the pain.
You grasp for it,
You gasp a bit,
You slowly go insane.

I'm sorry, but the time has come
To face the music, chum...

BART: Morose! Don't you think we could use a little levity right about now? A little light entertainment?

EDDIE: Maybe you're right.
(*He sings a gleeful song.*)
Dadaldedum, dedada, I'm sorry, chum.
Dedeldede, da da, your time has come.

BART: Morose!

EDDIE: Is that light enough for you?

BART: A person would assume that this man does not enjoy my company. In fact, if we were to jump to any conclusions, we might even think that he'd rather be on his own. But I know for a fact that with a little coaxing, he'll change his tune. There's nothing like a friend, is there Eddie? Nothing like it in the whole world. Someone to look after you when you're sick. Never leave you. And you'd never leave, would you, Eddie?

EDDIE: No.

BART: No.

WE'RE ALL WE'VE GOT

EDDIE: *I'm a lucky guy.*
I'll tell you why.
Because I've got a friend.
Someone to be
A mon ami
Until our travels end.
And if I want a confidant–
Somebody by my side–
I know you will see me through.
In you I can confide.

How could I live without you?
There's something about you.
It could be your heart of gold.
Or maybe that gun you hold so close
Mr. Gross...

Oh, we're quite the pair.

BART: *You're so right there.*

EDDIE: *A couple of confrêres.*

BART: *He cares!*

EDDIE: *It's quite the kinship...*

BART: *Thick and thinship – in all our affairs.*

EDDIE: *The gun is just a symbol, not a thing he would abuse...*

BART: *Unless...*

EDDIE: *Provoked, I guess*
But what the hell–
It's something to amuse.

BART: *Well...*

EDDIE: *But...*

BART: *What?*

EDDIE: *We're in this together.*
And whether we like it or not

EDDIE & BART: *We're all we've got.*

BART: *The whole shot!*

EDDIE: *He may be just a touch dictatorial.*

BART: *But...*

EDDIE: *What? Oh – such a nice guy.*

BART: *Well, I try.*

EDDIE: *And perhaps we don t see eye to eye*

BART: *Or at all.*

EDDIE: *But...*

BART: *But what?*

EDDIE: *But we're having a ball.*

BART: *Is that all?*

EDDIE: *Is there something that I haven't said?*

BART: That you're glad I'm alive.

EDDIE: Yes I'm glad you're not dead.

EDDIE & BART: Oh, we're pleased to see
Camaraderie
Is once again the trend.
Old fashioned sociality–
It's good to have a friend.

Companionship will guide us through,
Will help us stay alive.

EDDIE: He's at the wheel...

BART: He's at my heel...

EDDIE & BART: Together we'll survive!

(*As the crescendo is reached, BART cocks the gun and fires at EDDIE. Blackout.*)

ACT TWO

(*BART is tending to EDDIE's gunshot wound as they sing:*)

BOMBS AWAY

BART: Can you imagine the astonishment
When the big one went?
All the laughing and the music stopped
In a deadly silence, when it dropped.
What a blasted accident.

EDDIE: If I could have seen your face,
I'd have said goodbye.
But the light's so bright you lose your sight.
In a holocaust, the words are lost.
And I only heard the cry.

BART: What an ironically amusing twist
For the evolutionist.
From a protoplasmic nuclei
We develop and diversify
Into radiation mist.

EDDIE: Did you see the tragedy?
Did you wonder why?
Why we had to self-annihilate?
Was it sad regret or was it hate?
Or did we simply die?

BART: How disconcerting for the human race
To erase mankind.
Who'd believe that so deserved a fate
Could be thus achieved by means so great
They would leave it all behind?

(*BART is studying the condition of EDDIE's wound.*)

BART: Well, this looks pretty serious, Morose. It looks to me like we won't be going anywhere for a few days. Well, don't get all uptight about it. Look at it this way – this place is as good as any. I suppose you're wondering right about now why I had to go and shoot your foot.

EDDIE: I was sort of wondering. Yes.

BART: Well, let me put it this way – there are certain things that are beyond the realm of our understanding. One of them is man's violent disposition. Why, I recall, not too long ago, in the psychiatric unit of one of our penal institutions, where I had an opportunity to spend several months – meeting a very well-educated member of the upper class. Lived in a huge mansion on Marine Drive. And why would they go and lock him away, you ask. Because it seems that he went and decapitated his next-door neighbour with a pair of electric hedging sheers. Later, in consultation with one of the resident psychiatrists, he revealed that all of this had transpired over who the hedge belonged to that separated their properties. The neighbour wanted the hedge cut down, and he wanted it left as it was. Needless to say, the psychiatrist was astounded.
"You're an intelligent man," he said, "Couldn't you come to some kind of agreement? A compromise? Perhaps cut down half of the hedge, and leave the other half standing?"
"We could have," said the man, "But it wasn't a question of property. It was a question of honour. I had to be on my guard, you see... just in case he got any funny ideas about wandering over the property line, and having an affair with my wife."
"Why would you assume that?" asked the psychiatrist.

"Why not," answered the man, "I was having an affair with his."
So you see, my good man, violence often precludes any measure of conciliation... even in the best of circles.

EDDIE: Well, I thought we were friends. I thought we'd come to an agreement about that. You wanted a partner for your cabaret.

BART: We are friends, Eddie.

EDDIE: You shot me in the foot!

BART: Yes. But if we were enemies, I would have shot you in the head. But I didn't.

EDDIE: Yes. Thanks.

BART: Mind you, there comes a time in any friendship when things start to fall apart. When you start seeing the other side of a person. Where on the one hand you seem like a perfectly nice guy, on the other hand you just never know. You might turn out to be as bad as me. And we can't have that, can we?

EDDIE: No.

BART: No. I'd have to kill you.

EDDIE: You've been saying that for three weeks.

BART: Yes, but... there's nothing else left to kill.

EDDIE: What would happen to your cabaret? Your show?

BART: Maybe that's how it ends, Morose. I make a speech to the audience, emphasizing the innate wickedness of mankind. Referring to history to back me up. And then to make my point absolutely crystal clear, I kill you. Yes. I can see it now. The lights fade. The moment is tense. I point the gun...

EDDIE: Wait. Don't you think it's a bit early? Wouldn't you like to describe some of the more entertaining circumstances surrounding the nuclear war?

BART: Haven't we done that?

EDDIE: No. We haven't told them about our travels. Or how we met in the first place. Remember?

(*EDDIE starts to play Travelogue. BART doesn't remember.*)

BART: Oh, yes! I remember. I remember the day I met Eddie Morose along the road. "Have you reached some sort of philosophical dilemma?" I asked him.

EDDIE: Not really.

BART: Would you care to elaborate on that answer, sir?

EDDIE: Not really.

BART: Are you at a point of personal crisis then?

EDDIE: No. Not really.

BART: Then why are you standing in the middle of the highway in your pajamas?

EDDIE: No particular reason.

BART: Not a friendly chap, I thought. Perhaps there's more to this than meets the eye, I thought. Tell me, are you going East or West?

EDDIE: That depends.

BART: Ah. A politician! Depends on what?

EDDIE: On which way you re going.

BART: Well I was going North.

EDDIE: Then I'm going South.

BART: But no sooner had he said this, than he began heading West. It was at this point that I paused for a moment to consider the two possible reasons for this apparent contradiction. The first being that he was a liar. The second, that when it came to matters of direction, he didn't know where he was going. I decided that he was a liar. "Excuse me, sir," I said, "but

I don't like your attitude."

(*BART points the gun at EDDIE's head.*)

EDDIE: Is that a gun pointed at my head?

BART: Was he being unnecessarily superfluous, I wondered.

EDDIE: I don't have any money, if that's what you want.

BART: Obviously, my good man, you are not aware of the current monetary situation, vis-a-vis the recent collapse of our financial system. Even if you had a million dollars in your back pocket, it wouldn't be any good to me. Even if it was gold bullion, my friend. Everything of former value is now worthless. In fact, I knew a fellow, not unlike myself, who walked away with the entire Emily Carr collection from the Vancouver Art Gallery, and ended up having to trade it off for half a can of questionable-looking pork and beans. A sad comment on the state of the arts, I think. Times have changed. And with nothing of value to steal, criminals are being forced into other occupations. I've gone in to the entertainment business. I plan to open a cabaret. As soon as I find one. Entertain the masses, that sort of thing. It's especially true in these times of global annihilation, that people need a little fun in their lives, don't you think?

EDDIE: There's nobody left to entertain.

BART: It just so happens, my friend, that I've heard otherwise. I have it on good authority that some places were spared the inconvenience of nuclear war. And that's where I'm headed.

EDDIE: On whose authority did you hear this?

BART: A radical, I thought. On my authority, you half-dressed half-wit. And I'm sure you'll agree that I'm the one in authority here.

(*Using the gun again.*)

EDDIE: I see your point.

BART: It was then and there that Eddie Morose and myself came to our understanding. And so together, we headed off into the wilderness. To find our cabaret.

EDDIE: With a few diversions along the way.

THE TRAVELLING SONG

Oh we've travelled through it all.
Had a laugh. Had a ball.
Saw the worst of the absurd.
If not saw, at least we heard.
Heard of things to appall.
Make your epidermis crawl.

Oh, bombs away. Oh, bombs away,
Travelling everyday.
We saw the nuclear debris.
Heard the tales of tragedy.

BART: Where are we going?

EDDIE: Spain!

BART: *Bombs away!*
they bombed Seville the other day
but that's okay.
I hate the opera anyway.
And what's the fuss?
It didn't drop on us.
Can you figure it? Figure it? Figure it?
In Seville the civilians are in a fit.
Throughout Spain radiation is in the air.
And it's plain all the Spanish will lose their
  hair.
If it rains.
And rain it will,
So who the hell needs Barbers in Seville?

Bombs away,
Oh, bombs away–
Things are in a fix;
Though they signed a non-aggression pact.
Can you simply pull a magic act
From a bag of tricks?

Picasso,
He could have painted quite the scenes.
From what I hear, Iberia
Was blown to smithereens.
Guernica. What was Guernica? A few Guernicans?

*Compared to much more modern means
Of obliterating all the Spanish genes.*

(*BART has a rose.*)

BART: Fleures! Fleures para los muertos!

(*He tosses it to the ground. There is an explosion.*)

EDDIE: I'd like to sing a short lament.
*I saw Madrid, when I was just a kid,
But I didn't see Barcelona.
But now Spain's been blitzed
And my eyesight is fritzed anyway – Olé.*

(*BART tries to stop EDDIE but he continues.*)

BART: Bravo!

EDDIE: *I would have loved to see a bullfight
But there's no bulls and I've no eyesight.*

BART: Bravo!

EDDIE: *I once knew a Señorita–
Her name was Lolita
She was a flamenco dancer
But now she's a cancer casualty. Si, si.*

BART: Gratia. (*stops EDDIE from continuing*) Yes, folks. Spain is gone, but not forgotten. Why, who could forget Pisarro? Certainly not the Incas. Cortez? Certainly not the Aztecs. Franco? Certainly not the Spaniards – you can bet. If there were any Spaniards to forget.

EDDIE: And now what about France?

BART: Paree?

EDDIE: Oui, oui!

BART: *With a soupçon of atomic chemistry
You can make sauce Bordelaise out of Paris.*

*I saw Paris in the springtime,
But it vanished in the Fall.*

(*EDDIE plays the Marseilles'.*)

*How gastronomic to cook the French.
It's a modern neutron recipe
Without the mess and without the stench.*

*Bombs away, oh, bombs away!
Au revoir, Paree.
though they promised not to use the bomb
Can you stop a war from going on
With a limited arms recipe?*

This could use a little salt.
This could use a little Salt II.

*No matter what you do to change the taste,
It still ends up a sticky paste.*

EDDIE: Maintenant, mes amis
La lament du Paris...

*I saw the Seine
When I was seventeen,
But I didn't see the Champs d'Elysées.
Now I'm blind anyway
And the Champs d'Elysées is finis–
C'est la vie.*

BART: Magnifique!

EDDIE: *I would have loved to see the Metro
now I can only see it retrospectively–
Oui, oui–*

*I once knew a girl from Paris–
A wealthy young heiress
With long hair of gold.
But now she is old and heirless–
Oui, oui, yes, yes–*

(*EDDIE is again interrupted.*)

BART: We won't forget France, Ladies and Gentlemen. Even if we wanted to, we couldn't. Why, who could forget Marie Antoinette? Not to mention Cardinal Richelieu. Or Maurice Chevalier. And when we look back fondly on the works of Zola, Camus, and Sartre, we'll remember with a hushed reverence – what it meant to be truly – depressed.

EDDIE: And now we must do England.

BART: England?

EDDIE: Oh yes they'd love it.

BART: Really?

Good bye, good bye–
remember not to cry
When you see old Britannia flying by.
They were hit–
never realized
Oh, oh, oh, the English were surprised.
There goes Picadilly
There goes London Zoo
Say good bye to Lady Di and Charlie
And Charlie's little Willie, too.
There goes Leicester
And Manchester
And a little bit of Wales.
Is that Hampshire?
That's for damn sure.
Goodness, how Britannia sails!
What's that blimp, sir?
That's Westminster
And behind it Regent's Park.
It's a blitz to end them all.
Look sir, there goes old St. Paul
But this time it's on the mark.

Bombs away, oh, bombs away–
Goodbye Dear Old Sod
You've been blitzed before Londonium
But it wasn't with Plutonium
In a missile from abroad.

So much for England
Bloody pity, too
That the sun has finally
Set on you.

EDDIE: And now we present The English Lament.
I saw Big Ben
When I was only ten
But I didn't see
East Croydon.

Now England's gone to dust
And my eyesight can't be trusted
Anyway – I say.

I would have loved to see the seaside
But I can't see, and there is no tide.
I once knew a Bobbie.
His name was young Robbie.
He was one of London's finest.
But now he is minus his head
And dead, dead, dead, he's dead...

(*BART is deteriorating rapidly.*)

BART: I think it's time for the finale, Morose.

EDDIE: No! What about Russia?

BART: You know, my friend, a person would assume that you had an aversion to self-sacrifice. Don't think of it as death. Think of it as art.

EDDIE: But we can't talk about the nuclear war without at least mentioning Russia. And the US, or Pakistan, or Israel, or South Africa, or Argentina.

BART: But we'll be here all night!

(*EDDIE sings:*)

Heard of things to appall.
Make your epidermis crawl.
Oh, bombs away, oh bombs away,
Travelling everyday.
We saw the nuclear debris.
We heard the tales of tragedy.

(*EDDIE plays the Volga Boat Song. BART sings:*)

In Leningrad the scene is just as mad.
Each Bolshevik is either dead or sick.

(*Nutcracker.*)

Moscow had some lovely parts.
The Bolshoi and the Moscow Arts,
The Kremlin and the People's GUM,
And Lenin's tomb.

Tchaikowsky could have written
About how Moscow was smitten.
What was 1812 compared to modern doom?

Boom. Boom.

(*Kalinka.*)
Boom. Boom. (Etc....)

BART: *Too bad! Comrade!*
Tak chto! Ho, ho!

EDDIE: Tepyer mei presentski
Po Ruski Lamentski

*I saw Kiev
When I was just eleven
But I didn't see
Kirgizskaya.*

BART: Stop! I'm getting travel sickness. (*He is starting to lose even more of his light grip on reality.*) It's time for the finale. It's getting late. I see the dawn creeping up over the hills.

EDDIE: It's not dawn.

BART: How the hell would you know?

EDDIE: Because, I can hear coyotes. Owls. Crickets.

BART: Crickets?

EDDIE: Sssh. Listen.

BART: (*whispering*) What about the finale?

EDDIE: No, why don't you put down your gun and go to sleep? (*As Eddie plays a chord, Bart begins to fall asleep. EDDIE sings:*)

DESERT SONG

*Close your eyes.
Daylight is still just a dream.
Don't open your eyes–
Night skies are not what they seem.*

*Though the fires are burning,
They're still miles from here.
So don't worry, this desert's the best place.
Oh, the air here is cool.
Close your eyes, rest your head–
And the coyotes will sing of the dead.
Singing: Oooooo*

*Though we're tired and lost
And forgotten it seems,
This is no time to think about crying.
Oh, the morning will find us
So go to your dreams
And the night owl will sing of the dying.
Singing: Oooooo.*

*Though the angel of Death
Has no mercy tonight,
The Angel of Sleep is forgiving.*

*So don't worry, don't grieve.
Close your eyes, it's alright–
Now the night wind will weep for the living.
Singing: Oooooooo.*

*Don't open your eyes–
Night skies are not what they seem.*

(*EDDIE quietly leaves the piano, in search of the gun.*)

EDDIE: Gross? Gross?

(*Finding the gun, Eddie exits. Bart wakes to find Eddie gone. He looks about.*)

BART: Morose? Morose ? Morose! Where are you? Morose? Alright. I won't shoot you. Look. I was just kidding anyway. Honest. I couldn't kill a guy like you. There wouldn't be any fun in it. Morose! I won't ever use the gun again. I'll get rid of it if you want... (*He sees the gun is missing.*) Look, Morose. I think it's time we discussed this whole thing anyway. Morose! Eddie? (*He realizes that Eddie has left him.*) You can't do this to your friend. The one who's looked after you all these weeks, inspired you with various insights, introduced you to a bit of culture. Morose! I won't have this. I'll die first. No, I won't. I won't die, Morose! I don't need you, Morose. The show will go on.

(*BART approaches the audience, ingratiatingly. He is the performer once again, even though he's fading quickly.*)

There was a housewife from Vancouver
Who cleaned everything with a Hoover.
But in the nuclear blitz
She was sprayed into bits
And no vacuum could ever remove her.

In Richmond a lovely school teacher
Of remarkably fine facial feature.
Needed no makeup on
But after the bomb
She turned into a hideous creature.

A fellow named Tom from North Van
Wanted a nice even tan.
So the nuclear bomb
Radiated young Tom
And now he's a very dark man.

We haven't finished the travelogue...
Wait, Morose – We haven't done the United States, yet... or Canada.
Canada, Morose. What kind of Canadian are you?

O Canada,
Our home and native land.
You always thought
They'd ignore a place so bland.

This land is wasteland,
And that's for certain,
Despite the findings
Of Pierre Berton

(*The tapping of a cane can be heard. EDDIE is returning. BART plays dead.*)

EDDIE: Gross? Gross, where are you? Look, I've changed my mind. I'm not going to leave you to die on your own. You may not be the best person in the world to get stuck with, but you're still more or less a human being. (*He stumbles into BART and crouches down to him.*) Gross? (*Thinking Gross is dead, EDDIE sits, dejected.*) Oh, no.

(*BART stirs.*)

Gross! You're alive!

BART: Morose?

EDDIE I thought you were dead. I thought I might be too late.

BART: No. You're just in time.

EDDIE: Listen.

BART: Come a little closer. I can't quite hear you.

EDDIE: Listen, Gross, I'm not going to leave you. I thought about it, and I decided what's wrong with the world. If people would have got together in the end, this whole thing might never have happened.

BART: Just a little closer.

EDDIE: You can't just ignore people. Leave them to die. Even if they deserve to.

(*BART grabs the gun out of EDDIE's hand. He pulls the trigger, but nothing happens.*)

EDDIE: What are you doing?

BART: What do you think I'm doing, you jerk. I'm trying to blow your brains out!

(*The gun doesn't fire.*)

EDDIE: Well, there's no point trying to do that.

BART: Alright. Where are the bullets?

EDDIE: I buried them.

BART: You what?

EDDIE: They're gone, Gross. I thought it would be better to get rid of them.

BART: Is this some kind of symbolic gesture?

EDDIE: No. I just didn't like having them around. I didn't like the way they divided us as friends.

BART: You didn't. Oh, well, in that case I understand completely. (*shouting*) You *idiot*! Wait till I get my hands on you!

EDDIE: I figured our relationship would be more equal this way. More democratic.

BART: More democratic? That's not how democracy works, you myopic miscreant. Don't you understand the basic principles of representative government? I'm representing your interests. The gun was for your own protection. Now how am I supposed to defend you?

EDDIE: Let's put it this way, Gross. If I hadn't buried those bullets, you would have killed me by now.

BART: That's beside the point. Can't you carry on a political discussion without getting personal about it? You just go and dig up those bullets, Morose. Before we're ambushed.

EDDIE: No, don't you see? If nobody had any bullets, we wouldn't have to worry about it. We could all just be friends.

BART: Oh, what a great idea! Tell that to your enemies.

EDDIE: I haven't got any enemies. Oh, if only I'd realized it sooner. I could have had a lot more fun. Maybe gone into social work. But it's never too late. I've still got you.

BART: Great! That's great! We're going to have a ball! The murdering hordes can attack us. But we'll just laugh in the face of adversity. Offer them a beer.

EDDIE: That's more like it, Gross. Now you're talking like a real human being.

THE ARGUMENT

BART: *Asshole!*
The guy's an asshole!
Have you considered, my dear friend,
How this scenario will end?
I guess you didn't
I guess you think it's okay
To wait for someone less "humanitarian"
To come and blow us both away.
Like two sitting ducks.
Your philosophy sucks
What can I say?

EDDIE: *That's okay.*
I don't mind.
I have faith in humankind.

BART: *That just comes from being blind,*
You shithead,
You stupid birdbrain.
So tell me what we stand to gain
From faith in humankind when we are dead?

EDDIE: *We're not dead, we're alive.*
And together we'll survive.

BART: What's all this optimistic jive? Did you read it in a book somewhere? No, listen to me, if you need a philosophy. I'm the one with the ideas around here. If I had a few bullets in this thing, I'd tell you about it.

(*BART sits, brooding.*)

EDDIE: If everybody would have just got together in the end it would have been different. They might have still been here. Who knows? You and me could have met under different circumstances. Maybe even opened a cabaret together. We could have been surrounded by real people.

LAST CALL

(*EDDIE sings sweetly.*)
I used to drink all alone.
I sat in the bar on my own.
I'd sit by the wall
Until the last call
And then, quietly, I'd go home.

But if this were a cabaret
I wouldn't just drift away.
I'd stand and I'd drink
A last round, I think,
To friendship and amitié.

(*Chorus.*)

Last Call–
Last chance of all,
Forget all your sadness and sorrow.
Let's drink a last beer
As friends while we're here
And maybe we'll be here tomorrow.

I was a reclusive breed.
I brought a bestseller to read.
I hid in my book
Away from the looks
I didn't want life to impede.

But if I could change the plot,
Unliterary, or not,
I'd drink one last time
To all humankind
And thank God for friends
I've got.

(*Chorus.*)

BART: (*He rises, a new man.*) Morose, I think I'm quite moved. I feel a change going through me. Now, it may be that I have to puke again, but on the other hand, it could be that I'm feeling the warm glow of philanthropy...

(*He sings.*)

I used to be quite the wit.
I laughed at the crimes I'd commit.
I couldn't care less for
Human distress–
I just couldn't give a shit.

But if I could recompense,
I'd discard my malevolence.
I'd put down my gun
And toast everyone
With kindest of sentiments.

Last Call–
Last chance of all,
Forget all your sadness and sorrow.
Let's drink a last beer
As friends while we're here
And maybe we'll be here tomorrow.

(*EDDIE and BART sing together: Last Call chorus. The lights fade and BART assumes a darker tone.*)

BART: On the other hand, I think we've managed to simplify things just a bit. I'm not sure I'm entirely satisfied with the way things have worked out. From a purely logical perspective.

EDDIE: What's wrong with ending up as friends?

BART: Well, I think it's just a bit naive. A bit contrived. I mean, I don't know if anyone's prepared to accept optimism as a reasonable possibility. Especially after we went and blew up the whole fucking planet. Let's get serious here. What happened to good old-fashioned pessimism?

EDDIE: But, I thought you went through some sort of change.

BART: Like from an insect into a butterfly?

EDDIE: Yes.

BART: The point is, Morose, that a butterfly is still an insect. Furthermore, how is it that of all the places you could have accidentally stepped, including off the edge of a cliff, that you just happened to walk into my gun?

EDDIE: Just lucky, I guess.

BART: Well, I don't think luck should play such a major part in the final outcome. Do you? So let's try the whole thing again, shall we? From where you got the gun. Just for the sake of argument.

EDDIE: Alright.

(*EDDIE plays the end of Desert Song, and they re-enact the scene, with BART sleeping and EDDIE rising from the piano to go for the gun.*)

EDDIE: Gross? Gross?

(*As EDDIE approaches, BART lifts his head to watch. Just as EDDIE reaches the gun and is about to pick it up, BART takes it and points it at EDDIE's head.*)

BART: Looking for this? What are you trying to do, Morose? Huh? Just get back. Go on. Get back. That's it. That's it. Trying to kill me, Morose?

(*EDDIE returns to the piano.*)

EDDIE: No.

BART: Don't lie to me. I'm aware of your potential violence. If you're anything like me, you've got some very sick ideas churning around in that little head of yours.

EDDIE: I'm not a violent person. It's not in my nature.

BART: It's in everyone's nature, Morose. Now I'm not necessarily saying that you're capable of violence in the traditional sense. In fact, I'm willing to bet that the sight of blood made you sick. But you take a gun... this gun, for example. This compact little instrument of death. Why, the technology is amazing. Death is right here at your fingertips. You don't have to go out and find a club to bash my brains in with. You don't have to chisel an axe, or carve a spear, or forge a piece of iron into a sword, or boil any oil, or even mess around with gunpowder. All you have to do is pull the trigger. Just move your finger a fraction of an inch. Anybody can do that. Even you.

(*He sings:*)

THE SHOT

BART: You think you're so different from me.

EDDIE: But I am.

BART: But your vision of humanity is a sham,
And you're blind to the violent half of your mind,
If you think you're entirely void of all vice.
It's a nice sentiment, but deceptively nice, you'll find.

EDDIE: *I am basically quite a nice guy.*
Wouldn't hurt anybody or try.
How can you think that I
Would want you to die?
When it comes down to murder, I'm awfully shy.

BART: Just listen, and I'll tell you why...
You never know
What lurks behind the mask
Of common decency.
"Could it be wickedness?" you ask.
And I say "Yes" It's wickedness.
Remember before the Nuclear War?
while they all sat,
Discussed humanity,
Over another beer,
They never knew their own insanity.
They thought they were a peaceful lot.
Did you think you were somewhat unique?

EDDIE: *In a sense.*

BART: From the pattern of historical violence,
Then you're wrong.
You've lived violently all along.
How do you think we got where we did in the end?
No, my friend, not with what you pretend in a song–

You looked about.
You saw the quiet calm.
But underneath it all:
A time bomb.
And did you know when it would blow? No!

And so you went
About your own routine.
Just kept the peace,
And kept your nose clean, my friend.
But never sure
Who would be murdered in the end
Or who would be the murderer–
But never sure.

EDDIE: *And the clock ticks away.*
You wait for the bullet.

BART: *A hand on the trigger*
And you could just pull it.

EDDIE: *And you never know quite*
When the end is in sight.

BART: *It may never be time*
But it may be tonight.

EDDIE: *And the clock ticks away*
Every minute's an hour.
Is it now?

BART: *No not quite.*

EDDIE: *So you wait, never sure.*
Drink a beer very fast.
It could be just one more
Or it could be your last.
And the clock ticks away
Every minute's a year.
Resurrecting the past
Just to bury your fear
And your doubt.
Is it now?

BART: *Just about.*

EDDIE: *And they flicker the lights*
And they call the last call
And you see what's ahead
But your back's to the wall.
And you're starting to sweat
Just a bit. Is it now?

BART: *No. Not yet.*

EDDIE: *So you sit and you wait.*
Drink a beer. Contemplate.
Wonder who is to blame.

EDDIE & BART: *But you know you're the same as your worst enemies.*

BART: *Cause if you had a gun, I'd be down on my knees.*

EDDIE: *And there's safety, you think, While you sit in the bar. But the clock can strike Wherever you are,*

BART: *Wherever you are.*

EDDIE: *You're in the same spot Because, ready or not,*

BART: *Ready or not,*

EDDIE: *Here comes the... Comes the...*

BART: *Here comes the... shot.*

(BART *aims the gun. There is a silent explosion. Blackout. When the lights come up again, the two actors sing the epilogue.*)

*That's the way the story ends.
What more can be said?
Either they were life-long friends
Or they died instead as enemies.
Pick whichever one you please
Of these possibilities.
Though it's just a cabaret,
That's what life is anyway.
But it wasn't just their show–
Take any scenario,
Any one they're all the same.
It takes two to play the game.
One who's armed but cannot see
In authority.
One who's blind to tyranny,
Though he sees things democratically.
And there is another thing
About which we'd like to sing.
Blindness is a state of mind
Largely that of humankind
No one ever had a gun
Just for looks or just for fun.
No one ever made a bomb
Just to have around.
Not with bombs enough to cover
Every inch of ground
Bombs don't grow, no bombs are made
Made by people, I'm afraid–
People just like you and I,
People who don't really want to die–
And if that's too obscure,
There's always this one hitch:
Bombs don't drop, and that's for sure,
Without us to pull the switch.*

(*The actors sing a reprise of* Last Call Chorus.)

(*The end.*)

DIVING

BY

MARGARET HOLLINGSWORTH

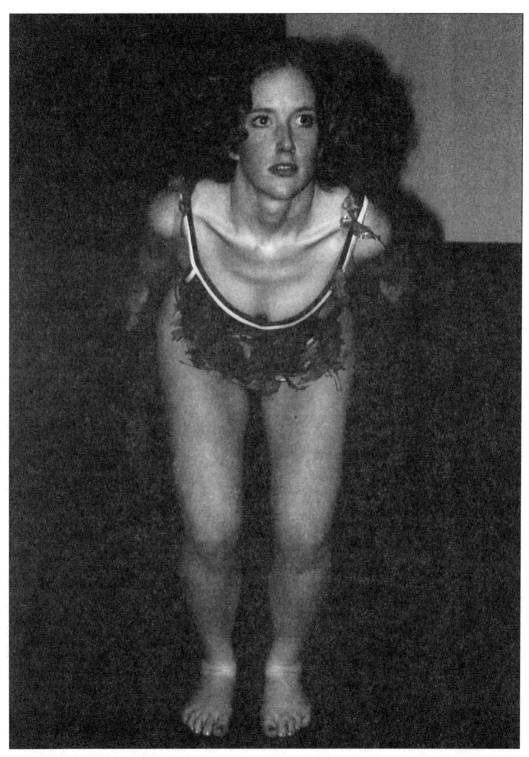

Angela Gordon as Viveca

Photographer: Theresia Reid

ALIEN – LIKE AN EAGLE: MARGARET HOLLINGSWORTH'S *DIVING*

Margaret Hollingsworth is best known for her full-length plays *Ever Loving* and *War Babies*, both of which premiered at the Belfry Theatre in Victoria. In the latter work, Esme, a playwright, says, "You know what theatre's best for? Showing pain." For Hollingsworth that pain has been especially women's, and it has to do with their physical displacement. For her women are frequently, like Hollingsworth herself, immigrants to Canada, and must negotiate existence in an alien world often determined by male structures of power; a world metaphorically (and sometimes literally) at war.

The three war brides in *Ever Loving* meet in the present at a candlelit dinner at that most romantic of places, Niagara Falls, but, as they travel back in time, crossing Canada to their waiting husbands and nominal homes, reality and disillusion set in. As a survival mechanism, her women create an energetic, inner world of fantasy, sometimes work and family related, as in her early plays *Bushed* and *Operators*, sometimes eroticized as in *Alli Alli Oh*, *Islands*, and *In Confidence*. In all of these the pain of displacement, enacted in stories of restless travel, of constantly looking over one's shoulder, gives her work a strong diasporaic feel. For Hollingsworth, British Columbia is both enervating and dangerous: a simultaneous lure, rich in its cultural mix and free from the class system of her native England; and threat, a place of emptiness and erasure.

In a colonized society, such as British Columbia's, the settlers' desire for a new, local identity is tempered with a crushing vulnerability: Hollingsworth's women characters have an obsessive, defining fear of going native. Making a home in a colonial place involves absorption into local life and customs, which some find threatening, degenerate: Esme sees her husband, with whom she is pregnant, as an "alien [being]... he feels like the enemy." Making a home then becomes highly problematical. Hollingsworth has lived in the province on and off during the 1970s and 80s, and for the past ten years. Asked whether she herself has found a home here, she recently told an interviewer: "No. Still looking. It may not be possible to find home, except perhaps where I started from. That's what I'm considering now. It's not something I look at lightly. Actually, it terrifies me" (Tatton).

Margaret Hollingsworth was born in London, England. An only child, she wrote plays from an early age, plays she put on in her back yard; at age 18 she won a national playwriting competition. She came to Canada in 1968, moving to Thunder Bay, Ontario, where she completed a degree in psychology, then worked as a librarian in the city's public library system. Four years later, she moved to Vancouver, where she completed a Master's degree at the University of British Columbia in theatre and creative writing. At present she teaches dramatic writing at the University of Victoria. Recent successful work has included *Blowing Up Toads* (later renamed *Commonwealth Games*), staged by Alberta Theatre Projects in 1996, a year-long run of *In Confidence* in Berlin in 2000, and upcoming stagings of two new plays, *O Positive* and *Deep Song*, in London.

In 1974 she became involved with the fledgling New Play Centre, which workshopped and staged several of her early plays. *Diving* was staged there in 1983, under the direction of Larry Lillo.

Diving demonstrates Hollingsworth's remarkable diversity and skill as a playwright. She has written one-acts, full-lengths, and monologues, in such a variety of dramatic form that her work is difficult to categorize. Her characters are housewives, labourers, writers; all are sharply drawn and unromanticized. They are familiar people who live in unexpected places: a remote logging camp, British Columbia's Gulf Islands, a wealthy Victoria suburb. Her stories are about arriving, settling, and leaving: flight amounts to a major theme in her work. *Diving*, with its image of a lonely woman poised precipitously on a diving platform, seems the perfect metaphor for Hollingsworth's opus.

Diving could almost be termed a work of performance art: using the central image/presence of a woman autobiographer performing herself in an empty space, a blank canvas, it bares the female psyche in an act of self-creation. Viveca, thin, emaciated, wearing clogs and wrapped in a towel, looks and acts like a waif – or a refugee. She nervously waits, removes the towel revealing a ridiculous bathing suit decorated with (real) maple leaves, then takes tentative steps toward a diving board as an anonymous male voice prompts her with, "Dive Viveca!" This is the unsettling image of a woman in an alien place: she is taking a lesson or a test, but her hesitations seem to doom her to failure – although, interestingly, we never actually see any trace of a diving board, nor do we see the origin of the voice. Their absence is telling.

If Viveca's outer world is alien, dominated by structures of control symbolized by the male voice, the stairs, the diving platform, and the pool, her inner world is not, for here she has a measure of power drawn from an eternal, mythic spirit connected to British Columbia – in the images of the eagle and the salmon. Clearly, she is unconventional, perhaps "challenged" in the conventional sense, as shown in her literal and symbolic association with the dog. But it is very much her world: here, in an associative inner monologue, Viveca freely moves out of an oppressive home and, like the eagle of her fantasy, ascends to her fifteenth floor apartment where she stands, triumphantly, dangerously, on the balcony rail. In this world she shows no fear and little wasted emotion; diving is an act of natural fulfillment, like the salmon completing the life cycle. This is the world of Viveca as sustained, enduring woman.

When the outer world returns at the end of the play, Viveca is renewed, clearly more in control. The "command" of the male voice is now gone, thus raising questions not so much about the truth of the forgoing "lesson," but about the varying, painful states of Viveca's self-construction in an alien world.

J.H.

Selected Bibliography:

- Brissenden, Connie ed. *West Coast Plays*. Vancouver: New Play Centre/Fineglow, 1975. Contains Hollingsworth's play *Operators*.
- Hodkinson, Yvonne. *Female Parts: The Art and Politics of Women Playwrights*. Montreal: Black Rose Books, 1991. Contains a discussion of the dramatic work of Hollingsworth, especially *Ever Loving* and *Islands*.
- Hollingsworth, Margaret. "Collaborators." *Canadian Theatre Review* 69 (Winter 1991): 15-19. The playwright discusses issues in directing women's scripts.
- Hollingsworth, Margaret. "Drama Bums." *Theatre Memoirs*. Toronto: Playwrights Union of Canada, 1998. The playwright reflects on her experience of playwriting in British Columbia.
- Peake, Linda M. Review of *Willful Acts*, in *Theatre History in Canada*, 8,1 (Spring 1987): 126-9.
- Rudakoff, Judith. "Margaret Hollingsworth Interview." *Fair Play: 12 Women Speak*, Judith Rudakoff and Rita Much, eds. Toronto: Simon & Pierre, 1990.
- Tatton, Carren. "Margaret Hollingsworth [interview]". *Questionable Activities*, Vol. III, Judith Rudakoff, ed. Toronto: Playwrights Union of Canada, 1998.
- Zimmerman, Cynthia. "Margaret Hollingsworth [interview]." *The Work: Conversations With English-Canadian Playwrights*, Robert Wallace and Cynthia Zimmerman. Toronto: Coach House Press, 1982.
- Zimmerman, Cynthia. "Margaret Hollingsworth: Feeling Out of Context." *Playwriting Women: Female Voices in English Canada*. Toronto: Simon & Pierre, 1994.

Diving
by Margaret Hollingsworth

Diving was first produced by the New Play Centre, Vancouver, in March 1983 with the following cast:

Viveca   Wendy Gorling

Directed by Larry Lillo

ACT ONE

The stage is completely bare.

VIVECA enters. She is thin, almost scrawny. She wears a pair of clogs. She carries a bag. She looks around, scared. Kicks off her clogs. Stops, thinks – has she forgotten something? She remembers. She takes a small box from between her breasts, careful not to uncover herself. She opens the box and takes earplugs out. Inserts plugs in ears. She puts the box down carefully next to the clogs which she lines up with precision. She shivers.

A male voice is heard offstage.

MALE VOICE: Dive Viveca.

VIVECA looks up to where the male voice comes from. She takes the earplugs out gingerly. Listens. The voice is silent. She puts one earplug back. She shades her eyes and looks out over the audience. She seems to be looking over a vast, deep body of water. She smiles nervously. She takes off her towel. She is wearing an absurd swimsuit decorated with maple leaves. She folds the towel very carefully, trying to make the edges perfect. She places it next to the shoes, the box and the bag. She remembers her nose clamp which she has left in a locker offstage and puts her foot into one of her clogs, meaning to go and get it.

MALE VOICE: Viveca!

She hastily withdraws her foot. She walks over to the stairway which leads up to the diving platform. (The structure is imaginary.) She puts her hands on the rails and takes one step up. She smiles upward, waiting for approval from the voice which does not come. She looks fearfully over the pool. She takes a tentative step, pulling herself up with her arms. She practises the diving position, very nervous.

VIVECA: I've been watching eagles. They don't close their eyes when they dive. They transfer the salmon from their beak to their claws. (*A long silence, as though she has forgotten herself.*) My mother says that swimming makes you bulge in all the wrong places. (*feels her forearms, covers her breasts*) She wants me to be a dog trainer. She says there's a future in breeding. She has three English sheepdogs. (*A pause. She goes up one step.*) I prefer eagles. She used to take the dogs down to the beach and throw sticks in the water. Retrieve! They never got their feet wet. I'd jump in and paddle out and bring the sticks back. In my hand – not in my mouth, in my hand. (*shows how, spluttering, half drowning*) No one told me it was easier in bare feet. Some things you learn by experience. An eagle never has to learn. But an eagle doesn't wear shoes in the first place. (*laughs*) Dogs she'd say, dogs are sensible. (*She looks up to see if anyone will notice if she dashes down the steps. Takes a tentative step down.*)

MALE VOICE: Dive Viveca!

VIVECA goes back to where she was on the steps. Goes a few steps higher.

VIVECA: I moved out of her house and I rented an upstairs apartment. No animals allowed it said. It was written up there on the entrance. By the mail slots. "Sorry no pets." That meant no snakes, no lizards, no small furry creatures. Not even a cricket in a cage. (*Pause.*) It was a lovely apartment. Just one room, but on the 15th floor – and a balcony. And there was a supermarket down below, and a car park and all these small cars like cockroaches coming and going, but what I could see most was the sky. (*She looks out into the distance over the heads of the audience.*) I used to stand on the balcony. (*She raises her arms.*) Once they called the fire truck and they shouted at me through a megaphone, and they brought my mother and she let herself in with the spare key. Apparently there's a rule about standing on your balcony– (*She goes up two* *more steps, very proud. Looks around.*) My mother gave me a dog for my birthday. It was a very small dog, she said no one would notice it. It used to whine, and when the caretaker asked about the noise I told him it was me. He told me I should see someone. He used to come to my door and listen and I'd watch him listening through the peephole – the pink top of his head, or a pink chin or his ring finger with no ring. When I went down the hallway I used to whine outside his door. (*She moves up a couple of steps.*) Then I moved to the "Y". I left the dog behind. It didn't have a name. I called it dog. Dog come here, Dog fetch, Dog jump. Over the balcony, down to the parking lot. (*She laughs.*) Dive dog!

MALE VOICE: Dive Viveca! (*She looks up fearfully.*)

VIVECA: But he didn't. Dogs don't.

MALE VOICE: Dive! (*She runs up three more steps.*)

VIVECA: They have a pool at the "Y". No pets allowed. Dog followed me. He had to stay outside. He sat by the steps till I came out, and then he walked as far as the dry cleaning shop and sat outside till I finished work. That's how stupid dogs are. Fetch dog. Sit dog. Laugh dog. Obey! Eagles don't.

MALE VOICE: Dive! (*She walks up another step petulantly.*)

VIVECA: No one ever tells me what to do.

MALE VOICE: Dive Viveca.

VIVECA: Mrs. Martin at the shop says I'm one of those born lucky people who just don't need to be told anything. So why does she keep telling me? (*Long pause. She stares out over the pool, shivers suddenly, backs down a step. The MALE VOICE clears its throat and VIVECA races up several steps.*) It's high up here. (*looks up at platform*) But not too high. (*Pause.*) Salmon. Salmon leap high up falls. I know, I've seen them. And in October they flap in the shallows and leap up and get caught in low branches, and there they stay, skeletons with their eyes pecked out. But before – before, the water's so thick with swimmers that you could walk on it, and banks lined with black crows, waiting. And fishermen at the falls with lures. And then the salmon are born again and there's no more river to swim up so they turn around and swim and swim down and dive down the falls. Isn't that right? It's called a life cycle.

MALE VOICE: Dive Viveca.

VIVECA makes up her mind. Walks up the last steps, reaches the platform, walks along the length of it, balancing. Goes to the edge and looks down. Draws her breath. Retreats almost losing her balance. Stretches her body. Stretches her arms. Stands on tiptoe. Breathes deep.

VIVECA: Like an arc, like a bridge, like a hammock with the wind under it. (*arches her body, and says playfully*) Dive dog.

MALE VOICE: (*commanding*) Viveca!

VIVECA: Dog!

MALE VOICE: Viveca! (*VIVECA laughs.*) Dive! (*VIVECA barks and MALE VOICE continues in a warning manner.*) Viveca (*She whimpers.*) Dive!

VIVECA: (*She gets ready, stands in perfect position, poised.*) Dog, dog, where are you?

MALE VOICE: Now!

VIVECA: Yes?

MALE VOICE: Yes.

VIVECA: Yes.

MALE VOICE: Yes!

VIVECA: Now!

She dives, lights snap off. Blackout. A spot roams around the stage looking for her and finds the skeleton of a salmon dangling at the level where VIVECA's head was. A disembodied male soprano voice sings "Oh For the Wings of a Dove." The lights and music fade to black and then the lights come up full. VIVECA enters briskly, no longer wearing leaves. She wears a jaunty maple-leaf patterned swimsuit and carries the towel over her shoulder. She hums a pop tune as she prepares to enter the water while putting in her earplugs and kicking off her clogs. She takes a tape recorder from her bag, switches it on and adjusts her nose clamp while she listens. The voice on the tape is the same MALE VOICE, but the note of command has gone.

MALE VOICE: Lesson two. (*snatch of pop music*) Now that you have mastered the preliminary exercise, stand waist deep in the water. Extend the arms above the head and bend forward at the waist; bend the knees slightly and focus your eyes on the bottom of the pool.

VIVECA tries but is confused. She bends, rewinds the tape. The MALE VOICE is reduced to gibberish. It starts again and VIVECA follows the instructions as the lights go down. Half light lingers on her briefly as she stands, staring at bottom of the pool.

Fade.

The end.

Ten Ways to Abuse an Old Woman

By

Sally Clark

Joan Orenstein as The Old Woman

Photographer: Taxi Entertainment

AUDACIOUS COMI-TRAGEDY: THE WAYS OF SALLY CLARK'S PLAYS

In her childhood, Sally Clark experienced a cultural awakening: "I saw Canadian plays performed on a regular basis at the Vancouver Playhouse. Previously, I had assumed that only British and American writers could be playwrights. I saw the premieres of George Ryga's *The Ecstasy of Rita Joe* and James Reaney's *Colours in the Dark*. Watching these plays performed with full production values made a huge impression on me. I saw that theatre was not some desecrated, imported art form but a live art that we could create for ourselves" (Preface 23). In the wake of Canada's Centennial celebrations and at the dawn of the Trudeau era, the personal revelation of Sally Clark was concomitant with the emergence of a post-colonial indigenous theatre that was part of a broader national cultural burgeoning. Little did the young Clark know she would not only advance the cause pioneered by Ryga and Reaney, but she would also be part of a generation that forged a further erosion of barriers – those standing in the way of female playwrights.

While she may have been enthralled with theatre as a young spectator, it was painting, not writing, that first attracted Clark as a creator when she left Vancouver (where she had lived since her birth in 1953) for Toronto in 1973. However, when her visual arts studies at York University failed to meet her expectations, she signed up for a theatre class, where she began a lasting friendship with fellow student and future theatre company founder Sky Gilbert. The two went on to produce their one-act plays together, and Clark was re-infected with the theatre bug, although she returned to her study of painting, this time at The Three Schools of Art. When that school dissolved as the result of provincial government cutbacks in the early 1980s, Clark began her theatre career in earnest.

Lost Souls and Missing Persons premiered at Toronto's Theatre Passe Muraille in 1984; *Trial* was produced in a 1985 Tamahnous Theatre production (later rewritten and changed to *The Trial of Judith K.*, produced in 1989); *Moo*, which was initially co-produced in 1988 by Calgary's Alberta Theatre Projects and Victoria's Belfry Theatre; *Jehanne of the Witches*, which premiered in 1989 at Tarragon Theatre, Toronto; *Sleeproom* (co-written with John Mighton, Robin Fulford, and Daniel MacIvor) for Theatre Passe Muraille in 1994; *Saint Frances of Hollywood*, an Alberta Theatre Projects production in 1994; and *Wasps*, which premiered at Toronto's Factory Theatre's Studio Café in 1996.

Clark has been playwright-in-residence at the Shaw Festival, Theatre Passe Muraille, Buddies in Bad Times Theatre, and Nightwood Theatre. She received the Floyd S. Chalmers Canadian Play Award for *Moo* in 1990; from France, the Henri Langlois International Short Film Festival Special Prix du Jury in 1992 for the film version of *Ten Ways to Abuse an Old Woman*, and, from Charleston, South Carolina, the Worldfest Original Dramatic Show Bronze Award in 1994 for the film "The Art of Conversation".

Ratsoy: What sparked the idea for *Ten Ways to Abuse an Old Woman*?

Clark: I wrote the title. I just had the title sitting on my desk for a while. Quite often, that's how I write plays. The title comes to me.

Ratsoy: And things just take shape from the title?

Clark: Yes. My friend Sky Gilbert had a Rhubarb! Festival for Buddies in Bad Times Theatre in Toronto. I had already written *Lost Souls and Missing Persons*, and it was looking like it was going to be produced, but prior to its production Sky said, " Why don't you do something short? Write a half-hour play." The idea was rooted in wanting to write a half-hour play for the Rhubarb! and submitting it for a deadline. I then wrote the title down and thought about it.

Ratsoy: Is there something that stands out for you about the play's premiere?

Clark: I had a lot of fun. I directed it, and I remember being pretty nervous. We weren't given much money, so I had to be stage manager as well. So, because I was performing such stage managing functions as finding costumes and organizing props, I came to the conclusion that directing was a lot of work.

Clark's work is characteristically black, mordant, audacious, feminist in an unorthodox sense, and comi-tragic. Like Morris Panych and John Lazarus, Clark has a magnetic attraction to the absurdities of life and a propensity to surprise, even alarm the reader with an injection of razor-sharp humour into the bleakest of situations. In *Moo*, for example, the situation of a protagonist who has been committed to a mental institution under false pretenses by a ne'er-do-well husband evokes serio-comic responses as the play indicts patriarchal institutions and power hierarchies. Clark's debt to Franz Kafka is patent in *The Trial of Judith K.*, a re-writing of the Czech's *The Trial* from the point of view of a female loans officer who wakes up on her thirtieth birthday to find herself nude and two officers ready to arrest her for an unidentified crime.

Ratsoy: I'm wondering, because I think both *Moo* and *Ten Ways to Abuse an Old Woman*, in particular, are quite outrageous plays, if you've ever received an outraged response to either of the plays or to the film version of *Ten Ways to Abuse an Old Women*.

Clark: Not that I'm aware of. I've had people tell me there's going to be an outraged response and anticipate one, but as far as I'm aware, no one has been outraged. A *Globe and Mail* critic said *Moo* wasn't politically correct and anticipated upset on the part of audiences. But I've never received an angry letter.

The filmed version of *Ten Ways to Abuse an Old Woman* was really popular in France. The Henri Langlois International Short Film Festival Special Prix du Jury is a big prize. It was great; the French kept showing it. A French neuro-psychologist wanted to use it as a study for Alzheimer's.

Feminist revisionist history informs a trio of Clark's plays. *Jehanne of the Witches* examines the story of the much-recorded Joan of Arc through the prism of the seldom-explored close friendship between Joan and Gilles De Rais, a playwright, a founder of French theatre, and the man on whom the tale of Bluebeard is based. Clark's choice of the name "Jehanne" reflects the pagan focus of the play: her original title was Jehanne la Pucelle; she was renamed Jeanne d'Arc by the Christians. Through De Rais' construction of a play about Joan, Clark calls attention to the process of theatrical invention and the arbitrary nature of identity by having Francois, the boy selected as actor, played by the same actress who plays Jehanne. *Saint Frances of Hollywood* explores the tragic life of Frances Farmer, the strong-willed socialist movie star who was hounded by the American government, ostracized by the Hollywood community, repeatedly institutionalized, and eventually lobotomized. Here, too, Clark's inclusion of scenes from plays and movies, including a clip of "Come and Get It," a movie in which Farmer starred, serves, in typical postmodern fashion, to remind the reader/viewer of the constructed nature of the play. *Life Without Instruction*, about Artemesia Gentileschi, the seventeenth-century painter who charged her instructor, Agostino Tassi, with rape, and who suffered public humiliation and torture at the ensuing trial, parallels that narrative with the Biblical story of Judith and Holofernes in a play-within-a play format that, as Artemesia re-constructs the Biblical tale, underscores both Clark's reconstruction of Artemesia's own story and the arbitrariness of recorded history. The three protagonists are independent-minded, defiant, subversive characters who are in a doomed struggle against the power structures of their respective times. Clark incorporates relatively large casts of characters and such techniques as time juxtapositions and trials (mock or "real") as metaphors for patriarchal judging to lend mythic qualities to these historical figures. Yet each female protagonist is neither helpless victim nor flawless heroine. There is little room for the mawkish in the incisive milieu of Sally Clark's plays.

Early in her career, Clark told Judith Rudakoff, "I think I'm writing tragedies. But I think they're funny" (78). This observation would prove to hold true for much of her subsequent work, and is certainly germane to *Ten Ways to Abuse an Old Woman*. The abruptness of the title, with its echoes of popular how-to manuals designed to expedite and simplify matters in a frenetically-paced, complex society, is reinforced by the brevity of the play itself, the fragmentary, vignette-like scenes and the jarring ending – all of which reflect the fragmentary nature of life itself. The relative anonymity of the setting—while references to the Bay and the French television station tell us this is Canada, geographical and time markers are otherwise vague—fosters a sense of dislocation, heightened by the prominence of the television. The television also serves to point to the absence of meaningful human interaction: in the opening scene, the mother is watching a programme delivered in a language she cannot understand and the daughter is engaged with the soap opera, but no real communication occurs. Not only is the dialogue between mother and daughter littered with non sequiturs, but the interaction between Margery and George, for example, is also basically uncommunicative and apparently aimless. The old woman's utterances may be preposterous and out of context, but those of the other characters are only slightly less absurd. The mother becomes a yardstick: an exaggeration for the satirist's purpose of emphasizing widespread inanity and vacuity. Closure is at once tentative and blunt as Clark undercuts the catastrophic ending of traditional tragedy with a touch of ambiguity and with mundane circumstances that evoke the comic in their suddenness.

Ratsoy: You have used the word "provocative" to describe Morris Panych's plays, and that is a word that could certainly also be used to describe your plays. Is that what you think a play should do, or your plays should do – be provocative, be subversive?

Clark: I think we should make people feel something. To me, theatre is about big themes, large events: it is a big experience, not a small one. Sometimes it gets reduced to people who are bereft of interesting conversation in their lives going to the theatre to hear other people talk. I think theatre should be really exciting. Big things should happen.

The reason those spectacles (such as the Andrew Lloyd Webber works) did so well is that people were crying out for something like that. They hadn't had it in theatre. There should be an element of spectacle to theatre and it should evoke large emotions.

For a time, I think, theatre just concentrated on thought, diction, and character and surrendered plot and ignored the other elements Aristotle said constitute a play.

Sally Clark's contributions to the live art she first experienced at the Vancouver Playhouse began with *Ten Ways to Abuse an Old Woman* and continued with plays set in heterogeneous places and times. The quality of the body of her bold, sharply comic, and fatalistic work puts her among the foremost feminist playwrights in Canada today. Although the settings for the great majority of her work are far removed from Vancouver, and Clark has spent more of her adult life in Toronto than in the city of her birth, in one important sense she and her work are never far from home. As Clark told Judith Rudakoff, "Whatever I write about and my sensibilities are Vancouver-based; you can never escape your background and it forms the root of what you're writing" (86).

G.R.

Selected Bibliography:

- Clark, Sally. Telephone Interview. 20 Dec. 2000.
- Clark, Sally. "Preface/Introduction to *Ten Ways to Abuse an Old Woman.*" *Windsor Review* 30:1 (Spring 1997): 23-5.
- Donnelly, Pat. "Playwright Sally Clark Making Her Mark in Quebec." *The Montreal Gazette* 22 April 1993.
- Hood, Sarah B. "The Word and the Flesh: New Worlds in Canadian Playwriting." *Performing Arts* 32: 4 (Winter 1999/2000): 20-24. The work of Clark and several other playwrights is examined in light of the question "What is a Canadian play?"
- Kirchhoff, H.J. "Playwright's Life a Series of Stages." *The Globe and Mail* 2 Aug. 1991.
- Ratsoy, Ginny. "Dramatic Discourse at Talonbooks: Narratives on the Publisher-Author Relationship." *Canadian Theatre Review* 101 (Winter 2000): 25-28. Four playwrights—including Clark, Joan Macleod, and John Gray—discuss the process of play publication.
- Rudakoff, Judith and Rita Much. *Fair Play. Twelve Women Speak: Conversations with Canadian Playwrights.* Toronto: Simon and Pierre, 1990. 73-86.
- "Ten Ways to Abuse an Old Woman." Dir. Sally Clark. Canadian Film Centre, 1992.

Ten Ways to Abuse an Old Woman
by Sally Clark

Ten Ways to Abuse an Old Woman was first produced in Toronto at Buddies in Bad Times Theatre's Rhubarb! Festival, in 1983, with the following cast:

Old Woman	Maja Ardal
Daughter	Patricia Hamilton
George	Paul Brown

Directed by Sally Clark

CHARACTERS

OLD WOMAN
DAUGHTER, aged 50
HUSBAND, aged 50

Note: The DAUGHTER and the HUSBAND also play GUEST 1 and GUEST 2 in the party scene.

NOTE ON PUNCTUATION

Capitals with a period means the person is speaking loudly, but is not necessarily angry. Capitals with a "!" indicate some anger or frustration. Capitals with a "!!" indicate lots of anger or frustration.

SCENE ONE

OLD WOMAN is watching television. It is blaring away on the French station.

DAUGHTER: (*walks in*) Mother.

OLD WOMAN pays no attention.

DAUGHTER: MOTHER!!!

OLD WOMAN: Yes.

DAUGHTER: DO YOU SPEAK FRENCH?

OLD WOMAN: Pardon?

DAUGHTER: FRENCH!! DO YOU SPEAK FRENCH!!!

OLD WOMAN: No.

DAUGHTER: WHY DO YOU HAVE THE TV ON?

OLD WOMAN: Oh. Do I?

DAUGHTER: YES. IT'S ON THE FRENCH STATION. AND YOU DON'T SPEAK FRENCH, DO YOU?

OLD WOMAN: No.

DAUGHTER: THEREFORE, YOU DON'T WANT TO WATCH FRENCH TV. THEREFORE, YOU DON'T NEED THE TV ON. (*snaps it off, walks out*) Honestly, the things I go through.

OLD WOMAN sits, gazing at blank set, holds out remote switch, tries to turn TV on. It won't go on.

SCENE TWO

OLD WOMAN and her DAUGHTER.

DAUGHTER: Here's a funny story...

OLD WOMAN starts laughing.

DAUGHTER: You're laughing.

OLD WOMAN: (*laughing softly, gives a sudden start, pulls herself abrupt*) Oh.

DAUGHTER: You're laughing and I haven't told you the story yet.

OLD WOMAN: (*looks cowed*) Oh.

DAUGHTER: I haven't told you the story and you're sitting there laughing. Don't laugh. I'll tell you when it's time to laugh. Are you ready, Mother?

OLD WOMAN: Pardon?

DAUGHTER: ARE YOU READY, MOTHER?

OLD WOMAN: Yes, I'm ready.

DAUGHTER: I saw Mrs. Gillespie, today...

OLD WOMAN: Who?

DAUGHTER: Mrs. Gillespie. Our neighbour. You never liked her.

OLD WOMAN: Oh. Didn't I?

DAUGHTER: Honestly, Mother, can't you even remember who you disliked!

OLD WOMAN: (*muses*) Mrs. Gillespie.

DAUGHTER: Well, she was in the Bay buying a hat. I bumped into her. And this will make you laugh–

OLD WOMAN laughs.

What's the point. What's the goddamn point of anything these days!

OLD WOMAN laughs.

SHUT UP!!!

OLD WOMAN glances fearfully at DAUGHTER then stares off into space.

SCENE THREE

OLD WOMAN and DAUGHTER in kitchen. There are three hard-boiled eggs on the counter. OLD WOMAN hands daughter a hard-boiled egg.

DAUGHTER: No eggs for me, thank you, Mother.

OLD WOMAN: Wouldn't you like a hard-boiled egg?

DAUGHTER: No, thanks. I don't like hard-boiled eggs.

OLD WOMAN: But you used to like hard-boiled eggs.

DAUGHTER: Actually, Mother, I've never liked hard-boiled eggs. I ate them five years ago when I went on that grapefruit and hard-boiled egg diet, but I didn't like them then, and I don't like them now. I've never liked hard-boiled eggs.

OLD WOMAN: Pardon?

DAUGHTER: No. Thank you..

OLD WOMAN: Pardon?

DAUGHTER: Forget it.

OLD WOMAN: Wouldn't you like a hard-boiled egg?

DAUGHTER: NO! I WOULDN'T!!

OLD WOMAN: There's no need to be rude.

DAUGHTER: Sorry, Mother.

OLD WOMAN: I've cooked three.

DAUGHTER: Yes. I know. You always cook three.

OLD WOMAN: What am I going to do with them?

DAUGHTER: Put them in the fridge with the rest of the hard-boiled eggs.

OLD WOMAN: Pardon?

DAUGHTER: Forget it.

OLD WOMAN: (*mashes up egg on a plate; sets it on the floor; calls*) Butchie! Butchie!

DAUGHTER looks up.

Butchie! Butchie!!

DAUGHTER: The dog's dead, Mother.

OLD WOMAN: Pardon?

DAUGHTER: The dog's dead and his name was Fred. Butch died years ago. There hasn't been a Butchie in this house for at least ten years and Fred's dead.

OLD WOMAN: (*hurt and accusing*) Who's going to eat his egg?

DAUGHTER: I don't know, Mother. Someone better eat his egg. I'm sure as hell sick of eating his egg. Maybe we should buy another dog and let him eat his egg. I honestly don't know, Mother.

OLD WOMAN: Pardon?

SCENE FOUR

OLD WOMAN and her DAUGHTER. They are eating hard-boiled eggs and watching the soap opera.

SOAP OPERA: "I love you, Karen. Nothing in the world could ever make me change what I feel about you."

OLD WOMAN: Look at the sky.

DAUGHTER: Mmmm?

SOAP OPERA: "Oh Donald, you don't know what you're saying. If you only knew the truth."

OLD WOMAN: Look at the sky.

DAUGHTER: Yes. (*looks*) What about it?

OLD WOMAN: It's very blue, today.

SOAP OPERA: "The truth." Karen: "Yes, the truth – Oh Donald. You think I'm just a nice woman who used to be a nun and is now having a bit of a hard time in life but it's more than that. It's much much more than that."

OLD WOMAN: Isn't it blue?

DAUGHTER: Yes, Mother. It's blue. It's been blue for some time.

SOAP OPERA: "You see, Donald... how can I tell you. I don't think I can tell you." Donald: "Trust me." Karen: "Oh, can I really trust you? Can I really? The last man I trusted was Father Ignatius. He was a good man. A fine man."

OLD WOMAN: Look at the sky.

DAUGHTER looks at OLD WOMAN.

SOAP OPERA: "Were you in love with Father Ignatius?" Karen: "We had a spiritual bond that went far beyond Christ and the Church and my vocation as a nun." Donald: "I see."

OLD WOMAN: Isn't this a lovely room. It's very unusual for a kitchen.

DAUGHTER: It's not a kitchen, Mother.

SOAP OPERA: "Oh, Donald, how can I tell you this other truth."

OLD WOMAN: Oh. (*laughs*) Heh heh heh.

DAUGHTER: It's a living room.

SOAP OPERA: Donald: "You mean what you have to tell me is not about Father Ignatius?" Karen: "Oh no, that was over years ago. I hardly think about him, now."

OLD WOMAN: It's very unusual. The people who live here have gone to great lengths to make it attractive.

SOAP OPERA: "But do you remember Marco Pane?"

DAUGHTER: We live here, Mother.

OLD WOMAN: Pardon?

SOAP OPERA: "Marco Pane??!"

DAUGHTER: We are the people who live here. There are no other people who live here. At least, none that I know of. Do you know of some? Are there any little munchkins here you'd like to introduce me to? In particular, the ones who've made this room so very attractive. I'd like to meet them. I've heard so much about them. I might as well meet them.

SOAP OPERA: (*simultaneously*) "Yes. Marco Pane." Donald: "Oh God, Karen. Marco Pane!" Karen: "No no, you don't understand, Donald." Donald: "I think I understand plenty." Karen: "No no, you don't." Donald: "Yes yes, I do. Oh God, Karen, Marco

Pane." Karen: "But it's not that way. It's not that way at all."

OLD WOMAN: Pardon?

SOAP OPERA: "Then tell me. Explain yourself."

OLD WOMAN: This room has lovely high ceilings.

DAUGHTER: Yes. It does. If you don't mind, Mother, I think I'll watch the soap opera.

SOAP OPERA: "Marco Pane was a friend of the other man – the man I want to tell you about." Donald: "Good God, you mean there's another one."

OLD WOMAN: Doesn't this room have lovely high ceilings?

DAUGHTER: Mmmmmhmmmm.

SOAP OPERA: "Yes. Floyd Dick." Donald: "Floyd Dick?!"

OLD WOMAN: You'd never know it was a kitchen.

SCENE FIVE

OLD WOMAN is padding about, singing softly to herself.

DAUGHTER: (*enters*) Mother.

OLD WOMAN continues singing.

MOTHER!

OLD WOMAN: Who?

DAUGHTER: YOU!! MOTHER!!!

OLD WOMAN: Oh.

DAUGHTER: (*in loud deliberate tones*) DO YOU KNOW WHERE THE CLOTHESPINS ARE?

OLD WOMAN: The what?

DAUGHTER: THE CLOTHESPINS.

OLD WOMAN: The what?

DAUGHTER: THE CLOTHESPINS!!!

Long, long pause as OLD WOMAN stops to think.

OLD WOMAN: Why, I think they're in the dryer.

DAUGHTER: (*starts toward dryer; stops*) NO. NOT THE CLOTHES!! THE CLOTHESPINS!!

OLD WOMAN: The what?

DAUGHTER: Forget it. Just forget it. I'll find them myself.

OLD WOMAN: The what?

DAUGHTER: FORGET IT.

OLD WOMAN: What?

DAUGHTER: THE CLOTHESPINS!!!! THE LITTLE THINGS THAT GO PINCH PINCH. YOU USE THEM TO HANG UP THE CLOTHES!!!

OLD WOMAN: Ooooh. (*Long pause.*) Oh my. Now, dear me. Oh. I wonder. Clothespins. Oh, where could they be? (*Pause.*) Why, I don't know where they could be. Do you know where they are?

DAUGHTER: (*hysterically*) NO NO NO NO NO NO NO!!!!

OLD WOMAN: There's no need to shout. (*exits*)

SCENE SIX

Phone rings. OLD WOMAN is passing by the phone.

OLD WOMAN: (*picks it up*) Hello. (*Pause.*) No. This is her mother. (*Pause.*) Yes. (*Pause.*) Yes. (*Pause.*) Oh yes. (*laughs softly, puts phone down*)

DAUGHTER: *(enters)* Was that the phone?

OLD WOMAN *ignores her.*

Mother, did you hear the phone?

OLD WOMAN *laughs; walks away.*

SCENE SEVEN

OLD WOMAN *sits quietly at a table, playing solitaire, nodding happily to herself.*

DAUGHTER: *(enters)* Mother.

OLD WOMAN *pays no attention.*

MOTHER?

OLD WOMAN *does not respond.*

MOTHER!!!!

OLD WOMAN: *(raises head slowly)* Yes.

DAUGHTER: Mother – WHY DON'T YOU PUT YOUR HEARING AID IN?

OLD WOMAN: Oh heh heh heh.

DAUGHTER: WELL, WHY DON'T YOU?

OLD WOMAN: Mmmm heh heh heh.

DAUGHTER: Come on, we'll put it in together. Where is it?

OLD WOMAN *points vaguely; continues playing solitaire.* DAUGHTER *puts it in.* OLD WOMAN *makes agonized faces.*

IS IT IN? *(shouts into ear)* DOES IT HURT? AM I HURTING YOU?

OLD WOMAN *taps on aid.*

Oh sorry, I forgot. I don't have to shout now, do I?

OLD WOMAN *continues playing solitaire.*

Isn't that better, Mother?

OLD WOMAN *nods vaguely.* DAUGHTER *exits.* OLD WOMAN, *as though she suddenly remembered something, reaches in ear, pulls out hearing aid and places it in box.*

(returns) I've got so many things to do today. I'm going to have to leave you alone for a while. You'll be all right alone, won't you, Mother? Now, there's no need to make lunch.

OLD WOMAN: *(continues playing solitaire)* Heh heh heh heh.

DAUGHTER: So, you won't have to boil any eggs. All right? NO EGGS. Can't think of anything else to tell you. Oh, no need to put the dishwasher on. OK? There're no dishes in it so there's no need to put it on. Don't forget to watch the soap opera and be sure to tell me what happens. Well, watch it anyway and try to remember something.

OLD WOMAN: Heh heh heh.

DAUGHTER: *(looks puzzled)* Well, goodbye, dear. *(kisses her and leaves)*

OLD WOMAN: *(pads out to kitchen; offstage)* Butchie! Butchie!

SCENE EIGHT

OLD WOMAN, *in best dress, playing solitaire at the table.* GEORGE *is sitting, reading the newspaper.* DAUGHTER *enters, stops, looks at* OLD WOMAN.

DAUGHTER: Mother! Mother, look at you.

OLD WOMAN *looks flustered.*

Your best dress. Why are you wearing your best dress?

OLD WOMAN: The party.

DAUGHTER: The party's not for three days. If you wear your best dress now, you won't have anything to wear for the party.

OLD WOMAN: Oh.

DAUGHTER: Look! You've spilled tomato on it, already.

OLD WOMAN: Oh.

DAUGHTER: *(looks at OLD WOMAN's feet)* Why are you wearing those shoes?

OLD WOMAN: I like them.

DAUGHTER: But you know they pinch your feet and make your ankles swell.

OLD WOMAN: Oh.

DAUGHTER: Take them off. Oh Mother, your feet are purple.

OLD WOMAN: Are they?

DAUGHTER: Yes. Those shoes are too tight and they cut off your circulation and your feet are purple.

OLD WOMAN: I can't feel anything.

DAUGHTER: Of course, you can't feel anything. There's no circulation there. Blood hasn't gone down to your feet for at least a day. You never walk.

OLD WOMAN: Oh.

DAUGHTER: George.

GEORGE: Mmmm.

DAUGHTER: George, Mother's feet are purple again.

GEORGE: Mmmm.

DAUGHTER: Doesn't anyone care except me. Nobody looks at her feet but me. She doesn't even look at her feet. You could chop them off and she'd never notice.

OLD WOMAN puts feet back into shoes.

DAUGHTER: TAKE THOSE SHOES OFF!!

OLD WOMAN: Pardon?

DAUGHTER: Christ.

SCENE NINE

OLD WOMAN and her DAUGHTER. They are dressed up and sipping drinks. DAUGHTER takes a sip of her drink. OLD WOMAN watches her; takes a sip of her drink. DAUGHTER takes another sip. OLD WOMAN drinks some more.

DAUGHTER: Now, it's a party, Mother, so you don't need to drink your gin right away. This isn't a race. The guests haven't arrived yet so you should have some gin left for when they get here.

OLD WOMAN drinks feverishly.

It's just habit, you know, Mother. I don't even think you like gin, any more. You just got used to drinking it. (*Pause.*) Lots of it. It could be water. Wouldn't make any difference. Except, because it's gin, you drink too much. Then, you don't feel like eating and you pass out at the table. I don't want you to pass out tonight, Mother.

OLD WOMAN finishes glass.

You're not getting any more till the guests come.

OLD WOMAN: Is it time for wine, yet?

DAUGHTER: No. That's with dinner. You'll have to wait till dinner before you get wine.

OLD WOMAN: And after dinner?

DAUGHTER: After dinner, you go to bed.

OLD WOMAN: Oh.

SCENE TEN

Party. The OLD WOMAN is sitting in a chair. She is wearing her best dress and drinking a glass of gin.

GUEST 1: *(approaches)* Why hello, Mrs. Stone.

OLD WOMAN: Hello.

GUEST 1: And how are you, today?

OLD WOMAN: Very well. Thank you.

GUEST 1: You're looking well.

Pause.

OLD WOMAN: (*smiles*) This room has lovely high ceilings.

GUEST 1: Yes. It does.

OLD WOMAN: They've made it very attractive.

GUEST 1: Oh? Did you have men in? Did they raise the ceiling?

OLD WOMAN laughs.

Amazing the things you don't notice. To me, this room looks the same as it always has. You know – I really should pay more attention. Always too busy, though. Rush rush rush – know what I mean? Say, your glass is empty. Would you like me to get you another drink?

OLD WOMAN: Oh yes please. Pretty please.

GUEST 1 leaves.

OLD WOMAN: You'd never know it was a kitchen.

GUEST 2: Mrs. Stone, you're looking absolutely wonderful.

OLD WOMAN: Isn't this a lovely room?

GUEST 2: Now don't be coy, Mrs Stone. You have to learn to take a compliment.

OLD WOMAN: It has lovely high ceilings.

GUEST 2: Ha! Changing the subject again. Here – let me get you a drink. (*leaves*)

GUEST 1: (*returns with drink*) Here you are Mrs. Stone.

OLD WOMAN: Why thank you. That was very fast. (*takes a sip*)

GUEST 1 leaves. OLD WOMAN wolfs down drink, places empty glass in line-up of empty glasses beside the chair.

GUEST 2: (*returns with drink*) Here you are Mrs. Stone.

OLD WOMAN: Oh? (*takes glass*) Thank you.

DAUGHTER enters.

GUEST 2: Your mother's looking wonderful tonight, Margery. Real old trooper. And what a sense of humour she's got.

DAUGHTER: She has?

GUEST 2: Cracking them wild all the time. We had a nice long chat.

DAUGHTER: You did?

GUEST 2: Now, don't be surprised. You take that poor old mother of yours for granted, Margery. She's a gem. A real gem.

DAUGHTER: She is.

GUEST 2: But you know, dear. I think those shoes she's wearing are too tight.

DAUGHTER: Oh.

SCENE ELEVEN

Dark room. OLD WOMAN is sitting in the room, staring straight ahead of her.

DAUGHTER: (*enters room, switches on light, screams*) Christ! You scared me. (*Pause.*) Mother? (*no response*) Mother, are you all right?

OLD WOMAN: Yes.

DAUGHTER: What are you doing here? We're all outside.

OLD WOMAN: I don't want to get sun poisoning.

DAUGHTER: But the sun went down ages ago. (*Pause.*) Do you want the TV on?

OLD WOMAN: No. Thank you.

DAUGHTER: Don't you want the light on?

OLD WOMAN: No. Thank you.

DAUGHTER: Well, come outside. Why are you sitting here all by yourself?

OLD WOMAN: I like it here and I'm very happy. (*laughs softly*)

SCENE TWELVE

DAUGHTER and GEORGE.

DAUGHTER: She has got to go.

GEORGE: Yes.

DAUGHTER: I mean it, George. It's like living with a zombie. A pleasant well-behaved zombie, but a zombie nonetheless.

GEORGE: What does she do, exactly?

DAUGHTER: She sits and laughs all day.

GEORGE: She laughs.

DAUGHTER: Yes. She's very jolly.

GEORGE: What about?

DAUGHTER: Who knows?

GEORGE: You need to go out more.

DAUGHTER: I can't go out because God knows what I'll find when I get home. She still does things, you know.

GEORGE: Like what?

DAUGHTER: She boils eggs.

GEORGE: So, what's the harm in that?

DAUGHTER: Someone has to eat all those eggs.

GEORGE: Yes.

DAUGHTER: You still haven't grasped it, have you? She boils eggs and someone has to eat all those eggs. Have you had a hard-boiled egg recently?

GEORGE: Are you all right?

DAUGHTER: Have you?

GEORGE: No.

DAUGHTER: I have. I have three per day. Sometimes, four. Every time I leave her alone, she's out there boiling eggs. I hate hard-boiled eggs. I positively loathe hard-boiled eggs.

GEORGE: Why don't you stop buying eggs?

DAUGHTER: Simple as that, eh? Just stop buying eggs.

GEORGE: Well.

DAUGHTER: Well, what am I going to do when I have to cook something? What am I going to do about that! I have to go out and get an egg, right? You can't buy just one egg. You have to buy a whole dozen.

GEORGE: Sometimes, half a dozen.

DAUGHTER: Yes. Yes. Sometimes half a dozen. That's five eggs, though. Five eggs for her to boil.

GEORGE: So, hide the eggs.

DAUGHTER: Hide the eggs. And where do you hide eggs? Can't hide them outside 'cause they'll go bad. Have to hide them in the fridge. Right?

GEORGE: Yes.

DAUGHTER: First place she'll look.

GEORGE: I see. (*Pause.*) Well, don't eat them.

DAUGHTER: It won't stop her. Nothing will stop her. She'll just continue boiling eggs. But, it's all right. The problem's solved. I know what to do.

GEORGE: I think you should go have your cholesterol checked.

SCENE THIRTEEN

Dinner. OLD WOMAN, DAUGHTER and GEORGE are sitting around a table. They are eating hard-boiled eggs. The OLD WOMAN is eating with the plate on her lap.

GEORGE: Pass the salt, please.

DAUGHTER passes it.

OLD WOMAN: (*sweetly*) Would you like mayonnaise?

GEORGE: No.

OLD WOMAN: They're much nicer with mayonnaise.

GEORGE: I DON'T WANT MAYONNAISE.

OLD WOMAN looks puzzled, bends down to eat food from plate on her lap.

DAUGHTER: Why don't you put your plate on the table, Mother?

OLD WOMAN continues, oblivious.

MOTHER.

OLD WOMAN continues eating.

MOTHER!

OLD WOMAN: Mmmm?

DAUGHTER: WHY DON'T YOU PUT YOUR PLATE ON THE TABLE?

OLD WOMAN: Oh. (*laughs softly*)

DAUGHTER: WELL?

OLD WOMAN looks at her.

WHY NOT?

OLD WOMAN: I'm very happy, thank you, dear.

DAUGHTER: I know that. We all know that.

OLD WOMAN: We're all in this world to be happy. Ho ho ho.

GEORGE: That's it! You're right, enough's enough. She has got to go!

OLD WOMAN: Because what sort of place would it be if people weren't happy.

GEORGE: People aren't happy.

OLD WOMAN: What?

GEORGE: PEOPLE AREN'T HAPPY.

OLD WOMAN: Oh. That's too bad. We're all in this world to be happy. Ho ho ho.

GEORGE: People aren't happy, goddamn it. You're happy.

OLD WOMAN: Yes. I am happy.

GEORGE: Well, you're the only person who is happy. The only person in the whole wide world. Besides, you weren't happy ten years ago.

OLD WOMAN: Oh. Wasn't I?

GEORGE: No. You weren't. And you weren't happy twenty years ago when Charlie died.

OLD WOMAN: Who?

GEORGE: Charlie. Your husband.

DAUGHTER: My father.

OLD WOMAN: (*muses*) Charlie.

DAUGHTER: My God, George, she's forgotten Charlie.

GEORGE: She can't have forgotten Charlie. She was madly in love with Charlie. When he died, we never heard the end of it. Every year, on his birthday, she went into mourning. We'd try and snap her out of it and then along would come the wedding anniversary and she'd be right back at it again. Then, she'd come out of it for a while and we'd hit the day that Charlie died. She can't have forgotten Charlie.

DAUGHTER: (*watches OLD WOMAN*) I think she has. Mother? (*no response*) MOTHER.

OLD WOMAN: Yes.

DAUGHTER: Don't you remember Charlie?

OLD WOMAN: Charlie.

DAUGHTER: CHARLIE. YOUR HUSBAND. MY FATHER. Charlie died and you were very unhappy. For years.

OLD WOMAN: (*mulls it over*) But, I'm happy now.

DAUGHTER: Yes, yes, you're happy, now. It's because you don't have a brain anymore. You're just an old shell who used to be my mother. You laugh and smile at everything. Of course, you're happy.

OLD WOMAN: (*thinks it over*) I could be crabby.

DAUGHTER: Yes, you could be crabby. You could be a thousand things. What a pity you're no longer my mother. You're so sweet. You've become so bloody sweet.

OLD WOMAN: Yes.

DAUGHTER: Well – Goddamn it, my mother may have been many things but she was never sweet. She was never sweet, was she, George?

GEORGE: No. She was an old bitch.

DAUGHTER: Now, wait a minute.

GEORGE: Sorry, dear. No. She was never sweet.

DAUGHTER: So, why is she sweet? What's happened to her? Does brain rot do this to you? Do you become inanely benign with each passing year?

OLD WOMAN: I could be crabby.

DAUGHTER & GEORGE: SHUT UP!

SCENE FOURTEEN

OLD WOMAN at a table.

OLD WOMAN: Who do I write the cheque to?

DAUGHTER: To Timmy.

OLD WOMAN: Who?

DAUGHTER: Timmy. Your grandson.

OLD WOMAN: And what's it for?

DAUGHTER: Christmas.

OLD WOMAN: Oh. (*Pause.*) What's the date?

DAUGHTER: Christmas. Christmas, Mother and when does Christmas come?

OLD WOMAN: December?

DAUGHTER: And when in December?

OLD WOMAN: (*thinks it over*) The twenty-fifth.

DAUGHTER: So, you write the cheque for December twenty-fifth. Christmas Day because it's for Christmas. (*exits then re-enters*) And that's the last time I'm going to tell you. (*exits*)

OLD WOMAN: Oh. (*pause; to herself, writing cheque*) December twenty-fifth. Nineteen. (*Pause.*) Nineteen. (*looks around for newspaper, finds one, checks paper, shows puzzlement* *over date*) Nineteen... Two oh oh. Two. Two... (*goes back*) Nineteen ninety-nine. (*smiles*)

SCENE FIFTEEN

DAUGHTER and GEORGE in bed. GEORGE sits up with a start.

DAUGHTER: Mmmmmm.

GEORGE: Ssssh.

DAUGHTER: (*still sleepy, murmurs*) What's wrong?

GEORGE: Ssssh. Do you hear something?

DAUGHTER: Mmmmm?

GEORGE: Yes, I can hear it. She's going downstairs. What's she going downstairs for?

DAUGHTER: (*half asleep*) How should I know? Who's going downstairs?

GEORGE: Your mother.

DAUGHTER: Oh. (*Pause.*) What's she going downstairs for?

DAUGHTER suddenly sits bolt upright.

GEORGE & DAUGHTER: Did you hide the eggs?

DAUGHTER: Wait. I hear water running. Oh no.

GEORGE: What?

DAUGHTER: She's putting the dishwasher on.

GEORGE: What!

DAUGHTER: I didn't let her do it today, so she's doing it now.

GEORGE: You didn't tell me about that.

DAUGHTER: No.

OLD WOMAN: (*offstage*) Butchie! Butchie!

SCENE SIXTEEN

Dark room. OLD WOMAN is sitting in the dark, staring straight ahead of her. DAUGHTER and GEORGE walk into room, switch on light to reveal OLD WOMAN, sitting motionless.

DAUGHTER: (*screams*) Christ! She's done it again. Honestly, George, she does that all the time. Just sits alone in the dark.

GEORGE: She's very quiet.

DAUGHTER: Doesn't have her hearing aid in.

GEORGE: Still, she's just staring.

DAUGHTER: Oh, she goes into trances all the time.

GEORGE: Oh.

DAUGHTER & GEORGE start to leave. GEORGE stops, looks back.

Do you think she's dead?

DAUGHTER: No. She's not dead.

GEORGE: How can you tell?

DAUGHTER: I just know, that's all.

GEORGE waves hand in front of OLD WOMAN's face. No response.

GEORGE: I don't know, honey.

DAUGHTER: It's all right, dear. She does this all the time.

GEORGE: She seems dead.

GEORGE snaps fingers in front of OLD WOMAN's face. No response.

DAUGHTER: We'll put a blanket over her and leave her till tomorrow morning.

DAUGHTER & GEORGE put a blanket over the OLD WOMAN.

DAUGHTER: Goodnight, Mother.

GEORGE: Yeah, goodnight Mother.

They turn off the light and leave.

The end.

UNDER THE SKIN

BY

BETTY LAMBERT

l to r
Alana Shields as Maggie, Wendy van Riesen as Renee, Dwight McFee as John

Photographer: Glen Erikson

BETTY LAMBERT'S TRENCHANT SOCIAL CRITICISM: *UNDER THE SKIN*

Although her early forays into writing were in the genres of poetry and the short story (she published her first poem at thirteen and won scholarships to the Banff School of Fine Arts for her short stories at nineteen), Betty Lambert was, as Joel Kaplan put it, "a playwright to her fingertips" (128). Born in Calgary on August 23, 1933, Lambert, by the age of eighteen, was attending the University of British Columbia (UBC) and working as a copywriter for a Vancouver radio station and, by twenty-two, had completed her first play, received a BA, and begun teaching at the newly-opened Simon Fraser University, where she remained for many years. Her first staged work, *The Riddle Machine* (1966), written for children, was performed in Montreal at Expo '67, and many of her plays, including *Grasshopper Hill*, which won the 1980 ACTRA Award for best radio play, were produced by CBC radio and television.

Of the approximately sixty plays Lambert wrote before her untimely death in November of 1983, the most noteworthy fall in the categories of satire or tragedy. Trenchant social criticism informs the comedies *Sqrieux-De-Dieu* (1975), a frequently produced commentary on upper-class Vancouver, and *Clouds of Glory*, set on a thinly disguised Simon Fraser University campus on the eve of the 1970 invocation of the War Measures Act. *Jennie's Story* dramatizes the effects of an Alberta law, in effect from 1928 to 1971, that condoned, without their consent, the sterilization of women deemed to be feeble-minded. A condemnation of church and state, the play is also a moving and poetic examination of what Lambert told Bonnie Worthington was the "major focus" of her plays: "women relating to each other" (62).

Ratsoy: What was your impression of Betty Lambert as a playwright and a person?

Pamela Hawthorn (first director of *Under the Skin*): I thought that she was a very fine playwright. I think that she was just entering the period of her mature work when she died. In the last ten years of her life, which is the working period in which I knew her best, she was quite prolific, and she wasn't showing any signs of not continuing.

Hers was a very intense personality, overwhelmingly so in some ways, and I think that is in the play. She was a committed artist; there's no question about that. And in order to get her to do any work on her material once she thought it was done you had to have all your soldiers in a row.

Ratsoy: How much of Betty Lambert is there in the character of Maggie? They were both professors and single mothers.

Hawthorn: I don't know; I don't want to play amateur psychologist. But the level of intensity, the level of guilt, and the passion – I think those come from who Betty was.

Ratsoy: One of the ways we're viewing this anthology is as a chronicle dating from the period in which BC theatre came into its own. Do you see Lambert as pioneering the field for women in British Columbia?

Hawthorn: You can't leave Gwen Ringwood, as a figure, a mentor, and a writer, out of the picture. Ringwood was ahead of professional theatre. In terms of the burgeoning of professional theatre that started to happen here, yes, I would think that Betty is probably the most significant woman writer of the period.

Lambert's novel, *Crossings*, first published in 1979 and set in BC, shares with her best plays a hard-hitting, no-holds-barred approach. Protagonist Vicky Ferris, a writer, examines the events in her life that have led to her self-destructive behaviour and present-time misalliance with Mik, a violent ex-convict. Unlike *Under the Skin*, *Crossings* eschews linearity and realism: Vicky's recollections aren't chronological and the novel is devoid of such conventions as chapter separations. Aretha Van Herk called *Crossings* "*the* Canadian novel about the growth and development of a woman/writer" (285).

Under the Skin is based on an actual event that took place in British Columbia in 1976 and received media attention again in January of 2001, when the victim, by then a 38-year old mother of five, went public to call attention to a rash of child abductions in the Vancouver area at that time and to persuade the justice system to deny the perpetrator his second parole request. The perpetrator's request was denied on January 20, 2001. Abby Drover, a Port Moody adolescent, spent 181 days locked in an eight-foot square dungeon under a work bench in a garage just three houses away from her home. Her captor, Donald Hay, was a suspect in her disappearance from the beginning, but, despite numerous visits to the garage, police failed to notice the underground room, and Hay's common-law wife neglected to alert them to it. It was only when his wife called police after Hay threatened suicide that they saw him emerge from the room and rescued Abby, who had lost one quarter of her body weight during her ordeal. Although Lambert's play is faithful to the event in many elements, she changed several details: most saliently, Abby's mother was not a professor, she and Hay's wife weren't close friends, and Lambert leaves Emma's fate unclear. These modifications allow Lambert to project herself into the scenario, to focus on the relationship between the two female characters, and to give us an ambiguous resolution. It is also noteworthy that Lambert chose to universalize the event by minimizing references to place names and instead depict a ubiquitous, generic suburb. Clearly, Lambert's purpose here is not documentary rendering.

Both the socialist leanings that Lambert developed in her teen years as a result of her own impoverished youth and the feminism that she began to embrace in her twenties inform *Under the Skin*, the title of which—highlighting the unsettling and uncomfortable—would seem to encapsulate the body of her most memorable writing. Canada's particular class system is scrutinized in Renee's preoccupation with grammar and her inferior education and in John's attitude and actions toward both women. The detailed set descriptions—down to the refrigerator that ejects ice cubes—with which the play opens clearly limn the trappings of a vacuous, materially preoccupied suburbia. Yet money cannot compensate for the abject feelings of inadequacy of the couple, and money keeps Renee in her prison; her denial of reality and acceptance of abuse are perpetrated in large measure by the fear that material insecurity instills in her. Renee is also economically vulnerable because of her motherhood, a situation compounded by the fact that, as she ages, she becomes a less enticing commodity. A rape victim who was also deserted by her first husband for a younger woman, she has assumed such a role of helplessness that she tells Maggie, "I can't make it without a man. I can't, I don't have your chances." In Lambert's microcosm, sexism knows no class: the chair of Maggie's department excuses a student guilty of plagiarism because "She's built like a brick shithouse." Lambert's depiction of John has been faulted by more than one critic. However, although the sole male character is so lacking in redeeming features as to be evil incarnate, the play is not a facile feminist diatribe. The women aren't let off easily: Renee is obviously complicit in her subjugation—even to the point of exhibiting masochistic tendencies—and duplicitous in her relationship with Maggie, and Maggie admits to a physical attraction toward John.

The influence of classical Greek drama is evident on several levels. Like much memorable drama, *Under the Skin* probes the dark side of the psyche in its exploration of evil. The play also provides penetrating insight into the complexities of friendship and relationships, both female-female and female-male, through its examination of one of the most horrendous losses that a human being can suffer. Maggie is certainly her creator's mouthpiece in her implication of the audience with her statement that "That's the basis of most dramatic literature. They love it when Oedipus falls down, you know, they get a secret nasty thrill when they know he's slept with his mother." The play arouses pity and fear, and features a villain and more than one victim; however, there are no clear heroes here, and Lambert eschews cathartic closure, opting instead for an ending that can be perceived of as disturbing as the rest of the play.

Part of the play's effectiveness lies in its understatement. Its chronological, realistic unfolding, coupled with the fact that there is very little on-stage physical violence, accentuates its psychological impact. *Under the Skin* is more a drama of ideas than of action. That the last two scenes take place on Halloween underscores the macabre circumstances played out, first, eerily near the dungeon and, finally, in the banal setting of the kitchen. Maggie's observation about the occasion ("All Saints' Eve. How we make the horrible ordinary. How we transform it, make it comic and cuddly. Human beings!") is especially relevant to the preceding scene, in which John attempts to rationalize his actions through reference to Dostoyevsky, the Bible, and Anne Frank. Equally chilling, given her new-found awareness, are Renee's automatic performance of routine duties such as sending the children out for the evening and the fact that she leads up to the revelation about Emma's capture by engaging Maggie in a conversation about innate individual selfishness.

Betty Lambert completed what was to have been a draft of *Under the Skin* less than two months before her death from lung cancer. According to Pamela Hawthorn, only a few minor changes were made to that draft for the initial production, and it is the production draft that is the published form of the play with which we are left. A complex study of multiple and multi-level abuse, a relentless scrutiny of patriarchy, class, friendship, sexuality, and the distortion of knowledge, *Under the Skin* has also been produced by Upstart Crow Theatre in both New York City and Hollywood, and by Toronto's Theatre Passe Muraille and Alumnae Theatre.

Ratsoy: After Lambert's death, you held the draft of *Under the Skin* for eighteen months before you decided to produce it. Why was there a delay, and what finally prompted you to produce it?

Hawthorn: I think her death is the answer to both of those questions. The whole mandate of the New Play Centre was to work with the playwrights on their material and produce their plays, and Betty was gone, so the idea of having a working playwright at your side was not possible. So that is why we sat on it as long as we did.

I think we produced it in the end for exactly the same reason: the fact that it was her last play and, although in my opinion a slightly unfinished play, in the end we decided that it should be done and we were the people most likely to do it.

Ratsoy: What stands out for you about the responses of the audience, cast, and crew when it was finally produced?

Hawthorn: It is a play that really affected the people who saw it in the original production. I guess the best word I can think of is "harrowing"; I think it was a harrowing experience for the audience, even though the play in one sense ended on an upward note.

Certainly for the three actors, the stage manager and myself—the five of us who lived together putting it together—it was a harrowing experience. I've directed an awful lot of plays in my life, and it was one of the very few that I took home every night and couldn't shake off, which for me, as a personality, was quite strange. But that was true for the three actors involved, too: it was a very absorbing and all-consuming kind of experience for all of us because it was so intense.

The power of *Under the Skin* is evoked in the responses of two critics to the Theatre Passe Muraille production. Vit Wagner wrote, "To understand the quality of tension created in Betty Lambert's disturbing play, *Under the Skin*, imagine the sensation of a rope tightening around your head at such a gradual rate that you hardly notice discomfort giving way to pain," and Mark Czarnecki called the play "an enduring cry of pain, a despairing judgment of humanity at its most tormented and malevolent" and commended Lambert for "transform[ing]what might otherwise be categorized as an isolated, demented crime into a savage portrait of the demonic forces at work beneath the surface of all human relationships."

Ratsoy: As a veteran of the British Columbia theatre scene, who, among other things, worked for almost nineteen years as Artistic/Managing Director of the New Play Centre, you are eminently qualified to address the question of whether there is a distinct British Columbia drama.

Hawthorn: My answer to that has always been, "No, I don't think there is." But now I will shade that and say that maybe its uniqueness is in the vast individuality of the people who have called this province home and who have written plays here. I mean, if you go from Sherman Snukal's *Talking Dirty* to Betty Lambert's *Under the Skin* you've got quite a stretch there.

G.R.

Selected Bibliography:

- Czarnecki, Mark. "Tragic Emotions Crawl Under the Skin." *Metropolis* 19 Jan. 1989.
- Dykk, Lloyd. "Social not-so-niceties." *Vancouver Sun* 7 Nov. 1985.
- Hawthorn, Pamela. "Introduction." *Jennie's Story* and *Under the Skin*. By Betty Lambert. Toronto: Playwrights Canada Press, 1987. 8-10.
- Hawthorn, Pamela. Telephone Interview. 16 Jan. 2001.
- Kaplan, Joel H. "Radio Active." *Canadian Literature* 110 (Fall 1986): 127-128.
- Lambert, Betty. *Crossings*. Vancouver: Douglas & McIntyre, 1989.
- Lambert, Betty. "Guilt." *Baker's Dozen: Stories by Women*. Ed. The Fictive Collective. Toronto: The Women's Press. 1984. 13-40.
- "Man Who Raped, Held Girl Captive Denied Parole." *Kamloops Daily News* 20 Jan. 2001.
- Moore, Kerry. " 'Obsessions' Used to Effect." *Vancouver Province* 7 Nov. 1985.
- Musgrove, Paul. " Rescued from Dungeon." *Vancouver Sun* 7 Sept. 1975.
- Nunn, Robert. "Review of *Jennie's Story* and *Under the Skin*." *Canadian Theatre Review* 60 (Fall 1989): 89-90.
- Stone-Blackburn, Susan. "Recent Plays on Women's Playwriting." *Essays in Theatre* 14.1 (Nov. 1995): 31-35.
- Twigg, Alan. *Vancouver and Its Writers: A Guide to Vancouver's Literary Landmarks*. Madiera Park, BC: Harbour, 1986.
- Van Herk, Aritha. "Double Crossings: Booking the Lover." *Amazing Space: Writing Canadian Women Writing*. Ed. Shirley Newman and Smaro Kamboureli. Edmonton: NeWest Press, 1986. 276-286. Van Herk examines violence as a narrative strategy in *Crossings*.
- Wagner, Vit. "Play's Subtle Reality Creeps Under the Skin." *The Toronto Star* 15 Jan. 1989.
- Wasserman, Jerry. "Underground: Review of *Jennie's Story* and *Under the Skin*." *Canadian Literature* 126 (Fall 1990): 172-3.
- Worthington, Bonnie. "Battling Aristotle: A Conversation Between Playwright Betty Lambert and Director Bonnie Worthington." *Room of One's Own* 8 (1983): 54-66.

Under the Skin
by Betty Lambert

Under the Skin was first produced by the New Play Centre at the Waterfront Theatre, Vancouver, B.C., in November, 1985, with the following cast:

Maggie Benton	Alana Shields
Renee Gifford	Wendy van Riesen
John Gifford	Dwight McFee

Directed by Pamela Hawthorn
Set Designed by Paul Ford
Stage Managed by Bill Leblanc

CHARACTERS

Maggie Benton: An assistant professor at the nearby university. Divorced. Comfortably off. Mother of Emma. Comes from secure class, and is initially unaware of Renee's fears and envies.

Renee Gifford: Pronounced Reenee. 36, thin, too made-up, too consciously feminine. Wracked with self-doubt. Sensual. Took an evening course but does not have a degree. Presently married to John. Her first husband, Nick, left her for someone younger; her children are Joanie, 9, and Dougie, 11.

John Gifford: About 40, good-looking in a squarish way – that is, he's square-set, not fat. Wears glasses. Looks something like the Reverend Jimmy Swaggart – has some of the same physical movements and the same intense self-absorption.

SETTING

We open on a set that is only partly revealed. It is the kitchen of the Gifford family. It is middle class and affluent. We see it from the vantage point of the workshop, which is down the hill. We see a patio on stilts, sliding glass doors that lead into the kitchen. A door leads offstage to a hallway, and upstairs, and to the front door.
The kitchen has all the latest equipment: a microwave, a waist-high oven, matching fridge, cuisinaire set, dishwasher. The cupboards and table and chairs are wooden, and finished with verithane. There is a degree of familiar clutter – Joanie and Dougie have put up their drawings on the fridge with magnetic buttons or ladybugs. The fridge ejects ice cubes. Things are clean but just a touch off – there's a kind of embarrassing tastelessness. There are, for instance, no pottery objects, such as Maggie would have – everything has a sort of Woolworth's glaze finish. Things are a bit too bright and shiny. The canister set is labelled, for example: coffee, tea, sugar, flour, and so on. A kitchen that tries too hard but doesn't quite make it. A bit like Renee herself.

TIME

181 days, from Spring to Fall.

SCENE ONE

From the kitchen people can see the sound, the greys and blues of a spring morning, the bright thin light of a morning of terror.

MAGGIE: (*sits at table*) So then he said, "Well, Mrs. Benton, we don't have unlimited manpower." I said, "Look, I called up yesterday and they told me she was off the computer printout." My god, the incompetence! I told him, I said, "Look, I phoned yesterday and she wasn't on the computer printout."

RENEE is making tea. She reaches up for cups and saucers from her built-in china cabinet. All the cups and saucers are single patterns – they don't match. They are displayed proudly through glass. There are also china knickknacks in the cabinet, and a wine decanter in the shape of a Mexican, a souvenir of her honeymoon.

You always look so – finished... in the morning. My god, I don't think I've showered for two days. (*smells herself*) Shh! Yech! "She was off the computer printout," I said.

RENEE: What did he say?

MAGGIE stares ahead of her. She is in a state of frenzy, trying to wrestle the world to her will. She is full of outrage, furious with the police, but beneath the outrage and the apparent grasp of the situation, she is living in terror. Occasionally she slips into that terror.

MAGGIE: He said... they didn't have unlimited manpower... he said they'd put her back on the printout.

RENEE: Well, so did you check yet to see if she's on it today?

MAGGIE: No. I didn't check it yet.

RENEE gives MAGGIE her tea. Goes to the wall phone. Listens to see if JOHN is on the phone in the workshop. Dials from a number written on a cute memo square, plastic, beside the phone. She checks one of the many hanging pots for wetness of soil as she waits.

RENEE: Have you heard from Graham again?

MAGGIE: No. I should go home in case he calls.

RENEE: Have your tea. I think you should eat – Hello? Yes, this is Mrs. Gifford, Mrs. John Gifford? I'm a neighbour of Mrs. Benton's? Yes. Yes. Apparently yesterday's printout of missing children did not contain Emma's name. I just wanted to make sure Emma's name is on today's printout. Yes, yes, I'll hold. They're checking.

MAGGIE: I can't believe the incompetence. I cannot believe the sheer incompetence. *(picks up stale old toast from a plate beside her and eats it)* I said, "Who is your superior?" You know what he did? He sighed. He sighed. He said, "Look, Mrs. Benton, we don't have unlimited manpower," and he sighed as if I were boring him. *(laughs)*

RENEE: Yes? Oh it is? Okay, thank you very much. You can understand how she feels. Yes, okay, yes. Thank you. Yes I will. *(hangs up)* He said would I keep an eye on you and I said I would.

MAGGIE: And when they were looking yesterday, they were making jokes. Didn't John say that when they were out in the bush they were making jokes about it?

RENEE: Not about that. Just jokes. People do that. To keep up their spirits.

MAGGIE: John said though, they were laughing. *(eats another piece of toast absently)*

RENEE: Let me make you some, fresh.

MAGGIE: No, I'm not hungry, I can't eat.

RENEE: *(annoyed)* They've done all they could, Maggie. John himself has been out every day. You've got good friends.

MAGGIE: Yes, I know. *(furious)* Why shouldn't they look? If it was their kid, I'd look. I'm not grateful, why should I be grateful? It's only what's human.

RENEE: They don't even know you, you're new here.

MAGGIE: I'm human, they owe me that, they owe Emma that, to look. Fuck them. I've been here four years!

RENEE: That's new to them. They've been out for a week, and she's probably just off with some guy she picked up with.

MAGGIE: What? Jesus Christ, Renee.

RENEE: I don't think you're in any position to take the name of the Lord in vain.

MAGGIE: "Some guy she picked up with"?

RENEE: You live in a dream world. Things like that happen.

MAGGIE: Not to people like us.

RENEE: Yes, to people like you, who says you're safe? Why should you be safe?

MAGGIE: We're talking about Emma, remember Emma? Emma with the big crush on the Holy Ghost? Emma whose big Bible was Anne Frank... (*hands over heart*) "I truly believe that everybody has some good in them" or crap like that while some SS was fucking her.... Oh Jesus! No, she'd phone me, if she met someone and she was off with him she'd phone me, say she had to save him or some shit, she'd phone me. Oh god. Oh god. She would have phoned me.

RENEE: You're blind about that girl. You're blind, she was asking for it. (*staring out front, towards the workshop*) The way she carries on, with John.

MAGGIE: She misses Graham.

RENEE: All right, I won't say anything. You're too upset right now. But you see, she'll phone from San Francisco, she'll ask for a ticket to fly home.

MAGGIE: I know I'm a burden to you.

RENEE: Oh god, it's been a terrible week, let me make you some food. Our nerves are all ragged. That's all. That's all it is. I had a bad night.

MAGGIE: I'll go home in a minute. I'll go home. I've got to take a shower. No, I don't want anything. Please don't make me anything. You've been good friends to me, I know I should feel grateful, I'm sorry I can't feel grateful, I think you should be good friends.

RENEE: (*staring out*) If it were Joanie I'd be mad.

MAGGIE: Yes, I thought I'd go mad at first. Isn't it funny.

RENEE: I said to Emma that time, I said, "Emma, for god's sake, you've got to use a feminine deodorant now you're menstruating because men can smell it."

MAGGIE: I've never in my life had to ask for favours. The police treat me as if I'm boring, a boring mother. I said, "Who is your superior?" and he sighed.

RENEE: And she should have worn a brassiere, just for practical reasons, your breasts start to sag and Emma was full-bosomed for her age.

MAGGIE: Don't do that.

RENEE: You need to eat. You've been picking at Joanie's leftovers.

MAGGIE: Do me a fucking favour and stop using the fucking past tense. Sorry. And I don't want eggs, for christ's sake, Renee, just let up on me, I don't wear a brassiere either, for christ's sake.

RENEE: You're swearing all the time now.

MAGGIE: I know. It's an alternative to screaming continuously.

RENEE: You were into a symbiotic relationship.

MAGGIE: (*laughs*) What's symbiosis anyway, I thought it was something to do with moss.

RENEE: Symbiosis is when you get so dependent on someone you can't live without them.

MAGGIE: I thought it had something to do with fungus. I thought the fungus lived off the tree and the tree got something from the fungus, and they were both better off.

RENEE: What would a tree get from a fungus?

MAGGIE: He sighed. He just gave this big sigh as if I were phoning about someone's dog peeing on my lawn.

RENEE has been boiling an egg and toasting bread. Getting it ready, cutting the toast into strips.

RENEE: John says he'd bet anything that Emma's just gone off with some guy.

MAGGIE: (*as RENEE serves it to her*) Why do you keep saying that? Emma's never in her life done anything remotely like that. My mother made egg toast that way. (*begins to eat* *hungrily*) I know I'm horrible, I know I'm ungrateful, I can't stand myself either. Yeah, Mom made them just like this, I'm glad she's dead, she'd die. (*laughs*) It'd kill her. (*laughs*) I didn't even want an egg.

RENEE: You may not have noticed, but Emma's growing up.

MAGGIE: She's only 12...

RENEE: She'll be 13 on Wednesday.

MAGGIE: (*overcome with terror, clutches herself*) Oh my god, oh my god.

RENEE comes over to hug her.

No, don't touch me, I can't stand it if anyone touches me, I'll go to pieces, don't.

RENEE, behind MAGGIE, draws back in disgust.

She's dead. She's dead.

RENEE: Don't be silly.

MAGGIE: That's what he said to me, that officer, "Mrs. Benton, you must prepare yourself for the worst." (*laughs*) How the fuck do you prepare yourself for the worst. I can't bear it.

RENEE: You've made that girl too much in your life.

MAGGIE is breathing hard.

Children leave us all some day.

MAGGIE: Not like this they don't.

RENEE: Well, at least you've eaten something. (*takes plate away from MAGGIE*)

MAGGIE: I didn't even think I was hungry.

RENEE: Sometimes I think it'll be nice when the kids go and John 'n' I are alone. John 'n' me, I mean.

MAGGIE: (*absently*) No, you were right the first time, it's John and I.

RENEE: Last time you said it was John and me.

MAGGIE: That's 'cause it was in the objective case, you said something something with John and I, and that should be John and me. A lot of people do that, they get upset about their fucking usage and over correct, like saying I feel badly.

RENEE: I thought that was right, I feel badly.

MAGGIE: No, it's I feel bad. Who gives a shit.

RENEE: Well I do, I don't want to sound like an illiterate.

MAGGIE: Christ, even my chairman says I feel badly. "Maggie, I can't tell you how badly I feel."

RENEE: (*putting dishes in washer*) Did I tell you how Dougie busted in on us last Sunday morning? (*laughs*) God! I was sure I'd hooked the door. I have this routine, go to the bathroom, put in my diaphragm, hook the door...

MAGGIE: They said she was on the computer printout, eh?

RENEE: I told you.

MAGGIE: I better go, Graham could phone.

RENEE: You'll have to go back to work, it's no use just waiting around the house, it's better to have a routine, it gives you something to hold on to.

MAGGIE: I know people have been good, I am grateful. (*tearful*) People have been really good. It's just the police seem so blasé... I said to that young one, the one who came the first night, "You never think this sort of thing will happen to you," and he just looked away as if I'd said something... disgusting. That's the thing, they make you feel so disgusting.

RENEE: When Nick and I broke up, Nick and me, I said, No way the kids're gointa be my life, I went out with John three months before I ever told him I had kids.

MAGGIE: (*flaring*) Why should I be made to feel disgusting! Fuck them!

RENEE: You better hold it down when John comes in, he can't stand a woman with a mouth, we'd go to his place, and I'd say I had to be home because all my stuff for work was there, in a way though it worked out, he got really jealous, thought I was married and had to get back to my old man. (laughs)

MAGGIE sits and stares.

Well, I've been lucky I guess.

MAGGIE: Sometimes I think just come and tell me she's dead. That way I know she's not suffering.

RENEE: Why do you keep on about that? Why should she be suffering? Kids run away... it's common knowledge kids run away with men... time means nothing to them... she's off with some guy... she isn't even thinking of you.

JOHN Gifford comes in through sliding doors. Goes to MAGGIE, embraces her. MAGGIE starts to cry. Holds onto his arm awkwardly.

JOHN: There there. There there. We're doing all we can.

RENEE looks on impassively.

She'll be found, she'll be found, Maggie, I know it. I feel it.

RENEE: (*neutral voice*) I've got your breakfast ready, it's in the oven. Juice?

JOHN, hugging MAGGIE, rocks her back and forth, kisses her hair. MAGGIE, head thrown back, gives herself to this comfort. JOHN looks down at MAGGIE's thrown back face. Moment of stillness. He bends down and kisses her full on the lips. RENEE turns abruptly and opens oven door. Puts on mitt. Reaches in for plate of pancakes and bacon. Places them on the table. JOHN now moves toward RENEE to kiss her on the lips. RENEE avoids him. Goes to fridge for juice. JOHN pulls her around firmly, smiles at her, kisses her on the lips.

JOHN: Good morning, Renee.

RENEE: (*looks at him*) Little early for it, isn't it?

JOHN: Hmmm. Think so?

RENEE: What's gotten into you?

JOHN: What's gotten into you lately? (*laughs; starts to eat with appetite*) I picked up the Fraser kids this morning. Hitch-hiking. Not a care in the world. Right out there. I stopped the van and told them to get in... I said, "You kids haven't heard about Emma Benton?" They won't hitch again in a hurry. Pass the syrup, would you?

RENEE: Oh those Fraser kids, they do what they want irregardless. I've told Joanie not to bring the girl over here anymore. Who needs it.

JOHN stares at the cupboard under the sink which RENEE has opened to get some cleanser.

JOHN: When are you going to clean that cupboard under the sink? God it bothers me... all that crud... you are really a scumbag housekeeper, Renee... my mother used to say, Look in a woman's cupboards if you want to know how she keeps herself.

RENEE: Oh your mother–

JOHN: Keep off my mother. (*mild*) Any coffee?

RENEE: (*pouring coffee*) Her cupboards are clean, oh yes, compensation...

JOHN: Quit that phony baloney crap. It's *regardless*.

RENEE: Pure compensation, over-compensation...

JOHN: My mother was a clean woman.

RENEE: Well, she's not so clean now.

JOHN: It's *regardless* not *irregardless*, ask the college professor here.

RENEE: (*sing-songy*) She's rotten... rotten... she is rotten... and the worms are crawling in her eyes...

MAGGIE gives a high laugh.

Sorry.

JOHN: You're sick.

RENEE: Sorry, Maggie, I didn't think...

MAGGIE: I should go.

JOHN: Give her a brandy.

RENEE goes toward the liquor cupboard.

MAGGIE: I should be home in case the police call. And Graham said he'd call.

RENEE pours the brandy into an ordinary glass, puts it in front of MAGGIE.

No, if I drink I won't be any good for the rest of the day.

JOHN: Maggie? I'm going to say something for your own good. Drink up. (*waits until she raises the glass to her lips*) Go back to work.

MAGGIE: I can't.

JOHN: You can.

MAGGIE: No. You don't know. They're so beautiful. You walk into a lecture room and there they are, so young and so beautiful and so full of life. All that joy. All that life.

RENEE: All the sex. 18-year-olds are nothing but walking bags of hormones.

MAGGIE: Yes. All that, yes, sensuality, that sheer joy at being alive and being able to move and laugh and sing. (*drinks*) I look at them sometimes and their sheer... beauty overwhelms me. The skin, pimples and all... it just radiates. Sometimes I come out of a lecture so high... just on them, the way they are. And every year they stay the same age and only I get older. I would see them all go up in flames in the fiery furnace, just to have her back. I would see them torn to pieces. I would see the world go mad. I would bring down the sky.

RENEE: You think I wouldn't. For Joanie and Dougie? You think I don't love them like that?

MAGGIE: I could kill.

RENEE: She's just off with some hulk. You didn't see her, she was always rubbing up against John.

JOHN: Keep your mouth off Emma. I'm telling you. (*to MAGGIE*) We're all just upset and worried.

MAGGIE: (*gets up*) Thank god for good friends, I do really... I mean to feel grateful... I will... it's just right now...

JOHN: 'sallright, no need to say a word. Anytime, Maggie, I'm here. (*walks her to sliding doors, arm around her shoulder*) Try to get some rest. And think about it, going back, work's the only salvation, it's an old clinker but it's true.

MAGGIE: Yes.

MAGGIE comes through the doors, onto patio, walks down steps and exits. JOHN watches her go. His gaze rests on the workshop. Turns and goes back into kitchen.

JOHN: Joanie's been mucking about with my things again, will you tell her to leave my stuff alone.

RENEE: She only borrowed a hammer.

JOHN: She put it back in the wrong place. I have everything exactly where I want it, everything has a place...

RENEE: Just to put a poster up, in her room.

JOHN: Are you listening to me? I don't think you're listening to me. I don't care what Joanie wanted the hammer for. She could have crucified the next door neighbour's cat for all I care. Does that penetrate your brain at all? I don't care what the hammer was used for. I do not like your brat using my things.

RENEE: Oh my, what a gruffy bear this morning. What a gruffy bear. Ooooh oh, he has the grumps this morning, he has, he has, oh my what a big Eeyore bear this morning.

JOHN: (*looking out the sliding doors*) You know what she said one day? (*short laugh*) She said "My mom's going to take me to get birth control when I'm sexually active." (*laughs*)

RENEE: What?

JOHN: Are you deaf?

RENEE: Who said that.

JOHN: Emma.

RENEE: Maggie was asking for trouble. That's all. Just asking for it.

JOHN: "Sexually active"!

RENEE: Maggie was always too free with that girl.

JOHN: Why don't you shut up.

RENEE: Grumpy bear this morning, grumpy bear.

JOHN: Just keep your brats out of my workshop. Oh yes, she said that, for all her big religious talk. "My mom's going to take me to get birth control when I'm sexually active." I said to her, Emma, you've got a big surprise waiting for you, the world isn't like that, everybody nice and good, the world is just waiting for people like you, everybody's out for number one.

RENEE: Oh kids get religious at that age. I wanted to be a nun when I was 13–

JOHN: I don't want to hear about how you wanted to be a nun. I've heard that story a thousand times. That is completely irrelevant. What are you trying to prove? Can't you keep your mind on the subject for two minutes?

RENEE: I was only saying that kids are often religious at that age, Emma was no different, it was just a phase...

JOHN: And you keep your mouth off Emma Do you hear me? You keep your filthy mouth off Emma. She's not like you, you're a born whore, do you hear me? Renee? Do you hear me? Do you understand me? Renee?

RENEE: Yes.

JOHN stares at her. RENEE turns and starts to put dishes in the washer. JOHN gets up, moves toward her, stands behind her.

I've got work to do.

JOHN pulls up her skirt and moves in to her, pushing her down over the washer.

Go to black.

SCENE TWO

The darkened kitchen. Late spring. A figure against the sliding doors, pounds on the jamb. The figure pounds again.

MAGGIE: (*calls*) Renee? Renee? Renee!

RENEE appears as a silhouette in the kitchen doorway, turns on the patio lights, recognizes—after a brief hesitation—MAGGIE. Goes to the sliding doors and opens them.

RENEE: What is it, what's happened?

MAGGIE: I heard her.

RENEE: What?

MAGGIE: I heard her, heard her crying out to me. I heard her calling me. "Momma, Momma." Somebody's hurting her.

RENEE: It was a dream.

MAGGIE: No. I wasn't asleep.

RENEE: You were asleep.

MAGGIE sits down at the table. She is disheveled, in an old robe.

I'll get you a drink. (*does so*)

MAGGIE: I heard her.

RENEE: It was only a dream. (*stares out at the workshop*)

MAGGIE: It was real, I could hear her. (*shaking*)

RENEE gives her the drink.

(*holding it*) Today one of my students came to see me. She wanted to complain against one of my TA's. He's not marking the essays. He's just giving grades. No comments. I said I'd mark it. That's the son of a bitch who faked his footnotes. (*brief laugh*)

RENEE: It's good you're back at work.

MAGGIE: Other people's children. I hate them. (*drinks*) I hate them for being alive and well.

RENEE: No, it's good for you to be back at work.

MAGGIE: People keep saying that to me. It's good I'm back at work. Whatshisname across the hall, he said, "You must have a steel trap for a mind." (*laughs*)

RENEE: You've got to think of yourself.

MAGGIE: Why is that?

RENEE sighs. MAGGIE gulps the drink, looks at RENEE.

Such a sigh. Why such a sigh? Am I disturbing you?

RENEE: Well, you make me... well, impatient. It's been two months.

MAGGIE: God yes, it's been two months, at least! I should be well over it by now.

RENEE sighs. MAGGIE puts down her drink; gets up.

Yes. You're right. It's boring. I should be able to handle it myself. (*starts for the sliding doors*)

RENEE: No. Don't go.

MAGGIE: (*pauses*) Were you asleep?

RENEE: No. No.

MAGGIE: Everything's so clean. For once in my life the house is completely organized. No mess at all.

RENEE: Life goes on.

MAGGIE: I feel I should be screaming down the street. I feel I should be tearing the world apart. The cherry blossoms're out. Everything's alive. I should pass and the grass should wither. (*laughs*) Everything hurts my eyes.

RENEE: Life goes on.

MAGGIE: (*laughs*) That's what's so unfair.

RENEE: I've never been one to brood. When Nick and I broke up, I said, That's that and I let him go. I went out and I met new men and I met John and I said Nick's over and done with. I opened my fingers and I let him go. I've shed enough tears for that bastard, I said. You're young, you're still attractive.

MAGGIE: Who are we talking about, what are we talking about, a child isn't a man, you can always get another *man*.

RENEE: You've had an education. You're independent. I never had the opportunities you've had, if something happened to John we'd be done for...

MAGGIE: Oh Renee, it's not the same–

RENEE: What do you know about it? What the christly hell... do you know about it. You've never had to struggle.

MAGGIE: I'd take a child over a man anytime, a man you can get anywhere, a child is... a child... you give birth to a child... what the fuck are we talking about... I put myself through university, it wasn't any free ride let me tell you...

RENEE: ...you've had it all given to you, how much did that chesterfield cost? And you didn't even think twice, you didn't even wait till the sales... you just bought it... saw it and bought it... you saw it and you wanted it... do you know how long it took me to get a kitchen like this? I was raped once you know.

MAGGIE: You never told me that.

RENEE: I don't tell you everything.

MAGGIE: What did you do about it?

RENEE: What could I do? I'd known him, we'd been to bed together, Nick was working nightshift then, and I started this thing with David. Then we broke up. One night he came to our place and he beat me up and raped me. I didn't dare scream because of the baby. That was Dougie. I was afraid to tell Nick. I couldn't tell Nick, how could I tell Nick? He'd have said I let him in on purpose. Well, I did let him in, he knocked on the door and I thought, Oh, it's just David and I let him in, you wouldn't think to look at him... I didn't get my period for three months, I was terrified I was pregnant. If I was pregnant I'd have had to tell Nick, he'd have had to sign the form, wouldn't he? And then I'd have had to tell him and he'd say I let David in, I asked for it.

MAGGIE: It's a nightmare. The whole world is a nightmare.

RENEE: But life goes on, you forget.

MAGGIE: Life goes on and on and on, and it has no business going on. –I could hear her crying out for me. Sometimes I think my ears are just dead to the sounds in the air. That the air, the real air, is alive with screams of pain and terror. The abattoir across the inlet. The screams of dying fish on hooks. All the suffering of the forest. And the deep deep sea. And that what I do, what we all do, is learn to close our ears to the real noise of the night.

RENEE: Shut up.

MAGGIE looks at her, astonished.

Just – shut – up.

MAGGIE: What is it? Renee? What is it?

MAGGIE gets up slowly. Holding her breath, crosses to RENEE. Takes her by the shoulders and shakes her once.

What is it?

RENEE: She's dead. Emma's dead. Face it. Emma's dead.

MAGGIE stares at RENEE and then howls. RENEE caught by her pain and by real affection and empathy, clasps her and rocks her, crying as well, rocking back and forth.

I know, I know, oh god, oh dear god, it's not true. It's not true.

JOHN enters through the sliding doors. He stands there, his back to us. The women look at him.

Go to black.

SCENE SIX

Mid-summer. On the patio. Deck chairs, table, umbrella shade, flowers in baskets and pots. MAGGIE and RENEE in summer clothes, drinking tall drinks. RENEE looks very good in shorts and top. MAGGIE is slumped in rumpled jeans and T-shirt. JOHN comes up from the garden, bare to the waist, in jeans.

JOHN: Whew! (*takes drink from RENEE and downs it*)

RENEE: (*archly*) Oh my, what a greedy bear, oh there he goes, stealing my honey! (*laughs at him*)

JOHN: Get me a drink.

RENEE: Oh no please... no please today... oh he hates to do the garden... he hates the sunshine... he hates nature... what a gruffy bear...

JOHN: Get me a drink, Renee, do I have to send you a telegram? Can you get it through your head I might be thirsty?

RENEE: My lord and master. Yes, sire. You command and I obey.

She gets up and archly wiggles herself in slave-like obeisance in front of him. Raises her hands and palms them prayerfully.

JOHN: Move! (*pulls up chair and sits down*)

RENEE: God, sometimes I could kill you. (*goes into kitchen through sliding doors*)

JOHN looks at MAGGIE. MAGGIE stares ahead of her. Drinks.

JOHN: You look like shit, Maggie. I'm telling you for your own good. You look like shit. Fix yourself up, for chrissake. When you going back to work?

MAGGIE: It's my research semester.

JOHN: So do some research.

MAGGIE: Get off my back, John.

JOHN: Forget it, forget her. She's off with some asshole, she's having the time of her life, she's not thinking about you, you'll get a phone call from Timbuctoo, bail me out, Mom...

MAGGIE: No. Not Emma. She wasn't like that.

JOHN: She was like that. She was like that. She was always out in the workshop, rubbing up against me. Oh it's natural, I guess, and she missed her dad. But she was asking for it, rubbing up against me. You know what she said one day, she said, "My mom's going to get me birth control pills when I'm sexually active." Sexually active!

MAGGIE: You think that was wrong.

JOHN: Was that true then? Did you actually say something like that? To a 12-year-old? Boy. Maggie. Shit.

MAGGIE: What're you going to tell Joanie?

JOHN: Joanie? What have I got to do with Joanie? She's not my kid. That's Renee's business.

MAGGIE: She's your kid now.

JOHN: (*suddenly enraged*) Joanie has nothing to do with me. I am nothing to her. We're not related.

MAGGIE: I'm sorry, I didn't mean anything.

JOHN: I didn't even know she *had* kids. Asked her to marry me, and then I find out. Shit.

MAGGIE: Well, you're her stepfather now.

JOHN: I never bargained for her brats. She pulled a fast one on me there.

RENEE: (*comes out with a drink for JOHN*) There you are oh Lord and Master. I told Maggie she has to get out of the house, all she does is sit and watch TV. (*sits down and drinks*) That's all I *can* do as a matter of fact. Can you believe it, Maggie, this old cheapskate won't even fix our TV. I've been after him for three weeks now. All it needs is for him to take it into Jenkins', but will he make the effort... nooooooh. (*drinks*)

JOHN: It's summer, what d'ya need TV for in the summer?

RENEE: Well, I like it at nights, when you're working.

JOHN: I've had the cable turned off anyway.

RENEE: You've what? You've what, John?

JOHN: The TV's busted, I had them turn off the cable for the summer.

RENEE: Aw John, aw John, aw. I *like* my TV.

JOHN: You like your fuckin' soaps.

RENEE: Oh what a gruffy bear he is this morning, oh my what a gruffy bear!

JOHN: Listen, I want you to tell Dougie to keep outa the workshop.

RENEE: Oh my, what a gruffy bear, what's the poor kid done now?

JOHN: He's been messing with my paint.

RENEE: Well, he was doing this sign for the circus. (*to MAGGIE*) You know, the kids're so cute, they got this circus going and Dougie was supposed to be the clown and he wanted to make this sign... a dime to get in...

JOHN: He moved my things. I have a place for everything and everything has a place.

RENEE: And Susie, from across the road? She's supposed to be the trapeze artist...

JOHN: Just keep your brats outa my workshop. Do you hear me, cunt?

RENEE: (*looks at MAGGIE quickly, laughs uneasily*) There's no need to talk to me like that. Not in front of Maggie.

JOHN: Maggie knows you're a cunt. Listen, Maggie? You know the other day, when you were talking to the police again? (*laughs*) And you said we live in the *cul de sac* off the highway? You know what Renee did after you left? She looked it up in the dictionary, only she didn't know how to spell it.

RENEE: I was telling Maggie, she'll turn up... she's just off with some guy... if it was anything else, we'd have heard. No news is good news, you've got to keep hoping.

MAGGIE: Emma wasn't like that.

RENEE: Mothers're the last ones, Maggie, she was always at John, rubbing up against him, wasn't she, John, you tell her...

MAGGIE: She was on this big religious kick. She was always quoting those last lines from Anne Frank at me, what are they... oh Jesus... "because in spite of everything... I still believe... (*choking*) ...that fucking people are really good at heart."

JOHN: Yeah but those aren't the last lines in the book.

MAGGIE: Yes, the last lines in that book, she was a little girl who hid out from the Nazis, in Holland, only they found her, and she kept this diary...

JOHN: I know the book you're talking about, Maggie, just because I'm married to a cunt doesn't mean I'm a cunt. I know the book and I'm telling you, those aren't the last lines in the book.

MAGGIE: Well, they're the last lines in the movie or something. Who gives a shit.

RENEE: I was on a religious kick when I was that age... it's sublimation...

JOHN: It's what?

RENEE: Sublimation.

JOHN: What's sublimation?

RENEE: Oh John, you know what sublimation is. (*laughs and looks at MAGGIE*)

JOHN: No I'm just an ignorant guy, Renee, I never went to no college course in psychology at night school.

RENEE: Well, sublimation is when you put your sex into something else...

JOHN: Oh, is that what that is.

JOHN throws a glance at MAGGIE who smiles weakly.

RENEE: Oh John, don't be such a bully...

JOHN: Me? I'm just trying to get an education, you know what it's like, living down the street from a college professor, I mean she just about pukes when she hears you going on sometimes, Renee, don't you know that?

MAGGIE: That's not true, John...

JOHN: She's laughing at you, for chrissake, Renee, don't you know that, you cunt?

Silence. MAGGIE starts to get up. JOHN pulls her down roughly.

Sit. Sit. Jesus. It's hot, it's just the heat and if it's not the heat it's the humidity.

JOHN laughs. RENEE and MAGGIE do not laugh.

MAGGIE: I'm not laughing at her.

JOHN: She makes you throw up, Maggie. She makes me throw up.

RENEE gets up abruptly and goes inside. MAGGIE twirls her glass around. Reaches into her pocket and takes out a cigarette package.

You want to kill yourself?

MAGGIE: Why do you do that? Why do you talk to her like that.

JOHN: She's illiterate.

MAGGIE: Oh for crying out loud. (*lights up*)

JOHN: You want cancer?

MAGGIE: What're you trying for, John, the Archie Bunker lookalike prize?

JOHN: That's how you see me, isn't it, a redneck bastard.

MAGGIE: You're the one with the hangup about class, John.

JOHN: Oh yeah? Listen, I see you, every time she drops some clanger, you wince, I see it.

MAGGIE: No you don't.

JOHN: I see you. When you first moved in, I saw you, this big polite act...

MAGGIE: Renee's my friend, she's been good to me, if it hadn't been for Renee these last months I would have gone insane.

JOHN: You looked at us like we were bugs... you looked at those plaques Renee's got in the kitchen like they was shit...

MAGGIE: They're just not my kind of thing.

JOHN: Oh. "Not your kind of thing," eh?

MAGGIE: No. People have different tastes, John.

JOHN: Your kind of thing is some old pot made by some hippie down in White Rock. Right?

MAGGIE: Right.

JOHN: You don't like me much, do you? Truth now, Maggie. Truth time.

MAGGIE: (*drinks, looks at him, smokes*) No.

JOHN: (*laughs*) But I turn you on, don't I?

MAGGIE: Yes.

JOHN: Yes. But you hate my guts.

MAGGIE: You're not important enough to hate, John. I merely despise your type.

JOHN: My type eh? What type is that, Maggie?

MAGGIE: Renee said it. The bully. The little bully. You push her around because she's helpless and can't do anything about it. You push her around but if anybody stands up to you you back down.

JOHN: You think I'd back down to you?

MAGGIE: I know it.

JOHN: (*long pause*) Fuck you, Maggie.

MAGGIE: Don't you wish, buster.

RENEE: (*comes out, all made up; brightly*) Listen, I've put some spare ribs on, let's all have spare ribs, never mind him, Maggie, he's such a gruffy bear when he hasn't had what he wants, you know... it was Dougie's fault wasn't it John? Dougie burst in this morning, I'd forgot the lock on the door, and Dougie bursts in this morning, you should have seen this gruffy bear... (*looks at JOHN and tentatively sits on his knee*)

JOHN: (*sits for a moment then shoves her off*) Get off me, you whore. (*gets up*) I'm going to the shop.

JOHN stalks off. RENEE looks after him, eyes wild.

Go to black.

SCENE FOUR

The fall. MAGGIE and RENEE in the kitchen. MAGGIE is wearing a new outfit: pants, top, boots. She has had her hair done. She smokes. RENEE looks drawn and haggard.

MAGGIE: And the chairman says he could understand that I was upset. Upset! I say, "Look, Benny, I've got an 18-page paper here, 17&1/2 pages of which are copied word for word from a book!" And Benny says I'm vindictive. He says, "However, I can understand what you are feeling." I said, "Look, Benny, this has nothing to do with Emma. This has nothing to do with the fact that Emma is still missing. That's irrelevant. This has to do with a simple case of fucking plagiarism. This fucking student has fucking well plagiarized her term paper, in a fourth year course, in Shakespeare..." "She didn't even copy from a good critic," he says. Thought that would make me laugh. Then he suggests I see a good doctor.

RENEE: What're they going to do about the student?

MAGGIE: Oh, I'm contracted to lecture to her. If Miss Shitface turns up on Monday, under the terms of my contract, I must lecture to her. "Listen," I told Benny, "If that bitch turns up in my class on Monday, I will puke all over her, direct from the podium." Then he says, "She's built like a brick shithouse." That's what he said– "built like a brick shithouse." The chairman of the English department! That's the sort of simile he uses for a woman.

RENEE: Maybe you shouldn't have expelled her from the class. Maybe that was a bit harsh.

MAGGIE: Harsh! Harsh! I'd like to string her up from her tits. How's about a drink, Renee?

RENEE: Oh yeah, sure. (*turns and gets bottle, etc. from cupboard*)

MAGGIE: You okay?

RENEE: Sure. Fine. Why?

MAGGIE: I don't know. You on a new diet again?

RENEE: No.

MAGGIE: No, people get away with everything these days, they're not wicked, they're just suffering from social maladjustment. Benny said something like that, he said the woman was emotionally disabled or something.

RENEE: Well, maybe she was! (*hands her a drink*)

MAGGIE: (*half-laugh*) Whaaat?

RENEE: You don't know why she did it. You don't know.

MAGGIE: I know. She wanted a good grade so she cheated. She thought it was worth the risk.

RENEE: Maybe it's not so simple, Maggie, maybe she was desperate. Maybe she couldn't write her essay and got desperate.

MAGGIE: Tough shit.

RENEE: Well, how would you know! You can always write whenever you want, maybe she needs your compassion

MAGGIE: Maybe she needs my boot in her butt. I said to Benny, "What has her being built like a brick shithouse got to do with anything?" And he kept calling her a girl. "The *girl* has emotional problems," he kept saying. I looked her up, she's twenty-fucking-eight.

RENEE: Well, maybe she does have emotional problems.

MAGGIE: You think that excuses her?

RENEE: Well, sometimes people don't always understand the things they get caught up in, and they just, you know, get caught up in them, and they just do it, they don't work it out, like, ahead of time, they just find themselves sort of in the middle of it.

MAGGIE: I don't know, it's like saying Hitler had a bad day.

RENEE: People get caught up in things!

MAGGIE: Then they should get un-caught. You get in a bad situation, you walk away. You just walk fucking... ay-way.

RENEE: Please stop using that word. It's bad in front of the children.

MAGGIE: The children are not present, Renee.

RENEE: Well, you don't watch your mouth even when they're here. I can't walk away! How can I walk away!

MAGGIE: I wasn't talking about John.

RENEE: Weren't you? He said you had a fight, he said you hate him. He says misery loves company, you'll try to get me to leave him, well, you can cut the crap, Maggie, just because you're lonely and frustrated...

MAGGIE: I've never interfered between you and John...

RENEE: Oh haven't you! Oh! haven't you... last week, when I was showing you that new dress, you got that look on your face, I could just tell what you were thinking–

MAGGIE: Because you were doing this cringing whelp act... you were cringing away–

RENEE: What... what act?

MAGGIE: Like a cringing whelp... a dog–

RENEE: That's another thing–

MAGGIE: "Oh John, I got this really cheap, see? See how cheap it was and I really do need it, oh you gruffy bear." Jesus–

RENEE: I do not sound like that!

MAGGIE: And you'd changed the sales tags – so he wouldn't know what you paid for the fucking dress!

RENEE: I do not sound like that!

MAGGIE: You sound like that!

RENEE: (*panting*) You don't understand.

MAGGIE: I understand.

RENEE: No. You don't. You don't understand.

MAGGIE: What is he, good in bed?

RENEE: Jealous?

MAGGIE: (*small laugh, gets up*) Maybe. That's it. Maybe. If a man came into me now he'll corrode in bile. He'd dissolve. I'm full of spleen. Sorry. Sorry. Sorry. It's none of my business. It's none of my business. People don't know about married couples. I don't know about you and John. What really goes on. I can't talk.

RENEE: (*still furious*) No. You can't.

MAGGIE: No, I can't. I don't know, maybe you're right, it's this thing affecting everything. It's true, I can't stand the way he treats you. That's true.

RENEE: You don't understand. I like it.

MAGGIE: Do you?

RENEE: Yes.

MAGGIE: Okay. Look, I'll water the plants, don't worry. I'll take care of things.

RENEE: All right.

MAGGIE: (*pauses, then goes and embraces her*) Have a good time, have a great holiday.

RENEE: (*stiffly, unyielding*) Thanks.

Go to black.

SCENE FIVE

The darkened kitchen. The hall light shines through into the kitchen. MAGGIE is at the sliding doors, key in lock. Opens doors, slides them back. She is in a housecoat. Switches on the light over the sink. Gets watering can and spray bottle from beside the sink. She measures hyponex into the watering can. Starts to water and spray plants. She moves about the house, then returns to the kitchen. Suddenly she bends over, grabs herself.

MAGGIE: It's like living with a stone at your centre. Emma? Emma? I wish they'd find you dead. Yes I do. I wish it would just be over. I wish I could bury you and it would just be finished. I want my life to start again. I'm sorry. I can't mourn you, I can't grieve. I've just become mean minded. Small and petty and mean minded. I resent everyone their life.

I resent Renee on a holiday in California, soaking up the sun, swimming. I resent her happiness. I resent her children. I grudge her that she has John to make love to at night. I grudge her that I can't love anyone until I know where you are. I grudge everything. I'm sorry. Be dead. Be something. I can't stand it any more.

MAGGIE turns and waters the plants. She then goes out and into the hall, presumably upstairs. RENEE comes in from the hall, carrying bags. Stares wildly around, as if expecting some terrible devastation. She looks wild, crazed. JOHN comes after her, carrying a polystyrene freezer container, and a food hamper.

JOHN: Why'd you run like that, you crazy or something? You coulda fallen and hurt yourself.

RENEE: She's watered the plants.

JOHN: She tells me to come home the middle a our friggin' vacation and that's why? She's afraid her friggin' lesbian friend's gonna forget ta water her friggin' plants?

RENEE: I was sick. I had to come home.

JOHN: She was sick. You are sick. You're crazy. I should have you put away in the funny farm. (*turns to go out, crosses to sliding doors*)

RENEE: Where're you going?

JOHN: To the car. To get the rest a our stuff. You left a lot a junk in the car.

RENEE: Don't wake Joanie, I'll get Joanie. I'll carry Joanie in.

JOHN: She's awake, she came in after me... she's upstairs.

RENEE: (*goes to hall, calls*) Joanie?! Joanie?! You in?! You upstairs?!

No answer. RENEE calls again.

Dougie?! Are you in, did you come in?

JOHN: They're dead on their feet, driving all day 'n' all night like maniacs.

RENEE stands there as if she can't remember what they have come home for. She reaches out to a plant, touches its leaf. It is still alive.

RENEE: She took care of my plants.

JOHN: Ladybird ladybird
Fly away home,
Your house is on fire
An' your children alone.

JOHN laughs as RENEE covers her ears.

You disgust me. You're old. You're getting old. You fill me with disgust. I can't touch you, you make me want to throw up.

JOHN turns and walks toward the sliding doors. MAGGIE comes in from the hall. RENEE gives a small scream. JOHN turns, stops.

RENEE: What are you doing here? What are you doing here!

MAGGIE: I was upstairs. I was watering your plants. What's happened? Has something happened?

RENEE: What did you say to them, what did you say?

MAGGIE: What? What?

RENEE: What did you say to my children?

MAGGIE: What? John?

JOHN comes back, shoves RENEE into a chair, gets her a drink, shoves it under her nose, forces her head back.

RENEE: (*drinks, chokes*) No. I don't want it.

JOHN: You're hysterical. Can you hear me? You're hysterical. We're halfway down the coast of California and she says we gotta come home. Ladybird, ladybird, fly away home...

RENEE: Stop it.

MAGGIE: Renee, what happened?

JOHN: Nothing happened.

RENEE: Nothing happened. We just drove and drove, farther and farther away. Away. We just kept on driving... (*laughs*) Now we're home.

MAGGIE: Was there an accident?

RENEE: My life is an accident. (*laughs again*)

JOHN: Drink that. Drink that all down.

RENEE: (*to MAGGIE*) Oh hate me, for god's sake, hate me.

MAGGIE: Oh Renee, I don't hate you.

MAGGIE crosses to her and tries to hug her, but RENEE cannot bear her touch.

I love you. You're my friend. I would have gone mad these months without you. You're my friend, my dear friend.

RENEE: No. No... (*sobs*)

MAGGIE: Why, why did you come home, what happened?

RENEE: Nothing. (*with terror*) Nothing happened. We just drove further and further away. I watched the signs going past... Sacramento... San Francisco... Carmel... I watched the signs going past... (*a long shuddering sigh*) I had to come home.

JOHN: She didn't like the signs. So she ruins a vacation. I guess it's the Change, I guess she's into the Change, you into the Change yet, Maggie?

RENEE: Why don't you check things out, John. Why don't you check things out. Maybe somebody's broken in. Maybe something's happened.

JOHN: (*small laugh*) Nothing's happened.

RENEE: You haven't checked your workshop, John, maybe something's gone, maybe something belongs to you is gone.

JOHN: Nothing's gone.

RENEE: Maybe it's gone.

JOHN: So, Maggie, sit down, have a drink, we haven't seen you in a long time, any word?

MAGGIE: What?

JOHN: Any word on Emma?

MAGGIE: You'd have heard first thing, John.

JOHN: Sure we would, sure we would, I know that. (*small laugh*)

MAGGIE sits down beside RENEE. Looks at JOHN. He goes to cupboard, pours a drink for MAGGIE.

You get it out of her, Maggie, you're her best friend, you get it out of her, why she decides to ruin a perfectly good vacation. Here.

JOHN hands MAGGIE the drink. She takes it cautiously.

What you two got going anyway, she can't leave you for a couple of weeks, what you two got going anyway, eh? (*laughs*) Oh don't give me that look, Renee, I heard about these intellectuals, they swing both ways, eh, Maggie, eh? You swing both ways, don't you?

MAGGIE looks at RENEE who hasn't touched her drink.

MAGGIE: Listen, are you okay? If you want I can stay for a bit.

JOHN: Ooooh ho ho ho, oooo, I get it, I get it, I can take a hint, oooh ho, yes, I can take a hint, don't mind me, I'm leaving, I'm leaving.

He goes to sliding doors. RENEE stares after him. Rigid.

I know when I'm not wanted, I know when I am not wanted, yes sir. I'll leave you two girls together for girl talk, yes sir, I will leave you two girls together for a little old heart to heart.

MAGGIE: Renee? What is it?

JOHN: What is it, Renee, tell your best friend in the world, eh? Why don't you, eh Renee? She's your best friend in the world. Maggie, you should watch out, people who come between husband and wife get their face punched out sometimes. (*holds up hand*) Unh, oh, no no, just kidding, eh? Just kidding. You know the kids missed Disneyland? The kids missed Disneyland. We got all the way to Santa Barbara almost and she says we gotta turn back. "We gotta turn back, we gotta go home." (*laughs*)

MAGGIE: Well, I'm glad you're back, I missed you.

JOHN: Missed me, Maggie?

MAGGIE: Missed you both. Having you here. You know, I came over every day to water your plants. It was scary. I felt I had to come. I don't know why. I just felt I had to come and check things. It was a bit freaky.

JOHN: So.

He walks over to the cupboard and opens it. Takes out a couple of chocolate bars. Reaches into drinks cupboard, takes bottle of vodka. RENEE watches him. JOHN takes down a package of chips. RENEE watches him.

Well, I got some stuff to do out in the workshop. (*goes to sliding doors, looks at RENEE, walks out, slides door back*)

MAGGIE: Listen, if you feel bad about what happened, before you left, don't – I've been a drain on you, I know. I've thought about it a lot while you've been gone. I'm too dependent on you, I know that, I'm going to be different. Listen, whatever the reason, I'm glad you're back. I missed you.

RENEE turns and looks at her.

What, what is it? Renee?

RENEE: You're a fool. You're a fool you stupid cunt. You disgust me.

MAGGIE: You're tired, you're exhausted, let me help you–

RENEE: Get out. You stupid whore. You cunt. Get out.

RENEE starts to laugh and then sob. MAGGIE puts her arm around RENEE and tries to help her from the room. RENEE pushes her away and goes into hall.

Go to black.

SCENE SIX

Mid-October. On the fridge, children's drawings of witches and jack-o'-lanterns are held up with magnetic buttons. RENEE comes in. It is early dusk. She comes to the sliding doors and looks out. Now she turns and goes to the fridge, starts to get vegetables out of the bin. She gets a piece of meat and she begins to pound it with a wooden mallet. She seasons it, puts it into a casserole. Puts in onions. Looks up, holds herself, comes again to the sliding doors and looks out. Picks up the telephone and presses the intercom button. Waits. Looks again to the sliding doors. Waits. Presses down the receiver button.

RENEE: Hi. It's me. Just about to put the meat into the microwave, thought I'd... (*listens*) John– (*listens*) John, the last week or so you've bitched about everything being overdone or cooked too much, I'm just about ready to put this stuff into the microwave, I thought I'd give you plenty of.... It's time to quit work! No, I did not. No, you did not. No. No, I never heard you tell me not to phone the shop. No. No. I told you, no. (*turns and stares out sliding doors*) No, this isn't some new idea she's put into my head. I said, I haven't seen Maggie in weeks. John, I know you're busy out there, what I want to know is, what are you doing? You haven't shipped out a chesterfield in a month! Okay, okay. I am minding my own business, I have to feed a family, don't I? Jenkins phoned again yesterday and said where was his armchair, that came in last August. You haven't even paid the hydro! I told you, Maggie hasn't even been here in... five weeks now. This is me, me, Renee talking. All I'm saying is, the dinner's going into the microwave, so could you be in here on time tonight?

She lifts her finger off receiver button. Presses intercom button. Waits. Looks toward sliding doors. Waits.

John? It's just me, I thought I'd tell you, dinner's going into the microwave now. I didn't think you'd mind just this once. Well, you haven't eaten your dinner the last few... all right, John. All right, all right, all right I won't, no I won't. I'm sorry. I'm... sorry.

Slowly she puts the receiver back onto the wall hook. Lifts receiver again. Dials three numbers. Puts receiver back onto hook. Puts casserole of meat into microwave. MAGGIE knocks at sliding doors. Slides them back.

MAGGIE: Hi.

RENEE: Oh. Hi.

MAGGIE: (*halfway in*) How are you?

RENEE: I'm all right. You?

MAGGIE: So so. Well, just thought I'd see how you were, saw your light on...

RENEE: Want a drink?

MAGGIE: Well...

RENEE: He's out in the shop.

MAGGIE: Well, maybe a quick one.

RENEE: Guess you've been pretty busy–

MAGGIE: I've been pretty busy...

They laugh. RENEE makes her a drink.

I've missed you.

RENEE: Yeah. Well. It's just one of those things. (*hands her the drink*) We really don't have that much in common. I took a couple a courses but John's right, I'm not in your league.

MAGGIE: John's not always right, Renee.

RENEE: Yeah, well, that's another thing; you always saying stuff like that, it could break us up, you know? John and I. John and me, which is it anyway?

MAGGIE: (*looks at her drink, puts it down*) Yeah. Well. Guess I better be going. (*starts for sliding doors*)

RENEE: How... are things?

MAGGIE: Shitty. Oh, I get up, I move, I go to work, I lecture, I even make jokes. Time goes by. I don't hear her screaming anymore.

RENEE: What?

MAGGIE: Sometimes at night I thought I heard her scream.

RENEE: Stay and have your drink.

MAGGIE: Was that what it was, my buttinsky stuff about John?

RENEE: Oh, you meant well

MAGGIE: No I didn't. Maybe I didn't. Maybe what happened has made me so paranoid about men. I don't know.

RENEE: Only it came to a choice kind of, between you and him, he.

MAGGIE: (*breaks into a laugh*) Him. It's him, you had it right the first time, why don't you just relax, you'll be okay, you have a feel for language, you know.

RENEE: Do I?

MAGGIE: Yes. You always pretend to be so stupid, Renee, it kind of pisses me off, if you want to know.

RENEE: Oh yes?

MAGGIE: Yes. I mean, if it's time for truth games, I might as well tell you, this habit you've got of putting yourself down all the time, and this invidious comparison stuff you're into about me, it really pisses me off.

RENEE: Invidious comparison. I don't know what that means.

MAGGIE: You know what it means. Look. If you wanted an education, a formal education, you could get one, what's stopping you? Don't put it off onto... no, I know what you're going to say... but this house practically runs itself and you could go in, even for day courses. John's always around anyway, you don't have to worry about Joanie and Dougie, there'd always be someone home for them.

RENEE: (*a shrill laugh*) You don't know what you're talking about.

MAGGIE: If you're that unhappy, leave him. Oh there I go again. Boy. Put my foot into it every time, it's just, I can't stand seeing you take it from him, I just can't stand it, it's horrible, it's so degrading. –I mean, have you got the TV fixed yet? No, no? There you are, you see? You were begging him to let you get it fixed how long ago, and just because he's out in the shop day and night doesn't mean you have to go without TV for you and the kids, I mean why doesn't he let you watch his set in the shop? I mean, it's crazy the way you have to beg for everything!

RENEE: What?

MAGGIE: The way you have to beg for everything, the way you have to cringe and grovel, and apologize for every blessed thing, you think I didn't hear you apologizing for spending so much on Joanie's school shoes.

RENEE: What TV?

MAGGIE: Your TV, haven't you got it fixed yet?

RENEE: No, you said he's got a TV in the shop, what TV?

MAGGIE: The one he took in last summer. He's got it hooked up to your cable line. I know because he bragged to me, he didn't have to pay twice, he knew how to hook it up, said he could hook it up to Pay-TV with some aluminum foil.

RENEE: John's got a TV in the shop?

MAGGIE: Oh, I don't know. I'm out of line I guess. I'm sorry. I said to myself, Keep your mouth shut, don't say a word, and here we are, right into it again.

RENEE: I didn't know about the TV.

MAGGIE: Well, he's gotta be doing something in there, he's in there day and night, isn't he? I guess he watches the TV in there.

RENEE: We have a good marriage. You have no right to say anything about our marriage.

MAGGIE: You have a rotten marriage.

RENEE: Get out of here. I didn't ask you in. I curse the day you moved next door. I curse you.

MAGGIE: What is it, Renee, tell me what it is.

RENEE: We were happy until you came. We were happy.

MAGGIE: He treats you like shit.

RENEE: He's right about you, you're green with envy.

MAGGIE: The day I envy you a man like that prick–

RENEE: You're dying for it.

MAGGIE laughs.

Don't you dare laugh at me, you big shot... you think you're perfect–

MAGGIE: Oh go to hell, go to hell. I've missed you, I've missed you terribly.

RENEE: Last week, Dougie was late home from school. The bus came and he wasn't on it. I was watching from the window, and I saw the bus come and drop off the Fraser kids, but Dougie wasn't on the bus. Joanie was going to be late because she had band practice, so I knew she'd be late, but Dougie was supposed to be on the bus. I phoned the school and Mrs. Duncan had kept him late. He'd thrown rocks during recess and she'd kept him late. She said she didn't know he was supposed to come home on the bus. She said it was inexcusable of her. She apologized. Dougie walked all the way home from school. He got here, he was half crying, he had ran all the way the last part, he knew I'd be worried sick about him. He had ran all the last part, he could hardly breathe.

MAGGIE: The terror.

RENEE: Yes. And that was just a few minutes. Less than 15 minutes before I got Mrs. Duncan on the phone. That was... and all these months, you...

MAGGIE nods, holding herself in.

It's true, I've always been jealous of you, it's true, you seemed to have it so good, you were so lucky, you were so free.

MAGGIE stiffens although RENEE does not notice.

MAGGIE: Fortune's child.

RENEE: (*unaware of the change*) Part of me was glad when you were brought down.

MAGGIE: That's the basis of most dramatic literature. They love it when Oedipus falls down, you know, they get a secret nasty thrill when they know he's slept with his mother.

MAGGIE laughs. RENEE steps away, realizes she's gone too far. The two women look at each other. The hostility re-flares.

RENEE: Well, I wouldn't know, I don't have your advanced knowledge of dramatic literature.

MAGGIE: (*closes her eyes*) Oh shit. Here we go again. I've lost my child, Renee. I've lost my child. My child could be anywhere, terrible things could be happening to her right now, while we fight out this old old story about who's got the better education... I don't believe you sometimes.

RENEE: I don't believe you walk in here, you haven't even stopped by in five weeks–

MAGGIE: Jesus, the last time I was here you called me a cunt.

RENEE: You bust in here, you try to get between me and John, what've you got against John anyway?

MAGGIE: Let's not get started.

RENEE: You've got something against him, you've looked down on him from the first, you have, I can remember that first night, after we'd been talking for a couple of weeks, and I invited you over–

MAGGIE: Emma and me.

RENEE: (*small smile*) Isn't it Emma and I?

MAGGIE: (*stares at her*) No, actually, that was the objective case.

RENEE: Oh was it?

MAGGIE: Yes, it was. Personally, I don't very much give a good fuck about the objective case, but it comes naturally to me, while the ablative absolute does not.

RENEE: Oooh ho.

MAGGIE: You want to know what I've got against John, you really want to know? That night, that night when we had dinner together, he put you down for every single thing you did, he put you down and he smiled this small little complicit smile at me as if I'd understand why he was doing it. This small little you-and-me-babe smile at me.

RENEE: What kind of smile?

MAGGIE: You-and-me-Babe, we-know-the-kind-of-dumb-bitch-we've-got-here smile.

RENEE: No, that other word. I don't understand what you say! You do it on purpose!

MAGGIE: What word?

RENEE: You know what word! How am I supposed to go out into the world? I can't make it without a man! I can't, I don't have your chances.

MAGGIE: Shit shit shit, Renee, that's shit and you know it's shit, and I won't have this envy, this rotten fucking envy, I won't let it eat away at you and me, I won't, I won't! (*goes to her, but angrily, and puts her arms around RENEE*)

RENEE: You're trying to bust us up. (*tries to resist MAGGIE's embrace*) It's true what he says, you're just trying to get in between us, you're making me think things about him, it's you... (*starts to sob*) Oh god, oh god.

MAGGIE is holding on grimly.

Oh god, oh god, oh I can't bear it. I can't stand it, Maggie, I can't live...

She buries her face in MAGGIE's breast. JOHN appears at sliding doors, watches. Opens the doors. MAGGIE starts, begins to draw back guiltily, then reaffirms her embrace of RENEE, and stares defiantly at JOHN. RENEE, at first, is unaware. JOHN comes in and stands silently, watching. Grins. RENEE, after a moment, senses his presence, and moves away. MAGGIE looks at her in fury.

It's almost ready. Dinner. I'll get you a beer.

She goes to fridge and gets JOHN a beer, opens it. Gets a glass. MAGGIE stands still, looks at JOHN. He grins at MAGGIE. RENEE holds out glass of beer to JOHN, who doesn't take it. RENEE puts it down on table beside the place setting.

MAGGIE: I'd better go then.

She comes toward sliding doors, but JOHN is in her way. She pauses.

Excuse me.

JOHN raises his hand abruptly. MAGGIE winces and cowers.

JOHN: (*laughs*) What's the matter, Maggie, I was just going to take off my cap. Didja think I was going to hit ya? She thought I was going to give her a knuckle sandwich, Renee. Didja see her? Jeezus, Maggie thought I was going ta give her an old knuckle sandwich, the old one-two, what's the matter, Maggie, got a guilty conscience? I was just taking off my cap, see?

MAGGIE: Just let me get by, please.

JOHN: I ain't stoppin' ya, Maggie, who's stoppin' ya? You can get by.

RENEE: Let her get by, John.

JOHN: Another country heard from – another cuntree heard from, get it, Maggie? You're the big professor, you should like wordplay, another cunt tree, get it?

MAGGIE: Why do you always do that, John? Talk like a moron when I'm here.

JOHN: (*laughs*) Do I talk like a moron, Maggie?

MAGGIE: Yes. You speak perfectly good English and then I come over and suddenly it's Dogpatch Time.

JOHN: Dogpatch Time, eh? That's pretty good, ain't it, Renee? Dogpatch Time.

RENEE: Let her go, John. Just let her go.

JOHN moves suddenly aside, with a sweep of his cap.

MAGGIE: I know you, John, I know you from when I was a kid in Winnipeg, there was this boy there, Norman Stewart, he used to grab the little ones and give them an Indian Wrist Burn.

MAGGIE exits. JOHN turns and watches her go. RENEE, behind him, closes her eyes. JOHN very casually closes the sliding doors. Crosses to table and sits down.

JOHN: Well? You said supper was going to be ready.

RENEE: (*with an effort, goes to microwave and gets out the food*) Oh. I'm sorry, I forgot the vegetables. She puts in the vegetable dish. Punches the computer. Puts the casserole on the table.

JOHN: No beer?

RENEE goes to table and gets the beer and lifts it toward him. He talks politely.

Thank you.

He refuses to take it. RENEE is forced to put it down beside him on the table beside his hand.

Well. So you and your friend have made up, eh? That's good. I like for you to have friends. Bosom buddies again eh? (*small laugh, lifts casserole dish*) My my, what's this?

RENEE: Lasagna.

JOHN: Lasagna. My my. Lasagna. What'd the kids have?

RENEE: They ate before.

JOHN: I didn't ask when they ate, Renee, I asked what did they eat? There's a grammatical distinction. There's a semantic distinction, which I am sure your dear friend Maggie could elucidate upon. What did they eat, the children?

RENEE: Peanut butter sandwiches.

JOHN: Peanut butter sandwiches. And I get lasagna. Excuse me, Renee, but this is not really anything so fancy as lasagna, this is hamburger and macaroni. No. Come here and look at it, Renee, this is hamburger and macaroni.

RENEE: (*as bell dings*) The vegetables are ready.

JOHN: It never fails to amaze me how you cannot understand what I am saying to you. Did I inquire about the state of the vegetables? Did I? Did I.

RENEE: No.

JOHN: No, I asked you to kindly step over here and look at this dish, which you claim is lasagna. Step over here, Maggie.

RENEE crosses to table.

Bend over and look at it, Maggie.

RENEE: Please.

JOHN: Look at it, Maggie.

RENEE: My name is Renee.

JOHN grabs her by the neck and pushes her face into the casserole.

JOHN: That is shit. This is shit, that's what it is, you give me shit to eat, you filthy bitch.

RENEE: You don't give me any money! (*backs away, teeth chattering, but ferocious*) You never give me any money, that's all I got in the freezer, that's why the kids don't even get hamburger, and you got a TV in the workshop!

JOHN: What?

RENEE: You heard me, you got a TV in the shop. (*grabs a tea towel and tries to wipe her face*)

JOHN: I got a what?

RENEE: (*standing against the sink*) If you touch me, I'll do something.

JOHN: I don't think I heard you right, Renee. I got a what in the shop?

RENEE: A TV.

JOHN: Oh? How you know that, Renee?

RENEE: I had to go in today. To get a washer.

JOHN: Oh yes? A washer? A washer for what?

RENEE: For the sink. For the bathroom sink. The tap in there.

JOHN: A washer. For the bathroom sink.

RENEE: I don't need to bother you for a washer put in, I can put one in myself. I don't need to worry you for that.

JOHN: Which tap is that, Renee?

RENEE: The one in the bathroom. It's leaking.

JOHN: I gathered it was the one in the bathroom. You told me that before.

RENEE: The one in the shower. The right one.

JOHN: The right one?

RENEE: I mean, hot, the hot one.

JOHN pushes back his chair. RENEE jumps. He crosses over to her and smiles.

JOHN: Don't give me any of your lies, Renee. You weren't in the shop.

RENEE: Yes, I was. I was.

JOHN: No, Renee, you were not.

RENEE: I saw it.

JOHN: (*backhands her casually*) No, Renee.

RENEE: (*falls to her knees*) Oh don't oh don't oh don't... the kids'll hear again... oh god...

JOHN kicks her in the stomach.

Oh don't John... I'm sorry... oh god...

JOHN: (*pulls her up by the hair*) Okay Renee? Okay? Now you tell me the truth, Renee. I have to do this when you lie to me. You know that. I have to hurt you when you lie to me, Renee, now you tell me.

He knees her in the chest. Catches her as she falls back, keeps her upright.

RENEE: Maggie.

JOHN: Ah. Maggie told you. Yeah. She saw me take it in.

RENEE: It isn't fair.

JOHN: What? Did I hear you make a comment?

RENEE: The kids don't have TV.

JOHN: You're an old whore, Renee, and I can do what I like with you and you'll take it, because you're an old whore and I'm the last chance you've got for a real man. That's true, isn't it? Renee?

RENEE: I'm not an... oooh.

JOHN: Yes, you are. Say it. (*pulls her hair back*)

RENEE: I'm... an old–

JOHN: Whore.

RENEE: Whore... and you're the last chance I got–

JOHN: For a real man.

RENEE: ...a real man...

JOHN: Now, Renee, I'm going to have to punish you, you know that, don't you? You know I've got to punish you now, don't you? Yes. Okay. Take it out. Go on. Take it out.

RENEE sobs. JOHN pulls her hair backwards until her face is close to his crotch.

Go on, Renee, don't make it hard on yourself. (*laughs*) Make it hard on me.

RENEE reaches up and unzips him.

That's a good girl. That's a good girl.

Go to black.

SCENE SEVEN

Halloween night. The workshop.

A very small area of the workshop is visible. We can see a bit of the work bench. The tools hanging on a perforated board. Nothing is out of place. There is a plastic filing cabinet arrangement for nuts, bolts, etc.

Immediately to one side of the work bench and lathe is a piece of the floor, painted a bright blue. On top of this floor area are plastic jugs filled with various fluids: oil for wood, paint thinner, etc.

Slowly, the lights are brought up on RENEE looking at the area, from the penumbra. RENEE looks at the workshop. She cannot see a TV.

She is wearing a housedress, and has made herself up carefully: neat and clean and ordinary-looking.

She comes into the light. Stands in front of the lathe. She touches the lathe, the tools, the filing cabinet of small items. Turns away, then turns back. She looks at the plastic jugs on the square of blue painted floor. The floor is painted a slightly brighter blue than the surrounding area. She turns away again. Can't think why she is bothered. Starts away. Stops. Turns back. Something else was there before. What was it? She looks around Yes, something else had stood there. She goes over to the jugs. She bends to lift one. It does not come away. It is glued to the piece of flooring which she sees now is a wooden plywood slab, fitted into the floor.

Behind her a silhouette... the figure of a man, as if in a doorway. RENEE straightens up. Does not turn.

JOHN: (*comes in*) Looking for something?

RENEE: You know that tarnish-free stuff? I was looking for that tarnish-free stuff...

JOHN: Why would I have tarnish-free stuff?

RENEE: I needed it for my rings. (*holds out her hands*)

JOHN: Gold doesn't tarnish.

RENEE: Not my wedding ring, this ring, the one Dougie gave me.

JOHN: The one Dougie gave you.

RENEE: It's turning my finger green! (*laughs, shows him*)

JOHN: (*refuses to look at her hand*) I don't like you messing around in the workshop.

RENEE: Where's the TV?

JOHN: What?

RENEE: Where's the TV, John?

JOHN: I took it back. I was watching it too much, I wasn't getting my work done. Listen, don't worry, I'll get the kids' TV fixed. I'll take it into the shop today. Is that what's bugging you?

RENEE: Is that Jenkins' armchair?

JOHN: Oh yeah. I had to wait for this part.

RENEE: You had a nightmare again last night.

JOHN: We got a good life, Renee, you and me, we got a good life for us 'n' the kids. We got our ups and downs but we're a lucky family, you know that? We got our health. I got this little business, it'll start picking up again, I know I'm good at what I do, I'm good with my hands, the thing is, you see, I'm really like everybody else. That's what you don't understand about me, Renee. I'm just like anybody else. I know you judge me, yes, you judge me, you have always judged me – but I am just like any man. Just like any man. I have my pride, Renee, you can't undermine a man's pride in his manhood, that's what you have done.

RENEE: How did I do that?

JOHN: A lot of couples, they can't talk things over like we can, they have a communication problem, we don't have a communication problem, we talk, you and I. A man sometimes has problems that way, that's all. It's quite natural. You ask any psychologist.

RENEE: I am not complaining about that, have I ever said anything about that?

JOHN: You're not an educated woman, Renee, you don't understand these things, a man goes through many stages in his life. Many stages in his life. There's a book called that *Stages in Life's Way* or something. By Kierkegaard. Have you read *Stage in Life's Way*, by Kierkegaard? Did you realize that if God exists, Renee, it is our duty to deny him? Have you read Heidegger? Have you read Jaspers? I'm an educated man. I've had to educate myself. You know Dostoyevsky once said that only if you could rape a 10-year-old girl could you say you were truly free. Free of all morality. It's conventional morality that holds us back, Renee. I married you although I knew you were a conventional woman.

RENEE: Why would anyone want to?

JOHN: I married you knowing full well there would be areas of my life you could not enter, areas in my life you could not understand, but you married me, you took an oath, for richer or poorer, for better or worse, we are one flesh, Renee. Why would anyone want to what?

RENEE: Rape a 10-year-old girl?

JOHN: You don't understand the concept, Renee. Listen, listen, you know what Maggie said that time about Emma–

RENEE: Emma?

JOHN: You know what she said, how Emma believed what Anne Frank believed, how she used to say those lines... "because in spite of everything, I still believe that people are really good at heart"? You know. Maggie quoted that to us, she said Emma believed that. But listen! Maggie said those lines were the last lines in the book. They're not. No. And I've heard that from other people too, people say that all the time, that those're the last lines in the book, but they're not. You know what Anne Frank talks about at the end of the book? No, those lines come earlier, a couple of chapters, I think, no, what she's talking about at the end of the book is how she can't be good, how she knows she can't ever really be a good person. People don't like to know that Anne Frank knew it, and what she says at the end of the book is she could be good, yes, she could be, "if only there weren't any people living in the world." Something like that, I haven't maybe got it exact I could be good if... "there weren't any other people living in the world." That's what it says at the very end of that book. You see? Do you see, Renee?

RENEE: She wasn't a good person? Anne Frank wasn't a good person? So it was okay what they did to her?

JOHN: It makes me tired sometimes, Renee, to try to make you understand a philosophical concept.

RENEE: You're trying to say Anne Frank wasn't a good person?

JOHN: That's right. Nobody is, Renee, that's what I am trying to convey to you.

RENEE: So she can be raped?

JOHN: What? What are you talking about? Anne Frank wasn't raped.

RENEE: You said this guy said you should rape a 10-year-old girl.

JOHN: On, no, that was just an example of the act that would be a defiance...would spit in the face of God, which is the duty of a free person. You see, Abraham should have given God the finger. You know. You have heard of Abraham, Renee.

RENEE: Yes.

JOHN: When he took up poor little Isaac to the mountaintop, and God said Kill your only son, and you can imagine how difficult that was. Sarah was 99 when she had him, how old was Abraham? I don't know, who cares, don't get me off the track, the point of all this is, Abraham should have refused to obey God.

RENEE: But there was a ram in the thicket.

JOHN: What–? Yes, but how did Abraham know that?

RENEE: He had faith.

JOHN: (*laughs*) A lot of good that did Anne Frank. Listen, if you want to know the truth about Emma, that was her trouble, she believed in people, she trusted people, Maggie taught her to trust people, that was her trouble. In a way, the person who teaches her that lesson is a saviour, an educator, yes, an educator, she could be grateful the rest of her life. Even Moses said you should rape the young girls. In Numbers. You didn't know that, did you? Oh yes, when they were going against some tribe, he said kill off all the older women, the ones who are dirty already. That means the ones that have done it with men. But then take the pure girls for yourself. Moses understood that that's what women really want. That's what you want, isn't it, Renee?

RENEE: I thought I did.

JOHN: Oh you did. You loved the rough and tumble, admit it.

RENEE: Yes. I admit it.

JOHN: Then you think you're a married woman, you get all respectable and you pretend you don't want it. But I remember.

RENEE: Only, it wasn't like it is now.

JOHN: Sure it is. You and I, we get along, Renee. You can't follow me everywhere, that's only natural, you don't have the education, and to tell you the truth, you're just not as bright as I am, but that's okay, I'll look after you. Only. Renee? Don't come into the workshop anymore, okay? Okay, Baby? I like to keep things a certain way. Anything you want you ask me for it, I'll get it. In fact, hey wait a minute – where is that tarnish-free? I did have it, I had it for something on that armoire I was doing – just a moment. Aha! (*gets the tarnish-free bottle and hands it to her*) You were right, kiddo, this time you were absolutely right, it was here all along!

RENEE: I can't believe anybody said that, rape a 10-year-old girl, I want to read that book where he says that.

JOHN: Okay. I'll get it for you. It's down in the basement.

RENEE: Where?

JOHN: Downstairs in the basement, in that box my mother sent over. I'll get it for you, but it's really a sort of metaphor you know. It doesn't mean literally.

RENEE: You took back the TV eh?

JOHN: Yes. Months ago.

RENEE: Okay. (*turns to go*)

JOHN: Don't worry, I'll take the one in the house in, I'll take it in this aft. The kids'll have it tonight.

RENEE: It's Halloween tonight. They'll be out tonight.

JOHN: Halloween eh? Jesus, time flies, doesn't it, it's quite warm still though, Indian summer eh?

RENEE: Yes. (*pauses*) That'd be nice though, John, if you could do that, for the kids. I miss it too, the TV.

JOHN: Okay okay. A promise is a promise. Okay?

RENEE: Okay.

RENEE goes out. JOHN looks after her. Turns and looks down at the jugs on the plywood slab. Now he looks out after RENEE.

Go to black.

SCENE EIGHT

Halloween night. The kitchen.

RENEE is preparing bowls of candies, apples, pennies, for the children. From the front room the sound of the TV can be heard.

RENEE: (*briskly*) Dougie? Joanie? Now you can listen to that TV anytime. You're going out tonight, do you hear me? I didn't put hours into those costumes for nothing. Now you get ready. I'm coming in and turning that TV off in 10 seconds. I'm not kidding. 10... 9... 8... 7... 6... 5... 4... 3... 2... 1!

The sound of the TV goes off. She turns back to get the bowls. As she goes out into the hall the ring of the doorbell is heard.

See? They've started already!

Door opens. Children's voices: "Trick or treat!"

(*off*) Well! Don't you look horrible! Oooh! You scare me sick. Oooh... what a face! Here, please take it and go away...

Laughter from children. Door shuts. RENEE reappears in kitchen.

Oh I forgot the pennies for Unicef. Joanie? Joanie, are the kids still taking pennies for Unicef? Joanie, answer me when I talk to you. (*goes into hall for a moment, comes back*) I thought they were.

She looks at telephone. Picks it up. Then puts it down firmly.

Okay. I'm coming. (*goes out, off*) Yes, that's good, yes, oh that bag's big enough, oh all right. (*comes back to kitchen, gets a big plastic bag, takes it out to hall*) Now I want you two sticking together, no, Dougie, I do not want you leaving your sister, No, listen to me! I don't care, you are not to leave your sister. Joanie? I am not listening to any of that, things're going to be different around here from now on, I'm not taking any lip from you, no! And back here by nine at the latest. Joanie, do you understand me? All right. All right.

Yes, you look lovely. Yes. I love you. Take care. Don't get sick!

Door opens.

Listen, don't bother Mrs. Webb, she's sick. Yes. She's dying. So don't go up to her place, okay? Okay.

Door shuts. RENEE comes back into the kitchen. Sits at the table. Gets up, goes to stove, puts on kettle. Doorbell rings. She goes out. Door opens.

Hello! Don't you look wonderful! Here you are.

Children's voices: "Trick or treat!" Door shuts. RENEE comes back. Sits at table. She stares out through the sliding doors. Kettle sings. She gets up and turns it off. She doesn't make tea. She stares out the sliding doors. Doorbell rings. She almost doesn't respond Then she does. We hear door open: "Trick or treat!"

Oh my! My goodness, oh that's really ugly, Bennie. Oh I'm sorry, it's not Bennie, I thought maybe it was Bennie Fraser from down the street, but you can't be Bennie, you're too disgusting.

Laughter. Door shuts. She comes back and stares out the sliding doors. She laughs. Goes to the telephone and speaks into it.

This is Mrs. John Gifford. 1600 Ashcroft Road. My husband is going to commit suicide. He's in his workshop. He's locked himself in with a gun. 1600 Ashcroft Road. That's just off the highway. A sort of lane. A cul de sac. Never mind. You just turn off the highway about five miles from the park, going east. 298-6009. 20 minutes ago. Yes he did.

Hangs up the receiver. Goes and sits at the table. Folds her hands and rests them on the table. Stares out the sliding doors. MAGGIE appears at the sliding doors. RENEE starts, then sees who it is. MAGGIE knocks tentatively, then opens the doors.

MAGGIE: Hi! I thought I'd come help. I brought some stuff.

She has some Halloween goodies with her in a bag. She goes to RENEE's cupboards and takes down bowls to put her stuff in.

Listen. I've got an apology to make. Listen, Renee, I'm sorry, I think I set you up for something. I think when I left here the other night I got him mad and I knew he'd take it out on you. It's been bugging the hell out of me. I don't even know why I did it. I knew he'd take it out on you. He did, didn't he?

Doorbell rings.

Oh let me get it. I put out all the lights at my place.

She goes out into hall. Door opens: "Trick or treat!"

Hi! Oh my! Oh what a gruesome pair! Oh Jeez, Renee, you should see these two! Oh where did you get that! Yuck.

Laughter. Door shuts. RENEE all the time sits staring at the sliding doors, her hands clasped. MAGGIE comes back into the kitchen.

At first I thought I couldn't stand Halloween and then I thought, Oh Hell, I'll just go over to Renee's. Are the kids collecting for Unicef this year?

RENEE: Mmm-hmm.

MAGGIE: He did take it out on you, didn't he? And I knew it. Jesus, I'm such a shit.

RENEE: (*small laugh*) You did me a favour. Now he'll do anything for me. I've got something on him, now he can't do enough for me, he got the TV fixed.

MAGGIE: Oh. That's good. I guess. What did you have to pay for it?

RENEE: (*small laugh*) Plenty.

Doorbell rings.

Too much.

MAGGIE: (*going to the hall*) Let me get this one, eh?

RENEE: Too fucking much.

Children's voices: "Trick or treat!"

MAGGIE: (*off*) Ooooh.... You look wonderful. Just beautiful. My goodness. Oh you're a real stunner. Does your mother know you're out?

RENEE makes an hysterical sound. The first break she's made.

There you are. Bye now.

Door shuts. MAGGIE comes back to kitchen.

God, they're so cute. *Walpurgisnacht*. All Saints' Eve. How we make the horrible ordinary. How we transform it, make it comic and cuddly. Human beings!

RENEE: Wal what?

MAGGIE: *Walpurgisnacht*... it means night of the witches. Something like that.

RENEE: Oh.

MAGGIE: Night of the female bitches. Oh the old chthonic underpinnings of this society... I love Halloween really. I always did, as a child. We don't really have enough times to let go... ritual times of release... I guess Christmas is the time we really let go... remember how drunk we got last Christmas...? How disgusted Emma was with us?

RENEE: I remember John kissed you, under the mistletoe.

MAGGIE: Yes.

RENEE: You seemed to enjoy it.

MAGGIE: Well, you can be attracted to a man

RENEE: Then you got into this thing about open mortgages.

MAGGIE: Oh yes, Jesus.

Doorbell rings.

You want to go?

RENEE shakes her head. MAGGIE goes into hall. Opens door: "Trick or treat."

Aw... aw, Renee, you should see these ones... there's a ghost and a skeleton and a monster mummy... is that what you are, a monster mummy? Oh my... here you go....Bye now. Bye.

Door shuts. MAGGIE returns shaking her head.

Normalization of our deepest terrors. That's part of it.

RENEE: You started in about how you had this open mortgage and John didn't know what you were talking about. And he said he'd paid off more than half of the house and you said how long had he owned it and he said 10 years and you said if he didn't have an open mortgage that would probably be impossible. And he got out the contract and you showed him, he hadn't been paying off the... what did you call it... the principal? He hadn't been paying off the principal at all. He'd just been paying off the interest, keeping just ahead of it really, and you said unless he got himself an open mortgage he couldn't pay off at his own rate, he was at the mercy of the mortgage company, and he was furious with you, did you know that? And he went down to check it out and you were right, and he couldn't even get an open mortgage, there weren't any and he said you must have done something fast, no, pulled a fast one to get an open mortgage, and then you came over and he said, Show me, and you did, you showed him. God he hated you for that. And every month he would sign the damn cheque and he would figure it out, how much off the principal and it was only 18 dollars or something, it would drive him crazy. And then you bought that chesterfield. I think that's when he started to go down.

MAGGIE: Go down... what is it, Renee?

RENEE: Oh yes, he started slacking off on his work, you know, and he spent so much time out in the shop. But nothing was really getting done. Oh everything was tidy. He organized everything. He spent hours, days, organizing screws and bolts and stuff. It was crazy. That was about February. The thing was, I always knew about the shop, it was in the house description when we got the place, so I always knew.

Doorbell rings. RENEE gets up and goes out to hall. Door opens. Children's voices: "Trick or treat!"

Here you are.

MAGGIE gets herself a drink from cupboard. Gets ice cubes from fridge. Sound of door closing. RENEE reappears.

Get me one too, would you?

MAGGIE: Sure. (*makes her a drink*) You're in a mood tonight.

RENEE: Night of bitches. (*small laugh*)

MAGGIE: I don't get what you said just before, about the house description. You said something and I didn't quite–

RENEE: Tell me about Emma

MAGGIE: What?

RENEE: No, you think you know someone, you live beside them for a few years, but you don't know them, tell me about Emma, who was she?

MAGGIE: Emma was a 12-year-old girl. She hated it when I got the divorce. The sun rose and set on Graham. It didn't matter what I said or how I felt, and the truth is, Graham isn't a bad man, I just didn't want him anymore. And, and, and, she was religious... she had this big religious streak... probably connected with puberty... she prayed for people... she believed everyone has good in them... I don't know, I probably encouraged that... we had a talk once and I said if there's a choice... and you could choose between the one who fools and the one who's fooled, it's better to choose the one who's fooled, because then you've put your bet on humanity, and that is like inertia... it starts something... people respond to trust... oh god, I may have made her a walking target for some creep.

RENEE: How would you describe me, if somebody asked, if I were dead or something and somebody asked?

MAGGIE: (*sips drink*) Well. I'd say, you were my friend. Your name was Renee, short for Maureen, Gifford. You'd been married once before, had two kids. Were raped once. Met John, married him, but I guess that's just data isn't it? Well, I'd say you had a good sense of humour, and a quick wit, but you were frustrated, you felt inadequate about your education, you felt inferior to other people, and it niggled at you because you knew if you had a chance you'd be okay. No, I'd say you were a woman torn between things. Torn. Not knowing which way to go, and caught in the middle.

RENEE: Is that what you'll say?

MAGGIE: Well, it was a bit off the cuff, I'm sure I could work up something better if I had to do your eulogy. I'd say, Renee was a good friend to me.

RENEE: Is that what you'll say?

MAGGIE: You planning on going somewhere?

RENEE: In the end, we're all just part of someone else's scenario, aren't we? I'm real to you as the neighbour who stuck by you when your daughter went missing. That's what it comes to, I'm just a character in your scenario. Someone you tried to help out, because she wasn't liberated. Someone who had a yen for education but was "torn."

MAGGIE: Well, you asked for it quick. I... you mean more to me than that.

RENEE: But even with Emma, in the end it's not Emma who's real to you, it's what you said wrong to her, what you did wrong, that's what's real

MAGGIE: Oh Emma is real. Oh yes. Emma is real. Although sometimes now I can't remember how her face looked. She had a mole right here... (*indicates thigh*) I used to notice it when I did her diapers... and then of course in the last years she's been so modest, she never let me see her naked... I never saw it.... Sometimes I think her god wants me to curse him and die. But I won't, I won't, won't give her god that satisfaction, won't admit her god exists. Not even to curse him. A twist on Job. But you're right – she's becoming somebody in my scenario. Jesus I hate words like that.

RENEE: (*drinks*) I have all these vocabulary entries from my one venture into higher education.

MAGGIE: Oh, when your child is taken from you the world ought to end. The world ought to end. I ought to have died from the pain of it.

MAGGIE takes out pack of cigarettes and lights one. RENEE reaches over to the cupboard and pulls out an ashtray for her.

That's what's so surprising, I went on living. It's not as though I had hope left. No, it's not as though I have hope left. Not now. I think, by the summer, I knew she had to be dead. She would have called me. One night, that was the night you came back, I came over here to water your plants, I thought I heard her calling me, I think she must have died that night. She felt so close.

RENEE: Do you hate the person?

MAGGIE: There's a line in the Bible, something about, whoever hurts a child, better he should have a millstone around his neck and be cast into a pond or something. I guess I think that about him. Can you imagine, living with that, having done that, all your life? You'd be better off dead.

RENEE: What if it's a woman?

MAGGIE: A woman? No, it couldn't be a woman.

RENEE: Why not? Why not. Women are equal to men, aren't they?

MAGGIE: No, a woman couldn't hurt a child like that.

RENEE: I thought you were the big women's libber.

MAGGIE: No, it wouldn't be a woman. A woman would feel what it was like. She would feel... empathy. No. No woman would do that to a child. To another woman.

RENEE gives a small laugh. Doorbell rings. MAGGIE hesitates.

Want me to get that?

RENEE: Okay.

MAGGIE goes out to the door. Door opens. Murmur of male voices.

MAGGIE: (*re-enters*) It's the mounties.

RENEE: What do they say?

MAGGIE: They want to talk to you. Oh Jesus, the kids!

RENEE: (*gets up slowly, stands there*) You see what they want.

MAGGIE goes back into hall. Murmur of her voice and male voice.

MAGGIE: Mrs. Gifford asked me to take a message.

RCMP: Well, we've been out to the workshop, it was open, but there's no one inside.

MAGGIE: The workshop? Are the kids in the workshop?

RCMP: No, it was Mr. Gifford she was worried about, I understand.

MAGGIE: Mr. Gifford?

RCMP: Mrs. Gifford put in a call to us about half an hour ago, but we've checked and there's no one in the shop. The lights are on but there's no one around. Actually, maybe she should lock up, it's Halloween and the kids get up to things on Halloween.

MAGGIE: (*comes back into kitchen*) They say there's nobody in the shop.

RENEE: I phoned the police. I told them I thought he was going to kill himself in the shop.

MAGGIE: What? My god, what? Renee.

RENEE: That's what I told them. What are they doing now?

MAGGIE: They've gone.

RENEE: Gone! They can't go. Tell them to go back! (*gets up, grabs MAGGIE*) Go on, tell them to go back!

MAGGIE: But he's not there!

RENEE: (*runs out into hall*) He's there!

Door opens. Shuts. RENEE comes back.

They've gone. They drove away. (*starts to rock herself back and forth*) I want you to know... I loved him... I loved him. (*reaches for the telephone, dials*) Yes, this is Mrs. Gifford again. Yes, I called you before. Your men have just left. They were here and they just left. Get them back. No, stop them, and get them back. No, my husband's there. He's there. No, there's a trap door in the workshop. There's a room, under the shop. Yes, there's a sort of air raid shelter under the shop. He's got another room down below. It's a plywood slab painted blue. There are jugs of stuff on top of it. They're glued. They stay on the slab when you pull it up. It's a secret room. It's on the house description. Yes. Yes. Thank you. Yes, I'll hold.

RENEE does not turn. MAGGIE is staring at her. Puts down her drink. Gets up slowly. Turns and looks out toward us, through the sliding doors.

Yes, yes? John Gifford. Yes. Yes. Yes, that one. Mrs. Benton lives next door. Yes. Yes, yes, it's a secret bunker or something. A plywood slab, painted blue. There're jugs of stuff, turpentine or something, on top, but they're glued down, so when you pull up the slab they don't fall off.

MAGGIE: (*turns and looks at RENEE*) I hope you live a long time, Renee. I hope you have a long long life.

RENEE: Forgive me.

MAGGIE: Never.

She turns and goes to the sliding doors, slides them open, and runs out into the night toward the workshop.

RENEE: Yes. Yes, I'll hold on.

Dim spot on RENEE's face, hold briefly, then go to black.

The end.

SKIN

BY

DENNIS FOON

l to r
Thomas Hunt as Todd, Keeman Wong as Tuan, Zena Daruwalla as Phiroza, Lori Lewis as Karen

Photographer: David Cooper

A LONG WAY FROM FAIRY TALES: YOUNG PEOPLE SPEAK IN DENNIS FOON'S *SKIN*

British Columbia is fortunate in having a number of exceptional people who developed a strong theatre for young audiences. In theatres and parks, in school halls and gymnasiums, thousands of young people annually enjoy professional, highly innovative theatrical entertainment – more and more presented from the perspective of the young and addressing aspects of childhood that might make their parents blush. Typically, this theatre presents fifty minutes of ancient and modern performance styles, mixing elements of mask, dance, live music, and song with electronic sound and lighting effects, all laced with crisp, up-to-date dialogue. Although it is often invisible to the public and frequently underfunded, theatre for young people enjoys, as Dennis Foon has noted, special artistic freedom – freedom from the box office, from critics, and "freedom to test work on an audience in virtual laboratory conditions" ("Green Thumb in Context"). Unlike theatre for adults, children's theatre has long escaped the confines of the proscenium stage.

Sydney Risk's Everyman Theatre, Vancouver's first post-war professional company, mounted plays for both adult and school audiences in the late forties. Joy Coghill, a key member, had studied children's theatre at the Goodman Theatre in Chicago under Charlotte Chorpenning. She was appointed co-director, and by the early fifties Everyman was producing a regular season of what it termed "educational" plays, mainly adapted from fairy tales, such as *The Emperor's New Clothes* (Chorpenning) and *Hansel and Gretel* (written by company member Robin Terry).

Holiday Theatre, Canada's first professional theatre for young people, was founded in 1953 by Coghill and Mrya Benson, both former members of Everyman. Its repertoire in the early years also featured fairy tales and stories from literature, but by the mid-sixties, especially with the creative impetus of Canada's Centennial, plays on local themes by British Columbia writers were successfully mounted – for example, Eric Nicol's *The Clam Made a Face*. In this participation play, children, as though attending a Potlatch, sit inside the setting of a west coast longhouse, adopt Native names, and make appropriate sounds as the actors enact Kwakiutl origin stories. In 1974, in Victoria, Elizabeth and Colin Gorrie founded Kaleidoscope Theatre for Young People, mounting and touring productions of great theatricality, using the barest of set, costuming, and props. Some of their plays were written by regional writers such as George Ryga.

By the late 1970s, what Joyce Doolittle calls "the issue-play" had become the focus of many children's theatre companies; in these young audiences are presented with situations, sometimes very troubling ones, that directly affect their lives. Green Thumb Theatre for Young People, founded in 1975 by Dennis Foon and Jane Howard Baker, became a leader in this movement. Foon came to Vancouver in 1973 from his home in Detroit, where he attended the University of Michigan, to complete a Master's degree in playwriting at the University of British Columbia (among his classmates were others who would make their mark in playwriting – and their presence in this anthology: Margaret Hollingsworth, Morris Panych, and Colin Thomas).

For his graduating thesis, Foon wrote four one-act plays designed to explore the actor/audience relationship. One of them was a children's play, "about a group of vegetables on the lam from a spider," that he and a few others, including Jane Howard Baker, decided to stage, and with the help of a federal Local Initiatives Project Grant, Green Thumb Players was born. Coincidentally, there was a theatrical gap in Vancouver: the Playhouse Theatre, which had absorbed Holiday Theatre in the sixties, decided to drop children's productions from their repertoire. As for Foon, from the beginning he was committed to plays for young people:

> There was a simple concept from the outset, that I think helped make it work, despite our initial ignorance. That was the company's mandate: to develop and produce new Canadian plays for young people – I wanted to create a positive breeding ground for new work – and I wanted to learn, which meant I needed to hire people who were better than me.
> —*Theatre Memoirs* 22-23.

Foon became artistic director of Green Thumb, and excelled at working collaboratively with west coast artists and writers, whether in joint productions (for example, Axis Mime, Arts Club), with strong guest directors (Pamela Hawthorn, Brian Richmond), or good writers (Sheldon Rosen, Irene Watts, John Lazarus). In the early years he continued writing plays, some based on British Columbia stories. His *Raft Baby* tells the Moses-like tale about a trapper finding a baby floating down the Peace River in northeast British Columbia.

A "groundbreaking" work for Green Thumb was Joe Weisenfeld's *Hilary's Birthday*, a play about a nine-year old girl's problems with divorce and her mother's new boyfriend. Staged in 1979, it was the first time the company had used adults to play the roles of children, performed in a realistic manner dealing with tough, young people's issues. For Foon, it was the first play that truly reflected the concerns of his youthful audience; watching it, they were "utterly transfixed." After that, the company staged Campbell Smith's popular musical, *Juve*, about teenagers and performed by teenagers, for which Smith had interviewed hundreds of adolescents. Keenly aware of the long-term costs of child abuse, Foon, with Green Thumb, began to collaborate on a full-fledged theatre-in-education project, *Feeling Yes, Feeling No*, a sexual abuse prevention program in which actor/facilitators portrayed children and abusers, and there was audience participation and help available for potential or past victims. The highly successful program has since been staged in other centres in Canada and was made into a National Film Board Film in 1985.

According to Sarah Gibson-Bray, who completed her doctoral dissertation studying the plays of Foon, this work sparked Foon's child advocacy plays, in which he strives to fulfill three objectives: "to engage, to inform and to empower his young viewers" (150). The playwright was now using oral history, involving extensive interviewing of young people, vernacular language, pop music, youth fashion, and familiar settings to continue to explore and connect with his audience. He learned to depict youthful situations with understanding and accuracy, so much so that he encourages subsequent directors to revise his scripts to make them connect with contemporary audiences. With plays about real-life scenarios, controversial social issues, even taboo topics, Foon was now a long way from fantasy and fairy-tale: racism is the subject in *New Canadian Kid*, *Skin*, and *Invisible Kids*; family dysfunction and abuse in *Liars*, *Mirror Game*, and *Seesaw*; although with occasional works such as *The Hunchback of Notre Dame*, he was still capable of writing "traditional" plays.

In *Skin*, Foon has three schoolchildren recount their experiences as recent immigrants to Canada. Speaking simply, honestly, often directly to the audience, they powerfully evoke the often subtle operations of racism in Canadian society without the excessive dramatics of the "racial incidents" reported so loudly in the media. The play begins and ends with the actor/characters making a terse, affecting statement of shared humanity: "I have two arms." "Two legs." "I feel." In between, the three youths, two of them immigrants, from India and Vietnam, and one a First Nations person from British Columbia, tell of routine misunderstandings, blatant rejection, and racist denigration in a school hallway, a classroom, on a job, riding a bus, or merely shopping. As shown in *Skin*, Foon's power as a playwright is in the sureness of his theme: you really believe it is the young people who are speaking. They have integrity; their voices are understated, powerful. The truth is that Foon, now the parent of young schoolchildren himself, really cares, having become a vocal, articulate child advocate at numerous conferences and in his non-dramatic writing. As he stated in a study guide to teachers about *Skin*:

> My objective with the play is to have audiences better understand the life experiences of visible minority kids—to try to break through some of the stereotypes, to see how racial incidents affect the victims—and to trigger discussions on what we can do about problems when we see them.

Typical of Foon's approach, *Skin* began as a collaboration between many groups and individuals. Under the title Project One he developed the script with the cooperation and support of groups almost too numerous to mention: the Vancouver East Cultural Centre, International Briefing Associates, the Young People's Theatre of Toronto, Multiculturalism Canada, the United Church of

Canada, the City of Vancouver, and others. The play was developed through months of research, hundreds of interviews with young people in Vancouver and Toronto, a series of workshops, then finally completed under the deft hand of a master playwright – as evidenced in numerous awards the play has garnered: a nomination for the Governor General's Theatre for Young Audiences Award, a Jessie Award for Best Production for Young Audiences (1986), and a Chalmers Award for Best Children's play (1987).

Skin exists in two versions: one for Toronto and one for Vancouver. The script published here is the Vancouver version.

J.H.

Selected Bibliography:

- Doolittle, Joyce. "The West Coast's Hardy Perennial: Green Thumb." *Canadian Theatre Review* 37 (Spring 1983): 59-65. This issue also contains Foon's adaptation of Volker Ludwig's play *Trummi Kaput*.
- Fatkin, Grace Y.K. "Presentable Issues, Portraying Racism for an Adolescent Audience." *Canadian Theatre Review* 60 (Fall 1989): 20-25. A review of the two versions of *Skin*, written for Toronto and Vancouver; includes production photographs.
- Foon, Dennis. "The Problems of Success." *Canadian Theatre Review* 41 (Winter 1984): 25-31. The playwright reflects on the Vancouver International Theatre Festival for Young People and its changes over time.
- Foon, Dennis. *Skin & Liars*. Toronto: Playwrights Canada Press, 1988. The script of *Skin* in this publication is the Toronto version.
- Foon, Dennis. "Green Thumb – In Context." *Theatre Memoirs*. Toronto: Playwrights Union of Canada, 1998.
- Gibson-Bray, Sarah. "'To Engage, to Inform, and to Empower': Dennis Foon's Child Advocacy Drama." *On-Stage and Off-Stage, English Canadian Drama in Discourse*, Albert-Reiner Glaap and Rolf Althof, eds. St. John's, NF: Breakwater, 1996.
- Page, Malcolm. "Controversial Subjects in Plays for Schools: Green Thumb's *One Thousand Cranes*." *Canadian Theatre Review* 39 (Spring 1984): 15-22.

Skin
by Dennis Foon

Skin was first produced by Green Thumb Theatre in March, 1986, with the following cast:

Phiroza, Sabrina, White Girl	Zena Daruwalla
Karen, The Blonde, Sponsor, Mrs. Paul	Lori Lewis
Tuan, Shopkeeper	Keeman Wong
Todd, Mr. Lizard, Hunk, Cop, Lo	Thomas Hunt

Directed by Dennis Foon
Designed by Marti Wright
Masks by Catherine Hahn

CHARACTERS

Phiroza Mehta
Karen Williams
Tuan Hung Wong
Sabrina
Mr. Lizard
Lo
Todd
Tuan's Sponsor
Mrs. Paul
Tuan's Supervisor
Various mask figures

Skin may be performed by as few as four actors – the three principal characters and one male actor.

STAGING

In the original production, the set was made up of a series of platforms with silhouette cut-outs of human figures placed about the stage.
A set of lockers stood stage left. The lockers were used by Phiroza, Mrs. Paul and acted as Mr. Lizard's podium. He would always pop up from behind them and use them as his playing area.

SCENE ONE

ACTOR 1: I am five foot six inches tall.

ACTOR 2: I weigh 150 pounds.

ACTOR 3: I have two arms

ACTOR 4: Two legs

ACTOR 1: Two feet

ACTOR 2: Two ears

ACTOR 3: Two eyes

ACTOR 4: One nose

ACTOR 1: One mouth

ACTOR 2: Ten fingers

ACTOR 3: Ten toes.

ACTOR 4: I can taste

ACTOR 1: I can smell

ACTOR 2: I can see

ACTOR 3: I can hear

ACTOR 4: I can touch

ACTOR 1: My blood is red

ACTOR 2: My blood is red

ACTOR 3: My blood is red

ACTOR 4: My blood is red.

ACTOR 1: I breathe.

ACTOR 2: I think.

ACTOR 3: I feel.

ACTOR 4: I feel.

ACTOR 1: I feel.

ACTOR 2: I feel.

SCENE TWO

PHIROZA: My name is Phiroza Mehta. In Persian, Phiroza means Victorious. In Gudjerati, Mehta means Teacher. I was born in Bombay. It's on the West Coast of India. My dad worked for Air India and travelled all over the world. So when I was four years old, he and my mom decided to take the family and move. So we sat down in that fat jumbo jet and 25 hours later landed in Vancouver.

KAREN: My name is Karen Williams. Williams comes from hundreds of years ago when the white missionaries came to Canada. They couldn't pronounce our real names so they renamed us after the Kings and Queens of England. Only trouble was, they didn't treat us much like royalty. I am one of the Leelwat people who once were the caretakers of over a quarter of the land that's now called British Columbia. Our people have been given a different name by the Government of Canada: Band Number Three Hundred Fifty-Six. Not a bad name if you like numbers.

TUAN: My name is Wong Tuan Hung (pronounced: Wun Hungh Dwon). In Chinese, my name means many things. I was born in Hanoi, North Vietnam. My father is Chinese, my mother Vietnamese. When the conflict started between China and Vietnam, it was very hard for us to live. My parents thought it would be safer if we left the country for a while but they only had enough money to send my older brother, younger sister and me. My parents stayed behind.

When we left Vietnam there were 300 of us in a thirty meter boat. It was pretty crowded. When half of us slept, the other half stood to make room. We floated for over half a month. We kept asking ships from different countries to tow us to the mainland but they wouldn't get involved. Besides, they said, we weren't in any danger – the boat was still floating. But then it sank, so we were given help. About sixty people drowned, though. Including my older brother.

SCENE THREE

PHIROZA: When I was growing up we lived outside Vancouver and I was friends with everybody. At the elementary school I went to everybody played together. Most of the kids were born here but their grandparents came from other countries. But then we moved and I started going to a different school.

One of the actors explodes a paper bag (or other SFX).

PHIROZA: What did you call me?

SFX.

I'm from India.

SFX.

Listen, Pakistan and India are two different countries.

SFX.

I'm a Parsi, Parsis are Zoroastrians, one of the world's oldest religions... we even had an influence on the bible because...

SFX.

Look, I'm from Bombay, in the state of Maharashtra.

SFX.

Listen, there are a lot of states in India.

SFX.

They didn't care who I really was or where I really came from. Because as far as they were concerned, there was no such thing as *me* anymore.

SCENE FOUR

KAREN: When I grew up I didn't know very much about being Indian. I just figured we were all the same, that there weren't any real differences between us, you know, like customs and language. And that political stuff, like land claims – don't ask me. Ask my cousin, Sabrina. Now Sabrina really knew about Native Rights.

SABRINA: Hey, my dad took us to that new steak and lobster place last night.

KAREN: Oh yeah? That place costs a fortune doesn't it?

SABRINA: Nothing's too good for us. Besides, it was a special occasion, my dad got a raise at work.

KAREN: Great, how was it?

SABRINA: I don't know, nobody would serve us.

KAREN: What? Why?

SABRINA: I don't know, we checked our bows and arrows in at the door.

KAREN: Oh, come on, you always leave them at the door.

They laugh.

SABRINA: Well, when we walked in they were all staring at us, like what's this bunch of Native Indians doing here? But you know my dad, he doesn't care, he just led us in and we all sat down.

KAREN: So?

SABRINA: We just sat. We kept asking for service but nobody came.

KAREN: Maybe they were just busy.

SABRINA: There were a lot of empty tables.

KAREN: But with a new restaurant things can be slow.

SABRINA: 'Specially when Native people come around.

Anyways, my dad's gonna press charges.

KAREN: You're kidding. That didn't necessarily happen because you're Indian.

SABRINA: You really believe that, Karen?

KAREN: Yes, Sabrina. (*to audience*) Yes.

SCENE FIVE

PHIROZA: Sometimes I'm not sure which is worse—getting called names and pushed around—or just being invisible. It's amazing how people can make you feel like you're not really there.

Mask mime.

Music: upbeat. For example: Pointer Sisters' "Jump".

PHIROZA sits centre, perhaps with magazine, as if she is in some kind of waiting room.

Female mask figure (the BLONDE) enters, dancing. Her mask is simply a beautiful smiling teen model's face (bigger than life size) cut out of a magazine.

The BLONDE sits. PHIROZA smiles at her. The BLONDE looks at PHIROZA with her frozen grin, then looks forward, tapping to the music.

PHIROZA looks at her, trying to initiate a conversation but the blonde keeps looking forward, so PHIROZA goes back to her magazine in frustration.

Pause.

Another mask figure enters, dancing. A male.

His mask is also a full-size magazine cutout. A current teenage heartthrob, grinning. We'll call him HUNK.

He sees the BLONDE, does a few moves and sits next to PHIROZA.

PHIROZA smiles and nods at him. He glances at her, nods with his frozen smile.

PHIROZA smiles. They both look forward.

HUNK turns again. PHIROZA looks at him, smiling.

The BLONDE looks at HUNK.

PHIROZA, still smiling, turns and realizes that HUNK isn't looking at her, but at BLONDE.

PHIROZA sits uncomfortably.

Pause.

HUNK looks at BLONDE.

BLONDE looks at HUNK.

They stare at each other.

Pause. PHIROZA withers.

He nods.

She nods.

He shrugs.

She shrugs.

They both stand up.

She takes his arm and they exit, dancing.

PHIROZA: Believe me, you don't need science fiction to become the Invisible Man.

SCENE SIX

TUAN: My sister was 12, I was 16. We were taken to Hong Kong where we stayed in a camp with other refugees. It was hard in the camp. Many people were cruel to us because they thought we were Vietnamese. But we left Vietnam because they were hard on us for being Chinese. Sometimes it is very difficult to understand the way people behave.... But then a church in Canada sponsored us and we came to Vancouver. When we first came off the plane, our sponsors were there to meet us. But no one spoke Chinese or Vietnamese so it was very confusing.

The SPONSOR enters, a bit out of breath, she is late meeting the plane. She is holding a snapshot looking for someone. She sees TUAN. She carefully walks over, trying to see if the photo and face match. As she cranes to look, TUAN turns. She quickly turns away.

Slight pause.

The SPONSOR tries to sneak another look at TUAN, but he looks at her so she turns away.

The SPONSOR tries to sneak another look but this time TUAN catches her. She smiles.

SPONSOR: Are you Tuan?

TUAN, not understanding, just looks at her.

Tuan?

TUAN, hearing this appalling pronunciation of his name, tentatively points to himself.

TUAN: Tuan?

The SPONSOR, thinking that he might be TUAN, points to the snapshot.

SPONSOR: Tuan?

TUAN sees that it is him in the photograph and is delighted.

TUAN: Tuan!

The SPONSOR is relieved.

SPONSOR: Tuan! Hello, I am your sponsor.

TUAN, of course, does not understand and just looks at her.

Pause.

SPONSOR: (*loudly*) Hello! I am your sponsor!

TUAN just smiles and nods. Then, to audience:

TUAN: Why do people think you'll understand if they say it louder?

SPONSOR: (*very loud*) Me Sponsor. You Tuan!

TUAN: Our sponsors were very nice. They really wanted to help. But we were quite confused. Their house was different from any we had ever seen. And the food was strange. Our first day of school we were given lunchboxes. (*holds up a ridiculous lunchbox*) It seemed like an odd way to carry food. English classes take place in an annex outside the school. To get to the main office, I had to go through the front hallway. It was full of kids.

The other actors put on neutral masks. They sit upstage of TUAN. He enters their area. They look up. He stops. Speaks in English.

TUAN: Hello. Office?

Pause.

Office.

TUAN starts to cross.

The first figure quickly stands, blocking TUAN's path.

TUAN hesitates. The figure moves toward him, TUAN backs away.

The figure and TUAN stand face to face. Suddenly, the figure raises his arm and smashes TUAN's book out of his hands.

TUAN moves slowly away from the figure and picks up his book.

The figures stand watching him.

TUAN: That was my first and last visit to the front hallway.

The figures exit. TUAN starts to sit with his book.

Lo enters.

Note: most of the TUAN/LO scenes begin and end with them speaking in Cantonese together. The speeches are written in rough phonetics with an English translation in brackets.

LO: *Nay mo see ah mah.* [Are you okay?]

TUAN: *Mo see.* [No problem.]

LO: Are you alright?

TUAN: (*to audience*) This was Lo. Lo became my first friend in Canada. He was Chinese and from Vietnam, just like me. And he was someone I could really talk to – in my own language. *She na gnah mm shi da gow.* [They were just giving me a hard time.]

LO: Why didn't you fight?

TUAN: I've seen enough blood. I've seen enough death. We've both seen war.

LO: It's a war here too.

TUAN: Oh yeah? Where are the bombs? The bodies on the ground? You call this war?

LO: In a way. You think they like you?

TUAN: Those guys don't. But it's not the same for all of them.

LO: Yes it is. Half of them give us a hard time and the other half let them do it. Not one new student can walk through that hallway. They all walk around the block so they can sneak in the back door. And the teachers don't see a thing.

TUAN: Get off it.

LO: It's true.

TUAN: We've been through this before, Lo. There are a lot of people here on our side.

LO: And a lot who aren't.

TUAN: So?

LO: You've got to stick up for yourself. I push you, you push me back. (*He pushes TUAN.*)

TUAN: Lo, quit playing games.

LO: (*pushing TUAN again*) Those guys are gonna waste you.

TUAN: No chance.

LO: I'll teach you.

LO goes to push TUAN again, but this time TUAN suddenly attacks him, locking LO's arm in a hold, with his hand at LO's throat.

TUAN: I know how to fight. You know I know how to fight.

LO: (*breaking the hold, they both leap into fighting stances*) Then come on!

TUAN: (*breaking from his fighting stance*) No.

LO: What's stopping you?

TUAN: After all I've been through to get here, I can't afford to get into trouble now – I have to work. I have to get my parents out of Vietnam.

LO: Then you have to fight. My whole family is depending on me to save them too – and I will. What about you?

TUAN: I'll help them. I have to. But I don't have to fight. *Ngoh mh sai tong koyee day dah gow.* [I don't have to fight.]

LO: *Ho-ah.* [Okay.]

Suddenly, with a shout, LO leaps into a fighting stance, startling TUAN. He then relaxes from the stance and they both laugh.

Joy geen. [See you around.]

LO exits.

SCENE SEVEN

PHIROZA: I guess it was last June, all of a sudden it was summer. It was just the crummiest weather and out of nowhere: Sun. I put on my shorts and shades, got on my old bike and headed for the beach... so I'm on this quiet street when I pass these guys and the biggest one of them, who looks like the Terminator yells at me: "Hey you—Blah, Blah!" I was paralyzed for a second, scared. I was minding my own business, what did I do? Then something snapped. What right did he have to ruin my day? So then I looked him right in the eye, and as loud as I could yelled: "Blah blah yourself!" They just froze. Six evil looking guys with their mouths dropped open and eyes bugged out, like this: (*demonstrating*) I guess they were a little surprised.

SCENE EIGHT

KAREN: I always did alright in school. Some of my teachers ignored me and some were really nice. Except for one – Mr. Lizard. (*pronunciation Lee-zard*)

Mr. LIZARD slowly enters, his green clawed hands emerging first. He wears a sport jacket and tie, and has a very green lizard mask. He sees a fly. Swats it out of the air and gulps it down. He then sees KAREN.

LIZARD: Do you have the answer, Miss Williams?

KAREN: Three point seventeen.

LIZARD: I can't hear you.

KAREN: Three point seventeen.

LIZARD: No. Three point one seven.

KAREN: Same thing.

LIZARD: Don't get smart with me, young lady. Out. You. Go.

KAREN: Or he'd...

LIZARD: Wakey, wakey, Miss Williams.

KAREN: Pardon me, Mr Lizard?

LIZARD: You were snoring like a lawn mower.

KAREN: No I wasn't–

LIZARD: Out. You. Go.

KAREN: Mr. Lizard always singled me out, I didn't know why. He considered me a loser.

LIZARD: You, Miss Williams, will never amount to anything.

KAREN: Why?

LIZARD: Because you're not very bright.

KAREN: What do you mean by that?

LIZARD: You don't have what it takes.

KAREN: That's not fair.

LIZARD: It's an objective assessment.

KAREN: No it's not.

LIZARD: Are you being smart with me, young lady?

KAREN: Yes, I'm being smart. I'm a lot smarter than you think.

LIZARD: Out. You. Go.

SABRINA: He does that to all the Native kids. He used to do the same thing to me.

KAREN: Really, Sabrina?

SABRINA: The old Lizard of Oz used to pick on me all the time too.

KAREN: He did?

SABRINA: All he figured I was good for was my art work. Come to think of it, a lot of my teachers figured I was destined to be an artist.

KAREN: You? You flunked finger painting.

SABRINA: Funny, isn't it? But everybody thought I had some special qualifications. Every year I painted the mural and got stuck doing beadwork.

KAREN: Why?

SABRINA: Why do you think? Funny, though, nobody ever encouraged me to be a scientist. Anybody ever encourage you?

KAREN: No. Not really.

SABRINA: But everybody figures you must be a natural wood carver, right?

KAREN: What are you saying?

SABRINA: Why are you taking all vocational courses?

KAREN: Because my counsellor told me to.

SABRINA: If your counsellor thought it was a good idea, would you jump in a lake? You're smart – smart enough to go to university. Why aren't you taking academic classes?

KAREN: 'Cause I'm not good enough.

SABRINA: That's what they've been telling Native people for centuries. And that might be what Mr. Lizard thinks. But I know how smart you are.

KAREN: I'm not that smart.

SABRINA: You're no Einstein, but you're smart enough to go to university. You could. You should.

KAREN: No way.

(*to audience*) But I wondered about that. Why was I doing what I was doing? I never knew if I could make it in academic courses because I never tried... but what if I did? Why not? I had nothing to lose.

SCENE NINE

TUAN: My sponsors helped me find work. Every night and on weekends I would clean office buildings. It was hard to do that and study for school too, but I had to send money to my parents. They wanted to leave Vietnam to come and be with us. And I needed money so my sister and I could eat.... Once, just before I finished work at midnight, my supervisor came around.

He mops.

MRS. PAUL: Hi, Tuan.

TUAN: (*not stopping work*) Hi, Mrs. Paul.

MRS. PAUL: How're you doing tonight?

TUAN: (*still mopping*) Okay. Thank you.

MRS. PAUL: Your sister, how's your sister?

TUAN: Sister good. Thank you.

MRS. PAUL: You're a great worker, Tuan. I wish I had five workers like you.... Hey, take a break.

TUAN doesn't understand, keeps mopping.

MRS. PAUL: Tuan.

She takes the mop to stop TUAN.

Tuan, I have to tell you something. Here.

MRS. PAUL hands TUAN an envelope.

TUAN: Thank you.

He opens it.

MRS. PAUL: Severance pay. And your separation certificate, though you don't have enough weeks to collect UIC.

TUAN: I don't understand.

MRS. PAUL: You're fired.

TUAN: I don't understand.

MRS. PAUL: No more job. You're through. No more work.

TUAN: No work?

MRS. PAUL: Right, right, you get it.

TUAN: Why no work?

MRS. PAUL: You're good, son, you're one of my best men. It's nothing personal.

TUAN: Personal?

MRS. PAUL: Forget it, just forget it. It's not up to me.

TUAN: Up to me?

MRS. PAUL: Look, the guy who owns this building complained.

TUAN: Complain?

MRS. PAUL: ...Look, don't make this any harder for me, kid, I already feel like a total jerk... I can't afford to lose this contract, so that's it, okay?

TUAN: Why no work?

MRS. PAUL: ...Good luck, kid.

MRS. PAUL exits.

SCENE TEN

PHIROZA: So for a long time I just plugged along, things were fine. I figured I could handle just about anything. And then one day...

TODD enters. He sees PHIROZA who is looking at her notebook. He checks his breath, sprays with a mouth freshener. Checks his hair, sprays it too. PHIROZA looks. He stops, smiles sheepishly.

TODD: Hi.

PHIROZA: Hi.

TODD: ...Is your name Phiroza?

PHIROZA: Yeah.

TODD: I'm–

PHIROZA: (*before he can get it out*) Todd.

TODD: ...Yeah.

Embarrassed silence.

...You're Italian, right?

PHIROZA: Maybe.

TODD: Greek?

PHIROZA: Try again. (*to audience*) So how long can I keep up this guessing game? I liked him, I wanted him to like me. So then I did something really dumb. I guess at the time I thought it was sort of funny. But it wasn't.

TODD: Spanish?

PHIROZA: No. (*beat*) Ready?

TODD: Yeah.

PHIROZA: My family comes from Persia.

TODD: Persia?

PHIROZA: It's called Iran now.

TODD: Iran? Far out.

PHIROZA: (*to audience*) It's not a total lie. Our people did come from Iran... when it was called Persia. 800 years ago.

TODD: You're really from Iran?

PHIROZA: Yeah, my whole family.

TODD: You know the Ayatollah Khomeini?

PHIROZA: Not personally. He came to power after we left Iran.

TODD: Who was in power?

PHIROZA: I can't remember. (*to audience*) It was 800 years ago. (*to TODD*) I'm pretty sure he's dead now.

TODD: Right. I'm pretty sure you're right.

PHIROZA: (*to audience*) We got along great. And if anyone ever gave us a rough time...

A horn honks (or other SFX).

TODD: She's from Persia, ya goof!

SFX.

Take your own advice, eh?

SFX.

PHIROZA: Hey, why don't you grow up?

Another SFX. PHIROZA and TODD just smile at each other, ignoring the taunt. They kiss.

PHIROZA: (*to audience*) So I didn't tell him the truth. Not then, anyway.

TODD: See you later, okay?

PHIROZA: Okay. Bye.

TODD exits.

I didn't want to tell him till I got to know him better. I thought it was an excellent tactic – for a while.

SCENE ELEVEN

KAREN quietly goes over to Mr. LIZARD's area and knocks. Pause. She knocks again. Mr. LIZARD suddenly pops up.

LIZARD: Yes, Miss Williams!

KAREN: I was thinking, sir–

LIZARD: Thinking? Thinking, Miss Williams, bravo!

KAREN: I was thinking about next semester, Sir, I want to start taking academic courses.

LIZARD: Pardon me?

KAREN: I want to stop taking vocational classes.

Pause.

LIZARD: Have you been drinking, Miss Williams?

KAREN: I do not drink, Mr. Lizard.

LIZARD: What, then, is responsible for this peculiar delusion?

KAREN: Nothing, Sir. It isn't a delusion.

LIZARD: Of course it is. Your work is mediocre at this level. How do you expect to succeed in an academic programme?

KAREN: By working harder.

LIZARD: There is a large difference, Miss Williams, between hard work and having what it takes.

KAREN: Are you saying I don't have what it takes?

LIZARD: Frankly, no. You do not.

KAREN: Well I think I do. (*to audience*) So I started working my butt off. It wasn't easy, but my grades started going up .

SABRINA: Hey, Karen, wanna go to a movie?

KAREN: Not tonight, Sabrina.

SABRINA: All you ever do is study.

KAREN: I've got a test on Monday.

SABRINA: I thought you weren't good enough to make it in school.

KAREN: Okay, okay, so you were right.

SABRINA: You just had to learn not to believe what they said about you.

KAREN: That I wasn't good enough?

SABRINA: Same thing they say to all Native people.

KAREN: Oh come on, Sabrina. People are people. Some are jerks and some are nice. They don't treat you different just cause you're Native.

SABRINA: You really think so?

KAREN: Yeah.

SABRINA: What about when people call you names?

KAREN: I just ignore them.

SABRINA: What about when guys come up to you on the street and ask you if you're for sale?

KAREN: I walk away.

SABRINA: And the stuff at school—everybody just assuming you're lazy and no good and your parents are drunks—you think every white person in this country goes through that too?

KAREN: I don't know.

SABRINA: Well, you're gonna, Karen. Whether you like it or not.

KAREN: Sabrina–

SABRINA exits.

SCENE TWELVE

TUAN: I had so little English, I didn't know what my supervisor was saying. But I knew what she meant. Now I know what she did was illegal. But when it happened I was upset, it didn't make sense. I needed to talk to someone.

LO enters. He grabs the separation certificate.

LO: *Keui mm iyu nay mieh la*? [What the hell is this?]

TUAN: *Mo gong jo lo.* [She fired me.]

LO: She fired you?

TUAN: Yeah, she fired me.

LO: Who cares, it was a stupid job anyway.

TUAN: Thanks, Lo, that makes me feel a lot better.

LO: I'm sure they liked how the work got done. They just didn't like who was doing it.

TUAN: They liked me. I know she liked me.

LO: Not enough to keep someone like us on the job. And you can't speak enough English to fight back so you're easy to mess around.

TUAN: I'll find another job, it's no big deal.

LO: What? Mopping floors?

TUAN: I don't mind it.

LO: Yeah, you're a real survivor.

TUAN: Aren't you?

LO: Maybe, but I won't mop floors. I'm a mechanic.

TUAN: You'll be okay. You'll get a job.

LO: Oh, sure, every time I apply for one, they say: you don't have Canadian experience. How am I supposed to get experience if nobody'll hire me? Or they say: Sorry, you don't speak enough English. But how often does a mechanic have to speak to a carburetor? Besides, most of the cars here are Japanese. I speak a little Japanese. If they need somebody to talk to a Toyota, I can do it.

TUAN: (*to audience*) But I knew Lo was in despair, he needed work so badly. Looking at it now, I think he was more upset about my bad fortune than even I was. Because in spite of everything, I still had hope. I had to earn money, so I didn't stop looking until I found another job. It wasn't much, but at least we could survive.

SCENE THIRTEEN

A tough masked figure, as in scene six, enters. He goes to PHIROZA's locker and scribbles on it.

As he exits, he shoves TUAN, who has been sitting on stage looking at the separation certificate.

SCENE FOURTEEN

TODD: Hey, Phiroza, get your stuff out of your locker and let's go.

PHIROZA: Just a second, Todd, just a sec... oh no.

TODD: What is it? (*stops at her locker and stares*) The jerks.

PHIROZA: Doesn't surprise me.

TODD: Do you know who wrote this?

PHIROZA: I think so.

TODD: Tell me. I'll kill the goofs.

PHIROZA: Perfect. You kill them, then their friends kill you. Then your friends kill their friends and then their friends' friends kill your friends and then your friends' friends kill their friends' friends and their friends' friends' friends kill...

TODD: Alright, alright. So what do you think we should do?

PHIROZA: I guess I'll move my locker.

TODD: Why should you have to do that? Put the same thing on their locker.

PHIROZA: Forget it. Why spread the pollution?

TODD: So you're just gonna let it happen?

PHIROZA: No, I could try talking to them.

TODD: Who?

PHIROZA: The guys who share the locker next to mine.

TODD: Oh, come on, they won't talk to you.

PHIROZA: Yeah, but I wonder what would happen. You know what the big one looks like? He's got this thing with his shoulders and he walks like this: (*She now plays both the JOCK and herself.*) With his chin stuck out and this kind of strut like he's the toughest dude in the world.

JOCK: Hey boys, look at this: (*He flexes his muscles.*) Not bad, eh? I been working out with the Nautilus. Hey, check out that chick. Watch this, boys: Hey, baby, what's happening? Wanna watch me drink a six pack? Two six packs? Hey come back, I love you.

PHIROZA: So then I say to him: Hey, why'd you do that to my locker?

Each time the JOCK speaks, he takes a different body builders' pose.

JOCK: What do you want?

PHIROZA: I want to know why you did that.

JOCK: I don't know what you're talking about.

PHIROZA: You do too. Now explain.

JOCK: I got nothin' to explain.

PHIROZA: You did it, now explain it.

JOCK: You want an explanation? It was something to do.

PHIROZA: Listen, if we would just learn to treat each other decently, we would be so much further ahead... just because I was born in–

She stops suddenly.

TODD: Go on, great, tell him where you were born.

She looks at TODD.

Go on, tell him where you were born – Phiroza? What is it?

PHIROZA: Nothing. Nothing!

TODD shrugs and exits.

It was great, perfect. He thought I was mad at him but I was really mad at myself for that stupid lie. I liked Todd a lot, wanted him to know who I was, who I really was. But instead I was covering up all the time, faking it. I couldn't believe I was doing this to him. Or myself.

SCENE FIFTEEN

TUAN: Sometimes late at night when I am mopping floors, I stop and listen. The empty building, so hollow. Buzzing of fluorescent tubes. Outside rain beats against windows. I feel... like I'm underwater. I think: around the corner, my brother will be standing. Waiting to grab the mop from my hands, shouting, "You're my little brother, why are you working when you should be sleeping? Give that mop to me, that is my job!" And I look at him, and his hair is still wet, wet like it was the last time I saw him. I want to say, "Did you swim, I thought you drowned. How did you find me here, in Canada, in this city, in this building right now? You didn't drown, you're alive and you made it all the way to me."

...And I walk down the corridor, turn the corner and look. The hallway goes on forever. It's so empty. No sound but the hum of lights. And the rain against windows.

SCENE SIXTEEN

The following is performed as a mask mime narrated by KAREN. The SHOPKEEPER, POLICEMAN and girl are Caucasian mask figures.

KAREN: I was in this store near school, looking at some magazines and this girl walked in. I saw her take some stuff: earrings, a bracelet, some hair clips. She shoved it in her purse and went for the door. Just then the storekeeper yells, "stop!" The girl starts running but it was the shop keeper's lucky day: A policeman was just walking in, she nearly bowled him over. He takes her to the counter and dumps out her purse. Out comes the earrings and bracelet and hair clips. He then tells the girl to apologize to the storekeeper and she does. The storekeeper accepts her apology. The girl says goodbye and leaves. Then:

Now the masked figures speak. Their smiling faces turn to frowns.

SHOPKEEPER: Wait. Don't let that girl go. I think she took something too.

KAREN: I was just standing here.

SHOPKEEPER: Every time her people come in here they walk out with half the stuff on my shelves.

COP: Open up your purse.

KAREN: But I was...

COP: Open it up!

He takes it from her and looks through it.

KAREN: See, I don't have anything.

COP: Don't get cheeky with me. You people are always mouthing off. You may not be in trouble now, but you'll end up just like the rest of them, drunk and living in the skids, hooking and stealing.

KAREN: I want your number. I'm gonna report you.

COP: Try it. You want to see harassment? Just cross the line once, baby, and you'll get it. I know just how to deal with your kind.

KAREN: (*to audience*) This is Canada. In 1986. But it happened, it really happened. I know most police aren't like that guy. But some are. And how many people are too? I started thinking about all times I've been bugged in stores– Can I help you? Can I help you? They all thought I was shoplifting. And all the people who've said to me: "you don't look like an Indian" What's an Indian supposed to look like? And walking down the street, the names little four- and five-year-olds have called me – where did they learn that stuff? I didn't teach it to them. Who did?

SCENE SEVENTEEN

TUAN: My younger sister always says that I work too hard, mopping floors or going to school. She wants to help earn money but I won't let her. She's too young and I promised my parents I'd take care of her. Besides, at least I had work.

LO: *Wai! A Dwon!* [Hey! Tuan!]

TUAN: *Gum yeh, nay hoy been doe a*? [It's late, Lo. What are you doing here?] Lo, it's late. What are you doing here?

LO: Going home.

TUAN: Good, we can walk together.

LO: Not that home.

TUAN: What do you mean?

LO: I'm going back to Vietnam.

TUAN: Going back? After all you went through to come to Canada?

LO: I thought it would be different.

TUAN: It is different, it's free.

LO: You call this free? Look at this.

TUAN: A letter. From your parents... they seem to be very impressed with you.

LO: And proud and happy. I spend all day looking for jobs when there aren't any and they think I'm a big success in Canada, making tons of money fixing monorail trains.

TUAN: You don't fix monorail trains.

LO: Don't tell them that. They're all ready to fly here to live in my five bedroom house as soon as I send them their plane tickets.

TUAN: You told them you have a five bedroom house?

LO: My room here is worse than anything I ever had in Vietnam... Tuan – I'm going home.

TUAN: You can't swim back to Vietnam.

LO: So?

TUAN: Maybe you need a holiday.

LO: What, take a cruise on the Love Boat?

TUAN: Well, no, go to Victoria or something.

LO: That's a good idea.

TUAN: I can lend you some money.

LO: I've got enough.

TUAN: Great. Let's get something to eat.

LO: Not right now. I've got a lot to do to get ready.

TUAN: Okay.

LO: ...Thanks for everything, Tuan. *Daw jah sai nay la.* [Thank you for everything] You've been a good friend.

LO starts to exit. TUAN stops him.

TUAN: *Wai. Nay yow mu see-ah?* [Hey, what's going on?]

LO shrugs.

LO: *Moh see.* [Nothing]

LO exits.

TUAN: We spoke the same language but I didn't understand what he was saying. If really knew I would have held onto him, not let him walk off alone. I would have run to his room, locked his windows... but I didn't understand and I let him walk away... let him die. His apartment building was too tall. The lights in the city shimmer so much at night they're like light on the water. It all looks so soft and inviting. He must have floated like a leaf in the wind just above the waves. Then one drop of water touches it and it never leaves the sea again. But it wasn't water, it was the sidewalk. And he was not a leaf.

SCENE EIGHTEEN

LIZARD: Well, Miss Williams, you did it. You'll be taking a full academic programme next semester. Congratulations.

KAREN: Thank you, Sir.

LIZARD: I always knew you could do it.

KAREN: Pardon me?

LIZARD: I always knew you had it in you.

KAREN: You did?

LIZARD: I only pushed you because I could see your potential. I could see that little spark of intelligence still glowing. I nurtured it, I made it grow. And here you are. Congratulations.

KAREN: Don't congratulate me. You say you were just pushing us but all it did was make us feel stupid and worthless. Cause you do, you do think we're stupid. You never thought I could do it, you never did. But I made it anyway, in spite of you. So, Mr. Lizard, I have just one thing to say to you: OUT. YOU. GO!!

Music: Bob Marley's "I Shot the Sheriff."

SCENE NINETEEN

PHIROZA: So Todd kept thinking I was from Iran. But I was really sick of the lie. I had to be so careful about everything I said to him. I wanted him to meet my family – but what if he started asking my dad questions about life in Persia? I decided to tell him the truth but it wasn't going to be easy.

TODD: Hey, Phiroza, where'd you put my Springsteen tape?

PHIROZA hands him a card.

Thanks. What's this? A birth certificate? It's yours. Place of birth: Bombay, India. ...I thought you were from Iran.

PHIROZA: That's right, we're from Iran.

TODD: Then why does it say India?

PHIROZA: Because I grew up in India.

TODD: It says you were born in India.

PHIROZA: I lived in India till I was four.

TODD: And then you went back to Iran to be born?

PHIROZA: No, then I went to Canada.

TODD: I thought you said you were from Iran.

PHIROZA: I am.

TODD: So did you get born twice, once in Iran and once in India?

PHIROZA: No.

TODD: Let me see if I've got it. You were born in India, then you came to Canada but you're from Iran.

PHIROZA: You've got it.

TODD: I do? Ever been to Iran?

PHIROZA: Personally?

TODD: Yes, personally.

PHIROZA: I was one of the Parsi people who came from Iran to India.

TODD: When?

PHIROZA: When?

TODD: Yeah, when.

PHIROZA: Oh, about... eight (*She mumbles.*) years ago.

TODD: Eight years ago?

PHIROZA: Not exactly.

TODD: Eight how many years ago.

PHIROZA: Hundred.

TODD: Eight hundred years ago? You went from Iran eight hundred years ago and came to India and were born and came to Canada when you were four?

PHIROZA: Because I was born again, like reincarnation.

TODD: I think you're the first older woman I ever went out with.

PHIROZA: I'm the same age as you.

TODD: Right. I see. You were born in this life, so this is the life that counts, right?

PHIROZA: Right.

TODD: So in this life, you were born in India, right?

PHIROZA: ...Right.

TODD: And in this life, you're Canadian, right?

PHIROZA: ...Right.

TODD: ...Right. So that makes you

PHIROZA: ...Indo-Canadian.

TODD: Right.

PHIROZA: Right... sorry for putting you on for so long. I should have told you sooner but the longer I waited, the harder it got to tell you, and I didn't know what to say.... Sorry.

Slight pause.

Do you want to break up?

TODD: Nah.

PHIROZA: For sure?

TODD: Yeah... cause I have a confession to make too.

PHIROZA: You do?

TODD: Yeah.

PHIROZA: What is it?

TODD: Well... you know I told you I was in Grade Twelve, supposed to graduate this year...

PHIROZA: What grade are you in!

TODD: I was afraid to tell you...

PHIROZA: What grade!

TODD: ...Three.

PHIROZA: What? How old are you?

TODD: Seven. You wanna break up?

PHIROZA: Get out of here!

TODD: I am, I'm seven years old. These are new teeth, see?

PHIROZA: You nut!

TODD: You wanna break up?

PHIROZA: No, I like younger men.

TODD: Oh, whew!

PHIROZA: You like older women?

TODD: Oh yeah.

PHIROZA: Whew!

PHIROZA: (*to audience*) Hey, that wasn't so bad, I could have told him the first day we met. I guess I knew from the start how he felt about me. I just wasn't sure how I felt about myself.

SCENE TWENTY

KAREN: Sometimes I wonder – was Mr. Lizard telling the truth? Did he treat me that way on purpose? Or was he what I thought he was? He did treat Sabrina the same way. I guess it's like everything else in this country – hard to see. I just take academic courses now and I'm doing okay, even if it is a lot of work. Some of my friends give me a hard time – but the ones who are my real friends understand, they're happy for me. So I think I'm going to go to university. Maybe I'll train to be a teacher. Or a lawyer. I don't know, I haven't decided yet. But I will.

TUAN: When I found out Lo was dead, it was such a puzzle. Why should I live and Lo die? We were so much the same – why not me? I remember he always said that I was a survivor. He'd laugh, tease me... now, I just wish he was a survivor too. By next year I will have enough money to bring my parents here. I'm glad they'll be safe. They are very excited, but as for me, I don't want to think about the future. For me, it is as hard to look forward as it is to look back. So I live for today. For each moment. And live as best I can.

PHIROZA: My name is Phiroza Mehta. I was born in Bombay, India...

KAREN: My name is Karen Williams. I was born near Lillooet, British Columbia...

TUAN: My name is Wong Tuan Hung. I was born in Hanoi, North Vietnam...

PHIROZA: My dad worked for Air India and travelled all over the world...

KAREN: The white missionaries couldn't pronounce our Indian names, so they renamed us after the Kings and Queens of England. Only trouble was, they didn't treat us much like royalty.

The end.

NO` XYA`
(OUR FOOTPRINTS)

BY

DAVID DIAMOND

WITH
HAL B. BLACKWATER
LOIS G. SHANNON
MARIE WILSON

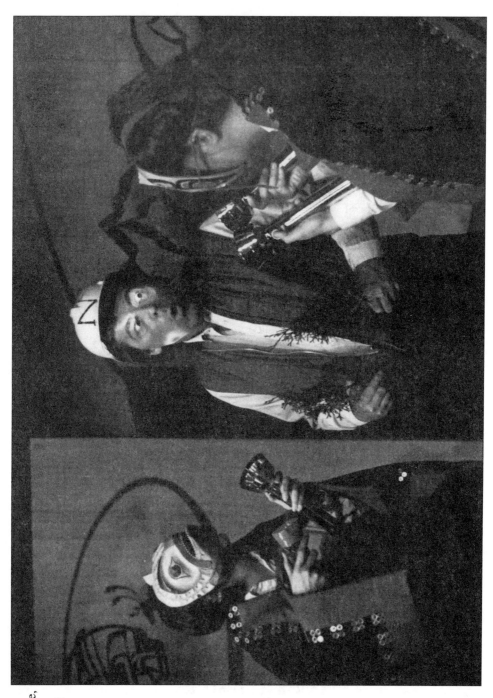

l to r
Sylvia-Anne George,
Edward J. Astley,
Sherri-Lee Guilbert

Photographer:
Chris Cameron

COLLAPSING BOUNDARIES: HEADLINES THEATRE AND
NO` XYA` (OUR FOOTPRINTS)

At the end of an article recounting the tour of Headlines Theatre's *Out of the Silence*, David Diamond, explaining the unorthodox approach of eliciting audience intervention during performance, reminds his readers of the origins of theatre and in doing so provides the philosophy behind the company he has been artistic director of since 1984:

> I know that there are those who will say it is not theatre, it is therapy. No. It is the root of theatre. Theatre used to be ordinary people singing, dancing and telling stories. It used to be the way individuals in a community expressed their fears, hopes and desires. Today, people have become merely consumers of culture. With projects like *Out of the Silence*, we are doing what I believe all good theatre should do – entertain and challenge, stimulate our senses, and be a tool with relevance to our everyday lives. (24)

From its inception in 1981 Headlines Theatre has worked consistently to effect social change through a focus on contemporary issues. The company was, in fact, born out of a concern about a housing crisis in Vancouver; their first production, *Buy, Buy Vancouver*, played to a non-mainstream audience, attracted then Mayor Mike Harcourt's attention, and was eventually performed for politicians, activists, and developers at the Chateau Laurier in Ottawa. Subsequent Headlines productions have dealt with such topics as militarism, economic policy, race relations, family violence, AIDS, biodiversity, and criminalization of youth, and have been staged around the world in such varied venues as schools and universities, government offices, corporate headquarters, restaurants, youth detention centres, and network and community cable television stations. Headlines Theatre has facilitated play creation as a means of problem solving among particular work groups, added talkback sessions to many of their productions, led empowerment workshops for young people, and developed an interactive television process involving on-air interventions by a viewing audience.

The variety of distinctions bestowed upon the troupe attests to their success in reaching diverse audiences: Diamond was recently awarded an Honourary Doctorate of Letters degree by the University College of the Fraser Valley (largely for his work with Headlines Theatre) and the company has received the Jessie Award for Innovation in Theatre, the Hometown USA Award (won over almost 2000 other entrants from all over North America), the Canadian Healthy Environment Award, appointment as resident theatre company of the Vancouver School District, Mosaic's Human Rights Award, and official recognition at the seventh International Festival of the Theatre of the Oppressed in Rio de Janeiro as a centre of the Theatre of the Oppressed in British Columbia.

Ratsoy: Where are you from, and how did you end up in British Columbia?

Diamond: I'm from Winnipeg, but as a student in the University of Alberta's drama department in Edmonton I could, lying in my little room on a cold clear night, pick up Vancouver radio, and it seemed so exciting there. There was that as well as the fact that I had my Equity card almost before I graduated with a Bachelor of Fine Arts degree. I went from school to do the first four shows for Northern Light (a new Edmonton theatre company) in 1975, and then I did some television and a show at the Citadel: it was all seeming too easy. I decided I needed to go where nobody knew me, and prove myself to myself, and Vancouver had an allure. When I came to Vancouver in 1976, I hit the tail end of Fourth Avenue's heyday, and I saw the water and the mountains and said, "I'm home."

The Rio de Janeiro honour was especially befitting: Headlines' "Theatre for Living" philosophy is a direct outgrowth of Diamond's study in Paris under Brazilian Augusto Boal, who developed a political theatre called "Theatre of the Oppressed" in the 1960s. Headlines' website identifies Boal's influence on Diamond as seminal in the direction of the company: Headlines moved from making theatre for communities to making theatre *with* communities.

Ratsoy: How did you meet Augusto Boal?

Diamond: The first time I met Boal was in 1984 in Paris. The Headlines collective dissolved that year. The Canada Council agreed to send me to Europe to visit different political theatre companies, although at the time I had never directed anything in my life. Rummaging through a bookstore before I left, I came across a book by a guy named Paulo Freire, whom I didn't know, called *Pedagogy of the Oppressed*. I liked the title so I bought it. I was travelling through Europe and visiting different political theatre companies and reading this book, and it was blowing my mind. While Headlines' work had been successful, I felt like there was a piece missing. The company had been really good at doing theatre *for* people, but how did one go about doing it *with* them? And *Pedagogy of the Oppressed* was answering all of that in theoretical ways. And then I got to Manchester to a theatre conference and Chris Vine was giving a demonstration of something called Forum Theatre by a guy named Augusto Boal. I saw that what Boal was doing was what I was reading about in *Pedagogy of the Oppressed*. And some phone calls got made. It turned out Boal was in exile in France and was doing a training session the next month. And I and a number of other very excited people went over to Paris. I made a number of lasting friendships, including one with Boal.

In addition to involving non-actors in performance, the troupe's collaborative philosophy has resulted in alliances with a long list of British Columbia theatre practitioners and a multidisciplinary approach that has engaged artists from other disciplines. For example, Colin Thomas's *Flesh and Blood* was produced by Headlines, and *Last Call* director Sue Astley, along with other Tamahnous members such as Suzie Payne, has worked with the company. Diamond worked with more than one hundred BC youth as background for *Ice: Beyond Cool*, the dance/theatre production that John Lazarus wrote for Judith Marcuse's DanceArts Vancouver, and film director Nettie Wild (a founding member of Headlines, now on the Board of Directors) and folksinger Bob Bossin have also been involved with Headlines projects. As it breaks down barriers between performer and spectator, Headlines Theatre also rejects as artificial boundaries between art forms, between art and ceremony, and between cultures.

In Canada recently, drama has been an efficacious genre delivering a history of First Nations/Crown relations and thereby showcasing the inseparability of the public and the private domains: Margo Kane's *Moonlodge*, Daniel David Moses's *Almighty Voice and His Wife,* and Tomson Highway's *Dry Lips Oughta Move to Kapuskasing*, for example, manage to both unfold specific stories and provide a remarkably full yet succinct historical and cultural context. *NO` XYA`* does the same: it delineates the land grabs, the outlawing of traditional ceremonies, the devastation of smallpox, measles, and alcohol, and the havoc caused by the federal policy of residential schools. It chronicles not only a region, but also the country: here, in contemporary issues such as logging policy and land claims disputes, is a history of the conquest writ small.

As early as 1887, a delegation of Chiefs from Northwest British Columbia, south of the Alaska panhandle, approached the provincial legislature to press for a treaty for the return of their traditional lands. They were turned away. In 1991, in the landmark *Delgamuukw et al. vs. The Queen* court case, BC Supreme Court Justice Allan MacEachern dismissed the claim of the Gitxsan-Wet'suwet'en Hereditary Chiefs to Aboriginal rights to an area of their traditional territories approximately the size of New Brunswick. However, he did find that the Gitxsan and Wet'suwet'en were entitled to the use of unoccupied crown land in the territory they claimed for aboriginal subsistence activities. Although the subsequent appeal of the case was unsuccessful, in 1997 the Supreme Court of Canada acknowledged Aboriginal title, ordered a new trial, and ruled that oral history should be accepted in court. The Supreme Court also encouraged the BC government and the Gitxsan-Wet'suwet'en to negotiate settlement outside the court system. In May of 2000, the Nisga'a, neighbours of the Gitxsan, received Royal assent in the form of the Nisga'a Treaty (the first treaty made in BC between the provincial government and First Nations people since Treaty No. 8 was signed a hundred years earlier) which provided them with approximately 2000 square kilometres of land, over $200 million in provincial and federal payments, and a form of self-government.

The approach, from inception through production, of Headlines Theatre to *NO` XYA`* (*Our Footprints*) illustrates its respect for and sensitivity to First Nations cultures. Typically, the play's initiators sought to engage audiences usually alienated from mainstream Canadian theatre and relied on extensive interviewing. This was a collaborative project developed with and for the people it is about. The research, initial writing, and subsequent rewriting for new tours were done in Kispiox in association with the Gitxsan and Wet'suwet'en Hereditary Chiefs and other individuals in the area: the play was authored by David Diamond with Hal B. Blackwater, Lois G. Shannon, and Marie Wilson. The sets, properties, and costumes also originated from the area. According to Alan Filewod, who first anthologized the play, the troupe respected wishes that one sacred song, which they received permission to sing in performance, be omitted from the written text, and *NO` XYA`* met with the approval of tribal elders. A representative of the chiefs attended each local performance and toured Canada and New Zealand with the show.

Ratsoy: How many times has *NO` XYA`* been performed?

Diamond: More than 110 performances in Canada and twenty or so in various Maori communities in New Zealand.

Ratsoy: What sort of reception did it get in New Zealand?

Diamond: Doug Cleverley, who was Headlines' administrator at the time, put together the New Zealand tour. Only one of us could go to New Zealand; somebody had to be here to hold down the fort. Because he worked so hard, I said that he should go. He went and tour managed. I flew out for the performances in Rotorua. I know stories about how wonderfully it was received in other communities but I witnessed it myself in Rotorua. It was a very profound tour for everybody – for the cast and for Ardythe Wilson (Skanu'u), who represented the Gitxsan and Wet'suwet'en chiefs and travelled with the show and went into ambassadorial meetings with the Maori. I sat in on one of those meetings, and it was remarkable. These were real strategy sessions around land claims – nuts and bolts stuff. And also, I think, it was a very strong experience for the Maori, who experienced this Gitxsan and Wet'suwet'en play, that, as I heard from them over and over again, came from another part of the world but told their story.

Playing the Pacific Province begins with a play written about a Native woman by a white man and ends with a work written by a Native woman about Native women. *NO` XYA`* (which falls close to the middle chronologically, at a time when the Canadian literary and theatrical establishments were finally beginning to listen to Native voices) illustrates the spirit of cooperation between cultures in both its process and its product and, as it interrogates Western beliefs in, for example, ownership, the primacy of economic growth, patrilineality, and the nuclear family, it, as Filewod remarks, "rests on the premise that the white colonizer can participate in and learn from Native traditional culture" (xi).

Ultimately, the play is more about commonalities than differences. As the text emphasizes the dispossession inherent in the narratives of both aboriginal and settler groups (there is both pathos and irony in the fact that the Scots immigrated to Canada as a result of being stripped of their land), points to similarities in the creation stories of the two cultures, and bestows upon the female representatives of each group the role of conciliator, *NO` XYA` (Our Footprints)* underscores the injustices and deficiencies in the status quo to Native *and* non-Native alike.

Fittingly, given its explicit message about the importance of all peoples acting in harmony with each other and the earth, the play, which was performed by a cast of Native and non-Native actors, is a harmonious fusion of elements of aboriginal and western cultures; for instance, it relies heavily on both written documentation and First Nations oral testimony and, as reviewer Michael Scott observes, blends "ancient Tsimshian narrative elements with moments of suburban psycho-drama" in "remarkable theatre" that "creates its own feast hall and offers glimpses of centuries-old rituals played out there." *NO` XYA`* also incorporates Native spiritual beliefs in transformation and the close relationship between humans and animals as it elides conventional time barriers.

The ending of *NO` XYA` (Our Footprints)* not only reflects the Gitxsan and Wet'suwet'en Feast Halls tradition, as the cast member states, but it also mirrors aboriginal beliefs in the circularity of existence: there isn't definite closure. Furthermore, this "conclusion" embodies David Diamond and Headlines Theatre's belief in direct involvement of the audience: in a device that breaks down conventional barriers between art and audience, the play, by inviting the audience to speak and to "act on" the message of the production, carries on beyond the script.

G.R.

Selected Bibliography:

- Crook, Barbara. "The Healing Stage: Headlines Theatre Plays a Key Role in Helping Native Canadians Reclaim Their Confidence After Years of Suffering Under the Residential School System." *The Vancouver Sun* 2 Mar. 1996. Examines Headlines Theatre workshops held across the province.
- Crook, Barbara. "The Play's the Thing to Catch the Conscience of a Community: Headlines Theatre Presents Plays About the Real Issues Affecting B.C." *The Vancouver Sun* 28 Apr. 1995.
- Diamond, David. "Making Headlines: On the Road with *Out of the Silence*." *Theatrum* 33 (April/May 1993): 21-24.
- Diamond, David. "The Squeegee Report." *Canadian Theatre Review* 103 (Summer 2000): 60-69. Diamond outlines Headlines' experience with Legislative Theatre; the company employed "squeegee kids" in a play, staged at Firehall Arts Centre, designed to stimulate questions about criminalization of youth and provoke Vancouver city council to action.
- Diamond, David. Telephone Interview. 10 Apr. 2001.
- Filewod, Alan. *New Canadian Drama 5: Political Drama*. Ottawa: Borealis Press, 1991. Includes the playscript of *NO` XYA`*.
- Freire, Paulo. *Pedagogy of the Oppressed*. Trans. Myra Bergman Ramos. New York: Seabury Press, 1970.
- Headlines Theatre Website. www.headlinestheatre.com .
- Read, Nicholas. "Playing to Kill, Disarmingly." *The Vancouver Sun* 6 Mar. 1982. Examines the efforts of both Morris Panych (with *Last Call*) and Headlines Theatre to increase public awareness about nuclear disarmament.
- Scott, Michael. "Headlines' *NO` XYA`* is Remarkable Theatre." *The Vancouver Sun* 4 Nov. 1987.

NO` XYA` (Our Footprints)
by David Diamond
with Hal B. Blackwater
Lois G. Shannon
Marie Wilson

NO` XYA` (Our Footprints) premiered in Kispiox, British Columbia, on September 9, 1987 and then toured the province. In 1988, it completed an extensive Canadian tour, and in 1990 played to five Maori communities before a final one-week run at the James Cowan Theatre in Vancouver. The cast/crew was made up of the following:

Edward J. Astley (Guusii'mas+)
Caribou dancer, Francis/Frank Larry, Bishop Dentenwill, Fisheries Officer

Hal B. Blackwater (Liigii Bin Ban/Frog)
Core research/writing, Choreographer, Gyat/James, Nahwodai, Salmon dancer, Guu Hadixs

Sylvia-Anne George (Fireweed)
Guu Hadixs, Hanakx/Marianne

Sherri-Lee Guilbert (Xsim duus+)
Salmon dancer, Helena/Helen Indian Agent, Guu Hadixs

Doug Cleverley (Guukxws Wiltxw+)
Tour Manager, voice of Guu Hadixs

Paul Williams
Technical director, Stage manager

Ardythe Wilson (Skanu'u/Fireweed)
Representative of the Gitxsan and Wet'suwet'en Hereditary Chiefs, sound tape production

+ These Gitxsan names were given by Chief Baasxya laxha (Bill Blackwater Sr.) in Anspayawx (Kispiox) BC in 1987.

The characters in *NO` XYA` (Our Footprints)* are composites based on real people. No character is intended to portray any person in particular.

ACKNOWLEDGEMENTS

The playwright acknowledges and thanks all the following in Gitxsan and Wet'suwet'en Territory and Vancouver who contributed to the success of the project: Gitxsan Chief Baasxya laxha (Bill Blackwater Sr./Wolf); Gitxsan Chief Bistay'i (Violet Smith/Fireweed); Ray Cournoyer; Marvin George (Frog); Wet'suwet'en Chief Gisdaywa (Alfred Joseph/Wolf); Haa mats sha (Fred Wilson Haisla Nation/Beaver); Maasgaak (Don Ryan/Fireweed); Maas Likiniswx (Ken N. Mowatt/Frog); Don Monet; Lois G. Shannon; Vernon Stephens (Wolf); Gitxsan Chief Wii'Elaast (Jim Angus Wolf); Gitxsan Chief Wii Mukwilixsw (Art Wilson/Wolf); Marie Wilson (Fireweed); Martin Keeley; Honey Maser; Patricia LaNauze; Helga Sermat; Theresa Marshall.

Clans of the Gitxsan and Wet'suwet'en: Fireweed, Beaver, Frog, Wolf and Eagle.

SETTING

Full upstage is a masking flat. Both left and right are angled flats. All of these have large Gitxsan designs on them. Downstage right is a long bent-box upended so that it stands about four feet tall. This is where the Guu Hadixs Chief's regalia is draped when not being worn so that it is a constant presence onstage. The regalia bears the crest of the Salmon. Any actor can play Guu Hadixs. There is also a bird rattle on the box. On the floor is a totem pole on which images will be hung as the pole is raised in stages during the play.

Centre stairs provide access to the stage. Entrances and exits are made from behind the flats and through the aisles in the seating area.

ACT ONE

The audience has been brought in to the sounds of taped voices of elders singing in Gitxsan[1] and Wet'suwet'en[2]. The doors close. The room goes dark. We hear traditional Gitxsan whistles from the front and back of the room. In the dark and over the speakers:

GUU HADIXS: The doors are closed.

In 1984 the Gitxsan and Wet'suwet'en Hereditary Chiefs began a court action against the Provincial Government of British Columbia and the Federal Government of Canada. The Chiefs claim uninterrupted ownership of and jurisdiction in their ancestral territories stretching back to time out of memory.

Welcome now to a part of what some people call British Columbia that is truly: Super... Natural.

We hear the whistles again. Drums begin underneath. A war rhythm, which builds to a crescendo throughout this section. Lights up on GUU HADIXS (the actress playing Hanakx/Marianne). No amplification.

Many years ago there was a clearing, with wooded areas on both sides. It was the sight of a fierce and bloody battle. Two warring camps would meet in this clearing, fight, and then retreat to rest, each to their own side. They were very evenly matched. They fought for a long time until each side had only a few warriors left alive.

The drums reach their crescendo and stop.

Suddenly, many white birds flew overhead and landed on the clearing which was the battlefield.

Two actors run a long white cloth from the back of the theatre and over the heads of the centre section of the audience. A few white down feathers drift from the cloth and onto the audience. The cloth comes to rest in front of the stage.

As the warriors watched the birds danced. Crossing over each other and moving forward. Crossing over each other and moving back.

The actors simulate this, running the cloth halfway up the audience and back.

Their fine white feathers covered the field.

The warriors, seeing this, lay down their weapons and danced also. Danced into what was once their battleground. Danced and rejoiced at the simplicity of the peace they made.[3]

Actors running the cloth have left it at the foot of the stage where it will remain until the end of the play, and exit.

The down is used today to bring peace into a space where an important event is about to unfold.

Welcome now to that long ago place. Welcome to Gawa-Gyani, the battleground where peace was made.

GUU HADIXS blows a little bit of down from her palm. Whistle. Lights up to half on rest of the stage. A Chief enters. He carries a carved cane and wears a button blanket. During the following narration he walks the perimeter of the stage, pounding the cane down on the four corners. Each time the cane hits the ground the Chief and GUU HADIXS shake their rattles.

The Gitxsan and the Wet'suwet'en peoples are made up of many Clans which include: Fireweed, Beaver, Frog, Wolf and Eagle. They live in a territory that covers 22,000 square miles. (*cane/rattle*)

They are bordered on all sides by different nations: The Nisga'a, Tsimsian, Haisla, Tahltan, Noo'tsinii, Chilcotin, and Sekani. (*cane/rattle*)

The Chiefs of the Gitxsan and the Wet'suwet'en walk the land and become one with the spirits and life forms there. (*cane/rattle*)

They place their canes in the earth—merging the power of the land, the animals and themselves—creating a bond of respect with all life that will never be broken. (*cane/rattle*)

In this way they mark off their territories as their own.

The Chief comes to centre stage and pounds the cane onto the ground. Rattle. GUU HADIXS keeps rattling until he exits up the aisle. Lights up full.

I am a Chief of the Salmon People. My name is Guu Hadixs. It means "good swimmer".

Sounds of the forest begin on tape.

The Dance of the Salmon. Two dancers, both in full salmon mask and robe. Sockeye and Coho. During the following they come up the aisles from the back of the house interacting with the audience.

Like the Gitxsan and Wet'suwet'en the Salmon People are also made up of many families: Spring, Sockeye, Pink, Coho and Steelhead. Every year we journey up the rivers and streams to our homes, each family to our own schedule. Each family to our own place.

Our streams are not deep so we must plan our journeys wisely. We do not want to get into each other's way.

And so the Springs share their name with the season in which they travel. The Sockeye— here is one now—the Sockeye travel in middle summer with the Pinks close behind. The Coho here enjoy the rays of the late summer sun and the hardy Steelhead choose to journey in the early autumn.

At this point in the dance the fish begin to use the centre stairs as a waterfall.

One place we all gather together every year is the large rock in the canyon of the river that is called "Watsonquah".[4] It is here that our whole family has a very big reunion, splashing and jumping in the foaming water. Then, together, we travel up the waterfalls and through the rocky streams to our homes. There we select a mate and lay our eggs.

Then we die. We leave our bodies as nourishment for all the life in and around the river.

We see the salmon spawn and die.

In exchange for this, the people along the shores treat us with respect, returning our remains to the river, and protecting the beds of stones where our eggs are resting.

Dance of the Salmon ends. Sound out. Dancers remove their masks and exit.

"The people know what the animals do, what the needs of the salmon, the beaver, the caribou and others are, because long ago their ancestors married the animals, learned all their ways, and passed on the knowledge from one generation to another."[5]

Whistle. Nahwodai[6] appears in a full buckskin outfit. The Dance of the Hunter and the Caribou.

A hunter dreams. A hunting dream. An animal encountering dream.

Rattle.

Nahwodai wakes. In the waking world he cleanses himself outside and he cleanses himself inside so that he is acceptable to the animal. Then he travels the path of his dream.

The sound of a heartbeat on the drum. The Caribou enters in full mask and skin.

Nahwodai asks the animal for food so that his family may eat.

He makes promises:

He will not hunt in the spring, so the animals may bear their young in peace.

He will take only what he needs.

He will waste nothing.

The kill will be swift.

We see the kill. Nahwodai takes the mask and skin from the Caribou dancer and carries it off over his head.

In exchange the Caribou promises to return and to keep providing food, clothing and tools for Nahwodai and his family.

It is through this mutual respect that the bond between the animals and the people continues.[7]

Dancer exits. Lights down on stage except GUU HADIXS. Forest sounds fade out.

In these ways, linked with the life around them since time out of memory, the Gitxsan and Wet'suwet'en govern themselves.

GUU HADIXS rattles. We hear the voice of Chief Gisdaywa[8] speaking place names in Wet'suwet'en.

The land is full.

The first totem image is hung on the pole. This is a processional ceremony done to the slow beat of a drum. The image is of a human with a walking cane (an image of jurisdiction). The pole is raised to the 1/3 position. The voice-over stops. Lights down from full stage to GUU HADIXS regalia. We hear a song in Gitxsan on tape.[9] Sweeping begins. Lights down on GUU HADIXS Regalia and up on centre section. HELENA enters. She has a dress on that is turn of the century. She sweeps for a while humming a 1910 tune and then sweeps out onto the porch. She hesitates and then sweeps the dirt off the porch.

HELENA: Oh! There were never anything like eagles at home.

You would think that with all there is to do there would be no time to think, let alone get lonely.

Helena pulls a line across the stage, attaching it from one side wall to the totem and begins hanging laundry.

We came to Hazelton on the railroad, you know. Days and days it took to cross this wild country – and before that endless days on a ship – coming from Scotland.

Francis had found an advertisement. It said that people here were making one thousand, two thousand percent profits on land – buying for $50 and selling for $1,200 more than that two years later.[10]

How could a youngest son whose parents' house had been burned to the ground – who had been driven off their own land to make room for the raising of sheep pass up an opportunity like that? He could not. Neither could I.

It must be difficult for my family to imagine me here. I had never built a fire in my life before. Never had to look for water.

Do you know how many pots of snow it takes to wash your hair? Thirteen. If you're going to rinse it. Then you use it to wash the dishes. Then you use it to wash the floors.

The flies do go to sleep when the sun goes down and sometimes in the evening after a very full day Francis and I sit out on the porch. We look over at Rocher Deboule Mountain and watch the moon. It is the same moon I have always known yet somehow – somehow in the midst of everything it makes me feel that I've found home in this huge and empty land. And that for the first–

FRANCIS: Helena! Helena!

FRANCIS enters running up the aisle from the back of the theatre.

HELENA: What?!

FRANCIS: Get into the house!

HELENA: Why?

FRANCIS: Get into the house! I will deal with this!

HELENA: What? Francis, deal with... oh!

FRANCIS has by now come up onto the porch. GYAT and HANAKX are approaching with baskets of berries.

FRANCIS: Helena!

HELENA: Stop ordering me about. We have no idea what they want.

GYAT: Yug Umahl Hadi'takxw![11] [Yu gu mach hadidach. *They may be violent!*][12]

HANAKX: Ha'w ji luu bagoyt kwihl he'n. [Ha ji lew bagat kle hen. *Don't be silly.*]

GYAT: Hana<u>k</u>x! [Hannach! *The character's name which means "woman".*]

HANA<u>K</u>X comes up the stairs and onto the porch. She puts a basket of berries onto the ground in front of HELENA. She extends her palms upward in a gesture of friendship.

HANA<u>K</u>X: Ha'wo [Ha wuh. *Welcome.*]

HELENA: Thank you.

HANA<u>K</u>X rejoins GYAT.

HANA<u>K</u>X: Wo-gya-ana [Whu ge ana. *There. You see?*]

GYAT: Neem gya'aw ts'a'aw<u>x</u> sdisda? [Nim ge'ach tsawach sdisda? *Did you see her shoes?*]

HANA<u>K</u>X: Gyat! [Get! *The character's name which means "man".*]

HANA<u>K</u>X smacks him playfully. GYAT laughs and runs away. HANA<u>K</u>X chases after him. HELENA picks up the basket of berries.

HELENA: Berries. Huckleberries. It is a present.

HELENA exits. FRANCIS watches where they have gone for a moment and then exits as well. Lights down centre section. Sound of the forest. HANA<u>K</u>X becomes GUU HADIXS. FRANCIS re-enters. He takes off his vest. He starts pounding fence posts into the ground. Lights up on the fence area and GUU HADIXS. Sound out.

GUU HADIXS: The newcomers were like white driftwood on the beach. They were thought of as poor relatives who were far away from home, and who would respect our home.

GYAT arrives. He has the cane from the previous territory walking scene.

Then the fences started appearing.

FRANCIS works. GYAT pounds the cane onto the ground. Lights down on GUU HADIXS.

FRANCIS: Why hello!

Lovely day.

Not bad for a first fence... what do you say?

That is a lovely cane. Is it very old? May I see it?

GYAT moves away.

Oh. Very beautiful. And it is all done by hand.

You know, a lot of the people back home think Helena and I have been, well, reckless moving out into all this wilderness. But the fact is – the fact is there just wasn't enough land to go around. Here, all we have to do is lay a claim, fence it off, and it's ours!

FRANCIS resumes his work pounding posts.

GYAT: The people from my House hunt all over there.

FRANCIS: Really? Well, I would be very much obliged if I could accompany you on a hunting expedition some day. I cannot seem to sneak up on the big ones the way you people do.

GYAT: Our berry grounds are here.

FRANCIS: Yes. So they are.

Well, you can still pick berries. We'll share them with you. All you have to do is ask.

GYAT: I think this is not a fence.

FRANCIS: Pardon me?

GYAT: I think this is not a fence. I think it is a trap. Like my trap for salmon.

GYAT turns to go.

FRANCIS: Wait! Before you go... I... here.

He holds out a bottle of rum.

GYAT: My grandmother says if we drink that it will turn us white.

FRANCIS: Your grandmother is a silly old woman. Take it.

GYAT exits. FRANCIS takes a drink. He finishes the fence. He puts up a no trespassing sign and exits. Lights down on fence, up centre section. HANAKX and HELENA enter to pick berries. HANAKX has two berry pickers[13], HELENA has an apron.

HELENA: Hannak.

HANAKX: Hanakx.

HELENA: Hannach.

HANAKX: Hanakx.

HELENA: Hanna-ck.

HANAKX: Hanakx.

HELENA: Hannakch.

This continues until they both start to laugh.

I think I will have to keep calling you Marianne.

MARIANNE: Yes, I am afraid you will.

They start to pick berries.

HELENA: Ow!

MARIANNE: You must be careful of your hands. Here. Like this.

MARIANNE shows HELENA how to use the berry picker.

Tell me another of your legends, Helena.

HELENA: They are not legends, Marianne, they are the truth. From the Bible.

MARIANNE: We have virgin birth, also, you know.

HELENA: What?

MARIANNE: Swallow the needle of a Fir tree and you bear a child. You had a big flood. So did we!

HELENA: You have a legend about a big flood?

MARIANNE: They are not legends, Helena. They are Ada'ox. Histories handed down. They are the truth.

HELENA: Of course. I thought James was coming with you today.

Marianne? Marianne, is something wrong?

MARIANNE: No. Nothing is wrong.

HELENA: Well, where is James?

MARIANNE: I am not supposed to tell. It is a secret.

HELENA: A secret! I will not tell anyone. I promise.

MARIANNE: No.

HELENA: Please?

MARIANNE: No.

HELENA: You can trust me, Marianne, we're friends, aren't we?

MARIANNE: Yes, but I...

Gyat – James is with his uncle. At a meeting. His uncle is a Chief and is preparing to travel to Ottawa. To meet the Crown. All the Chiefs are going together.

HELENA: But what does this have to do–

MARIANNE: James will be Chief when his Uncle dies so there is a great deal to talk about.

HELENA: James is going to be a Chief?

MARIANNE: Yes. His uncle was visited in a dream by a spirit just before James was born. The spirit was a great hunter and a Chief many years ago. The spirit said that James would be his uncle's own grandfather come back to life. James will inherit this Chief's name.

HELENA: Hm.

MARIANNE: It is the names that are handed down, generation to generation. Through the mother.

You call yourself by your husband's name. Why is that?

HELENA: When a woman marries she gives up her own name, and the family calls itself by the name of the father.

MARIANNE: But what of your name, your land and position? Do you lose them?

HELENA: I did not have any land or position to lose.

MARIANNE: But what of your family? Your mother and your sisters?

HELENA: Francis and I will start a new family.

MARIANNE: Without your mother and sisters?

HELENA: Yes.

MARIANNE: Is this what it means to be Christian?

HELENA: Oh! No!... well...

MARIANNE: Our lands are handed down through our Houses: aunt to nephew, uncle to niece, mother to son or daughter – always through the mother's side. They are never divided up.

Now the settlers – some of the newcomers have burned our houses to the ground. They have built new houses for themselves where ours were.

This is the reason the Chiefs are going to Ottawa. The Crown wants us to be farmers on small pieces of land, and to divide those pieces up from father to son. Soon I think we will have nothing left. Just like what happened to you.

HELENA: Surely no one here would force you to do that.

MARIANNE: Oh yes. The messengers of the Crown would. The Indian Agents would.

From the front and back of the theatre we hear: "I have the honour to state... I have the honour to state... I have the honour to state".... MARIANNE and HELENA break their scene, and get out of this scene's costume pieces. MARIANNE and JAMES get button blankets. FRANCIS becomes DENTENWILL. HELENA becomes the INDIAN AGENT. They all join the continuing chorus until:

INDIAN AGENT: Blast you all, I have got the honour to state!

DENTENWILL exits.

Quotes from the letters of R.E. Loring. Indian Agent. 1888 to 1912.

"I have the honour to state that there is something feverish and unwholesome in the air."[14]

"Indians are preparing for a big secret meeting, (with) covert threats of bloodshed against whites made to take place before Christmas, if no answer soon be given to Kapelano deputation before Premier Sir Wilfrid Laurier in Ottawa. Would advocate to give Indians early advice that their grievances be investigated sometime during May next. Navigation closed. Reply by wire."[15]

MARIANNE: The police told us, "The law is the British law, not the Indian law... if ever we (went) against the Crown's authority, although we might kill a great number of whites, the Crown's soldiers would hunt us down like rabbits."[16]

INDIAN AGENT: "I have the honour to state, that we have last year a visit by the Right Reverend A. Dentenwill, OMI, DD, Bishop of New Westminster, BC, and by Father Morice. Through the seemingly irresistible magnetism of the Right Reverend's charming personality, the honourable gentleman caused the destruction by fire of those ceremonial paraphernalia, which still bound the inhabitants of two villages to the customs and ideas of prehistoric days and prevented them from entering into the spirit of full civilization."[17]

Bishop Dentenwill, if you please:

DENTENWILL enters in Bishop's robe rolling out a large barrel.

DENTENWILL: Come around me, children, come around. Come around.

"If you have real heathenness and have become Christian go and have your heathen regalia and all throw them into the fire." [18]

GYAT and MARIANNE do not respond.

INDIAN AGENT: Have you lost your families to measles and smallpox?

DENTENWILL: Have you lost your families to measles and smallpox?

INDIAN AGENT: Yes.

MARIANNE: Yes.

DENTENWILL: Then come to the Lord! Come children! Come! Into the fire!

MARIANNE approaches the barrel. She hesitates. The INDIAN AGENT helps her remove her robe. MARIANNE slowly folds her robe up and holds it over the barrel.

GYAT: Hanakx!

DENTENWILL: "Do you burn them without regretting?" [19]

INDIAN AGENT: Yes.

DENTENWILL: Yes.

MARIANNE: Yes.

MARIANNE dumps her robe into the barrel. DENTENWILL looks into the barrel and then at GYAT.

DENTENWILL: "When the fire burns good all the fire goes right up to Heaven and you have taken (them) all from your houses. But when the fire refuses to burn there are some left!" [20]

Let us pray!

All except GYAT bow their heads. DENTENWILL leads them in a Latin prayer of which we only hear the first few words.

In Domine patre...

GYAT: "The priests taught us to close our eyes to pray. When we opened them, our land was gone." [21]

DENTENWILL & INDIAN AGENT: Amen!

DENTENWILL, GYAT and MARIANNE exit.

INDIAN AGENT: "I have the honour to state that an improved condition of affairs prevails here. The general health of the Indians of the district continues to remain excellent. Those in any way lacking are the old who have lost the power to adopt new methods, and, in the evolution of things will soon have passed away." [22]

INDIAN AGENT exits taking barrel.

Lights down leaving stage right section. The sound of the river. GYAT re-enters. He is very agitated. Almost immediately we hear MARIANNE calling after him.

MARIANNE: Gyat! Gyat!

She enters.

Gyat. They do not see the same things!

GYAT: They see the same as me. They could see the trees to rip them out by their roots!

Everything is gone. My traps – all my traps. Not one of them came to ask permission!

MARIANNE: And they will not.

GYAT: This will make them understand. (*a knife*)

MARIANNE: No!

GYAT: The punishment for what they have done is death. By our own law, Hanakx!

We hide our Feasts away in secret. Are we so powerless? Have we forgotten everything?

MARIANNE: This is not power. This will only bring more of them. And they will have guns.

GYAT: Then we will have guns.

MARIANNE: Is this the little boy who is going to be a Chief?

GYAT: They have emptied my mother's land! Burned it. Taken everything from it. Pushed my traps into the earth and twisted them into–

They have emptied my mother's land. I am supposed to take care of it. I will not be a Chief.

MARIANNE: You will be a Chief.

GYAT: An empty Chief. With no power.

MARIANNE: You will be a Chief. It is expected of you. And you will not go out and kill white people just because they are ignorant. It will not teach them anything. They will be followed by more of the same.

GYAT: I will not be a Chief. There is nothing left.

MARIANNE: We must understand them, Gyat. It is the only way.

GYAT slowly puts the knife back into its sheath. He sings a Song of Mourning.[23] *MARIANNE stays with him throughout this, looking out over the river. Sound of the river out. Lights come up on the Guu Hadixs regalia. When the song is finished a drum starts. The second Totem image is placed. It is an image of mourning.*[24] *Under this, on tape, is the voice of Chief Baasxya laxha*[25] *speaking place names in Gitxsan. The pole is raised to the 2/3 position. All the actors exit. The actor playing FRANCIS returns in a down vest and a hard hat.*

LARRY: One hundred and ten truck loads a day. That's how much timber we can get out of this place if we work hard enough. One hundred and ten truck loads a day. You ever seen a loaded logging truck? That's a lot of wood.

I'm Larry Weevil. New Star Timber. I feel sorry for these people, I do. No, no, I really do. A way of life has ended, and I understand that.

I always had a hankerin' for the backwoods. I lived in harmony with the forest, the fish and the animals. I spent months on end living off the forest and I loved it like a mother. I worked with Indian people and we spoke the same language, if you know what I mean. We were close to the earth.

But we live in a different time now. We live in a global economy. It's like my cousin Fletcher says, he says, Larry, he says, "Spiritual values are not a luxury we can afford any more. Those trees out there are not a forest. They're a bank. We have got to learn to make the best use of our resources." Pretty impressive, eh?

So here. Plant a tree.

LARRY goes out into the audience and hands out a few seedlings, improvising on the following:

Go ahead. Its cheap. Plant a tree for Fletcher and me.

Sounds of clear cut logging. LARRY returns to the stage.

The sound of money! You see, "resources by themselves are not wealth. A tree that's standing someplace back in the bush does nobody any good, except maybe some squirrel that chews pine cones off it. Until some enterprising businessman comes along and builds a road to that tree and builds a mill to manufacture it and flies out to Japan and China and Argentina and tries to find customers for that tree, that tree has absolutely no value."[26]

We're talking corporate survival here.

    If you clear cut the forest:

    (so) the trees are all down
    the birds fly away
    the animals are gone

(and) the soil flows down
into the river
and onto the gravel
where the salmon spawn,
then there's no more salmon
all down the river
and that makes it easier
to clear cut the forest

This repeats three times and builds in intensity from a quiet discovery to something of a Hallelujah song and dance number. Near the end of the third time everything goes black and the clear-cut sounds stop.

LARRY: Hey! What's goin' on?

Gitxsan whistle. The two salmon from the dance of the salmon start coming slowly from backstage, then around the sides to the front with high beam flashlights. In the dark and over the speakers we hear:

GUU HADIXS: A hunter dreams. A hunting dream.

LARRY: What?

GUU HADIXS: An animal encountering dream.

LARRY: Who is that?

GUU HADIXS: Larry.

LARRY: Who is that?

GUU HADIXS: Larry.

Gitxsan whistle. Synthesizer sounds in.

GUU HADIXS: It's your mother.

LARRY: You're not my mother!

GUU HADIXS: It's time.

LARRY: Time for what?

GUU HADIXS: You didn't think you could just take and take and never give anything back, did you?

LARRY: Cut the crap! Who are you?

He sees the two salmon with the flashlights almost upon him.

What the... O my god.

GUU HADIXS: Larry.

LARRY: What?!?

GUU HADIXS: Larry.

LARRY: What!!!!!!

Lights up low on GUU HADIXS regalia.

GUU HADIXS: I'm a salmon.

By this time the two salmon have reached LARRY and are on either side of him. We see his face by the lights of the flashlights.

LARRY: NO!!!!!!! NO!!!!!!! IT CAN'T BE!!!!!

LARRY tries to get through the Salmons' blockade.

Let me through here! Let me through!

GUU HADIXS: Larry.

LARRY: Huh?

GUU HADIXS: We have your front end loader, Larry.

LARRY: No–

GUU HADIXS: –and we are not going to let you through without asking permission any more.

LARRY: Fellas, please – I'll join your task force, I'll do anything–

GUU HADIXS: How can you learn, Larry, to live at peace with the Earth?

LARRY: I dunno. I want to share, I really do – I just – I just don't want to get ripped off! What are you going to do with me?

GUU HADIXS: What do you think?

LARRY: No. No. Please. DON'T TURN ME INTO A TREE!!!!!

The flashlights go out. Blackness. Synthesizer sounds stop.

GUU HADIXS: Perhaps, in two hundred years, when Larry is a mature tree, he will understand.

LARRY and the two salmon exit. Lights up full on the GUU HADIXS regalia.

GUU HADIXS: As the earth moves to make the necessary corrections that will heal itself, so do the Chiefs of the Gitxsan and the Wet'suwet'en. February 11, 1988: The first blockade to stop illegal logging in the territory. Many more actions will follow.

Welcome to Gawa-Gyani... today.

Lights up centre section and down on GUU HADIXS regalia as JAMES enters in modern dress.

JAMES: My grandfather has taught me very many things. He says I am the spirit of his Great Uncle who was one of the Chiefs who travelled to Ottawa in the early 1900s.

My Grandfather lost both his parents to smallpox when he was quite young, about eleven I guess. And so he went off to residential school.

His grandmother, she didn't want to let him go, but the local priest said he could arrange it. All my grandfather's friends and cousins were there so... I guess he sort'a talked his grandmother into it.

I'm like him a lot. We both really love to swim. He says when he was a kid at home, any time he wanted he'd go to the river or this little pond and swim all day long. But when he got to the residential school... well, here was the school playground and at the bottom there was a lake and right before the lake there was this fence. Right here.

Wednesdays and Sundays they'd go for walks. Out in the country. All in a line. With the whole row of disciplinarians in the back, he says. The kids used to speed up... a half mile ahead, and they'd go in the bush. Just running. So, he says, if there was a little rabbit in the area it was caught right away. All these kids hollerin' "rabbit, rabbit, rabbit", and everybody runnin' through the bush. Sometimes they'd roast it right where they were.

Of course that sort of thing wouldn't go unpunished.

They made the kids line up for everything. Line up to eat, line up to go to bed, line up to go to church, to go to class. If you got caught whisperin', or talkin' your own language or even if you went out of the buildin' without permission, you got sent to the shoe room.

The shoe room was where the kids got lickin's. They had a strap. A woven fibre. A belt off a threshing machine. They made the kids roll up their sleeves so the belt would hit them up to here. It's nice and soft, I guess. Of course, some kids got lickin's every day.

Now, if it was me I'd run away. My grandfather says kids did, except if they got caught they'd get brought back and tied to a bed and beat with a leather harness.

Those little kids were really penned in. They'd get there at five years old and sometimes not leave 'till they were sixteen.[27]

Something the church never thought about, though, was that they were all meetin' kids from all over the northern part of the territory. Kids from Atlin, Telegraph Creek, Fort Ware, Fort St. James... a lot of them are Chiefs or leaders now. And they all have this in common. And it ties them together – the residential schools. And now they're teachin' their grandchildren. I bet you the Church never thought about that.

JAMES exits. Instrumental on tape using Gitxsan whistles and synthesizer during scene change. Lights up on full stage to reveal a kitchen. The "no trespassing" sign is struck from the fence. HELEN is sweeping and listen-

ing to the radio. The music is interrupted by the Northern Native Broadcasting sound logo.

"We interrupt normal programming for a special Northern Native Broadcasting report:

The Gitxsan and Wet'suwet'en Hereditary Chiefs whose House territories are situated within the Kispiox watershed set up a roadblock today prohibiting all unauthorized resource use.

A spokesperson for the Chiefs stated that the blockade has been put up to protect the resource base for future Gitxsan, Wet'suwet'en and non-Indian generations. He stated that although the Chiefs sympathize with the loggers and millworkers, they want to give the forest a rest, to stop the war on the trees and speed up justice. The Chiefs will allow no unauthorized logging, hunting or fishing in the Kispiox valley until further notice."

HELEN listens to this with interest as FRANK enters calling from the back of the auditorium.

FRANK: Helen...

This is one of a series of blockades in the area already underway. More are planned.

FRANK: Helen!

HELEN: Frank?

The Chiefs maintain that local residents, farmers and others will not be obstructed and that essential services will be maintained.[28]

HELEN turns the radio off.

HELEN: Oh you poor thing. I heard on the–

FRANK: You heard?

HELEN: On the radio.

FRANK: Already?!

HELEN: Its been up for most of the day–

FRANK: The blockade.

HELEN: Yea.

FRANK: Well, there's more.

He gives her a letter which she reads while he gets a beer.

Those damn Indians!

HELEN: Oh my God.

FRANK: What are we gonna to do now?

HELEN: We'll be–

FRANK: What are we gonna do?!

HELEN: We'll be OK. You'll have unemployment, won't you? I could look for work.

FRANK: Yeah. Great.

HELEN: It won't be forever.

FRANK: They've got the road to the house under – under blockade for chrissake – you'd think the police would do something – and now they've taken away my job! Damn them!

HELEN: Hey, c'mon.

FRANK: Damn them!

HELEN: Calm down, Frank.

FRANK: Don't tell me what to do!

FRANK smashes a chair.

HELEN: You think we need new furniture? You know what I think? I think we should sit down, finish our beers, and I'll give you a nice special. Hmm?

FRANK: No.

HELEN: C'mon. It'll make you feel a lot better.

FRANK: Helen...

HELEN: C'mon.

FRANK: They've blockaded the road.

HELEN: I know. C'mon.

She takes him to a chair and takes off his boots. HELEN gives FRANK a foot massage. FRANK grunts and groans while she plays him like an instrument.

Did they say anything at the mill today about–

FRANK: No. They don't know.

HELEN: Well, it'll all work out. You'll see.

FRANK: The whole valley's shut down.

HELEN: The blockade isn't going to last forever.

From the mid-point in the hall we hear MARIANNE and JAMES.

MARIANNE: Helen!

HELEN: This whole thing will cool off.

FRANK: Oh...

MARIANNE: Helen!

HELEN: Everything will loosen up.

FRANK: Oh!

HELEN: C'mon Frank–

MARIANNE: (*to JAMES*) Come on, you said you would.

JAMES: It's not a good time to be doing this.

HELEN: The mill will start up again, you'll see.

MARIANNE: She's my friend.

JAMES: Its not her I'm worried about.

MARIANNE: Helen–

HELEN: In a few weeks–

MARIANNE: Anybody home?

JAMES: You see? I told you.

HELEN: That's Marianne and James.

MARIANNE: Their lights are on.

FRANK: Oh no. Not now.

MARIANNE: Let's just go to the door.

HELEN: I'm not turning them away, Frank.

MARIANNE: Helen.

HELEN: All this stuff that's going on isn't because of them.

MARIANNE: Helen?

HELEN: You be good. And go easy on the beer, OK?

MARIANNE: You in there?

HELEN: Hi!

MARIANNE: Hi.

JAMES: Hi.

MARIANNE: Didn't you hear us call?

HELEN: Uh, no.

MARIANNE: Can we come in?

HELEN: Sure. Yes. Come on in. Nice to see you.

JAMES: Hi, Frank.

MARIANNE: Our VCR broke down. Wanna watch a movie?

HELEN: A movie? A movie sounds great. You guys want some tea?

MARIANNE: Sure.

JAMES: Yes, please. Have any trouble gettin' home tonight, Frank old buddy?

I'll set this up. (*the tape*)

JAMES exits to the other room.

FRANK: (*to JAMES*) You grew up on reserve, didn't you?

HELEN: Frank?

FRANK: Oh, am I being rude? You want a beer? Anybody want a beer? Can I have another beer?

JAMES re-enters.

You grew up on reserve, didn't you?

JAMES: Yeah. Mostly.

FRANK: You ever worked your land?

JAMES: You mean my backyard?

FRANK: I mean worked your land. Got out there and broke your back to clear it – to do something with it – to make it into something.

JAMES: Not the way you're thinkin' about it.

FRANK: Well I have – the way I'm thinkin' about it. I've got sweat drops over every square inch of that ground out there and I won't have it taken away from me.

HELEN: We got notice today they're closing the mill down.

MARIANNE: Another one?

HELEN: Everyone's laid off.

MARIANNE: God, they're closing down so many mills.

FRANK: Whaddya mean they? I had to get through a damn military zone just to get to my house! Why are you people trying to take away my land?

JAMES: Nobody's takin' anyone's land away, Frank.

FRANK: You think I can make the payments on this place without a job?

JAMES: We're not the reason you got laid off from your job.

FRANK: I got friends gettin' up at two thirty in the morning, every morning, to get into line-ups just hoping to get a run of logs for their trucks. They're drivin' eight hundred miles a day. Don't tell me you're not the reason. You're shuttin' down the whole industry.

MARIANNE: We've got friends who work in the mill. They're losing their jobs, too. Its happening to everyone.

FRANK: The difference is I gotta deep down desire to have a better way of life than just movin' from one sweat job to another sweat job – so I applied my body to this land. Into helping develop it. Into making it into something.

MARIANNE: It's not necessary to make the land into anything.

FRANK: Why not? Why do you think the good Lord gave us dominion over the earth?

MARIANNE: It says in the bible that dominion–

HELEN: Frank–

FRANK: All this – OK – I'm sorry.

Look. You know I'm not a racist, right? I like you two. We have meals together. But all this stuff about letting the land do what it wants. Your whole reserve isn't doing anything with your land.

JAMES: O come on. You don't know what you're talkin'–

FRANK: –So what do you want mine for?

JAMES: Nobody's ever said anything about taking away your precious land!

We had all this. 22,000 square miles. Native people walked every inch of this land. We survived on it. We made a living on it.

FRANK: I never had to chase any Indians off this land so I could live on it.

HELEN: Well, there wasn't anyone living on this very spot when we got here–

FRANK: Whose side are you on, anyway?

MARIANNE: Of course you never had to chase anyone away, Frank. One of the first things the settlers did when they moved into this territory was burn our grandparents' houses to the ground to make room for their own farms. It was the middle of winter.

HELEN: Well, my grandparents were running away – they'd been burned off their own land back in Scotland.

MARIANNE: Is that an excuse for what people like them did here?

What do you think it feels like for me to drive past places that I know used to belong to my family? To know the connections. The pain is reversing itself. It's got to. Of course its gonna hurt. It's hurting all of us. But maybe it's time.

JAMES: The difference is if it hurts too much or if it gets too inconvenient you can just pack up and leave. We can't.

HELEN: Neither can we.

JAMES: You left someplace else to come here. If you wanted you could leave here and find a job someplace else.

HELEN: Our grandparents may have come from somewhere else, but this is our home now every bit as much as it is yours.

James. My life is here. My friends are here. I want my children to grow up here.

JAMES: But you don't belong here.

HELEN: That's not fair. We're here. If we're messing something up, fine, tell us. But in order to do that you're going to have to see us for the people we are. And the people we are are your friends.

JAMES: Well why don't you start acting like it?

MARIANNE: Look. It's not the blockade, Frank, it really isn't. It's because the decisions about what happens here are being made in Victoria and Ottawa and Japan.

A train 900 miles long full of trees leaves these territories every year.

FRANK: Oh, here we go. Little Greenpeacer. What is everyone supposed to do? Pack up and leave? Go on welfare?

JAMES: You didn't lose your job because of us or because of the blockade. There's too many mills, Frank. There's just too many mills.

You people see the trees and you think it's endless. You think you can build as many mills as you like and cut down all the trees and that's going to mean lots of jobs forever and ever. But what happens when there's no more trees? They were closin' down mills long before the blockades started.

FRANK: Yea, but not because there are too many mills. There's lots'a trees. You've closed down everything north of the Babine River! Too much interference, that's what there's too much of. Too many old men living in some happy hunting ground fantasy from the past who know nothing about world economics.

JAMES: You're talkin' about something you don't understand! I'm gonna be one of those "old men" one day, and you're crazy if you think they're living in the past. They've trained all their lives to be Chiefs and they've got a responsibility to their Houses—to their Clans—to protect their territories today. Even for people like you.

And in case you hadn't noticed, paleface, Chiefs come in male and female.

FRANK and JAMES' fight becomes physical.

MARIANNE & HELEN: Stop it! Both of you! Frank! That's enough! Stop it!

Pause.

MARIANNE: Helen. You make payments to the bank, right?

HELEN: While we can, yeah.

MARIANNE: Well, if the time comes that you can't make the payments the bank will take your land, right?

HELEN: That's right.

MARIANNE: Well we make payments, too. All kinds of them. All through our lives. In the Feast Hall. And our families have been doing that for thousands of years. Even when it was made illegal.

We have an obligation to take care of our land. It's like what happened to Joe's family. They sold their trapping rights to a logging company that clearcut the land, you remember? They had that land taken away from them in the Feast Hall. They were disgraced.

FRANK: My land is being taken away from me because I work in the mill?

MARIANNE: No! No. The fight isn't with you, Frank, you're stuck in the middle. The Chiefs have always said they won't take anyone's land away. But our laws have got to be the laws on our own land. Don't you see? Otherwise it's all going to be turned into real estate.

JAMES: But the land is not real estate. It's not for sale. It is our equal partner, and as equal partners all we can do, the land and us, is try to take care of each other.

MARIANNE: Our grandparents did it. We're trying to do it, and hopefully our grandchildren will have a chance to try to do it, too.

FRANK: Great. What about our grandchildren?

MARIANNE: Your grandchildren, too, if that's what you want. But you'll have to contribute in the Feast hall.

FRANK: But I still won't own my own land, will I?

HELEN: Maybe it isn't really possible for anyone to do that–

FRANK: Oh, come into the 1990s, Nellie. The traditional ways don't work in the modern world.

JAMES: Yes they do. They're workin' now. All around us.

MARIANNE: What's the matter, Frank, you want a master plan?

FRANK: That and my job back. You bet I do.

MARIANNE: I feel sorry about your job. And lots of other people's jobs. But maybe this'll force us – finally force us to discover what the master plan is together.

Pause.

HELEN: Good. Anybody wanna watch a movie?

JAMES: That's what we came here for... Jeez.

HELEN: Anybody want some popcorn?

MARIANNE: (*to FRANK*) Popcorn's Indian food, y'know.

FRANK: If everything is so friendly why block the road?

JAMES: Court, maybe. Hell, we've gone to a foreign court in a foreign territory to ask for something back that we never gave away. Court turns things into arguments.

FRANK: Hey! I'll take you to court, then. I'll sue for lost wages! How would you like that?

Aw, it's just as screwy as what they're doin'. You don't believe that there's a single judge in all of Canada who's going to be crazy enough to go down in history as the one who gave British Columbia back to the Indians, do you? It's not going to happen.

JAMES: It'll happen. Eventually it will have to happen. Because by your own laws we never signed anything away.

I recognize, Frank, that in the eighty or so many years that your family's been here you've learned to love the land so much that you are prepared to fight for it. That's good. You just think, though, what we might be prepared to do.

JAMES is leaving.

HELEN: James, please don't go away mad.

JAMES: There's going to be a brown hand signing your cutting permits, Frank old buddy. I'd start dealing with that if I were you.

JAMES goes.

MARIANNE: If we don't sort this out it'll be up to our children. If they don't, it'll have to be their children. Why can't we work together now to change things for the better?

FRANK: By attacking my land?!

MARIANNE: Never mind.

She exits.

FRANK: Oh Jesus!

HELEN goes out after her. Forest sound.

HELEN: Marianne, Wait!

I'm sorry.

MARIANNE: Helen, there is nothing for you to be sorry about. Nothing.

HELEN: I–

They embrace.

MARIANNE: Will you be OK?

HELEN: Yea. I'll be fine.

MARIANNE: I've got to go after my hothead husband. He's just like his grandfather. I'll call you.

She goes. HELEN goes back onto the porch. She looks out at Rocher Deboule Mountain.

She goes back into the house. Sound out. She puts the makings of popcorn away. She clears the table.

FRANK: Don't you start goin' Native on me Helen. Please. Not now.

HELEN: Can't you see what's happening all around us? Everything's changing, Frank. It's not James who's holding onto the past, it's you.

FRANK: Oh, hogwash. Dammit, I have a right to own private property. It's a basic–

FRANK & HELEN: –fundamental right!

HELEN: Your grandparents had their little piece of private property divided and used up so much back in Scotland there was nothing left. That's why they came here in the first place. Do we – do you have to do the same thing? Where else is there to go?

FRANK: That's just it. There is nowhere else to go. We have got to make a stand. It's a matter of everyone being equal.

HELEN: When you say "everyone being equal" does that mean everyone acting white?

FRANK: I don't know. Maybe it does.

HELEN starts to leave. FRANK grabs her.

Where are you going? Helen?

She goes.

Helen!

Everyone else is special. The French are special. The refugees are special. The Indians are special. Women are special. Christ.

Lights down. The sound of the river. The kitchen is struck. Lights up stage right. The actress playing HELEN becomes GUU HADIXS. JAMES enters and crawls under the fence. The "no trespassing" sign is now old. He has his fishing net with him. He mends the net and then prepares to throw it during the scene.

JAMES: ...the words just came tumbling out of my mouth.

Angry words. They scared me.

Lights up on GUU HADIXS.

GUU HADIXS: Why were you afraid?

JAMES: I don't want to be a Chief, there's too much at stake. I don't want the responsibility.

GUU HADIXS: There was a large rock in the canyon at Hagwilget. Do you remember?

JAMES: My mother remembers. That means I remember.

GUU HADIXS: It was a place where we all came together. So many of us, on our way back to our birth places. We jumped and danced in the foaming water, getting ready to tackle the falls. It was a place to celebrate life and the death that always precedes birth.

Those of us who were too tired to continue would come to the shore there and give ourselves to your people.

Why did they explode the rock at Hagwilget?

JAMES: The Department of Fisheries said the rock was stopping your journey up the river. It was how they explained the decrease in numbers.

GUU HADIXS: Did the Department of Fisheries not think our decrease in numbers had anything to do with the large boats at the mouth of the river?

JAMES: No.

GUU HADIXS: Do they not think now that artificially manufacturing our children will weaken us even more?

JAMES: No.

GUU HADIXS: We no longer celebrate at Hagwilget. Another link in the chain is broken. Soon it will all collapse.

Our laws are being broken even by our own people!

JAMES: But how am I to know when I am ready to become a Chief?

GUU HADIXS: It is not your decision to make.

Your task now is to seek knowledge of yourself. Self-knowledge is the first step along the secret path to self-control. Discovering self-control will bring you self-power. When you have achieved self-power, controlled power, the people will see that you are worthy of a Chief's Robe.

Your Robe of Power will come to you alive, containing the strength of many Chiefs before you. It will give you the courage to lead with authority and responsibility.

The Fisheries OFFICER enters with a rifle.

OFFICER: Hey! You down there!

Lights out on GUU HADIXS.

What are you doing?

JAMES: Just minding my own business.

OFFICER: You have a permit for that net? It's Saturday you know.

JAMES looks out for GUU HADIXS but she is gone.

Do you have a permit for that net?

JAMES: No.

OFFICER: One: There is no fishing Friday at 6 PM to Sunday at 6 PM. If you had a permit you'd know that. Two: There are quotas on the number of fish that can be taken–

JAMES: My family was fishing here long before anyone invented the paper your permit is printed on! We have our own quotas, and if someone wants to hunt or fish on our land they get permission from us!

OFFICER: Is that so?

JAMES: Yes. The salmon have a schedule that they keep to. And our schedule is the salmon's schedule.

OFFICER: Well, the Department of Fisheries has a schedule, too, and that schedule is enforced by the Crown.

JAMES: Where the hell is this damned crown everyone keeps talking about?

JAMES throws the net.

OFFICER: It's the Crown, wise guy, that says now I'm gonna take that net away from you and burn it.

JAMES: Like hell you are. I've got a smoke house. I have people to feed.

We hear the chug of the rifle being readied. Sound of river stops. JAMES and the Fisheries OFFICER freeze in place. MARIANNE enters to centre section.

MARIANNE: The Government of British Columbia has systematically burned our houses to the ground as recently as 1983. Now the Crown burns our nets in the same way it burned our grandparents' robes years ago. They take the nets away with shotguns that are meant to kill.

JAMES exits. The Fisheries OFFICER gathers up the net and exits.

It costs $1,100 to buy new fishing nets. But for some of us the price of applying for permits to an outside Government to fish on our own land is even more costly. So we go to our family... to my Clan for fish.

We are able to do this because the fences, the residential schools, the death imported in blankets, the robe burnings, the continued disrespect for the land, the denial of our economic and justice systems, even the apartheid practises of the Canadian Government, none of these have accomplished what they were intended to do. Our system of governing ourselves is intact.

We have not travelled this long journey, accepting newcomers into our home and teaching them ways to survive only to be told that we may dance our dances and carve our carvings but that we should not believe we can govern. Or that we never have.

BC Supreme Court Chief Justice McEachern is concerned that our Ada'ox, our oral histories, are nothing but anecdotes.[29] Is the truth only the truth if it is written on white paper?

"Our Ada'ox are like a windmill. They go around and around. They go from one generation to another and no one changes them" [30] with the stroke of a pen.

James wanted to go out and beat heads after that day on the river, but he did not. He governed himself. Self-Government is personal. It is individual. It is being responsible. Ourselves. All of us.

And so we stop them. We set up blockades and sometimes we take their equipment away from them. If we do not do this, when the court case is over there will be nothing left.

And we state what is in all our hearts. The true law. Not a law that someone somewhere else has invented. Not a law that changes every four or five years. But the eternal law. The law of the Earth.

We fish... without permits... together.

Lights up on full stage. The actors enter in sequence as they speak for the first time. They all wear button blankets. #4 has a drum.[31]

#1: We select a site near the village of Gitwangak on the banks of the Skeena River. It's known for being a place of international gatherings, and it is called–

#2: Ankiis. It has a good view of the river from both directions. And a bridge for the media, if they want it.

#3: We have a lot of committed souls. Gitxsan, Wet'suwet'en, Nisga'a from up the Nass River, Russian, Ukrainian.

#2: The people from the Church.

#1: Portuguese, French, Irish, Sockeye and Coho.

#4: The Department of Fisheries rents a Huey helicopter to fly their troops around in–

ALL: –And we build a smoke house.

#1: It is what we stand for.

#3: We teach the children to fish.

#4: We feed the hungry.

#2: We learn you don't have to be Indian to practise self-government.

#1: We obey the laws and time-tables of the Earth, building up instead of tearing down. To those people who want to provide an artificial timetable for our lives to work by we say:

ALL: You will not do it.

#3: Our power is the land.

#2: The land is ours–

#1: –and we know it.

A drum rhythm begins. All the actors dance the final dance as JAMES becomes GUU HADIXS, Chief of the Salmon People. After the dance, two of the actors go to the Guu Hadixs bent box. One takes the Robe and the other takes the Headpiece. The Robe is placed on JAMES. The Headpiece is placed on JAMES. He is given the cane. Down is placed in the Headpiece. Then the final totem image, a salmon, is placed on the pole and it is raised to the full upright position. There is drumming. The cast yell exclamations in Gitxsan throughout. During the pole raising we hear Chief Baasxya laxha and Chief Gisdaywa alternating Gitxsan and Wet'suwet'en place names. The Drumming stops. The lights change to isolate the centre section and Guu Hadixs comes down centre as the other actors take up their final positions. Guu Hadixs pounds the floor four times with the cane as the place names fade out.

GUU HADIXS: There are human footprints in soft earth at Goosley Lake. Footprints intact since time out of memory.

Not so many years ago we would stand with our feet in these footprints, and wait for the sun. When it rose behind the peak of Ghil là duz dii tii` Mountain we would know it was time to go home.

And so we would travel along trails, like the salmon in the rivers... like the caribou in the forest... meeting friends who would join the procession... linking up from hundreds of miles apart... each of us in time to the natural rhythms and laws of the Earth.[32]

Do you see the sun?

Come home with us now. Whether you are Gitxsan or Wet'suwet'en,

This builds into choral speaking as GUU HADIXS is joined by:

#3: Haida or Nisga'a, (*Maori*)

#2: English or French,

#4: European or Asian, brown or red, white, yellow or black. Come home with us now–

GUU HADIXS: To Gawa-Gyani. To the battleground where peace was made.

The white cloth flies back out over the audience's heads.

These are No` Xya` – our footprints. Stretching back to time out of memory.

May we walk gently together.

The actors come back to the stage from their different parts of the room and sing a chorus in Gitxsan. It repeats twice.

ALL: Gulla wak gulla nox dim na still newm ja guen.
Gulla wak gulla nox dim na we lak' newm ja guen.[33]

The actors bow. Three of the actors start to hand buttons out to the audience that say: "I'VE BEEN TO GAWA-GYANI".

CAST MEMBER: Thank you for witnessing what was said and done here tonight. We are very honoured to be in _____ territory.[34]

It is tradition in both the Gitxsan and Wet'suwet'en Feast Halls to give gifts, and so we would like to give each of you a gift now. If we miss you for some reason please pick one up at the door.

As is also the tradition in the Feast Hall, we would like to ask you, our honoured guests, to speak. To share your truth and understanding about ancestral land and self-government with us. We have Skanu'u (Ardythe Wilson)[35], here tonight who is representing the Gitxsan and Wet'suwet'en Hereditary Chiefs to respond to any questions you might have.

We are going to take a short break first so you can stretch and gather your thoughts. Before we break, we would like to thank our sponsors for this evening: (*s/he does*)

Oh. For those of you who got trees – please, take them home, put them in the fridge, plant them tomorrow, and then protect them for generations to come, OK?

Thank you and please come back so we can talk.

The end.

FOOTNOTES

[1] Courtesy of 'Ksan Performing Arts.
[2] Courtesy of Wet'suwet'en Chief Hoogit (Joseph George) and Wet'suwet'en Chief Gisdaywa (Alfred Joseph).
[3] Story of Gawa-Gyani told by Gitxsan Chief Baasxya laxha (Bill Blackwater Sr.) 1987.
[4] Known today as the Bulkley River.
[5] Wet'suwet'en elder, 1924. From *Proud Past*, P. 15.
[6] "Hunter" in Wet'suwet'en.
[7] Information on the Hunter from Gitxsan Chief Tkawok (James Morrison) 1987.
[8] Wet'suwet'en Chief Gisdaywa (Alfred Joseph).
[9] A Breath song sung by Gitxsan Chief Antgulilbix (Mary Johnson).
[10] *Northwest Digest Magazine*, Nov/Dec 1954 P.2 letter from Enoch R.L. Jones referring to 1908-9.
[11] Translations into Gitxsan courtesy of Gitxsan Chief Wiists'akxw (Russell Stevens).
[12] Gitxsan (phonetic [English translation]).
[13] These are small wooden boxes, open on one end with nails as sharp "teeth" and a handle on top.
[14] R.E. Loring. *Mountain to Mountain* P. 35.
[15] R.E. Loring, Indian Agent, October 30, 1908.
[16] Magistrate N. Fitz Stubbs, August 8, 1888 to Gitxsan Chiefs.
[17] R.E. Loring, Indian Agent, January 19, 1894.
[18] Right Reverend A. Dentenwill, 1903, from the Gitxsan and Wet'suwet'en Hereditary Chiefs' archives.
[19] Right Reverend A. Dentenwill, 1903, from the Gitxsan and Wet'suwet'en Hereditary Chiefs' archives.
[20] Father Morice at Dentenwill event, 1903, from the Gitxsan and Wet'suwet'en Hereditary Chiefs' archives.
[21] Gitxsan Chief Baasxya laxha (Bill Blackwater Sr.) 1987.
[22] R.E. Loring, Indian Agent, May 31, 1912.
[23] This is a sacred song used by permission of Gitxsan Chief Ma'uus (Jeff Harris Jr.) and cannot be reproduced in any manner.
[24] This image used by permission of Gitxsan Chief Ts'iibaasaa (Stanley Wilson)
[25] Gitxsan Chief Baasxya laxha (Bill Blackwater Sr.).

[26] Peter Weeber, Westar Lumber, CBC Documentary "This Empty Land", from a meeting in Smithers, BC.

[27] This story was told by Wet'suwet'en Chief Gisdaywa (Alfred Joseph).

[28] From a press release on the Kispiox blockade issued by the Office of the Gitxsan and Wet'suwet'en Hereditary Chiefs October 30, 1989.

[29] From BC Supreme Court Chief Justice McEachern's writings on the court case (1987).

[30] Gitxsan Chief Gyolugyet (Mary McKenzie) in BC Supreme Court. Transcript page # 236.

[31] #1 is the actor who plays James. #2 is the actor who plays Helen. #3 is the actor who plays Marianne. #4 is the actor who plays Frank.

[32] Story told by Wet'suwet'en Chief Gisdaywa (Alfred Joseph).

[33] "Come brother come sister let's walk together now. Come brother, come sister, we'll understand each other now". (Chorus by Gitxsan Chief Baasxya laxha [Bill Blackwater Sr.]).

[34] This will change every night depending on whose territory the play is being performed in.

[35] Skanu'u, (Ardythe Wilson) was representative of the Gitxsan and Wet'suwet'en Hereditary Chiefs for the New Zealand tour (1990). On the national tour of Canada (1988) this position was filled by Wet'suwet'en Chief Gisdaywa (Alfred Joseph). On the Provincial and Lower Mainland tours in British Columbia (1987) this position was filled by Marie Wilson.

The Hope Slide

by

Joan MacLeod

Sarah Orenstein as Irene

Photographer: Lydia Pawelak

DOMESTICATING SOCIAL ISSUES: JOAN MACLEOD AND *THE HOPE SLIDE*

One of only a few playwrights represented in this anthology who was born and raised in British Columbia, Joan MacLeod was cognizant early in her career of the centrality of place—cultural and geographical space—in both her writing and her identity. In a 1989 interview with Rita Much, she stated, "The place where my plays take place is always important.... I never would have thought that until I moved out here [Toronto], and now I realize how West Coast I am. I mean, probably even the way I'm sitting on this chair is West Coast" (201). In her life, the most mundane of individual acts takes on place identity. In her art, by melding construction of place with social issues, MacLeod domesticates those issues.

The indigenous operates on a multiplicity of levels in MacLeod's work. First, the domicile itself—private space—figures as the central setting: the monologue in *Jewel* is delivered from a mobile home near the Peace River; in *Toronto, Mississippi*, a middle-class Toronto home is the setting; in *Amigo's Blue Guitar*, the interior and exterior of a home on an island near Vancouver provide focus; in *Little Sister*, the girls' washroom of a Vancouver high school functions as a home away from home for teenagers; in *2000* both the indoors and the outdoors of a suburban Vancouver house are the sites of origin; and in *The Hope Slide* it is from a stranger's home in the Kootenays that Irene reviews her life. Significantly, these are personal and personalized, not societal venues. The domain of the MacLeod play is not the public cabaret of Panych, the courtroom of Ryga, the anonymous suburb of Lambert, or the bars of Clements.

The larger place—the geographical, cultural, and political space surrounding the private domicile—intrudes on, and is, in fact, inseparable from the private space. MacLeod's plays are replete with the identifiers of their respective real-life counterparts. Those set in British Columbia—the great majority—are informed by both geographical landmarks such as the Lions Gate Bridge, the Pacific National Exhibition grounds, and the Peace Arch, and cultural signifiers – from Doukhobors, Terry Fox, and Chief Dan George to bathtub races, loggers, and tree planters. Grounded in place, the plays construct a symbiotic space/identity relationship.

Even the monologue that is the *modus operandi* of *Jewel* and *The Hope Slide* can be seen as a form with a particular indigenous appeal. Theatre scholar Renate Usmiani argues convincingly that the solo performance enjoys a prevalence in Canadian theatre because of its ability to foreground both isolation and the search for identity, its kinship to the novel (long a more privileged genre in Canada, and one in which a not inconsiderable number of dramatists also write), its complementarity with plays which do not follow the traditional narrative pattern, and its particular ability to convey a political message. In sum, Usmiani states, "The monologue represents an effective tool in the struggle of post-colonial literatures to reflect the dilemmas of their society" (14).

In none of MacLeod's plays, monologue or otherwise, does domesticity elide political content. Each explores clearly political issues that are domestic in the sense that they affect individuals and that they are clearly delineated as Canadian social/political problems. Her works invariably examine the search for individual identity through community, and she pins that pursuit to issues that include corporate inhumanity, societal complicity in eating disorders, feminism, the devastation of urbanization, racial and religious intolerance, class differences, and treatment of the mentally challenged.

Ratsoy: Do you think of yourself as a BC playwright?

MacLeod: Yes, very much in what I write about. The landscape informs what I do. I'm a BC girl through and through. But I'm also a BC girl who is really glad I lived in Toronto for eight years. I'm really happy to have come of age as a playwright in Toronto, so that affects who I am. But BC landscape informs all that I am. Absolutely.

Born in Vancouver in 1954, MacLeod attended two Vancouver area colleges, the University of British Columbia, and the University of Victoria. She was captivated by the craft of writing at a young age, initially attracted to poetry and the novel. While studying at the Banff School of Fine Arts, MacLeod fell into drama at the encouragement of fellow students who were writing in the genre. Although playwriting has been her focus ever since, she continues to write poetry and prose fiction and to teach writing of all three genres at Kwantlen University College in Vancouver. The poetic side of MacLeod is most apparent in *Jewel* (in which she could be seen as making the bridge from poetry to drama) and *The Hope Slide*, and the novelist is, perhaps, most evident in her use of the monologue form. Although MacLeod spent eight years in Toronto (and several terms as playwright in residence at the city's Tarragon Theatre), has been a writer-in-residence in England, and enjoys periodic work terms at the Banff School, she calls Bowen Island, a twenty-minute ferry ride from West Vancouver, home, and the house in which she lives with her husband and daughter features a view of the ocean that is, even by British Columbia standards, stunning.

Ratsoy: What other hats have you worn besides playwright, and how many of those hats are comfortable to you?

MacLeod: I wear different hats as a writer. I write and publish poetry and prose, also. I feel equally at home in all three forms, although theatre is what I do best. As a novelist, dialogue comes easily to me; I have a feel for that. My plays are always being called poetic. Poetry is natural to me. Maybe I'm more imagistic than some playwrights are. Whatever genre I write in, it feels poetic. I've also acted, but that was purely by accident. I'm not an actor.

MacLeod's 1985 adaptation, *The Secret Garden*, won a Dora Mavor Moore Award for outstanding new revue/musical. *Jewel* began life at the Banff Centre the same year, but the revised and expanded version of the play, premiered at Tarragon Theatre in 1987, was Canada's entry in the Prix Italia (the international television and radio awards) in 1988, and was adapted for CBC radio under the title *Hand of God*. *Toronto, Mississippi* premiered at the same theatre in the same year, and *Amigo's Blue Guitar*, which garnered the Governor General's Literary Award for Drama in 1991, also debuted at Tarragon (in 1990). *Little Sister*, which took the Chalmers Canadian Play Award in the category of Theatre for Young Audiences, premiered in 1994, and the Great Canadian Theatre Company of Ottawa commissioned *2000*. *The Shape of a Girl*, based on the disturbing 1997 murder in Victoria of Reena Virk by fellow teenagers, had its initial production in Calgary in 2001 with Alberta Theatre Projects in association with Vancouver's Green Thumb Theatre. Although none of MacLeod's plays has premiered in her home province, they have enjoyed considerable popularity in BC, across Canada, and throughout the world: *Jewel*, for example, has been translated into four languages, and in 1989 *Toronto, Mississippi* was the second most produced play in Canada.

MacLeod's plays are experientially based: she drew on her early work experience in a pipeline camp when she crafted *Jewel*; a subsequent job as a life-skills teacher with the mentally challenged infuses *Toronto, Mississippi*; and her work to sponsor and help refugees resettle had a direct bearing on *Amigo's Blue Guitar*. It is *The Hope Slide*, however, that most directly reflects MacLeod's own life. In addition to the occupation of artist, MacLeod shares with Irene elements of the personal and cultural background which suffuses the play: she, too, had a childhood curiosity about both the Doukhobors and the Hope Slide and she, too, lost a close friend to AIDS. *The Hope Slide* is also, perhaps not surprisingly given the complex interplay of the personal and political that characterizes her work, the MacLeod play most rooted in British Columbia culture and history and, arguably, the most overtly sociopolitical. In addition to scrutinizing this country's treatment of nonconformity on an individual and group level, the play reminds us of appalling conditions on BC reserves and of the internment in the province of Japanese Canadians during World War Two, and protests contemporary ills such as the devastation of the environment and cutbacks to the arts. *The*

Hope Slide also yokes the personal, the political, and the geographical: the Doukhobors' plight, the natural disaster, Walter's death, and Irene herself are irrevocably linked by proximity – by shared geographical and cultural space.

Ratsoy: What sparked the idea for *The Hope Slide*?

MacLeod: I remember this really well. I had just opened *Amigo's Blue Guitar* in Toronto and I was doing a reading tour of the Kootenays. I was just exhausted. The plane I was on was supposed to go to Castlegar, but it landed in Penticton because of snow. We were bussed to Castlegar in what felt like the middle of the night but was probably six in the evening. It was pitch black in January and very snowy, and I realized I had started to look for Doukhobor houses. All of a sudden I remembered a lot of false, negative information about Doukhobors from my childhood . When I returned home and started researching, I began uncovering stories that I found just amazing – stories that were quite different from the newspaper articles and books I remembered. For me, any information that I have that is a little personal and that grabs and intrigues me is usually good terrain for writing.

The young Irene is at once fully individuated and representative of both distinct BC stereotypes and the postcolonial situation. In equal measure idealistic and jaded, she is non-conforming yet desirous of a community. Idealizing the marginalized group, she is rejected by them and disillusioned when the reality of their domicile doesn't meet her expectations. Although she professes rebellion against mainstream society, as represented by the high school, it is a necessary component in her impulse to perform. The mass of contradictions that is the adolescent Irene is, in part at least, reconciled in the adult Irene through her "legitimized" performance as an actor and through her recapitulation of her—and the Doukhobors'—story.

Ratsoy: I'd like to talk about space, geography, and realism. Often, when writing about Canadian literature in general, critics and scholars equate faithfulness to place with realism. Do you think that holds water with your plays? Do you think that a play that is deeply set in a specific region tends to be realistic?

MacLeod: No, I don't think so. When I moved to Toronto, our landscape in BC became exotic to me: almost surreal and so extreme and overpowering that the only way I knew to write about that was poetically. It is a great excuse for heightened language.

Ratsoy: So you are talking about landscape engendering something that is quite the opposite of realism?

MacLeod: Yes. For me, the landscape has that effect; there's nothing kitchen sink about it.

The Hope Slide is a testament to the power of story – specifically, to the ability of theatre to function as protest. It is a message monologue that, through humour, varying modes of dialogue, an engaging protagonist, juxtaposition of chronology, and the use of a play-within-a play structure, eludes such potential pitfalls of the form as didacticism and tedium. It is a regional drama with a vigor that is universal. Reviewers—both "at home" and abroad—were laudatory of *The Hope Slide*. In the *Globe and Mail*, H. J. Kirchoff wrote that the play "displays the apparently effortless command of language and the playwright's craft that is characteristic of MacLeod drama," and in the *Toronto Star*, Vit Wagner praised both Sarah Orenstein's "stirring performance" and MacLeod's "thought-provoking, intricate monologue." Of a production at Edinburgh's Traverse Theatre,

Stephen Chester wrote, "The different voices provide a rich mosaic, setting high comedy so seamlessly against moments of deep pathos that you become aware that this is great writing from an author confident enough in her art to avoid any deliberate verbal pyrotechnics."

Joan MacLeod's plays lay open both the insider—one who with confidence evokes place in the form of markers and historical detail—and the outsider: Marjorie is not from the Peace River, and has returned there in an attempt to find home; Katie, the protagonist in *Little Sister*, is ever the outsider, longing to escape to Toronto; Nanny in *2000* is not at peace until she can escape from the house of the urban planners and get back to nature with the Mountain Man; and not only is the young Irene patently in search of a home in the form of an idealized community, but the Irene in the present time of the play is a stranger in the house.

G.R.

Selected Bibliography:

- Chapman, Geoff. "Unpredictable MacLeod Brings Rich Writing to Real-Life Worries." *Toronto Star* 5 Mar. 1992.
- Chester, Stephen. "Thunderstruck." *List: Glasgow and Edinburgh Events Guide* 8-21 Apr. 1994.
- Derksen, Celeste. "Drama: Review of *The Hope Slide / Little Sister*." *Malahat Review* 115 (June 1996): 111-114.
- Derksen, Celeste. "B.C. Oddities: Interpellation and/in Joan MacLeod's *The Hope Slide*." *Canadian Theatre Review* 101 (Winter 2000): 49-52. Derksen examines stereotypes and perceptions of British Columbia through the prism of *The Hope Slide*.
- Hunt, Sarah B. "Review of *The Hope Slide*." *Theatrum* 29 (June 1992): 40.
- Kirchhoff, H. J. "The Reincarnations of Joan MacLeod." *The Globe and Mail* 28 Mar. 1992.
- Lawless, Jill. "Volatile Geography Brings Out Poet in MacLeod." *Now* 5-11 Mar. 1992.
- MacLeod, Joan. "Being Fearless." *In 2 Print* 10 (Winter 1998): 8-9. This autobiographical essay offers encouragement to teenage writers.
- MacLeod, Joan. Personal interview. 5 Nov. 2000.
- Rudakoff, Judith and Rita Much. *Fair Play. Twelve Women Speak: Conversations with Canadian Playwrights*. Toronto: Simon and Pierre, 1990. 190-207.
- Thomas, Colin. "Playwright Revisits Teenage Passion." *Georgia Straight* 8-15 Jan. 1992.
- Usmiani, Renate. "Going it Alone: Is Canadian Theatre the Sound of One Voice Talking?" *Theatrum* 28 (April 1992): 13-18.
- Wagner, Vit. "*Hope Slide*: Well-crafted, Beautifully Articulated." *Toronto Star* 11 Mar. 1992.

The Hope Slide
by Joan MacLeod

The Hope Slide was first produced by the Tarragon Theatre, Toronto, in March 1992, with the following cast:

Irene   Sarah Orenstein

Directed by Glynis Leyshon
Set & Costumes Designed by Sean Breaugh
Lighting Designed by W.F. Gosling

PRODUCTION NOTE

The Hope Slide takes place during one night in the Kootenays, a remote and mountainous area four hundred miles east of Vancouver, in 1990. During this night Irene travels from 1962 to 1967, from North Vancouver to the Doukhobor prison outside the town of Hope, from the turbulent Kootenays of the early sixties to the other side of Hope where a mountain collapsed in 1965.

ACT ONE

Lights up on the adult IRENE, thirty-seven years old. It is the middle of the night, in the Kootenays, January 1990. IRENE is sitting in a comfortable chair, wrapped up in a quilt.

IRENE: My first version of girlie pictures were these grainy photographs of Doukhobor women that my brother cut out of the *Vancouver Sun* and kept in a drawer behind his socks. This long line of big bums and kerchiefs. We were United Church so all this was pretty exotic, sexy as hell. When I was very little I thought Doukhobor meant untidy but then I started thinking they were true heroes because they didn't send their kids to school and when they were really pissed off they burnt down the school altogether. School was always a horrible place for me. My marks were terrible; I had the attention span of a flea.

Wanna play teenager? This used to be my favourite game. We'd roll up our skirts, smoke cherry bark and run around kissing one another. Wanna play Teenage Doukhobor? It's the same idea only the one who's it has to take off her pants. I was a very religious child. I used to light Kleenexes on fire and pray that Elvis would come, come to my house for supper. My parents would be out and all our furniture would be different.

In the seventies my friend Walter and I lived communally in the country and at first we attempted to organize our community on Doukhobor philosophy. We would have a meeting every Sunday, we would share household chores, men and women side by side, and any money made outside our quarter section would go into a communal kitty. The system began to break down when none of us wanted to work at regular jobs, in fact none of us wanted to work period. Walter's definition of housework included braiding his hair. Walter was also completely in love with this really obnoxious guy called Peter who was one of our house-mates. This divided us further. Then there was this poor cat who froze to death in a well, who later showed up as a shoulder bag and beret. This was a simpler time, a hopeful time. I was working with puppets—everyone was working with puppets—I still bought all my footwear at the House of Clogs.

January 1990 and I am travelling through Doukhobor country, through the Kootenays. I am a full-fledged actor, I am an actor on tour, solo, bringing my own one-woman show to small places – three voices for the price of one. The characters I play were real people, ghosts I have stolen and made speak. Doukhobors. These are hard times and I am proud to be working. I am billeted with English teachers in interior towns; I eat surf 'n' turf with the head of the Chamber of Commerce. I arrive by bus, one AM, exhausted and dying for a cigarette.

"I hope you like kids," a nervous mother asks while handing me a towel. "Absolutely," which is true. "Our little ones are up pretty early." I assure her that I am both an early riser and heavy sleeper – both lies.

I am exhausted but hyper, lying in a top bunk between Wayne Gretzky sheets – staring at a *No Smoking* sign the size of my head. I climb down the ladder and into their strange livingroom. Through the window the great terror of mountains at night, a river beginning to freeze. I love my country – so beautiful and wild. My country is disappearing.

When the Doukhobors lived here they tried to create a heaven on earth. Forty of them living under one roof, families sleeping in long narrow beds, toe-to-toe. Everything was shared and because of this they prospered. As a girl they were heroes to me – model anarchists and rebels. Their expulsion from Russia I linked directly with my being expelled from junior high school. Truant officers were the bane of their existence – well, me too. I envied the Doukhobors many things but most of all I envied they had a community.

I have a community now, I have the theatre, and my community is under attack. The Minister of Revenue has just suggested a more "hands on" approach to funding the arts. I suggest we all lay our hands directly on the Minister of Revenue. But this is nothing compared to the real enemy. The moon is full, the stars close and sharp-looking, metallic, explosive. I prop open the sliding glass door so that I can sneak a cigarette. The air is very cold and clean. I am tired and I realize stupidly that I am down here because I am afraid to sleep, for the first time in years I am afraid of the dark. No more. No more funerals. Although I know many young men who look ahead with remarkable bravery, for many of my friends hope has become a threatened species, with a bowed head and awkward feet, cold and trembling. Terrified.

IRENE is fifteen, and, at first glance, conservatively dressed. She is wearing a scarf knotted at the side of her neck, a large locket, a cardigan that is on backwards. Her skirt is inside out. Her socks are worn over her shoes. She is standing behind a table. On the table is a loaf of bread, a cellar of salt, and a clear pitcher of water. IRENE is delivering her Social Studies project on the Doukhobors to her grade nine class, showing slides of the Doukhobors and project props throughout.

My name is Irene Dickson, Division Three, Grade Nine. My project is called The Doukhobors: Friend or Foe? I wish to thank the Audio-Visual Club for use of the overhead projector, although I would like to take this opportunity to point out that it's not as if they personally own the equipment, it's supposed to be for our use but I do digress. My project contains many interesting elements but no handouts. Let us begin. The Doukhobors: Friend or Foe?

The Doukhobors came to be around the middle of the eighteenth century, utopian peasants whose beliefs went back to a bunch of groups that parted company with the Orthodox Church in Holy Russia as part of the Great Schism.

The Doukhobors settled by the Molochnaya River, the Milky Waters and, depending on the mood of the current Tsar and their neighbours, lived as Martyrs under terrible persecution or as Happy Communal Farmers. Their refusal to bear arms, i.e., fight and kill, and their refusal to register their marriages, births, deaths, etc. and so forth meant they were in extreme trouble more often than not. And so... on January 20th, 1899, the steamer the *Lake Huron* arrived in Halifax with the first of four shiploads of passengers. All in all seven thousand four hundred and twenty-seven Doukhobors came to Canada which was the majority of their numbers. The second boatload contained seven hundred children with Count Sergei Tolstoy, son of the extremely famous writer, in charge. Count Leo Tolstoy, the writer to whom I just referred, now dead of course, nominated the Doukhobors for the Nobel Peace Prize. They didn't win but this was still a high honour to be nominated. With the royalties from his last novel, *Resurrection*, and with help from the Quakers, as in porridge, the Doukhobors' passage from Russia to Canada was made. Although he himself was extremely wealthy Leo Tolstoy had spent a large portion of his life dreaming of anarchist Christian peasants and when he heard of the Doukhobors he felt he had hit the nail on the head. The Halifax paper described the new immigrants as follows: "People of the purest Russian type, large and strong, men and women both being of magnificent physique with a bright kindly sparkle to their eyes." I also want to add that this is about the last nice thing I have found in the newspapers about the Doukhobors during my research which has been both personal and exhaustive and goes right from the eighteenth century until 1967 – i.e., now. I know you are all well aware that I did live with the Doukhobors for a short time last year but that experience is personal, untouchable and purely mine.

The Doukhobors settled in Saskatchewan and in practically no time their communities were thriving. The government says okay to no military service but insists that the Doukhobors register their lands in individual names which the Doukhobors will not do because they share everything. So... some Doukhobors stay in Saskatchewan and the rest go out to BC with their great leader Peter Veregin in charge.

Doukhobors are very different from say, the United Church—which is the faith my parents have forced on me, or the Catholics who I disagree with on several issues, i.e., everything—in that the Doukhobors have no icons, no fasts and no festivals, no churches and no priests. They are pacifists and refuse to bear arms for any cause. Their stories and beliefs are passed on orally through their psalms—the *Living Book*. Traditional schools and written law are not only stupid to them but terrifying. The only law is God's law and to bow before the laws of man is to unite with Satan. All teachers, of course, are instruments of the devil. The Sons of Freedom believed that higher education, i.e., junior high school included, quote – turns you into a truly insane animal. End quote.

Their only obvious symbols of faith are the loaf of bread, the cellar of salt and the jug of water. When I come into the meeting hall, into the sobranya, I recognize in each one of you the divine spark. And I bow.

IRENE bows to several individuals in the audience.

You're supposed to bow back. Your participation is an integral part of my project.

IRENE begins to sing.

"Fortunate is he who loves all living creatures
The pulse of creation beats dear to his heart
For whom all in nature is kindred and near
Man and bird, flower and tree, none to him stand apart."

1903. The first stirrings of the group called Svobodniki or Freedomite or Sons of Freedom. Sixty men, women and children wander from village to village, reminding their sisters and brothers to reject all material things: they nibble the leaves off young trees, eat the grass, they set their animals free and give any money they might have to the authorities. They believe absolutely that God will provide for them and to show their simplicity and innocence they "go in the manner of the first: Adam and Eve" – i.e. naked. I would like to point out that naked is innocent to them not dirty.

Alright grade nine. How many of you are wearing a wristwatch? If I had some dynamite I could show you a simple method for making a bomb using only your watch, a stick of dynamite and a little common sense. Making of bombs is what they call black work and in 1923 the first of many schools in BC was burnt to the ground. Burnings, like nudity, at first meant a return to simplicity and purity but now became a form of protest.

This black work was often spur of the moment, they would be gripped by a sudden and mad inspiration and, like myself, worked best without a plan.

Basically this is how it all works: you want me to send my kids to school and I say no because I know school is evil and that you are going to teach my children a load of crap. So. You have this early-morning raid of truant officers in my village and gather my children and take them to the government school in New Denver – as in the place where the Japanese were locked up during the war. I steal my kids back and just as a little insurance, I burn down the local school. A solution, a simple solution. I also might set my own house on fire just to show you I don't care about material things. If my Doukhobor neighbours are getting a little too greedy I might burn down their house too so that they can get back to basics. If you have still missed the point I might just take all my clothes off or blow up a bridge. These are called the "upside down" days, demonstration to follow now. Because the RCMP, disguised as Doukhobors—fat chance—infiltrated their meetings, the leaders would wear their clothes in weird ways and this meant reverse all statements I am telling you – i.e., (*slowly building to a frenzy*) ...If I am telling you to go out and love your brother, your brother and our principal Mr. Miller in particular, you know because my shirt is on backwards that I really mean, *burn*, go on, do it, light a fire under this school or perhaps under Mr. Miller's house.

IRENE turns around, showing her backwards sweater.

Do not set fire to the offices of any newspapers. I mean the *Vancouver Sun* in particular even though they have made a blackout on Doukhobor matters, refuse to publish our concerns.

IRENE begins to strip.

Keep your shirt on at all times. (*undoing her buttons*) Do your buttons up, right to the top. Running around naked? That is for children, that is for the little child.

She throws her sweater off and lights a match.

There are certain dead heroes that I wish to bring to your attention! Harry Kootnikoff killed by fire, Paul Podmorrow by hunger, Mary Kalmakoff swallowed by the earth!

I protest the death of these people! Heroes, victims, outlaws one and all! I protest we are sent home early and say prayers for Kennedy and Churchill and we are ignoring those dying in our own backyard. These are dark days, terrible times loom ahead! I protest the silence. "My heart is full of courage, brave to do something to make change, upheaval!"

These are the words of Paul Podmorrow who starved to death on a hunger strike!

IRENE's shirt is pulled up revealing a white cotton bra, her skirt is pulled down revealing waist-high underwear. A bell sounds, meaning "stop." IRENE continues to yell over the chaos.

On behalf of him I call you to arms! I call you to fight goddamn you, fight goddamn you, fight goddamn you! *Fight!*

Blackout.

The adult IRENE appears.

I was always predicting the end of the world. The end of the world has been predicted a million times except in my case it almost happened. January 9, 1965. A wrinkle in the surface, part of the world heaved and buckled, let go for a moment and perhaps wanted to give in altogether. A mountain collapsed and threatened to bury a town just outside Vancouver. A mountain collapsed and threatened to bury the town of Hope. I didn't understand then that things are always changing, never steady. A shoreline shifts, rivers erupt, mountains fall. I thought death was only violent or accidental. Something for the very old and sick, the weak. I didn't understand then that people my own age might die, that young lives could be so painful.

Well. I understand it now.

IRENE lights a candle and speaks in the voice of Mary Kalmakoff, twenty-four years old, 1965.

I am pushing out against something. It is thin but tough – a strong piece of skin or good cotton sheet. And then I am through, above the buried car. I see my friends beside it – blood-spattered and still. I have special sight: I can see through the dark, the snow. It is three AM, January, and we were driving through the mountains. Avalanche I am thinking now, this is an avalanche because snow has come right through the roof, filled up the convertible. Everything is still. I push through the rocks and snow and boulders of ice as though they are air. I travel through all this cold like a vein of boiling water. My skin should be scraped raw but it is clear, white and warm.

Stupid. I am pushing the wrong way, a stupid little mole that means to rise up and out of the mountain but instead aims for the heart, the centre of the earth. Then suddenly I am in the air again and tumbling down, the mountain tumbles with me and I understand what has happened, the mountain has cracked – its whole face and front side fallen, buried the road and the valley, left the mountain half-gone and naked. It seems fetal, ridiculous, unborn. I understand now too that I am dead and never to be found. Lost outside the town of Hope. Me. Mary Kalmakoff, twenty-four years old, unmarried. Employee of the Penticton Fruit Growers. Religion – Doukhobor.

IRENE is fifteen. A few months later. She is talking to her truant officer.

First off I want it made perfectly clear that reporting to you, Miss Toye, a truant officer-slash-psychologist, is a complete violation of my rights and all I hold sacred and dear. The form in front of you was signed under duress, a condition of my being allowed back into school that I was forced to agree to. I was backed into a corner, the pen practically jammed into my hand. Although I am not against education *per se* I believe attendance should be voluntary.

My understanding, Miss Toye, is that I am to report to and talk to you, my truant officer-slash-warden, personally once a month and that if I am absent from school without a phone call and note from my mother or the queen mother or God himself then I am going to be expelled again. I agree to these conditions although it is with a heavy heart that I am agreeing. I also agree to keep my clothes on at all times, even in gym class I will wear my shorts over my stupid dress to avoid causing any further rioting amongst the members of my class. But although I am no longer allowed to protest publicly, I want you to know Mary Kalmakoff, Harry Kootnikoff and Paul Podmorrow are still heroes to me, unsung martyrs whose song I intend to keep alive come hell or high water.

These were real people who died an unjust and horrible death. How'd you like a mountain to fall on your head, Miss Toye? Or a bomb to explode in your lap? How'd you like to go on a hunger strike to get publicity but once you died nobody paid attention? The newspaper didn't even say it was sad. And this is absolutely the saddest thing that I think has ever happened but I do digress.

I would like you to write down right now that I, Irene Dickson, am absolutely thrilled to be back in school and that the idea of doing grade nine all over again is extremely exciting to me. I am turning over a new leaf, knuckling under, and disappointment is no longer a part of my life. I see this September as a new starting point on the rocky and difficult road of the life of *me* – Irene Dickson. You got all that?

What are you writing down? Everything on the form in front of you is totally true.... Except the part about my parents being divorced. It was an experiment I devised to see if people treat you any better if you come from a broken home. They don't. My parents get on like a house on fire, always have. The part about future occupation is true: dancer-slash-actress-slash-mayor of a great city. Present occupation: spirit wrestler. Meanness and forgiveness are growing inside me at an equal rate and creating an unholy war.

If you're going to write stuff down about me I think it is my right to see it.... Does it say there I have these theories? – i.e., last year I predicted North Van was going to slide into the ocean and settle like Atlantis under the Lions Gate Bridge. I also have several theories on hitchhiking, sex and friendship, drunken boys, the end of the world and, of course, the Doukhobors. Take your pick.

...Okay don't take your pick. Wanna talk about sex? No problem, anything goes here, I am an open book. Perhaps you are under the mistaken impression, along with the rest of this place, that Walter Dewitt is my boyfriend. That Walter Dewitt and I are doing it. Well, we're not. I do not see Walter in that way. He is my friend, my best friend, as a matter of fact, my only friend. You know Walter. He is very skinny and very bright, highly goofy. And like myself highly persecuted, my tribe. Walter and I believe friendship is the absolute highest state of being.

Pause.

I like your hair. I believe women should have long hair, another one of my theories. In pre pre-historic times our hair was long so that babies, our babies could hold on while we ran through the trees being chased by God knows what. Babies are born knowing how to hold but now they've lost it and have to be taught. No. They come out knowing but then they forget and have to be taught. I don't know. But something has happened with regard to babies and their ability to hold on in this century.

I don't mean I don't ever think about sex. I think about it often. Perhaps constantly. Not the actual act of sex which is as yet unknown to me but I do think of my policies regarding sex: i.e., do everything but, you know, as many times as you want with whoever you want just *keep your hymen intact*. When I first learned of my hymen and the importance of keeping it untouched, in place, I imagined it this big shield I could hold out front and ward off guys with, rather like a Viking would have. It's a great word, hymen – hymn and amen and hyena all rolled into one. This big bouncy kangaroo thing that laughs its guts out. I mean I know it isn't that and I know it isn't something that you carry with a spear but I used to also worry that my time will come, I will meet *him* and it will be perfect and holy and wild but... what if my hymen didn't break? What if guys just sort of bounced off it? This tough old piece of skin pulled tight as a drum, a bongo drum barring the way to heaven.

What if it leaves men in pain? Pain is something they cannot bear nearly as well as us. They also have a great deal of trouble touching their own eyes.

Don't write that down! Just write down stuff like I am knuckling under. I love that kind of crap. I am knuckling under. I know, I know. Our time is up. Tell me about it.

IRENE pulls up her scarf, bandit style, lights a match and speaks in the voice of a Doukhobor boy, Harry Kootnikoff, seventeen.

Harry Kootnikoff, that is me and I am dead now. Killed by fire. Poof...

IRENE pulls down the scarf, blows out the match.

This is the true story of what happened. I am with four friends. The day is February 16, 1962. This is the plan – we play crib for a while, then we go to the movie in Trail, maybe meet a girl, have a good time, then blow up the post office in Kinnaird at midnight and call it a night. I am seventeen. I know dynamite as a good friend since I am ten. I am the bomb-builder, the man in charge, me. We go to a movie and while I watch I have some of the bomb in the pocket of my coat and some of the bomb waiting in the back of our car. The Mounties pull us over, take the back seat right out and find nothing.

We know how to hide, us Doukhobors – hide dynamite, fuses, ourselves. When I am six *bang* my brother Frank pulls me out of my bed, I am on the floor. Quick, quick now my mother is pushing shoes on my feet, wrapping a blanket around us both and out the door! The devil is here. He has arrived in our village with the sun and brought his army. Frank has my hand, we run and run through the wood behind our house, branches slap into my face. We can hear dogs barking and the motor from the devil's bus. We lie in a ditch, cover ourselves with boards and leaves. My heart is loud.

Frank holds my hand, he covers my mouth with his other hand because I am crying. "Baby, baby, don't be a baby!" A spider grabs the end of my finger and bites into my arm.

Nyet! Nyet! I am dragged out by my foot, then picked up and carried by the waist. I bite the devil above his knee. "Jesus Christ!" he yells then ties me onto a seat in his bus. Mother, my mother, where is my mother? Other kids crying around me too. And yes. There she is, standing in front of the bus, her nightgown up and over her head. She is naked except for her boots and singing to me. The other mothers sing and strip too. The horn on the bus drowns out the singing, the driver of the bus laughs at her, my mother, then we are gone. I will not be allowed to live in my house again for six years. But now, here we are, I am a man, riding in the back of the car with the bomb being built in my lap. I have a careful hand, careful touch and maybe it's a bump in the road but all of a sudden all is white and loud and I am pushing through, pushing through something strong but thin. It is my own head and here I am flying above the scattered car, my friends blood-spattered and still. I understand I am gone now, dead.

IRENE speaks as an adult.

I don't know how to imagine someone building a bomb. I just think of someone wrapping a present, all the careful tucks and folds, the sticky tape pulling at the hair on the back of your hand. Then an enormous red bow that is nearly impossible to tie, a slip knot that springs from the loop and explodes. Here. You hold this one. Poof. I press my hand against the sliding glass door. My hand is steady. I breathe and my breath is a grey oval on the glass – going, going, gone. But I am here, alive. Alive and kicking, acting, travelling, smoking up a storm. This past month I buried a friend. But this is not why I am afraid of the dark, no sir. I have buried him so deep he can't surface.

Where are the Doukhobors now? They are in split-level houses with satellite dishes; they are in the cities, impossible to spot in a crowd. The Sons of Freedom are nearly gone – some went to South America, a few are still in prison. Gilpin, the last Freedomite village, is just shacks now—poor, forlorn—like some of the reserves way up north.

But I keep looking for them, watching for a flash of eyes at night, peering out, looking for a distant fire between the trees. Black work. They used to say they were making a pillar of fire to join the earth to heaven. I need them now, a pack of rebels, lighting a fuse, making a protest, making a pillar of fire for all to see.

IRENE is fifteen, speaking to her truant officer again, one month later.

Miss Toye? Did you ever kidnap a Doukhobor kid? Because if you did this relationship is over, finito, done just one month after it's begun.... Well, good. And a very good morning to you too. Undoubtedly you are aware that during the month of September my attendance was flawless, I have become a model student, a beaten and sheep-like citizen of the world. In this time of great change and protest, I am silent. 1967 is a dark year in the life of me, Irene Dickson. But you are my refuge, Miss Toye. Between these four walls I feel free to speak my mind, my fears, my theories and beliefs – i.e., oftentimes when I am sitting there in class, trying to mind my own business, I am suddenly aware that I have large white antlers growing out of my head. They're all mossy and delicate. If I bump into anything you can bet it would hurt. I have to move through the halls carefully, getting anything out of my locker is murder. The sheer weight of these antlers, Miss Toye, my truant-officer-slash-game warden, makes me sleepy and, needless to say, totally incapable of fitting in.

You know if I was a true Doukhobor I'd hate your guts. I'd know all teachers, truant officers, counsellors, government etc. and so forth are corrupt through and through. I wouldn't trust you as far as I could spit but I do digress.

Wanna play teenager? Wanna play teenage Doukhobor? It is a game of my invention combining the basic elements of Doctor and Hide 'n' Seek. What if the one who's it takes off all her clothes, puts on a blindfold and everybody hides. Except everybody doesn't hide. Everybody sneaks back and makes a circle around you, a circle of gasoline. And when you yell "A hundred! Ready or not!" Whoosh! Up it goes, flames everywhere, and everyone's gone except your dog who's going nuts and half the world's gotta hear you screaming blue murder but nobody comes. Then finally this kid shows up, he watches you for a moment, calm as anything, then disappears and comes back with the garden hose and you're standing there bare-naked while he quietly smothers the fire that is raging around you. For months afterwards you wake up choking because you think your mattress has caught fire. You also think that brown thistles are growing in your throat.

Doukhobor means spirit-wrestler. There are three kinds. The Independent, the Community and the Sons of Freedom. The first two are highly normal and integrated and all. The Sons of Freedom are the ones you read about, highly persecuted – not unlike myself, my tribe. They keep only what is needed: i.e., eternal life and the golden rule. They avoid church, state, schools, regulations, authority, war. They cannot harm another living creature because the spirit of God is inside – watch me breathe.

I would like to live in a Doukhobor kitchen. They live very simply. I would like to be with them, living there again. Sitting on a hard wooden chair, drinking a glass of cold clear water. I think they are very fine human beings and that people who make fun of them are the ones who should be in jail. Perhaps people don't know how good the Doukhobors started out. Perhaps people don't know that Count Leo Tolstoy was their very good friend. And me too. Although I lived with them for only a short time, I, like Leo Tolstoy, am, and forever more shall be, a friend.

The boy who rescued me was Walter Dewitt. He had just moved into our neighbourhood. This was summer, 1963, the year of the great hunger strike. Paul Podmorrow said, "My heart is full of courage, brave to do something to make change, upheaval." He became my hero, Walter became my friend.

I thought Paul was beautiful, blue eyes and blond hair, a scarf at his neck but it was his determination, his sense of purpose and conviction that made him shine. I had a newspaper picture of him above my bed, and a chart, a calendar marking off the days. I never thought anyone would really die.

Walter, you know, he's a man of science. That's what he calls himself. He believes very much in the space age and in technology. He also knows the human body. And calm as anything he'd explain malnutrition and the process of starving. Then he'd get back to work: he's always making highly complicated plans to build a great city. He will design it, I will be in charge. All the buildings will be round, the cars will run on air and nobody will have to work anymore.

At night that summer we'd take the bus over the Lions Gate Bridge and wait for the nine o'clock gun. You know the nine o'clock gun, it's a cannon, or at least it was a cannon, now it's phony. I mean it goes off every night but it's just noise, a blank, an incredible sound that can be heard even here, bouncing around the mountains on the North Shore. Waiting for the nine o'clock gun is excruciating and a favourite pastime of various families and dogs and kids. Several stupid people, i.e., my brother and his friends, imitate the blast while they wait and these boys, they practise dying for all the hillside to see. But Walter and me are quiet, there is an understanding that if we are still enough maybe it won't happen. The rule is we aren't allowed to look at our watch or the gun itself.

But I can always tell when it's going to happen by looking at Walter. He gets this very weird look like he's seeing something, seeing something coming that no one else can see. I don't know how to tell if it's something great or something scary or just something boring. Walter? What is it? What do you see?

Bang! The ground rumbles underneath us. Our heads are alive with noise then splitting with the silence.

Look, Miss Toye, there in the distance, do you see them? Doukhobors, two of them, wearing black pants and suspenders. They're coming, they're coming. They're coming for me. They mean to save me, rid me, deliver me from the hands of strange children. They each hold a candle in one hand, a gallon of gas in the other. There is this roaring sound. It is the sound of everything being blown to smithereens. It is the sound of freedom.

IRENE ties her kerchief around her neck, and speaks in the voice of Paul Podmorrow, twenty-two years old, delirious.

My prison is small. Bars at the door, bars at my bed. Don't come near me, doctor, teacher, devil. Don't talk to me, touch me, teach me words. I am a child of God, a child of my mother, my mother. Where is my mother? Paul! She is calling me in for supper, she is wrapping her big arms around me. But I am here, now, and this is a prison and I am a man. "We openly declare to all that we are on a hunger strike until death. The government refuses to investigate our matters and we protest." And now the devil is trying to stick a tube for feeding inside of me. I want to fight him but my arms are made of feathers and the fight is going out of me.

And then I am floating, above my bed and up, pushing through the walls, the ceiling, carried on the warm air of August above my prison and over the town of Hope. I have special sight. See the other Doukhobors, hundreds of them camped outside our prison, my brothers and sisters, singing psalms, making their breakfast, making a protest for all to see. They do not know yet what has happened to me – Paul Podmorrow, dead and gone now, child of God, child of the earth, Son of Freedom.

IRENE speaks as an adult.

This boy was a hero to me. When the strike started I would wake up in the middle of the night, knowing he was hungry. I had been dreaming him: when he opened his mouth thin blackbirds escaped. When he put his hand in mine it seemed drowned, yellow and puffed up. He never spoke but if he did it would be in a whisper. Sometimes he'd bring me gifts: a bright green bug cupped in his hands, a bowl of salt. What if his muscles came back strong as diamonds? What if he just stood up and walked straight through the bars and out the door? What if death's already in there, inside him? Come into his house like a goddamn rat. The angels of God are good thoughts. Each living thing a church where he lives. Watch me breathe. Leaders. The Doukhobors were always looking for a leader, someone to take them home, away from here. They knew this place was just temporary, borrowed, their footprints barely formed before they would vanish. Poof. I am lost, lead me out. Take me by the hand, away from here.

IRENE at fifteen is talking to her truant officer, one month later.

"Lighten up. These are the best days of your life." My friend Stan is always saying stuff like that to me, stuff designed to make me feel better that usually makes me feel like jumping off the nearest roof. Stan is the daytime security guard at the Marine Building which means he does zip. He is supposed to rid the building of kids like me but he doesn't. You know the Marine Building, right downtown, very old and sort of like the Empire State Building, like King Kong's going to be up top waving someone like you, Miss Toye, around in his fist. I consider its lobby to be my second home, my home away from home, my sanctuary. Stan is sixty-seven and used to be a farmer so he knows a thing or two about force-feeding. Stan believes no matter what that the government should've kept Paul Podmorrow alive. I don't know. I mean Stan is no intellectual but I do grant him his point of view.

Do you have a problem, Miss Toye? Exactly what is your problem? ...One day. I only missed one day of school. And I didn't *do* anything. I'm trying to come clean here. I just hitched over town and hung out with Stan at the Marine Building, end of story. When the strains of life and grade nine are too much for me, to the Marine Building I go. I am trying to explain to you, Miss Toye, some of the issues with which my mind grapples – life and death issues. Grapple, grapple.

And sometimes these issues keep me away from school and I don't like it any better than you. I was *not* running away again. I learned my lesson last year. I do not run away anymore. I face the trials of life head on. Even when I am deserted by all, I stand my ground. Antlered and weary, Irene Dickson, that is me.

Stan thinks I'm seventeen and that I'm a junior temp secretary for MacMillan Bloedel just up the street. I have no idea why I'm such a liar. I just am. I told the guy who gave me a ride home that I'm the youngest ever law student at UBC. I mean *the truth* is a very important issue to me but I mean in a general sort of way.

Okay, alright, I want to get this out. I also want you to swear yourself to secrecy, undying secrecy, Miss Toye. Agreed? I lied to you and everyone else about living with the Doukhobors. I didn't actually live with them. I just sort of visited last summer. Briefly. Very briefly. I went all the way up there, to the Kootenays, eight hours in a semi but the Doukhobors were not all that happy to see me. Or to be more precise they ordered me off their land which is a complete joke because they aren't supposed to own it in the first place.

But I just keep banging on the door, I am crying and making a fair amount of noise. Probably when they can't stand it any longer, they do let me in.

They are not proper Doukhobors. They are eating canned ham and watching "Car 54" on television. The world is full of phonies. These particular phonies have phoned the police to come get me.

I spend a terrible night in the home of the chief of police of Grand Forks. We're eating breakfast; the whole family is exhausted because I was awake the whole night and not exactly quiet about it. Despair is far too quiet a word for how I usually feel.

"Hey, you wanna see a real Doukhobor village?" The police chief is tapping me on the shoulder. And I say okay, that'd be alright, I'm pretty excited even. So off we go.

We drive for half an hour; very pretty country, snow-capped mountains etc., you expect to see Heidi and the whole gang around every corner. I am thinking of turning myself over to the Doukhobors, seeking asylum as they say. He parks the car in the middle of nowhere.

There is a gnarled old orchard and part of a barn. "Right up there," the chief points. A chimney, the black foundations of a house. "Used to be forty or more all crammed together under one roof, kids, husbands and wives, everyone married to one another and switching around...." There is fireweed everywhere, other black marks on the ground that must have been woodsheds, stables.... The horseflies are glinting like fish and biting me. It's a stupid place and it's horrible, too quiet. It is the saddest and stupidest place on earth.

IRENE sings the first four lines from "Goodnight Irene".

God I hate that song. Goodnight Irene, Irene goodnight, goodnight Irene. It is the most depressing song ever written but most of the world is nuts about it including my mother. How'd you like to be named after the most depressing song ever written, except even worse no one knows it's depressing, they sing along like it was Rudolph the Red-Nosed Reindeer. No one ever pays attention to anything. Undoubtedly everything you are currently writing down is unimportant.

IRENE sings the chorus of "Goodnight Irene".

My parents come that afternoon to pick me up. They're not angry, it's way worse than that. They're just *very disappointed.* They have brought Walter with them as a way of cheering me up.

He has this little booklet thing with him on the Hope Slide which he must've bought on the way up. He reads to me from it: "When Bill the trucker kissed his wife goodbye that cold and dark January morning, he took a bag lunch of corned beef on brown, his favourite, and said, "See you later." Little did he know that tonnes and tonnes of rock would cut short his journey and his life."

Well, the real thing is even worse than the book. We stop to look at it on the way home. The road just stops and there's this huge pile of rocks and mashed up trees. You can't imagine it. It goes on for miles. But the worst part is the mountain that fell down, highly unnatural, like this big foot just kicked its face off.

Walter finds it all fascinating. "This is the end, this is the beginning of the end," I tell Walter. "Irene, give it a rest." Walter is sifting through the rocks and explaining – "There were two small earthquakes creating a crack in the surface. It is an act of nature. It doesn't *mean* anything."

"Mary Kalmakoff is buried here. She might be right under our feet." Walter is ignoring me. "Hers was the only body not found. Don't you find it rather interesting that ten miles on one side of Hope is the prison built specially for the Doukhobors, the place where Paul Podmorrow starved to death. And here, ten miles on the other side of Hope a mountain falls down and a Doukhobor girl is buried. Don't you find stuff like that incredibly weird?" "Not particularly," Walter tells me.

"Did you know the Doukhobors don't seek converts? They don't care who you are. They just want to be left alone. Walter! I'm talking to you. I'm trying to tell you they didn't want me, I wasn't allowed in, and I want in, somewhere... I want to be right in the middle of something. I feel as though all great events in history happen just before I arrive."

"You could never be a Doukhobor anyway," Walter tells me. "Why?" Walter is carving his name into the rock, sometimes I really hate him. "Because, Irene. You're just too bossy." I promise then and there to never speak to Walter Dewitt again for the rest of my life. But on the other side of Hope, Walter starts talking to me:

"We will build a city. A great and wonderful city. A dome will protect us from the elements, from war, from all possible danger." And then Walter looks out the window and he sees that city. I can tell by his face that once again he is seeing what's invisible to me. What is it? What do you see?

IRENE lights four candles. She speaks as an adult.

Harry Kootnikoff killed by fire, Paul Podmorrow by hunger, Mary Kalmakoff swallowed by the earth, Walter Dewitt – a loss of hope.

When we were small, Walter always played at my house because Walter had one of those mothers who made you work when you visited. These mothers are famous within neighbourhoods, known and marked and avoided at all costs. When we were teenagers and went to his summer place to sneak beer and carry on, there was always a job that involved the septic tank, hoes and shovels. Septic tanks will always remind me of hangovers but I do digress.

So we'd be thirteen or so, and I'm supposed to go to Walter's house for the first time in ages because he has promised me his mother is out and we can't go to my house because I have ordered Walter off my property for a month, I can't remember why. I ring his doorbell and there's Walter, wearing cut-offs and his moonshiner sweatshirt.

There are these marble balls, just inside the front door, when you come in. Two of them (*makes a head-sized circle with her hands*) about so big. I don't know what they're supposed to be but Walter kicks off his runners and stands on one of these balls and starts rolling all over the wall-to-wall, up and down the halls. Incredible balance. "What do you think you're doing?"

He replies all calm and normal that he always uses these balls as a method of transportation within his own house. He was a real nutcase, Walter.

When Walter is dying I come running, come flying across the country and into his arms, arms held down by tubes and drugs and disease. For thirty years Walter has been my friend, my brother – sometimes I rescue Walter and sometimes Walter rescues me. I am part of a group of women—although we have boyfriends, husbands, lovers—the men we call in the middle of the night, the men we share the midnight scotch with, the friends of our childhood—they are often men who love other men and our men are dying.

Walter? He is almost gone, eighty-eight pounds, his skin puffed up and yellow. The name of his illness is unspeakable, ever since Walter was tested, he has refused to let us even mention the name of his disease. I am muzzled, frantic, and I hate it. Fight goddamn you, fight. I am a stupid girl who still believes that if I yell loud enough this won't happen. But it is happening all around us, the unimaginable, a mountain has fallen, hope is threatened, that nine o'clock gun was loaded all along. What if your muscles came back, strong as diamonds? What if I just picked you up and carried you out of here...

Walter is leaving, pushing through. Decisions have been made, made bravely. For him hope is gone, but we are here and with you now, a little bit longer please. I rub Walter's legs, feel the pulse drain out and he is gone.

Hope. It is a thing that is ever-changing but it's here, available. It is not soft. These days it has a dollar sign and a voice that is relentless, out on the street and howling. We are here, now, right in the middle of something. Fight. Hope ignites us into action. Makes a pillar of fire for all to see.

IRENE removes her shirt, fire suddenly comes up through a grate in the floor.

I protest the deaths of these young men. My heart is full of courage, brave to make change, upheaval. I protest the deaths of these young men. My friends, my heart, my beautiful brothers.

The fire goes out. IRENE wraps herself up in a quilt.

If I could sleep for twelve hours the world would be a better place. I am in a stranger's house, watching thin clouds cover the Kootenay moon, the stars, these are kind strangers, opening up their home to me. I will go back to my room. Tomorrow I will fly over the Hope Slide. It is getting more and more difficult to see the slide from the air, green covers the mountains, brave young trees planting themselves in impossible places, the lost highway now covered by shrubs and moss and all manner of living things. But I still remember the way it looked in the beginning, when the slide first happened, and that is something that can't be covered over. That memory is locked in and has affected now forever the way that I see. You can't really bury your friends, not ever.

Remember what I said about Walter and his incredible balance? This highly weird kid who could do something so special?

IRENE extends both arms, balances herself on invisible marble balls, looks ahead. She looks up. One arm reaches forward.

Walter? What is it? What do you see?

The end.

MOTHER TONGUE

BY

BETTY QUAN

l to r
Alannah Ong as Mother, Kameron Louangxay as Steve, Laara Ong as Mimi

Photographer: Deborah Dunn

ORIGINS AND LANGUAGE IN BETTY QUAN'S *MOTHER TONGUE*

Betty Quan's career as a dramatist coincides with the first period in which significant numbers of Chinese Canadian writers were making inroads into the literary establishment. Although Chinese immigration to Canada began in the middle of the nineteenth century, discriminatory and exclusionary policies and practices on the part of successive Canadian governments until after the end of the Second World War prevented full participation in mainstream Canadian society. The result was that Chinese Canadians were, as critic Lien Chao states, "collectively silenced" (ix). Bennett Lee and Jim Wong-Chu date literary writing in Chinese in Canada from "the time early arrivals inscribed poems on the walls of the quarantine cells where they were detained upon entry" (2) and point to subsequent works written in Chinese and, thus, exclusively to a Chinese-reading audience; however, apart from the late nineteenth and early twentieth century journalism of Edith Eaton, a Chinese Eurasian whose pen name was Sui Sin Far, Chinese Canadian writing for the mainstream, English-speaking audience was virtually non-existent for that first century.

Even as late as the 1960s, literature by Chinese Canadians and literature about Chinese Canadians was scarce. A rare exception is Saskatchewan-born Fred Wah, whose background is one-quarter Chinese. Wah, one of the founders of *Tish*, an influential Vancouver poetry movement of the 1960s, published his first poetry collection in 1965, and was awarded the Governor General's Award for Poetry in 1986 for *Waiting for Saskatchewan*. Although, as reflected in George Ryga's *The Ecstasy of Rita Joe* and Sharon Pollock's *The Komagata Maru Incident*, the 1960s and 1970s marked a period of increasing interest in those outside the ethnic majority on the part of Canadian writers, there is a curious dearth, given their importance in the country's history, of Chinese Canadian characters. Poet F. R. Scott and novelist Margaret Laurence provide striking exceptions. Scott's terse "All Spikes But the Last," written in 1957, manages to indict both the federal government's history of mistreatment of Chinese Canadians and fellow poet E. J. Pratt's exclusion of Chinese Canadians from "Towards the Last Spike," his epic on the building of the CPR. Laurence's canonical *The Stone Angel* features, near its end, the character Sandra Wong, who is instrumental in the growth of protagonist Hagar Shipley in her last days.

To be written about—as the other—is quite a different matter than writing oneself into a literature. Substantial ground was broken when, in Vancouver in 1976, a group of native-born Chinese Canadians jointly organized with Japanese Canadians a writers' workshop, from which emerged in 1979 *Inalienable Rice: A Chinese & Japanese Canadian Anthology*. The following decade saw mainstream interest in several important writers of Chinese descent, including Denise Chong, Sky Lee, Paul Yee, Evelyn Lau, and playwright Winston Christopher Kam, whose *Bachelor-Man* was staged in November, 1987, by Toronto's Theatre Passe Muraille. At the beginning of the 1990s, another anthology ushered in a decade of unprecedented growth of Chinese Canadian writers: *Many-Mouthed Birds: Contemporary Writing by Chinese Canadians* includes stories and poetry by writers whose careers began in the 1980s as well as some, most notably Wayson Choy and Larissa Lai, who would begin to leave their mark in the 1990s. The century closed with the publication of *Swallowing Clouds: An Anthology of Chinese-Canadian Poetry*, which focuses on such new voices as Andy Quan, Rita Wong, and Glenn Deer.

Into the twenty-first century, stage productions written by playwrights of Chinese ancestry that reflect historical and contemporary aspects of Chinese Canadian life are establishing a presence. Edmontonian Marty Chan, in addition to producing works at the Edmonton Fringe Festival, has had considerable success with *Mom, Dad, I'm Living with a White Girl*, which was premiered in 1996 by Cahoots Theatre Project/Theatre Passe Muraille and continues to be produced throughout the country. In 2001, *Gold Mountain Quest* by Richmond Gateway Theatre artistic director Simon Johnston premiered at the Arts Club Theatre in Vancouver. As Scott's poem did almost half a century earlier, the play (which featured an entirely non-white cast, including Laara Ong) deconstructs historical mythology around the building of the national railroad by focusing on the Chinese labourers who endured slave-like status and conditions to forge the tracks through British Columbia. Betty Quan herself authored a play—an adaptation of Paul Yee's children's book—about the building of the railway: *Ghost Train*, which premiered in the spring of 2001 at Toronto's

Young People's Theatre, examines the event from the viewpoint of a girl who arrives in Canada from China to find her father among the railway workers.

Although she is still in the early stages of her career, Quan, a University of British Columbia graduate, has had a broad base of experience in literary fields. She has worked as a book reviewer and a book marketer, has extensive credits in radio and television, and is in the process of publishing a picture book about a young girl's first reaction to the death of a family member. Quan also adapted two important Canadian novels for performance: Margaret Atwood's *The Robber Bride* in 1995 for CBC Radio's "Morningside," and Joy Kogawa's *Naomi's Road* (itself an adaptation for children of Kogawa's *Obasan*) in 1996 for Toronto's Young People's Theatre. *Nancy Chew Enters the Dragon* (1991) for Nightwood Theatre, *The Dragon's Pearl* (1995) for Young People's Theatre, and *Fault Lines* (1996) for Richmond Gateway Theatre are among her stage plays.

Ratsoy: Where were you born, what was your major at UBC, and how did you begin playwriting?

Quan: I was born in Vancouver, and received a Bachelor of Fine Arts degree, with my focus being Creative Writing. While at UBC, I got interested in dramatic writing, especially radio drama. After university, and having moved to Toronto, I continued to write plays and got involved with a theatre company, Cahoots Theatre Projects. I then subsequently got a commission to write a radio drama for the CBC, which got the whole thing rolling.

Fault Lines, a comedy set in contemporary Richmond, BC, brings together a white family and a newly-arrived Chinese couple, the Chans, who are experiencing an uneasy reunion with their son, who preceded them to Canada and has become very westernized. *Vancouver Sun* reviewer Tim Carlson commended Quan's facility with language and symbols in *Fault Lines*, which garnered the theatre company a Jessie Award for community outreach.

Mother Tongue, a nominee for the Governor-General's Literary Award for Drama in 1996, was workshopped by Toronto's Cahoots Theatre Projects as part of the theatre's "Lift Off 1994" series, held at Tarragon Theatre's Extra Space. An excerpt from the work, entitled "One Ocean," was subsequently aired on CBC Radio's "Morningside" Series. *The Georgia Straight* reviewer Colin Thomas deemed the play's first full stage production "a poetic and often moving exploration of the aching desire to overcome separations" and its author "a playwright worth following." Toronto's Factory Theatre staged *Mother Tongue* in April and May of 2001.

It is not surprising that the script, published by Scirocco in 1996, received favourable notice from scholarly journals. *Mother Tongue* is a very literary play, one which reads exceptionally well from the page. Ric Knowles noted that *Mother Tongue* "shifts delicately between past and present, memories and monologues, allowing the audience to hear and understand what the characters feel but cannot always express," and Celeste Derksen praised the work as "a quiet, intricate drama" and "a truly fascinating document." Quan provides detailed, evocative stage directions, and her flashbacks effectively render the importance of the past (the mother's youth, the father's death, and Steve's illness) on the present.

Ratsoy: Plays are, obviously, above all else meant to be seen. How important is publication to you?

Quan: With the exception of a few Canadian plays and playwrights, a new play doesn't often receive more productions post premiere, so publication is important because it provides an extended life for a play, so there is an opportunity for the play to be re-discovered. Also, having a book in front of one helps validate playwriting as a literary form.

Intergenerational conflict is an age-old focus of story, and the cultural complications of that conflict when the immigrant experience is added to the mix are rich fare for drama, as demonstrated by such productions as H. Jay Bunyan's 1981 play, *Prodigals in a Promised Land*, which examines the struggles of a Caribbean family in Toronto, and the aforementioned Marty Chan's *Mom, Dad, I'm Living With a White Girl*, which, as its title suggests, centres on conflicts over intergenerational/inter-racial relationships, an issue Vancouverite Mina Shum also explores in her 1994 film, *Double Happiness*. *Mother Tongue* examines the compounding of traditional difficulties between generations of Chinese Canadians because of linguistic differences, further heightens the tension through the deafness of Steve, the younger member of the younger generation, and accentuates the isolation of each character through heavy use of monologues. Thus, post-modern concerns about the limitations of language as a tool of communication are underscored as three languages—Chinese, English, and American Sign Language—are used and only one character is relatively fluent in all three. Mimi, the elder child, is clearly the conduit for the communication that does occur; her plans to leave Vancouver provide the point of attack for the play's action.

Ratsoy: How did *Mother Tongue* begin for you: was it with an image or a theme, or in some other way entirely?

Quan: *Mother Tongue* began as a phrase: "It's like liquid. Drowning…" I had no idea where the phrase would lead, but subsequently it became the first line of Steve's first monologue in the play.

Quan's script is remarkable for its compact intricacy. She deftly juxtaposes the Chinese myth of the jingwei bird with the family's past, present, and future. In the manner in which she unveils the tale, Quan also affirms the bonding power of storytelling: each family member (including the dead father) knows the story and has some role in its retellings. It is significant that the affirmative final scene, which closes with silent but nonetheless definite communication between the two characters left behind, highlights the tale's theme of unity.

The play is at once steeped in traditional Chinese symbols and rituals such as oranges, kites, incense, and Chingming, and is reflective of the contemporary Canadian milieu as the family gathers around the television at dinner. Employment Insurance forms need to be completed, and a female architecture major contemplates travel across the country to continue her studies. Bennett Lee's generalization certainly applies to *Mother Tongue*: "Ethnic minority writers have an experience of at least two cultures, one functional and mainstream, the other perhaps more suppressed and rooted in historical memory. This awareness of duality, the potential conflict arising from the friction between the two worlds and the powerful influence of the secondary culture lurking offstage account for what is fresh and energetic and unique about much of this literature. Chinese-Canadian writers are no exception"(7). The cultural hybridity of *Mother Tongue* is at the core of both the tension of the action and the appeal of the work.

Quan's approach to ethnic issues is powerful in its understatement. The play is rare in an era of focus on postcolonial issues in that there is a conspicuous absence of mention of overt racism in the script. It might, in fact, be argued that concern with familial communication supplants ethnic issues. However, such an argument overlooks two vital facts: the play's central characters do not form part of the dominant ethnic group (as their creator does not) and the mother is clearly disempowered by her inability to speak a dominant tongue. Although Quan's realm is the private rather than the obviously political, one has only to examine the mother's financial situation, for instance, for evidence of the inseparability of the two domains.

The apparently simple title is fraught with meaning. The term "mother tongue" has two denotative meanings: one's native language and a language to which other languages owe their origin. Its connotations in the context of the play are manifold: it underlines the centrality of language, it reminds us that the mother (unnamed and identified only by her birthing role) is the originator, it underscores the role of language as the originator of communication, and it suggests giving birth to (and through) language.

Both in *Mother Tongue* and on the Canadian literary scene, the long silence is over. As Lien Chao states, "A full-fledged, contemporary Chinese Canadian literature has entered the Canadian literary landscape with its own heroes and heroines, ghosts and devils, tragedies and comedies.... As a minority literature, Chinese Canadian literature—like other such literatures—raises a resistant voice against European cultural hegemony in Canadian literature" (xiv). It will be interesting to witness the ongoing contribution that Betty Quan's words—subtle but potent—make to the postcolonial discourse.

G.R.

Selected Bibliography:

- Beauregard, Guy. "The Emergence of 'Asian Canadian Literature': Can Lit's Obscene Supplement?" *Essays on Canadian Writing* 67 (Spring, 1997): 53-75.
- Birnie, Peter. "Fool's Gold." *Vancouver Sun* 14 Apr 2001. A review of Simon Johnston's *Gold Mountain Guest*.
- Birnie, Peter. "Raising Curtain, Lowering Barriers." *Vancouver Sun* 14 Apr 2001. Examines attempts by Vancouver theatres to attract non-white audiences.
- Birnie, Peter. "Stage White." *Vancouver Sun* 14 Apr 2001. Discusses limited casting opportunities in Vancouver for actors of colour.
- Carlson, Tim. "Review of *Fault Lines*." *Vancouver Sun* 26 Oct. 1996.
- Chao, Lien. "Anthologizing the Collective: The Epic Struggles to Establish Chinese Canadian Literature in English." *Writing Ethnicity: Cross-Cultural Consciousness in Canadian and Quebecois Literature*. Ed. Winfried Siemerling. Toronto: ECW Press, 1996. 145-170. An interesting examination of both Chinese Canadian literature and the politics of anthologizing.
- Chao, Lien. *Beyond Silence: Chinese Canadian Literature in English*. Toronto: Tsar, 1997.
- Chinese Canadian Writers Workshop. *Inalienable Rice*. Vancouver: Powell Street Revue, 1979.
- Crook, Barbara. "*Mother Tongue* Loses In Translation on Its Way to Stage." *Vancouver Sun* 21 Feb. 1995.
- Derksen, Celeste. "Review of *Mother Tongue*." *Canadian Theatre Review* 94 (Spring, 1998): 79-80.
- Gill, Alexandra. "Culture Clash Beyond Words." *The Globe and Mail* 9 May, 2001. Gill interviews Quan, prior to the Factory Theatre production of *Mother Tongue*, about the origins of the play.
- Knowles, Ric. "Review of *Beyond the Pale*." *University of Toronto Quarterly* 67.1 (Winter, 1997-8): 73.
- Lee, Bennett and Jim Wong-Chu (eds.). *Many – Mouthed Birds*. Vancouver: Douglas & McIntyre, 1991.
- Ng, Maria N. "Chop Suey Writing: Sui Sin Far, Wayson Choy, and Judy Fong Bates. "*Essays on Canadian Writing* 65 (Fall 1998): 171-186. Ng argues that contemporary Chinese Canadian writing is often stereotyped and artificially homogeneous.
- Quan, Andy and Jim Wong-Chu. *Swallowing Clouds: An Anthology of Chinese Canadian Poetry*. Vancouver: Arsenal Pulp Press, 1999.
- Quan, Betty. E-Mail Interview. 5 Jan. 2001.
- Quan, Betty. "The Play's the Thing... But How to Sell It?" *Quill & Quire* 60.11 (November, 1994): 19-21. In the role of literary journalist, Quan examines play publishing.
- Quan, Betty. "Review of *Many-Mouthed Birds*." *Quill & Quire* 57.10 (October, 1991): 27.
- Thomas, Colin. "Review of *Mother Tongue*." *The Georgia Straight* 24 Feb. to 3 Mar. 1995.
- Yhap, Beverly. "Performing Asian Canadian in Vancouver." *Canadian Theatre Review* 85 (Winter, 1995): 5-8.

Mother Tongue
by Betty Quan

Mother Tongue premiered at the Firehall Arts Centre in Vancouver in February, 1995, with the following cast:

Mother	Allanah Ong
Mimi	Laara Ong
Steve	Kameron Louangxay
Father	Michael Hirano

Directed by Donna Spencer
Costumes Designed by James Glen
Set Designed by Neil Fleming
Lighting Designed by Neil Fleming and James Proudfoot
Sound & Music Designed by Ted Hamilton
Movement Consultant: Lee Su-Feh
American Sign Language Consultant: Astrid Evensen-Flanjak
Assistant Directed by Michael Hirano
Stage Managed by Damon Fultz and Amadea Edwards

CHARACTERS

MOTHER: 53, widowed parent of STEVE and MIMI; has a Chinese accent (but not pidgin English); also speaks Chinese (Cantonese).
STEVE: 16, no Chinese accent (at age 11 lost his hearing so is fluent in American Sign Language).
MIMI: 21, STEVE's sister, no Chinese accent; speaks some Cantonese and when speaking with Steve, occasionally mixes in signed words.
FATHER: 30s, has a Chinese accent. (FATHER can be a physical presence on stage but always in shadow; alternatively, his dialogue may be done as voiceover.)

SETTING

The Chan family home in Vancouver, BC.

NOTES

When parenthesis appear (E) means the next line is in English. (C) means the next line is in Chinese/Cantonese. (ASL) refers to the text being signed, not spoken.

STEVE's signed dialogue attempts to follow the linguistic principles of American Sign Language. It is recommended that a member of the Deaf community or a certified sign language interpreter be consulted.

In the moments when MOTHER speaks Chinese, I have not provided a translation from the English to Chinese; rather I have written her dialogue/monologues in English. This is to allow the actress playing the part flexibility with the character and how much Chinese she wants to, or is able to, use.

Blindness cuts people off from things.
Deafness cuts people off from people.
—Helen Keller

SCENE ONE

Voiceover montage like a sea of voices ebbing and flowing, cutting and intercutting, reverberating. The stage remains dark.

MOTHER: A long time ago.

STEVE: Listen.

MIMI: A story.

MOTHER: Like a bird in your hand I was until you set me free–

STEVE: –across the sky–

MIMI: –across the ocean.

MOTHER: The wave became a blanket. And the little girl died.

MIMI: (*C*) Father? Come back! Come back!

STEVE: Did I stop hearing her?

MOTHER: It was my favourite story.

MIMI: Our favourite story. He would tell it to me.

STEVE: All my senses were swimming inside a seashell.

MIMI: Sometimes when I dream, I dream in Chinese.

STEVE: The ghost of your voice is inside me.

MOTHER: He called you his little jingwei.

STEVE: Listen to my hands as I speak to you.

MIMI: Sign.

STEVE: Sign.

MIMI: Speak.

STEVE: Speak.

MIMI: Hear.

STEVE: Listen to me. Please.

MOTHER: I am my language. I speak Chinese. Your voices. Your words. You drown me out.

STEVE: Silence. Silence.

Suddenly, the voices are cut off.

SCENE TWO

Lights up. MIMI and STEVE are doing homework. MOTHER prepares dinner. STEVE signs to MIMI.

STEVE: (*ASL*) University go you? Ontario. Letter I see room your.

MIMI: Again, please. You what?! Steve! You read my letter. (*She looks over her shoulder to make sure MOTHER doesn't hear.*) Don't.

STEVE: (*ASL*) Don't understand she.

MIMI: She can so understand. Even a little bit is enough. Snoop. What's the sign for snoop? (*ASL fingerspells*) S-N-O-O-P. (*resumes*) Yes, you. What were you doing going through my stuff?

MOTHER: (*C*) Mimi, come help me with dinner.

MIMI: Okay, wait a minute. Well?

STEVE: (*ASL*) Pencil search I.

MIMI: You were looking for a pencil.... That doesn't excuse the fact that you opened my letter.

STEVE: (*ASL*) Go?

MIMI: I don't know. Queen's is a good university and they have one of the best architecture departments...

STEVE: (*ASL*) Money, find where you? Expensive!

MIMI: It's a scholarship. You know Mother can't afford to send me. She thinks a bachelor's degree is enough. And you still have a couple more years left at the deaf institute.

STEVE: (*ASL*) Up-to-now you not-yet out Vancouver you. This will first time.

MIMI: I know it'll be my first time out of Vancouver alone.

STEVE: (*ASL, trying to scare her*) Jails. Many have. K-I-N-G-S-T-O-N.

MIMI: Fingerspell that again please.

STEVE: (*ASL, fingerspells*) J-A-I-L-S. K-I-N-G-S-T-O-N.

MIMI: (*reads out spelling*) J-A-... jails K-I-... Kingston. Oh stop it about the jails, will you?

STEVE: (*ASL*) Five.

MIMI: Really, there's five in Kingston? How do you know?

STEVE: (*ASL*) Decide finish you?

MIMI: I still have time to decide. And I have to talk to her.

STEVE becomes agitated.

STEVE: (*ASL*) Letter hide you. Not right.

MIMI: Wait, Steve! I'm the one who should be mad. I was going to tell you. Honest! I would never let you down. Never.

STEVE: (*ASL*) Liar. Remember?

MIMI: You won't let me forget that, will you?

MOTHER: (*C*) Mimi! Help set the table!

MIMI: Coming!

MIMI makes her exit. As her back becomes turned, STEVE reaches out to her and speaks as a deaf person would. It is barely understood and the way the words are modulated indicate he has not spoken for some time. MIMI hears him, but exits still.

STEVE: Don't go, Mimi. Come back. Come back. Don't go. Don't leave me all alone.

STEVE becomes bathed in a blue light. He turns to the audience. At first he tells his story silently, only mouthing the words. It is as if the audience has become deaf. STEVE then places his hand against his throat and speaks.

It's like liquid. Drowning. When I would go swimming, I would do the backstroke. I'd immerse my head in the water and listen to the swirling, swirling echo. It was a game I used to play – no one can hear underwater, can they? But now, it's not a game. Not anymore. There: the waves of air... circulating. It's like that inside my head. Air floats inside me. The sound of ether rising. (*places hands over his ears*) I feel my voice coming from inside my body. The thought becomes articulation, the movement of the throat, the exhalation of air as it forms into sounds as it forms into words. Air forming into sounds I can't hear. Into words I can't speak. Into sentences no one will listen to.

SCENE THREE

Dinner; they eat in front of the TV.

MOTHER: (*C*) Good?

MIMI: Yes.

MOTHER: (*C*) Some more?

MIMI: (*E then repeat in C*) I'm full.

MOTHER: (*C*) Maybe Steve wants more. You ask him.

MIMI: He's right there.

MOTHER: (*C*) Ask him. Mimi.

MIMI: One day you'll have to learn how to sign.

MOTHER: (*E*) I have to learn English. (*C*) Too late now.

MIMI: It's never too late to start. Who knows, I might not always be here. I mean, I know there's a Chinese sign language but Steve and I learned American Sign, so maybe, I mean I can write stuff down...

MOTHER: (*C*) I don't understand what you're talking about.

MOTHER gestures towards STEVE again, wanting MIMI to ask him if he wants more dinner.

MIMI: You have to learn English one day.

MOTHER: (*C*) Ask Steve.

MIMI touches STEVE to get his attention.

MIMI: (*ASL*) Food more want you?

STEVE: (*ASL*) Finish. Enough.

MIMI: No – you tell her. She's right there. Go on.

STEVE and MOTHER look at each other. STEVE shakes his head. A moment of silence. MIMI tries to conciliate, as usual.

MIMI: Mother, remember when you would tell us stories?

MOTHER: (*C*) I remember.

MIMI: We were young.

MOTHER: (*E then repeat in C*) Before all the trouble.

STEVE's inner voice is not heard by the others.

STEVE: I remember your voice, Mother. This, this is the sign for Mother.

MIMI looks at STEVE and sees the meaning of his signing.

(*He signs as he speaks it.*) A thumb on the chin with the fingers extending out. I've showed it to you before. Look, Mother. Please.

MOTHER: (*C*) What? What? I don't understand. Mimi?

MIMI: He's saying...

STEVE: (*inner voice spoken aloud*) Tell us a story, and I will read your lips. English or Chinese. I don't care. Just look at me when you talk. (*ASL*) Look-at-me. Look-at-me.

MIMI understands but does not translate full message.

MIMI: Steve says the same thing: tell us a story. Like you used to.

MOTHER: (*C*) I know a good one. A favourite. (*E*) My father used to tell it to me when I was a little girl. (*C*) You'll remember this one, Mimi.

MIMI: The emperor and his daughter.

MOTHER: (*C*) Yes, that's right. (*E*) Your father used to tell it too.

MIMI: Why don't you sit here, Steve, so you can see better? Oh, wait–

MIMI goes to the kitchen, returning with sliced up oranges. During her absence, silence; it is obvious that STEVE and MOTHER are uneasy with each other.

MOTHER: (*C*) Not from the fridge?

MIMI: I know you don't like them cold.

MOTHER: (*C*) So sweet. (*E*) Soon, we eat the oranges from *bi sin*. (*beat, then C*) A long time ago–

MIMI: (*ASL*) Long-time-ago.

MOTHER: (*C*) What does that mean?

MIMI: A long time ago.

STEVE: (*ASL*) Long-time-ago. Story. Yes. Understand.

MOTHER begins the motion of the hand sign, but stops and stares ahead.

MOTHER: (*C*) A long time ago there was an emperor who had a young daughter. They loved each other very much. But although his power could touch all corners of the land, the emperor could see only as far as the shoreline that divided his kingdom with the sea. Beyond that shoreline, his vision was limited, like a kite held high in a strong breeze – he could see the shape, but not the colours.

FATHER's voice is heard only by MIMI. His voice blends into MOTHER's and when he stops, MIMI takes over. The effect is like a chorus.

FATHER: A long time ago...

MIMI: (*C*) Father?

FATHER: There was an emperor who had a young daughter. They loved each other very much. Tell it, Mimi, my jingwei. A long time ago.

MOTHER & MIMI: (*Talking in unison, but with MOTHER speaking C and MIMI speaking E. MIMI's voice takes over the story until only she speaks it.*) A long time ago. It was my favourite. A story.

MIMI: About the Jingwei bird and why she is always dropping sticks and stones in the ocean. When I was small, I used to pretend I was that little bird. I would soar through our garden with arms for wings. Father. Tell me about the Jingwei. Yes, like you used to do when I was small. Like a bird in your hand

I was until you set me free across the sky, across the ocean. Such a long time ago, yet so close I can still see it unfolding before me. Father? Tell me a story. Like you used to do.

FATHER: A long time ago.

STEVE: (*ASL*) Long-time-ago.

FATHER: A long time ago there was an emperor who had a young daughter. They loved each other very much.

MIMI: But although his power could touch all corners of the land, the emperor could see only as far as the shoreline that divided his kingdom with the sea.

FATHER: Beyond that shoreline, his vision was limited, like a kite held high in a strong breeze – he could see the shape, but not the colours.

MIMI: (*as Jingwei*) Father, look at the waves, so tall they must be hiding something behind them. I will take my boat for a ride.

FATHER: (*as Emperor*) Not so far, not so far.

MIMI: (*as Jingwei*) Don't worry, Father. I'll be careful.

FATHER: (*as Emperor*) Why don't you wait a while? I'll join you. We can journey to the horizon together, where the sea meets the sun.

MIMI: (*as Jingwei*) When? When can we do this? (*laughs*) You're always promising such things, Father! I'll go out on my own first. On my own adventure. Then, I'll show you what I've seen.

STEVE: (*ASL*) Come, when you?

FATHER: (*as Emperor, laughs*) When?

STEVE: (*ASL*) When?

MIMI: (*as Jingwei*) What does that matter? We have all the time in the world.

MOTHER: (*C*) The sun was warm upon the little girl's face–

FATHER: –and the salty breeze off the water tempted the little girl to travel farther and farther. To see what hid behind the tall waves of the sea.

MIMI: Far far far away she went, when suddenly–

FATHER: (*as Sea God*) Who dares come this far upon the ocean of my reign?

MOTHER: (*C*) The Sea God's bad temper came upon the little girl.

STEVE: (*ASL*) Drown. Water. Waves.

FATHER: The water became a blanket that covered her. And the little girl died.

MIMI: (*gets onto her knees*) Died? I don't remember her dying. Is that right? I thought the water changed her into a bird. Like magic.

FATHER: I would tell you that when you were small. When you didn't understand death.

MIMI: Like I do now.

A dreamlike light surrounds MIMI.

Sometimes when I dream, I dream in Chinese. Not the pidgen Chinese I've developed but the fluent, flowing language my father used to coo as he walked with me, hand in hand. There is this one dream. I am walking with my father in the alleyway behind our house. I am seven years old. This is just before my father... before.... My father and I are holding hands and in perfect Cantonese talk about the snow peas in the garden that are ready for picking. Father doesn't know it, but for the past week I've been hiding amongst the staked vines, in the green light, gorging on the snow peas until there can't be anymore left. I'm about to tell him this—air my confession—when we come across a large kitchen table propped against the side of the garage. "A race, my little jingwei!" my Father says. "I'll go through the tunnel and we'll see which way is faster. One, two, three, GO!" We run; him in the tunnel, me on the gravel. I finish first and wait, expecting to meet him and rejoin hands. But he doesn't come out of the shadows. My extended hand is empty. I wait and wait and wait. I start screaming, (*C*) "Father! Father! Come back! Please come back! Father!" (*E*) And then, I wake up.

Moment returns to the real. MIMI is visibly upset.

MOTHER: (*continuing the story, C*) A wave came over the little girl and her boat, and the ocean pulled her down. Down to where the Sea God lived. And that day, she died.

MIMI: (*repeating, simultaneously signing to STEVE*) A wave came over the little girl and her boat, and the ocean pulled her down. Down to where the Sea God lived. And that day, she died. (*to MOTHER*) When (*C*) Father (*E*) told that story, I don't remember him saying that the little girl died.

MIMI turns away from STEVE.

I thought everything had to have a happy ending.

MOTHER: (*starts to clear up some of the dishes – E*) Story not over.

STEVE: (*ASL*) Crying, why?

MOTHER: (*C*) Mimi, my little jingwei, why are you crying?

MIMI: Please, don't call me that.

MOTHER: (*C*) What, jingwei? But I don't mean anything by it. (*E*) It's a pretty name. (*C*) My father used to tell the jingwei story to me when I was a little girl. Before I came here. (*E*) It's a good story. It was my favourite story. Just like you.

STEVE: (*ASL*) Mother tell her?

MIMI: (*signs and speaks*) Not now. Later.

MOTHER: (*C*) What are you talking about?

STEVE: (*ASL*) When? When?

MIMI: (*ASL*) Stop. When ready I.

STEVE: (*ASL*) Wrong.

MIMI: (*ASL*) My problem.

STEVE exits.

MOTHER: (*C*) Why does he leave like that, without a word? Always he does that!

MIMI: (*lying*) He said he was going upstairs.

MOTHER: (*C*) When? I didn't hear him.

MIMI: (*used to this conversation, but nevertheless lying*) He signed it.

MOTHER: (*C*) He doesn't talk anymore, Mimi. Never.

Offstage SFX: water running in the bathtub.

MIMI: It embarrasses him. You should understand that by now. Steve can't hear what he's saying. He thinks he might sound stupid. I've got an essay due tomorrow. Do you want me to help with the dishes?

MOTHER shakes her head. MIMI exits. MOTHER cleans up. Her inner voice speaks. MOTHER is awash in light like smoking red incense.

MOTHER: (*C then repeat in E*) A long time ago. I was 18, I left China for Canada. Alone. We were rich. Capitalists. (*E*) But the war had brought the Japanese, followed by Mao's government. Every night, we turned off the lights, closed the curtains, and we waited. Waited for the knock at the door, for someone to come and in the name of the Red Army take away everything we had. Everything I had... I arrived in Vancouver in 1959, without a word of English, wearing my hairspray and makeup and high heels, eager and excited. But I didn't fool anyone. Only myself. More than twenty years gone and I sometimes wonder why I ever came at all. My husband dead and me alone. None of my own family here to comfort me. No. There are my children. But I often feel as if I bore strangers who have my eyes, my skin, my hair, but whose souls have been stolen by invisible spirits. I wonder, when I am dead, if my children will remember to honour me on

Chingming. Will they follow tradition? Clean my grave, bring flowers, burn incense? Will they pay me tribute as I have done to ancestors they do not know? Yes, there are my children.

MOTHER moves out from her inner voice. She calls.

Mimi? Steve? (*as if talking to herself*) Is anyone home? Or is it just me?

SCENE FOUR

MIMI does homework. She drifts into sleep. MIMI's own dreamscape light fades up as she begins to dream.

MIMI: For years I've been sorry. Make a fist and circle it on my chest. Sorry.

MOTHER: (*C*) Don't forget, Mimi. I have to work late. (*E*) Overtime pays good! Take Steve to the doctor.

MIMI: He's 11 years old! (*to MOTHER*) He can go to the doctor himself.

MOTHER: (*C*) He's too sick to go by himself.

STEVE: Yeah, Mimi. I'm too sick to go by myself.

MOTHER: (*C*) Such a high fever!

STEVE: If my temperature gets any higher, I'll burn up! I'll spontaneously combust. (*He makes exploding noises.*)

MIMI: But there's a game. At the school. You know I've never been to one.

STEVE: Boys will be playing.

MIMI: Shut up, Steve. (*to MOTHER*) Why can't you go?

MOTHER: (*C*) I have to work overtime!

MIMI: But all my friends will be there.

STEVE: Boys.

MOTHER: (*C then repeat in E*) Mimi, you're too young for a boyfriend.

STEVE: I'll go to the doctor by myself.

MIMI: You're really not that sick, Steve.

STEVE: Forget it. Your friends are more important than me.

MIMI: Don't be such a baby. OKAY! I'll take you to the doctor.

MOTHER: (*C*) Don't forget.

STEVE: She'll forget.

Simultaneously.

(*ASL*) Tell her.

MOTHER: (*C*) Tell him.

STEVE and MOTHER repeat their separate languages as MIMI is driven under the weight of their words.

SCENE FIVE

MOTHER pays tribute to ancestral shrine.

MOTHER: (*C then repeat in E*) Husband, Father-in-Law, Mother-in-Law. Three cups for you each to drink from. Fragrance of incense and smoky tea. Chingming, the end of the second moon. Take care of my family. I'm burning money for you to spend in heaven.

MOTHER burns spirit money; sets out an offering of oranges. STEVE watches, trying to gather courage to move closer. Because her back is turned to him, MOTHER is unaware of his presence, and STEVE cannot see what she is saying.

(*C then repeat in E*) Obey and serve one's parents when they are alive. Bury them with honour when they are dead. Respect them always. If family does not pay tribute to the dead, they will bring evil upon those still living.

STEVE exits.

(*E*) Five years ago, I didn't burn enough spirit money. Cups were full. Incense burned. But not enough spirit money for you to buy more time in heaven. I gave you all I had – but it wasn't enough. Since then, you have made me remember. Every day, I see the evil you brought upon my son. The oranges here are sweet. Eat them and fill them with your luck. I will give them to my children.

SCENE SIX

STEVE in a blue light.

STEVE: It's nice. The water. Six months after... after I lost my hearing, I wasn't allowed to swim. Or take a plane ride; not that I'd be going anywhere. Not that any of us are going anywhere. Except for Mimi. (*beat*) I missed the water. Being in the water. Mother was probably glad though. She hated it when I went swimming. Thought I would catch a fever, leaving the pool without drying my hair. Maybe, maybe she was right. I remember when I was a baby. Even before I was born. Floating – rotating around and around in my mother's stomach like the earth around the sun. I could hear her voice too. I remember hearing my mother laughing and singing. But not anymore. Did she stop being happy? Or did I stop hearing her?

STEVE steps out of his light briefly.

(*ASL*) M-I-M-I stay. Please.

STEVE repeats the sign for please as the lights fade down on him.

SCENE SEVEN

MOTHER is in the living room, sewing. MIMI enters, back from school.

MIMI: Is anybody home?

MOTHER: (*C*) Here, Mimi. I got some (*E*) piece work (*C*) from the factory. (*E*) Pockets. (*C*) All day I've been sewing pockets. You'll have to mark for UIC.

MIMI: I'll work on the UIC statement tonight. Is Steve home yet?

MOTHER: (*C*) I don't know.

MIMI: Have you seen him?

MOTHER: (*C*) In his room.

MIMI: Then why didn't you say... (*sighs*)

MOTHER gestures at the burning incense.

MOTHER: (*C*) The incense is very fragrant, isn't it?

MIMI: Moon festival?

MOTHER: Chingming. (*C*) Have you forgotten already?

MIMI: No, I remember. I just get all of them confused, that's all.

MOTHER explains the festival; it's a lecture MIMI knows.

MOTHER: Chingming. (*E*) Not same as Moon Festival. Chingming. Time to remember all our dead family. (*C*) We'll go to the cemetery and bring your father flowers.

MIMI: What day do you want to go to the cemetery?

MOTHER: (*C*) Why? Are you busy? Too busy to visit your father's grave?

MIMI: It's not that. I just thought that if we went Sunday, we could go (*C*) drink tea.

MOTHER: (*C*) Drink tea! But we don't have enough money. (*E*) Next time. (*C*) We'll go next time.

MIMI: When?

MOTHER: (*E*) Next time. (*C*) Remember how your Father loved to go drink tea? Every Sunday, early in the morning, we'd take the bus to Chinatown?

MIMI: Father loved the shrimp dumplings.

MOTHER: (*C*) Shrimp dumplings. Pork dumplings. Sticky rice.

MIMI: (*E then repeat in C*) Pork with black bean sauce.

Together, in C, MIMI and MOTHER imitate Father.

MIMI & MOTHER: Hurry! Eat while it's still hot.

They laugh. MOTHER looks at her watch; realizes it's time to make dinner.

MOTHER: (*E*) I remember when your father died, you were just seven, and Steve, Steve was just two. (*C*) Still a baby. He doesn't remember your father, does he?

MIMI: He remembers him a bit; I don't know.

MOTHER: (*C*) Sometimes during the night, you'd wake up screaming. You had terrible nightmares. Do you remember?

MIMI: Yes.

MOTHER: (*C*) Nightmares about your Father. Do you still have them? Mimi?

MIMI: (*lying*) It doesn't matter. I don't have nightmares about him anymore.

MOTHER: (*C*) Your Father holding his chest. And me holding the two of you. (*E*) Too young to have a heart attack.

MIMI: Lucky the doctor was Chinese.

MOTHER: (*C*) I was so scared. I didn't know what was happening.

MIMI: It was the same for Steve, Mother. Remember? When he got sick? We were all scared. We all didn't know what was happening.

MOTHER: (*E*) I didn't understand Steve's doctor. Lucky I have you, Mimi.

MOTHER begins chopping vegetables.

(*E*) For Chingming we can't eat meat. (*C*) We'll eat jai.

MIMI: Buddha's Feast.

MOTHER: (*C*) Good: you remember the tradition. One day – you'll make jai for me.

STEVE enters the room to grab a snack. He looks at MIMI then exits.

MIMI: I'll cook jai for you. One day. (*beat*) I've got some good news. Mother – stop for a moment; I have to talk to you. You know I'll be getting my bachelor's degree soon. That's why we should go (*C*) drink tea. (*E*) Celebrate.

MOTHER: (*C*) Now you can get good job. Make lots of money. (*E*) Good daughter – take care of your mother and brother. (*E then repeat in C*) No more pockets to sew.

MIMI: I was thinking about going into post-graduate studies. Study architecture. Go to school for a few more years.

MOTHER: (*C*) Too expensive.

MIMI: I got offered a scholarship. They'll pay. For everything.

MOTHER: (*C*) Mimi! That's so good!

MIMI: My professor says that only two students got it.

MOTHER: (*C*) I'm so proud of you! Such a smart girl!

MIMI: It's at Queen's University.

MOTHER doesn't understand most of what MIMI is saying, but MIMI looks happy, so MOTHER is happy for her.

MOTHER: (*C*) Good. Good.

MIMI: They say it's one of the best universities in the country. They have an excellent architecture program. I'll design things, Mother. I'll make buildings like Arthur Erickson, the man who designed the courthouse over at Robson Street, or the American, Frank Lloyd Wright.

MOTHER: (*C*) Good.

MIMI: They have a beautiful campus. Lots of very old buildings. Tall and wide and open.

MOTHER: (*C*) Such a smart girl.

MIMI: Queen's is in Ontario.

MOTHER: (*C*) But that's so far away.

MIMI: It's only a three hour difference. (*mumbles*) By phone.

MOTHER: (*C*) Three hours. Are you trying to fool me?

MIMI: You know I can't write Chinese, but we can talk on the phone.

MOTHER: (*E*) Long-distance. (*C*) No money for that. Piece work can't pay! UI can't pay!

MIMI: There'll be one less mouth to feed without me around–

MOTHER: –Mimi–

MIMI: –plus the scholarship will pay for my room and board at Queen's. I won't really need any money except for my textbooks. Maybe I'll take a part time job. I'll pay for the telephone calls, then you–

MOTHER: (*C*) UI forms, who'll take care of those?

MIMI: I've showed Steve how to do them.

MOTHER: (*C*) He won't know how to do it!

MIMI: He's been doing them already. You just haven't noticed because I've been coming to you for the signatures.

MOTHER: (*C*) And when the UI runs out, we'll be on (*E*) welfare. (*beat, C*) What if there's trouble?

MIMI: What kind of trouble?

MOTHER: (*E*) People phone, they come to the door. (*C*) I never understand what they're talking about!

MIMI: Steve can take care of that too.

MOTHER: (*C*) He can't hear them.

MIMI: He doesn't need to hear them. They can phone on the TTY line. They can write down what they want.

MOTHER: (*C*) Someone breaks into the house, he can't hear them.

MIMI: Mother, you're worrying too much.

MOTHER: (*C then repeat in E*) You're too young to leave home, Mimi. Young women should only leave home to get married.

MIMI: You were 18 when you came to Canada all by yourself.

MOTHER: (*C*) But that was different.

MIMI: How? How was it different? You came here. I want to go to Ontario.

MOTHER: (*E*) I didn't want to come here! (*C*) Inflation because of all the trouble with Mao Zedong. (*E*) My father only had enough money to send me. A cousin—someone from my father's family—met me at the airport. (*C and repeat in E*) My first day, no sightseeing, nothing. My first day I started working.

MOTHER holds out her hands.

(*C*) Look at my hands, Mimi. I've been working since I was 18 years old. (*E*) I worked hard. Saved enough to sponsor my mother and father. (*C and repeat in E*) I was too late.

MIMI: I'm 22. I'll go to Queen's, study hard. And when I finish, I'll become a great architect and buy you a new house. I'll build you and Steve a new house. In Shaughnessy!

MOTHER: (*C*) No, you get scholarship here.

MIMI: The scholarship is not for here.

MOTHER: (*C*) What about Steve?

MIMI: He's deaf, not retarded. If you would only just listen...

MOTHER: (*C*) No. You listen. I am the Mother!

MIMI: Then act like one!

MIMI is surprised by her words; MOTHER reacts as if she's been slapped in the face.

MOTHER: (*C*) Who works hard, day and night? I put food on the table; you're going to an expensive university, and Steve needs special things. (*E*) Where do you think the money comes from? (*C*) Ever since your father died!

MIMI: I know, Mother! I know! But look at us. Look at you. When father died.... And Steve.... What are you afraid of?

MOTHER: (*She mimes the action of her words, of her fear. C.*) In China, every night we would turn out the lights, draw the curtains. We waited for the knock at the door. It could be a friend, a neighbour – wearing a Red Army badge, ready to take everything away from us. To take everything away from me.

MIMI: You're not in China anymore. The Red Army won't be knocking at the door. I'm here, Steve's here–

MOTHER: (*C*) Taking everything away from me. (*E*) And now they're taking you away from me too!

MIMI: I loved him too. But I can't be him, Mother. I can't always protect you. Mother.

MOTHER: (*C*) He called you his jingwei bird.

MIMI: Don't call me that! (*C*) Mother. (*E*) You came all the way across the Pacific Ocean. All by yourself. That's farther than I have to go.

MOTHER: (*C*) I had no choice!

MIMI: Then let me choose what I want to do!

MOTHER: (*C then repeat in E*) My family never came to Canada, your father died young, and Steve... now you. (*C*) You're going to leave me too.

MIMI: I'm not leaving you! I just want–

MOTHER: (*C*) Bi sin, Mimi. Go, pay tribute to your paternal grandfather and grandmother. Bi sin. You should've done that when you first came in. (*E*) Bow to your family.

MIMI: (*C*) Mother.

MOTHER: Chingming.

MIMI exits. MOTHER resumes food preparation.

MOTHER: (*to herself, C*) Eat jai. Bean sprouts. Bean thread noodles. (*E*) Ginger, garlic, onions. Tofu to remember how Buddha did not eat meat. Rice wine, mushrooms, onions. Onions.

MOTHER stops. She begins to silently cry.

SCENE EIGHT

STEVE is doing homework. MIMI enters, fresh from her argument with MOTHER.

STEVE: (*ASL*) Know now, Mother, she?

MIMI nods.

(*ASL*) University, can't?

MIMI: I'm going. I don't care what she says.

STEVE: (*ASL*) Not fair.

MIMI: (*ASL*) Don't. Please.

STEVE: (*speaks as a deaf person would*) Can't go. Not fair.

MIMI: I'm going to come back! I promise!

STEVE: (*speaks as a deaf person would*) Forget it. Don't bother!

STEVE gestures at his ears, doing the signs for listen and for deaf. He then points at MIMI accusingly. MIMI exits. STEVE faces the audience as if facing a mirror. He practices enunciating words. He speaks as if a deaf person would who is unused to speaking.

My name is Steve Chan. (*He is getting angry.*) My name is Steve Chan. I cannot hear you. My sister, sister, sister (*The deaf have particular difficulty with sibilant words. This frustrates STEVE.*) Sister! Sister!

STEVE puts his hand over his throat, we move into his inner voice.

I remember the last voice I heard. It was my mother, screaming my name. Steve! Steve! And she was crying. I was eleven. I remember that because we were reading *White Fang* in school and I decided I wanted to have a wolf/dog. I was making up a speech inside my head, about getting a dog, and how I could convince my mother that I should have one for my birthday. I'm always making up speeches inside my head. It was cold outside, and I already had a cold. I was supposed to wait for Mimi. She was supposed to take me to the doctor. She never showed up. I went home with a temperature. By evening my fever shot up. Everything was moving in slow motion. My mother with the cold wet cloth, trying to keep me cool, Mimi asking the paramedic questions and translating as best she could to my mother. Sixteen and already my sister was a mother. I fainted, and when I finally woke up, all my senses were swimming inside a seashell. Liquid had filled up my mouth and my ears. I lay back, trying to breathe. I thought I would drown in all that liquid. But there was nothing there, no water, no blood. Just a hole. A hole.

Each character moves into his/her individual lights, eg. STEVE's blue light, MOTHER's red, MIMI's dream light. Their inner voices speak to one another but they are physically unaware of each other. The overall effect is like that of Scene One.

MOTHER: Chinese.

MIMI: English.

STEVE: (*ASL*) Sign language.

MIMI: The little girl drowned.

MOTHER: Not understand.

STEVE: I cannot hear you.

MIMI: I can't do this. Not anymore.

MOTHER: Bow to your family.

MIMI: Inside me, it's been asleep for so long. What does it feel like to wake up from inside?

MOTHER: That is the way it works. In Chinese.

MIMI: Let me open the windows. Just a crack.

STEVE: (*ASL*) Please. Please.

MIMI: Let me pull back the curtains. Can I?

STEVE: I... can... not–

MOTHER: (*C*) Cannot.

STEVE: (*ASL*) Can't.

MIMI: Let me see what's outside.

STEVE: (*ASL*) Sign. Speak. Hear. Listen. Silence.

MIMI moves into the centre, her hand outstretched to STEVE who has moved to one side while MOTHER stands at the opposite side. For a moment, MIMI's hands touch both MOTHER and STEVE's hands. She fails to join all hands. STEVE and MOTHER recede into the darkness. MIMI's dream light fades up.

FATHER: The little girl's soul became a small bird called Jingwei. Continue. (*beat*) Mimi.

MIMI: Angry was the spirit in that bird, angry at the sea it was for taking her away from her beloved father. And every day the jingwei would carry in her beak stones and twigs from the Mountains of the east and ahead, flying west, she would drop her small stones and twigs into the sea. Finally, the Sea God noticed what the jingwei was trying to do.

She expects to hear her FATHER's voice again, but is greeted by silence.

(C) Father? (E) How do I finish the story? Where are you? Are you here, with me? Did you come back across the ocean to find me? Did you fly away like a kite in the breeze? So high up you can see the shape, but not the colours? Can you see me? You're so far away but all I have to do is pull you home. Father. Father. When I finish building a bridge, will you cross it? Even if the stones are loose, and the twigs are breaking. Will they cross it? Father? Will they cross it? Don't let me do this alone. Please. (*beat, C*) Father? (*E*) How big is the ocean?

SCENE NINE

MIMI and STEVE say goodbye to one another. Off, MOTHER watches them.

MIMI: (*ASL and E*) All the bills have been paid. The cheque-book's in the desk. Mother's supervisor at the factory said there might be some work next week. I gave her our TTY number. Once you get the dates, tell Mother.... (*STEVE looks questioning.*) Call me collect then if she doesn't understand and I'll–

MIMI becomes overwhelmed. STEVE puts his fingers against his lips: shhh. MIMI understands. Her mouth moves but makes no sound. STEVE presses his fingertips against MIMI's throat.

MIMI: (*ASL and E*) And the Sea God said. "Silly jingwei, my sea is wider and deeper than your limited imagination. You can never fill me up in a million years." To that the jingwei replied, "But I can. Every day for a million years I will do this. Every day until one day. Until one day... (*begins to fade down*) Until one day.... Until one day..."

STEVE: (*speaking as a deaf person would*) And the small bird flew back to land, only to return with another small stone or twig to drop into the sea.

MIMI smiles and gently pulls STEVE's hand from her neck. MIMI turns and moves into the shadows where she picks up a suitcase. She doesn't turn around. MOTHER moves forward, as if trying to reach MIMI. MOTHER also moves into the shadows. STEVE is alone. Lights fade down on him.

SCENE TEN

STEVE and MOTHER are at the kitchen table. They are bent over their food, avoiding eye contact. MOTHER speaks as she gets other dishes out. With STEVE's face bent down, he cannot see that MOTHER is speaking to him.

MOTHER: (*C then repeated E*) Can you understand me? When I try to speak English to you, can you understand me? In this ocean I am swimming and I am underwater and I cannot speak. What? I can't hear you. I am my language; I speak Chinese. Your language is not Chinese. Your voices, your words. I cannot understand. You drown me out.

MOTHER is seated, with her head bent down. When STEVE does his monologue in English, he speaks from his inner voice. The ASL, however, is directed at MOTHER.

STEVE: (*E then repeat in ASL*) Move your lips. Look at me. I can remember the sound. Say my name. I can hear the memory of how you used to say my name. Inside me. Look at me. Just because I can't hear anymore doesn't mean I've forgotten how to listen. If only you would just speak to me. The ghost of your voice is inside me. My mind hears you. It hears you, Mother.

During the ASL repeat, STEVE gets more angry. He tries to get MOTHER's attention, almost throwing his signs at her. MOTHER's head remains bent. He dares her to look at him.

STEVE: (*speaking as a deaf person would*) Mother. (*C*) Mother.

MOTHER looks up at him, finally. She looks back down. STEVE exits to another space. His inner voice speaks.

Can you see the words as they float in the air? My hands release them – out, out to be heard. Can you see the wind? The branches bending, the wind's fingers drumming against the window. There – thunder. The vibration crosses my spine. I can hear it. Yes, there's lightning. Music, music touches the floorboards, rises through my feet. My body hears all these sounds. Listen to my hands as I speak to you. Listen to me. Please.

SCENE ELEVEN

MOTHER goes to the shrine.

MOTHER: (*C then repeat in E*) I was born in 1940: the Chinese year of the dragon, the highest sign. (*E*) Steve was also born in the year of the dragon: 1976. It is considered great honour to be born a dragon. We have tempers like fire and generosity like liquid which pours from our mouths and fingertips. Dragon – *loong*. That is the Chinese word. The Chinese also call someone who cannot hear loong. Someone who cannot hear. *Loong*. I do not know why. When Chinese people pray to the dragon, for rain, for good luck, for happiness, they throw birds into the water. The dragon feeds on the meat of swallows and sparrows. Birds who make sweet sound. Birds who have sweet flesh. Birds are sacrificed to our dragons, the *loong*. Are you that little bird, Mimi, my jingwei? (*to herself*) Loong.

MOTHER takes one of the oranges from the shrine.

SCENE TWELVE

STEVE is huddled in his room, alone. MOTHER enters.

STEVE: (*ASL and speaks simultaneously*) Brother none. Sister 1. Father dead. Mother have. Family my.

STEVE looks up. Sees MOTHER. She holds one of the oranges from the shrine.

MOTHER: (*C*) Her soul became a small bird called jingwei. Angry was the spirit in that bird, angry at the sea she was. And everyday, that bird would pick up pebbles and twigs in her beak and drop them into the water.

MIMI: (*Her voice flows with that of MOTHER, but an echoing translation.*) Her soul became a small bird called jingwei. Angry was the spirit in that bird, angry at the sea she was. And everyday, that bird would pick up pebbles and twigs in her beak and drop them into the water.

STEVE: (*ASL and speaks simultaneously*) Together. Separate. Hearing person. Deaf person. Sign. Speak. See. Hear.

MIMI appears in spotlight which recedes towards the end of her speech. She holds a bird cage, opens it. SFX *of a bird in flight.*

MIMI: And the Sea God said, "Silly creature, you can never fill me up in a million years." "But I can," said the jingwei. "Every day for a million years I will do this. Every day until one day there will be no more water between me and my family. I will build a bridge, a bridge that they can walk across. That my family can walk across." And the small bird flew back to the land, only to return with another pebble or twig to drop into the sea.

Lights fade down on MIMI. STEVE signs "sister." He huddles and cries silently. He signs "mother." He signs again. MOTHER enters STEVE's light. STEVE is finishing the motion of the sign for "mother" with his fingers stretched out to her. MOTHER moves forward. Her hand holds out the orange. STEVE is hesitant to take it. MOTHER reaches out again, this time using her other hand to force STEVE to face her. Lights out.)

The end.

SEX IS MY RELIGION

BY

COLIN THOMAS

Patrick McIntyre as Jim

Photographer: Tim Matheson

CROSSOVERS: COLIN THOMAS AND *SEX IS MY RELIGION*

The theatre critic plays a singular role. On one level, as one of many spectators, the critic is integral to the play's success yet at one remove from its action. However, because theatre is fundamental to the critic's livelihood—because of the materiality inherent in the involvement (not to mention the reciprocal nature of the material dependence)—the relationship takes on an added dimension: the theatre critic is at once without and within. When the professional critic is also a professional playwright (and former professional actor) the complexities accrue. Perhaps it is to Colin Thomas's dual role as long-time theatre critic for the *The Georgia Straight* and acclaimed playwright that we may ascribe his ability to see through several lenses simultaneously and thereby produce work that defies easy classification – that fits apparently contradictory categories.

Born in Manitou, Manitoba, Colin Thomas moved with his family to various small Manitoba towns and spent several years in Winnipeg before his father, a member of the RCMP, was transferred to New Westminster in the late 1960s, when Colin was fifteen. Thomas completed a degree in theatre at UBC and studied acting at the Bristol Old Vic for a year. After a career as an actor, he turned his hand to writing plays for young people, an endeavour in which he has had remarkable success. Thomas has won the Chalmers Children's Playwriting Award three times – for *One Thousand Cranes* (which draws parallels between the bombing of Hiroshima in World War II and the nuclear threat of the 1980s), *Two Weeks, Twice a Year* (which examines the effects of his parents' divorce on a young man during two stages of his life), and *Flesh and Blood*. These plays, which have been mounted by most major Canadian children's theatre companies, have been produced in Germany, the USA, Austria, Japan, Hong Kong, the former Soviet Union, and Australia, and translated into French, Japanese, and German.

Ratsoy: You were an actor first. How did the transition to playwright happen?

Thomas: I worked with Touchstone Theatre; I wasn't a founding member, but I was in the first batch of actors. And I worked a lot with Green Thumb. Then I was part of a group hired by the Burnaby Parks and Recreation Department. Theresa Goode, who was coordinating the project, asked if I would write a play for us to perform, and *Burnaby Barnaby* was the result. Brian Linds wrote one scene and I basically wrote the rest. That's when I discovered that I really, really enjoyed writing for kids. By the second summer that we performed *Burnaby Barnaby*, we had little groupies who dressed like the characters and chanted along; it was like *The Rocky Horror Picture Show* for the daycare set. I also wrote *Tough Cookies* for Burnaby Parks and Rec. Then Dennis Foon asked me to write a show about the nuclear fears of children. That turned into *One Thousand Cranes*, which was a very big success.

Flesh and Blood (1991), commissioned to educate high school students and the general community about AIDS by British Columbia's (Social Credit) Ministry of Health (which subsequently withdrew funding because, an official told Thomas, they didn't want to "deal with the social issues surrounding AIDS"), marks a transition in Thomas's playwriting career: this play resonates with adults as much as with young people. While it succeeds in reaching out to an adolescent audience, as its successful productions at Toronto's Theatre Direct and Vancouver's Headlines Theatre attested, the drama is complex, sophisticated, and nuanced enough to easily engage on an adult level. *Flesh and Blood* was also an adventitious prequel to *Sex Is My Religion*.

Each play features a gay man with AIDS named Jim who is the offspring of a deserting father and a Christian fundamentalist mother. By turns harsh, harrowing, tender, humorous, and blunt, both plays are impressive for their penetrating examination of family dynamics. At *Flesh and Blood*'s core is the relationship between two brothers; revolving around that centre are their respective partnerships: twenty-six-year-old Jim's with Ralph and seventeen-year-old Allan's with Sherri-Lee. The play explores the turns in the brothers' relationship when Jim, who has been a surrogate father to Allan, somewhat belatedly (his disease is at an advanced stage) informs his brother of his illness. *Flesh and Blood* is so richly rendered that its lessons about safe sex and homophobia, neatly integrated into the drama, are dynamic without being didactic. As reviewer Robert Cushman wrote, " *Flesh and Blood* is a good play trying to pass itself off as social tract.... The play is moral all right, but its morality is not simple."

In his introduction to *Making, Out: Plays by Gay Men* (which includes *Flesh and Blood*), Robert Wallace calls attention to the range of plays in his anthology as he interrogates the notion of a "gay play." It is imperative to bear in mind that the voices of gay playwrights are polyphonic (each a product of unique experiences), that gay and lesbian playwrights do not necessarily always (or ever) produce gay-themed work, that heterosexual playwrights may write gay-themed plays, and that even terms such as "gay themed" are fraught with ambiguity.

Although gay dramatists who have created overtly gay characters have become vital players in Canadian theatre, acceptance has been gradual. John Herbert's gritty indictment of Canada's prison system, *Fortune and Men's Eyes*, (which debuted in New York City in 1967 and went on to international acclaim and film adaptation) did not receive a major production in his home town of Toronto until 1975. Michel Tremblay, probably Canada's most renowned playwright, is widely acknowledged for his depiction of historically marginalized groups (working class, joual-speaking women, for example, in the groundbreaking 1968 work, *Les Belles-Soeurs*) and interpreted in the context of Quebecois cultural and political struggle. Two of Tremblay's earliest works, *La Duchesse de Langeais* (1969), a monologue delivered by a transvestite, and especially *Hosanna* (1973), a powerful play about a gay transvestite hairdresser's confrontation of his multi-layered identity confusion (after his emulation of Elizabeth Taylor in her role as Cleopatra is met with derision within his social circle), had, by the late 1970s, frequent production at home and abroad.

Concomitant with the beginnings of limited mainstream acceptance of gay work was the founding of what became North America's largest gay and lesbian company, Toronto's Buddies in Bad Times Theatre, in 1979. Sky Gilbert's influence as co-founder and long-time artistic director of the company has been inseparable from his prominence as a playwright (of such widely produced works such as *Drag Queens on Trial* and *Drag Queens in Outer Space*) and his role as indefatigable promoter of the rights of gay artists in Canada. The last two decades of the last century saw emergence into the mainstream of important work by Robert Lepage, Brad Fraser, Daniel MacIvor, and Michel Marc Bouchard, among others. The work of these playwrights has been published in single-copy format and in a variety of mainstream anthologies. Furthermore, Robert Wallace's collection has been joined by another gay-focused work: *Rhubarb-orama! Plays and Playwrights from the Rhubarb! Festival*, edited by Franco Boni, anthologizes selected works from Buddies in Bad Times Theatre's annual Rhubarb! Festival (which premiered Sally Clark's *Ten Ways to Abuse an Old Woman*).

While production and publication opportunities for gay work by gay writers were increasing in other major centres across the country, production possibilities in Vancouver were limited, even as late as the early 1990s. In response, a half-dozen playwrights joined forces in early 1993 to plan a theatrical event they first called *The HIV Project*. Two and a half years later, *Plague of the Gorgeous*, five plays by Out West Performance Society (billed as Vancouver's first professional gay theatre company) played to exceptional critical acclaim. "The writing, direction and acting are at their absolute peak" wrote reviewer Barbara Crook, who praised the collective for "remarkable use of language and dramatic form, unparalleled honesty of emotion and some of the best performances this theatre community has ever witnessed." Rosalind Kerr assessed the appeal of the ensuing anthology: "They reveal interesting intersections between lived and fantasized experiences, capturing the painful dichotomies between gay/lesbian and queer representations" (87). The scope of the collection is also noteworthy: the works range from Gordon Armstrong's science fiction satire *Plague of the Gorgeous* to *Remembering Shanghai,* Peter Eliot Weiss's affectionate take-off on Noel Coward's *Private Lives*.

Ratsoy: Is it still difficult to get gay-themed work produced in Vancouver?

Thomas: There is much less ghettoization of gay culture these days. It's hip to be queer. But I think it is still helpful to have companies and events that provide venues for individual communities and concerns. A lot of good work came out of the Women in View Festival, for instance. I miss it. Out West is attempting a revival. I have no idea how successful that will be but I wish the company well. I remember how thrilled I was when *Plague of the Gorgeous* went up and was so popular. I got to experience in my own town what I had only experienced in theatres in other cities, like at Buddies in Toronto: a real celebration of queer community and work. So, even though the ghettoization is breaking down, I still think there's plenty of room for queer companies and events.

Sex Is My Religion, Colin Thomas's contribution to *Plague of the Gorgeous and Other Tales*, examines the lives of Marge, a Christian fundamentalist, and Jim, her gay son who has AIDS. In a disorienting, remarkable, and highly effective use of dual monologues, Jim assumes the character of Marge – that is, Jim becomes Marge; he doesn't simply act as he thinks Marge would – and vice versa. This technique is, as journalist Zsuzsi Gartner noted, "a twist that goes far beyond mere theatrical device." The monologues underscore the isolation of each character (the two are outwardly estranged, and the monologue does not evolve to dialogue) at the same time as the switch foregrounds the inextricability of familial links and emphasizes the fluidity of gender and familial roles.

Ratsoy: How did *Sex Is My Religion* evolve from *Flesh and Blood?*

Thomas: I started to write *Sex Is My Religion* because there was a possibility that *Flesh and Blood* might be turned into a TV movie. In the theatre, the audience will excuse the mother's absence because they implicitly understand the realities of casting. But on television, you have to meet her; there's no reason why you shouldn't. So I started to write in her voice as a way of getting to know her. Usually, when I'm writing, I can tell whether what's coming out is any good or not, but I couldn't tell with this stuff. So I said to a friend of mine, "Just listen to this." I started reading and I was overwhelmed by feelings that seemed to come out of nowhere. I could hardly get through it because I was sobbing and sobbing. That was a complete surprise; I had no idea that what I had written was so emotionally important to me. I was reading the speech in which Marge talks about her husband holding her nose when she was pregnant. Then I went from wondering where all that feeling came from to thinking that the material was really overwritten and purple. It was a long time before I could tell whether or not I liked it. But now I do. I like it a lot.

Each monologue progresses in a linear fashion: each character's life, from childhood to the present, is sketched. In tandem with the role reversal, the chronological approach amplifies the parallels in the two lives. Both characters have been passive—more acted upon than acting—and out of fear of self-dissolution resort to extremes bordering on addictions. The play's title, in fact, conflates those obsessions. Although Marge's religious fanaticism would seem antithetical to Jim's sexual obsession, the monologues reveal the similarities in what leads each character to his/her extremes. The concept of mirror images is played out in a striking visual pun.

Crook judged *Sex Is My Religion* "unforgettable" and Patrick McIntyre and Meredith Bain Woodward's performances "stunning" and praised Thomas's writing for "soar[ing] through a dizzying range of emotions and images." Critic Chris Dafoe saw the 1996 production at the Playhouse (with McIntyre and Woodward, who won a Jessie Award in the community-recognition category for her performance, reprising their roles) as "a simple yet lovely play" and Vit Wagner, in a review of the Buddies in Bad Times production (starring Clinton Walker and Ellen-Ray Hennessy) applauded the simplicity and theatricality of the reversal and the play in its entirety. *Sex Is My Religion* has also been produced in Houston, Texas, by The Group and transformed into dance by John Alleyne, artistic director of Ballet British Columbia.

G.R.

Selected Bibliography:

- Armstrong, Gordon, Colin Thomas, Stuart Blackley & Kevin Gregg, Lisa Lowe, and Peter Eliot Weiss. *Plague of the Gorgeous and Other Tales.* Winnipeg: Scirocco Drama, 1996. Weiss's introduction provides an overview, from conception to fruition, of the theatrical collaboration behind the anthology.
- Armstrong, Gordon. "Top Boys: Canadian Gay Plays: Getting it On." *Theatrum* 31 (Winter 1992/93): 16-21. Examines the six plays anthologized by Robert Wallace in *Making, Out: Plays by Gay Men*.
- Boni, Franco, ed. *Rhubarb-O-Rama: Plays and Playwrights from the Rhubarb! Festival.* Winnipeg: Blizzard Publishing, 1998. Contains 20 plays (including Sally Clark's *Trial of a Ladies' Man*) produced from 1979-1998 and includes interviews with Buddies' co-founders Sky Gilbert, Matt Walsh, and Jerry Ciccoritti, as well as twenty other playwrights, producers, and directors.
- Carnie, Morag, and Anton Wagner. " Gay and Lesbian Theatre." *Canadian Theatre Encyclopedia.* www.canadiantheatre.com/g/gayandlesbiantheatre.html 23 Mar. 2001.
- Crook, Barbara. "Gorgeous Way to Come Out." *The Vancouver Sun* 30 June 1995.
- Cushman, Robert. "Morality Not Simple in Moral Theatre Direct Play." *The Globe and Mail* 9 Apr. 1991.
- Dafoe, Chris. "A Small, Quiet Gem About Fractured Connections." *The Globe and Mail* 10 July 1996. A review of the Playhouse theatre production of *Sex Is My Religion*.
- Gartner, Zsuzsi. "*Sex* Promotes a Potent and Poignant Empathy." *The Georgia Straight* 4-11 July 1996.
- Kerr, Rosalind. "In Review: *Plague of the Gorgeous & Other Tales*." *Canadian Theatre Review* 92 (Fall 1997): 87-97.
- Rintoul, Harry. "Review of *Plague of the Gorgeous & Other Tales*." *Prairie Fire* 17:4 (Winter 1997): 130-131.
- Thomas, Colin. Telephone Interview. 2 Apr. 2001.
- Wagner, Vit. "Drama at its Most Elemental." *Toronto Star* 21 Mar. 1997.
- Wallace, Robert, ed. *Making, Out: Plays by Gay Men*. Toronto: Coach House Press, 1992. Includes plays by David Demchuk, Ken Garnhum, Sky Gilbert, Daniel MacIvor, and Harry Rintoul.

Sex Is My Religion
by Colin Thomas

Sex Is My Religion premiered at the Gastown Theatre in June, 1995, with the following cast:

Marge	Patrick McIntyre
Jim	Meredith Bain Woodward

CHARACTERS

Sex Is My Religion consists of two monologues, which are performed by two different actors. In the first, JIM plays the role of his mother, MARGE. In the second, MARGE plays the role of JIM.

SCENES

Part One: Sacrifice   Part Two: Eternity

1. Cow Song
2. Blueberry
3. Leaves
4. Robins
5. Fever
6. Sacrifice

7. Brooch
8. Dairy Queen
9. Gun
10. Shit
11. Eternity

PART ONE: SACRIFICE

There's a table and a chair onstage. On the table, there's a necklace, an inexpensive string of costume jewellery.

JIM enters. He sits on the chair and puts on the necklace. As he does so, he becomes his mother, MARGE.

Cow Song

MARGE: I am not a monster. I know that Jim has told you.... To hear him tell it, you'd think that everything that... all the different things he's struggling with are exactly my fault.

Well, they're not. He's an adult, isn't he? Would you say that Jim is an adult? Yes. Well, he has to take responsibility for himself.

Yes, my son and I were close. What's wrong with that?

Oh, don't tell me. I know what the implication is. Like the mother's love is always at fault. You tell me: how can love be a fault? You just look around you at the world and you *tell* me: do you think all the problems out there are because people love their children *too much*? I don't think so.

Lonely. My own childhood. I would have to say lonely, since you ask.

Well, for one thing, my parents were always fighting. And my mother was not the most stable individual in the world.

Well, if you want the whole story, my mom and dad came from Poland. They weren't poor, though; they had land. And that land was like a gold mine, my dad used to tell me. But just after they got married, he got involved in a bunch of crazy debts—gambling and drinking—and he had to sell everything off – the farm buildings and everything. And the first house they had here was a shack. And my mom had me right away. And then the other kids.

When I look at those pictures now... she was just so young.

She used to sing, you know. Good enough for the opera her friends said. But all of a sudden, she's digging in the dirt, tearing up her hands.

There's...

I remember the first night she came home... late for dinner. We were just all sitting there in the kitchen, like we couldn't manage by ourselves, and my dad asked her where she'd been and why wasn't dinner on the table. And she said she'd been walking along the railroad tracks. And he said dinner was late. And she said she decided to just lie down and wait for the train to come. And he didn't say anything. And she said next time maybe she'd wait a little longer. My father yelled at us kids to be quiet, but we hadn't made a sound.

I remember one time she went to this dress-up party at the church and she was a chrysanthemum. Spent two weeks making this pink petal dress out of *crêpe* paper. I looked at her when she was in it and I thought she was prettier than anything on the prairie.

She could play the violin, too. Did I mention that? And juggle oranges.

But then she'd have down spells and she'd disappear. I was terrified that if I put a foot out of line, all of a sudden I wouldn't have a mother. That's a terrible thing to do to a child.

I don't say that in judgement of her.

You know what's funny? In all of that, I never cried.

But I'll tell you what I did do. I'd go out to the barn with the cows and I'd lean my head against whichever one was my favourite at the time—in milking position, with my head on her side—and I'd make this sound I called "opera singing". Just a high, sad sound, really – something a little girl might think of as opera. And I just kept doing that till I was sure she was home.

BLUEBERRY

MARGE: Men? What are you getting at? Well, you know what most men are like – and even boys...

Well, they think their penises are awfully interesting, don't they? The way they're always showing them off.

(*laughing*) Did I shock you? I suppose you thought you knew everything about me once you knew I was Christian. Well, there's a lesson in that, then, isn't there?

Well, really! I can't have been more than six years old when Steve Chika asked if I wanted to go see some blueberries out behind the school. So, of course, I went with him and, when we got back there, he pulled down his pants and squeezed the end of his penis till it turned blue. I couldn't tell by his expression if I was supposed to laugh or run away.

And he was just the first of many. Most of the rest didn't have Steve's *savoir faire*.

My father? Absolutely not! But I suppose I would put him in the same category as the others. You know: "Not to be trusted." But, no, no, he was more of a distant figure.

LEAVES

MARGE: Jim thinks that I don't know anything about... well, about what he would probably call the sexy side of life. But do you know what's ironic? It was Jimmy who kept me alive when I was going through... all of that.

Well, I won't pretend my husband and I had healthy marital relations. I will tell you that he thought he owned sex, that he owned me. And I don't think that's right. He made me do things and say things.... But I believe that God has forgiven me for the things I did, because, the person I was then, I didn't have a choice. And that's all I have to say on the subject.

Other ways, though, I will tell you that he was mean.

When I was pregnant with Jimmy—and I was having trouble with that pregnancy—when I was asleep, he used to clamp his fingers over my nose and mouth, so I would wake up all the time suffocating. And he used to think that was really funny. And if I told him it wasn't, he'd just laugh all the harder.

Anyway – my mom had died years earlier, but, when I was pregnant, and my husband was being so mean and all, I was.... Well, let's just say I was at a very low point. And I found myself going for walks, out by the railway tracks, like I was looking for her. My mother. And then one day this idea came into my head that I should just lie down – just like she was always talking about doing.

So I lay down. And then I looked up at the trees along the tracks. It was spring, so, of course, there were new leaves.

I'm almost ashamed to tell you how much that moved me. That leaves... come back. It sounds like nonsense, doesn't it? But, nonsense or not,

I can only tell you that I started to feel my body as part of... I can only call it "the miracle of the leaves" – my belly, my breasts – unfolding and ripening. And I put one hand on my breasts and one hand on him—on Jim in my belly—and I started to sing to him. Just like I used to sing to those old cows, come to think of it. And it started off sad, like it was then, but before long, I was standing up and I was singing and it was...

By the time I got home, I was crying flat out and singing all these crazy things at the top of my lungs.

And you know something funny? I realized that, as I was walking along, I had my hand out like this. Like I was holding onto somebody's hand—or reaching—and I didn't know at first who that somebody was. But I know now that God had brought someone who would, you know – walk with me.

Robins

MARGE: Well, those first few years, my husband had me so low it.... You know what I was afraid of? Dissolving. And it started to happen, too. I'd look at my hand and it was almost like I could see molecules floating right off.

You think I'm crazy now, don't you? Well, maybe I was, almost. But then Jimmy would look at me with such... effort. And it was like he brought me into focus.

Once... let me tell you... I remember once there were robins nesting in our garage—Jimmy was very little—and some of the neighbour kids were in there trying to get at the nest with a broom. And the poor mother robin was just frantic. She couldn't get out and she couldn't stop it. And of course the nest was destroyed and her eggs were smashed. And I don't know if Jimmy was excited by the bird flying around or what. He may have thought that was exciting, but when the eggs were smashed, he started to scream. And he couldn't stop.

Of course, I came running and when he finally started to choke out a few words, it was like he was confessing he'd been an accomplice to murder. Beautiful blue eggs. On the cement.

I think he thought I could put them back together. And when I couldn't he just kept talking about the dead babies and the poor mother.

So I said that we should have a funeral and God would take care of them. I wasn't even in the church then. I just knew that it would feel better. And he got to work. He made a little coffin for the eggs out of a Birks box, and he dug a hole and put the coffin in it. He was organizing the whole thing and the other kids were just following along like they were in his congregation or something. So we had a little service. And then he asked me to sing. There were all these little faces looking up at me. And I wasn't in the church then, so I didn't know any hymns or anything. The only sad song I could think of was "Hang Down Your Head, Tom Dooley," so I sang that. And they seemed satisfied.

I'm sure he thought I could make the dead rise again.

It scared me sometimes.

Well, I guess any parent...

Fever

MARGE: Have you seen him?

How's he doing?

I'm sorry. I know.

I know.

Yes, I try to lead him to God. *Because he led me.*

Well, if I tell you, will you listen?

Okay. Alright. God called me... Jim's first sickness, when he was a little boy.

When I couldn't.... When my husband... left us... I don't know if you'll be able to understand this. (*short laugh*) I still have scars I got from that man, but, when my husband left us... I Did Not Know Who I Was. You follow me? And Jim got very sick. Pains in his joints. Fever. He had to be hospitalized. We didn't know what was wrong. The doctors told me it might be leukemia.

And I had to leave that child in the hospital every day. By the time I left he'd be screaming. Panicking. But I had to leave him. They were very, very strict. I had to do it. I had no choice.

Do you know there were children in that hospital who never ever got a visit from anybody? There was a little girl in Jimmy's room. Marta. She had leukemia, but she was much, much worse, and so, when I looked at her, I thought I could see.... Her parents were from out of town and I think there were younger children, but still.... How could you... *leave* a child... all alone... to suffer like that?

It wasn't enough for either of them, but I did what I could.

When Marta.... Well, I was sure Jimmy was next, so when Marta died, I thought she might as well just take me with her. Her bed...

I went to find a quiet room, and the only one available just happened to be the chapel. So I went in and I said—I *thought* to no one—I said: "I give up. I just give up."

And there was something in the silence.... It was like there was nothing of me left, so I just opened my heart and let it in. And all of the grief of all of the parents who had ever sat in that hospital chapel flooded into me. I thought it would kill me. It was so big I thought it would tear me apart. But it didn't, because, at the same time, I felt all of their love, too, and that love... healed me. Do you know what I mean? But it wasn't like any human love, really, because there was no end to it. That's when I knew it must be God.

Do you know what it means to be touched by Him? Because if it can happen to me, it can happen to anyone. Because that's when I realized that we are *all* children. Who have been... left. The whole human race! Not just Marta. Or Jimmy. Not just me. It's like we've all been left here in this beautiful garden, our planet, but we're frightened because we can't find our parents. So we try to invent them. We make up things like politics and philosophy and science. And willpower and sanity. But they can't really comfort us because they're not our true parents. And it's only when we completely give up, when we think that we're totally alone and abandoned, that our *true* father—God—comes to save us.

I prayed all night. That Jimmy wouldn't die from leukemia. And that I would find some rest.

And the next day... *the next day* the doctors told me that Jimmy didn't have leukemia after all! They said they'd made a mistake! They said that it was sub-clinical rheumatic fever but that he was already over the worst of it and he would probably be fine. And he was. Within a month, he was... perfect. Healthy.

Now that was a miracle to me. You can believe what you want. But I know that, through my child's suffering, the Lord spoke. And after that, I was so grateful, so willing, so *eager* to accept His word, His teachings. The discipline of His church.

And yes, I want to bring that kind of salvation to Jim. I want to save him from all his... struggle. Wouldn't you? Wouldn't you save him from his struggle if you could?

Wouldn't you?

SACRIFICE

MARGE: You think it's easy, don't you? That faith is somehow supposed to be for stupid people—oh, yes, you do—or the coward's way out. Well, you tell me: do you think it's easy having your only son turn his back on you when he's dying? The Lord brought me faith with the life of my son and now He is testing me with the life of my son.

Our pastor says faith is the hardest kind of love there is. And he's right.

It was our pastor who told me about Abraham and Isaac. He said.... When God told Abraham to take Isaac to the top of the mountain, and to sacrifice his young son, Isaac, instead of the sacrificial lamb, Abraham went with a heavy heart, but he did as his Lord commanded, and he bound Isaac's hands behind him, and he laid him on the sacrificial stone.

And if God must take Jim, I open my heart to God and I say, "Tear him out. Tear him out, Lord. He was yours before he was mine."

But at the last minute, God spared Isaac. He spared him. And I pray that God might spare Jim. One more time.

Jim has been... too proud for faith. But perhaps in the cruelty of his illness, there is also a gift: that Jim will open his heart to his true Father.

So I pray for him.

Oh, but I *do* talk to him. I have his picture on the fridge and I talk to him every day. But he talks to the dogs when he comes home more than he talks to me. And he hasn't been home for more than a year now.

No.

No, not even on the phone anymore.

He's the one who won't talk to me, you know. No matter what he told you.

MARGE takes off the necklace and becomes JIM once again.

JIM puts the necklace on the table.

The light fades.

PART TWO: ETERNITY

MARGE enters, wearing the necklace from "Part One: Sacrifice." She sits, removes the necklace, and puts it on the table.

She is now her son, JIM.

BROOCH

JIM: What'd she tell you?

Did she tell you how AIDS is God's punishment? How I brought it on myself? Prob'ly not. That'd be a bit too rude for company.

So with you. I wonder. Did she quote from Corinthians this time or did she lead from her strength? Did she cry? Bet she cried. Bet she came up with some really good reasons for crying. That's usually how she starts off if she doesn't know you that well. 'Cause if you know her better, see, you know she's been crying for the last thirty years and AIDS is just this really prime opportunity to pump up the volume.

It's always all about how hard it is for her.

Oh yeah. I know she loved me. And I loved her, too.

Well, there are a couple of things, I guess.

I remember once I was out in our backyard and I was screaming 'cause the only truck I had to play with didn't have any wheels. And I guess Mom musta seen me from the kitchen or something, because she came out, but—let me tell ya—she didn't look like she'd been doing the dishes. When she came out the back door it was like the light was different on her or something. She was wearing this dress that I'm sure I never saw before or since—it was sort of like mother of pearl—you know? Iridescent. And she came out and sat down beside me in the dirt. In that dress. And she said my truck didn't need wheels. That it was a flying truck.

I thought she looked like Jackie Kennedy. Only prettier. I guess you could say I was just completely in love with her.

You want to know the other thing I remember? Do you? I guess it's like my first—sexual—memory.

She used to take me into bed with her 'cause I used to wet the bed and she didn't want to change the sheets in the middle of the night. And I remember being awake—'s about six I think—I don't even know if this is real or a dream. But I remember being completely under the covers and I slid down till I was by my mother's ass. It was exciting, but I didn't know why. I knew about sex, but my ideas were pretty vague. But it was really hot and sweaty down there. It was scary too. And I knew I wanted to do something but I didn't know what.

So I hatched this plan. I slid out of bed and I got this brooch from her dresser. Scottish. Used to be my grandmother's brooch. And I slid back in beside her, then down under the covers. Back down there. And I got this brooch in my hand. And I pricked her flesh. Three times.

It was like being drunk and almost ready to throw up.

Maybe she didn't wake up because maybe it didn't happen.

On that day she came out and played with my truck? She didn't have on any shoes, you know. I guess it's because she didn't have any shoes to go with the dress and she didn't want to put on anything ugly. Most of the time—when she had the energy—I think she tried really, really hard to make everything perfect. And so did I. But I think she just got exhausted. And so did I.

DAIRY QUEEN

JIM: It was like, when I hit puberty, all of a sudden I was Clifford Olson to her or something. So one night I just split.

Sixteen.

My cousin's in Chilliwack.

Got this best friend, Steve, for a while. 'S great. Like I'd had sex with guys before. And a coupla girls, but I was always terrified they'd get pregnant. Anyway, we used to go on double dates together—Steve had a car—and after we'd dropped the girls off, Steve and I'd go park ourselves. It'd always start with something like – Steve'd grab his crotch and say somethin' like, "Christ!" and I'd say, "Yeah. No kidding."

And he'd say, "Fuckin' Evie!" 'cause his girlfriend's name was Evelyn. And I'd say, "Yeah. Fuckin' Bev." And he'd say, "You as horny as I am?" and I'd say, "Whadd*you* think?" And then: "If you were Evelyn, you know what I'd do?" "What?" And he'd start undoing my shirt and kissing me and feeling my chest. Sometimes we'd neck for hours. And then I'd blow him. Great, eh? Only problem was he never reciprocated. But I just kinda thought that was normal.

And then I started sucking off some of our other friends. And then I noticed that I was the only one doing the sucking.

It started to dawn on me that I might be the kind of guy they were talking about when they made jokes about fags.

One day I was at the Dairy Queen and I saw this guy there. Real queen. Almost a transvestite. Tight sweater. Big hair. Make-up even. I could feel the middle draining right outta me. I thought: "Jesus Christ. Is this who I am?"

Anyway, I moved to Vancouver. Started fucking everything in sight. We were party boys, eh? No regrets though. I made some great friends, then. Really good guys. We took care of one another.

GUN

JIM: Do I miss my father? How could I? I woulda shot him if I'd had a gun.

SHIT

JIM: I'm not the only one. Everybody in our family's addicted to something. Except my Mom.

But with Mom – it's like she's a Christ junkie, you know what I mean? After a while, it started getting like that with me and sex.

The worst? You don't wanna know! Well, people have done worse things, but...

Well, sometimes I can't get to sleep without using the phone lines, eh? And this one time this guy comes on—I said I really like being told what to do—and he asks if I've got sex toys.

He tells me to put on the tit clamps. He tells me to fuck myself with the dildo. Then he starts getting into shit.

Are you ready for this? Like he wants to hear the sound of the dildo in my ass.

He wants to hear me shit. In a bowl. In the bedroom. And I do it. He wants to hear me piss in the bowl. In my house. And I do it. And he wants me to get the shit on myself. And the thing is that I'm really turned on by this. It's vibrating, like way down inside me, like rock and roll, like a truck on the highway.

And he's getting really turned on and telling me what a hot man I am. And he comes.

And then he hangs up and I go into the bathroom. And that's when I start to feel like an accident just happened and I haven't felt the impact yet.

I'm panicking. My heart is racing. Like there's shit all over everything and it's just too scary. It's like I don't know who I am 'cause it's pretty obvious I'll do anything. And everything looks really weird. It's like the real world is trying to get back in, but I'm fighting it, so it's like my wall is way too blue, the lights are way too bright. And I finally just fall over in the middle of my hallway with my forehead on the rug. And I just try to keep breathing while the panic passes through me.

Eternity

JIM: Dissolving. That's what I'm afraid of. I mean, sometimes I feel like I'm gonna go crazy. And that feels like I'm dissolving. You know... (*singing*) "I fall to pieces."

And sometimes, with this disease, I'm afraid I'm gonna start... I mean, what happens if I start to get sick and nobody wants to have sex? It'd be like starting to disappear before you're dead.

Sorry. I don't usually talk like this. I been doing pretty good for about a year now. That kind of stuff doesn't scare me so much anymore.

Well, sometimes Christmas used to be pretty bad.

Well, 'cause I used to love it so much.

Well, it's a fag's dream, right? As far as I was concerned it was all about decorating. Me and my mom used to do the whole tree ourselves. Wouldn't let anybody else touch it. And she'd put on these – like "The Tammy Wynette Christmas Album" – and we'd sing along. She had a great voice. Sang on the radio a coupla times.

So I'd miss her then.

It's all fake anyway. Christmas.

But that's not the point. The point is...

I wanna tell you this 'cause it's the whole thing, really. On about December 21st, I'm at the beach, cruising—kind of—but really just trying to stop feeling shitty. When this kid comes up. Can't be more than about nineteen. Sweet face, but not really my type. I was into guys who looked a bit more like they were out on parole, if you know what I mean. But this kid won't take no for an answer. I even tell him I'm not really into sex, it's too late, I got work in the morning. Blah, blah, blah. But he says, fine, he'll give me a massage. And I figure: What the hell? He's warm, right?

And when we get back to my place, his mouth... tastes like the freshest fruit—like plums—you know what I mean? And he's got these eyes like—Pan or something—like he belongs in the forest, but really kind.

And I start to get down to the deed, you know – but he pushes me away, says he promised me a massage.

And he takes my clothes off very slowly. Then he's naked, too. 'S got this tattoo way down the bottom of his spine that looks like a kind of primitive symbol for eternity. Eternity and this beautiful boy's ass.

Then he covers me with these... hands. These... hands. I don't know how to say it except they were kind. And he's got one hand on my cock, and the other hand's moving around the rest of my body.

But I'm getting really nervous about something and I tell him I just don't feel like it. And he asks what's the matter and I tell him a bit about my mom and Christmas an' that. And he asks me if I love her and I tell him I hate her guts. And he says, "Try this. Try remembering a time when you loved her." And I say, "What are you, a shrink? Doogie Howser or something?" And he laughs and says, "What've you got to lose?" I don't even have to think about it and I'm back in my backyard and my mother's in that dress. He's lit candles in the room and it's like – the memory's so real I can smell it. Like she smelled real fresh. And he says, "Thank her, then leave."

And I do. I thank my mother. 'Cause in a way, she saved my life, right? Like, without her, I woulda been toast. So I thank my mother and I kiss her on the forehead. Then I leave her in the backyard. Still beautiful.

And then I'm really relaxed. And Lee—his name's Lee—keeps massaging. Sort of murmuring to me all the time, planting ideas in my head. It's like he's a shaman, you know? Like he's got magic. And then he says, "Try this." And he tells me to open my heart, to remember all the men I've fucked.

And I start to remember them. Donald. And Alex. We've all got these men, right?

And the amazing thing is this kid's holding my hand so it's like I can touch those men again for a minute. Say good-bye. You know?

And he keeps massaging. Tells me to see my father. And I do. Tells me to keep breathing. And I do.

And Lee—his name is Lee—tells me to forgive my father, and because this boy—this angel—is protecting me, I find out what it's like, for a minute, to forgive him.

He keeps massaging, then, "Hold your breath," he says. I have no idea what this is about, but I am too far gone by now to ask why, so I breathe deep, like I've been dying of thirst and he's offering water, and I clench every muscle in my body to hold that breath in. And it's like I go inside myself. Like the night sky and all the stars are inside my head and my chest and my belly. And then I'm floating in the sky, and part of it, too. Eternity flows in through the soles of my feet and out through the top of my head. And I know that my body is no more substantial than an outline, and even if that outline disappeared, I'd still be here, still connected.

It's like it's all one thing right? So I don't have to be afraid of dissolving.

"Breathe out," he says. And my mind is flooded with the beautiful parts of men. Lips. Necks. Ears, beards, forearms. Beauty that's around me every day and I don't even know I know it.

Lee tells me that I am excellent at sex because my heart is open. And he tells me he thinks people die the way they have sex.

Then he wraps me up in my blankets, kisses me on the forehead. And he's gone.

I see him every now and again on the street. Give him money sometimes when he's behind on his rent. But it's not like that; he's as sweet as ever.

Like I always knew sex was... my religion. But I didn't know how to make it a good thing before.

JIM places his hand on his mother's necklace.

My mother? Are you kidding? What could I tell her that I've just told you? She has no idea what I've been through. She couldn't begin to imagine.

JIM puts the necklace on and transforms back into MARGE.

MARGE exits. The lights fade.

The end.

The Unnatural and Accidental Women

By

Marie Clements

l to r
Adele Kruger as A Barbershop Woman, Peter Hall as The Barber

Photographer: Andree Lanthier

CIRCLES OF COMMUNITIES: LIFE AND ART IN THE CREATION AND PRODUCTION OF MARIE CLEMENTS' *THE UNNATURAL AND ACCIDENTAL WOMEN*

Ojibway writer Drew Hayden Taylor believes that more Canadian Native writers are attracted to playwriting than to other genres because drama is most akin to storytelling – to the oral tradition that is central to First Nations' cultures. Canadian drama certainly has been significantly altered and enriched by the works of contemporary Canadian Native playwrights such as Taylor, Margo Kane (with whom Marie Clements trained and worked), Tomson Highway, and Daniel David Moses. Although it would be fallacious to overstate the commonalities among such diverse writers, it is enlightening to examine some common threads in recent First Nations drama. Spiritual figures such as the Trickster figure, pivotal to traditional First Nations narrative, are, when transferred to the stage, dynamic surrealistic/expressionistic devices, as is the circularity of the traditional storytelling mode. These playwrights typically lay bare the landscape of the oppressed by fusing with tragedy elements of subversive humour that serve to intensify rather than attenuate the dramatic impact. Canadian First Nations dramatists also often meld elements of traditional First Nations' culture with contemporary mainstream popular culture, the result of which is, as Robert Nunn asserts, a hybridity that "is not evidence of being half-way to absorption, but on the contrary is a powerful form of resistance to absorption" (95).

While incorporating these elements into her work, Marie Clements has maintained an originality that arises, in part at least, out of her focus on multiple female protagonists in highly individuated urban landscapes. In the surrealistic *Now Look What You Made Me Do*, for example, two versions of the same Metis woman—on the cusp of adolescence and in early adulthood—cope with abusive relationships (with father and lover respectively) with support from an older friend and prostitute and various members of a self-help group. Clements' condemnation of the world of this play, replete with societal ills, is made all the more powerful by explicit reference to the "real world": by citing such locations as North Vancouver, the Riverdale Hospital, the Army and Navy store, and by integrating the larger British Columbia landscape through reference to such vocations as logging, Clements involves, if not incriminates, the larger society.

The Unnatural and Accidental Women also grounds itself in this way and thus forces its audience to examine its own complicity in the systems under attack. In this case, additional layers add to the immediacy: *The Unnatural and Accidental Women* was inspired by actual publicized events, and the theatre is linked to its community: where the play was first produced is in the very neighbourhood in which those events took place.

Over the course of more than two decades in Vancouver's east end, as many as ten women—most of them First Nations—who had previously been seen in the company of Gilbert Paul Jordan, a local barber, were found dead with extraordinarily high blood alcohol readings. Despite striking similarities in their deaths, coroners' reports listed cause of death as "unnatural and accidental." Finally, Jordan was convicted of manslaughter in 1988 for one of the deaths. Released from prison in 1994, Jordan, by June 2000, was facing four criminal charges, including providing a noxious substance—alcohol—to a woman he was charged with sexually assaulting. The Crown stayed the proceedings and Gilbert, out of jail for only a few days, was free for an extensive interview that appeared on the front page of *The Vancouver Sun* on the day *The Unnatural and Accidental Women* opened at the Firehall Arts Centre. By closing night, Gilbert was arrested and imprisoned awaiting trial for violating his parole by drinking heavily in a hotel with a woman who was trying to flee from him.

The Firehall Arts Centre has long been an integral part of the east-end Strathcona neighbourhood in which most of these events took place. By 1975 it was clear that the heritage building was no longer suitable as a firehall, and it was soon resurrected as a centre for the arts. By 1983 the Firehall Theatre Society was formed to administer the renovated building, which by then was serving as a venue for Axis Mime and Touchstone Theatre. Programmer Donna Spencer transformed the venue into a producing theatre and became the company's artistic director. She has also ensured that the Firehall Arts Centre maintains its connection to its community. In 1986 (Vancouver's centennial year), for example, she produced a collective creation, *Opening Doors*, which grew out of an oral history of the area. Firehall Arts Centre's mandate—"to promote, present and produce theatre and contemporary dance that reflects the cultural diversity of Canada"—reflects the historic and current demographics of the area, which has traditionally served immigrant and ethnic minority peoples. Among the plays the company has produced in the last decade are Betty Quan's *Mother Tongue*, George Ryga's *The Ecstasy of Rita Joe*, Marty Chan's *Mom, Dad, I'm Living with a White Girl*, and Drew Hayden Taylor's *Only Drunks and Children Tell the Truth*, *Someday*, and *alterNatives*. Spencer, who is currently artistic producer of both the Firehall Arts Centre and the Dancing on the Edge Festival, won the 1990 Jessie Award for multicultural innovation in theatre and the 2000 Cultural Harmony Award from the City of Vancouver.

Ratsoy: Do you think of yourself as a British Columbia playwright?

Clements: I don't usually, unless I'm somewhere else. Then I think west coast writers definitely have different perspectives from those on the east coast.

Hoffman: To what extent would you say this is a BC play? The imagery—the sound of buzz saws and falling timber—certainly seems to me very British Columbian.

Clements: It is, in the sense that the land and the evolution of this specific area is the environment of the play – from the trees to the hotels and to the oldtimers who felled those trees. In that way, it goes to this place and time where these women are now standing where the trees used to stand.

Ratsoy: How about on the Canadian scene as a whole? Does your work have much in common with, for example, Tomson Highway's plays?

Clements: I think there are similarities, but being from different genders and different environments reflects the way we think, the way we experience the world and tell a story. I've always seen my own work, my first impulse, in terms of visual compositions incorporating text, rhythms, and languages as layers.

Hoffman: Do you have a personal background in pre-contact First Nations performance?

Clements: Most of my Native family are Metis, from the North. It's a different tradition and a different perspective coming from the clash of contact. My own personal thoughts of pre-contact First Nations performance comes from an understanding, a spirituality or philosophy, that performance is a First Nations living art that has expressed itself from the inside out. The background is inside.

Marie Clements was drawn to performance as a nine-year old who studied song, dance, and voice. Before pursuing a theatrical career, she studied broadcasting at Mount Royal College and Arts Management at Simon Fraser University, then worked in a variety of capacities, including reporter, for radio. Her theatre training has included graduation from Spirit Song Theatre (where she won Best Actor Award) and instruction in a variety of techniques including authentic movement, the Grotowski Method, and mask work. Among Clements' extensive acting credits are roles in the Arts Club production of Tomson Highway's *Dry Lips Oughta Move to Kapuskasing*, CBC Radio's production of *The Ecstasy of Rita Joe*, Calgary's Maenad Theatre's production of *Urban Tattoo*, and Firehall productions of *Age of Iron* and Wendy Lill's *Sisters*. She has also danced with, among others, the Karen Jamieson Company and been employed as a publicist, workshop facilitator, and instructor. Following the premiere of *The Unnatural and Accidental Women*, Marie Clements became playwright-in-residence at the National Theatre School.

Her first produced play, *Age of Iron*, workshopped by Toronto's feminist Nightwood Theatre and produced in 1993 at The Firehall Arts Centre, received two Jessie Award nominations and was excerpted in Playwrights Canada Press's *Taking the Stage: Selections from Plays by Canadian Women*. Between 1994 and 1996, *Dirty Dog River*, a one-act puppet show designed to educate young people about AIDS, toured more than fifty communities across the country. *The Girl Who Swam Forever*, after workshopping at both the Playwrights Theatre Centre and UBC's Dorothy Somerset Theatre, was produced (under the title *The Town Twice Remembered*) at the Shadbolt Centre Theatre, and *Now Look What you Made me Do*, published in Blizzard Press's *Prerogatives: Contemporary Plays by Woman*, was workshopped at various companies (including the New Play Centre under the direction of John Lazarus) and had its Canadian premiere at Maenad Theatre. *Urban Tattoo*, a one-woman piece starring Clements, was read and staged at venues across North America and in England, premiered in 1998 at The Women in View Festival, and subsequently toured Canada, the US, and Europe.

Hoffman: At which point did this play become a possibility? Was it your own idea, as opposed to a commission or a suggestion?

Clements: It came from the four-page spread I read in *The Vancouver Sun* in 1988. It was quite a detailed story of Gilbert Paul Jordan's career and of these events. I guess what really put me over was that it was a huge spread on him and maybe half a page of all of his victims, and very little of them as human beings – just basically their last traced days.

Hoffman: Your play certainly shows the victims. You don't see Jordan until quite well in to the play.

Clements: Yes. He's in and around things but he's certainly not the main point of the story.

The Unnatural and Accidental Women underwent script development at both Banff Playwrights Colony and the Playwrights Theatre Centre in Vancouver. It also had a staged reading, directed by Kate Weiss, at the Women in View Festival and was published as a work-in-progress in the Winter, 2000 issue of *Canadian Theatre Review*, themed "Staging the Pacific Province."

The Unnatural and Accidental Women invites comparison with *The Ecstasy of Rita Joe* and *Under the Skin*, both of which also were born from newspaper accounts of actual events in the Vancouver area and feature female protagonists pitted against a patriarchal society. Lambert's play, however, unfolds in a realistic, linear fashion; it adapts a classical dramatic structure to its feminist, modern purposes. The comparison to Ryga's play, on the other hand, can be extended to structure: the mixture of naturalism and expressionism in a circular unfolding imparts a multi-faceted texture to both works. Clements builds on the foundations laid by her stage antecedents by (re)creating multiple protagonists, by incorporating humour into a horrifying situation, and by individuating place. Clements' attention to place—the meticulousness with which she delineates a site—has an actuating effect. The audience is in the discourse.

Yet, although the play pays documentary-like attention to, for example, the old Woodwards building, Hastings Street, and the various hotels in the area, its lush theatricality and multi-dimensionality preclude didacticism. The profuse and deft visual elements alone are mesmerizing, and Clements effectively brings together musical elements as apparently disparate as aboriginal chants, barbershop quartets, and American blues. (As reviewer Peter Birnie noted, the chanting circle with which the first act culminates is especially beautiful and powerful.) Strange though it may seem, given the horror of the events surrounding the deaths of these women, *The Unnatural and Accidental Women* is often celebratory. Marie Clements clearly succeeds in commemorating the women and in connecting their lives to each other and to the audience, and she takes the documentary to rarely explored places as she does so.

The Unnatural and Accidental Women is a rich, tough amalgam—incorporating, for example, traditional oratory, Biblical narratives, Western fairy tales, Hollywood movies, the Cree language, a host of verbal and visual puns—that spans vast time periods and imparts strong feminist, spiritual, environmental, and anti-imperialist messages. In short, it is a strong example of postcolonial literature, as was further demonstrated when the play expanded the community outreach aspect of the Firehall Arts Centre. Audience members phoned, mailed, and faxed the playwright, the administration, and the acting and technical crews; talk-back sessions were instituted; and the comment book placed in the company's lounge was well used. Like *The Ecstasy of Rita Joe*, *The Unnatural and Accidental Women* proved the efficacy of theatre as a medium of social comment and community discourse.

G.R.

Selected Bibliography:

- "An Unnatural Feeling." *Firehall News*. Winter, 2000/2001.
- Beatty, Jim. "The Demon Barber." *The Vancouver Sun* 4 Nov. 2000.
- Birnie, Peter. "Natural Gem is No Accident." *The Vancouver Sun* 9 Nov. 2000.
- Chamberlain, Adrian. "The Making of the *Urban Tattoo*." *Victoria Times Colonist*. 4 Mar. 1999.
- Clements, Marie. Personal Interview. 3 Nov. 2000.
- Firehall Website. http://www.firehall.org/society.html .
- Gilbert, Reid. "'Shine on us, Grandmother Moon': Coding in Canadian First Nations Drama." *Theatre Research International* 21:1 (Spring 1996): 24-32.
- Nunn, Robert. "Hybridity and Mimicry in the Plays of Drew Hayden Taylor." *Essays on Canadian Writing* 65 (Fall 1998): 95-119.
- Sarti, Robert, Chris Rose, and Kim Pemberton. "Death by Alcohol." *The Vancouver Sun* 22 Oct. 1988.
- Taylor, Drew Hayden. "Alive and Well: Native Theatre in Canada." *Journal of Canadian Studies* 31:3 (Fall 1996): 29-37.
- Thomas, Colin. "Review of *The Unnatural and Accidental Women*." *The Georgia Straight* 10 Nov. 2000.

The Unnatural and Accidental Women
by Marie Clements

The Unnatural and Accidental Women premiered from November 2 to November 25, 2000 at the Firehall Arts Centre, with the following cast:

Valerie	Columpa Bobb
Mavis	Gloria May Eshkibok
The Barber	Peter Hall
Aunt Shadie	Muriel Miguel
Rebecca	Michelle St. John
Ron	Bill Croft
Victoria	Tasha Faye Evans
Verna	Sophie Merasty
The Woman	Michelle Olson
Rose	Christine Willes
The Barbershop Women	Dolores Dallas, Adele Kruger, Odessa Shuquaya

Co-Directed by Donna Spencer and Marie Clements
Set and Lighting Designed by Robert Gardiner
Set and Lighting Assistant: Kyla Gardiner
Slide/Visual Designer: Michelle Nahanee
Musical Composition: ULALI
Arrangement: Simon Kendall
Costumes Designed by John Powell
Assistant Costume Designer: Lynn Hill
Sound Designed by Noah Drew
Assistant to the Directors: Fif Fernandes
Stage Managed by Deborah Ratelle

CHARACTERS

Rebecca (ages 4 and 30): Mixed blood/ Native – a writer searching for the end of a story.
Rose (age 52): English immigrant – a switchboard operator with a soft heart, but thorny.
Aunt Shadie (age 52): Native - mother qualities of strength, humour, love, patience.
Mavis (age 42): Native – a little slow from the butt down, but stubborn in life and memory.
The Woman (age 27): Native – looks and moves like a deer.
Valerie (age 33): Native – a big beautiful woman proud of her parts.
Verna (age 38): Native – sarcastic but searching to do the right thing, the right way.
Violet (ages 27 and 5): Native – an old spirit who grows younger to see herself again.
The Barbershop Women: A beautiful, sexy threesome that can move and sing.
    Marilyn (age 25): Native
    Penny (age 30): Native
    Patsy (age 40): Native
The Barber (ages 30s and 60s): White – short, balding, nice and creepy.
The Logger, The Man, The Romantic Partner, The Pillow, The Dresser, The Man's Shadow, The Airline Steward.
Ron (age 35): A cop – handsome, with a nice body and a good sense of humour.
SFX voices:
Evan (age 8): Valerie's oldest son, wise and angry.
Tommy (age 5): Valerie's youngest son, naive and sweet.
The Operator: A polite but repetitive telephone recording.
Fatherly Male Voice: The Woman's adopted father.
"Can I buy you a drink?": The Barber's Voice.

SETTING

Act One: Scenes involving the women should have a black-and-white picture feel that is animated by the bleeding-in of colour as the scene and their imaginations unfold. Colours of personality and spirit, life and isolation, paint their reality and activate their own particular landscape within their own particular hotel room and world. Their deaths are a drowning-down of hopes, despairs, wishes. The killer is a manipulative embodiment of their human need. Levels, rooms, views, perspectives, shadow, light, voices, memories, desires. Rebecca's journey through Act One should be a growing up through memory. Being in a memory, but present in time. Walking. Seeing. Time going by. Life – colour of memory and the searching. Aunt Shadie and Rose are on the top level from the beginning. In their own spaces and places. They are in their own world. Happy hunting ground and/or heaven. Elements: Trees falling, falling of women, earth, water flowing/transforming.

Act Two: Scenes in Rebecca's apartment are present and in Kitsilano, but reflect the symptoms of urban isolation even without being on Hastings Street. Flow: Scenes of hearing, shadow-seeing, consciousness, unconsciousness of what is around us/within us.

DEATH BY ALCOHOL
THE VANCOUVER SUN
OCTOBER 22, 1988

"She was found lying nude on her bed and had recent bruises on her scalp, nose, lips, and chin.... There was no evidence of violence, or suspicion of foul play," noted Coroner Glen McDonald."

"...a native Indian, had been drinking continuously for four days before she died.... Coroner Larry Campbell concluded her death was 'unnatural and accidental.'"

"...drank enough to kill her twice. That's the conclusion of a coroner's inquiry into the native Indian woman's death. She was found dead, lying face down on a foam mattress with a blanket covering her, in Jordon's barbershop.... At the time of her death, Coroner Campbell said there was no indication of foul play."

"To get the blood-alcohol reading that... had at the time of her death, experts say she would have had to drink about 40 ounces of hard liquor all at once. The mother of four died at Jordon's barbershop.... Coroner Mary Lou Glazier concluded... death was 'unnatural and accidental.'"

"'She had the highest blood level-alcohol reading of all the women.' ...He believes Jordon was finally stopped because he killed his daughter, who was not an alcoholic and who has family that insisted police look into her death. 'He picked the wrong person. She was someone that someone cares about.' ...No coroner's report has been issued."

ACT ONE

SFX: A collage of trees whispering in the wind.

SLIDE: THE UNNATURAL AND ACCIDENTAL WOMEN

SFX: The sound of a tree opening up to a split. A loud crack – a haunting gasp for air that is suspended. The sustained sound of suspension as the tree teeters.

SLIDE: FALLING BACK - Beacon Hotel

Lights dim up on a small room covered with the shadows of tree leaves and limbs. Lights up on a LOGGER looking up at a tree, handsaw in hand. He shouts across time.

LOGGER: TIM-BER...

AUNT SHADIE: Re-becca...

A big woman suddenly emerges from a bed of dark leaves. Gasping, she bolts upright, unfallen. Nude, she rises leaving the image of herself in the bed. She follows the sounds and images of the trees.

SLIDE: Rita Louise James, 52, died November 10, 1978 with a 0.12 blood alcohol reading. No coroner's report issued.

SFX: Real sound of REBECCA slamming a glass of beer on her table.

SFX: The sound of trees moving in the wind increases.

SLIDE: TIMBER

Lights fade up on REBECCA as she sits, and thinks, and drinks at a round table with a red terry cloth cover. She takes her pen and writes in her journal.

The logger continues sawing...

SFX: Sound of a long saw sawing under softly in lengths.

AUNT SHADIE walks through the forest, covered by the leaves/branches, in them.

REBECCA: Everything here has been falling – a hundred years of trees have fallen from the sky's grace. They laid on their backs trying to catch their breath as the loggers connected them to anything that could move, and moved them, creating a long muddy path where the ends of trees scraped the ground, whispering their last connection to the earth. This whispering left a skid. A skid mark. A row. Skid Row.

The LOGGER lays down his saw and picks up a chain saw...

SFX: Sound of a chain saw under.

Throughout – a blizzard of sawdust chips swarms the backdrop, covering AUNT SHADIE and tree parts. One by one, the trees have been carved into a row of hotels.

REBECCA: Hotels sprung up instead of trees – to make room for the loggers. First, young men sweating and working under the sky's grace. They worked. They sweated. They fed their family for the Grace of God. And then the men began to fall. First, just pieces.

AUNT SHADIE: Fingers...

REBECCA: ...chopped down to the palm.

AUNT SHADIE: Legs...

REBECCA: ...chopped up to the thighs.

AUNT SHADIE: Years...

REBECCA: ...went by. You never knew what might be fallen. A tree. A man. Or, a tree on its way down deciding to lay on its faller like a thick and humorous lover, saying...

AUNT SHADIE: "Honey, I love you – we are both in this together. This is love till death do us part – just try and crawl out from under me."

REBECCA: Some of the men survived their amorous lover. Rows of men sweet-talked that last fallen tree into moving an inch to get that human limb out. Maybe just a leg – or part of it. Whispering...

AUNT SHADIE: "God, if you just do this for me. Jesus, just get this log off me... and...

REBECCA: Well, a whole crew of men sitting in their rooms drinking and thinking of the weight of that last tall love.

The logger finishes and looks around and looks right at REBECCA. REBECCA mouths "I love you" to him silently.

The LOGGER cups his ear and shouts towards her.

LOGGER: Eh? (*He waves his hand "never mind" and continues.*)

REBECCA: Saying "Eh"?

The logger continues the buzz with the chain saw. Wood chips blizzard on the backdrop. The chain saw buzzes under transforming to a bar saw.

AUNT SHADIE: (*laughs*) Saying "Eh?" a lot. Could you repeat that? Their voices yelling over the sound of the power saw buzzing thirty years ago, or was it last year? Never mind, the buzz rings in their ears just as the sawdust used to rest in their belly buttons after a hard day's work. Honest work. A tree for...

REBECCA: ...a thumb.

AUNT SHADIE: A tree for a...

REBECCA: ...leg.

AUNT SHADIE: A tree for their...

REBECCA: ...hearing.

AUNT SHADIE: An honest trade made between a logger and his trees. No malice between the two – just an honest respect for the give and take of nature.

SFX: The full buzz of a bar under.

The woodchip blizzard clears, and crudely made stumps that look like bar stools remain behind her and deepen the look of the bar – The Empress Hotel. AUNT SHADIE walks across the bar but is also covered by it, in it.

REBECCA: Now the loggers sit like their lovers, the trees – they sit like stumps, and drink, and think. And think the world has gone to shit. They think of a time when cutting down a tree was an honest job, a time when they all had their good-looking limbs, a time when they were respected by the tallest order, a time when drinking was not an addiction.

AUNT SHADIE turns up a flight of stairs as we watch her shadow ascend.

AUNT SHADIE: And the woman. Oh the women strolled by and took in their young sun-baked muscles and happy cash.

REBECCA turns back to her journal.

REBECCA: If you sit long enough, maybe everything becomes clear. Maybe you can make sense of all the losses and find one thing you can hold on to. I'm sitting here thinking of everything that has passed, everyone that is gone, and hoping I can find her, my mother. Not because she is my first choice, but because she is my last choice and... my world has gone to shit.

She looks around the room and raises her glass.

Cheers...

Lights up on the same hotel room, as AUNT SHADIE takes two old suitcases out from under her bed. She lies them on the bed and opens them slowly, hesitantly. Cree words spill out everywhere. She opens and closes the sound and begins to laugh. Affectionately, she snaps them shut, picks them up and walks towards the door and up. The suitcases get heavier and heavier as she rises.

SLIDE: THE SWITCHBOARD – Reception

AUNT SHADIE walks towards small lights that fade up and down. As she approaches, lights fade up on the back of ROSE sitting at her switchboard. Her lobby is a 1960s hotel. ROSE is dressed conservatively in 1960s attire. The switchboard beeps and lights. She connects throughout. AUNT SHADIE huffs herself forward.

AUNT SHADIE: Excuse me.

ROSE: (*not looking at her*) Can I help you?

AUNT SHADIE: Yeah sure. I'm looking for a place to leave my baggage for awhile.

ROSE: I'm sorry, I can't do that.

AUNT SHADIE: Why, because I'm In...

ROSE: ...naked. Yes, that's it. You'll have to register first. I can't be taking just anybody's baggage now, can I? Can you write your name?

AUNT SHADIE: Listen, I'm naked not stupid.

ROSE: Oh. Well, I'm just trying to help you people out.

AUNT SHADIE: Why don't you look at me when you say that?

ROSE turns slowly around revealing a black eye and bruises on her face.

Wow, they sure dragged you through it.

ROSE: Humph. (*ROSE looks away from AUNT SHADIE's nakedness.*)

AUNT SHADIE: Haven't you ever seen anybody nude before?

ROSE: Not up front.

AUNT SHADIE: I'm not sure if I should feel sorry for you or not. Well, I went to bed wearing clothes, and then I woke up naked as a jailbird.

ROSE: I woke up naked once.

AUNT SHADIE: What, a million years ago?

ROSE: Pardon me?

AUNT SHADIE: I said, good for you.

ROSE: Aren't you cold?

AUNT SHADIE: Of course, I'm cold.

ROSE: Here, put this on.

ROSE takes a big beige cardigan from her chair and hands it to her.

AUNT SHADIE: Now I feel ugly.

ROSE: It's from England.

AUNT SHADIE: Like I said, now I feel ugly.

ROSE: It's the same one the Queen wore on her inaugural visit to Canada.

AUNT SHADIE: Like I said, ugly. (*looking at the sweater*) Ugly. For a Queen, you'd think she'd dress better. It's almost like she's punishing herself. If I had all her money, I wouldn't be wearing all those dowdy dresses. Just once I'd like her to wear a colour. Something not beige or plaid. Something blue maybe. Something that gives her colour: Red!

ROSE: Mothers of countries do not wear red.

AUNT SHADIE: She's a mother alright. Always did love those white gloves though. They remind me of white swans, especially when she waves. It's kinda pretty actually.

ROSE: My mother always wore gloves. She used to say a lady wasn't a lady unless she wore gloves.

AUNT SHADIE: Hmm. My mother wore mitts. They were white though, and furry. Big rabbit mitts. When my mother waved, it wasn't so much pretty as it was sad.

ROSE: Waving can be sad.

AUNT SHADIE waves like a Queen.

Where you going?

AUNT SHADIE: I'm dying for a smoke.

ROSE: What about registering?

ROSE watches as Aunt Shadie signs her name.

Rita Louise James.

AUNT SHADIE: There, you satisfied?

ROSE: Just doing my job.

AUNT SHADIE: What's that?

ROSE: I'm taking account.

AUNT SHADIE: Reminds me of the government. Taking count but not accountable.

She picks up her suitcases and begins to leave.

ROSE: You're going like that?

AUNT SHADIE: (*looks down on herself*) Why not?

ROSE: You sure you don't want me to find you some pants?

AUNT SHADIE: It's alright. There's a good draft...

ROSE: Oh please.

AUNT SHADIE: ...and frankly, if the pants look anything like the cardigan, I might as well be dead.

ROSE: Suit yourself.

AUNT SHADIE: I always have.

AUNT SHADIE keeps on walking. Lights fade on ROSE. AUNT SHADIE stops and sits on her suitcases. She reaches inside one of them and pulls out a pack of tobacco and rolls a cigarette. She reaches in and picks up an outfit from when she was a housewife. She smells the material and closes her eyes in memory. The clothes talk to her and she to them. She drapes them over her body and smokes her thinking smoke. Lights fade leaving a bright butt and smoke rising up.

SLIDE: *Rose Doreen Holmes, 52, died January 27, 1965, with a 0.51 blood alcohol reading. "Coroner's inquiry reported she was found nude on her bed and had recent bruises on her scalp, nose, lips and chin. There was no evidence of violence, or suspicion of foul play."*

Lights fade up on Rose, as she affectionately touches her switchboard. It responds with light flashes and beeps and muffled voices.

ROSE: I've always been right here. No matter where I am, I am in between people connecting. I like to think I'm the one who connects them, but mostly I like to think that they have to go through me. If nothing else, it gives me a place. A place in the making, the flashes of being... the feeling of feeding that beeping energy into a whole that understands it, and soothes it, into a gentle darkness. A small whimper when it enters—a connection between the here and there—a giant light it becomes. It begins and ends with the beeping, but it goes through me. I wait for the cry like a mother listening, hoping to slot the right thing into its void – hoping to be the one to bring about the pure answer. Again, the pure gentle darkness that says I have listened and you were lovely, no matter how loud your beeping cry becomes, no matter how many times I wanted to help but couldn't. There is something maternal about it, the wanting to help, the trying, going through the motions on the switchboard, but in the end just being there always it seems just listening to voices looking for connection, an eternal connection between women's voices and worlds.

ROSE leans over and nosily watches AUNT SHADIE enter REBECCA's world.

Everybody always thinks that the switchboard operator is listening into their conversations, and they're not always wrong. The tricky thing is to act like you don't know a thing. I swear on the Queen, it's a tricky thing.

AUNT SHADIE enters dressed as a young housewife. She is carrying her suitcases and a folded piece of paper. She sets the suitcases down and places a paper on the table. She turns to leave, but stops as REBECCA picks it up.

SLIDE: RUNNING SHOES

SFX: Sound of wind in the trees.

Backdrop gradually brings in close-ups of Hastings Street when it was the centre of shopping. The Army and Navy, Woolworth's – late 1960s/70s

REBECCA: My Dad – The Character was still full-limbed but hard-of-hearing when he died. Still asking "Eh?" after every sentence I spoke, but quick to hear the sound of change falling to the ground. Death was no big surprise for him. The thing he couldn't get out from under was the day she left. I found him holding a piece of paper she had put on the kitchen table. He held it for a long time and then simply folded it and put it in his pocket. "Where's Mom?" I asked.

SFX: Sound of tree falling and landing.

He said, "She went for a walk." I thought maybe she had gone to the IGA or something. Somebody was always having to go to the IGA. When she didn't return and he didn't move, I started complaining about the big fact that I was supposed to get new running shoes today. I was supposed to go downtown today. I was supposed to get a hamburger today... milkshakes, fries and ketchup at Woolworth's. It was supposed to have been a great day, and now we had to wait. I was getting pissed off, because I was getting tired of going to The Salvation Army for smelly clothes, and I felt like I was gonna be normal like everyone else when Mom said we could go to The Army and Navy and get something new, something that smelled good, something that nobody had ever worn. Blue suede running shoes – three stripes on either side. I had to have them. It was unbearable, and my Dad just standing there, and my Mom deciding to go to IGA. I thought it was a master plan. Both of them against me being normal. I started yelling – the injustice too great. My Dad just stood there like he didn't hear anything. "Get in the truck," he said. We went. I ate hamburgers and floats and fries and everything I could see in the posters of food on the walls of the Woodworth's cafeteria on Hastings Street. We went to The Army and Navy. We went home. No Mom. Again.

"Where's Mom?" again. He said, "She left us. I didn't know anything was wrong." He sat down. I took my running shoes off. I would never wear them again. Nothing was going to be normal.

REBECCA takes the running shoes off and kicks them. AUNT SHADIE turns around and silently picks them up, putting them properly under her chair. She exits.

Fade out.

SFX: Sound of car streams, transforming into the tide.

SLIDE: FOUR DAYS: DAY 1 – Glenaird Hotel

SFX: Sound of tide hitting the edge of the island/bed.

The hotel room is an ocean of blue. The bed an island. The lone woman sits on her island. She is wet and holds a white pillow that shapes her different needs. The comfort of a child, a lover. The woman reaches over and grabs a drink from the table beside her. She places it down and in... in her own drinking rhythm. The ocean gets deeper in its colour.

Rhythms of a drinking room: 1) Tide – Time. 2) Light vs. Shadow. 3) Drinking Rhythm.

SFX: Sound of the tide begins to increase and finally sprays to telephone static.

SLIDE: I'M SCARED TO DIE I

A click of light on. MAVIS sits in a huge beaten-up armchair. Her hotel room matches the chair. It is beaten and slightly tinged with hues of brown. As she sits, MAVIS leafs through her address book looking and reminiscing about each entry. She urgently picks up the phone and dials. A light flashes up on the switchboard, and we hear ROSE speak in the darkness.

MAVIS: Hi, Mona? It's me.

SFX: Weird static and otherworldly connection.

ROSE: I'm sorry, you've reached the operator.

MAVIS: The operator? I didn't want any operator. I dialed the numbers myself. I'm more than capable of calling a long-distance number.

ROSE: I'm sure you are. At any rate, you've reached the operator. (*very polite*) Can... I... help... you?

MAVIS: Well, I guess if you're just sitting on your ass you could put me through – save me the time of letting my fingers do the walking.

ROSE: I'm sorry, I can't do that.

MAVIS: Are you gonna help me or not?

ROSE: Well, to be honest... no one's ever reached me on the phone before, and I just don't know if it's house policy or not.

MAVIS: What kind of house are you in where people call and you don't help them?

ROSE: Don't raise your voice to me. I'm just following rules.

MAVIS: Whose rules?

ROSE: Management.

MAVIS: (*covers the receiver with her hand*) Bitch!

ROSE: Pardon me?

MAVIS: I said, isn't that rich.

ROSE: I'll put this call through just this once as a special favor, but this is highly unusual.

MAVIS: Sure... whatever.

SFX: Sound of real telephone connection.

(*ring*) Hi, Mona. I just thought... (*ring*) ...got to thinking of you and thought I'd call. Actually, I just thought I'd call cause (*ring*) I wondered if you and Bill might be coming into town sometime. You know, change of scenery and all.... (*ring*) Doing good here, though (*ring*) just would be nice to hear your voice. I'll try back later, okay. (*ring*) We'll talk about all sorts of things. What I need is a good laugh. (*ring*) You know, a laugh so hard liquid comes from your nose like that time.... (*ring*) Well, anyways, here I am going on.... Just would be nice to talk about some old times maybe. (*ring*) I'd like that. I'd... like... that...

She slowly places the receiver to her chest.

SFX: Sound of telephone ringing empty.

MAVIS looks back at her address book. Picks it up, and begins tracing names and thinking on each entry. Lights fade.

SFX: The telephone starts to buzz like a chainsaw under.

SLIDE: REBECCA – Hastings Street

The backdrop gives us a close-up of Pigeon Square. The buildings become smaller like stumps of logs. REBECCA sits at her table drinking. She holds a harmonica in her hand.

SFX: Sound of harmonica takes over the buzz of the chainsaw.

When she hears the sound of the harmonica, she gets up. A man enters and sits on one of the stumps. He watches her.

REBECCA: I'm dancing in Pigeon Square. It's not a dream, it's a memory. I'm four years old, and I don't have to ask why they call it Pigeon Square. There's pigeon shit everywhere. At four a genius... I know. A row of old men are sitting like stumps... smoking, laughing, tilting their heads back in a chuckle or a slug of rum. They are talking to The Character – my Dad. He's playing the harmonica. I'm pretending I'm a dancer. We don't know who's pretending more. Me, or him. But my feet are hitting the squares like I know what I'm doing, and he's hitting all the notes they can hear. They take their pennies out and splash them down around my dancing feet. The coppers fall... it is the most beautiful sound you can imagine, because you see I am very special, and talented, and the "poor bastards," as my father would say, are happy, clapping. I bow. My Dad takes my hand. We say goodbye. Some of them touch my cheek like they remember a daughter, some smile and wave a mitt, not a glove...

The man finishes clapping, and reaches up to her...

REBECCA: ...and one reaches his glove to surround my braid. My Dad – The Character, takes his hand and says to the man in the clearest logger voice "I could kill you" "Enough." The man lets go of my braid. My father, in the clearest voice "I love you" squishes my shoulder in a hug and says, "It's time to get the chain for the power saw. It should be fixed by now."

REBECCA turns back to the table and takes a drink. The man gets up and leaves.

REBECCA: It should be fixed by now.

SFX: Sound of rhythmic clapping echoes, and start of laughing.

SLIDE: THE BARBERSHOP QUARTET 1 – Barbershop

SFX: The real sound of a man laughing drunkenly.

Lights up on the interior of a barbershop. It is old and worse for wear. Mirrors reflect back. MARILYN sits in one of the barber chairs, her back to us. Her hair flows over the back of the chair as the BARBER cleans and preps his utensils. He exits briefly. MARILYN looks closely into the mirror, as a reflection of herself as MARILYN à la Farrah Fawcett looks back at her, becoming larger and more beautiful in the mirror. MARILYN à la Farrah Fawcett begins to sing softly. She enjoys her hair dream. The BARBER enters dressed in hyper whites and drapes a white cape over her, and her hair dream. He turns the barber light on, and it begins to slowly rotate – a red and white swirl. He places a bottle between her legs and tenderly begins to braid her hair in one long braid. He suddenly grabs her braid roughly and takes his scissors to cut it. She grabs it back in a tug of war.

MARILYN: Enough.

He leans over her and grabs the bottle. He brings it to her lips tenderly. She drinks. It spills.

BARBER: Down the hatch, baby.
Twenty bucks if you drink it right down.
Down the hatch, baby.
Right down – finish it right down.

She gulps and they laugh. He starts to twirl the barber chair faster and faster.

Fade out.

SLIDE: *ROOM 23, WHEN YOU'RE 33 – Clifton Hotel*

Lights up on an old beat-up room. It is animated by an old DRESSER with an ugly personality. Small and battered, it has three drawers with a mirror on the top. VALERIE stands in front of the mirror thinking about 23-year-old tits and adjusting her tits in her shirt.

DRESSER: You have a nice set.

VALERIE: Oh, shut up.

DRESSER: Really.

VALERIE: Why... don't... you... shut up?

DRESSER: Why don't you make me?

VALERIE: Just shut your drawers.

DRESSER: Make me.

She takes her shirt off and is trying to get her bra off. It's stubborn.

VALERIE: If I have to tell you again, you're gonna get it.

DRESSER: Get what?

VALERIE: A big fat punch in the chest.

DRESSER: Valerie. Pick a drawer – any drawer.

The DRESSER displays each drawer.

VALERIE: Pick it yourself. Can't you see I'm busy here?

DRESSER: Too busy to pick a drawer.

VALERIE: Too busy to pick my nose.

DRESSER: Too busy to pick your ass.

VALERIE: Too busy to pick your ass.

They laugh.

DRESSER: Pick a drawer.

VALERIE: What do I get?

DRESSER: What do you want?

VALERIE: Nice lingerie.

DRESSER: What colour?

VALERIE: Red.

DRESSER: What do I get?

VALERIE: You get to watch me put it on.

DRESSER: Maybe you're not my type.

VALERIE: Eeeeee – an uppity dresser. I got a real problem if you're my type, don't I? What is your type, old squat one?

DRESSER: A tall chest with two big knobs.

VALERIE: You're a pig of a dresser.

DRESSER: You're a pig.

VALERIE: Come over here and say that.

DRESSER: You come over here and say that.

VALERIE: Pig!

DRESSER: Whore!

VALERIE: I'll knock your drawers off.

DRESSER: Why don't you just get my drawers off?

VALERIE: That's no way to talk to a lady.

DRESSER: What lady? I don't see any LAY-DEE.

The mirror of the dresser starts to reflect a man's face.

VALERIE: And I don't see any-BODY. So shut up!

DRESSER: Okay, baby. Okay. Do you want to see what's in my drawers?

VALERIE: Probably skid marks.

DRESSER: Come on, baby... take a peek.... Come on, baby. That's it, baby.

She draws closer to the top drawer. It slides open slowly. She leans over to look in. A hand comes out and squeezes her tit.

VALERIE: Fuckin pig !

DRESSER: Let go! You fuckin whore!

She squeezes the drawer on his hand.

VALERIE: Say Valerie is the prettiest one of them all.

DRESSER: Val-er-ie is the pretti-est? ...CHUG of them all.

VALERIE: That's a bad dresser.

She squeezes the drawer harder on his hand.

He screams.

DRESSER: Valerie is the prettiest lay-dee of them all.

VALERIE: And smart.

DRESSER: ...and smart.

VALERIE: And she still has a great set of tits.

DRESSER: ...and she still has a great set of tits.

She lets go of his hand, and it shrinks back into the drawer. She turns.

VALERIE: I had two sons, you know... and I still have great tits.

DRESSER: Yah, you're a regular Hollywood dairy cow.

VALERIE: What did you say?

DRESSER: I said, you're a real Pocahontas.

VALERIE: Fuck you.

DRESSER: WHORE!

VALERIE: PIG!

She kicks him in the drawers. He groans. He moves towards her, they wrestle, and fall on the floor wrestling. Fade out.

SFX: Sound of the tide. A slower rhythm..

SLIDE: FOUR DAYS: DAY 2 – Glenaird Hotel

It is dark. The WOMAN stands on her bed/island and clicks on the light hanging from the ceiling. A pillow is propped up like a person next to her. The light of the light bulb sways slowly, back and forth. As she listens, she lifts the drink to her mouth and places it down slowly in her drinking rhythm. Repeats gesture, listening.

SFX: Voice-over – a fatherly male voice.

"Once upon a time, a very long time ago, there was a deer who lost its mother, because someone shot its mother. Something like the story of Bambi, except that the little fawn was adopted by a human family that loved it. And then someone said that the fawn that grew to a deer should be with its own kind, so the father of the human family, who lived on the mainland, took a ferry and dropped the deer on an island miles away and hoped it would be happier. Well, the deer wasn't happy without the only family it had ever known, and it swam all the way back to its human family, and everything was going great, everything was going great, until it ate some lettuce from the neighbour's garden, and the neighbour shot it dead."

Rhythms of a drinking room: 1) Tide – Time. 2) Light vs. Shadow. 3) Drinking Rhythm. 4) Conversations – recent and past.

The hanging light stills. Fade out.

SFX: *Sound of tide blends into the electronic sound of static.*

SLIDE: *I'M SCARED TO DIE II*

Lights fade up on MAVIS sitting in her chair. She sits in the exact same spot and manner. She is leafing through her address book. She finds a name and stops and smiles. Slowly, she runs her hand over herself, not so much sexually but as if remembering sex. She picks up the phone and dials him. Lights fade up on ROSE's switchboard.

MAVIS: Hello, John... it's me...

ROSE: It's me, Rose – your operator. What number were you calling?

MAVIS: This is an emergency, if you have to know. Big Nose.

ROSE: You don't have to be rude – I was just trying to be helpful. I have a very demanding job, and I don't need this static from you...

MAVIS: Well, I have a lot better things to do than talking to people I didn't want to talk to.

ROSE: Listen, Madame.

MAVIS: Don't use that tone with me.

ROSE: Don't think that all I do all day is sit on my big fanny and wait for people to talk to me like this – people who have no appreciation for the fine art of communication.

MAVIS: It gets pretty damn bad when you can't even make a phone call without having a conversation with someone you don't want to talk to. Nose.

Rose: And about that nose business. I don't have a big nose. If the facts be known, I have quite a fine upturned nose, and if you're referring to the fact that I asked you who you were calling – well, that has nothing to do with nosiness and everything to do with...

MAVIS: I'm asking you for nothing – but for you – to *shut up* – and put me through to who I need to talk to – and not have to go through – this talk... talk... talk. Cluck.... Cluck.... Cluck...

ROSE: Practicality, every time I pick up the phone...

MAVIS: ...like a goddamn BEAKY chicken!

A long, hurt silence.

ROSE: I'll thank you very much to refrain from making comments about my features.

MAVIS: Don't think that, just because you use bigger words than me and you went to reception school or something, that makes you better than me.

ROSE: I'm just doing my job, and that's all you can ask out of anybody – is a person do the job they were meant to do, and I try to do my job a million times a day.

MAVIS: Like you know it all, when you don't know me and you don't give a damn how I'm feeling or what I'm worried about or why I can't get off my ass and just leave my room.

ROSE: ...a million times a day.

MAVIS: I'm so scared I can't move.

ROSE: ...a million times a day...

MAVIS: I can't breathe.

ROSE: I get this static a million times a day...

MAVIS: I listen.

ROSE: ...times a day...

MAVIS: I cry.

ROSE: ...from the static of nothing.

MAVIS: A million times a day.

ROSE: I want...

MAVIS: I reach out for it.

ROSE: ...and nothing.

ROSE plugs her through. A surprising click for everyone.

SFX: Voice-over – "I'm sorry, the number you have reached has been disconnected. Please call your operator..."

MAVIS tries to talk over the recording as if nothing is wrong.

MAVIS: Hey, John. It's me. Remember me? Mavis. Mavis Gertrude Jones. Played baseball real good. You know, you used to say I had the best arm on the team. You know, you used to say I was the smartest person you'd ever met, because I was always reading those *Britannica Encyclopedias* with the letters on them. You used to say I had the best body in town – just kidding... and a pretty good bannock maker too. The queen of bannock making.

SFX: Voice-over – "I'm sorry, the number you have reached has been disconnected. Please call your operator and..."

MAVIS: I miss your smile. I remembered your smile the other day. Going into a piece of that bread and coming out all greasy, with butter and lard – all sassy. You could always make me smile... make me feel safe with those big brown arms of yours. John? Anyways, I remembered those big arms of yours, and I was thinking I'd really like to borrow them for a few weeks. I know, that seems silly, but I'd really like to have that feeling with me right now. Just until I can get away from this feeling. Shake it away with your big arms wrapped right around me. John? John.

Arms of the brown armchair extend like real arms and curl around her. She hugs them and love-coos in comfort.

MAVIS: Thank you, John. You always were sweet to me. Sweet Johnnie.

She love-coos to herself and Johnnie's arms, and finally falls asleep.

SFX: Soft sound of pigeons cooing grows underneath.

Pigeon wings mix and blur and land on the backdrop behind. AUNT SHADIE slowly emerges from them and walks towards REBECCA's table. She sits down silently.

SLIDE: WHITE BIRDS – Hastings Street

The Huge "W" of the Woodward's building is brightly lit red and appears above it all.

REBECCA: My mother. I see her in half-looks everywhere. I call it seeing the white bird look. This white is not the colour of skin, but the flutter of hope.

Women's white birds. Sometimes you witness it, and it makes you cry. Sometimes I see it across a coupled room, and when I do see it - I see my mother's chin bending down limp to her chest.

A young AUNT SHADIE's chin drops down to her chest. REBECCA looks in her direction.

Not to look at me, though the crease in her neck makes it possible for her to look at me, with tenderness, or to look at her man with tenderness, or to look at anything smaller than her, with tenderness. But to bend that long neck down, till her beak reaches her collar bone, and sits for a long time before it comes up. It sits so long, you ask: "What's wrong, Mom? What's wrong?"

AUNT SHADIE doesn't answer.

So long that your heart starts to beat, because something is wrong, so wrong, and nobody will speak. Not your Dad – The Character, who spoke words and made this bird-killing silence.... And finally, she lifts her head... finally she lifts her head, but something is gone. Something dead sits in her eyes, and rests itself on the tone of her voice, when my Dad – The Character asks, irritated: "Jesus, Rita. What's wrong now?"

AUNT SHADIE raises her chin slowly. Smiles faintly.

She slowly smiles oddly. "Nothing." My Dad – The Character continues talking, as if nothing has died. But I saw it flutter and die. "Are you alright, Mom? Mom?"

AUNT SHADIE rises and slowly walks away.

She is silent, and gets up and walks to the washroom, or we leave the restaurant, or she goes to the other room, and that hope dies without him even knowing it had anything to do with him. A man kills enough. A woman keeps on walking.

REBECCA gets up and watches her leave.

SLIDE: SWITCHBOARD – Reception

Lights up on AUNT SHADIE as she arrives at the reception counter. She is putting trapper clothes over her young housewife clothes. She leans on the reception counter, putting on a parka and rabbit mitts. ROSE's face is no longer bruised. AUNT SHADIE lays the sweater on the desk.

AUNT SHADIE: Thanks for the sweater.

ROSE: You're welcome, Rita.

AUNT SHADIE: You're welcome, Rose. Call me Aunt Shadie. Everybody else does.

ROSE: Alright, Aunt Shadie. Where did you get the clothes?

AUNT SHADIE: I found them in my baggage.

AUNT SHADIE begins to leave.

ROSE: Nice gloves.

AUNT SHADIE: Mitts.

She looks proudly at her mitts.

I used to be a real good trapper when I was young. You wouldn't believe it now that I'm such a city girl, but before when my legs and body were young and muscular, I could go forever. Walking those traplines with snowshoes. The sun coming down sprinkling everything with crystals, some floating down, and dusting that white comforter with magic. I would walk that trapline like a map, knowing every turn, every tree, every curve the land uses to confuse us. I felt like I was part of the magic, that wasn't confused. The crystals sticking to the cold, and the cold sticking to my black hair, my eyebrows, my clothes, my breath. A trap set. An animal caught. Red. If it squirmed, I would take my rifle and shoot it as fast as I could. Poor thing. I hate to see an animal suffer. *Meegwetch*, and thank you.

ROSE: It sounds barbaric.

AUNT SHADIE: Shopping at the Woodward's food floor is barbaric. You never know what you are eating. Even if it says ground hamburger meat on the package, how do you know it is ground hamburger? What is ground ham-burger? And why do they have to grind it? Everybody just eats it. No one questions where it came from. Must be the big hamburger animal. That big "W" in the sky doesn't stand for Woodward's, but for "what." WHAT did I just eat?

ROSE takes out a pair of long, white gloves and puts them on.

ROSE: I like that swan metaphor.

AUNT SHADIE: The what for? Swans are the great hamburger animal?

ROSE: Don't be silly. Gloves look like swans.

AUNT SHADIE: Well, actually, if I was to really think about it.... probably more like skinned rabbit mitts.

ROSE: I like the swans.

AUNT SHADIE: Did you ever feel like hugging a swan?

ROSE: Yes, I have.

AUNT SHADIE: You? You have hugged a swan.

ROSE: Yes, I have. I have an appreciation for animals too, you know.

AUNT SHADIE: No, I mean. I'm sure you do in your own polite way, but... a swan.

ROSE: It felt good.

AUNT SHADIE: You got me kinda worried here. What kind of hug was it?

ROSE: Just a quick peck on the cheek. But it wasn't a kiss. I just walked up to it real quiet, foot by foot, and placed my arms around it just for a second. Nice swan.

AUNT SHADIE: Have you ever hugged a swan so much you almost squished it?

ROSE: No, I haven't actually. What kind of animal lover do you think I am?

AUNT SHADIE: Every time I see a swan, I feel like hugging it hard. The kind of hug where you just can't stand how much you love it, or feel for it, and you're hugging and hugging it, and you just get carried away.

ROSE: How many swans have you hugged?

AUNT SHADIE: I never hugged a swan. I just figured anything that beautiful wouldn't want to be hugged. My nephews... yes... my daughter when she was small, my parents when they were old, my pillow when I was lonely... myself when I was stupid.

ROSE: How many things have you squished while hugging?

AUNT SHADIE: I never really squished anything. I was just trying to get across to you that feeling of loving something so much you could squish it. I think everybody should have that feeling at least once.

ROSE: Hugging till you squish, or being squished?

AUNT SHADIE: Both. But...

ROSE: What?

AUNT SHADIE: It makes you kinda want to be the squished one, doesn't it?

ROSE: Yes... yes, it does actually. Tea?

AUNT SHADIE: Sure.

REBECCA moves from her table and slots some coins into the juke box.

SLIDE: FOUR DAYS: DAY 3 – Glenaird Hotel – CONT.

As the lyrics of the song fade, the music remains under. She waltzes to it and to the voice-over of a conversation.

SFX: *Sound of the tide fades up and eventually takes over.*

SFX: *In a convincing male voice, like music...*

MALE VOICE: "You move so beautifully."

She steps.

WOMAN: Thank you. (*She stumbles.*)

MALE VOICE: "You have the most beautiful brown skin."

She steps.

WOMAN: Thank You. (*She stumbles.*)

MALE VOICE: "You don't have to be scared. I would never let anybody hurt you."

She steps and loses her balance. She takes her face out of her pillow's shoulder and looks down. She looks down at her legs as if something is wrong with them. The silhouette of a deer's legs and hooves look back from the floor. She begins to cry, confused. The pillow becomes a man, dressed like a pillow. He lifts her chin slowly, and dries her tears. Lights out.

Rhythms of a drinking room: 1) Tide – Time. 2) Lights vs. Shadow. 3) Drinking Rhythm. 4) Conversations – recent and past. 5) Music/Movement – romantic.

SFX: *The phone rings.*

SLIDE: I'M SCARED TO DIE III

MAVIS wakes in a start and picks up the phone.

MAVIS: It's okay, Johnnie... it's probably just my operator. You need your rest. Hello, who is it?

ROSE: It's Rose.

MAVIS: Rose who?

ROSE: Rose – you know very well, Rose who.

MAVIS: What do you want?

ROSE: I thought I'd call and check in with you. I heard somebody breathing funny on your line.

MAVIS: I just got company that's all.

ROSE: What kind of company?

MAVIS: Man company. He just kinda showed up out of the brown.

ROSE: Humph. I never did trust a man that just showed up.

MAVIS: Well, some of my best romances came from men that just showed up.

ROSE: Suit yourself... as long as nothing is wrong.

MAVIS: Listen, Rose, I appreciate your worry. It's just been nice and peaceful for a change. I just been having a creepy feeling, and that's why I don't go out much. But with John here it's not so bad.

ROSE: What kind of creepy feeling?

MAVIS: (*softly*) Death.

ROSE: Mavis, I can't hear you when you talk soft like that.

MAVIS: (*louder*) Nothing.

ROSE: Mavis, I think there's...

MAVIS: My sister. It's my sister.

ROSE: You're scared of your sister?

MAVIS: Isn't everyone?

ROSE: Why don't you to talk to her? I'm not doing anything anyway.

MAVIS: Sure. I'll be brave. (*She adjusts herself.*) Put me through, Rose. Meegweetch.

ROSE: Fine, just put me through... no, thank you... no, that's great of you, Rose... thanks for taking the time to.... Well, McWitch to you too!

MAVIS: *Meegweetch*, Rose. *Meegweetch*. It means "Thank You."

Click of call going through. It rings and...

Hi, Laverne. It's me... Ma...

SFX: Answering machine.

MACHINE: "Hi. You've reached Laverne..."

MAVIS: Laverne?

MACHINE: "We're not in right now, but if you leave a message we'll get back to you as soon as possible, or you can reach us on the pager at (204) 266-4325, or fax us at (204) 266-5646, or at work at (204) 456-1425, or just leave a message after the beep, I guess."

MAVIS: Gawd. Hi... it's me. Mavis... your sister. Yeah, it's been a long time, but I was thinking of you and... I'm doing real good. I just thought I'd call and say... it's good to hear your voice, even if it's on the answering machine. It sounds like you got a lot of stuff... Laverne. You know when someone wants your chair, your place? Not like our mother, or an elder, or someone we know, but when someone you don't like wants your place, and you can feel them thinking about it... just waiting for you to get up... concentrating on you getting up so they jump in your place, and never give it back. I can feel someone getting closer and closer, inch by inch, stepping closer, and pretty soon they'll be in my seat. Breathing where I should be sitting. I know that sounds weird, but it's just a feeling.

SFX: Answering machine clicks off.

ROSE: I wouldn't call if I'd been drinking or anything. I love you... I didn't mean to sound stupid.

SLIDE: THE BARBERSHOP QUARTET II – Barbershop

SFX: The sound of MARILYN singing softly.

The interior of the barbershop flares up. The red and white swirl of the barber light is twirling. PENNY sits drunkenly in the barber chair as a beautiful MARILYN à la Farrah Fawcett emerges. Reaching her hands out to PENNY, she begins to clear PENNY's hair from her face gently. PENNY looks into the mirror and sees herself as PENNY à la Pat Benetar. They both laugh. The BARBER enters dressed in hyper barber white. He places a white cape over PENNY, and her hair dream. The BARBER takes the bottle and places it between her legs and begins to braid her hair in one long braid. MARILYN's song gets strained as she reaches for the bottle in an effort to take it from them. The BARBER grabs it and raises it to PENNY's lips seductively. He moves to climb on top of her.

BARBER: Down the hatch, baby.
Twenty bucks if you drink it right down.
Down the hatch, baby.
Drink it right down.

Fade out.

SLIDE: KEEP ON WALKING – Hastings Street

Lights up below on REBECCA as she walks. Backdrop of Hastings Street. Signs in windows advertising for help. AUNT SHADIE's face appears in the images.

REBECCA: Where do women walk to when they have been fallen? Sure, you could say some of them walk on to something better. They leave their bastardly husbands, get a job, and free themselves from suffocating domesticality. They learn to type, or waitress, or become your chambermaid, your housekeeper, your cleaner, your babysitter and pretty soon it feels like this new-found freedom is not so free – the man's face has just changed. If they can stand this, they stay. If not, one day they just keep walking.

SLIDE: THE WRONG ROOM – Balmoral Hotel

VERNA: ...one fuckin day at a time.

Lights up on VERNA sitting on her bed in the hotel room. A bottle of wine sits on the bedside table eyeing her. She fondles the bottle wanting to take a drink but touches a toy plane in her lap instead. She talks to her ex-husband on the phone...

Yeah. I'm serious. I got a gift for him... for his birthday. If you come and pick me up... maybe we could take the kid for Chinese food, and I could give him his present then. Yeah, I'll be downstairs out in front waiting. I'll be down there... I told you..

SLIDE: ROOM 23, WHEN YOU'RE 33 – Clifton Hotel

The room is dishevelled. VALERIE is lying on the floor, the dresser is lying on the floor. They are both trying to get themselves back together.

DRESSER: You have a nice set.

VALERIE: Oh, shut up.

DRESSER: Really.

VALERIE: Why don't you shut up?

DRESSER: Why don't you make me?

VALERIE: I made you already.

DRESSER: I made you already.

VALERIE: No reason to be a sore loser.

DRESSER: Pick a drawer.

VALERIE: Go away.

DRESSER: Go on, pick a drawer. I'll bet you'll like this drawer.

His bottom drawer slides open. The TOMMY drawer speaks.

SFX: Voices of her two sons.

TOMMY: Mommy?

VALERIE: Tomm...

TOMMY: Mommy.

VALERIE: Tommy.

TOMMY: Hey, Mom.

VALERIE: Hey, Tom. Tom... what are you doing in there?

TOMMY: Mom, I'm a real good dancer now. I can even dance better than Evan.

His second drawer opens. The EVAN drawer.

EVAN: Yeah, right.

TOMMY: I can.

EVAN: Like hell!

VALERIE: Don't swear.

EVAN: Don't tell me what to do.

VALERIE: I'm your mother.

EVAN: Yeah, right.

VALERIE: How are things?

TOMMY: Good.

EVAN: How do you think things are?

TOMMY: When are you coming home?

EVAN: Probably never.

VALERIE: Soon... real soon.

EVAN: Soon... liar.

TOMMY: When are you coming home? It's been a long time now.

VALERIE: It's hard to come right now. But soon. I'm gonna get this job and soon...

TOMMY: How soon?

EVAN: Soon. Liar.

TOMMY: How long is soon?

VALERIE: I can picture you in my head.

EVAN: Take a picture – it lasts longer.

VALERIE: Maybe, I could take a couple days off...

EVAN: ...drinking.

VALERIE: ...working. And we could get together...

EVAN: Soon.

VALERIE: Just me, and my two little men.

TOMMY: Mom?

EVAN: Mom?

VALERIE: Yeah?

The drawers don't respond. She gets real close to the drawers.

VALERIE: Yeah, I'm listening. I'm right here. I'M RIGHT HERE.

DRESSER: Yeah. Here you go, bitch!

The DRESSER lets her have it with the drawers. One of the drawers slams her head, the other her stomach and legs – it buckles her. It keeps punching her till she lies on the floor semi-conscious.

The dresser slowly opens the TOMMY drawer.

TOMMY: Mommy?

She barely wakes.

VALERIE: I'm coming... I'm coming.

She crawls to the DRESSER. The top drawer slams her in the head. She slumps down, her head on the TOMMY drawer.

The DRESSER's hand comes out of the top drawer and reaches down across her chest fondling her breasts. Lights out.

SLIDE: *Valerie Nancy Homes, 33. Died November 19, 1986 with a 0.04 blood alcohol reading. "Jordon arrived at the Vancouver police station with his lawyer to report the death. He said he and Homes had been drinking for two days."*

SLIDE: FOUR DAYS: DAY 4 – Glenaird Hotel – CONT.

SFX: Sound of the tide starts under. The slowest rhythm. The distorted sound of love whispers between a man and a woman.

The light bulb fades up slowly on the ocean that has become the room. The WOMAN is lying flat on her bed. A pillow lies on top of her. Her hand over the side of the bed holds a drink. She drinks and floats, making a slow swimming motion with her pelvis.

SFX: Voice-over – A fatherly male voice- faster, more emotional.

FATHERLY MALE VOICE: "Someone had told her a story, a very, very long time ago, about a deer who lost its mother, because someone shot its mother. Something like the story of Bambi, except that the little fawn was adopted by a white family that loved it, and then someone said that the fawn that grew to be an Indian girl should be with its own kind, so the father of the white family, who lived on the mainland, took a ferry and dropped the Indian girl on an island miles away, and hoped she would be happier. Well, the Indian girl wasn't happy without the only family she had ever known, and she swam all the way back to her white family, and everything was going great... everything was... going... great..."

The pillow on top of her becomes the man dressed as a pillow. He grinds into her, adding a violence to the swimming sex rhythm. She is totally disconnected to what is happening, staring straight up to the story.

WOMAN: ...every thing was going great, until she decided that she really didn't belong anywhere. So she decided it would be better to surrender to the ocean, to just let go, than to swim so hard, for so long, just to get to the mainland and be shot by a neighbour over a head of lettuce. (*She laughs.*)

Blackout.

SFX: Sound of the glass hitting the floor.

Rhythms of a drinking room: 1)Tide – Time. 2) Light vs. Dark. 3) Drinking rhythm. 4) Conversations – recent and past. 5) Music-Movement-romantic. 6) Sex.

Lights fade.

SLIDE: THE BARBERSHOP QUARTET III – *Barbershop*

SFX: Sound of MARILYN and PENNY singing softly.

The interior of the barbershop flares up. The red and white swirl of the barbershop light is circling. MARILYN a la Farrah Fawcett and PENNY a la Pat Benetar reflect out towards PATSY as she falls from the chair and begins to crawl away. The BARBER dressed in whites follows after her with the scissors. The scissors make a chopping noise as he grabs her braid. The red and white swirl of light intensifies the struggle. The song of MARILYN and PENNY intensifies as they call to her.

BARBER: Down the hatch, baby.
Twenty bucks if you drink it right down.
Down the hatch, baby.
Right down. Finish it right down.
Down the hatch, baby.
DRINK IT – DROWN.

The Barber emerges from the swirl with Patsy's braid. He covers her body on the floor with his white cape. He turns and leaves, as

WOMAN's reflections in the mirror begin to multiply and become surreal.

SLIDE: KEEP ON WALKING – Hastings Street – CONT.

The backdrop of windows of the hotel buildings. AUNT SHADIE's face appears in and out of the images.

REBECCA: One might walk here. One story among a rooming house full of walking stories. I've come to find her story. My mother. My mother's one story. I walk through these streets. I walk through the women standing on legs like stilts. No pantihose, but varicose seams everywhere, blue and yellow on their plastic skin. Skirts hiked up and shirts hiked down, their faces hollowed to a pout.

SLIDE: THE WRONG ROOM – Balmoral Hotel – CONT.

VERNA: I'll be down there – I told you. Okay, thirty minutes. Yes – I said thirty minutes. Right out in front. THIR-TEE minutes. (*She hangs up.*) Ree-tard. (*She starts talking to the plane.*) My son'll like you. Almost spent my whole skinny cheque. I hope he likes you. I hope he likes me. I hope he's not mad. My son has a temper just like his mother.

The plane lifts from her hand, and its wings wave a "yes." VERNA laughs. She takes the plane and opens the door to go out. She forgets her purse and lets the plane idle.

SFX: *Buzz of plane flying.*

VERNA: You stay here.

She turns to get her purse, and the plane is flying down the hallway. She calls to it.

It's not like you have to hold my hand – just wait up for me, will yah?

She loses sight of the plane as it descends down the stairwell. She follows it a flight behind. Floor 7.

SFX: *Sound of plane descending.*

SFX: *A slight whispering. A male voice that grows louder under and...*

MALE VOICE: "Can I get you a drink?"

SLIDE: I'M SCARED TO DIE IV

Lights up on MAVIS sitting in her chair with JOHN's arms wrapped around her tightly.

SFX: *Sound of phone ringing.*

MAVIS picks it up.

MAVIS: Rose?

Lights up on ROSE plugging into MAVIS' line but getting a busy signal.

SFX: *Voice-over – the phone beeps an aggressive, electronic:*

VOICE: "Can – I – get – you – a – drink?"

Lights down on ROSE.

MALE VOICE: No. It's downstairs. I can't seem to transfer a call to you. She says she's your sister. Do you want to come and take it down here?

MAVIS: Laverne? My sister.

MALE VOICE: Do you want to come and take it down here?

MAVIS: (*puts her hand over the receiver*) My chair? Laverne. My chair? Laverne. Aahhh shit, I was just getting comfy. Okay, I guess I'll be right down.

She gently kisses JOHNNIE's arms and moves them gently to the side. She looks suspiciously around the room and murmurs under her breath.

MAVIS: You even think of sitting in my chair and I'll kick your ass.

She drops the receiver and runs for the door and exits.

SFX: *Sound of quick footsteps down a flight of stairs.*

MAVIS: (*offstage*) Laverne? Goddamn it! (*slams phone*)

SFX: *Sound of quicker steps up a flight of stairs.*

MAVIS: (*mumbling up*) My sister... my ass...

She emerges in the doorway. Her chair has been turned around to face her. A man sits in it.

Get out of my chair!

MAN: Can I get you a drink?

MAVIS: Where is John?

MAN: John who?

SFX: *Voice-over – sound of static from the receiver and...*

VOICE: "If you need help, just hang up and dial your operator... if you need help, just hang up and dial your operator."

Lights fade.

SLIDE: *Mavis Gertrude Jones, 42. Died November 30, 1980 with a 0.34 blood alcohol reading. An inquiry concluded Jones' death was "unnatural and accidental."*

VERNA follows the plane down floor 6.

SFX: *Descent of plane.*

SFX: *Louder. A Male voice that grows louder and louder...*

MALE VOICE: "Can I get you a drink?"

SLIDE: KEEP ON WALKING – Hastings Street – Cont.

Backdrop of close-up of grocery store. Faces/bottles. AUNT SHADIE's face appears and disappears.

REBECCA: I walk through the elderly and the mentally ill and people stir-fried on Chinese cooking wine. I walk, and when I get tired I stop for a pack of smokes at the corner store and look at the Aqua Velva people in front of me in line. They are not blue. I then look at the Aqua Velva bottles all lined up pretty on the shelf next to the Aspirin. The most normal of refreshments to sell. I look into the woman punching the figures into the till. She could be my mother except that she is Asian. I look for some kind of clue that allows a hardworking woman that's worked hard all her life to ring up a bottle of Aqua Velva and sell it to an old man who is not "The Aqua Velva Man" but "Man with Huge Red Nose." She rings it in, all business, no trace of remorse. She stocks it for him – refreshment meeting cologne. Seller meeting buyer. It stinks, and I need a drink that isn't blue.

REBECCA exits.

AUNT SHADIE stands in front of the barbershop mirror. Three slides emerge, and three women stand behind the images of their slides. They begin to emerge from the barbershop mirror as AUNT SHADIE calls to them in song and they respond, in song, in rounds of their original languages.

The women in the Barbershop call to each fallen woman, in each solitary room. The women respond and join them in song and ritual as they gather their voice, language, and selves in the barbershop.

Throughout, the song floats in and out of each scene, submerging under some, and taking over others, flowing like a river. Each call and response a current. It grows in strength and intensity to the end of Act One where all their voices join force.

AUNT SHADIE: Do I hear you sister like yesterday today.
Ke-peh-tat-in/jee/ne-gee-metch
Das-goots/o-tahg-gos-ehk
Ahnotes/ka-kee-se-khak

SLIDE: *Marilyn Wiles, 40. Died December 04, 1984 with a 0.51 blood alcohol reading. An inquiry at the time concluded Wiles' death was "unnatural and accidental."*

Patsy Rosemary Forest, 25. Died July 03, 1982 with a 0.43 blood alcohol reading. At the time of her death, the coroner said there was no indication of foul play.

Penny Florence Ways, 45. Died June 08, 1985 with a 0.79 blood alcohol reading. The coroner concluded her death was "unnatural and accidental."

VERNA follows the plane down floor 5.

SFX: Descent of plane.

SFX: Louder. A Male voice that grows louder under and...

MALE VOICE: "Can I get you a drink?"

Lights dimly up on VIOLET.

"Can I get you a drink?

WOMEN: Do I hear you sister like yesterday today.
*Ke-peh-tat-in/jee/ne-gee-metch
Das-goots/o-tahg-gos-ehk
Ahnotes/ka-kee-se-khak*

Under water – under time
*Ee-tam-pehg/eetam-ehg
Te-pi-he-gun*

SLIDE: VIOLET – Niagara Hotel

VIOLET, as she sits on the floor of her hotel room. Her focus upwards. The shadow of a man casts itself long on the walls. Her face reaches him mid-groin.

VIOLET: I've swallowed it all. I've swallowed it all... downtown, right between my lips. I didn't know if it was the neck of the bottle I was swallowing or his penis. Both have that musty kind of smell at the opening of it. Like it has been around for a while, waiting for the next set of lips but not cleaning in between deaths. Musty – you never know where it's been. I swallowed. Man's fingers weaved in my hair pulling down and up, down and up, down and up so many times I didn't know if it was the salt that filled me or the sting of the vodka. I don't even drink usually.

VIOLET's head falls down.

SLIDE: Violet Leslie Taylor, 27. Died October 12, 1987 with a 0.91 blood alcohol reading. "She had the highest blood alcohol reading of all the women." No coroner's report has been issued.

WOMEN: Do I hear you sister like yesterday today.
*Ke-peh-tat-in/jee/ne-gee-metch
Das-goots/o-tahg-gos-ehk
Ahnotes/ka-kee-se-khak*

Hear your words right next to mine
*Ee-pee-ta-man/ke-ta-yaur-e
Win/me-too-nee/o-ta*

VERNA follows the plane down floor 4.

SFX: Descent of plane.

MALE VOICE: "Can I get you a drink?"

WOMEN: Do I hear you sister like yesterday today.
*Ke-peh-tat-in/jee/ne-gee-metch
Das-goots/o-tahg-gos-ehk
Ahnotes/ka-kee-se-khak*

SLIDE: FOUR DAYS: THERE IS NO DAY FIVE – Glenaird Hotel

SFX: No sound.

The light bulb fades up. No movement. The WOMAN lays flat on her bed, alone in the hotel room. Clothes up when they should be down. No pillow. The light becomes brighter and brighter revealing an ocean floor in low tide.

Light clicks out.

Rhythms of a drinking room: None.

WOMEN: You are not speaking and yet I touch your words.
*Ee-ka/ee-I-am-e-en/maga-e-tagh-in-a-man/
  ke-ta
Ya-mi-win*

SLIDE: Brenda A. Moore, 27. Died September 11, 1981 with a 0.43 blood alcohol reading. Coroner's report concluded her death was "unnatural and accidental."

VERNA is on floor 3. She stops and listens for the buzz of the plane. Nothing but the sound of a man's voice coming from ROOM 315. VERNA approaches it slowly.

MALE VOICE: "Can I get you a drink? Can I get you a drink – a drink? Can I get you a drink?"

WOMEN: So the river says to me drink me feel better.
Kwa-ne-ka-isit-/se-pe-h
Me-knee-qua-sin/me-thwa-ya

Like the river must of said to you first
Tas-koch-e-to-key/ka-key-e
Tisk/ne-s-tum

Below lights up on REBECCA as she sits at a table in The Empress Hotel.

VERNA enters room 315. The man dressed as an airline pilot seats her. Her son's plane buzzes around her head as he hands her a drink.

PILOT: Can I get you a drink?

REBECCA looks up from her small, red, terry-clothed table. She motions two glasses.

SFX: *The plane sputters and sputters and smashes to the ground.*

Lights out.

SLIDE: Verna Deborah Gregory, 38. Died September 25, 1986 with a 0.63 blood alcohol reading. Gregory's death was ruled "accidental as a result of acute alcohol poisoning."

WOMEN: Drink me – feel better.
Me-knee-qua-sin/me-thwa-ya

There is no sadness just the war of a great thirst
Moi-ch/ke-qua-eh/ka-quat-ta-keye-ta-mo-win

SLIDE: VIOLET – Niagara Hotel – Cont.

Lights fade dimly up on VIOLET as she detaches from her shadow. She leaves herself there with the man. She becomes smaller and more childlike, as she backs away and finally sits back on a swing and just stares, watching her woman self there with the man. Her body begins to become purple as AUNT SHADIE moves tenderly behind her and begins to swing her.

VIOLET: It was the back and forth of it. Like being on a swing when I was a girl. My father pushing the swing into the sky. Back and forth, that's where my mind went from the past and up from the past and up and up... I thought if I got any higher the swing would wrap around the pole and I would choke, but I went up after the last push, and after the last... my legs pumping the air for flight.

WOMEN: Do I see you sisters like yesterday today.
Ke-peh-tat-in/jee/ne-gee-metch
Das-goots/o-tahg-gos-ehk
Ahnotes/ka-kee-se-khak

AUNT SHADIE stops the swing and takes VIOLET's hand. They turn and begin to walk into a shadowy forest.

SFX: *Loud sound of pool balls being broken.*

The women suddenly turn their attention, song and focus on the bar. VERNA leads them into the bar.

VIOLET suddenly turns with the sound of the pool balls being broken and looks towards all the women walking in the bar.

VIOLET: Can I go with them?

AUNT SHADIE: No, you're too young. Besides, I need someone to walk with me.

VIOLET: Heh? Who's that?

ROSE walks towards the two.

WOMEN: See you as if you were sitting right here next to me.

Ee-wa-pa-me-tan/tas-koots
Ota-e-iy-ya-pee-in

Below, the BARBER gets up, and VERNA follows him as he walks towards REBECCA, who rummages through her purse, takes out some money and leaves it on the table. She looks for something she thinks she's lost and dismisses it. She grabs her journal from the table just as VALERIE goes to look through it.

WOMEN: Under the water – under the earth.
Eetam pehg/etam-as-keke

AUNT SHADIE: I'll introduce you to uppity. That's Rose.

VIOLET: And I'm Violet.

AUNT SHADIE: Exactly. And I'm poopoo ka ka. Anyways...

ROSE reaches them and hugs VIOLET.

WOMEN: My bodies floating where all the days are the same.
Ne-eow/e-pa-pam-mau-ho
Tehk/eddie-tah-to-ke-sik
Kow/pe-ya-kwun-nohk

REBECCA walks towards the exit where RON is playing pool and MAVIS is making him look good.

WOMEN: Long and flowing like a river.
E-ke-knock/aqua/e-pe-mow-
Ho-teak/tas-kooch/se-pe-h

VIOLET: She's squishing me.

AUNT SHADIE: She's hugging you.

VIOLET: No, she's squishing me.

AUNT SHADIE: Hugging – squishing. It's all the same thing.

VIOLET: The same what?

AUNT SHADIE: Love.

MAVIS bumps RON and he stumbles into REBECCA, who drops her journal.

Newspaper clippings of the women fall to the floor. The women slowly pick them up, look at themselves and then slowly place their clipping back into REBECCA's journal.

WOMEN: My root – my heart.
Weh-geese/ne dee

The BARBER reaches her table and looks down, as VERNA places REBECCA's wallet on the table. He looks around and puts it in his jacket. He watches as REBECCA begins to exit.

The WOMEN shift all their energy towards the BARBER.

Lights begin to fade.

WOMEN: My hair drifts behind me
Nes-ta-ga-yah/e-pim-mow
How-te-key

Lights out.

ACT TWO

SFX: A distorted radio-sounding version of "Natural Woman" by Aretha Franklin drifts in and through. The women's voices pick it up softly.

SLIDE: THE MORNING AFTER – Rebecca's Apartment – Kitsilano

It is dark in the bedroom. The neon face of the clock on the bedside table shows 4:08. It clicks.

A figure stirs in bed. A blue hue splashes down on white sheets and a figure underneath. REBECCA awakens.

REBECCA: I remember drinking something blue, or was it thinking something blue? All I know right now is... I have to pee. That means I have to get up, which means you have to... get up. Get up, I dare you. Get up.

Her body doesn't move.

I'd like to lay here for an eternity, but I feel like I've eaten a squirrel and I need something to wash it down, and something to scrape it off my tongue. Don't feed the squirrels – eat them. Brilliant. Okay, I'm getting up, which means we're getting up.

The women sit or stand in the darkness. They can be vaguely seen, but REBECCA cannot really see or really hear them. MAVIS her Chair Ass sits.

REBECCA's body gets up, protesting. She stumbles through her bedroom. She makes walking, stumbling curses. She stubs her toe on the foot of the bed.

REBECCA: Ahhwww... fuuuuuuuuuck, that hurts. Fuck you, bed.

MAVIS: Watch where you're going, big feet.

REBECCA: (*to herself*) Big Foot.

She walks through her bedroom into the hallway, not turning the lights on but doing the blind wall-feel.

VERNA: Right on my little toe. Not this way or that, but right on my baby toe.

VALERIE: This... is a handicapped zone.

MAVIS: Well, you better hope she doesn't park on your toe.

VALERIE: Oh yeah. Too late – she just parked on my toe with the corn. What the hell is this?

VERNA: It's the fuckin toe walk.

REBECCA walks into the wall, forehead first.

REBECCA: Fuuuuck ouch.... Fuck you, wall.

ALL: Fuck you, big head.

REBECCA: (*to wall*) What did you say?

Nothing. Silence.

That's what I thought you said.

VALERIE: (*mimicking*) That's what I thought you said.

REBECCA reaches the fridge and opens the door. A bright light filters through like a tunnel, revealing the insides of the fridge and the inside of her apartment. The women are all seated in a line. They are in various hues of shadow and dressed in white. Their hair is short.

REBECCA: Ouch! Shit, that hurts.

VALERIE: Wow, let there be light.

VERNA: And there was light... I remember that.

REBECCA squints inside her fridge. Picks up a carton and tilts it back in a drink. Picks up another carton and another and another.

VALERIE: Let there be skim milk.

VERNA: And there was none.

VALERIE: Let there be orange juice.

VERNA: And there was none.

VALERIE: Let there be water.

VERNA: And there was none. Shit, she's making me have to go to the bathroom.

REBECCA closes the fridge door. Darkness. She stumbles along to the bathroom. She sits down on the can and takes a pee. The sound of a long pee.

MAVIS: You think she could close the door.

VERNA: You think she could go for me?

REBECCA: Oh, that feels good.

REBECCA flushes the toilet.

MAVIS: At least she didn't do number two.

VERNA: At least she didn't do number two while reading a newspaper.

VALERIE: Only men do that.

VERNA: Women read novels.

MAVIS: Like what?

VALERIE: Well, real smart novels. They leave it in the can so they can make themselves look good.

MAVIS: Like what?

VERNA: I actually finished the whole AA bible. Not one day at a time but one shit at a time. It took me a year... if you were going to ask.

MAVIS: I wasn't going to ask, but since you answered – why did it take you so long?

VERNA: I kept having to introduce myself. There was always a big silence after I said, "Hi, my name's Verna." It left me kinda empty.

ALL: Hi, Verna.

VERNA: Thanks.

REBECCA gets herself to the front of the sink. The loud sound of her brushing her teeth. The sound of her taking a drink from the tap. She reaches over to turn the bathroom light on. When the bathroom lights blast on, the images of all three women reflect back in the mirror. REBECCA looks closely in the mirror.

The women scream in horror.

REBECCA: Wo-ow... I look like shit.

REBECCA turns off the light.

ALL: Speak for yourself.

The sound of REBECCA returning on her journey back to bed in the darkness.

MAVIS: Ouch...

VERNA: Ouch...

VALERIE: Fuck! Oh yeah... right on the same toe, why don't yah!

REBECCA crawls into bed. Grabs her pillow and pulls it closer to her. She pulls it closer and feels it. She feels it harder, her hand exploring it. It has legs. It has a butt. It has a penis.

IT moans.

REBECCA screams.

IT: Hey...

REBECCA: Oh, fuck me!

VERNA: Too late.

VALERIE: The penis talks.

REBECCA jumps out of bed and turns on the bedroom light.

IT: Hey, what did you do that for?

They squint at each other.

REBECCA: It's time to get up. I mean... I mean... it's time for you to get out. Leave.

MAVIS: That's cold.

VERNA: I like it. Thanks, and it's time to get up. Get in, get out... and it's time to leave. It's to the point. Move on.

REBECCA: Listen. I'm having a really bad morning.

IT: Well, you had a really good night.

REBECCA: If you say so.

IT: You said so.

REBECCA: That's really... special... but I have um... I have to get myself together here pretty soon and go to work. Work is good. Work.

IT: You don't work.

REBECCA: Everybody works. You're right. I don't work. I write. Writing is work, and I really should work or write and um... it's not easy to write when...

IT: You have a strange man in your bed.

REBECCA: I was going to say, when there are people around.

IT: Oh.

REBECCA: Are you strange?

IT: Okay... I'm not strange. I'm a stranger.

REBECCA: That's better. At least you're not weird.

IT: Who's to know?

REBECCA: Okay, if you weren't a stranger, would I know you were weird even if I knew you? I mean, does anybody ever know anybody's true weirdness?

IT: This is weird.

REBECCA: This is hurting my head, Ted.

IT: It's Ron.

REBECCA: I know... it was just a rhyming thing. Yeah, Ron... Ron (*to herself*) ...Ron with the nice butt leaning over the table.

MAVIS: Turn over, Ron. Turn over a new leaf.

REBECCA: You were playing... we ended up playing pool.

RON: You're surprised I'm here.

REBECCA: Well, no. I mean, yes... I mean, who wouldn't be surprised? A guy like you. A girl like me. Listen, I'm swimming here. Let's just call this a day. Okay, Ron. Thanks, it was great. Really. Ron. It was great. Great.

RON: What was great?

REBECCA: Oh, you know – the conversation, the beautiful dinner, your great car... your great suit, how you put yourself together, your great words, your greatness, your all-over greatness... your money... your tireless dick. Is that good? You are great. Great.

WOMEN: Tireless dick? Let's see the great dick.

RON: We didn't do it.

REBECCA: O-kay... it just looks like we did.

RON: Well, there was a point when that was an option, but...

REBECCA: What?

RON: You started crying.

REBECCA: People do that some times.

RON: When they're making love?

REBECCA: No, when they're fucking and it reminds them of love.

RON/WOMEN: Ouch.

REBECCA: Sorry.

Silence.

REBECCA: Listen... I don't mean to be rude...

MAVIS: ...maybe just a little peek...

REBECCA: ...but I'm really not at my best right now, and maybe you should just leave.

RON: What's your best?

REBECCA: Coffee, fresh-squeezed orange juice, eggs benedict, morning sex.

RON: Do you bring a lot of men home?

REBECCA: What, to mother? No, *Ron*, I don't bring a lot of men home. Actually, you are the first man I've thought to bring *home* in ten years. And really, what if I did? What if I liked sleeping with men? What if I enjoyed sleeping with men so much I slept with men? What then, *Ron*... would that make me a slut? Or better yet, maybe I should of let you buy me a steak and potato and a bottle of plaid wine, and you could at least feel decent...

He buries his head in the sheets.

Don't go to Sunday mass on me now, Ronny. (*he looks up*) I would get a good meal and a plaid wine, and you could feel like you deserved to fuck me. Fuck you, Ronny, and fuck the full meal deal.

RON: Are you finished?

REBECCA: I'm tired. I need a nap.

RON: Come here.

REBECCA: It's okay.

RON: Come here.

REBECCA: It's okay, I said.

RON: It's o-kay.

She goes towards him.

REBECCA: Okay. Don't you have a job?

RON: A day off.

REBECCA: Off?

RON: I'm a cop.

REBECCA: A cop.

RON: A problem?

WOMEN: A problem.

REBECCA: No, just weird. I don't usually do men with badges.

REBECCA and RON settle into each other and fall asleep. The WOMEN turn the lights off and walk into the living room. Lights up in the living room.

MAVIS: A cop.

VALERIE: You ever do a cop?

VERNA: Well, if I would have known they have nice butts and tireless dicks, I would of reconsidered.

MAVIS: A dick is a dick.

VALERIE: ...is a dick.

VERNA: Is a prick.

MAVIS: I always kinda fantasized about it though... kinda like a Harlequin Romance set in Canada. The Mountie, the horse and the Indian maiden.

VERNA: Exactly – the horse and the Indian maiden.

VALERIE: The Mountie would probably just be watching.

VERNA: You'd probably have a better time with the horse anyways...

MAVIS: You ever seen a horse's di...

VALERIE: Too much of a good thing.

MAVIS: You said that kinda fast.

VERNA: Maybe a Mountie with a dick the size of a horse.

MAVIS: Dream on.

VALERIE: I am.

VERNA: Thanks... now I'm getting all horny here. Let's make some tea and talk about our ex's or something... that should calm us down.

They follow each other into the kitchen. A kettle is set down and begins to heat. Lights out. Steam forms.

SLIDE: *VIOLET DREAMS*

Lights slowly up on a figure above REBECCA's bed. The lights are different hues of violet. VIOLET is on a swing, slowly swinging back and forth above REBECCA's bed. She drops small pebbles over them as she talks.

VIOLET: She's sleeping. Dreaming parts of worlds, yours and mine and hers. Dreaming and pressing into things... old memories and loves and waking in moments wondering where people ended and why even in sleep it hurts. Even in sleep, it occurs and reoccurs and you wake half here, half there, everything separated.

REBECCA: Everything not quite there, because you can't quite touch your own loss. Because it is so hollow.

VIOLET: So...

REBECCA: ...So far away – when you scream, it echoes.

VIOLET: Oh, Jesus, we have all died for our sins.

REBECCA: ...Oh, Jesus, you say...

VIOLET: ...We have all died for our sins.

REBECCA: There are great days when everything is perfect. Cool days on your skin, when the breeze hits you just right and you can touch and taste the lips of those you loved. Cool, beautiful days when a tint of colour touches you... just so. Just so.

VIOLET: ...Just so lovely.

VIOLET places a petal on REBECCA's lips.

REBECCA: You want to feel it on your lips forever. Just so. Just so until it ends, and all you can do is put your hand over your mouth. Gulping down the loss. Gulping down... down until you eat the scream. Blood vowels getting stuck between the sheets and pillows, between his legs and your throat, and all you want to do is say: Please help me. Please help me. Do you remember me? Because I remember me. I remember everything. Everything. Everything. And I can't breathe. And I would gladly die if I knew any better, but there is nothing to do but keep gulping silently. And it hurts my throat and god I want everything. I want to place my face in my mother's palm and say... and feel my lips on her lifeline and palm softness and whisper... I love you, you fucking bitch. I love you and where is everyone.

SFX: The women's kettle screams from the kitchen.

The violet lights slowly fade and cross-fade, bringing purple on...

SLIDE: SWITCHBOARD – Reception

AUNT SHADIE and ROSE move around a large family table, setting it for tea. They stop to notice the switchboard and get caught up in its flashing beauty. The calls are lighting up different hues of purple.

ROSE: It's so beautiful.

AUNT SHADIE: It gives me a headache.

ROSE: If you sit in a room and sit in a room... pretty soon... *(She listens.)* you can hear noises and voices coming through the wallpaper like a whole bunch of flowers sitting on a kitchen table. You become a part of that family of sounds just by hearing them. You can hear them eating and arguing, loving and fighting and breathing.

AUNT SHADIE: And snoring.

ROSE: And... snoring.

AUNT SHADIE: Is that why you became a switchboard operator?

ROSE: Partly.

AUNT SHADIE: The other part?

ROSE: It was a job, but after a while it made me a part of something bigger than my own loneliness. As if every time I connected someone I had found an answer.

AUNT SHADIE: I've heard her voice through the wall. As if I've had my ear to her as she's grown up. Just listening, not touching. Not able to soothe her, even when she was a child, because I wasn't there.

ROSE: Maybe she was listening back to you.

AUNT SHADIE: I didn't want her to see me the way he began to look at me. It wasn't that he said anything cruel, but men can be cruel with the twist of their face. I could feel myself disappearing, becoming invisible in his eyes;

and when I looked in the mirror, what I held good like a stone deep inside was gone. I could no longer see myself. In life, you see yourself in how the people you love see you, and I began to hate seeing myself through his eyes. I began to hate my reflection. The stone though... loved his strong arms and body, loved the way his body tanned to meet mine in the summer times, loved the way he used to love me. I thought my silence complimented his voice, thought my redness, my stone, gave him weight. I have this child – light and dark, old and new. I place my stone in her and I leave. I was afraid she would begin to see me the way he saw me, the way white people look up and down without seeing you – like you are not worthy of seeing. Extinct, like a ghost... being invisible can kill you.

ROSE: I see you, and I like what I see.

AUNT SHADIE: I see you – and don't worry, you're not white.

ROSE: I'm pretty sure I'm white. I'm English.

AUNT SHADIE: White is a blindness – it has nothing to do with the colour of your skin.

ROSE: You're gonna make me cry.

AUNT SHADIE: You better make us some tea then.

ROSE: That will help?

AUNT SHADIE: No, but it gives you something to do.

ROSE goes through her serious ritual of making tea. The violet lights fade and cross-fade to REBECCA's bed. They light up the bed like the bottom of a river, rocks scattered, rocks curled. VALERIE and VERNA have come back to the bed riverside. They are sitting around drinking tea, looking like large boulders. They laugh and sing softly. VIOLET eventually comes down from the swing, childlike.

SLIDE: SHE SLEEPS LIKE A ROCK

REBECCA: My heaviness has shifted – I'm all lopsided. Right now, I am deep down laying between friends, tumbling over each other, because we are round and hard and loving every minute of it, because it is so far down the only language we have to know has molded from the earth—its tears and blood, its laughter and love—gone solid. I hold it in my heart, it keeps me attached to the gravity of a perfect knowing.

VALERIE: A mother opens the heart of her child and places her rock inside the flesh. Inside, so no one – no man, no ugliness, will ever place its grabby hands on it.

VERNA: A mother buries its knowledge inside the child. *Kiss-ageeta-ooma.* (*Salish*) It drops inside the eternity of blood and earth. *Kiss-ageeta-ooma.* (*Salish*) I love you, silly face.

REBECCA: It makes me hit the riverbed like a rock. Water shining over me new, over me new, a new reflection of my true self, knowing I am heavy.

VALERIE: A mother opens the heart of her child and places her rock inside the flesh. A growing child takes a rock from the earth it walked from and places it in a leather pouch and hangs it around her neck. A woman walks heavy.

VIOLET: She sleeps like a rock.

VERNA: She sleeps like a rock.

VIOLET: She dreams like a rock.

VERNA: She dreams like a rock.

VALERIE: A woman walks heavy. A woman walks heavy. Like a rock molded from the earth—its tears and blood, its laughter and love—gone solid.

SLIDE: THE LIVING ROOM

MAVIS her Chair Ass is at REBECCA's desk. She goes through her phone book and dials a number. AUNT SHADIE picks up the phone from the switchboard.

MAVIS: Hi, Aunt Shadie.

AUNT SHADIE: Verna?

MAVIS: No, it's me... Mavis. We're a little late.

AUNT SHADIE: Get your ass home.

MAVIS: Don't yell at me – I'm the one who's considerate.

AUNT SHADIE: I tell you, Rose is making tea for everyone...

MAVIS: (*pinched operator's voice*) "To continue your call, please deposit more coins in the telephone or we'll have to..."

AUNT SHADIE: Don't even try that with me.

VERNA walks in from the bedroom.

MAVIS: Pardon me. You want to talk to Verna?

VERNA nodding her head – no, no, no.

Aunt Shadie wants to talk to you. Seriously.

VERNA: Hi, Aunt Shadie.

AUNT SHADIE: Like I was telling Mavis, get your asses home.

VERNA: We just got caught up. Like I told you, we'll be up there in thir-tee minutes. Seriously. Thirty minutes.

She screams out for VALERIE.

Hey, Valerie it's Pizza Hut. What kind of toppings do you want on your pizza. Here, you talk to them... I don't get what they're saying. They're talking too fast. Like you said, us Salish girls aren't so bright.

VALERIE marches in and grabs the phone. VIOLET follows.

VALERIE: We want everything. We want the special. Give us the special. Give us two specials. Hey, do you have any two-for-one specials?

VIOLET walks in from the bedroom.

VIOLET: Ham and pineapple.

AUNT SHADIE: You're gonna get something real goddamned special when you all get home.

VALERIE puts the receiver in her chest.

SFX: Muffled voice blabbing away.

VALERIE: I don't think this is Pizza Hut.

VIOLET: Why?

VALERIE: Because Pizza Hut just swore. You can never make Pizza Hut swear.

VIOLET: How do you know?

VALERIE: Because, sometimes when I'm bored, I phone them up and play with them.

VIOLET: Like how?

VALERIE: Well, I ask what they got and then I ask 'em if they have any pizza made with bannock and then I pretend I forget what they got and then I ask them what they got, what certain toppings are, and then anyways it goes on quite awhile. Indians aren't as much stupid as they are aggravating.

VERNA: It's not Pizza Hut, stupid. It's Aunt Shadie.

VALERIE: I thought I recognized her voice.

VERNA: Here, you talk to her. She won't yell at you, because you're a baby.

VERNA picks up the receiver, listens to it and pushes it on VIOLET. VERNA goes into another room.

VIOLET: Hi, Aunt Shadie. It's Violet. How are you? We're fine. We're all good. No, we're just hanging around. You know, talking and stuff. How's Rose?

AUNT SHADIE: Save it.

VIOLET: She said save it.

VALERIE: She's pissed.

AUNT SHADIE: Rose made tea for everyone, and now it's cold and...

VIOLET: (*to VALERIE*) Rose made tea for everyone and now...

VALERIE: Who cares? She's a weird duck anyways... she can take the Red Rose manifest destiny and shove it up her ass...

VIOLET: ...a teapot.

VALERIE: Exactly. Free the leaves, baby. Free the tea leaves of Canada. Say goodbye already... we'll be there as soon as we can.

VIOLET: Goodbye already... we'll be there as soon as we can. Aunt Shadie, sorry about the tea...

AUNT SHADIE: Just you hold it a...

Click of phone.

VIOLET: Sorry.

VALERIE: Where's Verna ? She's awfully quiet all of a sudden.

VIOLET: She's always quiet.

VALERIE: Just because a person doesn't say anything doesn't mean they're quiet. I can hear her thinking all the time. Where's Mavis? Now, her silence scares me. You know there's something wrong when you can't hear her talking.

They tiptoe around and peak in the bedroom. MAVIS is on the bed just about to pull the sheet off of RON's ass.

VALERIE: Mavis, you pervert.

MAVIS: I was just lookin', it's not like I was going to touch it or anything.

VALERIE: Go ahead, I dare you.

MAVIS: I dare you.

VALERIE: Shit, I wouldn't touch anything that beige.

VIOLET: Why?

VALERIE: Jesus, Violet, you don't want to be lookin' at that.

VIOLET: Why?

VALERIE: You might go blind.

MAVIS: I thought that's what happened when you masturbated.

VALERIE: Well, you should know.

MAVIS: Like... I... said. I thought that's what happened when you masturbated – I never heard of anyone going blind by touching a white ass.

VALERIE: You shouldn't say masturbate in front of the kid.

MAVIS: Masturbate, masturbate, masturbate. Why?

VIOLET looks at VALERIE intensely.

VALERIE: It's a big word... with a... lot of responsibility.

MAVIS: Number one, she's not a kid – she just seems like one.

VALERIE: Well, maybe this isn't an ass – it just seems like one.

MAVIS: Only one way to find out. Touch it.

VALERIE: You touch it.

MAVIS: No, you touch it.

VALERIE: Scared of the real thing? You've been dying for it for so long. Go crazy.

MAVIS: You go crazy.

VALERIE pinches it hard.

RON: Oh!

RON wakes up and looks around. The clock neons 6:30. He crawls out of bed. Walks around the living room and picks up a newspaper and walks to the bathroom and shuts the door.

MAVIS: Now he's gonna take a shit and stink up the place.

VALERIE: Let a guy into your bedroom, and he thinks he can take a big dump in your can.

MAVIS: I bet he turns on the fan.

Sound of the toilet flushing and bathroom fan turns on.

VALERIE: Like that's gonna help.

They wait. Silence. Smell. They both start waving their hands in front of their face like a fan.

Shiiiiiiiiiiit...

VIOLET starts looking for VERNA. VERNA wants to be alone and is sitting slumped down against a wall. VIOLET sits down next her.

VIOLET: Why do you think we're here?

VERNA: Is this the BIG question? Because, if it is... I'm not up to it, okay? Why don't you go ask "know it all" Mavis or something?

VIOLET: I'm asking you.

VERNA: And I'm telling you I don't know. I mean, why is anybody anybody? Why does anybody end up anywhere? Why does... I never figured it out, okay. I just don't know... if I knew I wouldn't be here or maybe I would. I just don't know.

VIOLET: Why don't you know?

VERNA: Why don't you shut up?

VIOLET: You don't have to be mean.

VERNA: (*in a whiny voice*) Why is the world mean? Why doesn't Mommy love me? Why is Daddy touching me there? Why? Why? I don't know. Why me?

VIOLET: Why aren't you nice ?

VERNA: (*raises her voice*) Why aren't you in bed?

VIOLET: Why are you yelling?

VERNA: I'm not yelling.

VIOLET: Why are you mad?

VERNA: Because I'm dead, and I'm still thirsty.

VIOLET: Thirsty?

VERNA leans over and screams at her silently.

VERNA: THIRSTY, you fuckin parrot. I'm thirsty for... for... my kids, my man. I'm thirsty, thirsty, thirsty, THIR-sty, THIRSTY, dehydrated, dry, parched, thirsty. Get IT?

VIOLET: You didn't have to get mad. (*She puts her head down and pouts.*)

VERNA: (*lowers her voice and gets up*) It's the only way I know how to get from here... to there.

VIOLET looks up, and VERNA has disappeared. VERNA makes her way to the Empress Hotel.

RON walks through all the women with coffee. They all stop and look at his parts.

SLIDE: THE MORNING AFTER – CONT.

RON walks into the bedroom with two cups of coffee. He hands one to REBECCA.

RON: I made some coffee. You don't have any cream. You have a carton, but you don't have any cream.

REBECCA: That doesn't surprise me.

RON: So.

REBECCA: So. Ron. How are you this morning?

RON: I feel like shit.

REBECCA: Well, since we're doing the true confession part of the morning – me too .

RON: You were talking in your sleep... and you pinched my ass.

REBECCA: I talk in my sleep, but it wasn't me that pinched your ass.

RON: I pinched my own ass.

REBECCA: Stranger things have happened. Maybe you were feeling hard done by.

RON: I am actually, but that's another story. What were you doing down there?

REBECCA: The Empress? Thinking and drinking. What were you doing down there?

RON: Drinking and playing pool. We usually go in after work and have a couple of beers. Why do you drink there?

REBECCA: Well, I don't always drink there, but it's a good place to go and think, and I can usually have a drink in quiet without some suit coming up and trying to dazzle me. The worst thing that can happen is an old beat-up suit will sit down and try and dazzle me, which is usually more sad than it is offensive. Besides, I am looking for someone.

RON: Who – Mr. Right?

REBECCA: I married Mr. Right. And divorced Mr. Right. So, now I'm looking for Mr. Fun.

RON: So, who are you looking for really?

REBECCA: I'm looking for my Mom. She went for a walk twenty years ago, and I haven't seen her since.

RON: And you think she's down there.

REBECCA: Yup.

RON: Why?

REBECCA: She was last seen down there.

RON: Why now?

REBECCA: Why now what?

RON: Why do you want to find her now?

REBECCA: I'm not mad anymore.

RON: Remind me not to make you mad.

REBECCA: Well, sometimes it helps to be mad.

RON: You think she's down there. Like living down there? It's not the greatest place to live.

REBECCA: No, really?

RON: I'm just saying the people that live down there are mostly drunks and junkies and Ind... First Na...

REBECCA: And what? You were going to say Indians. Oh, don't get all politically correct on me now...

RON: Okay, Indians. You got a thing for Indians?

REBECCA: Yeah, I got a thing for Indians. You got a thing against Indians?

RON: No, I was just saying...

REBECCA: Never mind. Save it for your job.

RON: What's that supposed to mean?

REBECCA: Listen. I'm not really into Education 101 this morning. So why don't you take your pale bum home.

RON: Let me guess... you're Indian.

REBECCA: Part Indian.

RON: Which part?

REBECCA: The good part.

RON: I thought you were Italian or something.

REBECCA: I thought you were white or something. And I was right. So we both win.

RON: It's just that you don't seem Indian.

REBECCA: That begs the question – what does an Indian seem like? Let me guess – you probably think that, if an Indian goes to university or watches TV, it makes them the same as every other Canadian. Only less. The big melting pot. The only problem is you can't melt an Indian. You can't kill a stone. You can grind it down to sand, but it's still there sifting through everything forever. There, you got it.

RON: Wow, and it's not even nine o'clock in the morning.

REBECCA: I haven't even finished my first cup of coffee.

RON: Since you're there, why do you think so many end up down there?

REBECCA: Since you asked, I don't think so many of them end up down there. I think so many people end up down there. Period.

RON: Why?

REBECCA: It's an accident. Something heavy falls on them. It might just be one thing... one thing and then everything seems to tumble down and pretty soon there is no getting up.

RON: What do you mean?

REBECCA: Like an accident – people drive by in their nice cars and stare at people on those streets, because they realize for a moment it could happen to them. So they might be saying "poor bastards," but what they're really thinking about is themselves and their own potential tragedy.

So these nice people finally look away and— to console themselves from that one conscious thought—think it couldn't happen to them. It's happening to "those" people. Even better if "those" people are mentally ill or brown or addicted to one thing or another. Because these nice people can park their nice cars in their nice driveways and open the doors to their nice homes and take a couple of nice valiums, or call up that nice Betty Ford and go for a nice little vacation "just to get away." They think they are safe. It doesn't matter where your room is – you still have to face the face.

RON: The room?

REBECCA: Yourself. Alone.

RON: So you're saying that's why people end up there.

REBECCA: Yes, they're alone and they know it but there's nothing more comforting than being with a group of people that know they are alone...

RON: ...It's like going to hear the Blues when you're feeling like shit. It makes you feel better.

REBECCA: (*She looks at him.*) Yeah...

RON: Gotcha.

REBECCA: Well, this has been a lot of fun, but I really have to get a move on.

RON: That means I have to leave.

REBECCA: That means – yeah... you have to leave. I have to get dressed. Day stuff.

RON: Can I give you a call?

REBECCA: Mmmmm?

RON: Maybe I could take you out for supper.

REBECCA: Steak and potato and a good red wine.

RON: Sure... make me an honest asshole.

REBECCA: Make me an honest woman. My life is kinda clustered right now but...

RON: But...

REBECCA: Yeah... maybe... I think I've told you too much.

RON: I don't think you've told me enough.

REBECCA: Well, I wouldn't have told you anything, but I didn't think I'd see you again.

RON: And now?

REBECCA: I've probably said too much.

Ron starts to get his clothes together and puts them on. He leaves. Rebecca rolls over to sleep.

SLIDE: THE LIVING ROOM – CONT.

The women are in different areas of the apartment touching and using REBECCA's things. VALERIE is going through REBECCA's laundry that's lying in a basket. She's pulling out different pieces of underwear and trying them on. MAVIS is sitting at REBECCA's desk playing with the phone. VIOLET has been in REBECCA's bedroom swinging on her swing and playing with REBECCA's pretty things. Gradually, the women pick what they want of REBECCA's clothing and make up and put them on.

MAVIS: She's gonna know you were in her drawers. Women always know when someone's been in their drawers.

VALERIE: So. Like, what's she gonna do about it?

MAVIS: The point is – you shouldn't be wearing her underwear. It doesn't even fit you.

VALERIE: It fits parts of me. And why don't you get off your ass and find out where Verna went?

MAVIS: I will after... I finish this one last call.

VALERIE: Who the hell are you talking to anyways?

MAVIS: Talked to my Aunt Bertha. She died when I was eight. She thought I'd forgotten all about her, but I said I always remembered her on account she told me I was beautiful when I was little. I always remember people who said I was beautiful.

VALERIE: Well, that's got to be real hard on your memory.

MAVIS: What?

VALERIE: I said, are you going to see where Verna is or do I have to?

MAVIS: You have to.

VALERIE doesn't leave but eavesdrops on MAVIS' conversation.

MAVIS: Hi... Dad. It's me. Mavis. Well, I just thought I'd call and say "hi." No reason. Like I said, I just got to thinking about you and thought – what the hell, I'll just give the old man a call just out of the blue. How have you been? (*She shrugs.*) How do I think you've been? Well, good I guess. Dad? Geez, he hung up on me.

VALERIE: What did you expect?

MAVIS: I thought he would of mellowed a bit in death.

VALERIE sniffs the air, and VIOLET tiptoes back into the room.

VALERIE: I think she's been into the perfume.

MAVIS: How do you know?

VALERIE: Can't you smell her coming?

MAVIS: Geez, she smells like an old whore.

VALERIE: What's that supposed to mean?

MAVIS: Just that she stinks I guess.

VIOLET: She's got lots of perfume.

VALERIE: We know.

VIOLET: I love perfume. I always wanted lots of perfume. That a drop could make you smell good all over, feel good all over, is kinda amazing.

VALERIE: That's the way I feel about lingerie. I got my first real bra when I was 12, you know one of those God-ugly white things from the Sears catalogue. The first day I come to the city, I went into a lingerie store – it was the most beautiful thing. Red and silk and satin and nylons and things that went up your butt and things that went down your butt and pulled things together and separated other things. That's a fuckin miracle happening if you ask me. I guess lingerie was my downfall.

MAVIS: How so?

VALERIE: I always wanted to show it to people.

MAVIS: Give me a pair of clean cotton undies any day.

VALERIE: What do you know about lingerie? You never get off your ass to appreciate anything on your ass.

MAVIS: Listen, Valerie... enough about my ass, okay?

VALERIE: Okay, okay – touchy, touchy.

MAVIS: ...and since you're worried about everybody's ass, go and see if Verna's in the can.

VALERIE moves towards the bathroom.

VALERIE: Probably reading her one-shit-at-a-time AA book. A capital-letter SOB story if you ask me.

VIOLET: She's not in there.

MAVIS: So now what?

VALERIE: Well, I guess we look good enough to go look for her.

They stop and look in REBECCA's mirror. They put on the finishing touches of make-up and scarves, etc. They look good. They turn to go.

VALERIE: Ready?

MAVIS: Ready.

They leave. VIOLET picks up some red lipstick and puts it on.

The phone rings. Lights up on REBECCA, as she mutters and gets up and picks up the phone. Lights up on AUNT SHADIE at the switchboard.

REBECCA: Hello?

AUNT SHADIE—recognizing REBECCA's voice—stops, breathes slowly and sits down, not able to answer, cradling the phone.

Answer, why don't you?

Nothing.

(*sarcastically*) I love you too.

REBECCA places the receiver down. Lights out on AUNT SHADIE. REBECCA enters the bathroom and starts the shower and gets in.

The phone rings. She wraps herself and stumbles towards it, dripping. She picks it up.

SFX: A male voice talking under.

REBECCA: Ahhhh... enough already. (*picks up phone*) Hello? Am I missing something? (*to herself*) Well, why don't we just play a little game. I'm not sure yet – why? Why didn't you just say that? I must of lost it when I was down there last night. Yeah, I'll be down this afternoon. How will I know you? Okay, yeah. I'll ask the bartender. You can tell me by the picture on my driver's license, or at least I hope you can. Thanks... yeah this afternoon. I'll be there – I told you. Thanks.

She hangs up the phone.

(*to herself*) Weirdo.

REBECCA searches through her laundry basket for her new underwear. She looks under things, the search continues.

REBECCA: Oh, that's great. I finally get a set of great underwear, and the dryer eats it. Here, underwear. Oh, this is not a good day. I should just go back to bed. Go back to bed. Okay, I can do it. Seventy dollars worth of gonch disappeared... feeling like shit.

The phone rings. It's RON.

Hello. I mean... (*sexy*) hel-lo. Just kidding. How you doing? I haven't seen you for at least a couple of hours. Dinner? What do you feel like eating? Steak. Perfect. No, great choice. How can I refuse when you say it like that? I have some running around to do today, but later tonight sounds good. Okay – see you then... there... whatever. Bye.

She gets up, walks past a mirror and looks in.

Feeling good... looking like shit... lost my wallet... talking to myself... and a slut to top it off. Perfect.

She walks into her bedroom. Stops suspiciously and looks at the bed's toes.

REBECCA: Don't even think about it if you want to live.

Lights down.

VIOLET makes her way slowly up the stairs.

SLIDE: SETTING THE TABLE

ROSE is going around the table placing plates.

ROSE: You smell pretty. Do you want to help?

VIOLET: Okay.

VIOLET picks up a pile of cutlery and begins handing it to her. AUNT SHADIE sits quietly by herself weaving snowshoes. She places her feet in each, testing them out. ROSE and VIOLET place the silverware in a setting ritual.

VIOLET: Why do you think we're here?

ROSE: That's a big question.

VIOLET: That's a big question – that's what everybody says.

ROSE: I spent most of life waiting for the big answer. Waiting to fall in love, waiting to have children, waiting to give.

VIOLET: Waiting for the right things to happen that would make everything alright.

ROSE: Waiting.

VIOLET: (*more like a woman than a child*) But not making a choice.

ROSE: Some times the right moment in time...

VIOLET: The right waiting is our own making...

ROSE: ...our knowing that everything has a time and a place.

AUNT SHADIE puts both snowshoes on and is practicing. Proud of her limbs and her snowshoe expertise.

AUNT SHADIE: That we've never forgotten.

VIOLET holds the last knife for a moment and then places it on the table in its setting. She turns to look at AUNT SHADIE. AUNT SHADIE nods and VIOLET walks back down like a woman.

SLIDE: THE EMPRESSES

The BARBER sits at a red terry-cloth table sipping beer. He is dressed in a suit, though shabby around the edges. VERNA is seated beside him, leaning into him, talking. The BARBER is scoping out the place and oblivious to her chatter.

VERNA: Listen, you moron. I'm talking to you. Oh bald one. Don't think I even went around with you because you are good-looking or nothing – you're ugly. Ugly... look at those glasses – four eyes – big eyes bulging out like you're looking at headlights or something. Big dumb.... Stupid.

VERNA slaps him upside the head. His glasses fall off. He picks them up and places them back on his head. The slap changes his focus. He looks through the bar where his barbershop slowly lights up. In a hunting hallucination, his instinct sharpens as he sees a flash of brown moving. He attempts to stumble up. VERNA sits him down roughly.

Not so fast, ree-tard. I got a few more things to get off my chest.

He staggers back down, his eyes fixated on an image coming through the mirrors of his barbershop. A forest forms in the mirrors. The flashes of brown become closer, getting clearer.

GILBERT: Okay, baby... that's it, baby... that's it.

VERNA: *Nee.chin whikth quan.knit to squaw.kwaw* – I already took the liquor.

He concentrates single-mindedly on his vision.

GILBERT: Oh, it is brown – the colour of my thirst.

VERNA: It's my drink – *tay squaw.kaw*

The brown blurs form into a beautiful projection of Marilyn, Penny and Patsy, who are dressed in their hair dreams, seductive and sensual. The projections accent their legs and limbs and eyes. VALERIE and MAVIS step into the image and slowly emerge from the mirror, beautifully in deer-like grace, in unison – part woman, part animal seduction. As they emerge, VIOLET follows behind them – high woman vogue. The following is a collage of images, song, language and movement. Intoxicating and potent.

Quaw.swhat.tus.at.na.ay.quee.quaw – as it reaches my stomach,
Yoh hat.toe.know.a.tone.nas.new.whakt – of my sacred beliefs.

VALERIE and MAVIS get closer to him, moving slow and sensual. They stop to apply lipstick seductively, suggestively, for him.

VERNA: Thirsty for living.

GILBERT: I watched.

They stop mid-lipstick.

VERNA: Thirsty.

WOMEN: I held my breath.

GILBERT: Like animals before her, she was there when I needed to take.

VERNA: Hungry.

The WOMEN seductively pour beer down his throat.

WOMEN: He was afraid of making a mistake.

VERNA: Hungry.

GILBERT: Like animals before her, I wished to look in her eyes...

He tries to pull VALERIE closer. VALERIE places her lips on his and feeds him beer.

VERNA: Hungry.

WOMEN: I saw the smallness.

VERNA: ...lies...

GILBERT: I took them before they could really see me.

VERNA: In desperation.

They sniff.

WOMEN: I smelt him.

VERNA: Hungry for me.

GILBERT: Like animals before her, there was a stillness.

He staggers for them. They pull away. Stop.

VERNA: My heart.

They stop and sigh.

WOMEN: ...a stillness...

VERNA: The real me.

WOMEN: ...a peacefulness...

VERNA: Waiting.

GILBERT: A gasp.

They pose and sigh.

VERNA: Waiting.

GILBERT: Expecting...

They moan seductively.

VERNA: ...to laugh at...

GILBERT: ...deliverance.

VERNA: ...Salvation.

They walk away slowly, beautifully, eyes on him.

WOMEN: There was only my God laughing when he said...

GILBERT: "...There are more ways than one to skin an animal."

WOMEN: There was only my God laughing when he said...

GILBERT: "...Everyone thinks it, they just don't do it."

WOMEN: There was only me laughing when he said...

GILBERT: Die. Die.

WOMEN: Only me.

VERNA: Seeing...

GILBERT: ...the look in their eyes.

VERNA: Pointing...

WOMEN: ...back...

VERNA: Leaving you...

GILBERT: ...wondering – can an animal laugh?

VALERIE and MAVIS and VIOLET slip back into the mirror and through the images of Marilyn, Patsy and Penny. The mirror reflecting many women.

WOMEN: Oh yes. Oh yes. Forever

GILBERT starts pounding his drinks, shaken.

GILBERT: I am a good and decent man. I am a good and good-living man.

MAVIS Her Chair Ass and VALERIE and VIOLET appear behind VERNA. VALERIE places her hand on VERNA's shoulder.

VALERIE: It's time to go, Verna – he's not worth it.

GILBERT: I am clean.

MAVIS: He's just a man.

GILBERT: I am.

VERNA: An ugly man to boot.

GILBERT: I am.

VIOLET: An ugly man to boot.

GILBERT: I am.

MAVIS: You should feel sorry for him.

GILBERT: Therefore, I am.

VERNA: Sorry? (*Pause.*) All I feel sorry for is his little dick and his ugly face. Besides, I'm tired of feeling sorry for white people.

GILBERT continues to get blasted.

MAVIS: Okay, enough of this ugly.

VERNA: What? You got something for him, Mavis?

MAVIS: I never had anything for him, Verna. I thought he was someone else.

VERNA: Well, that's easy to say now...

VALERIE: That's enough, Verna. We all thought he was someone we knew. Someone we needed. Okay, leave it alone.

VERNA: Skinny bastard.

MAVIS: We should go, Verna.

VERNA: You go.

VALERIE: We're not leaving you here, Verna.

VERNA: Why the hell not?

VALERIE: It would be too pitiful.

VERNA: You wanna make something out of this, Valerie?

VALERIE: Verna, you know I could make you in a minute.

VERNA gets up from her chair to challenge VALERIE.

VERNA: Make this...

MAVIS: Hello – it's her Rebecca.

VALERIE & VIOLET: Oh shitttttttttttttttttt....

REBECCA approaches them. The women back away slightly.

REBECCA: Excuse me?

WOMEN: Ahhhh... yeah?

GILBERT: (*hazy drunk*) Yeah? What do you want? (*He looks at her intensely.*) I mean... how can I help you? Miss.

REBECCA: Umm... the guy at the front said you were the one that had my wallet. I mean you were the one that found it. Remember, you told me to get the bartender to point you out.

GILBERT: Right... right. Mind isn't what it used to be. (*laughs*) Have a seat.

REBECCA sits.

I saw you in here last night. It must of fell from your jacket or something. I'm just glad I could help.

VALERIE: Help this, you fuckin pig! (*She squeezes her boobs together.*)

REBECCA: Well, thanks. It's always a big hassle when you lose your ID.

WOMEN: I'll say.

GILBERT: What's a nice girl like you hanging around a place like this?

MAVIS: Oh, that's original.

REBECCA: Just playing pool.

GILBERT: Can I buy you a drink?

VIOLET: No.

REBECCA: No, it's okay.

GILBERT: Seriously, you look like a lady that was lookin' for something.

He hands her over a beer. She watches the beer slide over.

REBECCA: O-kay.... We'll, it's a long story.

GILBERT: I got all the time in the world.

REBECCA: Really. I have been looking for my mother. She was last seen in this neighbourhood. Seems I just get close to where she last lived, or where she used to hang out, and I somehow miss her.

GILBERT: You gotta picture? I've been around here for a long time.

REBECCA shuffles in her purse and pulls a picture out. She shows it to him. All the women look at it.

VALERIE: Holy shit, she was beautiful.

MAVIS: Kinda looks like me when I was young.

VERNA: Yeah, right.

GILBERT: I think I know her. I think her name was – well... I don't know her real name, but they used to call her Aunt Shadie or something...

REBECCA: Aunt Shadie?

WOMEN: Aunt Shadie?!

GILBERT: Aunt Shadie. Come to think of it, I had a drink with her awhile back.

REBECCA: How long ago is a while back?

GILBERT: I lose track of time – you know how it is? Anyways, she left some things with me to hold for safe keeping... she said she was gonna try and look up a daughter she hadn't seen in awhile. I'm always tryin' to help some of these women out.

REBECCA: Really.

GILBERT: If you want, we can finish these off and head over to my Barbershop. I think I got something of hers there.

The BARBER watches her as REBECCA downs her beer. They get up, and he stumbles and tries to pull himself together. REBECCA looks around, she stops.

WOMEN: It's alright.

REBECCA: *(to herself, them)* It's alright.

Lights down.

SLIDE: WHEN SHE WAS HORNY AND WANTED SEX – The Barbershop

They enter the Barbershop. GILBERT walks around and shuts the blinds to his storefront. REBECCA walks around the shop, keeping her distance. He stares intensely at her.

REBECCA: It's a nice shop. Do you have a lot of clients?

GILBERT: Just my regulars. They like the service I've always given them.

REBECCA: I'm sure they do.

GILBERT: I'm good at my job. Been doing it for thirty years now.

REBECCA: Really?

GILBERT: You could say this has been my calling.

REBECCA: What do you like best about it?

GILBERT: I'm in control, and I know what they want.

REBECCA: What do they want?

GILBERT: That depends.

REBECCA: I love barbershops. Always loved them. Ever since I was a little girl I used to come with my Dad and watch him get shaved and have his hair cut.

She touches his utensils.

GILBERT: You used to have long hair?

REBECCA: Yeah, but I cut it because I... you wouldn't understand. I cut it to my shoulders a couple of months ago. It will grow, and I'll braid it like I used to when I was a kid.

GILBERT: Braids?

REBECCA: My Dad used to do it for me... he used to say I looked just like my Mom when he finished. I used to love that.

GILBERT: Can I braid it? I like women in braids.

REBECCA: No, it's alright. Thanks...

He grabs her hair from behind.

She grabs her hair back.

REBECCA: Enough.

GILBERT: (*He turns and says to himself:*) You fuckin uppity bitch.

REBECCA: Pardon me.

GILBERT: Pardon me? (*mimicking her*)

He gets out a bottle from his cupboard.

Do you want a drink?

REBECCA: Sure, I guess. Shouldn't you be working?

GILBERT: I am.

Long awkward silence.

REBECCA: So... can I see what you have of my mother's? I don't usually drink in the afternoon, so this is really a special treat. It really goes straight to my head...

GILBERT: Here, I'll just top you up.

REBECCA: Yeah...

She watches him pour the drink.

GILBERT: I'm just gonna go freshen up a bit. Don't want to be in the company of a beautiful young woman looking like I need to brush my teeth.

Gilbert exits to go to the bathroom.

REBECCA: And you're only worried about your teeth... fuckin scary.

She goes to pull out a drawer and then stops and looks at the red and white barber light. She stops for a long moment and breathes. She walks directly towards it, taking the bottom off the light. A handful of long black braids fall to the floor. She gasps and touches each one until she gets to her mother's. She picks her mother's braid up and buries her face in it and sobs. REBECCA hears GILBERT approaching. Shaken, she takes her jacket off and covers the braids and tries to get herself together.

REBECCA: Here, Gilbert, why don't you have a seat. I always found shaving men sexy. It makes me horny. Can I shave you, Gilbert?

GILBERT: I don't know... it's not usually how things work.

REBECCA: Things they are a changin'...

GILBERT: What?

REBECCA: Just a song I had in my head. Oh, come on.

GILBERT: Okay... you have to be careful.

REBECCA: I'll be gentle.

He reaches up to touch her. She grabs his hands.

You have beautiful hands. I've always loved men's hands. How they move. Your hands are so soft and white. I bet you've loved a lot of women.

GILBERT: I've had my share of women.

REBECCA: You're being modest.

GILBERT: Women have always taken to me. I know how to make a woman happy. I know what they want to hear.

He places his hands on her breasts.

REBECCA: Slow down, Gilbert. Slow down, we have lots of time. Would you like a drink? Can I buy you a drink? Can I get you a drink?

GILBERT: What do you mean?

REBECCA: I mean, can I pour you a drink?

GILBERT: Sure, I guess.

REBECCA: Here you go. You sure you don't want more? You look like you can handle your liquor.

GILBERT: I'm not scared of anything.

She pours him a heap.

REBECCA: Of course not. Okay, baby. Can I shave you?

GILBERT: You have to be very careful.

REBECCA: I'd never do anything to hurt you. Do want your bottle? Here, why don't I place it right here, so it can be close to you? Do you like that? It's right here so it can be close to you. Do you like that?

She grooves it into his crotch. He moans.

I'll just place this over you now. Like this?

She places his barbershop cape over him. It covers his body.

GILBERT: That's right.

REBECCA: That's right.

He grabs her hand. She keeps him from forcing her hand down.

GILBERT: That's right. Right down here... you fuckin...

REBECCA: Gilbert. Shhhhhhhh... just wait... just wait. Close your eyes and relax. Relax. I'm here, baby.

GILBERT: Yeah. I'll relax when I'm stuffing you with my...

REBECCA: Should I use this? (*She grabs the shaving cream bottle.*) So, I take it in my hand... spray it out like this? You tell me, you're the professional.

GILBERT: That's it. That's it. Jesus Christ, just do it.

REBECCA: Just close your eyes – let me do all the work.

She smoothes the foam over his face sensually.

GILBERT: Mmmmmm.

He closes his eyes. As she spreads the foam on his face, a forest reflects in the mirrors as it is being covered by billowing snow. A beautiful, crystallized snow scene.

A voice from the dark approaches through the landscape. It gets closer and closer. At first, just a movement and glimpses of brown.

AUNT SHADIE: I used to be a real good trapper when I was young. You wouldn't believe it, now that I'm such a city girl. But before, when my legs and body were young and muscular, I could go forever. Walking those traplines with snowshoes. The sun coming down, sprinkling everything with crystals, some floating down and dusting that white comforter with magic. I would walk that trapline...

REBECCA: I would walk that trapline...

AUNT SHADIE: ...like a map, my body knowing every turn, every tree, every curve the land uses to confuse us.

REBECCA: . . . like a map, my body knowing every turn, every lie, every curve they use to kill us.

REBECCA & AUNT SHADIE: I felt like I was part of the magic that wasn't confused.

REBECCA: The crystals sticking to the cold and the cold sticking to my black hair, my eyebrows, my clothes, my breath. A trap set.

REBECCA braces herself. She takes the razor and is about to cut his throat.

An animal caught.

The BARBER's eyes suddenly blaze open. He grabs her hand and they struggle with the blade. The blade draws closer to her neck and is about to cut her open.

AUNT SHADIE emerges from the landscape as a trapper. She stands behind REBECCA. She puts her hand over REBECCA's hand and draws the knife closer to the BARBER's neck. He looks up and panics as he sees AUNT SHADIE and the Women/trappers behind her. Squirming, they slit his throat.

AUNT SHADIE: Red.

They look at each other. Blood seeps on his white gown.

REBECCA: Red.

AUNT SHADIE: If it squirmed, I would put it out of its misery as fast as I could.

The trappers follow through, as REBECCA and her mother stare at each other. The trappers take the razor, wash it and replace it. REBECCA hands each woman their braids. The women leave in a line. Her mother remains standing. REBECCA reaches in her pocket and hands her mother her braid of hair.

AUNT SHADIE: Re-becca.

AUNT SHADIE raises her hand and touches her face.

REBECCA: *Meegweetch* and thank you.

AUNT SHADIE hugs her and falls behind the line of women/trappers. She falls in behind the rest of the trappers, as the lights fade on the landscape and the women tracking their way back.

SLIDE: THE FIRST SUPPER – NOT TO BE CONFUSED WITH THE LAST SUPPER

REBECCA watches the long line of women as they take their heavy trapping clothes off, their long, long hair spilling everywhere. They begin to sit down to a beautiful banquet à la the Last Supper. Lights fade on them, and the sound of their voices becomes the sound of trees.

SFX: *Sound of tree leaves moving in the wind.*

REBECCA exits from the barbershop. She walks in the wind and trees.

SFX: *The loud sound of a tree falling...*

She stops and listens to the sound.

The Barbershop is empty except for the BARBER in his chair. Barber lights swirl red and white throughout the barbershop. The red light intensifies and takes over the room. Fade out.

SFX: *The sound of the tree hitting the ground with a loud thud.*

REBECCA closes her eyes for a moment and then continues walking.

Fade out.

The end.

AGMV Marquis
MEMBER OF SCABRINI MEDIA
Quebec, Canada
2001